LEARN HOW THIS BOOK CAN HELP YOU UNDERSTAND U.S. HISTORY

See pages xxiv–xxix.

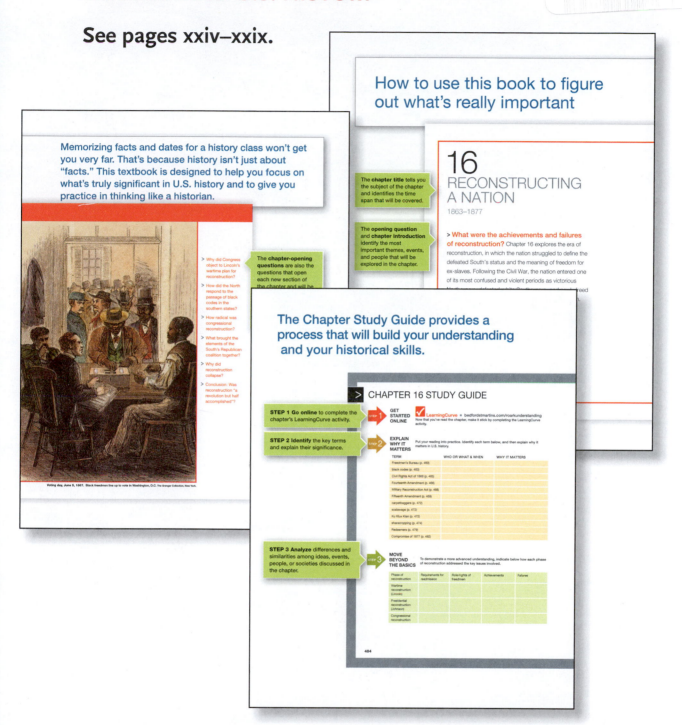

Memorizing facts and dates for a history class won't get you very far. That's because history isn't just about "facts." This textbook is designed to help you focus on what's truly significant in U.S. history and to give you practice in thinking like a historian.

> Why did Congress object to Lincoln's wartime plan for reconstruction?

> How did the North respond to the passage of black codes in the southern states?

> How radical was congressional reconstruction?

> What brought the elements of the South's Republican coalition together?

> Why did reconstruction collapse?

> Conclusion: Was reconstruction "a revolution but half accomplished"?

The **chapter-opening questions** are also the questions that open each new section of the chapter and will be

Voting day, June 5, 1867. Black freedmen line up to vote in Washington, D.C. The Granger Collection, New York.

How to use this book to figure out what's really important

The **chapter title** tells you the subject of the chapter and identifies the time span that will be covered.

The **opening question** and **chapter introduction** identify the most important themes, events, and people that will be explored in the chapter.

16
RECONSTRUCTING A NATION
1863–1877

> **What were the achievements and failures of reconstruction?** Chapter 16 explores the era of reconstruction, in which the nation struggled to define the defeated South's status and the meaning of freedom for ex-slaves. Following the Civil War, the nation entered one of its most confused and violent periods as victorious

The Chapter Study Guide provides a process that will build your understanding and your historical skills.

> CHAPTER 16 STUDY GUIDE

STEP 1 Go online to complete the chapter's LearningCurve activity.

GET STARTED ONLINE

✓ LearningCurve • bedfordstmartins.com/roarkunderstanding
Now that you've read the chapter, make it stick by completing the LearningCurve activity.

STEP 2 Identify the key terms and explain their significance.

EXPLAIN WHY IT MATTERS

Put your reading into practice. Identify each term below, and then explain why it matters in U.S. history.

TERM	WHO OR WHAT & WHEN	WHY IT MATTERS
Freedmen's Bureau (p. 463)		
black codes (p. 463)		
Civil Rights Act of 1866 (p. 465)		
Fourteenth Amendment (p. 466)		
Military Reconstruction Act (p. 468)		
Fifteenth Amendment (p. 469)		
carpetbaggers (p. 472)		
scalawags (p. 472)		
Ku Klux Klan (p. 472)		
sharecropping (p. 474)		
Redeemers (p. 479)		
Compromise of 1877 (p. 480)		

STEP 3 Analyze differences and similarities among ideas, events, people, or societies discussed in the chapter.

MOVE BEYOND THE BASICS

To demonstrate a more advanced understanding, indicate below how each phase of reconstruction addressed the key issues involved.

Phase of reconstruction	Requirements for readmission	Role/rights of freedmen	Achievements	Failures
Wartime Reconstruction (Lincoln)				
Presidential Reconstruction (Johnson)				
Congressional Reconstruction				

484

"The pedagogical tools in *Understanding the American Promise* are superior."
—Tim Myers, Butler Community College

Understanding
the
American Promise

A HISTORY

Understanding the American Promise

A HISTORY

SECOND EDITION

Volume I
To 1877

James L. Roark
Emory University

Michael P. Johnson
Johns Hopkins University

Patricia Cline Cohen
*University of California,
Santa Barbara*

Sarah Stage
Arizona State University

Susan M. Hartmann
The Ohio State University

Bedford/St. Martin's
Boston • New York

For Bedford/St. Martin's

Publisher for History: Mary V. Dougherty
Executive Editor for History: William J. Lombardo
Director of Development for History: Jane Knetzger
Developmental Editor: Kathryn Abbott
Senior Production Editor: Karen S. Baart
Assistant Production Manager: Joe Ford
Executive Marketing Manager: Sandra McGuire
Associate Editors: Jack Cashman, Jennifer Jovin
Editorial Assistant: Emily DiPietro
Production Assistants: Elise Keller, Kim Lester
Copyeditor: Linda McLatchie
Indexer: Leoni Z. McVey, McVey & Associates, Inc.
Photo Researchers: Pembroke Herbert and Sandi Rygiel, Picture Research Consultants, Inc.
Senior Art Director: Anna Palchik
Text Designer: Cenveo Publisher Services
Cover Designer: Donna Lee Dennison
Cover Art: Reuben Moulthrop (attr.), *Mrs. Daniel Truman and Child,* c. 1798–1810. Oil on
    canvas. Collection of the New York Historical Society, USA.
Cartography: Mapping Specialists, Limited
Composition: Cenveo Publisher Services
Printing and Binding: RR Donnelley and Sons

President, Bedford/St. Martin's: Denise B. Wydra
Director of Marketing: Karen R. Soeltz
Production Director: Susan W. Brown
Director of Rights and Permissions: Hilary Newman

Manufactured in the United States of America.

2 3 4 5 6   17 16 15 14 13

For information, write: Bedford/St. Martin's, 75 Arlington Street, Boston, MA 02116
(617-399-4000)

ISBN: 978–1–4576–3979–1 (Combined Edition)
ISBN: 978–1–4576–6414–4 (Loose-leaf Edition)
ISBN: 978–1–4576–3980–7 (Volume I)
ISBN: 978–1–4576–6415–1 (Loose-leaf Edition,
    Volume I)

ISBN: 978–1–4576–3982–1 (Volume II)
ISBN: 978–1–4576–6413–7 (Loose-leaf Edition,
    Volume II)
ISBN: 978–1–4576–6255–3 (High School Edition)

PREFACE: Why This Book This Way

Understanding the American Promise grew out of many conversations over the last decade among ourselves and with others about the teaching and learning of history. We knew that instructors wanted a U.S. history text that introduced students to overarching trends and developments but at the same time gave voice to the diverse people who have made American history. We also knew that instructors wanted a text demonstrating that history is a discipline rooted in debate and inquiry. At the same time, we knew that even though many students dutifully read their survey texts, they often come away overwhelmed and confused about what is most important to know. Because of the difficulty many students have understanding the most important concepts when they read a traditional U.S. survey text, a growing number of instructors thought that their students needed a brief text that did not overwhelm them with detail. Instructors also wanted a text that would help students focus as they read, keep their interest in the material, and encourage them to learn historical thinking skills.

With these issues in mind, we took a hard look at the introductory course from a number of different directions. We reflected on the changes in our own classrooms, reviewed state-of-the-art scholarship on effective teaching, consulted learning experts and instructional designers, and talked to students and instructors about their needs. We talked to people who are teaching online and listened to instructors' wish lists for time-saving support materials. *Understanding the American Promise* is a textbook designed to address these wide-ranging concerns. With the second edition, we again combine an abridged narrative with an innovative design and unique pedagogy orchestrated to work together to aid students' understanding of the most important developments while also fostering students' ability to think historically. A number of revisions and additions make the second edition an even better tool for this textbook designed for understanding.

Because, like other instructors, we are eager to ensure students read and assimilate this rich material, we are excited to announce that the second edition of *Understanding the American Promise* comes with **LearningCurve**—an adaptive game-like online learning tool that helps students master content. The second edition also introduces **LaunchPad,** a new robust interactive e-book built into its own course space that makes customizing and assigning the book and its resources easy and efficient. To learn more about the benefits of LearningCurve and LaunchPad, see the "Versions and Supplements" section on page ix.

An Inquiry-based Model Designed for Understanding

By employing innovative pedagogy, we believe that *Understanding the American Promise* helps students not only understand the book's major developments but also begin to grasp the question-driven methodology that is at the heart of the historian's craft. Each chapter opens with a **NEW chapter-opening question** that drives students toward the overarching themes of the chapter, followed by a **brief chapter introduction** that identifies in simple, straightforward terms the most important events and people to be discussed. **Section-opening headings** expressed as questions and **section-ending quick review** questions further model the kinds of questions historians ask and help students engage in inquiry-based reading and understanding.

Chapter Study Guides Designed for Active Learning

At the core of *Understanding the American Promise*'s unique pedagogical features are the revised **Chapter Study Guides** that provide a carefully structured four-step process to help students build deep understanding of the chapter material. In **Step One,** students go online to complete the LearningCurve activity to ensure that they have a grasp of the basic content and concepts of the chapter. In **Step Two,** students not only identify the chapter's key terms but also explain why each matters. In **Step Three,** they begin to apply their understanding of the chapter material through activities that ask them to consider comparison, change-over-time, or cause and effect. In **Step Four,** analytical and synthetic questions require students to engage in higher-order historical thinking. And, finally, in an active recitation exercise, students **answer the chapter-opening question** to fully realize their understanding of the chapter.

Visual Learning Aids

Throughout each chapter, a wide range of visual material keeps students' attention and reinforces important concepts. Some narrative material has been moved into **figures and tables** to call out and organize certain concepts visually and provide an alternative mode of learning. Two **map activities** per chapter engage students in reading maps and making connections and thus enhance geographical literacy. In total, there are over 165 maps in the book. A **visual activity** in each chapter reinforces the role of images as historical evidence. Many of the 300-plus images in the book are historical artifacts that underscore the importance of material culture.

Additional Pedagogical Features

The second edition includes several other helpful learning tools. As mentioned earlier, the NEW **LearningCurve online adaptive activity** is designed to prepare students for class by reinforcing their work reading the textbooks. **Section-based chronologies** of historical developments help students keep events in context as they read. Because students often have difficulty seeing the forest for the trees, innovative **chapter locators** at the foot of the page remind students of where they are in the chapter's larger progression of events and concepts. **Key terms** highlighted in the text and then defined in the margins further remind students of what's most important to know.

Updated Scholarship

In our ongoing effort to offer a comprehensive text that braids all Americans into the national narrative and to frame that narrative in a more global perspective, we updated the second edition in many ways. We have paid particular attention to the most recent scholarship and, as always, appreciated and applied many suggestions from our users that keep the book fresh, accurate, and organized in a way that works best for students.

Volume I draws on exciting new scholarship on Native Americans, leading to enhanced coverage of Pontiac's Rebellion in chapter 6 and more attention to Indians and their roles in the conflict between the British and the colonists in chapter 7. Chapter 9 expands the coverage of American interactions with Indians in the Southwest, adding new material on Creek chief Alexander McGillivray. Chapter 10 greatly increases the coverage of Indians in the West, with a new section devoted to the Osage territory and the powerful Comanche empire known as Comanchería.

Volume II also includes expanded attention to Native Americans — particularly in Chapter 17, where we improved coverage of Indian schools, assimilation techniques used by whites, and Indian resistance strategies. For the second edition, we also provide more coverage of women, African Americans, and the global context of U.S. history. In the narrative, we consider the ways in which the GI Bill disproportionately benefited white men after World War II. Chapter 16 includes new coverage of the Colfax massacre, arguably the single worst incidence of brutality against African Americans during the Reconstruction era. Chapter 27 provides new coverage of civil rights activism in northern states.

Because students live in an increasingly global world and need help making connections with the world outside the United States, we have continued our efforts to incorporate the global context of American history throughout the second edition. This is particularly evident in Volume II, where we have expanded coverage of transnational issues in recent decades, such as the U.S. bombing campaign in Vietnam and U.S. involvement in Afghanistan.

In addition to the many changes noted above, in both volumes we have updated, revised, and improved this second edition in response to both new scholarship and requests from instructors. New and expanded coverage areas include, among others, taxation in the pre-Revolutionary period and the early Republic, the Newburgh Conspiracy of the 1780s, the overbuilding of railroads in the West during the Gilded Age, the 1918–1919 global influenza epidemic, finance reform in the 1930s, post–World War II considerations of universal health care, Latino activism, the economic downturn of the late 2000s, the most recent developments in the Middle East, and the Obama presidency.

Acknowledgments

We gratefully acknowledge all of the helpful suggestions from those who have read or taught from the previous edition of *Understanding the American Promise*, and we hope that our many classroom collaborators will be pleased to see their influence in the second edition. In particular, we wish to thank the talented scholars and teachers who gave generously of their time and knowledge to review this book: Brittany Adams, *Irvine Valley College*; John Bradford Bowers, *Pueblo Community College*; Vincent A. Clark, *Johnson County Community College*; Jane Dabel, *California State University–Long Beach*; Diane Duray, *Howard Community College*; Michael J. Engle, *Pueblo Community College*; Keith A. Erekson, *University of Texas–El Paso*; Josh Fulton, *Valley Community College*; Jessica Gerard, *Ozarks Technical Community College*; Geoffrey R. Hunt, *Community College of Aurora*; Josh Lieser, *MiraCosta College*; Steven Lurenz, *Mesa Community College*; Jeffrey J. Malanson, *Indiana University-Purdue University–Fort Wayne*; Tim

Myers, *Butler Community College*; Marjorie Moss Nash, *Alvin Community College*; Brian D. Page, *Edison State College*; Jessica Patton, *Tarrant County College*; Carmen Reys-Johnson, *Northeast Lakeview College*; Norman Rodriguez, *John Wood Community College*; Mark Roehrs, *Lincoln Land Community College*; Nancy E. Shockley, *Oakland Community College*; Allen N. Smith, Jr., *Ivy Tech Community College*; Adam M. Sowards, *University of Idaho*; Michael A. Sparks, *Ivy Tech Community College*; Danielle J. Swiontek, *Santa Barbara City College*; David Tegeder, *University of Florida*; Joseph Thurman, *Jefferson College*; Kirk Walton, *Black Hawk College*; Laura Westhoff, *University of Missouri–St. Louis*.

A project as complex as this requires the talents of many individuals. First, we would like to acknowledge our families for their support, forbearance, and toleration of our textbook responsibilities. Pembroke Herbert and Sandi Rygiel of Picture Research Consultants, Inc., contributed their unparalleled knowledge, soaring imagination, and diligent research to make possible the extraordinary illustration program.

We would also like to thank the many people at Bedford/St. Martin's who have been crucial to this project. Developmental editor Kathryn Abbott managed the entire revision and supplements program. Her skill, good judgment, and deep commitment to the project are obvious on every page. Thanks also go to associate editor Jack Cashman, who oversaw the development of the supplements, associate editor Jennifer Jovin who assisted in creating some of the reading and study tools, and editorial assistant Emily DiPietro for her help coordinating the pre-revision review and preparing the manuscript. We are also grateful to Jane Knetzger, director of development for history; William J. Lombardo, executive editor for history; and Mary Dougherty, publisher for history, for their support and guidance. For their imaginative and tireless efforts to promote the book, we want to thank John Hunger, Sean Blest, Sandra McGuire, and Alex Kaufman. With great skill and professionalism, senior production editor Karen Baart pulled together the many pieces related to copyediting, design, and composition with the guidance of associate production director Elise Kaiser. Assistant production supervisor Joe Ford oversaw the manufacturing of the book. Designer Carie Keller, copyeditor Linda McLatchie, and proofreaders Kathleen Lafferty and Angela Morrison attended to the myriad details that help make the book shine. Leoni McVey and Associates provided the index. The book's gorgeous covers were designed by Donna Lee Dennison. New media editors Kimberly Hampton and Marissa Zanetti and media producers Rebecca Merrill and Michelle Camisa made sure that *Understanding the American Promise* remains at the forefront of technological support for students and instructors. President of Bedford/St. Martin's Denise Wydra provided helpful advice throughout the course of the project. Finally, Charles H. Christensen, former president, took a personal interest in *The American Promise* from the start, and Joan E. Feinberg, co-president of Macmillan Higher Education, encouraged us through each edition.

James Roark
Michael Johnson
Patricia Cohen
Sarah Stage
Susan Hartmann

VERSIONS AND SUPPLEMENTS

Adopters of *Understanding the American Promise* and their students have access to abundant extra resources, including documents, presentation and testing materials, the acclaimed Bedford Series in History and Culture volumes, and much more. See below for more information, visit the book's catalog site at **bedfordstmartins.com/roarkunderstanding/catalog**, or contact your local Bedford/St. Martin's sales representative.

Get the Right Version for Your Class

To accommodate different course lengths and course budgets, *Understanding the American Promise* is available in several different formats, including three-hole-punched loose-leaf Budget Books versions and e-books, which are available at a substantial discount.

- **Combined edition** (Chapters 1–31)—available in paperback, loose-leaf, and e-book formats
- **Volume 1: To 1877** (Chapters 1–16)—available in paperback, loose-leaf, and e-book formats
- **Volume 2: From 1865** (Chapters 16–31)—available in paperback, loose-leaf, and e-book formats

Any of these volumes can be packaged with additional books for a discount. To get ISBNs for discount packages, see the online catalog at **bedfordstmartins .com/roarkunderstanding/catalog** or contact your Bedford/St. Martin's representative.

▶ **NEW Assign LaunchPad—the online, interactive e-book in a course space enriched with integrated assets.** The new standard in digital history, LaunchPad course tools are so intuitive to use that online, hybrid, and face-to-face courses can be set up in minutes. Even novices will find it's easy to create assignments, track students' work, and access a wealth of relevant learning and teaching resources. It is the ideal learning environment for students to work with the text, maps, documents, video, and assessment. LaunchPad is loaded with the full interactive e-book and the *Reading the American Past* documents collection—plus LearningCurve, additional primary sources, videos, guided reading exercises designed to help students read actively for key concepts, chapter summative quizzes, and more. LaunchPad can be used as is or customized, and it easily integrates with course management systems. And with fast ways to build assignments, rearrange chapters, and add new pages, sections, or links, it lets teachers build the course materials they need and hold students accountable.

▶ **Let students choose their e-book format.** In addition to the LaunchPad e-book, students can purchase the downloadable *Bedford e-Book to Go for Understanding* *the American Promise* from our Web site or find other PDF versions of the e-book at our publishing partners' sites: CourseSmart, Barnes & Noble NookStudy, Kno, CafeScribe, or Chegg.

NEW Assign LearningCurve So You Know What Your Students Know and They Come to Class Prepared

As described in the preface and on the inside front cover, students purchasing new books receive access to LearningCurve for *Understanding the American Promise*. Assigning LearningCurve in place of reading quizzes is easy for instructors, and the reporting features help instructors track overall class trends and spot topics that are giving students trouble so they can adjust their lectures and class activities. This online learning tool is popular with students because it was designed to help them rehearse content at their own pace in a non-threatening, game-like environment. The feedback for wrong answers provides instructional coaching and sends students back to the book for review. Students answer as many questions as necessary to reach a target score, with repeated chances to revisit material they haven't mastered. When LearningCurve is assigned, students come to class better prepared.

Send Students to Free Online Resources

The book's Student Site at **bedfordstmartins.com/roarkunderstanding** gives students a way to read, write, and study by providing plentiful quizzes and activities, study aids, and history research and writing help.

▶ **FREE Online Study Guide.** Available at the Student Site, this popular resource provides students with quizzes and activities for each chapter, including multiple-choice self-tests that focus on important concepts, flashcards that test students' knowledge of key terms, timeline activities that emphasize causal relationships, and map quizzes intended to strengthen students' geography skills. Instructors can monitor students' progress through an online Quiz Gradebook or receive e-mail updates.

▶ **FREE Research, Writing, and Anti-plagiarism Advice.** Available at the Student Site, Bedford's **History Research and Writing Help** includes the textbook authors' **Suggested References** organized by chapter; **History Research and Reference Sources,** with links to history-related databases, indexes, and journals; **Build a Bibliography,** a simple Web-based tool known as The Bedford Bibliographer that generates bibliographies in four commonly used documentation styles; and **Tips on Avoiding Plagiarism,** an online tutorial that reviews the consequences of plagiarism and features exercises to help students practice integrating sources and recognize acceptable summaries.

Take Advantage of Instructor Resources

Bedford/St. Martin's has developed a rich array of teaching resources for this book and for this course. They range from lecture and presentation materials and assessment tools to course management options. Most can be downloaded or ordered at **bedfordstmartins.com/roarkunderstanding/catalog.**

▶ **Instructor's Resource Manual.** The instructor's manual offers both experienced and first-time instructors tools for preparing lectures and running discussions. It includes chapter-review material, teaching strategies, and a guide to chapter-specific supplements available for the text, plus suggestions on how to get the most out of LearningCurve and a survival guide for first-time teaching assistants.

▶ **Guide to Changing Editions.** Designed to facilitate an instructor's transition from the previous edition of *Understanding the American Promise* to the current edition, this guide presents an overview of major changes as well as of changes in each chapter.

▶ **Computerized Test Bank.** The test bank includes a mix of fresh, carefully crafted multiple-choice, short-answer, and essay questions for each chapter. It also contains volume-wide essay questions. All questions appear in Microsoft Word format and in easy-to-use test bank software that allows instructors to add, edit, re-sequence, and print questions and answers. Instructors can also export questions into a variety of formats, including Blackboard, Desire2Learn, and Moodle.

▶ *The Bedford Lecture Kit:* **PowerPoint Maps, Images, Lecture Outlines, and i>clicker Content.** Look good and save time with *The Bedford Lecture Kit.* These presentation materials are downloadable individually from the Instructor Resources tab at **bedfordstmartins.com/roarkunderstanding/catalog** and are available on *The Bedford Lecture Kit* **Instructor's Resource CD-ROM.** They provide ready-made and fully customizable PowerPoint multimedia presentations that include lecture outlines with embedded maps, figures, and selected images from the textbook and extra background for instructors. Also available are maps and selected images in JPEG and PowerPoint formats; content for i>clicker, a classroom response system, in Microsoft Word and PowerPoint formats; the Instructor's Resource Manual in Microsoft Word format; and outline maps in PDF format for quizzing or handing out. All files are suitable for copying onto transparency acetates.

▶ *Reel Teaching: Film Clips for the U.S. History Survey.* This DVD provides a large collection of short video clips for classroom presentation. Designed as engaging "lecture launchers" varying in length from one to fifteen minutes or longer, the fifty-nine documentary clips were carefully chosen for use in both semesters of the U.S. survey course. The clips feature compelling images, archival footage, personal narratives, and commentary by noted historians.

▶ *America in Motion: Video Clips for U.S. History.* Set history in motion with *America in Motion,* an instructor DVD containing dozens of short digital movie files of events in twentieth-century American history. From the wreckage of the battleship *Maine* to FDR's fireside chats to Oliver North testifying before Congress, *America in Motion* engages students with dynamic scenes from key events and challenges them to think critically. All files are classroom-ready, edited for brevity, and easily integrated with PowerPoint or other presentation software for electronic lectures or assignments. An accompanying guide provides each clip's historical context, ideas for use, and suggested questions.

▶ **Videos and Multimedia.** A wide assortment of videos and multimedia CD-ROMs on various topics in U.S. history is available to qualified adopters through your Bedford/St. Martin's sales representative.

Package and Save Your Students Money

For information on free packages and discounts up to 50%, visit **bedfordstmartins .com/roarkunderstanding/catalog** or contact your local Bedford/St. Martin's sales representative. The products that follow all qualify for discount packaging.

▶ *Reading the American Past,* **Fifth Edition.** Edited by Michael P. Johnson, one of the authors of *The American Promise*, and designed to complement the textbook, *Reading the American Past* provides a broad selection of over 150 primary-source documents as well as editorial apparatus to help students understand the sources. Available free when packaged with the print text and included in the LaunchPad e-book. Also available on its own as a downloadable PDF e-book or with the main text's e-Book to Go.

▶ **NEW Bedford Digital Collections @ bedfordstmartins.com/bdc/catalog.** This source collection provides a flexible and affordable online repository of discovery-oriented primary-source projects and single primary sources that you can easily customize and link to from your course management system or Web site. Package discounts are available.

▶ **The Bedford Series in History and Culture.** More than 120 titles in this highly praised series combine first-rate scholarship, historical narrative, and important primary documents for undergraduate courses. Each book is brief, inexpensive, and focused on a specific topic or period. For a complete list of titles, visit **bedfordstmartins.com/history/series.** Package discounts are available.

▶ *Rand McNally Atlas of American History.* This collection of more than eighty full-color maps illustrates key events and eras from early exploration, settlement, expansion, and immigration to U.S. involvement in wars abroad and on U.S. soil. Introductory pages for each section include a brief overview, timelines, graphs, and photos to quickly establish a historical context. Available for $5.00 when packaged with the print text.

▶ *Maps in Context: A Workbook for American History.* Written by historical cartography expert Gerald A. Danzer (University of Illinois at Chicago), this skill-building workbook helps students comprehend essential connections between geographic literacy and historical understanding. Organized to correspond to the typical U.S. history survey course, *Maps in Context* presents a wealth of map-centered projects and convenient pop quizzes that give students hands-on experience working with maps. Available free when packaged with the print text.

▶ *The Bedford Glossary for U.S. History.* This handy supplement for the survey course gives students historically contextualized definitions for hundreds of terms—from *abolitionism* to *zoot suit*—that they will encounter in lectures, reading, and exams. Available free when packaged with the print text.

▶ *U.S. History Matters: A Student Guide to World History Online.* This resource, written by Alan Gevinson, Kelly Schrum, and the late Roy Rosenzweig (all of George Mason University), provides an illustrated and annotated guide to 250 of the most useful Web sites for student research in U.S. history as well as advice on evaluating and using Internet sources. This essential guide is based on the acclaimed "History Matters" Web site developed by the American Social History Project and the Center for History and New Media. Available free when packaged with the print text.

▶ **Trade Books.** Titles published by sister companies Hill and Wang; Farrar, Straus and Giroux; Henry Holt and Company; St. Martin's Press; Picador; and Palgrave Macmillan are available at a 50% discount when packaged with Bedford/St. Martin's textbooks. For more information, visit **bedfordstmartins.com/tradeup.**

▶ *A Pocket Guide to Writing in History.* This portable and affordable reference tool by Mary Lynn Rampolla provides reading, writing, and research advice useful to students in all history courses. Concise yet comprehensive advice on approaching typical history assignments, developing critical reading skills, writing effective history papers, conducting research, using and documenting sources, and avoiding plagiarism—enhanced with practical tips and examples throughout—have made this slim reference a best seller. Package discounts are available.

▶ *A Student's Guide to History.* This complete guide to success in any history course provides the practical help students need to be effective. In addition to introducing students to the nature of the discipline, author Jules Benjamin teaches a wide range of skills, from preparing for exams to approaching common writing assignments, and explains the research and documentation process with plentiful examples. Package discounts are available.

▶ *Going to the Source: The Bedford Reader in American History.* Developed by Victoria Bissell Brown and Timothy J. Shannon, this reader's strong pedagogical framework helps students learn how to ask fruitful questions in order to evaluate documents effectively and develop critical reading skills. The reader's wide variety of chapter topics that complement the survey course and its rich diversity of sources—from personal letters to political cartoons—provoke students' interest as it teaches them the skills they need to successfully interrogate historical sources. Package discounts are available.

▶ *America Firsthand.* With its distinctive focus on ordinary people, this primary documents reader, by Anthony Marcus, John M. Giggie, and David Burner, offers a remarkable range of perspectives on America's history from those who lived it. Popular Points of View sections expose students to different perspectives on a specific event or topic, and Visual Portfolios invite analysis of the visual record. Package discounts are available.

BRIEF CONTENTS

CONTENTS

1 UNDERSTANDING ANCIENT AMERICA

BEFORE 1492 *2*

2 EUROPEANS ENCOUNTER THE NEW WORLD

1492–1600 *28*

15

THE CRUCIBLE OF WAR

1861–1865 *422*

16

RECONSTRUCTING A NATION

1863–1877 *456*

✔ **LearningCurve**
bedfordstmartins.com/roarkunderstanding

✔ **LearningCurve**
bedfordstmartins.com/roarkunderstanding

MAPS, FIGURES, AND TABLES

How to use this book to figure out what's really important

The **chapter title** tells you the subject of the chapter and identifies the time span that will be covered.

The **opening question** and **chapter introduction** identify the most important themes, events, and people that will be explored in the chapter.

16
RECONSTRUCTING A NATION

1863–1877

> **What were the achievements and failures of reconstruction?** Chapter 16 explores the era of reconstruction, in which the nation struggled to define the defeated South's status and the meaning of freedom for ex-slaves. Following the Civil War, the nation entered one of its most confused and violent periods as victorious Northerners, defeated white Southerners, and newly freed African Americans battled to shape the postwar South.

 **LearningCurve**
bedfordstmartins.com/roarkunderstanding
After reading the chapter, use LearningCurve to retain what you've read.

Memorizing facts and dates for a history class won't get you very far. That's because history isn't just about "facts." This textbook is designed to help you focus on what's truly significant in U.S. history and to give you practice in thinking like a historian.

Voting day, June 5, 1867. Black freedmen line up to vote in Washington, D.C. The Granger Collection, New York.

> Why did Congress object to Lincoln's wartime plan for reconstruction?

> How did the North respond to the passage of black codes in the southern states?

> How radical was congressional reconstruction?

> What brought the elements of the South's Republican coalition together?

> Why did reconstruction collapse?

> Conclusion: Was reconstruction "a revolution but half accomplished"?

The **chapter-opening questions** are also the questions that open each new section of the chapter and will be addressed in turn on the following pages. You should think about answers to these as you read.

Each section has tools that help you focus on what's important.

The **question in red** asks about the specific topic being discussed in this section. Think about the answer to this question as you read the section.

> ## How did the North respond to the passage of black codes in the southern states?

The Black Codes

Titled "Selling a Freeman to Pay His Fine at Monticello, Florida," this 1867 drawing from a northern magazine equates black codes with the institution of slavery. The ascension of Andrew Johnson to the presidency emboldered many southern states to pass laws severely restricting blacks' freedom. Granger Collection.

ABRAHAM LINCOLN DIED on April 15, 1865, just hours after John Wilkes Booth shot him at a Washington, D.C., theater. Chief Justice Salmon P. Chase immediately administered the oath of office to Vice President Andrew Johnson of Tennessee. Congress had adjourned in March and would not reconvene until December. Throughout the summer and fall, Johnson drew up and executed a plan of reconstruction without congressional advice.

Congress returned to the capital in December to find that, as far as the president and former Confederates were concerned, reconstruction was completed. Most Republicans, however, thought Johnson's plan made far too few demands of ex-rebels. They claimed that Johnson's leniency had acted as midwife to the rebirth of the Old South, that he had achieved political reunification at the cost of black freedom. Republicans in Congress then proceeded to dismantle Johnson's program and substitute a program of their own.

Johnson's Program of Reconciliation

Born in 1808 in Raleigh, North Carolina, Andrew Johnson was the son of illiterate parents. Self-educated and ambitious, Johnson moved to Tennessee, where he built a career in politics championing the South's common white people and assailing its "illegitimate, swaggering, bastard, scrub aristocracy." The only senator from a Confederate state to remain loyal to the Union, Johnson held the planter class responsible for secession.

A Democrat all his life, Johnson occupied the White House only because the Republican Party in 1864 had needed a vice presidential candidate who would

CHAPTER LOCATOR | Why did Congress object to Lincoln's wartime plan for reconstruction? | **How did the North respond to the passage of black codes in the southern states?**

462 CHAPTER 16 RECONSTRUCTING A NATION

The **chapter locator** at the bottom of the page puts this section in the context of the chapter as a whole, so you can see how this section relates to what's coming next.

peal to loyal, Union-supporting Democrats. Johnson vigorously defended states'
ights (but not secession) and opposed Republican efforts to expand the power of
e federal government. A steadfast supporter of slavery, Johnson had owned
ves until 1862, when Tennessee rebels, angry at his Unionism, confiscated
m. When he grudgingly accepted emancipation, it was more because he hated
nters than because he sympathized with slaves. "Damn the negroes," he said.
am fighting those traitorous aristocrats, their masters." The new president har-
ed unshakable racist convictions. Africans, Johnson said, were "inferior to the
ite man in point of intellect — better calculated in physical structure to
dergo drudgery and hardship."

Like Lincoln, Johnson stressed the rapid restoration of civil government in the
uth. Like Lincoln, he promised to pardon most, but not all, ex-rebels. Johnson
ognized the state governments created by Lincoln but set out his own require-
nts for restoring the other rebel states to the Union.

Republican senator Lyman Trumbull of Illinois declared that the president's
icy meant that an ex-slave would "be tyrannized over, abused, and virtually
nslaved without some legislation by the nation for his protection." Early in
66, the moderates produced two bills that strengthened the federal shield. The
t, the Freedmen's Bureau bill, prolonged the life of the agency established by
previous Congress. Arguing that the Constitution never contemplated a
stem for the support of indigent persons," President Andrew Johnson vetoed
bill. Congress failed by a narrow margin to override the president's veto.

The moderates designed their second measure, what would become the
vil Rights Act of 1866, to nullify the black codes by affirming African
ericans' rights to "full and equal benefit of all laws and proceedings for the
urity of person and property as is enjoyed by white citizens." The act required
end of racial discrimination in state laws and represented an extraordinary
ansion of black rights and federal authority. The president argued that the civil
nts bill amounted to "unconstitutional invasion of states' rights" and vetoed it.

In April 1866, an incensed Republican Party again pushed the civil rights bill
ough Congress and overrode the presidential veto. In July, it passed another
edmen's Bureau bill and overrode Johnson's veto. For the first time in American
tory, Congress had overridden presidential vetoes of major legislation. As a wor-
d South Carolinian observed, Johnson had succeeded in uniting the Republicans
probably touched off "a fight this fall such as has never been seen."

> CHRONOLOGY

1865
– Lincoln is assassinated;
  Andrew Johnson becomes
  president.
– Black codes are enacted.
– Thirteenth Amendment
  becomes part of Constitution.

1866
– Civil Rights Act.

Chronologies for each
major section show
the sequence of
events and underlying
developments in the
section.

Civil Rights Act of 1866
▶ Legislation passed by
Congress in 1866 that nullified
the black codes and affirmed
that black Americans should
have equal benefit of the law.
President Andrew Johnson
vetoed this expansion of black
rights and federal authority, but
Congress later overrode his veto.

Key terms in the margins
give you background on
important ideas and events.
Use these for reference
while you read, but also
think about which are
emphasized and why they
matter.

QUICK REVIEW <

When the southern states passed the black
codes, how did the U.S. Congress respond?

The **quick review**
helps you check
your recall of the
section before you
resume reading.

 LearningCurve
Check what you know.
bedfordstmartins.com
/roarkunderstanding

463

The Chapter Study Guide provides a process that will build your understanding and your historical skills.

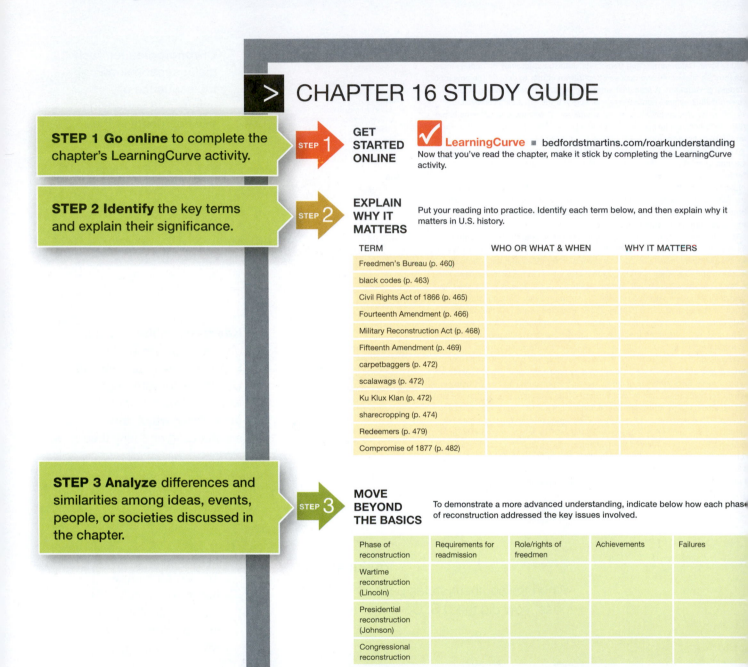

STEP 1 Go online to complete the chapter's LearningCurve activity.

STEP 2 Identify the key terms and explain their significance.

STEP 3 Analyze differences and similarities among ideas, events, people, or societies discussed in the chapter.

> CHAPTER 16 STUDY GUIDE

STEP 1

GET STARTED ONLINE

✓ **LearningCurve** ■ bedfordstmartins.com/roarkunderstanding
Now that you've read the chapter, make it stick by completing the LearningCurve activity.

STEP 2

EXPLAIN WHY IT MATTERS

Put your reading into practice. Identify each term below, and then explain why it matters in U.S. history.

TERM	WHO OR WHAT & WHEN	WHY IT MATTERS
Freedmen's Bureau (p. 460)		
black codes (p. 463)		
Civil Rights Act of 1866 (p. 465)		
Fourteenth Amendment (p. 466)		
Military Reconstruction Act (p. 468)		
Fifteenth Amendment (p. 469)		
carpetbaggers (p. 472)		
scalawags (p. 472)		
Ku Klux Klan (p. 472)		
sharecropping (p. 474)		
Redeemers (p. 479)		
Compromise of 1877 (p. 482)		

STEP 3

MOVE BEYOND THE BASICS

To demonstrate a more advanced understanding, indicate below how each phase of reconstruction addressed the key issues involved.

Phase of reconstruction	Requirements for readmission	Role/rights of freedmen	Achievements	Failures
Wartime reconstruction (Lincoln)				
Presidential reconstruction (Johnson)				
Congressional reconstruction				

484

STEP 4 PUT IT ALL TOGETHER Now, take a step back and try to explain the big picture. Remember to use specific examples from the chapter in your answers.

STEP 4 Answer the big-picture questions using specific examples or evidence from the chapter.

PRESIDENTIAL AND CONGRESSIONAL RECONSTRUCTION

► What role did the black codes play in shaping the course of reconstruction?

► What steps did Congress take between 1865 and 1869 to assist ex-slaves in their lives as freedmen? How effective were these actions?

SOUTHERN RECONSTRUCTION IN ACTION

► How did white Southerners respond during reconstruction? Consider both Democrats and Republicans in your response.

► How did southern African Americans attempt to shape their own lives during reconstruction?

THE END OF RECONSTRUCTION

► How and why did the decline of northern support for reconstruction help southern Democrats "redeem" the South?

► Why did white supremacy become the foundation of southern politics in the 1870s?

LOOKING BACKWARD, LOOKING AHEAD

► How did long-held racial views among whites, in both the South and the North, shape reconstruction?

► What were the lasting accomplishments of reconstruction? What were its most important failures?

> **IN YOUR OWN WORDS** Imagine that you must give an oral report to the class answering the following question: **What were the achievements and failures of reconstruction?** What would be the most important points to include and why?

ACTIVE RECITATION Explain how you would answer the chapter-opening question in your own words to make sure you have a firm grasp of the most important themes and events of the chapter.

> **Do it online at the Student Site** ■ bedfordstmartins.com/roarkunderstanding

Visit the FREE Student Site at **bedfordstmartins.com /roarkunderstanding** to do these steps online.

Understanding
the
American Promise

A HISTORY

1

UNDERSTANDING ANCIENT AMERICA

BEFORE 1492

> **How did ancient North American peoples shape the history of the continent before the arrival of Europeans in 1492?** Chapter 1 charts the history of Native American peoples from their migration out of Asia to the eve of European contact. It explores the development of distinct Native American cultures, as well as their shared characteristics.

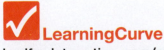

LearningCurve

bedfordstmartins.com/roarkunderstanding
After reading the chapter, use LearningCurve to
retain what you've read.

The Great Tenochtitlán. **Detail of the 1945 fresco by Mexican artist Diego Rivera. Charles and Josette Lenaris/Corbis.**

> When and why do historians rely on the work of archaeologists?

> How and why did humans migrate into North America?

> Why did Archaic Native Americans shift to foraging and hunting smaller animals?

> How did agriculture influence Native American cultures?

> What cultural similarities did native peoples of the Western Hemisphere share in the 1490s?

> Why was tribute important in the Mexican empire?

> Conclusion: How do we understand the worlds of ancient Americans?

> When and why do historians rely on the work of archaeologists?

Mississippian Wooden Mask

Sometime between AD 1200 and 1350, a Native American among the Mississippian people in what is now central Illinois fashioned this mask from red cedar. Influenced by the culture of Cahokia, the mask was probably used in rituals to depict the face of both worldly and supernatural power. The haunting visage evokes the long history of ancient Americans and their impressive achievements. Mask photograph: © 2002 John Bigelow Taylor, www.johnbigelowtaylor .com. Illinois State Museum, Springfield, Cat. No. 273.

> KEY FACTORS

Archaeologists
– Focus on physical objects such as bones, spear points, and pottery.

Historians
– Tend to focus more on written records.

ARCHAEOLOGISTS AND HISTORIANS share the desire to learn about people who lived in the past, but they usually employ different methods to obtain information. Both archaeologists and historians study artifacts as clues to the activities and ideas of the humans who created them. They concentrate, however, on different kinds of artifacts.

CHAPTER LOCATOR | When and why do historians rely on the work of archaeologists? | How and why did humans migrate into North America?

Artifacts That Archaeologists Study	Artifacts That Historians Study
bones	letters
spear points	diaries
pots	laws
baskets	speeches
jewelry/clothing	newspapers
buildings	court cases

The characteristic concentration of historians on writings and of archaeologists on other physical objects denotes a rough cultural and chronological boundary between the human beings studied by the two groups of scholars, a boundary marked by the use of writing.

Writing is defined as a system of symbols that record spoken language. Writing originated among ancient peoples in China, Egypt, and Central America about eight thousand years ago, within the most recent 2 percent of the four hundred millennia that modern human beings have existed. While those who inhabited North America in 1492 possessed many forms of symbolic representation, they did not use writing. Much of what we would like to know about their experiences and those of other ancient Americans remains unknown because they did not write about it.

Archaeologists specialize in learning about people who did not document their history in writing. They study the millions of artifacts these people created. They also scrutinize geological strata, pollen, and other environmental features to reconstruct as much as possible about the world inhabited by ancient peoples. This chapter relies on studies by archaeologists to sketch a brief overview of ancient America, the long first phase of the history of the United States.

Ancient Americans and their descendants resided in North America for thousands of years before Europeans arrived. While they created societies and cultures of remarkable diversity and complexity, their history cannot be reconstructed with the detail and certainty made possible by writing.

QUICK REVIEW <

Why must historians rely on the work of archaeologists to write the history of ancient America?

Why did Archaic Native Americans shift to foraging and hunting smaller animals?

How did agriculture influence Native American cultures?

What cultural similarities did native peoples of the Western Hemisphere share in the 1490s?

Why was tribute important in the Mexican empire?

Conclusion: How do we understand the worlds of ancient Americans?

LearningCurve
Check what you know.
bedfordstmartins.com
/roarkunderstanding

How and why did humans migrate into North America?

Clovis Spear Straightener

Clovis hunters used this bone spear straightener about 11,000 BP at a campsite in Arizona. Presumably, Clovis hunters stuck their spear shafts through the opening and then grasped the handle of the straightener and moved it back and forth along the length of the shaft to remove imperfections and to make the spear a more effective weapon. Arizona State Museum, University of Arizona.

> CHRONOLOGY

ca. 400,000 BP
– *Homo sapiens* evolve in Africa.

ca. 25,000–14,000 BP
– Glaciation exposes the Beringian land bridge.

ca. 15,000 BP
– Humans arrive in North America.

ca. 13,500–13,000 BP
– Paleo-Indians use Clovis points.

ca. 11,000 BP
– Mammoths become extinct.

NOTE: *BP* is an abbreviation used by archaeologists for "years before the present."

THE FIRST HUMAN BEINGS to arrive in the Western Hemisphere emigrated from Asia. They brought with them hunting skills, weapon- and tool-making techniques, and other forms of human knowledge developed millennia earlier in Africa, Europe, and Asia. These first Americans hunted large mammals, such as the mammoths they had learned in Europe and Asia to kill, butcher, and process for food, clothing, and building materials. Most likely, these first Americans wandered into the Western Hemisphere more or less accidentally in pursuit of prey.

African and Asian Origins

Human beings lived elsewhere in the world for hundreds of thousands of years before they reached the Western Hemisphere. They lacked a way to travel to the Western Hemisphere because millions of years before humans existed anywhere on the globe, North and South America became detached from the gigantic common landmass scientists now call Pangaea. About 240 million years ago, powerful forces deep within the earth fractured Pangaea and slowly pushed continents apart to their present positions (**Map 1.1**). This process of continental drift encircled the land of the Western Hemisphere with large oceans that isolated it from the other continents long before early human beings (*Homo erectus*) first appeared in Africa about two million years ago.

More than 1.5 million years after *Homo erectus* appeared, or about 400,000 BP, modern humans (*Homo sapiens*) evolved in Africa. All human beings throughout the world today are descendants of these ancient Africans. Slowly, over many millennia, *Homo sapiens* migrated out of Africa and into Europe and Asia, which had retained land connections to Africa, allowing ancient humans to migrate on foot. For roughly

CHAPTER LOCATOR | When and why do historians rely on the work of archaeologists? | **How and why did humans migrate into North America?**

6 CHAPTER 1 UNDERSTANDING ANCIENT AMERICA

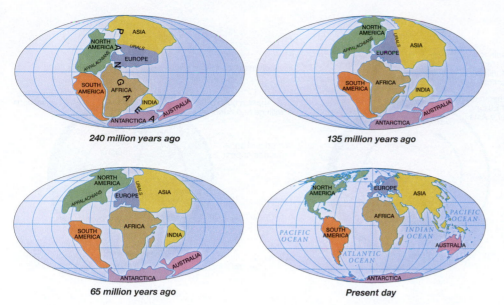

240 million years ago

135 million years ago

65 million years ago

Present day

MAP 1.1 ■ Continental Drift

Massive geological forces separated North and South America from other continents eons before human beings evolved in Africa 1.5 million years ago.

> **MAP ACTIVITY**

READING THE MAP: Which continents separated from Pangaea earliest? Which ones separated from each other last? Which are still closely connected to each other?

97 percent of the time *Homo sapiens* have been on earth, none migrated across the enormous oceans isolating North and South America from the Eurasian landmass.

Two major developments made it possible for ancient humans to migrate to the Western Hemisphere. First, people successfully adapted to the frigid environment near the Arctic Circle. Second, changes in the earth's climate reconnected North America to Asia.

By about 25,000 BP, *Homo sapiens* had spread from Africa throughout Europe and Asia. People, probably women, had learned to use bone needles to sew animal skins into warm clothing that permitted them to become permanent residents of extremely cold regions such as northeastern Siberia. A few of these ancient Siberians clothed in animal hides walked to North America on land that now lies submerged beneath the sixty miles of water that currently separate easternmost Siberia from westernmost Alaska. A pathway across this watery chasm opened during the last global cold spell—which endured from about 25,000 BP to 14,000 BP—when the sea level dropped and exposed a land bridge hundreds of miles wide called **Beringia** that connected Asian Siberia and American Alaska.

Siberian hunters roamed Beringia for centuries in search of mammoths, bison, and numerous smaller animals. As the hunters ventured farther and farther east, they eventually became pioneers of human life in the Western Hemisphere. Although they did not know it, their migrations revolutionized the history of the world.

Archaeologists refer to these first migrants and their descendants for the next few millennia as **Paleo-Indians**. They speculate that these Siberian

Beringia

Beringia
▶ The land bridge between Siberia and Alaska that was exposed by glaciation, allowing people to migrate into the Western Hemisphere.

Paleo-Indians
▶ Archaeologists' term for the first migrants into North America and their descendants who spread across the Americas between approximately 15,000 BP and 13,500 BP.

| Why did Archaic Native Americans shift to foraging and hunting smaller animals? | How did agriculture influence Native American cultures? | What cultural similarities did native peoples of the Western Hemisphere share in the 1490s? | Why was tribute important in the Mexican empire? | Conclusion: How do we understand the worlds of ancient Americans? | ✔ **LearningCurve** Check what you know. bedfordstmartins.com /roarkunderstanding |

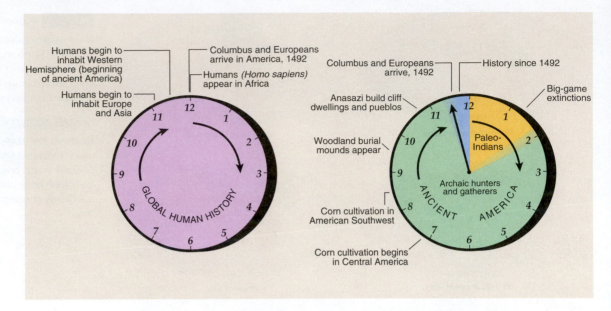

FIGURE 1.1 ■ Human Habitation of the World and the Western Hemisphere
These clock faces illustrate the long global history of modern humans (left) and of human history in the Western Hemisphere since the arrival of the first ancient Americans (right).

hunters traveled in small bands of no more than twenty-five people. How many such bands arrived in North America before Beringia disappeared beneath the sea will never be known.

When the first migrants came is hotly debated by experts. They probably arrived sometime after 15,000 BP. Scattered and inconclusive evidence suggests that they may have arrived several thousand years earlier. Certainly, humans who came from Asia—whose ancestors left Africa hundreds of thousands of years earlier—inhabited the Western Hemisphere by 14,000 BP.

Paleo-Indian Hunters

When humans first arrived in the Western Hemisphere, massive glaciers covered most of present-day Canada. Many archaeologists believe that Paleo-Indians probably migrated along an ice-free passageway on the eastern side of Canada's Rocky Mountains in pursuit of game. Other Paleo-Indians may have traveled along the Pacific coast in small boats, hunting marine life and hopscotching from one desirable landing spot to another. At the southern edge of the glaciers, Paleo-Indians entered a hunters' paradise teeming with wildlife that had never before confronted human predators armed with razor-sharp spears. The abundance of game presumably made hunting relatively easy. Ample food permitted the Paleo-Indian population to grow. Within a thousand years or so, Paleo-Indians had migrated throughout the Western Hemisphere.

Early Paleo-Indians used a distinctively shaped spearhead known as a **Clovis point**, named for the place in New Mexico where it was first excavated. Archaeologists' discovery of abundant Clovis points throughout North and Central America in sites occupied between 13,500 BP and 13,000 BP provides evidence that these nomadic

Clovis points
▶ Distinctively shaped spearheads used by Paleo-Indians and named for the place in New Mexico where they were first excavated.

CHAPTER LOCATOR | When and why do historians rely on the work of archaeologists? | **How and why did humans migrate into North America?**

CHAPTER 1
8 UNDERSTANDING ANCIENT AMERICA

hunters shared a common ancestry and way of life. At a few isolated sites, archaeologists have found still-controversial evidence of pre-Clovis artifacts that suggest the people who used Clovis spear points may have been preceded by several hundred years by a few non-Clovis pioneers. Paleo-Indians hunted mammoths and bison, but they probably also killed smaller animals. Concentration on large animals, when possible, made sense because just one mammoth could supply meat for months. In addition, mammoths provided Paleo-Indians with hides and bones for clothing, shelter, tools, and much more.

About 11,000 BP, Paleo-Indians confronted a major crisis. The mammoths and other large mammals they hunted became extinct. The extinction was gradual, stretching over several hundred years. Scientists are not completely certain why it occurred, although environmental change probably contributed to it. About this time, the earth's climate warmed, glaciers melted, and sea levels rose. Mammoths and other large mammals probably had difficulty adapting to the warmer climate. Many archaeologists also believe, however, that Paleo-Indians probably contributed to the extinctions in the Western Hemisphere by killing large animals more rapidly than they could reproduce. Whatever the causes, after the extinction of large mammals, Paleo-Indians literally inhabited a new world.

Paleo-Indians adapted to this drastic environmental change by making at least two important changes in their way of life. First, hunters began to prey more intensively on smaller animals. Second, Paleo-Indians devoted more energy to foraging—that is, to collecting wild plant foods such as roots, seeds, nuts, berries, and fruits. When Paleo-Indians made these changes, they replaced the apparent uniformity of the big-game-oriented Clovis culture with great cultural diversity adapted to the many natural environments throughout the hemisphere.

These post-Clovis adaptations to local environments resulted in the astounding variety of Native American cultures that existed when Europeans arrived in AD 1492. By then, more than three hundred major tribes and hundreds of lesser groups inhabited North America alone. Hundreds more lived in Central and South America. Hundreds of other ancient American cultures had disappeared or transformed as their people constantly adapted to environmental and other challenges.

QUICK REVIEW <

Why and how did Paleo-Indians adapt to environmental change?

| Why did Archaic Native Americans shift to foraging and hunting smaller animals? | How did agriculture influence Native American cultures? | What cultural similarities did native peoples of the Western Hemisphere share in the 1490s? | Why was tribute important in the Mexican empire? | Conclusion: How do we understand the worlds of ancient Americans? | LearningCurve Check what you know. bedfordstmartins.com /roarkunderstanding |

> Why did Archaic Native Americans shift to foraging and hunting smaller animals?

Folsom Point at Wild Horse Arroyo

In 1927, paleontologist J. D. Figgins found this spear point embedded between the fossilized ribs of a bison that had been extinct for ten thousand years. Subsequently named the Folsom point, this discovery stimulated archaeologists to rethink the history of ancient Americans and to uncover fresh evidence of their many cultures.

hunter-gatherer

▶ A way of life that involved hunting game and gathering food from naturally occurring sources, as opposed to engaging in agriculture and animal husbandry. Archaic Indians and their descendants survived in North America for centuries as hunter-gatherers.

Archaic Indians

▶ Hunting and gathering peoples who descended from Paleo-Indians and dominated the Americas from 10,000 BP to between 4000 and 3000 BP.

ARCHAEOLOGISTS use the term *Archaic* to describe the many different hunting and gathering cultures that descended from Paleo-Indians and the long period of time when those cultures dominated the history of ancient America—roughly from 10,000 BP to somewhere between 4000 BP and 3000 BP. The term describes the era in the history of ancient America that followed the Paleo-Indian big-game hunters and preceded the development of agriculture. It denotes a **hunter-gatherer** way of life that persisted in North America long after European colonization.

Like their Paleo-Indian ancestors, **Archaic Indians** hunted with spears, but they also took smaller game with traps, nets, and hooks. Unlike their Paleo-Indian predecessors, most Archaic peoples prepared food from wild plants by using a variety of stone tools. A characteristic Archaic artifact is a grinding stone used to pulverize seeds into edible form. Most Archaic Indians migrated from place to place to harvest plants and hunt animals. They usually did not establish permanent villages, although they often returned to the same river valley or fertile meadow year after year. In regions with especially rich resources—such as present-day California and the Pacific Northwest—they developed permanent settlements. Archaic peoples followed these practices in distinctive ways in the different environmental regions of North America (**Map 1.2**).

CHAPTER LOCATOR | When and why do historians rely on the work of archaeologists? | How and why did humans migrate into North America?

MAP 1.2 ■ Native North American Cultures

Environmental conditions defined the boundaries of the broad zones of cultural similarity among ancient North Americans.

> MAP ACTIVITY

READING THE MAP: What crucial environmental features set the boundaries of each cultural region? (The topography indicated on Map 1.3, "Native North Americans about 1500," may be helpful.)

CONNECTIONS: How did environmental factors and variations affect the development of different groups of Native American cultures? Why do you think historians and archaeologists group cultures together by their regional positions?

| **Why did Archaic Native Americans shift to foraging and hunting smaller animals?** | How did agriculture influence Native American cultures? | What cultural similarities did native peoples of the Western Hemisphere share in the 1490s? | Why was tribute important in the Mexican empire? | Conclusion: How do we understand the worlds of ancient Americans? | ✓ LearningCurve Check what you know. bedfordstmartins.com /roarkunderstanding |

> CHRONOLOGY

ca. 10,000–3000 BP
– Archaic hunter-gatherer cultures dominate ancient America.

ca. 5000 BP
– Chumash culture emerges in southern California.

ca. 4000 BP
– Eastern Woodland peoples practice agriculture and make pottery.

ca. 2500 BP
– Eastern Woodland cultures cultivate corn.

ca. AD 500
– Great Plains hunters begin to use bows and arrows.

Ancient California Peoples

Great Plains Bison Hunters

After the extinction of large game animals, some hunters began to concentrate on bison in the huge herds that grazed the plains stretching hundreds of miles east of the Rocky Mountains. For almost a thousand years after the big-game extinctions, Archaic Indians hunted bison with Folsom points, named after a site near Folsom, New Mexico. Like their nomadic predecessors, Folsom hunters moved constantly to maintain contact with their prey. Great Plains hunters often stampeded bison herds over cliffs and then slaughtered the animals that plunged to their deaths.

Bows and arrows reached Great Plains hunters from the north about AD 500. They largely replaced spears, which had been the hunters' weapons of choice for millennia. Bows permitted hunters to wound animals from farther away, arrows made it possible to shoot repeatedly, and arrowheads were easier to make and therefore less costly to lose than the larger, heavier spear points. Great Plains people hunted on foot. After Europeans imported horses in the decades after 1492, Great Plains bison hunters acquired them and soon became expert riders.

Great Basin Cultures

Archaic peoples in the Great Basin between the Rocky Mountains and the Sierra Nevada inhabited a region of great environmental diversity defined largely by the amount of rain. While some lived on the shores of lakes and marshes fed by the rain and ate fish, others hunted deer, antelope, bison, and smaller game. To protect against shortages in fish and game caused by the fickle rainfall, Great Basin Indians relied on plants as their most important food. Unlike meat and fish, plant food could be collected and stored for long periods. Many Great Basin peoples gathered piñon nuts as a dietary staple. Great Basin peoples adapted to the severe environmental challenges of the region and maintained their Archaic hunter-gatherer way of life for centuries after Europeans arrived in AD 1492.

Pacific Coast Cultures

The richness of the natural environment made present-day California the most densely settled area in all of ancient North America. The land and ocean offered such ample food that California peoples remained hunters and gatherers for hundreds of years after AD 1492. The diversity of California's environment also encouraged corresponding variety among native peoples. The mosaic of Archaic settlements in California included about five hundred separate tribes speaking some ninety languages, each with local dialects.

The Chumash, one of the many California cultures, emerged in the region surrounding what is now Santa Barbara about 5000 BP. Comparatively plentiful food resources — especially acorns — permitted Chumash people to establish relatively permanent villages. Although few other California cultures achieved the population density and village settlements of the Chumash, all shared the hunter-gatherer way of life and reliance on acorns as a major food source.

Another rich natural environment lay along the Pacific Northwest coast. Like the Chumash, Northwest peoples built more or less permanent villages. After about

CHAPTER LOCATOR | When and why do historians rely on the work of archaeologists? | How and why did humans migrate into North America?

5500 BP, they concentrated on catching whales and large quantities of salmon, halibut, and other fish, which they dried to last throughout the year. They also traded with people who lived hundreds of miles from the coast. Fishing freed Northwest peoples to develop sophisticated woodworking skills. They fashioned elaborate wood carvings that denoted wealth and status, as well as huge canoes for fishing, hunting, and conducting warfare against neighboring tribes.

Ozette Whale Effigy

This carving of a whale fin decorated with hundreds of sea otter teeth was discovered along with thousands of other artifacts of daily life at Ozette, an ancient village on the tip of the Olympic Peninsula in present-day Washington that was inundated by a catastrophic mud slide about five hundred years ago. The fin illustrates the importance of whale hunting to the residents of Ozette. Richard Alexander Cooke III.

Eastern Woodland Cultures

East of the Mississippi River, Archaic peoples adapted to a forest environment that included the major river valleys of the Mississippi, Ohio, Tennessee, and Cumberland; the Great Lakes region; and the Atlantic coast (see Map 1.2). Throughout these diverse locales, Archaic peoples pursued similar survival strategies.

Woodland hunters stalked deer as their most important prey. Deer supplied Woodland peoples with food as well as hides and bones that they crafted into clothing, weapons, and many other tools. Like Archaic peoples elsewhere, Woodland Indians gathered edible plants, seeds, and nuts. About 6000 BP, some Woodland groups established more or less permanent settlements of 25 to 150 people, usually near a river or lake that offered a wide variety of plant and animal resources. Woodland burial sites suggest that life expectancy was about eighteen years, a relatively short time to learn all the skills necessary to survive, reproduce, and adapt to change.

Around 4000 BP, Woodland cultures added two important features to their basic hunter-gatherer lifestyles: agriculture and pottery. Trade and migration from Mexico brought gourds and pumpkins to Woodland peoples, who also began to cultivate sunflowers and small quantities of tobacco. Corn, which had been grown in Mexico and South America since about 7000 BP, also traveled north and became a significant food crop among Eastern Woodland peoples around 2500 BP. Most likely, women learned how to plant, grow, and harvest these crops as an outgrowth of their work gathering edible wild plants. Cultivated crops did not alter Woodland peoples' dependence on gathering wild plants, seeds, and nuts.

Like agriculture, pottery probably originated in Mexico. Pots were more durable than baskets for cooking and the storage of food and water, but they were also much heavier and therefore were shunned by nomadic peoples. The permanent settlements of Woodland peoples made the heavy weight of pots much less important than their advantages compared to leaky and fragile baskets. While pottery and agriculture introduced changes in Woodland cultures, ancient Woodland Americans retained the other basic features of their Archaic hunter-gatherer lifestyle until 1492 and beyond.

Why did Archaic Native Americans shift to foraging and hunting smaller animals?

How did agriculture influence Native American cultures?

What cultural similarities did native peoples of the Western Hemisphere share in the 1490s?

Why was tribute important in the Mexican empire?

Conclusion: How do we understand the worlds of ancient Americans?

✓ LearningCurve
Check what you know.
bedfordstmartins.com
/roarkunderstanding

13

TABLE 1.1 ■ Archaic Indians at a Glance

Great Plains Bison Hunters	
Where they lived	East of the Rocky Mountains, in present-day eastern Colorado, northeastern New Mexico, North Dakota, South Dakota, Nebraska, Kansas, Oklahoma, Texas, Minnesota, Iowa, Missouri, Wisconsin, Michigan, Illinois, Indiana, and southwestern Canada
Lifestyle	Nomadic
How they acquired food	Hunting
What they ate	Bison
Technological developments	Acquired bow and arrow from the north; after Europeans' arrival, used horses to hunt
Great Basin Cultures	
Where they lived	Between the Rocky Mountains and the Sierra Nevada, present-day eastern California, Nevada, Idaho, Utah, Arizona, New Mexico, and Colorado
Lifestyle	Nomadic
How they acquired food	Fishing, hunting, and gathering
What they ate	Fish, deer, antelope, bison, smaller game, plants, and piñon nuts
Technological developments	None
Pacific Coast Cultures: Chumash and Northwest Peoples	
Where they lived	Chumash: around present-day Santa Barbara, California; Northwest peoples: present-day northern California, Oregon, Washington, and the west coast of Canada
Lifestyle	Village settlements
How they acquired food	Chumash: hunting and gathering; Northwest peoples: fishing
What they ate	Chumash: acorns; Northwest peoples: salmon, halibut, and other fish
Technological developments	Northwest peoples: elaborate wood carvings that denoted wealth and status; huge canoes for fishing, hunting, and conducting warfare against neighboring tribes
Eastern Woodland Cultures	
Where they lived	East of the Mississippi River, in the major river valleys of the Mississippi, Ohio, Tennessee, and Cumberland; the Great Lakes region; and the Atlantic coast
Lifestyle	Permanent settlements
How they acquired food	Hunting and gathering
What they ate	Deer, plants, seeds, and nuts
Technological developments	Agriculture and pottery

> ## QUICK REVIEW

Why did Archaic Indians shift from big-game hunting to foraging and smaller-game hunting?

CHAPTER LOCATOR | When and why do historians rely on the work of archaeologists? | How and why did humans migrate into North America?

Pueblo Bonito, Chaco Canyon, New Mexico About AD 1000, Pueblo Bonito stood at the center of Chacoan culture, which extended over more than 20,000 square miles in the region at the intersection of present-day Utah, Colorado, Arizona, and New Mexico. The numerous circular kivas show the significance of ceremonies and rituals to the people of Chaco Canyon. Richard Alexander Cooke III.

AMONG EASTERN WOODLAND PEOPLES and most other Archaic cultures, agriculture supplemented hunter-gatherer subsistence strategies but did not replace them. Reliance on wild animals and plants required most Archaic groups to remain small and mobile. But beginning about 4000 BP, distinctive southwestern cultures began to depend on agriculture and to build permanent settlements. Later, around 2500 BP, Woodland peoples in the vast Mississippi valley began to construct burial mounds and other earthworks that suggest the existence of social and political hierarchies that archaeologists term *chiefdoms*. Although the hunter-gatherer lifestyle never entirely disappeared, the development of agricultural settlements and chiefdoms represented important innovations to the Archaic way of life.

Southwestern Cultures

Ancient Americans in present-day Arizona, New Mexico, and southern portions of Utah and Colorado developed cultures characterized by agricultural settlements and multiunit dwellings called **pueblos**. All southwestern peoples confronted the challenge of a dry climate and unpredictable fluctuations in rainfall that made the supply of wild plant food very unreliable. These ancient Americans probably adopted agriculture in response to this basic environmental uncertainty.

About 3500 BP, southwestern hunters and gatherers began to cultivate corn, their signature food crop. The demands of corn cultivation encouraged hunter-gatherers to restrict their migratory habits in order to tend the crop. A vital consideration was access to water. Southwestern Indians became irrigation experts, conserving water from streams, springs, and rainfall and distributing it to thirsty crops.

pueblos

▶ Multiunit dwellings, storage spaces, and ceremonial centers — often termed *kivas* — built by ancient Americans in the Southwest for centuries, starting around AD 1000.

| Why did Archaic Native Americans shift to foraging and hunting smaller animals? | **How did agriculture influence Native American cultures?** | What cultural similarities did native peoples of the Western Hemisphere share in the 1490s? | Why was tribute important in the Mexican empire? | Conclusion: How do we understand the worlds of ancient Americans? | ✓ LearningCurve Check what you know. bedfordstmartins.com /roarkunderstanding |

15

Ancient Agriculture

Dropping seeds into holes punched in cleared ground by a pointed stick known as a "dibble," this ancient American farmer sows a new crop while previously planted seeds — including the corn and beans immediately opposite him — bear fruit for harvest. Created by a sixteenth-century European artist, the drawing misrepresents who did the agricultural work in many ancient American cultures — namely, women rather than men. The Pierpont Morgan Library/Art Resource, NY.

> VISUAL ACTIVITY

READING THE IMAGE: In what ways has this ancient farmer modified and taken advantage of the natural environment?
CONNECTIONS: What were the advantages and disadvantages of agriculture compared to hunting and gathering?

Pueblo Bonito
▶ The largest residential and ceremonial site, containing more than 600 rooms and 35 kivas, in the major Anasazi cultural center of Chaco Canyon in present-day New Mexico.

About AD 200, small farming settlements began to appear throughout southern New Mexico, marking the emergence of the Mogollon culture. Typically, a Mogollon settlement included a dozen pit houses, each made by digging out a pit about fifteen feet in diameter and a foot or two deep and then erecting poles to support a roof of branches or dirt. Larger villages usually had one or two bigger pit houses that may have been the predecessors of the circular kivas, the ceremonial rooms that became a characteristic of nearly all southwestern settlements. About AD 900, Mogollon culture began to decline, for reasons that remain obscure.

Around AD 500, while the Mogollon culture prevailed in New Mexico, other ancient people migrated from Mexico to southern Arizona and established the distinctive Hohokam culture. Hohokam settlements used sophisticated grids of irrigation canals to plant and harvest crops twice a year. Hohokam settlements reflected Mexican cultural practices that northbound migrants brought with them, including

CHAPTER LOCATOR | When and why do historians rely on the work of archaeologists? | How and why did humans migrate into North America?

the building of sizable platform mounds and ball courts. About AD 1400, Hohokam culture declined for reasons that remain a mystery, although the rising salinity of the soil brought about by centuries of irrigation probably caused declining crop yields and growing food shortages.

North of the Hohokam and Mogollon cultures, in a region that encompassed southern Utah and Colorado and northern Arizona and New Mexico, the Anasazi culture began to flourish about AD 100. The early Anasazi built pit houses on mesa tops and used irrigation much as their neighbors did to the south. Beginning around AD 1000, some Anasazi began to move to large, multistory cliff dwellings whose spectacular ruins still exist at Mesa Verde, Colorado, and elsewhere. Other Anasazi communities—like the one known as **Pueblo Bonito**, whose impressive ruins can be visited at Chaco Canyon, New Mexico—erected huge stone-walled pueblos with enough rooms to house everyone in the settlement. Anasazi pueblos and cliff dwellings typically included one or more kivas used for secret ceremonies, restricted to men, that sought to communicate with the supernatural world.

Drought began to plague the region about AD 1130, and it lasted for more than half a century, triggering the disappearance of the Anasazi culture. By AD 1200, the large Anasazi pueblos had been abandoned. Some Anasazi migrated toward regions with more reliable rainfall and settled in Hopi, Zuñi, and Acoma pueblos that their descendants in Arizona and New Mexico have occupied ever since.

Mexican Ball Court Model

The Mexica and other Mesoamerican peoples commonly built special courts (or playing fields) for their intensely competitive ball games. This rare model of a Mexican ball court, made between 2200 BP and AD 250, shows a game in progress, complete with players and spectators. A few ball courts have been excavated in North America, compelling evidence of the many connections to Mexico. Yale University Art Gallery. Stephen Carlton Clark, B.A. 1903, Fund.

Woodland Burial Mounds and Chiefdoms

No other ancient Americans created dwellings similar to pueblos, but around 2500 BP, Woodland cultures throughout the Mississippi River watershed began to build **burial mounds**. The size of the mounds, the labor and organization required to erect them, and differences in the artifacts buried with certain individuals suggest the existence of a social and political hierarchy that archaeologists term a **chiefdom**. Experts do not know the name of a single chief. But the only way archaeologists can account for the complex and labor-intensive burial mounds is to assume that one person—whom scholars term a *chief*—commanded the labor and obedience of very large numbers of other people, who made up the chief's chiefdom.

Between 2500 BP and 2100 BP, Adena people built hundreds of burial mounds radiating from central Ohio. In the mounds, the Adena usually included grave goods such as spear points and stone pipes as well as thin sheets of mica (a glasslike mineral) crafted into animal or human shapes. Sometimes burial mounds were constructed all at once, but often they were built up slowly over many years.

About 2100 BP, Adena culture evolved into the more elaborate Hopewell culture, which lasted about five hundred years. Centered in Ohio, Hopewell culture extended throughout the enormous drainage of the Ohio and Mississippi rivers. Hopewell people built larger mounds than did their Adena predecessors

burial mounds
▶ Earthen mounds constructed by ancient American peoples, especially throughout the gigantic drainage of the Ohio and Mississippi rivers, after about 2500 BP and often used to bury important leaders and to enact major ceremonies.

chiefdom
▶ Hierarchical social organization headed by a chief. Archaeologists posit that the Woodland cultures were organized into chiefdoms because the construction of their characteristic burial mounds likely required one person having command over the labor of others.

Why did Archaic Native Americans shift to foraging and hunting smaller animals?

How did agriculture influence Native American cultures?

What cultural similarities did native peoples of the Western Hemisphere share in the 1490s?

Why was tribute important in the Mexican empire?

Conclusion: How do we understand the worlds of ancient Americans?

✓ LearningCurve
Check what you know.
bedfordstmartins.com
/roarkunderstanding

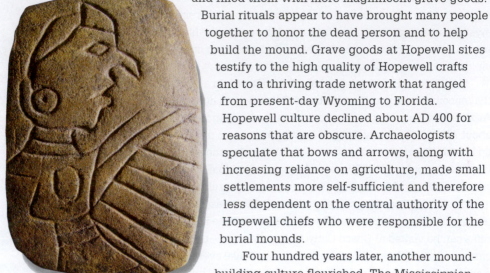

This stone tablet, excavated from the largest mound at Cahokia, depicts a bird-man whose sweeping wings and facial features — especially the nose and mouth — resemble a bird. Crafted around AD 1100, the tablet probably played some role in rituals enacted on the mound by Cahokian people. Similar birdlike human forms have been found among other Mississippian cultures. Cahokia Mounds Historic Site.

Cahokia

▶ The largest ceremonial site in ancient North America, located on the eastern bank of the Mississippi River across from present-day St. Louis, where thousands of inhabitants built hundreds of earthen mounds between about AD 800 and AD 1500.

and filled them with more magnificent grave goods. Burial rituals appear to have brought many people together to honor the dead person and to help build the mound. Grave goods at Hopewell sites testify to the high quality of Hopewell crafts and to a thriving trade network that ranged from present-day Wyoming to Florida. Hopewell culture declined about AD 400 for reasons that are obscure. Archaeologists speculate that bows and arrows, along with increasing reliance on agriculture, made small settlements more self-sufficient and therefore less dependent on the central authority of the Hopewell chiefs who were responsible for the burial mounds.

Four hundred years later, another mound-building culture flourished. The Mississippian culture emerged in the floodplains of the major southeastern river systems about AD 800 and lasted until about AD 1500. Major Mississippian sites, such as the one at **Cahokia**, included huge mounds with platforms on top for ceremonies and for the residences of great chiefs. Most likely, the ceremonial mounds and ritual practices derived from Mexican cultural expressions that were brought north by traders and migrants. At Cahokia, skilled farmers supported the large population with ample crops of corn. In addition to mounds, Cahokians erected what archaeologists call woodhenges (after the famous Stonehenge in England)—long wooden poles set upright in the ground and carefully arranged in huge circles. Although the purpose of woodhenges is unknown, experts believe that Cahokians probably built them partly for celestial observations.

Cahokia and other Mississippian cultures dwindled by AD 1500. When Europeans arrived, most of the descendants of Mississippian cultures, like those of the Hopewell culture, lived in small dispersed villages supported by hunting and gathering, supplemented by agriculture. Clearly, the conditions that caused large chiefdoms to emerge—whatever they were—had changed, and chiefs no longer commanded the sweeping powers they had once enjoyed.

> ### QUICK REVIEW

How and why did the societies of the Southwest differ from eastern societies?

CHAPTER LOCATOR | When and why do historians rely on the work of archaeologists? | How and why did humans migrate into North America?

18 CHAPTER 1
UNDERSTANDING ANCIENT AMERICA

Ancient American Weaving

This workbasket of a master weaver illustrates the technology of ancient American textile production. Found in a woman's grave in the Andes dating from one thousand years ago, the workbasket contains tools and thread for every stage of textile production. Weaving — like cooking, hunting, and worship — depended on human knowledge that survived only when passed from an experienced person to a novice. Museum of Fine Arts, Boston. Gift of Charles H. White, 02.680.

What cultural similarities did native peoples of the Western Hemisphere share in the 1490s?

ON THE EVE of European colonization in the 1490s, Native Americans lived throughout North and South America, but their total population is uncertain. Some experts claim that Native Americans inhabiting what is now the United States and Canada numbered 18 million to 20 million, while others place the population at no more than 1 million. A prudent estimate is about 4 million, or about the same as the number of people living on the small island nation of England at that time. The vastness of the territory meant that the overall population density of North America was low, just 60 people per 100 square miles, compared to more than 8,000 in England. Native Americans were spread thin across the land because of their survival strategies of hunting, gathering, and agriculture, but regional populations varied (**Figure 1.2**).

Eastern and Great Plains Peoples

About one-third of native North Americans inhabited the enormous Woodland region east of the Mississippi River; their population density approximated the average for North America as a whole. Eastern Woodland peoples clustered into three broad linguistic and cultural groups: Algonquian, Iroquoian, and Muskogean.

Algonquian tribes inhabited the Atlantic seaboard, the Great Lakes region, and much of the upper Midwest (**Map 1.3**). The relatively mild climate along the Atlantic permitted the coastal Algonquians to grow corn and other crops as well as to hunt and fish. Around the Great Lakes and in northern New England, however, cool summers and severe winters made agriculture impractical. Instead, the Abenaki, Penobscot, Chippewa, and other tribes concentrated on hunting and fishing, using canoes both for transportation and for gathering wild rice.

Why did Archaic Native Americans shift to foraging and hunting smaller animals?

How did agriculture influence Native American cultures?

What cultural similarities did native peoples of the Western Hemisphere share in the 1490s?

Why was tribute important in the Mexican empire?

Conclusion: How do we understand the worlds of ancient Americans?

✓ LearningCurve Check what you know. bedfordstmartins.com /roarkunderstanding

19

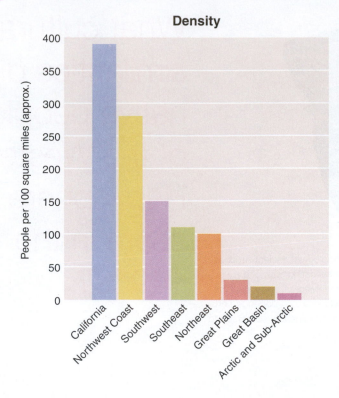

Density

People per 100 square miles (approx.)

California / Northwest Coast / Southwest / Southeast / Northeast / Great Plains / Great Basin / Arctic and Sub-Arctic

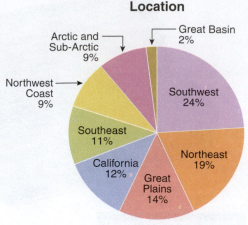

Location

Arctic and Sub-Arctic 9%
Great Basin 2%
Northwest Coast 9%
Southwest 24%
Southeast 11%
Northeast 19%
California 12%
Great Plains 14%

FIGURE 1.2 ■ Native American Population in North America about 1492 (Estimated)

Just before Europeans arrived, Native American population density varied widely, depending in large part on the availability of natural resources. The Pacific coast, with its rich marine resources, had the highest concentration of people. Overall, the population density of North America was less than 1 percent that of England, which helps explain why Europeans viewed North America as a relatively empty wilderness.

Inland from the Algonquian region, Iroquoian tribes occupied territories centered in Pennsylvania and upstate New York, as well as the hilly upland regions of the Carolinas and Georgia. Three features distinguished Iroquoian tribes from their neighbors. First, their success in cultivating corn and other crops allowed them to build permanent settlements, usually consisting of several longhouses housing five to ten families. Second, Iroquoian societies adhered to matrilineal rules of descent. Property of all sorts belonged to women. Women headed family clans and even selected the chiefs (normally men) who governed the tribes. Third, for purposes of war and diplomacy, an Iroquoian confederation—including the Seneca, Onondaga, Mohawk, Oneida, and Cayuga tribes—formed the League of Five Nations, which remained powerful well into the eighteenth century.

Muskogean peoples spread throughout the woodlands of the Southeast, south of the Ohio River and east of the Mississippi. Including the Creek, Choctaw, Chickasaw, and Natchez tribes, Muskogeans inhabited a bountiful natural environment that provided abundant food from hunting, gathering, and agriculture. Remnants of the earlier Mississippian culture still existed in Muskogean religion. The Natchez, for example, worshipped the sun and built temple mounds modeled after those of their Mississippian ancestors, including Cahokia.

Great Plains peoples accounted for about one out of seven native North Americans. Inhabiting the huge region west of the Eastern Woodland people and east of the Rocky Mountains, many tribes had migrated to the Great Plains within the century or two

CHAPTER LOCATOR | When and why do historians rely on the work of archaeologists? | How and why did humans migrate into North America?

20 CHAPTER 1 UNDERSTANDING ANCIENT AMERICA

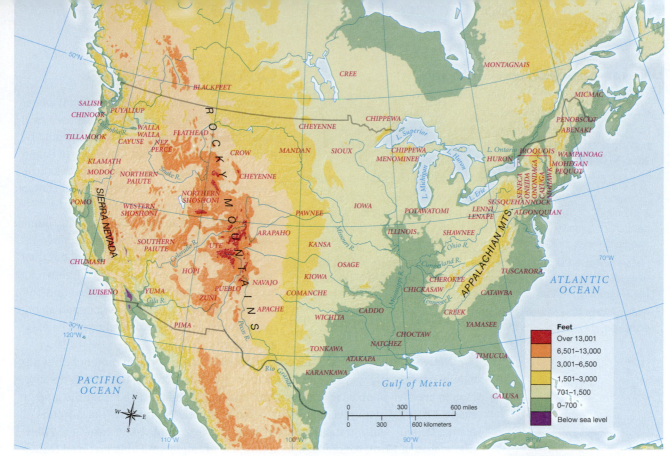

MAP 1.3 ■ Native North Americans about 1500

Distinctive Native American peoples resided throughout the area that, centuries later, became the United States. This map indicates the approximate location of some of the larger tribes about 1500. In the interest of legibility, many other peoples who inhabited North America at the time are omitted from the map.

before the 1490s, forced westward by Iroquoian and Algonquian tribes. Some Great Plains tribes—especially the Mandan and Pawnee—farmed successfully, growing both corn and sunflowers. But the Teton Sioux, Blackfeet, Comanche, Cheyenne, and Crow on the northern plains and the Apache and other nomadic tribes on the southern plains depended on buffalo (American bison) for their subsistence.

Southwestern and Western Peoples

Southwestern cultures included about a quarter of all native North Americans. These descendants of the Mogollon, Hohokam, and Anasazi cultures lived in settled agricultural communities, many of them pueblos. They continued to grow corn, beans, and squash using methods they had refined for centuries.

However, their communities came under attack by a large number of warlike Athapascans who invaded the Southwest beginning around AD 1300. The Athapascans—principally Apache and Navajo—were skillful warriors who preyed on the sedentary pueblo Indians, reaping the fruits of agriculture without the work of farming.

About a fifth of all native North Americans resided along the Pacific coast. In California, abundant acorns and nutritious marine life continued to support high population densities, but this abundance retarded the development of agriculture. Similar dependence on hunting and gathering persisted along the Northwest coast, where fishing reigned supreme.

| Why did Archaic Native Americans shift to foraging and hunting smaller animals? | How did agriculture influence Native American cultures? | **What cultural similarities did native peoples of the Western Hemisphere share in the 1490s?** | Why was tribute important in the Mexican empire? | Conclusion: How do we understand the worlds of ancient Americans? | ✔ LearningCurve Check what you know. bedfordstmartins.com /roarkunderstanding |

TABLE 1.2 ■ Native North Americans in the 1490s

- All native North Americans depended on hunting and gathering for a portion of their food.
- Most practiced agriculture. Agriculture sometimes supplemented hunting and gathering; at other times, hunting and gathering supplemented agriculture.
- All used bows, arrows, and other weapons for hunting and warfare.
- Evidence of artistic expression include drawings on stones, wood, and animal skins; woven patterns in baskets and textiles; designs painted on pottery, crafted into beadwork, or carved in effigies; songs, dances, religious ceremonies, and burial rites.
- Native North Americans did not have a writing system, did not use wheels or sailing ships, and did not have domesticated animals. Metal use was limited to copper.
- Native North Americans were able to adapt to local natural and social environments.

Cultural Similarities

Although North Americans may not have been as technologically advanced in weaponry as were Europeans during the 1490s, it would be a mistake to conclude that native North Americans lived in blissful harmony. Archaeological sites provide ample evidence of violent conflict. Skeletons, like those at Cahokia, bear the marks of wounds as well as of ritualistic human sacrifice. Religious, ethnic, economic, and familial conflicts must have occurred, but they remain in obscurity because they left few archaeological traces. In general, fear and anxiety must have been at least as common among native North Americans as feelings of peace and security.

Native North Americans not only adapted to the natural environment but also changed it in many ways. They built thousands of structures, from small dwellings to massive pueblos and enormous mounds, permanently altering the landscape. Their gathering techniques selected productive and nutritious varieties of plants, thereby shifting the balance of local plants toward useful varieties. The first stages of North American agriculture, for example, probably involved Native Americans gathering wild seeds and then sowing them in a meadow for later harvest. To clear land for planting seeds, native North Americans set fires that burned off thousands of acres of forest.

Native North Americans also used fires for hunting. Hunters often started fires to frighten and force together deer, buffalo, and other animals and make them easy to slaughter. Indians also started fires along the edges of woods to burn off shrubby undergrowth, encouraging the growth of tender young plants that attracted deer and other game, bringing them within convenient range of hunters' weapons. The burns also encouraged the growth of sun-loving food plants that Indians relished, such as blackberries, strawberries, and raspberries.

Because the fires set by native North Americans usually burned until they ran out of fuel or were extinguished by rain or wind, enormous regions of North America were burned over. In the long run, fires created and maintained a diverse and productive natural environment. Fires, like other activities of native North Americans, shaped the landscape of North America long before Europeans arrived in 1492.

> **QUICK REVIEW**

What common characteristics underlay Native American diversity?

CHAPTER LOCATOR | When and why do historians rely on the work of archaeologists? | How and why did humans migrate into North America?

Why was tribute important in the Mexican empire?

Mexican Tribute Account

This page from the *Codex Mendoza* records the tribute paid to the Mexican capital by the Xoconochco province, a tropical region near present-day Chiapas. In this case, the tribute includes, among many other things, two large strings of green stones, fourteen hundred bundles of rich feathers, and eighty complete bird skins. The tribute exacted by the Mexicans from other peoples was a significant part of their wealth and created the resentment that tributary peoples felt toward their overlords. Bodleian Library, Oxford, U.K., MS Arch.Self. A1.Fol.47r.

THE VAST MAJORITY of the 80 million people who lived in the Western Hemisphere in the 1490s inhabited Mesoamerica and South America, where the population approximately equaled that of Europe. Like their much less numerous counterparts north of the Rio Grande, these people lived in a natural environment of tremendous diversity. Among all these cultures, the **Mexica** stood out. Their empire stretched from coast to coast across central Mexico, encompassing between 8 million and 25 million people (experts disagree about the total population). Their significance in the history of the New World after 1492 dictates a brief survey of their culture and society.

The Mexica began their rise to prominence about 1325, when small bands settled on a marshy island in Lake Texcoco, the site of the future city of Tenochtitlán, the capital of the Mexican empire. Resourceful, courageous, and

Mexica

▶ A people whose empire stretched from coast to coast across central Mexico and who numbered as many as 25 million. The Mexican culture was characterized by steep hierarchy and devotion to the war god Huitzilopochtli.

c. AD 1325
- Small bands of Mexica settle on a marshy island in Lake Texcoco.

c. 1490
- Mexican empire stretches from coast to coast in central Mexico and encompasses between 8 and 25 million people.

AD 1492
- Christopher Columbus arrives in New World, beginning European colonization.

tribute

▶ The goods the Mexica collected from conquered peoples, from basic food products to candidates for human sacrifice. Tribute engendered resentment among the Mexica's subjects, creating a vulnerability the Spanish would later exploit.

cold-blooded warriors, the Mexica were often hired out as mercenaries for richer, more settled tribes.

The empire exemplified the central values of Mexican society and contributed far more to Mexican society than victims for sacrifice. At the most basic level, the empire functioned as a military and political system that collected **tribute** from subject peoples. The Mexica forced conquered tribes to pay tribute in goods, not money. Tribute redistributed to the Mexica as much as one-third of the goods produced by conquered tribes. It included everything from candidates for human sacrifice to textiles and basic food products as well as exotic luxury items such as gold, turquoise, and rare bird feathers.

Tribute reflected the fundamental relations of power and wealth that pervaded the Mexican empire. The relatively small nobility of Mexican warriors, supported by a still smaller priesthood, possessed the military and religious power to command the obedience of thousands of non-noble Mexicans and of millions of non-Mexicans in subjugated colonies. The Mexican elite exercised their power to obtain tribute and thereby to redistribute wealth from the conquered to the conquerors, from the commoners to the nobility, from the poor to the rich.

On the whole, the Mexica did not interfere much with the internal government of conquered regions. Instead, they usually permitted the traditional ruling elite to stay in power—so long as they paid tribute. Subjugated communities felt exploited by the constant payment of tribute to the Mexica. The high level of discontent among subject peoples constituted the soft, vulnerable underbelly of the Mexican empire, a fact that Spanish intruders exploited after 1492 to conquer the Mexica.

> The Mexica, at a Glance

- By the 1490s, the Mexica ruled an empire that covered more land than Spain and Portugal combined and contained almost three times as many people.

- Warriors were the most important members of society. The Mexica worshipped the war god Huitzilopochtli.

- Capturing prisoners in battle was considered the highest act of bravery; prisoners were sacrificed to Huitzilopochtli.

- The Mexica believed that human sacrifice fed the sun's craving for blood, which kept the sun aflame and prevented the fatal descent of everlasting darkness and chaos.

- Wealth collected from conquered peoples gave Mexicans the means with which to build the cities, temples, markets, and luxuriant gardens that so impressed the Spaniards upon their arrival in the New World.

> QUICK REVIEW

How did the conquest and creation of an empire exemplify the central values of Mexican society?

CHAPTER LOCATOR | When and why do historians rely on the work of archaeologists? | How and why did humans migrate into North America?

24 CHAPTER 1 UNDERSTANDING ANCIENT AMERICA

Conclusion: How do we understand the worlds of ancient Americans?

ANCIENT AMERICANS SHAPED the history of human beings in the New World for more than thirteen thousand years. They established continuous human habitation in the Western Hemisphere from the time the first big-game hunters crossed Beringia until 1492 and beyond. Much of their history remains lost because they relied on oral rather than written communication. But much can be pieced together from artifacts they left behind at camps, kill sites, and ceremonial and residential centers such as Cahokia and Tenochtitlán, the capital of the Mexican empire. Ancient Americans achieved their success through resourceful adaptation to the hemisphere's many and changing natural environments. They also adapted to social and cultural changes caused by human beings—such as marriages and deaths, as well as political struggles and warfare among chiefdoms. Their creativity and artistry are unmistakably documented in their numerous artifacts. Those material objects sketch the only likenesses of ancient Americans we will ever have—blurred, shadowy images that are indisputably human but forever silent.

When European intruders began arriving in the Western Hemisphere in 1492, their attitudes about the promise of the New World were heavily influenced by the diverse peoples they encountered. Europeans coveted Native Americans' wealth, labor, and land, and Christian missionaries sought to save their souls. Likewise, Native Americans marveled at such European technological novelties as sailing ships, steel weapons, gunpowder, and horses, while often reserving judgment about Europeans' Christian religion.

In the centuries following 1492, as the trickle of European strangers became a flood of newcomers from both Europe and Africa, Native Americans and settlers continued to encounter each other. Peaceful negotiations as well as violent conflicts over both land and trading rights resulted in chronic fear and mistrust. While the era of European colonization marked the beginning of the end of ancient America, the ideas, subsistence strategies, and cultural beliefs of native North Americans remained powerful among their descendants for generations and continue to persist to the present.

Why did Archaic Native Americans shift to foraging and hunting smaller animals?

How did agriculture influence Native American cultures?

What cultural similarities did native peoples of the Western Hemisphere share in the 1490s?

Why was tribute important in the Mexican empire?

Conclusion: How do we understand the worlds of ancient Americans?

☑ **LearningCurve** Check what you know. bedfordstmartins.com /roarkunderstanding

25

CHAPTER 1 STUDY GUIDE

 STEP 1

GET STARTED ONLINE

✓ **LearningCurve** ▪ bedfordstmartins.com/roarkunderstanding
Now that you've read the chapter, make it stick by completing the LearningCurve activity.

 STEP 2

EXPLAIN WHY IT MATTERS

Put your reading into practice. Identify each term below, and then explain why it matters in U.S. history.

TERM	WHO OR WHAT & WHEN	WHY IT MATTERS
Beringia (p. 7)		
Paleo-Indians (p. 7)		
Clovis points (p. 8)		
hunter-gatherer (p. 10)		
Archaic Indians (p. 10)		
pueblos (p. 15)		
Pueblo Bonito (p. 17)		
burial mounds (p. 17)		
chiefdom (p. 17)		
Cahokia (p. 18)		
Mexica (p. 23)		
tribute (p. 24)		

STEP 3

MOVE BEYOND THE BASICS

To demonstrate a more advanced understanding, describe the cultural differences of Native American peoples in 1492.

Indian peoples in 1490	Geography and climate	Economy and lifestyle (sources of food and material goods, economic organization, trade)	Social/political organization (religion, family structures, social hierarchy)
Southwestern cultures			
Eastern Woodland cultures			
Pacific coast cultures			
Great Basin cultures			
Great Plains cultures			

Now, take a step back and try to explain the big picture. Remember to use specific examples from the chapter in your answers.

THE FIRST AMERICANS

▶ When and how did humans first arrive in the Americas?

▶ Describe the lifestyle of the Paleo-Indians. How did they adapt to the extinction of mammoths and other large mammals around 11,000 BP?

AGRICULTURE AND ADAPTATION

▶ How did Archaic Indians differ from their Paleo-Indian ancestors?

▶ How did the advent of agriculture change the settlement patterns and social organization of some Indian groups?

NATIVE AMERICAN CULTURES IN 1490

▶ What factors shaped population density across North America?

▶ What set the Mexica apart from the other Indian cultures of North America?

LOOKING BACKWARD, LOOKING AHEAD

▶ What accounts for the diversity of Indian peoples on the eve of European contact?

> IN YOUR OWN WORDS

Imagine that you must give an oral report to the class answering the following question: **How did ancient North American peoples shape the history of the continent before the arrival of Europeans in 1492?** What would be the most important points to include and why?

 Do it online at the Student Site ■ bedfordstmartins.com/roarkunderstanding

2

EUROPEANS ENCOUNTER THE NEW WORLD

1492–1600

> ## What were the most significant effects of European exploration in the sixteenth century?

Chapter 2 examines the causes, course, and impact of European exploration of parts of the world previously unknown to them. It follows early Portuguese efforts to chart the coast of Africa and the Spanish establishment of a colonial empire in the New World. It then explores the many changes in both the New and Old Worlds that were a result of Europeans' encounters with Native Americans during the sixteenth century.

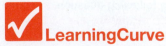

LearningCurve
bedfordstmartins.com/roarkunderstanding
After reading the chapter, use LearningCurve to retain what you've read.

Europeans Encountering Indians. Unknown artist, ca. 1700. Private Collection/Picture Research Consultants and Archives.

> What factors led to European exploration in the fifteenth century?

> What did Spanish explorers discover in the western Atlantic?

> How did Spaniards explore, conquer, and colonize New Spain?

> What impact did Spain's New World endeavors have in Europe?

> Conclusion: What promise did the New World offer Europeans?

> What factors led to European exploration in the fifteenth century?

> CHRONOLOGY

Mid-fourteenth century
- Black Death kills approximately one-third of Europe's population.

1415–1460
- Portuguese led by Prince Henry the Navigator use new navigational tools and techniques to aid maritime exploration.

1480
- Portuguese ships reach the Congo.

1488
- Bartolomeu Dias rounds Cape of Good Hope.

1498
- Vasco da Gama sails to India.

HISTORICALLY, THE EAST—not the West — attracted Europeans. Wealthy Europeans developed a taste for luxury goods from Asia and Africa, and merchants competed to satisfy that desire. As Europeans traded with the East and with one another, they acquired new information about the world they inhabited. A few people—sailors, merchants, and aristocrats—took the risks of exploring beyond the limits of the world known to Europeans. Those risks could be deadly, but sometimes they paid off in new information, new opportunities, and eventually the discovery of a world entirely new to Europeans.

Mediterranean Trade and European Expansion

From the twelfth through the fifteenth centuries, spices, silk, carpets, ivory, and gold traveled overland from Persia, Asia Minor, India, and Africa and then funneled into continental Europe through Mediterranean trade routes (**Map 2.1**). Dominated primarily by the Italian cities of Venice, Genoa, and Pisa, this lucrative trade enriched Italian merchants and bankers. The vitality of the Mediterranean trade offered merchants few incentives to look for alternatives. New routes to the East and the discovery of new lands were the stuff of fantasy.

Preconditions for turning fantasy into reality developed in fifteenth-century Europe. In the mid-fourteenth century, a catastrophic epidemic of bubonic plague

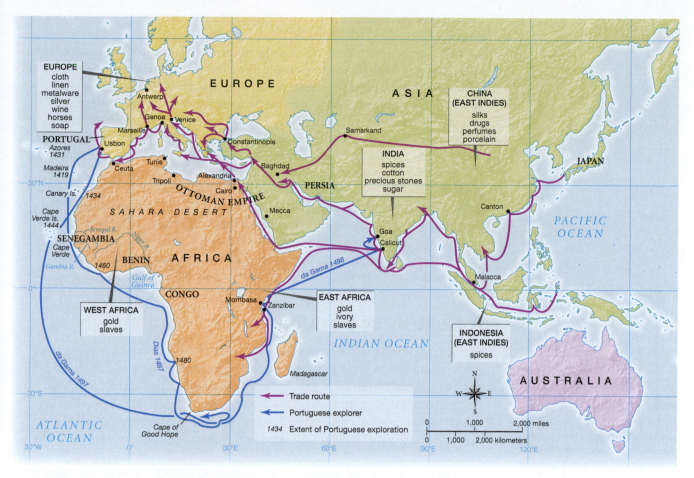

MAP 2.1 ■ European Trade Routes and Portuguese Exploration in the Fifteenth Century

Italian cities' domination of trade from Asia was slowly undermined during the fifteenth century by Portuguese explorers who hopscotched along the coast of Africa and eventually found a sea route that opened the rich trade of the East to Portuguese merchants.

(or the **Black Death**, as it was called) killed about a third of the European population. This devastating pestilence had major long-term consequences. By drastically reducing the population, it made Europe's limited supply of food more plentiful for survivors. Many survivors inherited property from plague victims, giving them new chances for advancement.

Understandably, most Europeans perceived the world as a place of alarming risks where the delicate balance of health, harvests, and peace could quickly be tipped toward disaster by epidemics, famine, and violence. Most people protected themselves from the constant threat of calamity by worshipping the supernatural, by living amid kinfolk and friends, and by maintaining good relations with the rich and powerful. But the insecurity and uncertainty of fifteenth-century European life also encouraged a few people to take greater risks, such as embarking on dangerous sea voyages through uncharted waters to points unknown.

Black Death

▶ An epidemic of bubonic plague that in the mid-fourteenth century killed about a third of the European population and resulted in increased food and resources for the survivors as well as a sense of a world in precarious balance.

What did Spanish explorers discover in the western Atlantic?

How did Spaniards explore, conquer, and colonize New Spain?

What impact did Spain's New World endeavors have in Europe?

Conclusion: What promise did the New World offer Europeans?

✔ LearningCurve Check what you know. bedfordstmartins.com /roarkunderstanding

In European societies, exploration promised fame and fortune to those who succeeded, whether they were kings or commoners. Monarchs hoped to enlarge their realms and enrich their dynasties by sponsoring journeys of exploration. More territory meant more subjects who could pay more taxes, provide more soldiers, and participate in more commerce, magnifying the monarch's power and prestige. Voyages of exploration also could stabilize the monarch's regime by diverting unruly noblemen toward distant lands. Some explorers were commoners who hoped to be elevated to the aristocracy as a reward for their daring achievements.

Scientific and technological advances also helped set the stage for exploration. The invention of movable type by Johannes Gutenberg around 1450 in Germany made printing easier and cheaper, stimulating the diffusion of information, including news of discoveries, among literate Europeans. By 1400, crucial navigational aids employed by maritime explorers were already available: compasses; hourglasses; and the astrolabe and quadrant, which were devices for determining latitude. The Portuguese were the first to use these technological advances in a campaign to sail beyond the limits of the world known to Europeans.

A Century of Portuguese Exploration

With only 2 percent of the population of Christian Europe, Portugal devoted far more energy and wealth to the geographic exploration of the world between 1415 and 1460 than all other European countries combined. As a Christian kingdom, Portugal cooperated with Spain in the Reconquest, the centuries-long drive to expel the Muslims from the Iberian Peninsula. The religious zeal that propelled the Reconquest also justified expansion into what the Portuguese considered heathen lands.

The most influential advocate of Portuguese exploration was Prince Henry the Navigator, son of the Portuguese king. From 1415 until his death in 1460, Henry collected the latest information about sailing techniques and geography, supported new crusades against the Muslims, sought fresh sources of trade to fatten Portuguese pocketbooks, and pushed explorers to go farther still.

Neither the Portuguese nor anybody else in Europe knew the immensity of Africa or the length of its coastline, which fronted the Atlantic for more than seven thousand miles. At first, Portuguese mariners cautiously hugged the west coast of Africa, seldom venturing beyond sight of land. By 1434, they had reached the northern edge of the Sahara Desert, where they learned to ride strong westerly currents before catching favorable easterly winds that turned them back toward land, which allowed them to reach Cape Verde by 1444.

To stow the supplies necessary for long sea voyages and to withstand the battering of waves in the open ocean, the Portuguese developed the caravel, a fast, sturdy ship that became explorers' vessel of choice. In caravels, Portuguese mariners sailed into and around the Gulf of Guinea and as far south as the Congo by 1480.

Fierce African resistance confined Portuguese expeditions to coastal trading posts, where they bartered successfully for gold, slaves, and ivory. Powerful African kingdoms welcomed Portuguese trading ships loaded with iron goods,

Reconquest

▶ The centuries-long drive to expel Muslims from the Iberian Peninsula undertaken by the Christian kingdoms of Spain and Portugal. The military victories of the Reconquest helped the Portuguese gain greater access to sea routes.

What factors led to European exploration in the fifteenth century?

weapons, textiles, and ornamental shells. Portuguese merchants learned that establishing relatively peaceful trading posts on the coast offered more profit than attempting violent conquest and colonization of inland regions. In the 1460s, the Portuguese used African slaves to develop sugar plantations on the Cape Verde Islands, inaugurating an association between enslaved Africans and plantation labor that would be transplanted to the New World in the centuries to come.

About 1480, Portuguese explorers, eager to bypass the Mediterranean merchants, began a conscious search for a sea route to Asia. In 1488, Bartolomeu Dias sailed around the Cape of Good Hope at the southern tip of Africa and hurried back to Lisbon with the exciting news that it appeared to be possible to sail on to India and China. In 1498, after ten years of careful preparation, Vasco da Gama commanded the first Portuguese fleet to sail to India. Portugal quickly capitalized on the commercial potential of da Gama's new sea route. By the early sixteenth century, the Portuguese controlled a far-flung commercial empire in India, Indonesia, and China (collectively referred to as the East Indies). Their new sea route to the East eliminated overland travel and allowed Portuguese merchants to charge much lower prices for the Eastern goods they imported.

Portugal's African explorations during the fifteenth century broke the monopoly of the old Mediterranean trade with the East, dramatically expanded the world known to Europeans, established a network of Portuguese outposts in Africa and Asia, and developed methods of sailing the high seas.

QUICK REVIEW

Why did European exploration expand dramatically in the fifteenth century?

| What did Spanish explorers discover in the western Atlantic? | How did Spaniards explore, conquer, and colonize New Spain? | What impact did Spain's New World endeavors have in Europe? | Conclusion: What promise did the New World offer Europeans? | ☑ **LearningCurve** Check what you know. bedfordstmartins.com /roarkunderstanding |

What did Spanish explorers discover in the western Atlantic?

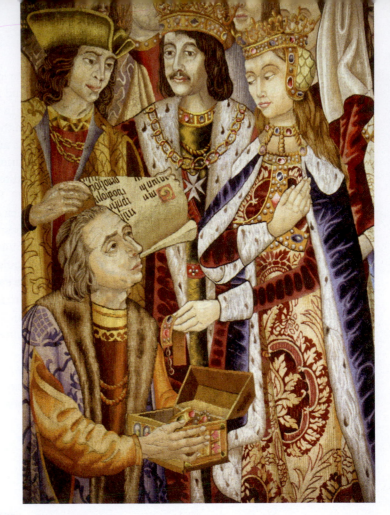

Spanish Tapestry This detail from a lavish sixteenth-century tapestry depicts Columbus (kneeling) receiving a box of jewels from Queen Isabella (whose husband, King Ferdinand, stands slightly behind her) in appreciation for his voyages to the New World. © Julio Conoso/Corbis Sygma.

THE PORTUGUESE AND OTHER experts believed that sailing west across the Atlantic to Asia was literally impossible. The European discovery of America required someone bold enough to believe that the experts were wrong. That person was Christopher Columbus. His explorations inaugurated a geographic revolution that forever altered Europeans' understanding of the world and its peoples, including themselves. Columbus's landfall in the Caribbean initiated a thriving exchange between the people, ideas, cultures, and institutions of the Old and New Worlds that continues to this day.

The Explorations of Columbus

Columbus went to sea when he was about fourteen and eventually made his way to Lisbon, where he gained access to maps and information about the tricky currents and winds in the Atlantic. Like other educated Europeans, Columbus

CHAPTER LOCATOR | What factors led to European exploration in the fifteenth century?

believed that the earth was a sphere and that theoretically it was possible to reach the East Indies by sailing west. With flawed calculations, he estimated that Asia was only about 2,500 miles away, a shorter distance than Portuguese ships routinely sailed between Lisbon and the Congo. In fact, the shortest distance to Japan from Europe's jumping-off point was nearly 11,000 miles. Convinced by his erroneous calculations, Columbus became obsessed with a scheme to prove he was right.

In 1492, after years of unsuccessful lobbying in Portugal, Spain, England, and France, Columbus finally won financing for his journey from the Spanish monarchs, Queen Isabella and King Ferdinand. They saw Columbus's venture as an inexpensive gamble: The potential loss was small, but the potential gain was huge.

After frantic preparation, Columbus and his small fleet—the *Niña* and the *Pinta*, both caravels, and the *Santa María*, a larger merchant vessel—headed west. Six weeks after leaving the Canary Islands, Columbus landed on a tiny Caribbean island about three hundred miles north of the eastern tip of Cuba.

Columbus claimed possession of the island for Spain and named it San Salvador, in honor of the Savior, Jesus Christ. He called the islanders "Indians," assuming that they inhabited the East Indies somewhere near Japan or China. The islanders called themselves **Tainos**, which in their language meant "good" or "noble." An agricultural people, the Tainos grew cassava, corn, cotton, tobacco, and other crops. Instead of dressing in the finery Columbus had expected to find in the East Indies, the Tainos "all . . . go around as naked as their mothers bore them," Columbus wrote. Although Columbus concluded that the Tainos "had no religion," in reality they worshipped gods they called zemis, ancestral spirits who inhabited natural objects such as trees and stones. The Tainos had no riches. "It seemed to me that they were a people very poor in everything," Columbus wrote.

What the Tainos thought about Columbus and his sailors we can only surmise, since they left no written documents. At first, Columbus got the impression that the Tainos believed the Spaniards came from heaven. But after six weeks of encounters, Columbus decided that "the people of these lands do not understand me nor do I, nor anyone else that I have with me, [understand] them." The confused communication between the Spaniards and the Tainos suggests how strange each group seemed to the other. Columbus's perceptions of the Tainos were shaped by European attitudes, ideas, and expectations, just as the Tainos' perceptions of the Europeans were no doubt colored by their own culture.

Columbus and his men understood that they had made a momentous discovery. In 1493, when Queen Isabella and King Ferdinand learned Columbus's news, they were overjoyed. With a voyage that had lasted barely eight months, Columbus appeared to have catapulted Spain into a serious challenger to Portugal, whose explorers had not yet sailed to India or China.

Columbus's First Voyage to the New World, 1492–1493

Tainos
▶ The Indians who inhabited San Salvador and many Caribbean islands and who were the first people Columbus encountered after making landfall in the New World.

Taino Zemi Basket
Crafted sometime between 1492 and about 1520, this basket is an example of the effigies Tainos made to represent zemis, or deities. The basket maker used African ivory and European mirrors as well as Native American fibers, dyes, and designs. Archivio Fotografico del Museo Preistorico Etnografico L. Pigorini, Roma.

| **What did Spanish explorers discover in the western Atlantic?** | How did Spaniards explore, conquer, and colonize New Spain? | What impact did Spain's New World endeavors have in Europe? | Conclusion: What promise did the New World offer Europeans? | ✓ LearningCurve Check what you know. bedfordstmartins.com /roarkunderstanding |

Treaty of Tordesillas
▶ The treaty negotiated in 1494 to delineate land claims in the New World. The treaty drew an imaginary line west of the Canary Islands; land discovered west of the line belonged to Spain, and land to the east belonged to Portugal.

Soon after Columbus returned to Spain, the Spanish monarchs rushed to obtain the pope's support for their claim to the new lands in the West. When the pope, a Spaniard, complied, the Portuguese feared that their own claims to recently discovered territories were in jeopardy. To protect their claims, the Portuguese and Spanish monarchs negotiated the **Treaty of Tordesillas** in 1494. The treaty drew an imaginary line eleven hundred miles west of the Canary Islands (**Map 2.2**). Land discovered west of the line (namely, the islands that Columbus discovered and any additional land that might be found) belonged to Spain; Portugal claimed land to the east (namely, its African and East Indian trading empire).

Isabella and Ferdinand moved quickly to realize the promise of their new claims. In the fall of 1493, they dispatched Columbus once again, this time with a fleet of seventeen ships and more than a thousand men who planned to locate the Asian mainland, find gold, and get rich. Before Columbus died in 1506, he returned to the New World two more times (in 1498 and 1502) without relinquishing his belief that the East Indies were there, someplace. Other explorers continued to search for a passage to the East or some other source of profit. Before long, however, prospects of beating the Portuguese to Asia began to dim along with the hope of finding vast hoards of gold.

Nonetheless, Columbus's discoveries forced sixteenth-century Europeans to think about the world in new ways. He proved it was possible to sail from Europe to the western rim of the Atlantic and return to Europe. Most important, Columbus's voyages demonstrated that lands and peoples entirely unknown to Europeans lay across the Atlantic.

The Geographic Revolution and the Columbian Exchange

Within thirty years of Columbus's initial discovery, Europeans' understanding of world geography underwent a revolution. An elite of perhaps twenty thousand people with access to Europe's royal courts and trading centers learned the exciting news about global geography. But it took a generation of additional exploration before they could comprehend the larger contours of Columbus's discoveries.

By 1500, European experts knew that several large chunks of land cluttered the western Atlantic. A few cartographers speculated that these chunks were connected to one another in a landmass that was not Asia. In 1507, Martin Waldseemüller, a German cartographer, published the first map that showed the New World separate from Asia; he named the land America, in honor of Amerigo Vespucci.

> **Early Voyages to the Americas**	
Explorer	**Voyage**
John Cabot	Reached Newfoundland in 1497 while searching for a Northwest Passage to Asia.
Amerigo Vespucci	Participated in a Spanish expedition that landed on the northern coast of South America in 1499.
Pedro Álvars Cabral	Commanded a Portuguese fleet bound for the Indian Ocean that accidentally made landfall on the coast of Brazil.

CHAPTER LOCATOR | What factors led to European exploration in the fifteenth century?

MAP 2.2 ■ European Exploration in Sixteenth-Century America

This map illustrates the approximate routes of early European explorations of the New World.

> **MAP ACTIVITY**

READING THE MAP: Which countries were most actively exploring the New World? Which countries were exploring later than others?

CONNECTIONS: What were the motivations behind the explorations? What were the motivations for colonization?

Two additional discoveries confirmed Waldseemüller's speculation. In 1513, Vasco Núñez de Balboa crossed the Isthmus of Panama and reached the Pacific Ocean. Clearly, more water lay between the New World and Asia. Ferdinand Magellan discovered just how much water when he led an expedition to circumnavigate the globe in 1519. Sponsored by Spain, Magellan's voyage took him first to the New World, around the southern tip of South America, and into the Pacific. Crossing the Pacific took almost four months, decimating his crew with hunger and

What did Spanish explorers discover in the western Atlantic?	How did Spaniards explore, conquer, and colonize New Spain?	What impact did Spain's New World endeavors have in Europe?	Conclusion: What promise did the New World offer Europeans?	☑ LearningCurve Check what you know. bedfordstmartins.com /roarkunderstanding

thirst. Magellan himself was killed by Philippine tribesmen. A remnant of his expedition continued on to the Indian Ocean and managed to transport a cargo of spices back to Spain in 1522.

In most ways, Magellan's voyage was a disaster. One ship and 18 men crawled back from an expedition that had begun with five ships and more than 250 men. But the geographic information it provided left no doubt that America was a continent separated from Asia by the enormous Pacific Ocean. Magellan's voyage made clear that it was possible to sail west to reach the East Indies, but that was a terrible way to go. After Magellan, most Europeans who sailed west set their sights on the New World, not on Asia.

Columbus's arrival in the Caribbean anchored the western end of what might be imagined as a sea bridge that spanned the Atlantic, connecting the Western Hemisphere to Europe. Somewhat like the Beringian land bridge traversed by the first Americans millennia earlier (see chapter 1), the new sea bridge reestablished a connection between the Eastern and Western Hemispheres. The Atlantic Ocean, which had previously isolated America from Europe, became an aquatic highway, thanks to sailing technology, intrepid seamen, and their European sponsors. This new sea bridge launched the **Columbian exchange**, a transatlantic trade of goods, people, and ideas that has continued ever since.

Spaniards brought novelties to the New World that were commonplace in Europe, including Christianity, iron technology, sailing ships, firearms, wheeled vehicles, and horses. Unknowingly, they also carried many Old World microorganisms that caused devastating epidemics of smallpox, measles, and other diseases that killed the vast majority of Indians during the sixteenth century and continued to decimate survivors in later centuries. European diseases made the Columbian exchange catastrophic for Native Americans. In the long term, these diseases helped transform the dominant peoples of the New World from descendants of Asians, who had inhabited the hemisphere for millennia, to descendants of Europeans and Africans, the recent arrivals from the Old World.

Ancient American goods, people, and ideas made the return trip across the Atlantic. Europeans were introduced to New World foods such as corn and potatoes that became important staples in European diets, especially for poor people. Columbus's sailors became infected with syphilis in sexual encounters with New World women and unwittingly carried the deadly bacteria back to Europe. New World tobacco created a European fashion for smoking that ignited quickly and has yet to be extinguished. But for almost a generation after 1492, this Columbian exchange did not reward the Spaniards with the riches they yearned to find.

Columbian exchange

▶ The transatlantic exchange of goods, people, and ideas that began when Columbus arrived in the Caribbean, ending the age-old separation of the Eastern and Western Hemispheres.

> **QUICK REVIEW**

How did Columbus's discoveries help revolutionize Europeans' understanding of global geography?

CHAPTER LOCATOR | What factors led to European exploration in the fifteenth century?

38 CHAPTER 2 EUROPEANS ENCOUNTER THE NEW WORLD

Cortés Arrives in Tenochtitlán This portrayal of the arrival of Cortés and his army in the Mexican capital illustrates the Spaniards' military advantages of horses, armor, and Indian supporters. Bibliothèque Nationale de France.

DURING THE SIXTEENTH CENTURY, the New World helped Spain become the most powerful monarchy in both Europe and the Americas. Initially, Spaniards enslaved Caribbean tribes and put them to work growing crops and mining gold. But the profits from these early ventures barely covered the costs of maintaining the settlers. After almost thirty years of exploration, the promise of Columbus's discovery seemed illusory.

In 1519, however, that promise was spectacularly fulfilled by Hernán Cortés's march into Mexico. By about 1545, Spanish conquests extended from northern Mexico to southern Chile, and New World riches filled Spanish treasure chests. Cortés's expedition served as the model for Spaniards' and other Europeans' expectations that the New World could yield bonanza profits for its conquerors while forced labor and deadly epidemics decimated native populations.

The Conquest of Mexico

Hernán Cortés, an obscure nineteen-year-old Spaniard, arrived in the New World in 1504. Throughout his twenties, he fought in the conquest of Cuba and elsewhere in the Caribbean. In 1519, the governor of Cuba authorized Cortés to organize an expedition of about six hundred men and eleven ships to investigate rumors of a fabulously wealthy kingdom somewhere in the interior of the mainland.

A charismatic and confident man, Cortés could not speak any Native American language. Landing first on the Yucatán peninsula with his ragtag army,

What did Spanish explorers discover in the western Atlantic?

How did Spaniards explore, conquer, and colonize New Spain?

What impact did Spain's New World endeavors have in Europe?

Conclusion: What promise did the New World offer Europeans?

✓ LearningCurve
Check what you know.
bedfordstmartins.com/roarkunderstanding

39

Cortés's Invasion of Tenochtitlán, 1519–1521

he had the good fortune to receive from a local chief the gift of a young girl named Malinali. She spoke several native languages, including Nahuatl, the language of the Mexica, the most powerful people in what is now Mexico and Central America (see chapter 1). Malinali, whom the Spaniards called Marina, soon learned Spanish and became Cortés's interpreter. "Without her help," wrote one of the Spaniards who accompanied Cortés, "we would not have understood the language of New Spain and Mexico."

In Tenochtitlán, the capital of the Mexican empire, the emperor Montezuma heard about some strange creatures sighted along the coast. The emperor sent representatives to bring the strangers large quantities of food. But along with the food, the Mexica also brought the Spaniards another gift, a "disk in the shape of a sun, as big as a cartwheel and made of very fine gold," as a Mexican recalled. Here was conclusive evidence that the rumors of fabulous riches heard by Cortés had some basis in fact.

In August 1519, Cortés marched inland to find Montezuma. Leading about 350 men, Cortés had to live off the land, establishing peaceful relations with indigenous tribes when he could and killing them when he thought it necessary. On November 8, 1519, Cortés reached Tenochtitlán, where Montezuma welcomed him and showered the Spaniards with lavish hospitality. Quickly, Cortés took Montezuma hostage and held him under house arrest, hoping to make him a puppet through whom the Spaniards could rule the Mexican empire. This uneasy peace existed for several months until one of Cortés's men led a brutal massacre of many Mexican nobles, causing the people of Tenochtitlán to revolt. Montezuma was killed, and the Mexica mounted a ferocious assault on the Spaniards. On June 30, 1520, Cortés and about a hundred other Spaniards fought their way out of Tenochtitlán and retreated about one hundred miles to Tlaxcala, a stronghold of bitter enemies of the Mexica. The Tlaxcalans—who had long resented Mexican power—allowed Cortés to regroup, obtain reinforcements, and plan a strategy to conquer Tenochtitlán.

In the spring of 1521, Cortés and thousands of Indian allies laid siege to the Mexican capital. With a relentless, scorched-earth strategy, Cortés finally defeated the last Mexican defenders on August 13, 1521. The great capital of the Mexican empire "looked as if it had been ploughed up," one of Cortés's soldiers remembered.

How did a few hundred Spaniards so far away from home defeat millions of Indians fighting on their home turf? For one thing, the Spaniards had superior military technology that partially offset the Mexicans' numerical advantages. They fought with weapons of iron and steel against the Mexicans' stone, wood, and copper. The muscles of Mexican warriors could not match the power of cannons and muskets fueled by gunpowder.

European viruses proved to be even more powerful weapons. Smallpox arrived in Mexico with Cortés, and in the ensuing epidemic thousands of Mexicans died and many others became too sick to fight. The sickness spread along the network of trade and tribute feeding Tenochtitlán, causing many to fear that their gods had abandoned them. "Cut us loose," one Mexican pleaded, "because the gods have died."

The Spaniards' concept of war also favored them. Mexicans tended to consider war a way to impose their tribute system on conquered people and to take captives for sacrifice. They believed that the high cost of continuing to fight would cause their adversaries to surrender and pay tribute. In contrast, Spaniards sought total victory by destroying their enemy's ability to fight.

Politics proved decisive in Cortés's victory over the Mexicans. Cortés shrewdly exploited the tensions between the Mexica and the people they ruled in their empire (see chapter 1). Cortés reinforced his small army with thousands of Indian allies who were eager to seek revenge against the Mexica. Hundreds of thousands of other Indians aided Cortés by failing to come to the Mexicans' defense. In the end, the political tensions created by the Mexican empire proved to be its crippling weakness.

The Search for Other Mexicos

Lured by their insatiable appetite for gold, Spanish **conquistadors** (soldiers who fought in conquests) quickly fanned out from Tenochtitlán in search of other sources of treasure. The most spectacular prize fell to Francisco Pizarro, who conquered the **Incan empire** in Peru. The Incas controlled a vast, complex region that contained more than nine million people and stretched along the western coast of South America for more than two thousand miles. In 1532, Pizarro and his army of fewer than two hundred men captured the Incan emperor Atahualpa and held him hostage. As ransom, the Incas gave Pizarro the largest treasure yet produced by the

conquistadors
▶ Term (literally meaning "conquerors") that refers to the Spanish explorers and soldiers who conquered lands in the New World.

Incan empire
▶ A region under the control of the Incas and their emperor, Atahualpa, that stretched along the western coast of South America and contained more than nine million people and a wealth in gold and silver.

> Unsuccessful Attempts to Secure New World Riches	
Conquistador	**Mission**
Juan Ponce de León	Sailed to Florida in 1521 to find riches, only to be killed in battle with Calusa Indians.
Lucas Vázquez de Ayllón	Explored the Atlantic coast north of Florida to present-day South Carolina; in 1526, established a small settlement on the Georgia coast named San Miguel de Gualdape, the first Spanish attempt to establish a foothold in what is now the United States. Sickness and hostile Indians destroyed the settlement.
Pánfilo de Narváez	Surveyed the Gulf coast from Florida to Texas in 1528. The expedition ended disastrously with a shipwreck near present-day Galveston, Texas.
Hernando de Soto	Searched for another Peru in southeastern North America in 1539. After his death in 1542, de Soto's men returned to Mexico.
Francisco Vásquez de Coronado	Starting in 1540, searched the Southwest and Great Plains of North America for the mythical Seven Cities of Cíbola, which turned out to be a small Zuñi pueblo. After two years, Coronado gave up searching for the riches that eluded him.
Juan Rodríguez Coronado	Sought wealth along the coast of California in 1542; died on Santa Catalina Island, offshore from present-day Los Angeles. His men sailed on to Oregon, where a ferocious storm forced them to turn back toward Mexico.

What did Spanish explorers discover in the western Atlantic?

How did Spaniards explore, conquer, and colonize New Spain?

What impact did Spain's New World endeavors have in Europe?

Conclusion: What promise did the New World offer Europeans?

✓ LearningCurve
Check what you know.
bedfordstmartins.com/roarkunderstanding

41

conquests: gold and silver equivalent to half a century's worth of precious-metal production in Europe. With the ransom safely in their hands, the Spaniards murdered Atahualpa. The Incan treasure proved that at least one other Mexico did indeed exist, and it spurred the Spaniards' search for others.

The probes into North America by de Soto, Coronado, and Cabrillo persuaded other Spaniards that although enormous territories stretched northward from Mexico, their inhabitants had little to loot or exploit. After a generation of vigorous exploration, the Spaniards concluded that there was only one Mexico and one Peru.

Spanish Outposts in Florida and New Mexico

Disappointed by the explorers' failure to discover riches in North America, the Spanish monarchy insisted that a few settlements be established in Florida and New Mexico to give a token of reality to its territorial claims. Settlements in Florida would have the additional benefit of protecting Spanish ships from pirates and privateers who lurked along the southeastern coast, waiting for the Spanish treasure fleet sailing toward Spain.

In 1565, the Spanish king sent Pedro Menéndez de Avilés to found St. Augustine in Florida, the first permanent European settlement within what became the United States. By 1600, St. Augustine had a population of about five hundred, the only remaining Spanish beachhead on North America's vast Atlantic shoreline.

More than sixteen hundred miles west of St. Augustine, the Spaniards founded another outpost in 1598. Juan de Oñate led an expedition of about five hundred people to settle northern Mexico, now called New Mexico, and claim the booty rumored to exist there. When Oñate and his companions reached pueblos near present-day Albuquerque and Santa Fe, he sent out scouting parties to find the legendary treasures of the region. Meanwhile, many of his soldiers planned to mutiny, and relations with the Indians deteriorated. When Indians in the Acoma pueblo revolted against the Spaniards in 1599, Oñate ruthlessly suppressed the uprising, killing eight hundred men, women, and children. Although Oñate's response to the **Acoma pueblo revolt** reconfirmed the Spaniards' military superiority, he did not bring peace or stability to the region. After another pueblo revolt occurred in the same year, many of Oñate's settlers returned to Mexico, leaving New Mexico a small, dusty assertion of Spanish claims to the North American Southwest.

Acoma pueblo revolt
▶ Revolt against the Spanish by Indians living at the Acoma pueblo in 1599. Juan de Oñate violently suppressed the uprising, but the Indians revolted again later that year, after which many Spanish settlers returned to Mexico.

New Spain in the Sixteenth Century

For all practical purposes, Spain was the dominant European power in the Western Hemisphere during the sixteenth century (**Map 2.3**). Portugal claimed the giant territory of Brazil under the Tordesillas treaty but was far more concerned with exploiting its hard-won trade with the East Indies than with colonizing the

CHAPTER LOCATOR | What factors led to European exploration in the fifteenth century?

42 CHAPTER 2 EUROPEANS ENCOUNTER THE NEW WORLD

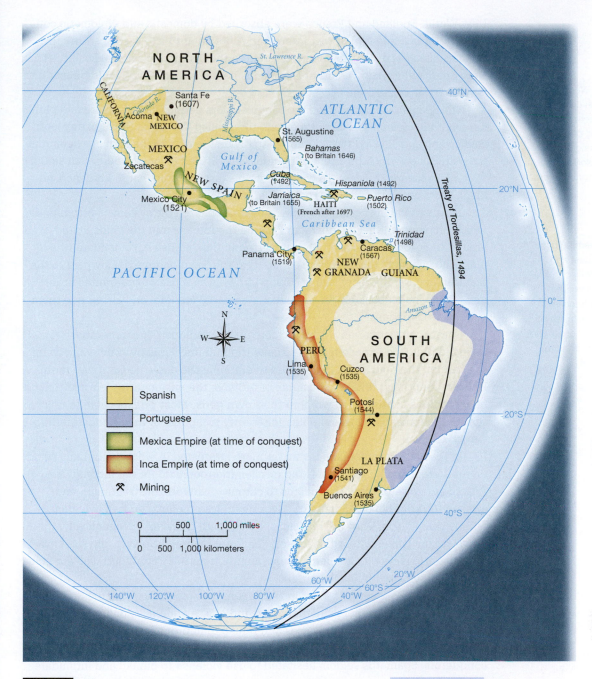

MAP 2.3 ■ Sixteenth-Century European Colonies in the New World

Spanish control spread throughout Central and South America during the sixteenth century, with the important exception of Portuguese Brazil. North America, though claimed by Spain under the Treaty of Tordesillas, remained peripheral to Spain's New World empire.

> **MAP ACTIVITY**

READING THE MAP: Track Spain's efforts at colonization by date. How did political holdings, the physical layout of the land, and natural resources influence where the Spaniards directed their energies?

CONNECTIONS: What was the purpose of the Treaty of Tordesillas? How might the location of silver and gold mines have affected Spain's desire to assert its claims over regions still held by Portugal after 1494 as well as Spain's interest in California, New Mexico, and Florida?

| What did Spanish explorers discover in the western Atlantic? | **How did Spaniards explore, conquer, and colonize New Spain?** | What impact did Spain's New World endeavors have in Europe? | Conclusion: What promise did the New World offer Europeans? | ✔ **LearningCurve** Check what you know. bedfordstmartins.com /roarkunderstanding |

New Spain

▶ Land in the New World held by the Spanish crown. Spain pioneered techniques of using New World colonies to strengthen the kingdom in Europe. Spain's colonial system would become a model for other European nations.

encomienda

▶ A system for governing used during the Reconquest and in New Spain. It allowed the Spanish encomendero (the "owner" of a town) to collect tribute from the town in return for providing law and order and encouraging "his" Indians to convert to Christianity.

New World. England and France were absorbed by domestic and diplomatic concerns in Europe and largely lost interest in America until late in the century. In the decades after 1519, the Spaniards created the distinctive colonial society of **New Spain**, which showed other Europeans how the New World could be made to serve the purposes of the Old.

The Spanish monarchy gave the conquistadors permission to explore and plunder what they found. The crown took one-fifth, called the "royal fifth," of any loot confiscated and allowed the conquerors to divide the rest. In the end, most conquistadors received very little after the plunder was divided among leaders such as Cortés and his favorite officers. To compensate his disappointed, battle-hardened soldiers, Cortés gave them towns the Spaniards had subdued.

The distribution of conquered towns institutionalized the system of **encomienda**, which empowered the conquistadors to rule the Indians and the lands in and around their towns. Encomienda transferred to the Spanish encomendero (the man who "owned" the town) the tribute that the town had previously paid to the Mexican empire. In theory, the encomendero was supposed to guarantee order and justice, be responsible for the Indians' material welfare, and encourage them to become Christians.

Catholic missionaries worked to convert the Indians. They fervently believed that God expected them to save the Indians' souls by convincing them to abandon their old sinful beliefs and to embrace the one true Christian faith. But after baptizing tens of thousands of Indians, the missionaries learned that many Indians continued to worship their own gods. Most priests came to believe that the Indians were lesser beings inherently incapable of fully understanding Christianity.

In practice, encomenderos were far more interested in what the Indians could do for them than in what they or the missionaries could do for the Indians. Encomenderos subjected the Indians to chronic overwork, mistreatment, and abuse. According to one Spaniard, "Everything [the Indians] do is slowly done and by compulsion. They are malicious, lying, [and] thievish." Economically, however, encomienda recognized a fundamental reality of New Spain: The most important treasure the Spaniards could plunder from the New World was not gold but uncompensated Indian labor.

The practice of coerced labor in New Spain grew directly out of the Spaniards' assumption that they were superior to the Indians. As one missionary put it, the Indians "are more stupid than asses and refuse to improve in anything." Therefore, most Spaniards assumed, Indians' labor should be organized by and for their conquerors. Spaniards seldom hesitated to use violence to punish and intimidate recalcitrant Indians.

Encomienda engendered two groups of influential critics. A few missionaries were horrified at the brutal mistreatment of the Indians. "What will [the Indians] think about the God of the Christians," Friar Bartolomé de Las Casas asked, when they see their friends "with their heads split, their hands amputated, their intestines torn open? . . . Would they want to come to Christ's sheepfold after their homes had been destroyed, their children imprisoned, their wives raped, their cities devastated, their maidens deflowered, and their provinces laid waste?" Las Casas and other outspoken missionaries softened few hearts among the encomenderos, but they did win some sympathy for the

CHAPTER LOCATOR | What factors led to European exploration in the fifteenth century?

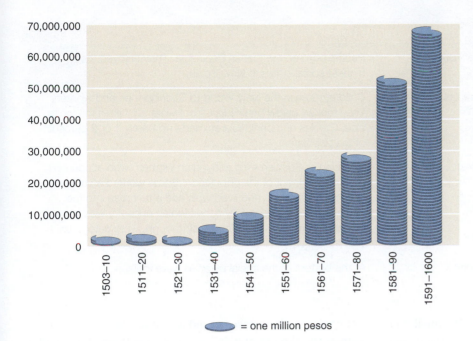

FIGURE 2.1 ■ New World Gold and Silver Imported into Spain during the Sixteenth Century, in Pesos

Spain imported more gold than silver during the first three decades of the sixteenth century, but the total value of this treasure was quickly eclipsed during the 1530s and 1540s, when rich silver mines were developed. Silver accounted for most of the enormous growth in Spain's precious-metal imports from the New World.

= one million pesos

Indians from the Spanish monarchy and royal bureaucracy. The Spanish monarchy moved to abolish encomienda in an effort to replace swashbuckling old conquistadors with royal bureaucrats as the rulers of New Spain.

In 1549, a reform called the *repartimiento* began to replace encomienda. It limited the labor an encomendero could command from his Indians to forty-five days per year from each adult male. The repartimiento, however, did not challenge the principle of forced labor, nor did it prevent encomenderos from continuing to cheat, mistreat, and overwork their Indians. Many Indians were put to work in silver mines. Mining was grueling and dangerous for the workers, but very profitable for the Spaniards who supervised them: During the entire sixteenth century, precious-metal exports from New Spain to Spain were worth twenty-five times more than the next most important export, leather hides (**Figure 2.1**).

For Spaniards, life in New Spain after the conquests was relatively easy. As one colonist wrote to his brother in Spain, "Don't hesitate [to come]. . . . This land [New Spain] is as good as ours [in Spain], for God has given us more here than there, and we shall be better off." During the century after 1492, about 225,000 Spaniards settled in the colonies. Virtually all of them were poor young men of common (non-noble) lineage who came directly from Spain. Laborers and artisans made up the largest proportion, but soldiers and sailors were also numerous. Men vastly outnumbered women.

The gender and number of Spanish settlers shaped two fundamental features of the society of New Spain. First, Europeans never made up more than 1 or 2 percent of the total population. Although Spaniards ruled New Spain, the population was almost wholly Indian. Second, the shortage of Spanish women meant that Spanish men frequently married Indian women or used them as concubines. The relatively few women from Spain usually married Spanish men, contributing to a tiny elite defined by European origins.

What did Spanish explorers discover in the western Atlantic?

How did Spaniards explore, conquer, and colonize New Spain?

What impact did Spain's New World endeavors have in Europe?

Conclusion: What promise did the New World offer Europeans?

☑ LearningCurve
Check what you know.
bedfordstmartins.com
/roarkunderstanding

45

> Social and Racial Hierarchy in New Spain	
Peninsulares	People born on the Iberian Peninsula. They enjoyed the highest social status in New Spain.
Creoles	Children born in the New World to Spanish men and women. They ranked below peninsulares but were still within the white elite. Creoles and peninsulares made up barely 1 or 2 percent of the population.
Mestizos	Offspring of Spanish men and Indian women, who accounted for 4 or 5 percent of the population. Some worked as artisans and labor overseers and lived well, and a few rose into the ranks of the elite, especially if their Indian ancestry was not obvious from their skin color. Most, though, were categorized with Indians.
Indians	At the bottom of the social pyramid were Indians.

creoles

▶ Children born to Spanish parents in the New World who, with the peninsulares, made up the tiny portion of the population at the top of the colonial social hierarchy.

The small number of Spaniards, the masses of Indians, and the frequency of intermarriage created a steep social hierarchy defined by perceptions of national origin and race. The society of New Spain, with *peninsulares* and **creoles** enjoying the highest status, established the precedent for what would become a pronounced pattern in the European colonies of the New World: a society stratified sharply by social origin and race. All Europeans of whatever social origin considered themselves superior to Native Americans; in New Spain, they were a dominant minority in both power and status.

The Toll of Spanish Conquest and Colonization

By 1560, the major centers of Indian civilization had been conquered, their leaders overthrown, their religion held in contempt, and their people forced to work for the Spaniards. Profound demoralization pervaded Indian society.

Adding to the culture shock of conquest and colonization was the deadly toll of European diseases. As conquest spread, the Indians succumbed to epidemics of measles, smallpox, and respiratory illnesses. They had no immunity to these diseases because they had not been exposed to them before the arrival of Europeans. By 1570, the Indian population of New Spain had fallen about 90 percent from what it had been when Columbus arrived, a catastrophe unequaled in human history.

For the Spaniards, Indian deaths meant that the most valuable resource of New Spain—Indian labor—dwindled rapidly. By the last quarter of the sixteenth century, Spanish colonists began to import African slaves. In the years before 1550, while Indian labor was still adequate, only 15,000 slaves were imported from Africa. The relatively high cost of African slaves kept imports low, totaling approximately 36,000 from 1550 to the end of the century. During the sixteenth century, New Spain continued to rely primarily on a shrinking number of Indians.

CHAPTER LOCATOR | What factors led to European exploration in the fifteenth century?

Español con India.
Mestizo.

Mestizo con Española.
Castizo.

Castizo con Española.
Español.

Español con Mora.
Mulato.

5

Mulato con Española.
Morisco.

6

Morisco con Española.
Chino.

7

Chino con India.
Salta atras.

Salta atras con Mulata.
Lobo.

Mixed Races

These eighteenth-century paintings illustrate forms of racial mixture common in sixteenth-century New Spain. In the first painting, a Spanish man and an Indian woman have a mestizo son; in the fourth, a Spanish man and a woman of African descent have a mulatto son. Can you detect any meanings of racial categories in the clothing? Bob Schalkwijk/INAH.

> VISUAL ACTIVITY

READING THE IMAGE: What do these paintings reveal about social status in New Spain?

CONNECTIONS: How do these paintings illustrate the power the Spaniards exercised in their New World colonies? What were some other aspects of colonial society that demonstrated Spanish domination?

QUICK REVIEW

How did New Spain's distinctive colonial population shape its economy and society?

What did Spanish explorers discover in the western Atlantic?

How did Spaniards explore, conquer, and colonize New Spain?

What impact did Spain's New World endeavors have in Europe?

Conclusion: What promise did the New World offer Europeans?

☑ LearningCurve
Check what you know.
bedfordstmartins.com
/roarkunderstanding

What impact did Spain's New World endeavors have in Europe?

Algonquian Ceremonial Dance

When English artist John White visited the coast of present-day North Carolina in 1585 as part of Raleigh's expedition, he painted this Algonquian ceremonial dance. This is one of the only likenesses of sixteenth-century North American Indians that were drawn from direct observation. Copyright © The British Museum.

THE RICHES OF NEW SPAIN HELPED make the sixteenth century the Golden Age of Spain. After Queen Isabella and King Ferdinand died, their sixteen-year-old grandson became King Charles I of Spain in 1516. Three years later, in 1519, just as Cortés ventured into Mexico, King Charles became Holy Roman Emperor Charles V. His empire encompassed more territory than that of any other European monarch. He used the wealth of New Spain to promote his interests in sixteenth-century Europe. He also sought to defend orthodox Christianity from the insurgent heresy of the Protestant Reformation. The power of the Spanish monarchy spread the message throughout sixteenth-century Europe that a New World empire could bankroll Old World ambitions.

The Protestant Reformation and the Spanish Response

In 1517, Martin Luther, an obscure Catholic priest in central Germany, initiated the **Protestant Reformation** by publicizing his criticisms of the Catholic Church. Luther's ideas won the sympathy of many Catholics, but they were considered

Protestant Reformation

▶ The reform movement that began in 1517 with Martin Luther's critiques of the Roman Catholic Church. The Protestant Reformation precipitated an enduring schism that divided Protestants from Catholics.

CHAPTER LOCATOR | What factors led to European exploration in the fifteenth century?

extremely dangerous by church officials and by monarchs such as Charles V, who believed that just as the church spoke for God, they ruled for God.

Luther preached a doctrine known as "justification by faith": Individual Christians could obtain salvation and life everlasting only by having faith that God would save them. Giving monetary offerings to the church, following the orders of priests, or participating in church rituals would not bring believers closer to heaven. The only true source of information about God's will was the Bible, not the church. By reading the Bible, any Christian could learn as much about God's commandments as any priest. Indeed, Luther called for a "priesthood of all believers."

In effect, Luther charged that the Catholic Church was in many respects fraudulent. Luther declared that the church had neglected its true purpose of helping individual Christians understand the spiritual realm revealed in the Bible and had wasted its resources in worldly conflicts of politics and wars. Luther hoped his ideas would reform the Catholic Church, but instead they ruptured forever the unity of Christianity in western Europe.

Charles V pledged to exterminate Luther's Protestant heresies. The wealth pouring into Spain from the New World fueled his efforts to defend the orthodox Catholic faith against Protestants, as well as against any other challenge to Spain's supremacy. As the most powerful monarch in Europe, Charles V, followed by his son and successor Philip II, assumed responsibility for upholding the existing order of sixteenth-century Europe.

American wealth, particularly Mexican silver, fueled Spanish ambitions, but Charles V's and Philip II's expenses for constant warfare far outstripped the revenues arriving from New Spain. The monarchy's ambitions impoverished the vast majority of Spain's population and brought the nation to the brink of bankruptcy. By the end of the sixteenth century, interest payments on royal debts swallowed two-thirds of the crown's annual revenues. In retrospect, the riches from New Spain proved a short-term blessing but a long-term curse.

Most Spaniards, however, looked upon New Spain as a glorious national achievement that displayed Spain's superiority over Native Americans and other Europeans. They had added enormously to their own knowledge and wealth. They had built mines, cities, Catholic churches, and even universities on the other side of the Atlantic. These military, religious, and economic achievements gave them great pride and confidence.

Europe and the Spanish Example

The lessons of sixteenth-century Spain were not lost on Spain's European rivals. Spain proudly displayed the fruits of its New World conquests. In 1520, for example, the German artist Albrecht Dürer wrote in his diary that he "marveled over the subtle ingenuity of the men in these distant lands [of New Spain]" who created such things as "a sun entirely of gold, a whole fathom [six feet] broad." But

1517
– Protestant Reformation begins in Germany.

1519
– Charles I of Spain becomes the Holy Roman Emperor Charles V.

1524
– Giovanni da Verrazano explores the Atlantic coast of North America for France.

1535
– Jacques Cartier explores the St. Lawrence River.

1576
– Martin Frobisher explores northern Canadian waters.

1578/1583
– Sir Humphrey Gilbert leads expeditions to Newfoundland.

1585
– Sir Walter Raleigh organizes expedition to settle Roanoke Island.

What did Spanish explorers discover in the western Atlantic?

How did Spaniards explore, conquer, and colonize New Spain?

What impact did Spain's New World endeavors have in Europe?

Conclusion: What promise did the New World offer Europeans?

☑ LearningCurve
Check what you know.
bedfordstmartins.com
/roarkunderstanding

49

Roanoke Settlement, 1587–1590

the most exciting news about "the men in these distant lands" was that they could serve the interests of Europeans, as Spain had shown. With a few notable exceptions, Europeans saw the New World as a place for the expansion of European influence, a place where, as one Spaniard wrote, Europeans could "give to those strange lands the form of our own."

France and England tried to follow Spain's example. Both nations warred with Spain in Europe, preyed on Spanish treasure fleets, and ventured to the New World, where they too hoped to find an undiscovered passageway to the East Indies or another Mexico or Peru. By the end of the century, however, England had failed to secure a New World beachhead.

TABLE 2.1 ■ France and England Follow Spain to the New World

Explorer (sponsoring country)	Destination and result
Giovanni da Verrazano (France)	The Atlantic coast of North America from North Carolina to Canada, to search for a Northwest Passage, 1524. Unsuccessful.
Jacques Cartier (France)	St. Lawrence River, 1535. Established colony in 1541, but it did not succeed.
Martin Frobisher (England)	In 1576, in another attempt to find a Northwest Passage, sailed to northern Canada, where he retrieved worthless "ore" that he thought was gold, causing the English to lose interest in the region and explore farther south.
Sir Humphrey Gilbert (England)	Led expeditions to Newfoundland in 1578 and 1583 to found colonies; vanished at sea.
Sir Walter Raleigh (England)	Organized expedition in 1585 to settle Roanoke Island off the coast of present-day North Carolina. More than one hundred settlers were sent to colonize Roanoke in 1587. The colonists disappeared between 1587 and 1590, leaving only the word *Croatoan* (whose meaning is unknown) carved in a tree.

> QUICK REVIEW

How did Spain's conquests in the New World shape Spanish influence in Europe?

CHAPTER LOCATOR | What factors led to European exploration in the fifteenth century?

Conclusion: What promise did the New World offer Europeans?

THE SIXTEENTH CENTURY in the New World belonged to the Spaniards who employed Columbus and to the Indians who greeted him as he stepped ashore. The Portuguese, whose voyages to Africa and Asia set the stage for Columbus's voyages, won the important consolation prize of Brazil, but Spain hit the jackpot. Isabella of Spain helped initiate the Columbian exchange between the New World and the Old, which massively benefited first Spain and later other Europeans and which continues to this day. The exchange also subjected Native Americans to the ravages of European diseases and Spanish conquest. Spanish explorers, conquistadors, and colonists forced the Indians to serve the interests of Spanish settlers and the Spanish monarchy. The exchange illustrated one of the most important lessons of the sixteenth century: After millions of years, the Atlantic no longer was an impermeable barrier separating the Eastern and Western Hemispheres. After the voyages of Columbus, European sailing ships regularly bridged the Atlantic and carried people, products, diseases, and ideas from one shore to the other.

No European monarch could forget the seductive lesson taught by Spain's example: The New World could vastly enrich the Old. Spain remained a New World power for almost four centuries, and its language, religion, culture, and institutions left a permanent imprint. By the end of the sixteenth century, however, other European monarchies had begun to contest Spain's dominion in Europe and to make forays into the northern fringes of Spain's New World preserve. To reap the benefits the Spaniards enjoyed from their New World domain, the others had to learn a difficult lesson: how to deviate from Spain's example. That discovery lay ahead.

While England's rulers eyed the huge North American hinterland of New Spain, they realized that it lacked the two main attractions of Mexico and Peru: incredible material wealth and large populations of Indians to use as workers. In the absence of gold and silver booty and plentiful native labor in North America, England would need to find some way to attract colonizers to a region that—compared to New Spain—did not appear very promising. During the next century, England's leaders overcame these dilemmas by developing a distinctive colonial model, one that encouraged land-hungry settlers from England and Europe to engage in agriculture and that depended on other sources of unfree labor: indentured servants from Europe and slaves from Africa.

What did Spanish explorers discover in the western Atlantic?

How did Spaniards explore, conquer, and colonize New Spain?

What impact did Spain's New World endeavors have in Europe?

Conclusion: What promise did the New World offer Europeans?

☑ **LearningCurve**
Check what you know.
bedfordstmartins.com
/roarkunderstanding

51

CHAPTER 2 STUDY GUIDE

 STEP 1 **GET STARTED ONLINE**

 LearningCurve ▪ bedfordstmartins.com/roarkunderstanding

Now that you've read the chapter, make it stick by completing the LearningCurve activity.

 STEP 2 **EXPLAIN WHY IT MATTERS**

Put your reading into practice. Identify each term below, and then explain why it matters in U.S. history.

TERM	WHO OR WHAT & WHEN	WHY IT MATTERS
Black Death (p. 31)		
Reconquest (p. 32)		
Tainos (p. 35)		
Treaty of Tordesillas (p. 36)		
Columbian exchange (p. 38)		
conquistadors (p. 41)		
Incan empire (p. 41)		
Acoma pueblo revolt (p. 42)		
New Spain (p. 44)		
encomienda (p. 44)		
creoles (p. 46)		
Protestant Reformation (p. 48)		

 **STEP 3** **MOVE BEYOND THE BASICS**

To demonstrate a more advanced understanding, consider the similarities and differences in the exploration and conquest of two explorers for Spain — Christopher Columbus and Hernán Cortés. What were the motivations behind each man's expeditions? How did these expeditions affect the peoples each encountered?

Explorer	Motivations	Impact on New World peoples	Benefits for Spain
Christopher Columbus			
Hernán Cortés			

PUT IT ALL TOGETHER Now, take a step back and try to explain the big picture. Remember to use specific examples from the chapter in your answers.

EXPANSION AND EXPLORATION

▶ Why was Portuguese maritime exploration focused on the west coast of Africa? What did Portugal hope to gain from such journeys?

▶ What was the Columbian exchange, and what were its consequences for both the peoples of the Americas and those from the Old World?

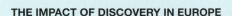

CONQUEST AND COLONIZATION

▶ Describe the government and society of New Spain. How did New Spain reflect the values, beliefs, and goals of the Spanish conquerors?

▶ How did Spanish conquest and colonization affect the peoples of the Americas?

THE IMPACT OF DISCOVERY IN EUROPE

▶ What role did New World wealth play in the clash between Protestants and Catholics in sixteenth-century Europe?

▶ What lessons did other European powers draw from Spain's experience in the New World?

LOOKING BACKWARD, LOOKING AHEAD

▶ How did the isolation of the peoples of the Americas before 1492 affect the course and consequences of European expansion in the New World?

▶ How did Spanish success in the New World influence European competition for control of the Americas?

> **IN YOUR OWN WORDS**

Imagine that you must give an oral report to the class answering the following question: **What were the most significant effects of European exploration in the sixteenth century?** What would be the most important points to include and why?

> **Do it online at the Student Site** ■ **bedfordstmartins.com/roarkunderstanding**

3

FOUNDING THE SOUTHERN COLONIES IN THE SEVENTEENTH CENTURY

1601–1700

> **What were the most important factors that shaped England's southern colonies in the seventeenth century?** Chapter 3 examines the establishment and growth of England's southern mainland colonies in North America over the course of the seventeenth century. It explores the early years of the Virginia colony, the rise of tobacco culture in the Chesapeake and its impact on the region's social and political environment, colonial relations among different groups of people, and the development of African slavery as the dominant labor force in the south.

LearningCurve

bedfordstmartins.com/roarkunderstanding
After reading the chapter, use LearningCurve to retain what you've read.

Scene from Captain John Smith, *A Generall Historie of Virginia* (1624), in which Pocahontas "saves" Smith's life. Bridgeman.

> What challenges faced early Chesapeake colonists?

> How did Chesapeake tobacco society take shape?

> Why did Chesapeake colonial society change in the late seventeenth century?

> Why did the southern colonies move toward a slave labor system?

> Conclusion: Why were export crops and slave labor important in the growth of the southern colonies?

What challenges faced early Chesapeake colonists?

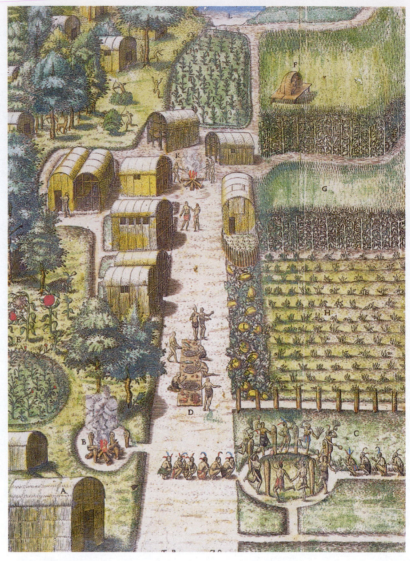

Secotan Village

This engraving was copied from an original drawing John White made in 1585 when he visited the village of Secotan on the coast of present-day North Carolina. The drawing shows daily life in the village, which may have resembled one of Powhatan's settlements. This drawing conveys the message that Secotan was orderly, settled, religious, harmonious, and peaceful—and very different from English villages. Princeton University Libraries, Department of Rare Books and Special Collections.

> VISUAL ACTIVITY

READING THE IMAGE: What does this image say about Indian life in Secotan?
CONNECTIONS: How did Indian society differ from the English tobacco society that emerged later?

IN 1606, England's King James I granted the Virginia Company more than six million acres in North America in hopes of establishing the English equivalent of Spain's New World empire. Enthusiastic reports from the Roanoke voyages twenty years earlier (see chapter 2) claimed that in Virginia "the earth bringeth foorth all things in aboundance . . . without toile or labour." Investors hoped to profit by growing some valuable exotic crop, finding gold or silver, or raiding

Spanish treasure ships. Their hopes failed to confront the difficulties of adapting English desires and expectations to the New World already inhabited by Native Americans. The Jamestown settlement struggled to survive for nearly two decades, until the royal government replaced the private Virginia Company, which never earned a profit for its investors.

The Fragile Jamestown Settlement

Although Spain claimed all of North America under the 1494 Treaty of Tordesillas (see chapter 2), King James believed that England could encroach on the outskirts of Spain's New World empire. In effect, his land grant to the **Virginia Company**, a joint-stock company, was a royal license to poach on both Spanish claims and the chiefdom of Powhatan, the supreme chief of the **Algonquian Indians** who inhabited the coastal plain of present-day Virginia.

English merchants had pooled their capital and shared risks for many years by using joint-stock companies for trading voyages to Europe, Asia, and Africa. The London investors of the Virginia Company, however, had larger ambitions: They hoped to found an empire that would strengthen England both overseas and at home. Richard Hakluyt, a strong proponent of colonization, claimed that a colony would provide work for swarms of poor "valiant youths rusting and hurtfull by lack of employment" in England. Colonists could buy English goods and supply products that England now had to import from other nations.

In December 1606, the ships *Susan Constant*, *Discovery*, and *Godspeed* carried 144 Englishmen toward Virginia. A few weeks after they arrived at the mouth of Chesapeake Bay on April 26, 1607, they went ashore on a small peninsula in the midst of the territory ruled by Powhatan and quickly built a fort, the first building in **Jamestown**. The fort showed the colonists' awareness that they needed to protect themselves. For weeks, the settlers and Algonquian warriors under the leadership of Powhatan skirmished repeatedly.

The settlers soon confronted dangerous, invisible threats: disease and starvation. During the summer, many of the Englishmen lay "night and day groaning in every corner of the Fort most pittiful to heare," wrote George Percy, one of the settlers. The colonists increased their misery by bickering among themselves, leaving crops unplanted and food supplies shrinking. "For the most part [the settlers] died of meere famine," Percy wrote; "there were never Englishmen left in a forreigne Countrey in such miserie as wee were in this new discovered Virginia."

Powhatan's people came to the rescue of the weakened and demoralized Englishmen. Early in September 1607, they began to bring corn to the colony for barter. Accustomed to eating food derived from wheat, English people considered corn the food "of the barbarous Indians which know no better." The famished colonists soon overcame their prejudice against corn. Indians' corn acquired by both trade and plunder managed to keep 38 of the original settlers alive until a fresh supply of food and 120 more colonists arrived from England in January 1608.

It is difficult to exaggerate the fragility of the early Jamestown settlement. One colonist lamented that "this place [is] a meere plantacion of sorrowes and Cropp of trobles, having been plentifull in nothing but want and wanting nothing but plenty." The Virginia Company sent hundreds of new settlers to Jamestown

Virginia Company
▶ A joint-stock company organized by London investors in 1606 that received a land grant from King James I in order to establish English colonies in North America. Investors hoped to enrich themselves and strengthen England economically and politically.

Algonquian Indians
▶ People who inhabited the coastal plain of present-day Virginia, near Chesapeake Bay, when English colonists first settled the region.

Jamestown
▶ The first permanent English settlement in North America, established in 1607 by colonists sponsored by the Virginia Company.

| How did Chesapeake tobacco society take shape? | Why did Chesapeake colonial society change in the late seventeenth century? | Why did the southern colonies move toward a slave labor system? | Conclusion: Why were export crops and slave labor important in the growth of the southern colonies? | ✓ **LearningCurve** Check what you know. bedfordstmartins.com /roarkunderstanding |

57

each year, each of them eager to find the paradise promised by the company. But most settlers went instead to early graves.

Cooperation and Conflict between Natives and Newcomers

Powhatan's people stayed in contact with the English settlers but maintained their distance. The Virginia Company boasted that the settlers bought from the Indians "the pearles of earth [corn] and [sold] to them the pearles of heaven [Christianity]." In fact, few Indians converted to Christianity, and the English devoted scant effort to proselytizing. Marriage between Indian women and English men also was rare, despite the acute shortage of English women in Virginia in the early years. Few settlers bothered to learn the Indians' language.

The miscommunication and misunderstandings between the settlers and Powhatan's people are illustrated by the story of the capture and release of Captain John Smith. In December 1607, Smith was captured by warriors of Powhatan. According to Smith, Powhatan "feasted him after their best barbarous manner." Then, Smith recalled, "two great stones were brought before Powhatan: then as many [Indians] as could layd hands on [Smith], dragged him to [the stones], and thereon laid his head, and being ready with their clubs, to beate out his braines."

Ætatis suæ 21. Aᵒ. 1616.

Matoaks als Rebecka daughter to the mighty Prince Powhatan Emperour of Attanoughkomouck als Virginia converted and baptized in the Christian faith, and Wife to the worᵗ Mʳ Thoː Rolff.

At that moment, Pocahontas, Powhatan's eleven-year-old daughter, rushed forward and "got [Smith's] head in her armes, and laid her owne upon his to save him from death." Pocahontas, Smith wrote, "hazarded the beating out of her owne braines to save mine, and . . . so prevailed with her father, that I was safely conducted [back] to James towne."

Historians believe that this episode happened more or less as Smith described it. But Smith did not understand why Pocahontas acted as she did. Most likely, what Smith interpreted as Pocahontas's saving him from certain death was instead a ritual enacting Powhatan's willingness to incorporate Smith and the white strangers at

Pocahontas in England

Shortly after Pocahontas and her husband, John Rolfe, arrived in England in 1616, she posed for this portrait dressed in English clothing. The portrait captures the dual novelty of England for Pocahontas and of Pocahontas for the English. The mutability of Pocahontas's identity is displayed in the identification of her as "Matoaks" or "Rebecka." National Portrait Gallery, Smithsonian Institution/Art Resource, NY.

CHAPTER LOCATOR | **What challenges faced early Chesapeake colonists?**

Jamestown into Powhatan's empire. By appearing to save Smith, Pocahontas was probably acting out Smith's new status as an adopted member of Powhatan's extended family.

After Smith returned to England about two years later, relations between Powhatan and the English colonists deteriorated into bloody raids. In 1613, the colonists captured Pocahontas and held her hostage at Jamestown. Within a year, she converted to Christianity and married a colonist named John Rolfe. After giving birth to a son named Thomas, Pocahontas, her husband, and the new baby sailed for England in the spring of 1616. There, promoters of the Virginia colony dressed her as a proper Englishwoman and arranged for her to go to a ball attended by the king and queen. Pocahontas died in England in 1617. Her son, Thomas, ultimately returned to Virginia.

Events like the capture of Pocahontas gave Powhatan's people good reason to regard the English with suspicion. Although the settlers often made friendly overtures to the Indians, they did not hesitate to use their guns and swords to enforce English notions of proper Indian behavior. When Indians refused to trade their corn to the settlers, the English pillaged their villages and confiscated their corn.

The Indians retaliated against English violence, but for fifteen years they did not organize an all-out assault on the European intruders, probably for several reasons. Although Christianity held few attractions for the Indians, the power of the settlers' God impressed them. One chief told John Smith that "he did believe that our [English] God as much exceeded theirs as our guns did their bows and arrows." Powhatan probably concluded that these powerful strangers would make better allies than enemies.

The English also traded with his people, usually exchanging European goods for corn. Native Virginians quickly recognized the superiority of the intruders' iron and steel knives, axes, and pots, and they eagerly traded corn for them.

But why were the settlers unable to feed themselves for more than a decade? First, as the staggering death rate suggests, many settlers were too sick to be productive. Second, very few farmers came to Virginia in the early years. Instead, most of the newcomers were gentlemen and their servants who, in John Smith's words, "never did know what a day's work was." Smith declared repeatedly that in Virginia "there is no country to pillage [as in New Spain]. . . . All you can expect from [Virginia] must be by labor."

The persistence of the Virginia colony created difficulties for Powhatan's chiefdom. Steady contact between natives and newcomers spread European diseases among the Indians, who suffered deadly epidemics. To produce enough corn for trade with the English required the Indian women to spend more time and effort growing crops. But from the Indians' viewpoint, the most important fact about the always-hungry English colonists was that they were not going away.

Powhatan died in 1618, and his brother Opechancanough replaced him as supreme chief. In 1622, Opechancanough organized an all-out assault on the English settlers. As an English colonist observed, "the savages . . . fell upon us murdering and killing everybody they could reach[,] sparing neither women nor children." In all, the Indians killed 347 colonists, nearly a third of the English population. But the attack failed to dislodge the colonists. Instead, in the years to come the settlers unleashed a murderous campaign of Indian extermination that

How did Chesapeake tobacco society take shape?

Why did Chesapeake colonial society change in the late seventeenth century?

Why did the southern colonies move toward a slave labor system?

Conclusion: Why were export crops and slave labor important in the growth of the southern colonies?

LearningCurve
Check what you know.
bedfordstmartins.com
/roarkunderstanding

pushed the Indians beyond the small circumference of white settlement. After 1622, most colonists considered Indians their perpetual enemies.

From Private Company to Royal Government

In the immediate aftermath of the 1622 uprising, the survivors became demoralized because, as one explained, the "massacre killed all our Countrie . . . [and] burst the heart of all the rest." The disaster prompted a royal investigation of affairs in Virginia. The investigators discovered that the appalling mortality among the colonists was caused more by disease and mismanagement than by Indian raids. In 1624, King James revoked the charter of the Virginia Company and made Virginia a **royal colony**, subject to the direction of the royal government rather than of the company's private investors, an arrangement that lasted until 1776.

The king now appointed the governor of Virginia and his council, but most other features of local government established under the Virginia Company remained intact. In 1619, for example, the company had inaugurated the **House of Burgesses**, an assembly of representatives (called burgesses) elected by the colony's male voters. Under the new royal government, laws passed by the burgesses had to be approved by the king's bureaucrats in England rather than by the company. Otherwise, the House of Burgesses continued as before, acquiring distinction as the oldest representative legislative assembly in the English colonies. Under the new royal government, all free adult men in Virginia could vote for the House of Burgesses, giving it a far broader and more representative constituency than the English House of Commons had.

The demise of the Virginia Company marked the end of the first phase of colonization of the Chesapeake region. From the first 105 adventurers in 1607, the population had grown to about 1,200 by 1624. Despite mortality rates higher than during the worst epidemics in London, new settlers still came. Their arrival and King James's willingness to take over the struggling colony reflected a fundamental change in Virginia. After years of fruitless experimentation, it was becoming clear that English settlers could make a fortune in Virginia by growing tobacco.

royal colony

▶ A colony ruled by a king or queen and governed by officials appointed to serve the monarchy and represent its interests.

House of Burgesses

▶ An organ of government in colonial Virginia made up of an assembly of representatives elected by the colony's male voters. It was established by the Virginia Company and continued by the crown after Virginia was made a royal colony.

> ## QUICK REVIEW

Why did Powhatan behave as he did toward the English colonists?

Smoking Club In Europe, tobacco smokers congregated in clubs to enjoy the intoxicating weed. This seventeenth-century print satirizes smokers' gatherings of fashionable men, women, and children who indulged their taste for tobacco. Emblems of the tobacco trade adorn the wall; pipes, spittoons, and other smoking implements are close at hand; and the dog cleans up after those who cannot hold their smoke. *Koninklijke Bibliotheek, The Hague.*

How did Chesapeake tobacco society take shape?

TOBACCO GREW WILD IN THE NEW WORLD, and Native Americans had used it for thousands of years before Europeans arrived. Many sixteenth-century European explorers noticed the Indians' habit of "drinking smoke." During the sixteenth century, tobacco was an expensive luxury used sparingly by a few in Europe. During the next century, English colonists in North America sent so much tobacco to European markets that it became an affordable indulgence used often by many people.

By 1700, nearly 100,000 colonists lived in the Chesapeake region, encompassing Virginia, Maryland, and northern North Carolina (**Map 3.1**). Although they differed in wealth, landholding, access to labor, and religion, they shared a dedication to growing tobacco. They exported more than 35 million pounds of tobacco in 1700, a fivefold increase in per capita production since 1620. Settlers lived by the rhythms of tobacco agriculture, and their endless need for labor attracted droves of English indentured servants to grueling work in tobacco fields.

Tobacco Agriculture

Initially, the Virginia Company had no plans to grow and sell tobacco. John Rolfe—future husband of Pocahontas—planted West Indian tobacco seeds in 1612 and learned that they flourished in Virginia. By 1617, the colonists had grown enough tobacco to send the first commercial shipment to England, where

> **CHRONOLOGY**

1612
– John Rolfe begins to plant tobacco in Virginia.

1617
– Colonists send the first commercial tobacco shipment to England.

1619
– First Africans arrive in Virginia.

1632
– King Charles I grants land for the colony of Maryland.

1634
– Colonists begin to arrive in Maryland.

How did Chesapeake tobacco society take shape?

Why did Chesapeake colonial society change in the late seventeenth century?

Why did the southern colonies move toward a slave labor system?

Conclusion: Why were export crops and slave labor important in the growth of the southern colonies?

☑ LearningCurve Check what you know. bedfordstmartins.com /roarkunderstanding

61

MAP 3.1 ■ Chesapeake Colonies in the Seventeenth Century

This map illustrates the intimate association between land and water in the settlement of the Chesapeake in the seventeenth century. The fall line indicates the limit of navigable water, where rapids and falls prevented travel farther upstream.

> MAP ACTIVITY

READING THE MAP: Using the notations on the map, create a chronology of the establishment of towns and settlements. What physical features correspond to the earliest habitation by English settlers?

CONNECTIONS: Why was access to navigable water so important? Given the settlers' need for defense against native tribes, what explains the distance between settlements?

it sold for a high price. After that, Virginia pivoted from a colony of rather aimless adventurers to a society of dedicated tobacco planters.

A demanding crop, tobacco required close attention and a great deal of hand labor year-round. Like the Indians, the colonists "cleared" fields by cutting a ring of bark from each tree (a procedure known as "girdling"), thereby killing the tree. Girdling brought sunlight to clearings but left fields studded with tree stumps, requiring colonists to use heavy hoes to till their tobacco fields. To plant, a visitor observed, they "just make holes [with a stick] into which they drop the seeds," much as the Indians did.

The English settlers worked hard because their labor promised greater rewards in the Chesapeake region than in England. One colonist proclaimed that "the dirt of this Province affords as great a profit to the general Inhabitant, as the Gold of Peru doth to . . . the Spaniard." Although he exaggerated, it was true that

CHAPTER LOCATOR | What challenges faced early Chesapeake colonists?

Tobacco Plantation This print illustrates the processing of tobacco on a seventeenth-century plantation. Workers cut the mature plants and put the leaves in piles to wilt (left foreground). After the leaves dried somewhat, they were suspended from poles in a drying barn (right foreground), where they were seasoned before being packed in casks for shipping. From "About Tobacco," Lehman Brothers.

a hired man could expect to earn two or three times more in Virginia's tobacco fields than in England. Better still, in Virginia land was so abundant that it was extremely cheap compared with land in England.

By the mid-seventeenth century, common laborers could buy a hundred acres for less than their annual wages—an impossibility in England. New settlers who paid their own transportation to the Chesapeake received a grant of fifty acres of free land (termed a **headright**). The Virginia Company granted headrights to encourage settlement, and the royal government continued them for the same reason.

A Servant Labor System

Headrights, cheap land, and high wages gave poor English folk powerful incentives to immigrate to the New World. Yet many potential immigrants could not scrape together the money to pay for a trip across the Atlantic. Their poverty and the colonists' crying need for labor formed the basic context for the creation of a servant labor system.

About 80 percent of the immigrants to the Chesapeake during the seventeenth century came as **indentured servants**. Instead of a slave society, the

headright
▶ Fifty acres of free land granted by the Virginia Company to new settlers who paid their own transportation to the Chesapeake and to planters for each indentured servant they purchased.

indentured servants
▶ Poor immigrants who signed contracts known as indentures, in which they committed to four to seven years of labor in North America in exchange for transportation from England, as well as food and shelter after they arrived in the colony.

How did Chesapeake tobacco society take shape?

Why did Chesapeake colonial society change in the late seventeenth century?

Why did the southern colonies move toward a slave labor system?

Conclusion: Why were export crops and slave labor important in the growth of the southern colonies?

LearningCurve
Check what you know.
bedfordstmartins.com
/roarkunderstanding

seventeenth-century Chesapeake region was fundamentally a society of white servants and ex-servants.

Relatively few African slaves were brought to the Chesapeake in the first half century after settlement. The first known Africans arrived in Virginia in 1619. The "20. And odd Negroes," as John Rolfe called them, were slaves captured in Angola in west-central Africa. A few more slaves trickled into the Chesapeake region during the next several decades. Men and women of African descent occasionally became indentured servants, served out their terms of servitude, and became free. A few slaves purchased their way out of bondage and lived as free people. These people were exceptions, however. Almost all people of African descent were slaves and remained enslaved for life.

Ideally, indentures allowed poor immigrants to trade their most valuable assets — their freedom and their ability to work — for a trip to the New World and a period of servitude followed by freedom in a land of opportunity. Planters

Bristol Docks This painting of the docks in Bristol, England, portrays a scene common at ports throughout the seventeenth-century Atlantic world. Tobacco flooded into Bristol in the seventeenth century while Bristol merchants also became active in the African slave trade, trading English goods on the West African coast for slaves, who were then taken to the New World to be sold to eager sugar and tobacco planters. © Bristol City Museum and Art Gallery/UK Bridgeman Art Library.

CHAPTER LOCATOR | What challenges faced early Chesapeake colonists?

reaped more immediate benefits. Servants meant more hands to grow more tobacco. A planter expected a servant to grow enough tobacco in one year to cover the price the planter had paid for the indenture. Servants' labor during the remaining three to six years of the indenture promised a handsome profit for the planter. Planters also profited because they received a headright of fifty acres of land from the colonial government for every newly purchased servant.

> ### > Features of Indentured Servitude in the Chesapeake

- The majority of indentured servants were white immigrants from England.
- Immigrants borrowed the costs of transportation from a merchant or ship captain in England in exchange for four to seven years of work in North America.
- Immigrants' labor was sold to planters upon arrival in the colonies. Planters paid twice the cost of transportation and agreed to provide food and shelter.
- At the end of the indenture, former servants received "freedom dues," usually a few barrels of corn and a suit of clothes.

About three out of four servants were young men between the ages of fifteen and twenty-five when they arrived in the Chesapeake. Typically, they shared the desperation of sixteen-year-old Francis Haires, who indentured himself for seven years because, according to his contract, "his father and mother and All friends [are] dead and he [is] a miserable wandering boy." Like Francis, most servants had no special training or skills, although the majority had some experience with agricultural work. A skilled craftsman could obtain a shorter indenture, but few risked coming to the colonies since their prospects were better in England.

Women were almost as rare as skilled craftsmen in the Chesapeake and more ardently desired. In the early days of the tobacco boom, the Virginia Company shipped young single women servants to the colony as prospective wives for male settlers willing to pay "120 weight [pounds] of the best leaf tobacco for each of them," in effect getting both a wife and a servant. The company reasoned that, as one official wrote in 1622, "the plantation can never flourish till families be planted, and the respect of wives and children fix the people on the soil." Nonetheless, women remained a small minority of the Chesapeake population until late in the seventeenth century.

The servant labor system perpetuated the gender imbalance. Although female servants cost about the same as males and generally served for the same length of time, planters preferred male servants, as one explained, because they were "the mor[e] excellent and yousefull Cretuers," especially for field work. Although many servant women hoed and harvested tobacco fields, most also did household chores such as cooking, washing, cleaning, gardening, and milking.

The Rigors of Servitude

Servants—whether men or women, white or black, English or African—tended to work together and socialize together. During the first half century of settlement, racial intermingling occurred, although the small number of blacks made it infrequent. In general, the commonalities of servitude caused servants—regardless of

How did Chesapeake tobacco society take shape?

Why did Chesapeake colonial society change in the late seventeenth century?

Why did the southern colonies move toward a slave labor system?

Conclusion: Why were export crops and slave labor important in the growth of the southern colonies?

☑ LearningCurve
Check what you know.
bedfordstmartins.com
/roarkunderstanding

65

their race and gender—to consider themselves apart from free people, whose ranks they longed to join eventually.

Servant life was harsh by the standards of seventeenth-century England and even by the frontier standards of the Chesapeake. Unlike servants in England, Chesapeake servants had no control over who purchased their labor—and thus them—for the period of their indenture. They were "sold here upp and downe like horses," one observer reported. But tobacco planters' need for labor muffled complaints about treating servants as property.

For servants, the promise of indentured servitude in the Chesapeake often withered when they confronted the rigors of labor in the tobacco fields. Severe laws aimed to keep servants in their place. Punishments for petty crimes stretched servitude far beyond the original terms of indenture. After midcentury, the Virginia legislature added three or more years to the indentures of most servants by requiring them to serve until they were twenty-four years old.

Women servants were subject to special restrictions and risks. They were prohibited from marrying until their servitude had expired. A servant woman, the law assumed, could not serve two masters at the same time: one who owned her indentured labor and another who was her husband. As a rule, if a woman servant gave birth to a child, she had to serve two extra years and pay a fine.

Harsh punishments reflected four fundamental realities of the servant labor system. First, planters' hunger for labor caused them to demand as much labor as they could get from their servants. Second, servants hoped to survive their servitude and use their freedom to obtain land and start a family. Third, since servants saw themselves as free people in a temporary status of servitude, they often made grudging, halfhearted workers. Finally, planters put up with this contentious arrangement because the alternatives were less desirable.

Planters could not easily hire free men and women because land was readily available and free people preferred to work for themselves on their own land. Nor could planters depend on much labor from family members because families were few, were started late, and thus had few children. And, until the 1680s and 1690s, slaves were expensive and hard to come by. Before then, masters who wanted to grow more tobacco had few alternatives to buying indentured servants.

Cultivating Land and Faith

Villages and small towns dotted the rural landscape of seventeenth-century England, but in the Chesapeake towns were few and far between. Instead, tobacco farms occupied small clearings surrounded by hundreds of acres of wilderness. Since tobacco was a labor-intensive crop that quickly exhausted the fertility of the soil, each farmer cultivated only 5 or 10 percent of his land at any one time. Tobacco planters sought land that fronted a navigable river in order to minimize the work of transporting the heavy barrels of tobacco onto ships. A settled region thus resembled a lacework of farms stitched around waterways.

Most Chesapeake colonists were nominally Protestants. Attendance at Sunday services and conformity to the doctrines of the Church of England were required of all English men and women. Few clergymen migrated to the

CHAPTER LOCATOR | What challenges faced early Chesapeake colonists?

Chesapeake, however, and too few of those who did were models of piety. Certainly, some colonists took their religion seriously. But on the whole, religion did not awaken the zeal of Chesapeake settlers, certainly not as it did the zeal of New England settlers in these same years (as discussed in chapter 4). The religion of the Chesapeake colonists was Anglican, but their faith lay in the turbulent, competitive, high-stakes gamble of survival as tobacco planters.

Settlement Patterns along the James River

The situation was similar in the Catholic colony of Maryland. In 1632, England's King Charles I granted his Catholic friend Lord Baltimore about 6.5 million acres in the northern Chesapeake region. Lord Baltimore intended to create a refuge for Catholics, who suffered severe discrimination in England. He fitted out two ships, the *Ark* and the *Dove*; gathered about 150 settlers; and sent them to the new colony, where they arrived on March 25, 1634. However, Maryland failed to live up to Lord Baltimore's hopes. The colony's population grew very slowly for twenty years, and most settlers were Protestants rather than Catholics. The religious turmoil of the Puritan Revolution in England (discussed in chapter 4) spilled across the Atlantic, creating conflict between Maryland's few Catholics—most of them wealthy and prominent—and the Protestant majority, most of them neither wealthy nor prominent. During the 1660s, Maryland began to attract settlers, mostly Protestants, as readily as Virginia. Although Catholics and the Catholic faith continued to exert influence in Maryland, the colony's society, economy, politics, and culture became nearly indistinguishable from Virginia's. Both colonies shared a devotion to tobacco, the true faith of the Chesapeake.

QUICK REVIEW

Why did the vast majority of European immigrants to the Chesapeake come as indentured servants?

| **How did Chesapeake tobacco society take shape?** | Why did Chesapeake colonial society change in the late seventeenth century? | Why did the southern colonies move toward a slave labor system? | Conclusion: Why were export crops and slave labor important in the growth of the southern colonies? | ✓ LearningCurve Check what you know. bedfordstmartins.com /roarkunderstanding |

> Why did Chesapeake colonial society change in the late seventeenth century?

Jamestown Church Tower

This modern-day photograph shows the remains of the tower of the Anglican church that colonists constructed in Jamestown beginning in 1639. Nearby is the foundation of an older church, built in 1617, that also served as the site of the first meeting of the Virginia general assembly or House of Burgesses, the first representative legislative body in English North America. The churches illustrate the importance that Virginia's leaders attached to maintaining the central English institution of worship and spiritual order in the fledgling colony. Courtesy of Preservation Virginia.

THE SYSTEM OF INDENTURED SERVITUDE sharpened inequality in Chesapeake society by the mid-seventeenth century, propelling social and political polarization that culminated in 1676 with Bacon's Rebellion. The rebellion prompted reforms that stabilized relations between elite planters and their lesser neighbors and paved the way for a social hierarchy that muted differences of landholding and wealth and amplified racial differences. Amid this social and political evolution, Chesapeake colonists' dedication to growing tobacco did not change.

Social and Economic Polarization

The first half of the seventeenth century in the Chesapeake was the era of the yeoman—a farmer who owned a small plot of land sufficient to support a family and tilled largely by servants and a few family members. A small number of elite planters had larger estates and commanded ten or more servants. But for the first

CHAPTER LOCATOR | What challenges faced early Chesapeake colonists?

several decades, few men lived long enough to accumulate fortunes sufficient to set them much apart from their neighbors.

Until midcentury, the principal division in Chesapeake society was less between rich and poor planters than between free farmers and unfree servants. Although these two groups contrasted sharply in their legal and economic status, their daily lives had many similarities. Servants looked forward to the time when their indentures would expire and they would become free and eventually own land.

Three major developments splintered this rough frontier equality during the third quarter of the century. First, as planters grew more and more tobacco, the ample supply depressed tobacco prices in European markets. Cheap tobacco reduced planters' profits and made saving enough to become landowners more difficult for freed servants. Second, because the mortality rate in the Chesapeake colonies declined, more and more servants survived their indentures, and landless freemen became more numerous and grew more discontented. Third, declining mortality also encouraged the formation of a planter elite. By living longer, the most successful planters compounded their success. The wealthiest planters also began to buy slaves as well as to serve as merchants.

By the 1670s, the society of the Chesapeake had become polarized. Landowners—the planter elite and the more numerous yeoman planters— clustered around one pole. Landless colonists, mainly freed servants, gathered at the other. Each group eyed the other with suspicion and mistrust. For the most part, planters saw landless freemen as a dangerous rabble rather than as fellow colonists with legitimate grievances. Governor William Berkeley feared the political threat to the governing elite posed by "six parts in seven [of Virginia colonists who] . . . are poor, indebted, discontented, and armed."

> CHRONOLOGY

ca. 1600–1650
– Yeoman farmers predominate in the Chesapeake region.

1644
– Opechancanough leads second uprising.

1660
– Navigation Act requires that colonial products be shipped only to English ports.

1661–1676
– No elections are called in the House of Burgesses.

1670
– House of Burgesses outlaws voting by poor men.

1676
– Bacon's Rebellion.

Governor William Berkeley

This portrait illustrates the distance that separated Governor Berkeley and the other Chesapeake grandees from poor planters, landless freemen, servants, and slaves. His haughty, satisfied demeanor suggests his lack of sympathy for poor Virginians, who, he was certain, deserved their lot. Courtesy of Berkeley Castle Charitable Trust, Gloucestershire.

How did Chesapeake tobacco society take shape?

Why did Chesapeake colonial society change in the late seventeenth century?

Why did the southern colonies move toward a slave labor system?

Conclusion: Why were export crops and slave labor important in the growth of the southern colonies?

☑ LearningCurve
Check what you know.
bedfordstmartins.com
/roarkunderstanding

Government Policies and Political Conflict

In general, government enforced the distinction separating servants and masters with an iron fist. Poor men complained that "nether the Governor nor Counsell could or would doe any poore men right, but that they would shew favor to great men and wronge the poore." Most Chesapeake colonists, like most Europeans, assumed that "great men" should bear the responsibilities of government. Until 1670, all freemen could vote, and they routinely elected prosperous planters to the legislature. No former servant served in either the governor's council or the House of Burgesses after 1640. Yet poor Virginians believed that the "great men" used their government offices to promote their selfish personal interests rather than governing impartially.

As discontent mounted among the poor during the 1660s and 1670s, colonial officials tried to keep political power in safe hands. Beginning in 1661, for example, Governor William Berkeley did not call an election for the House of Burgesses for fifteen years. In 1670, the House of Burgesses outlawed voting by poor men, permitting only men who headed households and were landowners to vote.

The king also began to tighten the royal government's control of trade and to collect substantial revenue from the Chesapeake colonies. A series of English laws funneled the colonial trade exclusively into the hands of English merchants and shippers. The **Navigation Acts** of 1650 and 1651 specified that colonial goods had to be transported in English ships with predominantly English crews. A 1660 act required colonial products to be sent only to English ports, and a 1663 law stipulated further that all goods sent to the colonies must pass through English ports and be carried on English ships manned by English sailors. Taken together, these navigation acts reflected the English government's mercantilist assumption that what was good for England should determine colonial policy.

Assumptions about mercantilism also underlay the import duty on tobacco inaugurated by the Navigation Act of 1660. The law assessed an import tax of two pence on every pound of colonial tobacco brought into England, about the price a Chesapeake tobacco farmer received. The tax gave the king a major financial interest in the size of the tobacco crop, which yielded about a quarter of all English customs revenues during the 1660s.

Navigation Acts
► English laws passed in the 1650s and 1660s requiring that English colonial goods be shipped through English ports on English ships with English sailors in order to benefit English merchants, shippers, and seamen.

Bacon's Rebellion

Colonists, like residents of European monarchies, accepted class divisions and inequality as long as they believed that government officials ruled for the general good. When rulers violated that precept, ordinary people felt justified in rebelling. In 1676, **Bacon's Rebellion** erupted as a dispute over Virginia's Indian policy. Before it was over, the rebellion convulsed Chesapeake politics and society, leaving in its wake death, destruction, and a legacy of hostility between the great planters and their poorer neighbors.

In June 1676, the new legislature passed a series of reform measures known as Bacon's Laws. Among other changes, the laws gave local settlers a voice in setting tax levies, forbade officeholders from demanding bribes or other extra fees

Bacon's Rebellion
► An unsuccessful rebellion against the colonial government in 1676, led by frontier settler Nathaniel Bacon.

CHAPTER LOCATOR | What challenges faced early Chesapeake colonists?

for carrying out their duties, placed limits on holding multiple offices, and restored the vote to all freemen. But elite planters soon convinced Governor Berkeley that Nathanial Bacon and his supporters among small planters and frontiersmen were a greater threat than the Indians.

When Bacon learned that Berkeley had branded him a traitor, he declared war against Berkeley and the other grandees. For three months, Bacon's forces fought the Indians, sacked the grandees' plantations, and attacked Jamestown. Berkeley's loyalists retaliated by plundering the homes of Bacon's supporters. The fighting continued until Bacon unexpectedly died, most likely from dysentery, and several English ships arrived to bolster Berkeley's strength.

The rebellion did nothing to dislodge the grandees from their positions of power. If anything, it strengthened them. When the king learned of the turmoil in the Chesapeake and its devastating effect on tobacco exports and customs duties, he ordered an investigation. Royal officials replaced Berkeley with a governor more attentive to the king's interests, nullified Bacon's Laws, and instituted an export tax on tobacco as a way of paying the expenses of government without having to obtain the consent of the tightfisted House of Burgesses.

In the aftermath of Bacon's Rebellion, tensions between great planters and small farmers moderated. Bacon's Rebellion showed, a governor of Virginia said, that it was necessary "to steer between . . . either an Indian or a civil war." The ruling elite concluded that it was safer for the colonists to fight the Indians than to fight each other, and the government made little effort to restrict settlers' encroachment on Indian land. Tax cuts also were welcomed by all freemen. The export duty on tobacco imposed by the king allowed the colonial government to reduce taxes by 75 percent between 1660 and 1700. In the long run, however, the most important contribution to political stability was the declining importance of the servant labor system. During the 1680s and 1690s, fewer servants arrived in the Chesapeake, partly because of improving economic conditions in England. Accordingly, the number of poor, newly freed servants also declined, reducing the size of the lowest stratum of free society. In 1700, when about one-third of the free colonists still worked as tenants on land owned by others, the Chesapeake was in the midst of transitioning to a slave labor system that minimized the differences between poor farmers and rich planters and magnified the differences between whites and blacks.

QUICK REVIEW

Why did Chesapeake colonial society become increasingly polarized between 1650 and 1670?

How did Chesapeake tobacco society take shape?

Why did Chesapeake colonial society change in the late seventeenth century?

Why did the southern colonies move toward a slave labor system?

Conclusion: Why were export crops and slave labor important in the growth of the southern colonies?

☑ LearningCurve
Check what you know.
bedfordstmartins.com
/roarkunderstanding

> Why did the southern colonies move toward a slave labor system?

Sugar Plantation

This portrait of a Brazilian sugar plantation shows cartloads of sugarcane being hauled to the mill, which is powered by a waterwheel (far right), where the cane will be squeezed between rollers to extract the sugary juice. The juice will then be distilled over a fire tended by the slaves until it has the desired consistency and purity. *Courtesy of the John Carter Brown Library at Brown University.*

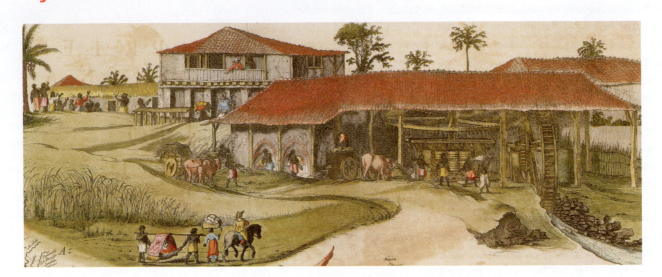

slavery

▶ Coerced labor. African slavery became the most important form of coerced labor in the New World in the seventeenth century.

ALTHOUGH FORCED NATIVE LABOR was common practice in New Spain, English colonists were unsuccessful in conscripting Indian labor. They looked instead to another source of workers used by the Spaniards and Portuguese: enslaved Africans. On this foundation, European colonizers built African **slavery** into the most important form of coerced labor in the New World.

During the seventeenth century, English colonies in the West Indies followed the Spanish and Portuguese examples and developed sugar plantations with slave labor. In the English North American colonies, however, a slave labor system did not emerge until the last quarter of the seventeenth century. During the 1670s, settlers from Barbados brought slavery to the new English mainland colony of Carolina, where the imprint of the West Indies remained strong for decades. In Chesapeake tobacco fields at about the same time, slave labor began to replace servant labor, marking the transition toward a society of freedom for whites and slavery for Africans.

CHAPTER LOCATOR | What challenges faced early Chesapeake colonists?

Religion and Revolt in the Spanish Borderland

While English colonies in the Chesapeake grew and prospered with the tobacco trade, the northern outposts of the Spanish empire in New Mexico and Florida stagnated. Only about fifteen hundred Spaniards lived in Florida, and roughly twice as many inhabited New Mexico, yet both colonies required regular deliveries of goods and large subsidies. One royal governor complained that "no [Spaniard] comes . . . to plow and sow [crops], but only to eat and loaf."

Instead of attracting settlers and growing crops for export, New Mexico and Florida appealed to Spanish missionaries seeking to convert Indians to Christianity. In both colonies, Indians outnumbered Spaniards ten or twenty to one. Royal officials hoped that the missionaries' efforts would pacify the Indians and be a relatively cheap way to preserve Spanish footholds in North America. The missionaries baptized thousands of Indians in Spanish North America during the seventeenth century, but they also planted the seeds of Indian uprisings against Spanish rule.

The missionaries followed royal instructions that Indians should be taught "to live in a civilized manner, clothed and wearing shoes . . . [and] given the use of . . . bread, linen, horses, cattle, tools, and weapons, and all the rest that Spain has had." In effect, the missionaries sought to convert the Indians not just into Christians but also into surrogate Spaniards.

The missionaries supervised the building of scores of Catholic churches across Florida and New Mexico. Adopting practices common elsewhere in New Spain, they forced the Indians both to construct these churches and to pay tribute in the form of food, blankets, and other goods. Although the missionaries congratulated themselves on the many Indians they converted, their coercive methods subverted their goals. A missionary reported that an Indian in New Mexico asked him, "If we [missionaries] who are Christians caused so much harm and violence [to Indians], why should they become Christians?"

The Indians retaliated repeatedly against Spanish exploitation, but the Spaniards suppressed the violent uprisings by taking advantage of the disunity among the Indians, much as Cortés did in the conquest of Mexico (see chapter 2). In 1680, however, the native leader Popé organized the **Pueblo Revolt**, ordering his followers, as one recounted, to "break up and burn the images of the holy Christ, the Virgin Mary, and the other saints, the crosses, and everything pertaining to Christianity." During the revolt, Indians desecrated churches, killed two-thirds of the Spanish missionaries, and drove the Spaniards out of New Mexico to present-day El Paso, Texas. The Spaniards managed to return to New Mexico by the end of the seventeenth century, but only by curtailing the missionaries and reducing labor exploitation. Florida Indians never mounted a unified attack on Spanish rule, but they too organized sporadic uprisings and resisted conversion.

The West Indies: Sugar and Slavery

The most profitable part of the English New World empire in the seventeenth century lay in the Caribbean (**Map 3.2**). The tiny island of **Barbados**, colonized in the

> CHRONOLOGY

1640s
– Colonists in Barbados begin to grow sugarcane with the labor of African slaves.

1663
– Royal charter is granted for the Carolina colony.

1670
– Charles Towne, South Carolina, is founded.

1670–1700
– Slave labor system emerges in Carolina and Chesapeake colonies.

1680
– Popé leads the Pueblo Revolt.

Pueblo Revolt
► An effective revolt of Pueblo Indians in New Mexico, under the leadership of Popé, against the Spaniards in 1680. Particularly targeting symbols of Christianity, the Pueblo Indians succeeded in killing two-thirds of the Spanish missionaries and driving the Spaniards out of New Mexico.

Barbados
► An island in the British West Indies. Colonized in the 1630s, Barbados became an enormous sugar producer and a source of wealth for England. The island's African slaves quickly became a majority of the island's population despite the deadliness of their work.

How did Chesapeake tobacco society take shape?

Why did Chesapeake colonial society change in the late seventeenth century?

Why did the southern colonies move toward a slave labor system?

Conclusion: Why were export crops and slave labor important in the growth of the southern colonies?

✓ LearningCurve
Check what you know.
bedfordstmartins.com
/roarkunderstanding

1630s, was the jewel of the English West Indies. During the 1640s, a colonial official proclaimed Barbados "the most flourishing Island in all those American parts, and I verily believe in all the world for the production of sugar." Sugar commanded high prices in England, and planters rushed to grow as much as they could. By midcentury, annual sugar exports from the English Caribbean totaled about 150,000 pounds; by 1700, exports reached nearly 50 million pounds.

MAP 3.2 ■ **The West Indies and Carolina in the Seventeenth Century**

Although Carolina was geographically close to the Chesapeake colonies, it was culturally closer to the West Indies in the seventeenth century because its early settlers — both blacks and whites — came from Barbados. South Carolina maintained strong ties to the West Indies for more than a century.

> MAP ACTIVITY

READING THE MAP: Locate English colonies in America and English holdings in the Caribbean. Which European country controlled most of the mainland bordering the Caribbean? Where was the closest mainland English territory?

CONNECTIONS: Why were colonists in Carolina so interested in Barbados? What goods did they export? Describe the relationship between Carolina and Barbados in 1700.

CHAPTER LOCATOR | What challenges faced early Chesapeake colonists?

Sugar transformed Barbados and other West Indian islands. Poor farmers could not afford the expensive machinery that extracted and refined sugarcane juice, but planters with enough capital to grow sugar got rich. By 1680, the wealthiest Barbadian sugar planters were, on average, four times richer than tobacco grandees in the Chesapeake. The sugar grandees differed from their Chesapeake counterparts in another crucial way: The average sugar baron in Barbados owned 115 slaves in 1680.

African slaves planted, cultivated, and harvested the sugarcane that made West Indian planters wealthy. Beginning in the 1640s, Barbadian planters purchased thousands of slaves to work their plantations, and the African population on the island mushroomed. During the 1650s, when blacks made up only 3 percent of the Chesapeake population, they had already become the majority in Barbados. By 1700, slaves constituted more than three-fourths of the island's population (**Figure 3.1**).

For slaves, work on a sugar plantation was a life sentence to brutal, unremitting labor. Slaves suffered high death rates. Since slave men outnumbered slave women two to one, few slaves could form families and have children. These grim

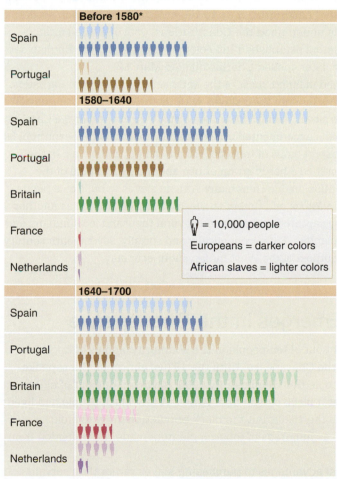

*Note: Before 1580, migration from Britain, France, and the Netherlands was negligible.

> GLOBAL COMPARISON

FIGURE 3.1 ■ Migration to the New World from Europe and Africa, 1492–1700

Before 1640, Spain and Portugal sent four out of five European migrants to the New World, virtually all of them bound for New Spain or Brazil. But from 1640 to 1700, nearly as many migrants came from England as from other European nations combined, a measure of the growing significance of England's colonies. From 1492 to 1700, more enslaved Africans than Europeans arrived in the New World. What might explain the shifts in the destinations of enslaved Africans? Were those shifts comparable to shifts among European immigrants?

How did Chesapeake tobacco society take shape?	Why did Chesapeake colonial society change in the late seventeenth century?	**Why did the southern colonies move toward a slave labor system?**	Conclusion: Why were export crops and slave labor important in the growth of the southern colonies?	✓ LearningCurve Check what you know. bedfordstmartins.com /roarkunderstanding

realities meant that in Barbados and elsewhere in the West Indies, the slave population did not grow by natural reproduction. Instead, planters continually purchased enslaved Africans. Although sugar plantations did not gain a foothold in North America in the seventeenth century, the West Indies nonetheless exerted a powerful influence on the development of slavery in the mainland colonies.

Carolina: A West Indian Frontier

The early settlers of what became South Carolina were immigrants from Barbados. In 1663, a Barbadian planter named John Colleton and a group of seven other men obtained a charter from England's King Charles II to establish a colony north of the Spanish territories in Florida. The men, known as "proprietors," hoped to siphon settlers from Barbados and other colonies and encourage them to develop a profitable export crop comparable to West Indian sugar and Chesapeake tobacco. The proprietors enlisted the English philosopher John Locke to help draft the Fundamental Constitutions of Carolina, which provided for religious liberty and political rights for small property holders while envisioning a landed aristocracy supported by bound laborers and slaves. Following the Chesapeake example, the proprietors also offered headrights of up to 150 acres of land for each settler, a provision that eventually undermined the Constitutions' goal of a titled aristocracy. In 1670, the proprietors established the colony's first permanent English settlement, Charles Towne, later spelled Charleston (see Map 3.2).

As the proprietors had planned, most of the early settlers were from Barbados. The Barbadian immigrants brought their slaves with them. More than one-quarter of the early settlers were slaves, and by 1700 slaves made up about half the Carolina population. The Carolinians experimented unsuccessfully to match their semitropical climate with profitable export crops of tobacco, cotton, indigo, and olives. In the mid-1690s, colonists identified a hardy strain of rice and took advantage of the knowledge of rice cultivation among their many African slaves to build rice plantations. Settlers also sold livestock and timber to the West Indies, as well as another "natural resource": They captured and enslaved several thousand local Indians and sold them to Caribbean planters. Both economically and socially, seventeenth-century Carolina was a frontier outpost of the West Indian sugar economy.

Slave Labor Emerges in the Chesapeake

By 1700, more than eight out of ten people in the southern colonies of English North America lived in the Chesapeake. Until the 1670s, almost all Chesapeake colonists were white people from England. By 1700, however, one out of eight people in the region was a black person from Africa. A few black people had lived in the Chesapeake since the 1620s, but the black population grew fivefold between 1670 and 1700 as hundreds of tobacco planters made the transition from servant to slave labor.

Planters saw several advantages to purchasing slaves rather than servants. Although slaves cost three to five times more than servants, slaves never became

CHAPTER LOCATOR | What challenges faced early Chesapeake colonists?

Tobacco Wrapper

This wrapper labeled a container of tobacco from the English colonies sold at Reighly's shop in Essex. The wrapper was much like a brand, promising consumers consistency in quality and taste. The wrapper illustrates tobacco growing in a field and harvested leaves ready to be packed into a barrel, ferried to the ships waiting offshore, and transported to Reighly's and other tobacconists in England. The Granger Collection, New York.

free. Because the mortality rate had declined by the 1680s, planters could reasonably expect a slave to live longer than a servant's period of indenture. Slaves also promised to be a perpetual labor force, since children of slave mothers inherited the status of slavery. And unlike servants, they could be controlled politically. A slave labor system promised to avoid the political problems such as Bacon's Rebellion caused by the servant labor system. Slavery kept discontented laborers in permanent servitude, and their color was a badge of their bondage.

The slave labor system polarized Chesapeake society along lines of race and status: All slaves were black, and nearly all blacks were slaves; almost all free people were white, and all whites were free or only temporarily bound in indentured servitude. Unlike Barbados, however, the Chesapeake retained a vast white majority. Among whites, huge differences of wealth and status still existed. By 1700, more than three-quarters of white families had neither servants nor slaves. Nonetheless, poor white farmers enjoyed the privileges of free status. They could own property, get married, have families, and bequeath their property and their freedom to their descendants; they could move when and where they wanted; they could associate freely with other people; they could serve on juries, vote, and hold political office; and they could work, loaf, and sleep as they chose. These

How did Chesapeake tobacco society take shape?

Why did Chesapeake colonial society change in the late seventeenth century?

Why did the southern colonies move toward a slave labor system?

Conclusion: Why were export crops and slave labor important in the growth of the southern colonies?

✓ **LearningCurve**
Check what you know.
bedfordstmartins.com /roarkunderstanding

77

privileges of freedom—none of them possessed by slaves—made lesser white folk feel they had a genuine stake in the existence of slavery, even if they did not own a single slave. By emphasizing the privileges of freedom shared by all white people, the slave labor system reduced the tensions between poor folk and grandees that had plagued the Chesapeake region in the 1670s.

In contrast to slaves in Barbados, most slaves in the seventeenth-century Chesapeake colonies had frequent and close contact with white people. Slaves and white servants performed the same tasks on tobacco plantations, often working side by side in the fields. Slaves took advantage of every opportunity to slip away from white supervision and seek out the company of other slaves. Planters often feared that slaves would turn such seemingly innocent social pleasures to political ends, either to run away or to conspire to strike against their masters. Slaves often did run away, but they were usually captured or returned after a brief absence. Despite planters' nightmares, slave insurrections did not occur.

Although slavery resolved the political unrest caused by the servant labor system, it created new political problems. By 1700, the bedrock political issue in the southern colonies was keeping slaves in their place, at the end of a hoe. The slave labor system in the southern colonies stood roughly midway between the sugar plantations and black majority of Barbados to the south and the small farms and homogeneous villages that developed in seventeenth-century New England to the north (as discussed in chapter 4).

> ## QUICK REVIEW

Why had slave labor largely displaced indentured servant labor by 1700 in Chesapeake tobacco production?

Conclusion: Why were export crops and slave labor important in the growth of the southern colonies?

BY 1700, the colonies of Virginia, Maryland, and Carolina were firmly established. The staple crops they grew for export provided a livelihood for many, a fortune for a few, and valuable revenues for shippers, merchants, and the English monarchy. Their societies differed markedly from English society in most respects, yet the colonists considered themselves English people who happened to live in North America. They claimed the same rights and privileges as English men and women, while they denied those rights and privileges to Native Americans and African slaves.

The English colonies also differed from the example of New Spain. Settlers and servants flocked to English colonies, in contrast to the Spaniards who trickled into New Spain. Few English missionaries sought to convert Indians to Protestant Christianity, unlike the numerous Catholic missionaries in the Spanish settlements in New Mexico and Florida. Large quantities of gold and silver never materialized in English North America. English colonists never adopted the system of encomienda (see chapter 2). Yet important forms of coerced labor and racial distinction that developed in New Spain had North American counterparts, as English colonists employed servants and slaves and defined themselves as superior to Indians and Africans.

By 1700, the remnants of Powhatan's people still survived. As English settlement pushed north, west, and south of Chesapeake Bay, the Indians faced the new colonial world that Powhatan and Pocahontas had encountered when John Smith and the first colonists had arrived at Jamestown. By 1700, the many descendants of Pocahontas's son, Thomas, as well as other colonists and Native Americans, understood that the English had come to stay.

Economically, the southern colonies developed during the seventeenth century from the struggling Jamestown settlement that could not feed itself into a major source of profits for England. The European fashion for tobacco provided livelihoods for numerous white families and riches for elite planters. But after 1700, enslaved Africans were conscripted in growing numbers to grow tobacco in the Chesapeake and rice in Carolina. The slave society that dominated the eighteenth-century southern colonies was firmly rooted in the developments of the seventeenth century.

A desire for land, a hope for profit, and a dream for security motivated southern white colonists. Realizing these aspirations involved great risks, considerable suffering, and frequent disappointment, as well as seizing Indian lands and coercing labor from servants and slaves. By 1700, despite huge disparities in individual colonists' success in achieving their goals, tens of thousands of white colonists who were immigrants or descendants of immigrants now considered the southern colonies their home, shaping the history of the region and of the nation as a whole for centuries to come.

How did Chesapeake tobacco society take shape?

Why did Chesapeake colonial society change in the late seventeenth century?

Why did the southern colonies move toward a slave labor system?

Conclusion: Why were export crops and slave labor important in the growth of the southern colonies?

LearningCurve
Check what you know.
bedfordstmartins.com
/roarkunderstanding

CHAPTER 3 STUDY GUIDE

STEP 1

GET STARTED ONLINE

✓ **LearningCurve** ■ bedfordstmartins.com/roarkunderstanding

Now that you've read the chapter, make it stick by completing the LearningCurve activity.

STEP 2

EXPLAIN WHY IT MATTERS

Put your reading into practice. Identify each term below, and then explain why it matters in U.S. history.

TERM	WHO OR WHAT & WHEN	WHY IT MATTERS
Virginia Company (p. 57)		
Algonquian Indians (p. 57)		
Jamestown (p. 57)		
royal colony (p. 60)		
House of Burgesses (p. 60)		
headright (p. 63)		
indentured servants (p. 63)		
Navigation Acts (p. 70)		
Bacon's Rebellion (p. 70)		
slavery (p. 72)		
Pueblo Revolt (p. 73)		
Barbados (p. 73)		

STEP 3

MOVE BEYOND THE BASICS

To demonstrate a more advanced understanding, detail the demographics (who lived in the Chesapeake colonies), economic structures (how people survived and thrived), the major political and sociocultural divisions within colonial Chesapeake society, and the causes of these divisions.

Date	Demographics	Economy	Political/social divisions within colonial society	Reasons for conflicts
1607				
1620				
1650				
1700				

PUT IT ALL TOGETHER

Now, take a step back and try to explain the big picture. Remember to use specific examples from the chapter in your answers.

JAMESTOWN AND THE CHESAPEAKE

▶ How did interactions with the Algonquians shape the Jamestown colony's early history?

▶ How did the development of tobacco cultivation transform the Chesapeake?

INDENTURED SERVITUDE AND BACON'S REBELLION

▶ What role did indentured servants play in the transformation of the Chesapeake in the early seventeenth century?

▶ What events led to Bacon's Rebellion, and why did Virginia erupt into violence in 1676?

SLAVERY

▶ What role did sugar play in the development of African slavery in the New World?

▶ How did the introduction of African slaves affect the development of Chesapeake society?

LOOKING BACKWARD, LOOKING AHEAD

▶ How did the seventeenth-century English colonies differ from their sixteenth-century Spanish counterparts?

▶ How did the introduction of African slaves contribute to the emergence of a distinct southern colonial society?

> ## IN YOUR OWN WORDS

Imagine that you must give an oral report to the class answering the following question: **What were the most important factors that shaped England's southern colonies in the seventeenth century?** What would be the most important points to include and why?

 Do it online at the Student Site ■ bedfordstmartins.com/roarkunderstanding

4

FOUNDING THE NORTHERN COLONIES

1601–1700

> **How did religious dissidents from England come to establish colonies in northern North America?** Chapter 4 explores the development of the northern colonies in the seventeenth century, examining the factors that gave each colony its unique character. It pays particular attention to the importance of religion in the evolution of New England and to England's attempts to control colonial trade.

LearningCurve
bedfordstmartins.com/roarkunderstanding
After reading the chapter, use LearningCurve to retain what you've read.

Thomas Smith, a New England mariner, created colonial America's oldest known self-portrait around **1680.** Worcester Art Museum.

> Why did the Puritans immigrate to North America?

> How did New England society change during the seventeenth century?

> What was distinctive about the middle colonies?

> What was the connection between the colonies and the English empire?

> Conclusion: Was there an English model of colonization in North America?

Why did the Puritans immigrate to North America?

Seal of Massachusetts Bay Colony

In 1629, the Massachusetts Bay Company designed this seal depicting an Indian man inviting English settlers to "come over and help us." Of course, such an invitation was never issued. The seal was an attempt to lend an aura of altruism to the Massachusetts Bay Company's colonization efforts. What does the seal suggest about English views of Indians? Courtesy of Massachusetts Archives.

Puritans

▶ Dissenters from the Church of England who wanted a genuine Reformation rather than the partial Reformation sought by Henry VIII. The Puritans' religious principles emphasized the importance of an individual's relationship with God, developed through Bible study, prayer, and introspection.

English Reformation

▶ Reform effort initiated by King Henry VIII that included banning the Catholic Church and declaring the English monarch head of the new Church of England but little change in doctrine. Henry's primary concern was consolidating his political power.

PURITANS WHO IMMIGRATED to North America aspired to escape the turmoil and persecution they suffered in England, a long-term consequence of the English Reformation. They also sought to build a new, orderly, Puritan version of England. Puritans established the first small settlement in New England in 1620, followed a few years later by additional settlements by the Massachusetts Bay Company. Allowed self-government through royal charter, these Puritans were in a unique position to direct the new colonies according to their faith. Although many New England colonists were not Puritans, Puritanism remained a paramount influence in New England's religion, politics, and community life during the seventeenth century.

Puritan Origins: The English Reformation

The religious roots of the **Puritans** who founded New England reached back to the Protestant Reformation, which arose in Germany in 1517 (see chapter 2). The English church initially remained within the Catholic fold. Henry VIII, who reigned from 1509 to 1547, saw that the Reformation offered him an opportunity to break with Rome and take control of the church in England. In 1534, Henry formally initiated the **English Reformation**. At his insistence, Parliament outlawed the Catholic Church and proclaimed the king "the only supreme head on earth of the Church of England." Henry seized the vast properties of the Catholic Church in England as well as the privilege of appointing bishops and others in the church hierarchy.

> CHRONOLOGY

1534
– English Reformation begins.

1558–1603
– Reign of Elizabeth I in England.

1603–1625
– Reign of James I in England.

1620
– Plymouth colony is founded by Pilgrims.

1629
– Massachusetts Bay Company receives a royal charter.

1630
– John Winthrop leads Puritan settlers to Massachusetts Bay.

Queen Elizabeth This sixteenth-century portrait of Queen Elizabeth celebrates the English victory over the Spanish Armada in 1588 (shown in the panels on either side of Elizabeth's head), which resulted in England's empire reaching North America (notice her right hand covering North America on the globe). © Bettmann/Corbis.

The fate of Protestantism waxed and waned under the monarchs who succeeded Henry VIII. In 1558, Elizabeth I, the daughter of Henry and his second wife, Anne Boleyn, became queen. During her long reign, Elizabeth reaffirmed the English Reformation and tried to position the English church between the extremes of Catholicism and Puritanism. Like her father, she desired a church that would strengthen the monarchy and the nation. By the time Elizabeth died in 1603, many people in England looked on Protestantism as a defining feature of national identity.

> **The English Reformation and Puritanism**

- Henry VIII took advantage of the Protestant Reformation in Europe to break with Rome and take control of the Church of England.

- Reformation brought political and religious turmoil to England; many English Catholics wanted to revoke the English Reformation, while other English people wanted a thorough Reformation.

- The Puritans wanted to eliminate what they considered the offensive features of Catholicism that remained in the religious doctrines and practices of the Church of England.

- Puritans wanted to do away with the rituals of Catholic worship and instead emphasize an individual's relationship with God, developed through Bible study, prayer, and introspection.

- All Puritans shared a desire to make the English church thoroughly Protestant.

How did New England society change during the seventeenth century?

What was distinctive about the middle colonies?

What was the connection between the colonies and the English empire?

Conclusion: Was there an English model of colonization in North America?

✔ **LearningCurve**
Check what you know.
bedfordstmartins.com
/roarkunderstanding

When Elizabeth's successor, James I, became king, English Puritans petitioned for further reform of the Church of England. James authorized a new translation of the Bible, known ever since as the King James Version. However, neither James I nor his son Charles I, who became king in 1625, was receptive to the ideas of Puritan reformers. James and Charles moved the Church of England away from Puritanism. They enforced conformity to the Church of England and punished dissenters. In 1629, Charles I dissolved Parliament—where Puritans were well represented—and initiated aggressive anti-Puritan policies. Many Puritans despaired about continuing to defend their faith in England and made plans to emigrate to Europe, the West Indies, or America.

The Pilgrims and Plymouth Colony

Separatists

▶ Protestants who sought withdrawal from the Church of England. The Pilgrims were Separatists.

One of the first Protestant groups to emigrate, later known as Pilgrims, professed an unorthodox view known as separatism. These **Separatists** sought to withdraw—or separate—from the Church of England, which they considered hopelessly corrupt. William Bradford, a leader of the Separatists, believed that America promised to better protect and preserve their community. Separatists obtained permission to settle in the extensive territory granted to the Virginia Company (see chapter 3). In August 1620, the Pilgrim families boarded the *Mayflower*, and after eleven weeks at sea all but one of the 102 immigrants arrived in present-day Massachusetts.

The Pilgrims drew up the Mayflower Compact on the day they arrived. They pledged to "covenant and combine ourselves together into a civil Body Politick, for our better Ordering and Preservation." The signers (all men) agreed to enact and obey necessary and just laws.

The Pilgrims settled at Plymouth and elected William Bradford their governor. That first winter, which they spent aboard their ship, "was most sad and lamentable," Bradford wrote later. "In two or three months' time half of [our] company died."

In the spring, Indians rescued the floundering Plymouth settlement. First Samoset and then Squanto befriended the settlers. Samoset arranged for the Pilgrims to meet and establish good relations with Massasoit, the chief of the Wampanoag Indians, whose territory included Plymouth. With the Indians' guidance, the Pilgrims managed to harvest enough food to guarantee their survival through the coming winter, an occasion they celebrated in the fall of 1621 with a feast of thanksgiving attended by Massasoit and other Wampanoags.

The Pilgrims persisted, living simply and coexisting in relative peace with the Indians. By 1630, Plymouth had become a small permanent settlement, but it failed to attract many other English Puritans.

TABLE 4.1 ■ Pilgrims and Puritans

Pilgrims	Puritans
Wanted to separate from the Church of England; called Separatists	Wanted to reform the Church of England
Settled in Plymouth in 1620	Settled in Boston in 1630
Led by William Bradford	Led by John Winthrop

CHAPTER LOCATOR | **Why did the Puritans immigrate to North America?**

The Founding of Massachusetts Bay Colony

In 1629, shortly before Charles I dissolved Parliament, a group of Puritans obtained a royal charter for the Massachusetts Bay Company. The charter provided the usual privileges granted to joint-stock companies, including land for colonization that spanned present-day Massachusetts, New Hampshire, Vermont, Maine, and upstate New York. A unique provision of the charter permitted the government of the Massachusetts Bay Company to be located in the colony rather than in England. This provision allowed Puritans to exchange their status as a harassed minority in England for self-government in Massachusetts.

To lead the emigrants, the Massachusetts Bay Company selected John Winthrop, a prosperous lawyer and landowner, to serve as governor. In March 1630, eleven ships crammed with seven hundred passengers sailed for Massachusetts; six more ships and another five hundred emigrants followed a few months later. Winthrop and a small group chose to settle on the peninsula that became Boston, and other settlers clustered at promising locations nearby (**Map 4.1**).

In a sermon to his companions aboard the *Arbella* while they were still at sea—probably the most famous sermon in American history—Winthrop proclaimed the cosmic significance of their journey. The Puritans had "entered into a covenant" with God to "work out our salvation under the power and purity of his holy ordinances," Winthrop declared. This sanctified agreement with God meant that the Puritans had to make "extraordinary" efforts to "bring into familiar and constant practice" religious principles that most people in England merely preached. To achieve their pious goals, the Puritans had to subordinate their individual interests to the common good. "We must be knit together in this work as

MAP 4.1 ■ New England Colonies in the Seventeenth Century

New Englanders spread across the landscape town by town during the seventeenth century. (For the sake of legibility, only a few of the more important towns are shown on the map.)

> **MAP ACTIVITY**

READING THE MAP: Using the dates on the map, create a chronology of the establishment of towns in New England. What physical features correspond to the earliest habitation by English settlers?

CONNECTIONS: Why were towns so much more a feature of seventeenth-century New England than of the Chesapeake (see also chapter 3)? How did Puritan dissent influence the settlement of New England colonies?

| How did New England society change during the seventeenth century? | What was distinctive about the middle colonies? | What was the connection between the colonies and the English empire? | Conclusion: Was there an English model of colonization in North America? | ✔ LearningCurve Check what you know. bedfordstmartins.com /roarkunderstanding |

one man," Winthrop preached. "We must delight in each other, make others' conditions our own, rejoice together, mourn together, labor and suffer together." The stakes could not be higher, Winthrop told his listeners: "We must consider that we shall be as a city upon a hill. The eyes of all people are upon us."

That belief shaped seventeenth-century New England as profoundly as tobacco shaped the Chesapeake. Winthrop's vision of a city on a hill fired the Puritans' fierce determination to keep their covenant and live according to God's laws, unlike the backsliders and compromisers who accommodated to the Church of England. Their resolve to adhere strictly to God's plan charged nearly every feature of life in seventeenth-century New England with a distinctive, high-voltage piety.

Unlike the early Chesapeake settlers, the first Massachusetts Bay colonists encountered few Indians because the local population had been almost entirely exterminated by an epidemic. And each year from 1630 to 1640, ship after ship followed in the wake of Winthrop's fleet, bringing more than twenty thousand new settlers.

Often, when the Church of England cracked down on a Puritan minister in England, he and many of his followers moved together to New England. By 1640, New England had one of the highest ratios of preachers to population in all of Christendom. Several ministers sought to carry the message of Christianity to the Indians and established "praying towns" to encourage Indians to adopt English ways. But the colonists focused far less on saving Indians' souls than on saving their own.

The occupations of New England immigrants reflected the social origins of English Puritans. On the whole, the immigrants came from the middle ranks of English society. The vast majority were either farmers or tradesmen. Indentured servants, whose numbers dominated the Chesapeake settlers, accounted for only about a fifth of those headed for New England. Most New England immigrants paid their way to Massachusetts. They were encouraged by the promise of bounty in New England reported in Winthrop's letter to his son: "Here can be no want of anything to those who bring means to raise [it] out of the earth and sea."

In contrast to Chesapeake newcomers, New England immigrants usually arrived as families. In fact, more Puritans came with family members than did any other group of immigrants in all of American history. Unlike immigrants to the Chesapeake, women and children made up a solid majority in New England.

As Winthrop reminded the first settlers in his *Arbella* sermon, each family was a "little commonwealth" that mirrored the hierarchy among all God's creatures. Just as humankind was subordinate to God, so young people were subordinate to their elders, children to their parents, and wives to their husbands. The immigrants' family ties reinforced their religious beliefs with the interlocking institutions of family, church, and community.

> QUICK REVIEW

What was a "little commonwealth," and why was it so important to New England settlement?

CHAPTER LOCATOR | Why did the Puritans immigrate to North America?

88   CHAPTER 4
FOUNDING THE NORTHERN COLONIES

How did New England society change during the seventeenth century?

David, Joanna, and Abigail Mason

In this 1670 painting, which depicts the children of Bostonians Joanna and Anthony Mason, the artist lavished attention on the young subjects' elaborate clothing and adornments: fashionable slashed sleeves, fancy lace, silver-studded shoes, necklaces for the girls, and a silver-headed cane for the boy. The portrait expresses the growing respect for wealth and its worldly rewards in seventeenth-century New England. Fine Arts Museums of San Francisco. Gift of Mr. and Mrs. John D. Rockefeller III.

THE NEW ENGLAND COLONISTS, unlike their counterparts in the Chesapeake, settled in small towns, usually located on the coast or by a river (see Map 4.1). Massachusetts Bay colonists founded 133 towns during the seventeenth century, each with one or more churches. Church members' fervent piety, buttressed by the institutions of local government, enforced remarkable religious and social conformity in the small New England settlements. During the century, tensions within the Puritan faith and changes in New England communities splintered religious orthodoxy and weakened Puritan zeal. By 1700, however, Puritanism retained a distinctive influence in New England.

> **CHRONOLOGY**

1636
– Rhode Island colony is established.
– Connecticut colony is founded.

1638
– Anne Hutchinson is excommunicated.

1642
– Puritan Revolution inflames England.

1649
– English Puritans win the civil war.

1656
– Quakers arrive in Massachusetts and are persecuted.

1662
– Many Puritan congregations adopt the Halfway Covenant.

1692
– Salem witch trials.

How did New England society change during the seventeenth century? | What was distinctive about the middle colonies? | What was the connection between the colonies and the English empire? | Conclusion: Was there an English model of colonization in North America? | ☑ LearningCurve Check what you know. bedfordstmartins.com /roarkunderstanding

89

Church, Covenant, and Conformity

Puritans believed that a church consisted of men and women who had entered a solemn covenant with one another and with God. Each new member of the covenant had to persuade existing members that she or he had fully experienced conversion.

Puritans embraced a distinctive version of Protestantism derived from **Calvinism**, the doctrines of John Calvin, who insisted that Christians strictly discipline their behavior to conform to God's commandments announced in the Bible. Like Calvin, Puritans believed in **predestination**—the idea that the all-powerful God, before the creation of the world, decided which few human souls would receive eternal life. Only God knows the identity of these fortunate predestined individuals—the "elect" or "saints." Nothing a person did in his or her lifetime could alter God's choice or provide assurance that the person was predestined for salvation with the elect or damned to hell with the doomed multitude.

Despite the looming uncertainty about God's choice of the elect, Puritans believed that if a person lived a rigorously godly life—constantly winning the daily battle against sin—his or her behavior was likely to be a hint, a visible sign, that he or she was one of God's chosen few. Puritans thought that "sainthood" would become visible in individuals' behavior, especially if they were privileged to know God's Word as revealed in the Bible.

The connection between sainthood and saintly behavior, however, was far from certain. Some members of the elect, Puritans believed, had not heard God's Word. One reason Puritans required all town residents to attend church services was to enlighten anyone who was ignorant of God's Truth. The slippery relationship between saintly behavior and God's predestined election caused Puritans to worry constantly that individuals who acted like saints were fooling themselves and others. Nevertheless, Puritans thought that **visible saints**—persons who passed the Puritans' demanding tests of conversion and church membership—probably were among God's elect.

Members of Puritan churches ardently hoped that God had chosen them to receive eternal life and tried to demonstrate saintly behavior. Their covenant bound them to help one another attain salvation and to discipline the entire community by saintly standards. Church members kept an eye on the behavior of everybody in town. By overseeing every aspect of life, the visible saints enforced a remarkable degree of righteous conformity in Puritan communities. Total conformity, however, was never achieved. Ardent Puritans differed among themselves, and non-Puritans shirked orthodox rules, such as the Roxbury servant who declared that "if hell were ten times hotter, [I] would rather be there than [I] would serve [my] master."

Despite the central importance of religion, churches played no direct role in the civil government of New England communities. Puritans did not want to mimic the Church of England, which they considered a puppet of the king rather than an independent body that served the Lord. They were determined to insulate New England churches from the contaminating influence of the civil state and its merely human laws. Ministers were prohibited from holding government office.

Puritans had no qualms, however, about their religious beliefs influencing New England governments. As much as possible, the Puritans tried to bring

Calvinism

▶ Christian doctrine of the Swiss Protestant theologian John Calvin. Its chief tenet was predestination, the idea that God had determined which human souls would receive eternal salvation. Despite this doctrine, Calvinism promoted strict discipline in daily and religious life.

predestination

▶ A doctrine stating that God determined whether individuals were destined for salvation or damnation before their birth. According to the doctrine, nothing an individual did during his or her lifetime could affect that person's fate.

visible saints

▶ Puritans who had passed the tests of conversion and church membership and were therefore thought to be among God's elect.

CHAPTER LOCATOR | Why did the Puritans immigrate to North America?

90 CHAPTER 4 FOUNDING THE NORTHERN COLONIES

public life into conformity with their view of God's law. For example, fines were issued for Sabbath-breaking activities such as working, traveling, playing a flute, smoking a pipe, and visiting neighbors.

Puritans mandated other purifications of what they considered corrupt English practices. They refused to celebrate Christmas or Easter because the Bible did not mention either one. They outlawed religious wedding ceremonies; couples were married by a magistrate in a civil ceremony. They banned cards, dice, shuffleboard, and other games of chance, as well as music and dancing. "Mixt or Promiscuous Dancing . . . of Men and Women" could not be tolerated since "the unchaste Touches and Gesticulations used by Dancers have a palpable tendency to that which is evil."

Government by Puritans for Puritanism

It is only a slight exaggeration to say that seventeenth-century New England was governed by Puritans for Puritanism. The charter of the Massachusetts Bay Company empowered the company's stockholders, known as freemen, to meet as a body known as the General Court and make the laws needed to govern the company's affairs. The colonists transformed this arrangement for running a joint-stock company into a structure for governing the colony. Hoping to ensure that godly men would decide government policies, the General Court expanded the number of freemen in 1631 to include all male church members. Only freemen had the right to vote for governor and other officials. When the size of the General Court grew too large to meet conveniently, the freemen agreed in 1634 that each town would send two deputies to the General Court to act as the colony's

How did New England society change during the seventeenth century?	What was distinctive about the middle colonies?	What was the connection between the colonies and the English empire?	Conclusion: Was there an English model of colonization in North America?	✔ LearningCurve Check what you know. bedfordstmartins.com /roarkunderstanding

91

legislative assembly. All other men were classified as "inhabitants," who had the right to vote, hold office, and participate fully in town government.

A "town meeting," composed of a town's inhabitants and freemen, chose the selectmen who administered local affairs. New England town meetings routinely practiced a level of popular participation in political life that was unprecedented elsewhere in the world during the seventeenth century. Almost every adult man could speak out and vote in town meetings, but all women—even church members—were prohibited from voting. This widespread political participation tended to reinforce conformity to Puritan ideals.

The General Court granted land for town sites to pious petitioners, once the Indians agreed to relinquish their claim to the land, usually in exchange for manufactured goods. Town founders then apportioned land among themselves and any newcomers they approved. Most family plots clustered between roughly fifty to one hundred acres, resulting in a more nearly equal distribution of land in New England than in the Chesapeake.

The physical layout of New England towns encouraged settlers to look inward toward their neighbors, multiplying the opportunities for godly vigilance. Most people considered the forest that lay just beyond every settler's house an alien environment. Footpaths connecting one town to another were so rudimentary that even John Winthrop once got lost and spent a sleepless night in the forest only half a mile from his house.

The Splintering of Puritanism

Almost from the beginning, John Winthrop and other leaders had difficulty enforcing their views of Puritan orthodoxy. In England, persecution as a dissenting minority had unified Puritan voices in opposition to the Church of England. In New England, the promise of a godly society and the Puritans' emphasis on individual Bible study led toward different visions of godliness. Puritan leaders, however, interpreted dissent as an error caused either by a misguided believer or by the malevolent power of Satan. As one Puritan minister proclaimed, "The Scripture saith . . . there is no Truth but one."

The case of Roger Williams provides an example of dissent and its consequences. In 1633, Williams became the minister of the church in Salem, Massachusetts, and stated his belief that the Bible shrouded the Word of God in "mist and fog." That observation led him to denounce the emerging New England order as impure, ungodly, and tyrannical. He disagreed with the New England government's requirement that everyone attend church services. He argued that forcing people who were not Christians to attend church was "False Worshipping" that only promoted "spiritual drunkenness and whoredom." He believed that to regulate religious behavior would be "spiritual rape" and that governments should tolerate all religious beliefs because only God knows the Truth. "I commend that man," Williams wrote, "whether Jew, or Turk, or Papist, or whoever, that steers no otherwise than his conscience dares."

New England's leaders denounced Williams's arguments and banished him for his "extreme and dangerous" opinions. In January 1636, he fled south to Narragansett Bay, where he and his followers established the colony of Rhode

Island, which enshrined "Liberty of Conscience" as a fundamental ideal and became a refuge for other dissenters.

Shortly after banishing Roger Williams, Winthrop confronted another dissenter, this time a devout Puritan woman steeped in Scripture and absorbed by religious questions: Anne Hutchinson. The mother of fourteen children, Hutchinson served her neighbors as a midwife and in 1634 began to give weekly lectures on recent sermons attended by women who gathered at her home. Hutchinson lectured on the "covenant of grace"—the idea that individuals could be saved only by God's grace in choosing them to be members of the elect. This familiar Puritan doctrine contrasted with the covenant of works, the erroneous belief that a person's behavior—one's works—could win God's favor and ultimately earn a person salvation.

The meetings at Hutchinson's house alarmed her nearest neighbor, Governor John Winthrop, who believed that she was subverting the good order of the colony. In 1637, Winthrop had formal charges brought against Hutchinson and denounced her lectures as "not tolerable nor comely in the sight of God nor fitting for your sex." He told her, "You have stept out of your place, you have rather bine a Husband than a Wife and a preacher than a Hearer; and a Magistrate than a Subject."

Winthrop and other Puritan elders referred to Hutchinson and her followers as **antinomians**, people who believed that Christians could be saved by faith alone and did not need to act in accordance with God's law as set forth in the Bible and as interpreted by the colony's leaders. Hutchinson nimbly defended herself against the accusation of antinomianism. Yes, she acknowledged, she believed that men and women were saved by faith alone; but no, she did not deny the need to obey God's law. "The Lord hath let me see which was the clear ministry and which the wrong," she said. How could she tell, Winthrop asked, which ministry was which? "By an immediate revelation," she replied, "by the voice of [God's] own spirit to my soul." Winthrop seized this statement as the

antinomians

▶ Individuals who believed that Christians could be saved by faith alone and did not need to act in accordance with God's law as set forth in the Bible. Puritan leaders considered this belief to be heresy.

How did New England society change during the seventeenth century? | What was distinctive about the middle colonies? | What was the connection between the colonies and the English empire? | Conclusion: Was there an English model of colonization in North America? | ☑ **LearningCurve** Check what you know. bedfordstmartins.com /roarkunderstanding

heresy of prophecy, the view that God revealed his will directly to a believer instead of exclusively through the Bible, as every right-minded Puritan knew.

In 1638, the Boston church formally excommunicated Hutchinson. The minister decreed, "I doe cast you out and . . . deliver you up to Satan." Banished, Hutchinson and her family moved first to Roger Williams's Rhode Island and then to present-day New York, where she and most of her family were killed by Indians.

The strains within Puritanism exemplified by Anne Hutchinson and Roger Williams caused communities to splinter repeatedly during the seventeenth century. Thomas Hooker, a prominent minister, clashed with Winthrop and other leaders over the composition of the church. Hooker argued that men and women who lived godly lives should be admitted to church membership even if they had not experienced conversion. In 1636, Hooker led an exodus of more than eight hundred colonists from Massachusetts to the Connecticut River valley, where they founded Hartford and neighboring towns. In 1639, the towns adopted the Fundamental Orders of Connecticut, a quasi-constitution that could be altered by the vote of freemen, who did not have to be church members, though nearly all of them were.

Other Puritan churches divided and subdivided throughout the seventeenth century as acrimony developed over doctrine and church government. Sometimes churches split over the appointment of a controversial minister. These schisms arose from ambiguities and tensions within Puritan belief. As the colonies matured, other tensions developed as well.

Religious Controversies and Economic Changes

A revolutionary transformation in the fortunes of Puritans in England had profound consequences in New England. Disputes between King Charles I and Parliament, which was dominated by Puritans, escalated in 1642 to civil war in England, a conflict known as the **Puritan Revolution**. Parliamentary forces led by the staunch Puritan Oliver Cromwell were victorious, executing Charles I in 1649 and proclaiming England a Puritan republic. From 1649 to 1660, England's rulers were not monarchs who suppressed Puritanism but believers who championed it.

When the Puritan Revolution began, the stream of immigrants to New England dwindled to a trickle, creating hard times for the colonists. They could no longer consider themselves a city on a hill setting a godly example for humankind. Puritans in England, not New England, were reforming English society. Furthermore, when immigrant ships became rare, the colonists faced sky-high prices for scarce English goods and few customers for their own colonial products. As they searched to find new products and markets, they established the enduring patterns of New England's economy.

New England's rocky soil and short growing season ruled out cultivating the southern colonies' crops of tobacco and rice that found ready markets in Atlantic ports. Exports that New Englanders could not get from the soil they took instead from the forest and the sea. By the 1640s, furbearing animals had become scarce unless traders ventured far beyond the frontiers of English settlement. Trees from the seemingly limitless forests of New England proved a longer-lasting resource.

Puritan Revolution

▶ English civil war that arose out of disputes between King Charles I and Parliament, which was dominated by Puritans. The conflict began in 1642 and ended with the execution of Charles I in 1649, resulting in Puritan rule in England until 1660.

CHAPTER LOCATOR | Why did the Puritans immigrate to North America?

94   CHAPTER 4   FOUNDING THE NORTHERN COLONIES

Masts for ships and staves for barrels of Spanish wine and West Indian sugar were crafted from New England timber.

The most important New England export was fish. Dried, salted codfish from the rich North Atlantic fishing grounds found markets in southern Europe and the West Indies. The fish trade also stimulated colonial shipbuilding and trained generations of fishermen, sailors, and merchants. But the lives of most New England colonists revolved around their farms, churches, and families.

Although immigration came to a standstill in the 1640s, the population continued to boom, doubling every twenty years. In New England, almost everyone married, and women often had eight or nine children. Long, cold winters minimized the presence of warm-weather ailments such as malaria and yellow fever, so the mortality rate was lower than in the South.

During the second half of the seventeenth century, under the pressures of steady population growth (**Figure 4.1**) and integration into the Atlantic economy, the red-hot piety of the founders cooled. After 1640, the population grew faster than church membership. Boston's churches in 1650 could house only about a third of the city's residents. By the 1680s, women were the majority of church members throughout New England. In some towns, only 15 percent of the adult men were members. This slackening of piety led the Puritan minister Michael Wigglesworth to ask, in verse:

> How is it that
> I find In stead of holiness Carnality;
> In stead of heavenly frames an Earthly mind,
> For burning zeal luke-warm Indifferency,
> For flaming love, key-cold Dead-heartedness. . . .
> Whence cometh it . . .
> that an honest man can hardly
> Trust his Brother?

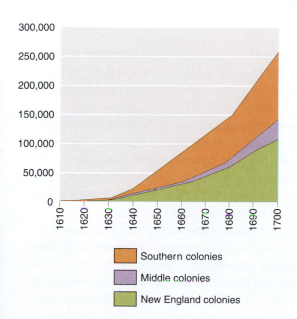

FIGURE 4.1 ■ **Population of the English North American Colonies in the Seventeenth Century**

The colonial population grew at a steadily accelerating rate during the seventeenth century. New England and the southern colonies each accounted for about half the total colonial population until after 1680, when growth in Pennsylvania and New York contributed to a surge in the population of the middle colonies.

How did New England society change during the seventeenth century? | What was distinctive about the middle colonies? | What was the connection between the colonies and the English empire? | Conclusion: Was there an English model of colonization in North America? | ✓ LearningCurve Check what you know. bedfordstmartins.com /roarkunderstanding

95

Most alarming to Puritan leaders, many of the children of the visible saints of Winthrop's generation failed to experience conversion and attain full church membership. Puritans tended to assume that sainthood was inherited—that the children of visible saints were probably also among the elect. As these children grew up during the 1640s and 1650s, however, they seldom experienced the inward transformation that signaled conversion and qualification for church membership. The problem of declining church membership and the watering-down of Puritan orthodoxy became urgent during the 1650s when the children of saints, who had grown to adulthood in New England but had not experienced conversion, began to have children themselves. Their sons and daughters—the grandchildren of the founders of the colony—could not receive the protection that baptism afforded against the terrors of death because their parents had not experienced conversion.

Puritan churches debated what to do. To allow anyone, even the child of a saint, to become a church member without conversion was an unthinkable retreat from fundamental Puritan doctrine. In 1662, a synod of Massachusetts ministers reached a compromise known as the **Halfway Covenant**. Unconverted children of saints would be permitted to become "halfway" church members. Like regular church members, they could baptize their infants. But unlike full church members, they could not participate in communion or have the voting privileges of church membership. The Halfway Covenant generated a controversy that sputtered through Puritan churches for the remainder of the century. With the Halfway Covenant, Puritan churches came to terms with the lukewarm piety that had replaced the founders' burning zeal.

Nonetheless, New England communities continued to enforce piety with holy rigor. Beginning in 1656, small bands of **Quakers**—members of the Society of Friends, as they called themselves—began to arrive in Massachusetts. Quakers believed that God spoke directly to each individual through an "inner light" and that individuals needed neither a preacher nor the Bible to discover God's Word. Maintaining that all human beings were equal in God's eyes, Quakers refused to conform to mere temporal powers such as laws and governments unless God requested otherwise. Women often took a leading role in Quaker meetings, in contrast to Puritan congregations, where women usually outnumbered men but remained subordinate.

New England communities treated Quakers with ruthless severity. Some Quakers were branded on the face "with a red-hot iron with [an] H. for heresie." When Quakers refused to leave Massachusetts, Boston officials hanged four of them between 1659 and 1661.

New Englanders' partial success in realizing the promise of a godly society ultimately undermined the intense appeal of Puritanism. In the pious Puritan communities of New England, leaders tried to eliminate sin. In the process, they diminished the sense of utter human depravity that was the wellspring of Puritanism. By 1700, New Englanders did not doubt that human beings sinned, but they were more concerned with the sins of others than with their own.

Witch trials held in Salem, Massachusetts, signaled the erosion of religious confidence and assurance. From the beginning of English settlement in the New World, more than 95 percent of all legal accusations of witchcraft occurred in New England, a hint of the Puritans' preoccupation with sin and evil. The most notorious witchcraft trials took place in Salem in 1692, when witnesses accused more

Halfway Covenant
▶ A Puritan compromise established in Massachusetts in 1662 that allowed the unconverted children of the "visible saints" to become "halfway" members of the church and to baptize their own children even though they were not full members of the church themselves.

Quakers
▶ Epithet for members of the Society of Friends. Their belief that God spoke directly to each individual through an "inner light" and that neither ministers nor the Bible was essential to discovering God's Word put them in conflict with orthodox Puritans.

CHAPTER LOCATOR | Why did the Puritans immigrate to North America?

96 CHAPTER 4
FOUNDING THE NORTHERN COLONIES

than one hundred people of witchcraft, a capital crime. Bewitched young girls shrieked in pain, their limbs twisted into strange contortions, as they pointed out the witches who tortured them. According to the trial court record, the bewitched girls declared that "the shape of [one accused witch] did oftentimes very grievously pinch them, choke them, bite them, and afflict them; urging them to write their names in a book" — the devil's book. Most of the accused witches were older women, and virtually all of them were well known to their accusers. The Salem court hanged nineteen accused witches and pressed one to death, signaling enduring belief in the supernatural origins of evil and gnawing doubt about the strength of Puritan New Englanders' faith. Why else, after all, had so many New Englanders succumbed to what their accusers and the judges believed were the temptations of Satan?

QUICK REVIEW <

Why did Massachusetts Puritans adopt the Halfway Covenant?

How did New England society change during the seventeenth century?	What was distinctive about the middle colonies?	What was the connection between the colonies and the English empire?	Conclusion: Was there an English model of colonization in North America?	LearningCurve Check what you know. bedfordstmartins.com /roarkunderstanding

What was distinctive about the middle colonies?

SOUTH OF NEW ENGLAND and north of the Chesapeake, a group of middle colonies were founded in the last third of the seventeenth century. Before the 1670s, few Europeans settled in the region. For the first two-thirds of the seventeenth century, the most important European outpost in the area was the relatively small Dutch colony of New Netherland. By 1700, however, the English monarchy had seized New Netherland, renamed it New York, and encouraged the creation of a Quaker colony in Pennsylvania led by William Penn. Unlike the New England colonies, the middle colonies of New York, New Jersey, and Pennsylvania originated as land grants by the English monarch to one or more proprietors, who then possessed both the land and the extensive, almost monarchical, powers of government (**Map 4.2**). These middle colonies attracted settlers of more diverse European origins and religious faiths than were found in New England.

From New Netherland to New York

In 1609, the Dutch East India Company dispatched Henry Hudson to search for a Northwest Passage to the Orient. Hudson ventured up the large river that now bears his name until it dwindled to a stream that obviously did not lead to China. A decade later, the Dutch government granted the West India Company—a group of Dutch merchants and shippers—exclusive rights to trade with the Western Hemisphere. In 1626, Peter Minuit, the resident director of the company, purchased Manhattan Island from the Manhate Indians for trade goods worth the equivalent

CHAPTER LOCATOR | Why did the Puritans immigrate to North America?

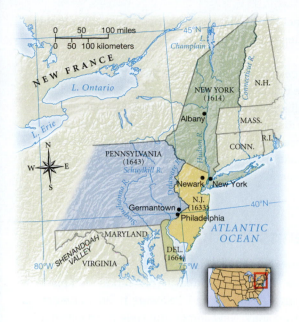

MAP 4.2 ■ **Middle Colonies in the Seventeenth Century**

For the most part, settlers in the middle colonies in the seventeenth century clustered along the Hudson and Delaware rivers. The geographic extent of the colonies shown in this map reflects land grants authorized in England. Most of this area was inhabited by Native Americans rather than colonists.

> **CHRONOLOGY**

1609
– Henry Hudson searches for a Northwest Passage.

1626
– Peter Minuit purchases Manhattan Island for the Dutch; New Amsterdam is founded.

1664
– English seize New Amsterdam and rename it New York.
– Colony of New Jersey is created.

1681
– Colony of Pennsylvania is founded.

New Netherland
▶ Dutch colony in present-day New York. New Amsterdam on Manhattan Island was its capital and colony headquarters.

of a dozen beaver pelts. New Amsterdam, the small settlement established at the southern tip of Manhattan Island, became the principal trading center in **New Netherland** and the colony's headquarters.

Unlike the English colonies, New Netherland did not attract many European immigrants. Like New England and the Chesapeake colonies, New Netherland never realized its sponsors' dreams of great profits. The company tried to stimulate immigration by granting patroonships—allotments of eighteen miles of land along the Hudson River—to wealthy stockholders who would bring fifty families to the colony and settle them as serflike tenants on their huge domains. Only one patroonship succeeded; the others failed to attract settlers, and the company eventually recovered much of the land.

Though few in number, New Netherlanders were remarkably diverse, especially compared with the homogeneous English settlers to the north and south. Religious dissenters and immigrants from Holland, Sweden, France, Germany, and elsewhere made their way to the colony. A minister of the Dutch Reformed Church complained to his superiors in Holland that several groups of Jews had recently arrived, adding to the religious mixture of "Papists, Mennonites and Lutherans among the Dutch [and] many Puritans . . . and many other atheists . . . who conceal themselves under the name of Christians."

The West India Company struggled to govern the motley colonists. Peter Stuyvesant, governor from 1647 to 1664, tried to enforce conformity to the Dutch Reformed Church, but the company declared that "the consciences of men should be free and unshackled," making a virtue of New Netherland necessity. The company never permitted the colony's settlers to form a representative government. Instead, the company appointed government officials who established policies, including taxes, that many colonists deeply resented.

In 1664, New Netherland became New York. Charles II, who became king of England in 1660 when Parliament restored the monarchy, gave his brother James, the Duke of York, an enormous grant of land that included New Netherland. The

How did New England society change during the seventeenth century?

What was distinctive about the middle colonies?

What was the connection between the colonies and the English empire?

Conclusion: Was there an English model of colonization in North America?

✔ LearningCurve
Check what you know.
bedfordstmartins.com/roarkunderstanding

99

duke quickly organized a small fleet of warships, which appeared off Manhattan Island in late summer 1664, and demanded that Stuyvesant surrender. With little choice, he did.

As the new proprietor of the colony, the Duke of York exercised almost the same unlimited authority over the colony as had the West India Company. Like the Dutch, the duke permitted "all persons of what Religion soever, quietly to inhabit . . . provided they give no disturbance to the publique peace, nor doe molest or disquiet others in the free exercise of their religion." This policy of religious toleration was less an affirmation of liberty of conscience than a recognition of the reality of the most heterogeneous colony in seventeenth-century North America.

New Jersey and Pennsylvania

The creation of New York led indirectly to the founding of two other middle colonies, New Jersey and Pennsylvania. In 1664, the Duke of York subdivided his grant and gave the portion between the Hudson and Delaware rivers to two of his friends. The proprietors of this new colony, New Jersey, quarreled and called in a prominent English Quaker, William Penn, to arbitrate their dispute. Penn eventually worked out a settlement that continued New Jersey's proprietary government. In the process, Penn became intensely interested in what he termed a "holy experiment" of establishing a genuinely Quaker colony in America.

Unlike most Quakers, William Penn came from an eminent family. Born in 1644, Penn trained for a military career, but the ideas of dissenters from the reestablished Church of England appealed to him, and he became a devout Quaker.

Despite his many run-ins with the government (he was jailed four times for his Quaker practices), Penn remained on good terms with Charles II. Partly to rid England of the troublesome Quakers, in 1681 Charles made Penn the proprietor of a new colony of some 45,000 square miles called Pennsylvania.

> Quakers in the New World

- Quakers believed in an open, generous God who made his love equally available to all people.
- Quaker leaders were ordinary men and women, not specially trained preachers; women were allowed to hold positions of religious leadership. They considered social hierarchy false and evil.
- Nearly eight thousand Quaker immigrants from England, Ireland, and Wales arrived in Pennsylvania between 1682 and 1685.
- Immigrants represented a cross section of the artisans, farmers, and laborers who predominated among English Quakers.

Toleration and Diversity in Pennsylvania

Quaker missionaries encouraged immigrants from the European continent, and many came, giving Pennsylvania greater ethnic diversity than any other English colony except New York. The Quaker colony prospered, and the capital city,

CHAPTER LOCATOR | Why did the Puritans immigrate to North America?

100 CHAPTER 4 FOUNDING THE NORTHERN COLONIES

Philadelphia, soon rivaled New York as a center of commerce. By 1700, the city's five thousand inhabitants participated in a thriving trade exporting flour and other food products to the West Indies and importing English textiles and manufactured goods.

Penn was determined to live in peace with the Indians who inhabited the region. His Indian policy expressed his Quaker ideals and contrasted sharply with the hostile policies of the other English colonies. As he explained to the chief of the Lenni Lenape (Delaware) Indians, "God has written his law in our hearts, by which we are taught and commanded to love and help and do good to one another . . . [and] I desire to enjoy [Pennsylvania lands] with your love and consent." Penn instructed his agents to obtain the Indians' consent by purchasing their land, respecting their claims, and dealing with them fairly.

Penn declared that the first principle of government was that every settler would "enjoy the free possession of his or her faith and exercise of worship towards God." Accordingly, Pennsylvania tolerated Protestant sects of all kinds as well as Roman Catholicism. All voters and officeholders had to be Christians, but the government did not compel settlers to attend religious services, as in Massachusetts, or to pay taxes to maintain a state-supported church, as in Virginia.

Despite its toleration and diversity, Pennsylvania was as much a Quaker colony as New England was a stronghold of Puritanism. Penn had no hesitation about using civil government to enforce religious morality. One of the colony's first laws provided severe punishment for "all such offenses against God, as swearing, cursing, lying, profane talking, [and] drunkenness . . . which excite the people to rudeness, cruelty, looseness, and irreligion."

As proprietor, Penn had extensive powers subject only to review by the king. He appointed a governor, who maintained the proprietor's power to veto any laws passed by the colonial council, which was elected by property owners who possessed at least one hundred acres of land or who paid taxes. The council had the power to originate laws and administer all the affairs of government. A popularly elected assembly served as a check on the council; its members had the authority to reject or approve laws framed by the council.

Penn stressed that the exact form of government mattered less than the men who served in it. In Penn's eyes, "good men" staffed Pennsylvania's government because Quakers dominated elective and appointive offices. Quakers, of course, differed among themselves. Members of the assembly struggled to win the right to debate and amend laws, especially tax laws. They finally won the battle in 1701 when a new Charter of Privileges gave the proprietor the power to appoint the council and in turn stripped the council of all its former powers and gave them to the assembly, which became the only single-house legislature in all the English colonies.

QUICK REVIEW <

How did Quaker ideals shape the colony of Pennsylvania?

How did New England society change during the seventeenth century?

What was distinctive about the middle colonies?

What was the connection between the colonies and the English empire?

Conclusion: Was there an English model of colonization in North America?

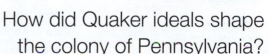

LearningCurve
Check what you know.
bedfordstmartins.com
/roarkunderstanding

> What was the connection between the colonies and the English empire?

Pine Tree Shilling

In violation of English rules that forbade colonies from issuing their own currency, John Hull, a wealthy Boston merchant and shipowner, began to mint coins in 1652. Shown here is one of his pine tree shillings, both sides boldly announcing its origins. Courtesy of the Museum of the American Numismatic Association.

PROPRIETARY GRANTS TO FARAWAY lands were a cheap way for the king to reward friends. As the colonies grew, however, the grants became more valuable. After 1660, the king took initiatives to channel colonial trade through English hands and to consolidate royal authority over colonial governments. Occasioned by such economic and political considerations and triggered by King Philip's War between colonists and Native Americans, these initiatives defined the basic relationship between the colonies and England that endured until the American Revolution (**Map 4.3**).

Royal Regulation of Colonial Trade

English economic policies toward the colonies were designed to yield customs revenues for the monarchy and profitable business for English merchants and shippers. Also, the policies were intended to divert the colonies' trade from England's enemies, especially the Dutch and the French.

The Navigation Acts of 1650, 1651, 1660, and 1663 (see chapter 3) set forth two fundamental rules governing colonial trade. First, goods shipped to and from the colonies had to be transported in English ships using primarily English crews. Second, the Navigation Acts listed colonial products that could be shipped only to England or to other English colonies. While these regulations prevented Chesapeake planters from shipping their tobacco directly to the European

CHAPTER LOCATOR | Why did the Puritans immigrate to North America?

MAP 4.3 ■ **American Colonies at the End of the Seventeenth Century**

By the end of the seventeenth century, settlers inhabited a narrow band of land that stretched from Boston to Norfolk, with pockets of settlement farther south. The colonies' claims to enormous tracts of land to the west were contested by Native Americans as well as by France and Spain.

> MAP ACTIVITY

READING THE MAP: What geographic feature acted as the western boundary for colonial territorial claims? Which colonies were the most settled and which the least?
CONNECTIONS: The map divides the colonies into four regions. Can you think of an alternative organization? On what criteria would it be based?

continent, they interfered less with the commerce of New England and the middle colonies, whose principal exports—fish, lumber, and flour—could legally be sent directly to their most important markets in the West Indies.

By the end of the seventeenth century, colonial commerce was defined by regulations that subjected merchants and shippers to royal supervision and gave them access to markets throughout the English empire. In addition, colonial commerce received protection from the English navy. By 1700, colonial goods (including those from the West Indies) accounted for one-fifth of all English imports and for two-thirds of all goods re-exported from England to the European continent. In turn, the

| How did New England society change during the seventeenth century? | What was distinctive about the middle colonies? | **What was the connection between the colonies and the English empire?** | Conclusion: Was there an English model of colonization in North America? | ✓ LearningCurve Check what you know. bedfordstmartins.com /roarkunderstanding |

colonies absorbed more than one-tenth of English exports. The commercial regulations gave economic value to England's proprietorship of the American colonies.

King Philip's War and the Consolidation of Royal Authority

The monarchy also took steps to exercise greater control over colonial governments. Virginia had been a royal colony since 1624; Maryland, South Carolina, and the middle colonies were proprietary colonies with close ties to the crown. The New England colonies possessed royal charters, but they had developed their own distinctively Puritan governments. Charles II, whose father, Charles I, had been executed by Puritans in England, took a particular interest in harnessing the New England colonies more firmly to the English empire. The occasion was a royal investigation following **King Philip's War**.

A series of skirmishes in the Connecticut River valley between 1636 and 1637 culminated in the Pequot War when colonists massacred hundreds of Pequot Indians. In the decades that followed, New Englanders established relatively peaceful relations with the more potent Wampanoags, but they steadily encroached on Indian land. In 1642, a native leader urged warring tribes to band together against the English. "We [must] be one as they [the English] are," he said; "otherwise we shall be gone shortly, for . . . these English having gotten our land, they with scythes cut down the grass, and with axes fell the trees, and their cows and horses eat the grass, and their hogs spoil our clam banks, and we shall all be starved."

Such grievances accumulated until 1675, when the Wampanoags, led by their chief Metacomet (whom the colonists called King Philip), attacked English settlements in western Massachusetts. Militias from Massachusetts and other New England colonies counterattacked the Wampanoags, Nipmucks, and Narragansetts in a deadly sequence of battles that killed more than a thousand colonists and thousands more Indians. The Indians destroyed thirteen English settlements and partially burned another half dozen. Mary Rowlandson, a minister's wife in Lancaster, Massachusetts, who was captured by Indians, recalled later that it was a "solemn sight to see so many Christians lying in their blood . . . like a company of sheep torn by wolves."

By the spring of 1676, Indian warriors ranged freely within seventeen miles of Boston. The colonists finally defeated the Indians, principally with a scorched-earth policy of burning their food supplies. But King Philip's War left the New England colonists with a large war debt, a devastated frontier, and an enduring hatred of Indians. "A Swarm of Flies, they may arise, a Nation to Annoy," a colonial officer wrote in justification of destroying the Indians; "Yea Rats and Mice, or Swarms of Lice a Nation may destroy."

In 1676, an agent of the king arrived to investigate whether New England was abiding by English laws. Not surprisingly, the king's agent found all sorts of deviations from English rules, and the monarchy decided to govern New England more directly. In 1684, an

King Philip's War

► War begun by Metacomet (King Philip), in which the Wampanoag Indians attacked colonial settlements in western Massachusetts in 1675. Colonists responded by attacking the Wampanoags and other tribes they believed conspired with them. The colonists prevailed in the brutal war.

King Philip's War, 1675–1676

CHAPTER LOCATOR | Why did the Puritans immigrate to North America?

104 CHAPTER 4 FOUNDING THE NORTHERN COLONIES

Wampanoag War Club This seventeenth-century war club was used to kill King Philip, according to the Anglican missionary who obtained it from Indians early in the eighteenth century. Although the tale is probably a legend, the club is certainly a seventeenth-century Wampanoag weapon that could have been used in King Philip's War. The heavy ball carved into the head of the club could deliver a fatal blow. Courtesy of the Fruitlands Museums, Harvard, Massachusetts.

English court revoked the Massachusetts charter, the foundation of the distinctive Puritan government. Two years later, in 1686, royal officials incorporated Massachusetts and the other colonies north of Maryland into the Dominion of New England. To govern the dominion, the English sent Sir Edmund Andros to Boston. Some New England merchants cooperated with Andros, but most colonists were offended by his flagrant disregard of such Puritan traditions as keeping the Sabbath. Worst of all, the Dominion of New England invalidated all land titles, confronting every landowner in New England with the horrifying prospect of losing his or her land.

Events in England, however, permitted Massachusetts colonists to overthrow Andros and retain title to their property. When Charles II died in 1685, he was succeeded by his brother James II, a zealous Catholic. James's aggressive campaign to appoint Catholics to government posts engendered such unrest that in 1688 a group of Protestant noblemen in Parliament invited the Dutch ruler William III of Orange, James's son-in-law, to claim the English throne.

When William III landed in England at the head of a large army, James fled to France, and William III and his wife, Mary II (James's daughter), became corulers in the relatively bloodless "Glorious Revolution," reasserting Protestant influence in England and its empire. Rumors of the revolution raced across the Atlantic and emboldened colonial uprisings against royal authority in Massachusetts, New York, and Maryland.

In Boston in 1689, rebels tossed Andros and other English officials in jail, destroyed the Dominion of New England, and reestablished the former charter government. New Yorkers followed the Massachusetts example. Under the leadership of Jacob Leisler, rebels seized the royal governor in 1689 and ruled the colony for more than a year. That same year in Maryland, the Protestant Association, led by John Coode, overthrew the colony's pro-Catholic government, fearing it would not recognize the new Protestant king.

But these rebel governments did not last. When King William III's governor of New York arrived in 1691, he executed Leisler for treason. Coode's men ruled Maryland until the new royal governor arrived in 1692 and ended both Coode's rebellion and Lord Baltimore's proprietary government. In Massachusetts, John

How did New England society change during the seventeenth century?

What was distinctive about the middle colonies?

What was the connection between the colonies and the English empire?

Conclusion: Was there an English model of colonization in North America?

✓ LearningCurve
Check what you know.
bedfordstmartins.com
/roarkunderstanding

105

Winthrop's city on a hill became another royal colony in 1691. The new charter said that the governor of the colony would be appointed by the king rather than elected by the colonists' representatives. But perhaps the most unsettling change was the new qualification for voting. Possession of property replaced church membership as a prerequisite for voting in colony-wide elections. Wealth replaced God's grace as the defining characteristic of Massachusetts citizenship.

Much as colonists chafed under increasing royal control, they still valued English protection from hostile neighbors. Colonists worried that the Catholic colony of New France to the north menaced frontier regions by encouraging Indian raids and by competing for the lucrative fur trade. Although French leaders tried to buttress the military strength of New France during the last third of the seventeenth century to block the expansion of the English colonies, most of the military efforts mustered by New France focused on defending against attacks by the powerful Iroquois. However, when the English colonies were distracted by the Glorious Revolution, French forces from the fur-trading regions along the Great Lakes and in Canada attacked villages in New England and New York. Known as King William's War, the conflict with the French was a colonial outgrowth of William's war against France in Europe. The war dragged on from 1689 until 1697 and ended inconclusively in both Europe and the colonies. But it made clear to many colonists that along with English royal government came a welcome measure of military security.

> **QUICK REVIEW**

Why did the Glorious Revolution in England lead to uprisings in the American colonies?

CHAPTER LOCATOR | Why did the Puritans immigrate to North America?

106 CHAPTER 4
FOUNDING THE NORTHERN COLONIES

Conclusion: Was there an English model of colonization in North America?

<

BY 1700, THE NORTHERN ENGLISH colonies of North America had developed along lines quite different from the example set by their southern counterparts. Emigrants came with their families and created settlements unlike the scattered plantations and largely male environment of early Virginia. Puritans in New England built towns and governments around their churches and placed worship of God, not tobacco, at the center of their society. They depended chiefly on the labor of family members rather than on that of servants and slaves.

The convictions of Puritanism that motivated John Winthrop and others to reinvent England in the colonies became muted, however, as New England matured and dissenters such as Roger Williams multiplied. Catholics, Quakers, Anglicans (members of the Church of England), Jews, and others settled in the middle and southern colonies, creating considerable religious toleration, especially in Pennsylvania and New York. At the same time, northern colonists, like their southern counterparts, developed an ever-increasing need for land that inevitably led to bloody conflict with the Indians who were displaced. By the closing years of the seventeenth century, the royal government in England intervened to try to moderate those conflicts and to govern the colonies more directly for the benefit of the monarchy. Assertions of royal control triggered colonial resistance that was ultimately suppressed, resulting in Massachusetts losing its special charter status and becoming a royal colony much like the other English North American colonies.

During the next century, the English colonial world would undergo surprising new developments built on the achievements of the seventeenth century. Immigrants from Scotland, Ireland, and Germany streamed into North America, and unprecedented numbers of African slaves poured into the southern colonies. On average, white colonists attained a relatively comfortable standard of living, especially compared with most people in England and continental Europe. While religion remained important, the intensity of religious concern that characterized the seventeenth century waned during the eighteenth century. Colonists worried more about prosperity than about providence, and their societies grew increasingly secular, worldly, and diverse.

☑ **LearningCurve**
Check what you know.
bedfordstmartins.com
/roarkunderstanding

CHAPTER 4 STUDY GUIDE

STEP 1 **GET STARTED ONLINE**

 LearningCurve ▪ bedfordstmartins.com/roarkunderstanding

Now that you've read the chapter, make it stick by completing the LearningCurve activity.

STEP 2 **EXPLAIN WHY IT MATTERS**

Put your reading into practice. Identify each term below, and then explain why it matters in U.S. history.

TERM	WHO OR WHAT & WHEN	WHY IT MATTERS
Puritans (p. 84)		
English Reformation (p. 84)		
Separatists (p. 86)		
Calvinism (p. 90)		
predestination (p. 90)		
visible saints (p. 90)		
antinomians (p. 93)		
Puritan Revolution (p. 94)		
Halfway Covenant (p. 96)		
Quakers (p. 96)		
New Netherland (p. 99)		
King Philip's War (p. 104)		

STEP 3 **MOVE BEYOND THE BASICS**

To demonstrate a more advanced understanding, compare and contrast the northern colonies—why they were settled, sociopolitical structures, and economic organization.

Colony	Reasons for settlement	Social/political structures (religion, family, legal system)	Economics (land use and distribution, industry, income, labor)
Plymouth			
Massachusetts Bay			
Rhode Island			
New Netherland/ New York			
Pennsylvania			

STEP 4 **PUT IT ALL TOGETHER** Now, take a step back and try to explain the big picture. Remember to use specific examples from the chapter in your answers.

NEW ENGLAND

▶ What kind of society did the early settlers of New England hope to create?

▶ What forces challenged Puritan domination of New England?

THE MIDDLE COLONIES

▶ How did the settlement of the middle colonies differ from that of New England?

▶ What explains the religious and ethnic diversity of the middle colonies?

THE EMPIRE

▶ How did the English crown seek to regulate colonial trade?

▶ How did the colonists respond to the English crown's efforts to assert political authority?

LOOKING BACKWARD, LOOKING AHEAD

▶ How did European colonization of the Americas in the seventeenth century differ from Spanish colonization in the previous century?

▶ How did the growth and development of English colonies in the seventeenth century set the stage for conflict between England and its colonies in the eighteenth century?

> **IN YOUR OWN WORDS**

Imagine that you must give an oral report to the class answering the following question: **How did religious dissidents from England come to establish colonies in northern North America?** What would be the most important points to include and why?

> Do it online at the Student Site ∎ bedfordstmartins.com/roarkunderstanding

5

THE CHANGING WORLD OF COLONIAL AMERICA

1701–1770

> **What were the most important changes in colonial North America between 1701 and 1770?** Chapter 5 examines the factors that resulted in regional differences in colonial North America, as well as the common experiences, assumptions, and attitudes that contributed to a growing sense of unity among British American colonists. These unifying trends helped prepare the foundation for what would become the United States of America in 1776.

LearningCurve

bedfordstmartins.com/roarkunderstanding
After reading the chapter, use LearningCurve to
retain what you've read.

> How did the North American colonies change in the eighteenth century?

> What changed in New England life and culture?

> What spurred the growth of the middle colonies?

> Why did slavery become the defining feature of the southern colonies?

> What experiences tended to unify the colonists in British North America during the eighteenth century?

> Conclusion: What was the dual identity of British North American colonists?

Chandler wedding tapestry. New England, artist unknown, 1756. Courtesy, American Antiquarian Society.

How did the North American colonies change in the eighteenth century?

New York City Street This painting depicts John Street, a residential neighborhood of New York City, in 1768, as recalled by the artist Joseph B. Smith in the early nineteenth century. Notice that fences separate house yards from the street, rather than houses from one another, hinting of friendly relations among neighbors. Old John Street United Methodist Church.

THE MOST IMPORTANT FACT about eighteenth-century British America is its phenomenal population growth: from about 250,000 in 1700 to over two million by 1770. The eightfold growth of the colonial population signaled the maturation of a distinctive colonial society. Colonists of different ethnic groups, races, and religions lived in varied environments under thirteen different colonial governments, all of them part of the British empire.

In general, the growth and diversity of the eighteenth-century colonial population derived from two sources: immigration and **natural increase** (growth through reproduction). Natural increase contributed about three-fourths of the population growth, immigration about one-fourth. Immigration shifted the ethnic and racial balance among the colonists, making them by 1770 less English and less white than ever before. Fewer than 10 percent of eighteenth-century immigrants came from England; about 36 percent were Scots-Irish, mostly from northern Ireland; 33 percent arrived from Africa, almost all of them slaves; nearly 15 percent had emigrated from the many German-language principalities (the nation of Germany did not exist until 1871); and almost 10 percent came from Scotland. In 1670, more than 9 out of 10 colonists were of English ancestry, and only 1 out of 25 was of African ancestry. By 1770, only about half of the colonists were of English descent, while more than 20 percent descended from Africans. Thus, by 1770, the people of the colonies had a distinctive colonial—rather than English—profile (**Map 5.1**).

natural increase

▶ The growth of population through reproduction, as opposed to immigration. In the eighteenth century, natural increase accounted for about three-fourths of the American colonies' population growth.

CHAPTER LOCATOR | **How did the North American colonies change in the eighteenth century?** | What changed in New England life and culture?

112 CHAPTER 5
THE CHANGING WORLD OF COLONIAL AMERICA

In 1770
- Colonial population had grown to two million, compared with 250,000 in 1700.
- About half of American colonists were of English descent, while more than 20 percent were of African descent.

MAP 5.1 ■ Europeans and Africans in the Eighteenth Century

This map illustrates regions where Africans and certain immigrant groups clustered. It is important to avoid misreading the map. Predominantly English and German regions, for example, also contained colonists from other places. Likewise, regions where African slaves resided in large numbers also included many whites, slave masters among them. The map suggests the diversity of eighteenth-century colonial society.

The booming population of the colonies hints at a second major feature of eighteenth-century colonial society: an expanding economy. The nearly limitless wilderness stretching westward made land relatively cheap compared with its price in the Old World. The abundance of land made labor precious, and the colonists always needed more. The insatiable demand for labor was the fundamental economic environment that sustained the mushrooming population. Economic historians estimate that free colonists (those who were not indentured servants or slaves) had a higher standard of living than the majority of people elsewhere in the Atlantic world.

QUICK REVIEW <

How did the North American colonies achieve the remarkable population growth of the eighteenth century?

| What spurred the growth of the middle colonies? | Why did slavery become the defining feature of the southern colonies? | What experiences tended to unify colonists in British North America? | Conclusion: What was the dual identity of British North American colonists? | LearningCurve Check what you know. bedfordstmartins.com /roarkunderstanding |

What changed in New England life and culture?

Boston Common in Needlework

Hannah Otis embroidered this exquisite needlework portrait of Boston Common in 1750, when she was eighteen years old. From the perspective of the twenty-first century, the scene gives few hints of city life. Otis populated the cityscape with more animals than people and more plants than paving stones. What features of this portrait would suggest a city to an eighteenth-century viewer? Photograph © 2012 Museum of Fine Arts, Boston.

THE NEW ENGLAND POPULATION grew sixfold during the eighteenth century but lagged behind the growth in the other colonies. Most immigrants chose other destinations because of New England's relatively densely settled land and because Puritan orthodoxy made these colonies comparatively inhospitable to those of other faiths and those indifferent to religion. As the population grew, many settlers in search of farmland dispersed from towns, and Puritan communities lost much of their cohesion. Nonetheless, networks of economic exchange laced New Englanders to their neighbors, to Boston merchants, and to the broad currents of Atlantic commerce. In many ways, trade became a faith that competed strongly with the traditions of Puritanism.

Natural Increase and Land Distribution

New England's population grew mostly by natural increase, much as it had during the seventeenth century. The perils of childbirth gave wives a shorter life expectancy than husbands, but wives often lived to have six, seven, or eight babies. The growing New England population pressed against a limited amount of land (see Map 5.1). Moreover, as the northernmost group of British colonies, New England had contested frontiers where powerful Native Americans, especially the Iroquois and Mahicans, jealously guarded their territory. The French (and Catholic) colony of New France also menaced the British (and mostly Protestant) New England colonies when provoked by colonial or European disputes.

CHAPTER LOCATOR | How did the North American colonies change in the eighteenth century? | **What changed in New England life and culture?**

114 CHAPTER 5 THE CHANGING WORLD OF COLONIAL AMERICA

During the seventeenth century, New England towns parceled out land to individual families. In most cases, the original settlers practiced **partible inheritance**—that is, they subdivided land more or less equally among sons. By the eighteenth century, the original land allotments had to be further subdivided, and many plots of land became too small to support a family. Sons who could not hope to inherit sufficient land had to move away from the town where they were born.

During the eighteenth century, colonial governments in New England abandoned the seventeenth-century policy of granting land to towns. Needing revenue, the governments of both Connecticut and Massachusetts sold land directly to individuals, including speculators. Now money, rather than membership in a community bound by a church covenant, determined whether a person could obtain land. The new land policy eroded the seventeenth-century pattern of settlement. As colonists spread north and west, they tended to settle on individual farms rather than in the towns and villages that characterized the seventeenth century. Far more than in the seventeenth century, eighteenth-century New Englanders regulated their behavior by their own individual choices.

partible inheritance
▶ A system of inheritance in which land was divided equally among sons. By the eighteenth century, this practice in Massachusetts had subdivided plots of land into units too small for subsistence, forcing children to move away to find sufficient farmland.

Farms, Fish, and Atlantic Trade

A New England farm was a place to get by, not to get rich. New England farmers grew food for their families, but their fields did not produce huge marketable surpluses. Instead of one big crop, a farmer grew many small ones. If farmers had extra, they sold to or traded with neighbors. Poor roads made travel difficult, time-consuming, and expensive, especially with bulky and heavy agricultural goods. The one major agricultural product the New England colonies exported—livestock—walked to market on its own legs. By 1770, New Englanders had only one-fourth as much wealth per capita as free colonists in the southern colonies.

As consumers, New England farmers participated in a diversified commercial economy that linked remote farms to markets throughout the Atlantic world. Merchants large and small stocked imported goods—British textiles, ceramics, and metal goods; Chinese tea; West Indian sugar; and Chesapeake tobacco. Farmers' needs supported local shoemakers, tailors, wheelwrights, and carpenters. Larger towns, especially Boston, housed skilled tradesmen such as cabinetmakers, silversmiths, and printers. Shipbuilders were among the many New Englanders who made their fortunes at sea.

Fish accounted for more than a third of New England's eighteenth-century exports; livestock and timber made up another third. The West Indies absorbed two-thirds of all New England's exports. Almost all the rest of New England's exports went to Britain and continental Europe (**Map 5.2**). This Atlantic commerce benefited the entire New England economy, providing jobs for laborers and tradesmen as well as for ship captains, clerks, merchants, and sailors.

Merchants dominated Atlantic commerce. The largest and most successful New England merchants lived in Boston at the hub of trade between local folk and the international market. The magnificence of a wealthy Boston merchant's home

What spurred the growth of the middle colonies? | Why did slavery become the defining feature of the southern colonies? | What experiences tended to unify colonists in British North America? | Conclusion: What was the dual identity of British North American colonists? | ✓ LearningCurve Check what you know. bedfordstmartins.com /roarkunderstanding

115

Major centers of trade

Major ocean trade route

MAP 5.2 ■ Atlantic Trade in the Eighteenth Century

This map illustrates the economic outlook of the colonies in the eighteenth century—east toward the Atlantic world rather than west toward the interior of North America. The long distances involved in the Atlantic trade and the uncertainties of ocean travel suggest the difficulties Britain experienced governing the colonies and regulating colonial commerce.

> MAP ACTIVITY

READING THE MAP: What were the major markets for trade coming out of Europe? What goods did the British colonies import and export?

CONNECTIONS: In what ways did the flow of raw materials from the colonies affect British industry? How did British colonial trade policies influence the Atlantic trade?

CHAPTER LOCATOR | How did the North American colonies change in the eighteenth century?

What changed in New England life and culture?

CHAPTER 5

116 THE CHANGING WORLD OF COLONIAL AMERICA

stunned John Adams, who termed it a house that seemed fit "for a noble Man, a Prince." Such luxurious Boston homes contrasted with the modest dwellings of Adams and other New Englanders, a measure of the polarization of wealth that developed in Boston and other seaports during the eighteenth century.

By 1770, the richest 5 percent of Bostonians owned about half the city's wealth; the poorest two-thirds of the population owned less than one-tenth. Still, the incidence of genuine poverty did not change much. About 5 percent of New Englanders qualified for poor relief throughout the eighteenth century. Overall, colonists were better off than most people in England.

New England was more homogeneously English than any other colonial region. People of African ancestry (almost all of them slaves) numbered more than fifteen thousand by 1770, but they barely diversified the region's 97 percent white majority. Most New Englanders had little use for slaves on their family farms. Instead, the few slaves concentrated in towns, especially Boston, where most of them worked as domestic servants and laborers.

By 1770, the population, wealth, and commercial activity of New England differed from what they had been in 1700. Ministers still enjoyed high status, but Yankee traders had replaced Puritan saints as the symbolic New Englanders. Atlantic commerce competed with religious convictions in ordering New Englanders' daily lives.

QUICK REVIEW

Why did settlement patterns in New England change from the seventeenth to the eighteenth century?

| What spurred the growth of the middle colonies? | Why did slavery become the defining feature of the southern colonies? | What experiences tended to unify colonists in British North America? | Conclusion: What was the dual identity of British North American colonists? | ✓ LearningCurve Check what you know. bedfordstmartins.com /roarkunderstanding |

What spurred the growth of the middle colonies?

Bethlehem, Pennsylvania

This view of Bethlehem, Pennsylvania, in 1757 dramatizes the profound transformation of the natural landscape humans wrought in the eighteenth century by highly motivated human labor. Founded by Moravian immigrants in 1740, in less than twenty years Bethlehem featured precisely laid-out orchards and fields in place of forests and glades. By carefully penning their livestock (lower center right) and fencing their fields (lower left), farmers safeguarded their livelihoods from the risks and disorders of untamed nature. Individual farmsteads (lower center) and brick town buildings (upper center) integrated the bounty of the land with community life. Few eighteenth-century communities were as orderly as Bethlehem, but many effected a comparable transformation of the environment. Print Collection, Miriam and Ira D. Wallack Division of Art, Prints, and Photographs, The New York Public Library. Astor, Lenox, and Tilden Foundations.

> **VISUAL ACTIVITY**

READING THE IMAGE: What does this painting indicate about the colonists' priorities?
CONNECTIONS: Why might Pennsylvanians have been so concerned about maintaining order?

I IN 1700, THE MIDDLE COLONIES of Pennsylvania, New York, New Jersey, and Delaware had only half the population of New England. But by 1770, the population of the middle colonies had multiplied tenfold and nearly equaled the population of New England. Immigrants—mainly German, Irish, and Scottish—made the middle colonies a uniquely diverse society. By 1800, barely one-third of Pennsylvanians and less than half the total population of the middle colonies traced their ancestry to England. New white settlers, both free and in servitude, poured into the middle colonies because they perceived unparalleled opportunities.

German and Scots-Irish Immigrants

Germans made up the largest contingent of migrants from the European continent to the middle colonies. By 1770, about 85,000 Germans had arrived in the colonies. Their fellow colonists often referred to them as **Pennsylvania Dutch**, an English corruption of *Deutsch*, the word the immigrants used to describe themselves.

Pennsylvania Dutch
▶ The name given by other colonists to German immigrants to the middle colonies; an English corruption of the German term *Deutsch*. Germans made up the largest contingent of migrants from continental Europe to the middle colonies in the eighteenth century.

CHAPTER LOCATOR | How did the North American colonies change in the eighteenth century? | What changed in New England life and culture?

118 CHAPTER 5 THE CHANGING WORLD OF COLONIAL AMERICA

Most German immigrants came from what is now southwestern Germany, where, one observer noted, peasants were "not as well off as cattle elsewhere." German immigrants included numerous artisans and a few merchants, but the great majority were farmers and laborers. Economically, they represented "middling folk," neither the poorest (who could not afford the trip) nor the better-off (who did not want to leave).

By the 1720s, Germans who had established themselves in the colonies wrote back to their friends and relatives, as one reported, "of the civil and religious liberties [and] privileges, and of all the goodness I have heard and seen." Such letters prompted still more Germans to pull up stakes and embark for the middle colonies.

Similar motives propelled the **Scots-Irish**, who considerably outnumbered German immigrants. The "Scots-Irish" actually hailed from northern Ireland, Scotland, and northern England. Like the Germans, the Scots-Irish were Protestants, but with a difference. Most German immigrants worshipped in Lutheran or German Reformed churches; many others belonged to dissenting sects such as the Mennonites, Moravians, and Amish, whose adherents sought relief from the persecution they had suffered in Europe for their refusal to bear arms and to swear oaths, practices they shared with the Quakers. By contrast, the Scots-Irish tended to be militant Presbyterians who seldom hesitated to bear arms or swear oaths. Like German settlers, however, Scots-Irish immigrants were clannish, residing when they could among relatives or neighbors from the old country.

In the eighteenth century, wave after wave of Scots-Irish immigrants arrived, culminating in a flood of immigration in the years just before the American Revolution. Deteriorating economic conditions in northern Ireland, Scotland, and England pushed many toward America. Most of the immigrants were farm laborers or tenant farmers fleeing droughts, crop failures, high food prices, or rising rents. They came, they told British officials, because of "poverty," the "tyranny of landlords," and their desire to "do better in America."

Both Scots-Irish and Germans probably heard the common saying "Pennsylvania is heaven for farmers [and] paradise for artisans," but they almost certainly did not fully understand the risks of their decision to leave their native lands. Ship captains, aware of the hunger for labor in the colonies, eagerly signed up the penniless German emigrants as **redemptioners**, a variant of indentured servants. A captain would agree to provide transportation to Philadelphia, where redemptioners would obtain the money to pay for their passage by borrowing it from a friend or relative who was already in the colonies or, as most did, by selling themselves as servants. Many redemptioners traveled in family groups, unlike impoverished Scots-Irish emigrants, who usually traveled alone and paid for their passage by contracting as indentured servants before they sailed to the colonies.

Redemptioners and indentured servants were packed aboard ships "as closely as herring," one migrant observed. Seasickness compounded by exhaustion, poverty, poor food, bad water, inadequate sanitation, and tight quarters encouraged the spread of disease. Unlike indentured servants, redemptioners negotiated independently with their purchasers about their period of servitude. Typically, a healthy adult redemptioner agreed to four years of labor. Indentured servants commonly served five, six, or seven years.

1733
- Benjamin Franklin begins publication of *Poor Richard's Almanack*.

1770
- The population of the colonies of Pennsylvania, New York, New Jersey, and Delaware has increased tenfold since 1700, largely the result of immigration.
- Germans make up the largest percentage of migrants from the European continent.
- The middle colonies' per capita consumption of imported goods from Britain has more than doubled since 1720.

Scots-Irish

▶ Protestant immigrants from northern Ireland, Scotland, and northern England. Deteriorating economic conditions in their European homelands contributed to increasing migration to the colonies in the eighteenth century.

redemptioners

▶ A kind of indentured servant. In this system, a captain agreed to provide passage to Philadelphia, where redemptioners would obtain money to pay for their transportation, usually by selling themselves as a servant.

What spurred the growth of the middle colonies?

Why did slavery become the defining feature of the southern colonies?

What experiences tended to unify colonists in British North America?

Conclusion: What was the dual identity of British North American colonists?

☑ LearningCurve
Check what you know.
bedfordstmartins.com /roarkunderstanding

119

"God Gives All Things to Industry": Urban and Rural Labor

An indentured servant in 1743 wrote that Pennsylvania was "the best poor Man's Country in the World." Although the servant reported that "the Condition of bought Servants is very hard" and that masters often failed to live up to their promise to provide decent food and clothing, opportunity abounded in the middle colonies because there was more work to be done than workers to do it.

Most servants toiled in Philadelphia, New York City, or one of the smaller towns or villages. Artisans, small manufacturers, and shopkeepers prized the labor of male servants. Female servants made valuable additions to households, where nearly all of them cleaned, washed, cooked, or minded children. From the masters' viewpoint, servants were a bargain. A master could purchase five or six years of a servant's labor for approximately the wages a common laborer would earn in four months.

Since a slave cost at least three times as much as a servant, only affluent colonists could afford the long-term investment in slave labor. Most farmers in the middle colonies used family labor, not slaves. Wheat, the most widely grown crop, did not require more labor than farmers could typically muster from relatives, neighbors, and a hired hand or two. Consequently, although people of African ancestry (almost all slaves) increased to more than thirty thousand in the middle colonies by 1770, they accounted for only about 7 percent of the total population and much less outside the cities.

Most slaves came to the middle colonies and New England after a stopover in the West Indies. Very few came directly from Africa. Slaves—unlike servants—could not charge masters with violating the terms of their contracts. A master's commands, not a written contract, set the terms of a slave's bondage. Small numbers of slaves managed to obtain their freedom, but no African Americans escaped whites' firm convictions about black inferiority.

Whites' racism and blacks' lowly social status made African Americans scapegoats for European Americans' suspicions and anxieties. In 1741, when arson and several unexplained thefts plagued New York City, officials suspected a murderous slave conspiracy and executed thirty-one slaves. Although slaves were certifiably impoverished, they were not among the poor for whom the middle colonies were reputed to be the best country in the world.

Immigrants swarmed to the middle colonies because of the availability of land. The Penn family (see chapter 4) encouraged immigration to bring in potential buyers for their enormous tracts of land in Pennsylvania. From the beginning, Pennsylvania followed a policy of negotiating with Indian tribes to purchase additional land. This policy reduced the violent frontier clashes more common elsewhere in the colonies. Few colonists drifted beyond the northern boundaries of Pennsylvania. Owners of the huge estates in New York's Hudson valley preferred to rent rather than sell their land, and therefore they attracted fewer immigrants. The Iroquois Indians dominated the lucrative fur trade of the St. Lawrence valley and eastern Great Lakes, and they vigorously defended their territory from colonial encroachment, causing most settlers to prefer the comparatively safe environs of Pennsylvania.

CHAPTER LOCATOR | How did the North American colonies change in the eighteenth century? | What changed in New England life and culture?

120 CHAPTER 5 THE CHANGING WORLD OF COLONIAL AMERICA

Patterns of Settlement, 1700–1770

Since the cheapest land always lay at the margin of settlement, would-be farmers tended to migrate to promising areas just beyond already improved farms. By midcentury, settlement had reached the eastern slopes of the Appalachian Mountains, and newcomers spilled south down the fertile valley of the Shenandoah River into western Virginia and the Carolinas. Thousands of settlers migrated from the middle colonies through this back door to the South.

Farmers made the middle colonies the breadbasket of North America. They planted a wide variety of crops to feed their families, but they grew wheat in abundance. Flour milling was the number one industry and flour the number one export, constituting nearly three-fourths of all exports from the middle colonies. Because farmers profited from the grain market in the Atlantic world with the steady rise of grain prices after 1720, the standard of living in rural Pennsylvania was probably higher than in any other agricultural region of the eighteenth-century world. The comparatively widespread prosperity of all the middle colonies permitted residents to indulge in a half-century shopping spree for British imports. The middle colonies' per capita consumption of imported goods from Britain more than doubled between 1720 and 1770, far outstripping the per capita consumption of British goods in New England and the southern colonies.

Marten Van Bergen Farm

This detail from a rare 1730s painting depicts the home of Marten and Catarina Van Bergen, prosperous Dutch colonists in New York's Hudson valley. The full-size painting, commissioned by the Van Bergens to hang over their fireplace mantel, is a panorama portraying the farm as a peaceable, small-scale kingdom governed by the couple and populated by their seven children, their slaves and indentured servants, and neighboring Native Americans. Rather than a place of fields and crops, which are absent from the painting, the farm is the locus of a happy, orderly family. Copyright © New York State Historical Association, Cooperstown, NY.

What spurred the growth of the middle colonies?

Why did slavery become the defining feature of the southern colonies?

What experiences tended to unify colonists in British North America?

Conclusion: What was the dual identity of British North American colonists?

✓ LearningCurve
Check what you know.
bedfordstmartins.com
/roarkunderstanding

121

Philadelphia stood at the crossroads of trade in wheat exports and British imports. Merchants occupied the top stratum of Philadelphia society. In a city where only 2 percent of the residents owned enough property to qualify to vote, merchants built grand homes and dominated local government. Many of Philadelphia's wealthiest merchants were Quakers. Quaker traits of industry, thrift, honesty, and sobriety encouraged the accumulation of wealth.

The lower ranks of merchants included aspiring tradesmen such as Benjamin Franklin. In 1733, Benjamin Franklin began to publish *Poor Richard's Almanack*, which preached the likelihood of long-term rewards for tireless labor and quickly became Franklin's most profitable product. The popularity of *Poor Richard's Almanack* suggests that many Pennsylvanians thought less about the pearly gates of heaven than about their pocketbooks. Poor Richard's advice that "God gives all Things to Industry" might be considered the motto for the middle colonies. The promise of a worldly payoff made work a secular faith. Quakers remained influential, but Franklin spoke for most colonists with his aphorisms of work, discipline, and thrift that celebrated the spark of ambition and the promise of gain.

> **QUICK REVIEW**

Why did immigrants flood into Pennsylvania during the eighteenth century?

CHAPTER LOCATOR | How did the North American colonies change in the eighteenth century? | What changed in New England life and culture?

CHAPTER 5

122   THE CHANGING WORLD OF COLONIAL AMERICA

Why did slavery become the defining feature of the southern colonies?

Charleston Harbor This 1730s painting of Charleston, South Carolina, depicts the intersecting currents of international trade and local commerce in the variety of vessels conveying goods and people between ship and shore. More African slaves arrived in Charleston than in any other North American port, yet no slaves appear in this painting. Colonial Williamsburg Foundation.

BETWEEN 1700 AND 1770, the population of the southern colonies of Virginia, Maryland, North Carolina, South Carolina, and Georgia grew almost ninefold. By 1770, about twice as many people lived in the South as in either the middle colonies or New England. As elsewhere, natural increase and immigration accounted for the rapid population growth. Many Scots-Irish and German immigrants funneled from the middle colonies into the southern backcountry. Other immigrants were indentured servants (mostly English and Scots-Irish). But slaves made the most striking contribution to the booming southern colonies, transforming the racial composition of the population. Slavery became the defining characteristic of the southern colonies during the eighteenth century, shaping the region's economy, society, and politics.

The Atlantic Slave Trade and the Growth of Slavery

The number of southerners of African ancestry (nearly all of them slaves) rocketed from just over 20,000 in 1700 to well over 400,000 in 1770. The black population increased nearly three times faster than the South's briskly growing white population. Consequently, the proportion of southerners of African ancestry grew from 20 percent in 1700 to 40 percent in 1770.

Southern colonists clustered into two distinct geographic and agricultural zones. The colonies in the upper South, surrounding the Chesapeake Bay, specialized in growing tobacco, as they had since the early seventeenth century. Throughout the eighteenth century, nine out of ten southern whites and eight out

> CHRONOLOGY

1711
– North Carolina is founded.

1732
– Georgia is founded.

1739
– Stono Rebellion, an uprising by slaves in South Carolina.

1770
– The southern colonies supply 90 percent of all North American exports to Britain.

What spurred the growth of the middle colonies?

Why did slavery become the defining feature of the southern colonies?

What experiences tended to unify colonists in British North America?

Conclusion: What was the dual identity of British North American colonists?

✓ LearningCurve
Check what you know.
bedfordstmartins.com
/roarkunderstanding

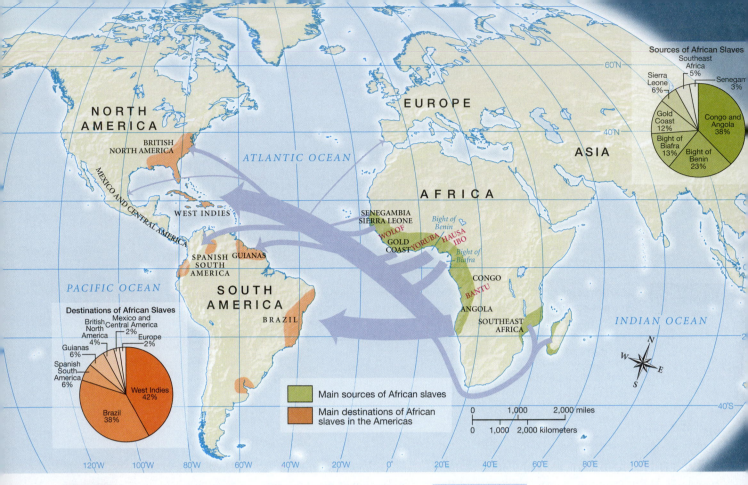

MAP 5.3 ■ The Atlantic Slave Trade

Although the Atlantic slave trade lasted from about 1450 to 1870, it peaked during the eighteenth century, when more than six million African slaves were imported to the New World. Only a small fraction of these slaves were taken to British North America. Most went to sugar plantations in Brazil and the Caribbean.

> **MAP ACTIVITY**

READING THE MAP: Where in Africa did most slaves originate? Approximately how far was the trip from the busiest ports of origin to the two most common New World destinations?
CONNECTIONS: Why were so many more African slaves sent to the West Indies and Brazil than to British North America?

of ten southern blacks lived in the Chesapeake region. The upper South retained a white majority during the eighteenth century.

In the lower South, a much smaller cluster of colonists inhabited the coastal region and specialized in the production of rice and indigo (a plant used to make blue dye). Lower South colonists made up only 5 percent of the total population of the southern colonies in 1700 but inched upward to 15 percent by 1770. South Carolina was the sole British colony along the southern Atlantic coast until 1732. (North Carolina, founded in 1711, was largely an extension of the Chesapeake region.) Georgia was founded in 1732 as a refuge for poor people from England. Georgia's leaders banned slaves from 1735 to 1750, but few settlers arrived until after 1750, when the prohibition on slavery was lifted and slaves flooded in. In South Carolina, in contrast to Georgia and every other British mainland colony, slaves outnumbered whites almost two to one; in some low-country districts, the ratio of blacks to whites exceeded ten to one.

CHAPTER LOCATOR | How did the North American colonies change in the eighteenth century? | What changed in New England life and culture?

TABLE 5.1 ■ Slave Imports, 1451–1870

Estimated Slave Imports to the Western Hemisphere	
1451–1600	275,000
1601–1700	1,341,000
1701–1810	6,100,000
1811–1870	1,900,000

The enormous growth in the South's slave population occurred through natural increase and the flourishing Atlantic slave trade (**Map 5.3** and **Table 5.1**). Slave ships brought almost 300,000 Africans to British North America between 1619 and 1780. Of these Africans, 95 percent arrived in the South and 96 percent arrived during the eighteenth century. Unlike indentured servants and redemptioners, these Africans did not choose to come to the colonies. Most of them had been born into free families in villages located within a few hundred miles of the West African coast.

Although they shared African origins, they came from many different cultures. They spoke different languages, worshipped different deities, observed different rules of kinship, grew different crops, and recognized different rulers. The most important experience they had in common was enslavement.

Captured in war, kidnapped, or sold into slavery by other Africans, they were brought to the coast, sold to African traders who assembled slaves for resale, and sold again to European or colonial slave traders or ship captains, who packed two hundred to three hundred or more aboard ships that carried them on the **Middle Passage** across the Atlantic and then sold them yet again to colonial slave merchants or southern planters.

Olaudah Equiano published an account of his enslavement that hints at the common experiences of millions of other Africans swept up in the slave trade. When he was eleven years old, Equiano was kidnapped by Africans in what is now Nigeria, who sold him to other Africans, who in turn eventually sold him to a slave ship on the coast. Equiano feared that he was "going to be killed" and "eaten by those white men with horrible looks, red faces, and loose hair." Once the ship set sail, many of the slaves, crowded together in suffocating heat fouled by filth of all descriptions, died from sickness. "The shrieks of the women and the groans of the dying rendered the whole a scene of horror almost inconceivable," Equiano recalled. Most of the slaves on the ship were sold in Barbados, but Equiano and some others were shipped off to Virginia, where he "saw few or none of our native Africans and not one soul who could talk to me." Equiano felt isolated and "exceedingly miserable"

Middle Passage

▶ The crossing of the Atlantic by slave ships traveling from West Africa to the Americas. Slaves were crowded together in extremely unhealthful circumstances, and mortality rates were high.

Olaudah Equiano

Created after he had bought his freedom, this portrait evokes Equiano's successful acculturation to eighteenth-century English customs. In his *Interesting Narrative*, Equiano wrote that he "looked upon [the English] . . . as men superior to us [Africans], and therefore I had the stronger desire to resemble them, to imbibe their spirit and imitate their manners." Library of Congress.

What spurred the growth of the middle colonies?	**Why did slavery become the defining feature of the southern colonies?**	What experiences tended to unify colonists in British North America?	Conclusion: What was the dual identity of British North American colonists?	✔ LearningCurve Check what you know. bedfordstmartins.com /roarkunderstanding

because he "had no person to speak to that I could understand." Finally, the captain of a tobacco ship bound for England purchased Equiano, and he traveled as a slave between North America, England, and the West Indies for ten years until he succeeded in buying his freedom in 1766.

> ### > The Deadly Middle Passage

- Eighty-five percent of slaves to the southern colonies came directly from Africa.
- Mortality during the Middle Passage varied considerably from ship to ship.
- On average, about 15 percent of the slaves died.
- In general, the longer the voyage lasted, the more people died.
- Smallpox, dysentery, and acute dehydration were leading causes of death.
- Men outnumbered women two to one.
- Children usually accounted for no more than 10 to 15 percent of the cargo.

new Negroes

▶ Term given to newly arrived African slaves in the colonies. Planters usually maintained only a small number of recent arrivals among their slaves at any given time in order to accelerate their acculturation to their new circumstances.

Normally, an individual planter purchased at any one time a relatively small number of newly arrived Africans, or **new Negroes**, as they were called. New Negroes were often profoundly depressed, demoralized, and disoriented. Planters expected their other slaves — either those born into slavery in the colonies (often called country-born or creole slaves) or Africans who had arrived earlier — to help new Negroes become accustomed to their strange new surroundings. Although slaves spoke many different languages, enough linguistic and cultural similarities existed that they could usually communicate with other Africans from the same region.

New Africans had to adjust to the physical as well as the cultural environment of the southern colonies. Slaves who had just endured the Middle Passage were poorly nourished, weak, and sick. In this vulnerable state, they encountered the alien diseases of North America without having developed a biological arsenal of acquired immunities. As many as 10 to 15 percent of newly arrived Africans died during their first year in the southern colonies. Nonetheless, the large number of newly enslaved Africans made the influence of African culture in the South stronger in the eighteenth century than ever before — or since.

While newly enslaved Africans poured into the southern colonies, slave mothers bore children, which caused the slave population in the South to grow rapidly. Slave owners encouraged these births. Thomas Jefferson explained, "I consider the labor of a breeding [slave] woman as no object, that a [slave] child raised every 2 years is of more profit than the crop of the best laboring [slave] man." Although slave mothers loved and nurtured their children, the mortality rate among slave children was high, and the ever-present risk of being separated by sale brought grief to many slave families. Nonetheless, the growing number of slave babies set the southern colonies apart from other New World slave societies, where mortality rates were so high that deaths exceeded births. The high rate of natural increase in the southern colonies meant that by the 1740s the majority of southern slaves were country-born.

CHAPTER LOCATOR | How did the North American colonies change in the eighteenth century? | What changed in New England life and culture?

126 CHAPTER 5 | THE CHANGING WORLD OF COLONIAL AMERICA

Slave Labor and African American Culture

Southern planters expected slaves to work from sunup to sundown and beyond. George Washington wrote that his slaves should "be at their work as soon as it is light, work til it is dark, and be diligent while they are at it." The conflict between the masters' desire for maximum labor and the slaves' reluctance to do more than necessary made the threat of physical punishment a constant for eighteenth-century slaves. Masters preferred black slaves to white indentured servants, not just because slaves served for life but also because colonial laws did not limit the force masters could use against slaves. Slaves often resisted their masters' demands, one traveler noted, because of their "greatness of soul" — their stubborn unwillingness to conform to their masters' definition of them as merely slaves.

Some slaves escalated their acts of resistance to direct physical confrontation with the master, the mistress, or an overseer. But a hoe raised in anger, a punch in the face, or a desperate swipe with a knife led to swift and predictable retaliation by whites. Throughout the southern colonies, the balance of physical power rested securely in the hands of whites.

Rebellion occurred, however, at Stono, South Carolina, in 1739. A group of about twenty slaves attacked a country store, killed the two storekeepers, and confiscated the store's guns, ammunition, and powder. Enticing other slaves to join, the group plundered and burned more than half a dozen plantations and killed more than twenty white men, women, and children. A mounted force of whites quickly suppressed the rebellion. The **Stono Rebellion** illustrated that eighteenth-century slaves had no chance of overturning slavery and very little chance of defending themselves in any bold strike for freedom. No other similar uprisings occurred during the colonial period.

Slaves maneuvered constantly to protect themselves and to gain a measure of autonomy within the boundaries of slavery. In Chesapeake tobacco fields, most slaves were subject to close supervision by whites. In the lower South, the **task system** gave slaves some control over the pace of their work and some discretion in the use of the rest of their time. A "task" was typically defined as a certain area of ground to be cultivated or a specific job to be completed. A slave who completed the assigned task might use the remainder of the day, if any, to work in a garden, fish, hunt, spin, weave, sew, or cook. When masters sought to boost productivity by increasing tasks, slaves did what they could to defend their customary work assignments.

Eighteenth-century slaves also planted the roots of African American lineages that branch out to the present. Slaves valued family ties, and, as in West African societies, kinship structured slaves' relations with one another. Slave parents often gave a child the name of a grandparent, an aunt, or an uncle. In West Africa, kinship identified a person's place among living relatives and linked the person to ancestors in the past and to descendants in the future. Newly imported African slaves usually arrived alone, like Equiano, without kin. Often slaves who had traversed the Middle Passage on the same ship adopted one another as "brothers" and "sisters." Likewise, as new Negroes were seasoned and incorporated into existing slave communities, established families often adopted them as fictive kin.

Stono Rebellion
▶ Slave uprising in Stono, South Carolina, in 1739 in which a group of slaves armed themselves, plundered six plantations, and killed more than twenty whites. Whites quickly suppressed the rebellion.

task system
▶ A system of labor in which a slave was assigned a daily task to complete and allowed to do as he or she wished upon its completion. This system offered more freedom than the carefully supervised gang-labor system.

What spurred the growth of the middle colonies? | **Why did slavery become the defining feature of the southern colonies?** | What experiences tended to unify colonists in British North America? | Conclusion: What was the dual identity of British North American colonists? | ✓ LearningCurve Check what you know. bedfordstmartins.com /roarkunderstanding

127

When possible, slaves expressed many other features of their West African origins in their lives on New World plantations. They gave their children traditional dolls and African names such as Cudjo, Quash, Minda, or Fuladi. They grew food crops they had known in Africa, such as yams and okra. They constructed huts with mud walls and thatched roofs similar to African residences. They fashioned banjos, drums, and other musical instruments, held dances, and observed funeral rites that echoed African practices. In these and many other ways, slaves drew upon their African heritages as much as the oppressive circumstances of slavery permitted.

Tobacco, Rice, and Prosperity

Slaves' labor bestowed prosperity on their masters, British merchants, and the monarchy. Slavery was so important and valuable that one minister claimed in 1757 that "to live in Virginia without slaves is morally impossible." The southern colonies supplied 90 percent of all North American exports to Britain. Rice exports from the lower South exploded from less than half a million pounds in 1700 to eighty million pounds in 1770, nearly all of it grown by slaves. Exports of indigo also boomed. Together, rice and indigo made up three-fourths of lower South exports, nearly two-thirds of them going to Britain and most of the rest to the West Indies, where sugar-growing slaves ate slave-grown rice.

Tobacco was by far the most important export from British North America; by 1770, it represented almost one-third of all colonial exports and three-fourths of all Chesapeake exports. Under the provisions of the Navigation Acts (see chapter 4), nearly all of the exported tobacco went to Britain, where the monarchy collected a lucrative tax on each pound. British merchants then re-exported more than 80 percent of the tobacco to the European continent, pocketing a nice markup for their troubles.

These products of slave labor made the southern colonies by far the richest in North America. The per capita wealth of free whites in the South was four times greater than that in New England and three times that in the middle colonies. At the top of the wealth pyramid stood the rice grandees of the lower South and the tobacco gentry of the Chesapeake. These elite families commonly resided on large estates in handsome mansions adorned by luxurious gardens, all maintained and supported by slaves.

CHAPTER LOCATOR | How did the North American colonies change in the eighteenth century? | What changed in New England life and culture?

128 **CHAPTER 5** THE CHANGING WORLD OF COLONIAL AMERICA

The vast differences in wealth among white southerners engendered envy and occasional tension between rich and poor, but remarkably little open hostility. In private, the planter elite spoke disparagingly of humble whites, but in public the planters acknowledged their lesser neighbors as equals, at least in belonging to the superior—in their minds—white race. Looking upward, white yeomen and tenants (who owned neither land nor slaves) sensed the gentry's condescension and veiled contempt. But they also appreciated the gentry for granting favors, upholding white supremacy, and keeping slaves in their place. Although racial slavery made a few whites much richer than others, it also gave those who did not get rich a powerful reason to feel similar (in race) to those who were so different (in wealth).

The slaveholding gentry dominated the politics and economy of the southern colonies. In Virginia, only adult white men who owned at least one hundred acres of unimproved land or twenty-five acres of land with a house could vote. This property-holding requirement prevented about 40 percent of white men in Virginia from voting for representatives to the House of Burgesses. In South Carolina, the property requirement was only fifty acres of land, and therefore most adult white men qualified to vote. In both colonies, voters elected members of the gentry to serve in the colonial legislature. The gentry passed elected political offices from generation to generation, almost as if they were hereditary. Politically, the gentry built a self-perpetuating oligarchy—rule by the elite few—with the votes of their many humble neighbors.

The gentry also set the cultural standard in the southern colonies. They entertained lavishly, gambled regularly, and attended Anglican (Church of England) services more for social than for religious reasons. Above all, they cultivated the leisurely pursuit of happiness. They did not condone idleness, however. Their many pleasures and responsibilities as plantation owners kept them busy. Thomas Jefferson, a phenomenally productive member of the gentry, recalled that his earliest childhood memory was of being carried on a pillow by a family slave—a powerful image of the slave hands supporting the gentry's leisure and achievement.

QUICK REVIEW <

How did slavery influence the society and economy of the southern colonies?

What spurred the growth of the middle colonies?

Why did slavery become the defining feature of the southern colonies?

What experiences tended to unify colonists in British North America?

Conclusion: What was the dual identity of British North American colonists?

LearningCurve
Check what you know.
bedfordstmartins.com
/roarkunderstanding

What experiences tended to unify the colonists in British North America during the eighteenth century?

George Whitefield

An anonymous artist portrayed George Whitefield preaching, emphasizing the power of his sermons to transport his audience to a revived awareness of divine spirituality. The woman below his hands appears transfixed. Her eyes and Whitefield's do not meet, yet the artist's use of light suggests that she and Whitefield see the same core of holy Truth. National Portrait Gallery, London.

THE SOCIETIES OF NEW ENGLAND, the middle colonies, and the southern colonies became more sharply differentiated during the eighteenth century, but colonists throughout British North America also shared unifying experiences that eluded settlers in the Spanish and French colonies.

> ### > Unifying Experiences in British North America

- All three British colonial regions had their economic roots in agriculture.
- Religion had declined in importance by the eighteenth century.
- White inhabitants throughout British North America became aware that they shared a distinctive identity as *British* colonists. They asserted their prerogatives as British subjects to defend their special colonial interests.
- The consumption of British exports built a certain material uniformity across region, religion, class, and status.

Commerce and Consumption

Eighteenth-century commerce whetted colonists' appetites to consume. Colonial products spurred the development of mass markets throughout the Atlantic world. Huge increases in the supply of colonial tobacco and sugar brought the price of

CHAPTER LOCATOR | How did the North American colonies change in the eighteenth century? | What changed in New England life and culture?

these small luxuries within the reach of most free whites. Colonial goods brought into focus an important lesson of eighteenth-century commerce: Ordinary people, not just the wealthy elite, would buy the things that they desired in addition to what they absolutely needed. Even news, formerly restricted mostly to a few people through face-to-face conversations or private letters, became an object of public consumption through the innovation of newspapers and the rise in literacy among whites. With the appropriate stimulus, market demand seemed unlimited (**Figure 5.1**).

The Atlantic commerce that took colonial goods to markets in Britain brought objects of consumer desire back to the colonies. British merchants and manufacturers recognized that colonists made excellent customers, and the Navigation Acts gave British exporters privileged access to the colonial market. By midcentury, export-oriented industries in Britain were growing ten times faster than firms attuned to the home market. When the colonists' eagerness to consume exceeded their ability to pay, British exporters willingly extended credit, and colonial debts soared. Imported mirrors, silver plates, spices, bed and table linens, clocks, tea services, wigs, books, and more infiltrated parlors, kitchens, and bedrooms throughout the colonies.

The dazzling variety of imported consumer goods presented women and men with a novel array of choices. In many respects, the choices might appear trivial: whether to buy knives and forks, teacups, a mirror, or a clock. But such small choices confronted eighteenth-century consumers with a big question: What do you want? As colonial consumers defined and expressed their desires with greater frequency during the eighteenth century, they became accustomed to thinking of themselves as individuals who had the power to make decisions that influenced the quality of their lives.

Religion, Enlightenment, and Revival

Eighteenth-century colonists could choose from almost as many religions as consumer goods. Virtually all of the many religious denominations represented some form of Christianity, almost all of them Protestant. Slaves made up the largest group of non-Christians. A few slaves converted to Christianity in Africa or after they arrived in North America, but most continued to embrace elements of indigenous African religions. Roman Catholics concentrated in Maryland as they had since the seventeenth century, but even there they were far outnumbered by Protestants.

The varieties of Protestant faith and practice ranged across a broad spectrum. The middle colonies and the southern backcountry included militant Baptists and Presbyterians. Huguenots, French Protestants who had fled persecution in Catholic France, peopled congregations in several cities. In New England, old-style Puritanism splintered into strands of Congregationalism that differed over fine points of theological doctrine. The Congregational Church was the official established church in New England, and all residents paid taxes for its support. Throughout the plantation South and in urban centers such as Charleston, New York, and Philadelphia, prominent colonists belonged to the Anglican Church, which received tax support in the South. But dissenting faiths grew everywhere, and in most colonies their adherents won the right to worship publicly, although the established churches retained official support.

Many educated colonists became deists, looking for God's plan in nature more than in the Bible. Deism shared the ideas of eighteenth-century European

> CHRONOLOGY

1730s
– Jonathan Edwards promotes the religious movement known as the Great Awakening.

1740s
– George Whitefield preaches religious revival in North America.

1754
– Seven Years' War begins.

1769
– American Philosophical Society is founded.
– First Spanish mission in California, San Diego de Alcalá, is established.

1770
– Spanish mission and presidio are established at Monterey, California.

What spurred the growth of the middle colonies?

Why did slavery become the defining feature of the southern colonies?

What experiences tended to unify colonists in British North America?

Conclusion: What was the dual identity of British North American colonists?

✓ LearningCurve
Check what you know.
bedfordstmartins.com
/roarkunderstanding

131

FIGURE 5.1 ■ Colonial Exports, 1768–1772

These pie charts provide an overview of the colonial export economy of the 1760s. The first two show that almost two-thirds of colonial exports came from the South and that the majority of the colonies' exports went to Great Britain. The remaining charts illustrate the distinctive patterns of exports in each colonial region. What do these patterns reveal about regional variations in Britain's North American colonies? What do they suggest about Britain's economic interest in the colonies?

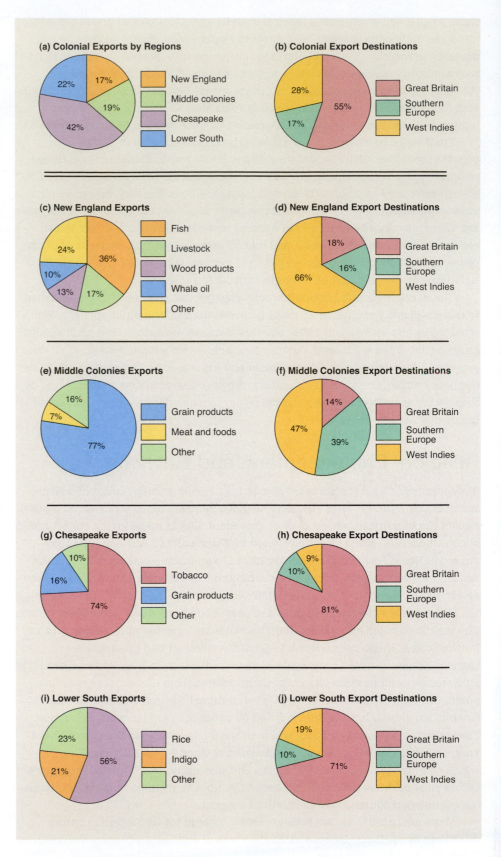

CHAPTER LOCATOR | How did the North American colonies change in the eighteenth century? | What changed in New England life and culture?

Enlightenment thinkers, who tended to agree that science and reason could disclose God's laws in the natural order. In the colonies as well as in Europe, Enlightenment ideas encouraged people to study the world around them, to think for themselves, and to ask whether the disorderly appearance of things masked the principles of a deeper, more profound natural order. Leading colonial thinkers such as Benjamin Franklin and Thomas Jefferson communicated with each other as they sought both to understand nature and to find ways to improve society.

Most eighteenth-century colonists went to church seldom or not at all, although they probably considered themselves Christians. A minister in Charleston observed that on the Sabbath "the Taverns have more Visitants than the Churches." In the leading colonial cities, church members were a small minority. Anglican parishes in the South rarely claimed more than one-fifth of adults as members. In some regions of rural New England and the middle colonies, church membership embraced two-thirds of adults, while in other areas only one-quarter of the residents belonged to a church. The dominant faith overall was religious indifference. As a late-eighteenth-century traveler observed, "Religious indifference is imperceptibly disseminated from one end of the continent to the other."

The spread of religious indifference, of deism, of denominational rivalry, and of comfortable backsliding profoundly concerned many Christians. A few despaired that, as one wrote, "religion . . . lay a-dying and ready to expire its last breath of life." To combat what one preacher called the "dead formality" of church services, some ministers set out to convert nonbelievers and to revive the piety of the faithful with a new style of preaching that appealed more to the heart than to the head. Historians have termed this wave of revivals the **Great Awakening**. In Massachusetts during the mid-1730s, the fiery Puritan minister Jonathan Edwards reaped a harvest of souls by reemphasizing traditional Puritan doctrines of humanity's utter depravity and God's vengeful omnipotence. In Pennsylvania and New Jersey, William Tennent led revivals that dramatized spiritual rebirth with accounts of God's miraculous powers.

The most famous revivalist in the eighteenth-century Atlantic world was George Whitefield. An Anglican, Whitefield preached well-worn messages of sin and salvation to large audiences in England using his spellbinding, unforgettable voice. Whitefield visited the North American colonies seven times, staying for more than three years during the mid-1740s and attracting tens of thousands to his sermons, including Benjamin Franklin and Olaudah Equiano. Whitefield's preaching transported many in his audience to emotion-choked states of religious ecstasy, as he wrote, with "most lifting their eyes to heaven, and crying to God for mercy."

The revivals awakened and refreshed the spiritual energies of thousands of colonists struggling with the uncertainties and anxieties of eighteenth-century America. The conversions at revivals did not substantially boost the total number of church members, however. After the revivalists moved on, the routines and pressures of everyday existence reasserted their primacy in the lives of many converts. But the revivals communicated the important message that every soul mattered, that men and women could choose to be saved, that individuals had the power to make a decision for everlasting life or death. Colonial revivals expressed in religious terms many of the same democratic and egalitarian values expressed in economic terms by colonists' patterns of consumption. One colonist noted the analogy by referring to itinerant revivalists as "Pedlars in divinity." Like consumption,

Enlightenment

▶ An eighteenth-century philosophical movement that emphasized the use of reason to reevaluate previously accepted doctrines and traditions. Enlightenment ideas encouraged examination of the world and independence of mind.

Great Awakening

▶ A wave of religious revivals that began in Massachusetts and spread through the colonies in the 1730s and 1740s. The movement emphasized vital religious faith and personal choice. It was characterized by large, open-air meetings at which emotional sermons were given by itinerant preachers.

What spurred the growth of the middle colonies?

Why did slavery become the defining feature of the southern colonies?

What experiences tended to unify colonists in British North America?

Conclusion: What was the dual identity of British North American colonists?

☑ LearningCurve
Check what you know.
bedfordstmartins.com
/roarkunderstanding

133

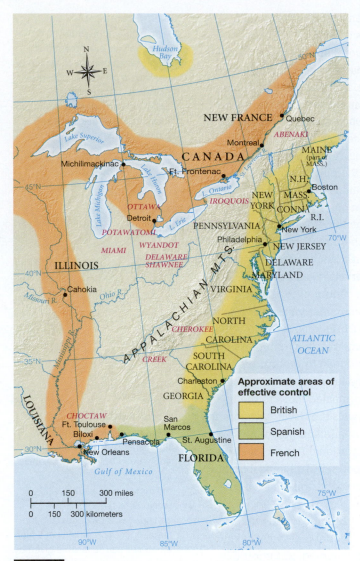

MAP 5.4 ■ Zones of Empire in Eastern North America

The British zone, extending west from the Atlantic coast, was much more densely settled than the zones under French, Spanish, and Indian control. The comparatively large number of British colonists made them more secure than the relatively few colonists in the vast regions claimed by France and Spain or the settlers living among the many Indian peoples in the huge area between the Mississippi River and the Appalachian Mountains. Yet the British colonists were not powerful enough to dominate the French, Spaniards, or Indians. Instead, they had to guard against attacks by powerful Indian groups allied with the French or Spaniards.

revivals contributed to a set of common experiences that bridged colonial divides of faith, region, class, and status.

Trade and Conflict in the North American Borderlands

British power defended the diverse inhabitants of its colonies from Indian, French, and Spanish enemies on their borders—as well as from foreign powers abroad. Royal officials warily eyed the small North American settlements of New France and New Spain for signs of threats to the colonies.

Alone, neither New France nor New Spain jeopardized British North America, but with Indian allies they could become a potent force that kept colonists on their guard (**Map 5.4**). Native Americans' impulse to defend their territory from colonial incursions competed with their desire for trade, which tugged them toward the settlers. As a colonial official observed in 1761, "A modern Indian cannot subsist without Europeans. . . . [The European goods that were] only conveniency at first [have] now become necessity." To obtain such necessities as guns, ammunition, clothing, and sewing utensils manufactured largely by the British, Indians trapped beavers, deer, and other furbearing animals. British, French, Spanish, and Dutch officials competed for the fur trade. Indians took advantage of this competition to improve their own prospects, playing one trader and empire off another. Indian tribes and confederacies also competed among themselves for favored trading rights with one colony or another, a competition colonists encouraged. The shifting alliances and complex dynamics of the fur trade struck a fragile balance along the frontier. The threat of violence from all sides was ever present, and the threat became reality often enough for all parties to be prepared for the worst.

Relations between Indians and colonists differed from colony to colony and from year to year. But the British colonists' nagging perceptions of menace on the frontier kept them continually hoping for help from the British to keep the Indians at bay and to maintain the essential flow of trade. In 1754, the British colonists' endemic competition with the French flared into the Seven Years' War (also known as the French and Indian War), which would inflame the frontier for years (as discussed in chapter 6). Colonists agreed that Indians made deadly enemies, profitable trading partners, and powerful allies.

CHAPTER LOCATOR | How did the North American colonies change in the eighteenth century? | What changed in New England life and culture?

134 CHAPTER 5 THE CHANGING WORLD OF COLONIAL AMERICA

The Spanish kept an eye on the Pacific coast, where Russian hunters in search of seals and sea otters threatened to become a permanent presence on New Spain's northern frontier. To block Russian access to present-day California, officials in New Spain mounted a campaign to build forts (called **presidios**) and missions there. In 1769, an expedition headed by a military man, Gaspar de Portolá, and a Catholic priest, Junípero Serra, traveled north from Mexico to present-day San Diego, where they founded the first California mission, San Diego de Alcalá. They soon journeyed all the way to Monterey, which became the capital of Spanish California. There Portolá established a presidio in 1770 "to defend us from attacks by the Russians," he wrote. The same year, Serra founded Mission San Carlos Borroméo de Carmelo in Monterey to convert the Indians and recruit them to work to support the soldiers and other Spaniards in the presidio. By 1772, Serra had founded other missions along the path from San Diego to Monterey.

One Spanish soldier praised the work of the missionaries, writing that "with flattery and presents [the missionaries] attract the savage Indians and persuade them to adhere to life in society and to receive instruction for a knowledge of the Catholic faith, the cultivation of the land, and the arts necessary for making the instruments most needed for farming." Yet for the Indians, the Spaniards' California missions had horrendous consequences, as they had elsewhere in the Spanish borderlands. European diseases decimated Indian populations, Spanish soldiers raped Indian women, and missionaries beat Indians and subjected them to near slavery. Indian uprisings against the Spaniards occurred repeatedly, but the presidios and missions endured as feeble projections of the Spanish empire along the Pacific coast.

Spanish Missions in California

presidios
▶ Spanish forts built to block Russian access to California.

Colonial Politics in the British Empire

The plurality of peoples, faiths, and communities that characterized the North American colonies arose from the somewhat haphazard policies of the eighteenth-century British empire. Unlike Spain and France—whose policies of excluding Protestants and foreigners kept the population of their North American colonial territories tiny—Britain kept the door to its colonies open to anyone, and tens of thousands of non-British immigrants settled in the North American colonies and raised families. The open door did not extend to trade, however, as the seventeenth-century Navigation Acts restricted colonial trade to British ships and traders. These policies evolved because they served the interests of the monarchy and of influential groups in Britain and the colonies. The policies also gave the colonists a common framework of political expectations and experiences.

Mission Carmel

This eighteenth-century drawing portrays a reception for a Spanish visitor at Mission Carmel in what is now Carmel, California. Lines of mission Indians dressed in robes flank the entrance to the chapel where a priest and his assistants await the visitor. The reception ritual dramatized the strict hierarchy that governed relations among Spanish missionaries, ruling officials, and the subordinate Indians. University of California at Berkeley, Bancroft Library.

What spurred the growth of the middle colonies?

Why did slavery become the defining feature of the southern colonies?

What experiences tended to unify colonists in British North America?

Conclusion: What was the dual identity of British North American colonists?

✓ LearningCurve
Check what you know.
bedfordstmartins.com
/roarkunderstanding

British attempts to exercise political power in their colonial governments met with success so long as British officials were on or very near the sea. Colonists acknowledged—although they did not always readily comply with—British authority to collect customs duties, inspect cargoes, and enforce trade regulations. But when royal officials tried to wield their authority in the internal affairs of the colonies on land, they invariably encountered colonial resistance. A governor appointed by the king in each of the nine royal colonies (Rhode Island and Connecticut selected their own governors) or by the proprietors in Maryland and Pennsylvania headed the government of each colony. The British envisioned colonial governors as mini-monarchs able to exert influence in the colonies much as the king did in Britain. But colonial governors were not kings, and the colonies were not Britain.

Even the best-intentioned colonial governors had difficulty developing relations of trust and respect with influential colonists because their terms of office averaged just five years and could be terminated at any time. Colonial governors controlled few patronage positions to secure political friendships in the colonies. Obedient and loyal to their superiors in Britain, colonial governors fought incessantly with the colonists' assemblies. They battled over issues such as governors' vetoes of colonial legislation, removal of colonial judges, and dismissal of the representative assemblies. But during the eighteenth century, the assemblies gained the upper hand.

Since British policies did not clearly define the colonists' legal powers, colonial assemblies seized the opportunity to make their own rules. Gradually, the assemblies established a strong tradition of representative government analogous, in their eyes, to the British Parliament. Voters often returned the same representatives to the assemblies year after year, building continuity in power and leadership that far exceeded that of the governor.

By 1720, colonial assemblies had won the power to initiate legislation, including tax laws and authorizations to spend public funds. Although all laws passed by the assemblies (except in Maryland, Rhode Island, and Connecticut) had to be approved by the governor and then by the Board of Trade in Britain, the difficulties in communication about complex subjects over long distances effectively ratified the assemblies' decisions. Years often passed before colonial laws were repealed by British authorities, and in the meantime the assemblies' laws prevailed.

The heated political struggles between royal governors and colonial assemblies that occurred throughout the eighteenth century taught colonists a common set of political lessons. They learned to employ traditionally British ideas of representative government to defend their own colonial interests. More important, they learned that power in the British colonies rarely belonged to the British government.

> QUICK REVIEW

How did culture, commerce, and consumption shape the collective identity of Britain's North American colonists in the eighteenth century?

CHAPTER LOCATOR | How did the North American colonies change in the eighteenth century? | What changed in New England life and culture?

136 CHAPTER 5 THE CHANGING WORLD OF COLONIAL AMERICA

Conclusion: What was the dual identity of British North American colonists?

DURING THE EIGHTEENTH CENTURY, a society that was both distinctively colonial and distinctively British emerged in British North America. Tens of thousands of immigrants and slaves gave the colonies an unmistakably colonial complexion and contributed to the colonies' growing population and expanding economy. People of different ethnicities and faiths sought their fortunes in the colonies, where land was cheap, labor was dear, and work promised to be rewarding. Indentured servants and redemptioners risked temporary periods of bondage for the potential reward of better opportunities in the colonies than in Europe. Slaves arrived in unprecedented numbers and endured lifelong servitude, which they neither chose nor desired but from which their masters greatly benefited.

None of the European colonies could claim complete dominance of North America. The desire to expand and defend their current claims meant that the English, French, and Spanish colonies were drawn into regular conflict with one another, as well as with the Indians upon whose land they encroached. In varying degrees, all sought control of the Native Americans and their land, their military power, their trade, and even their souls. Spanish missionaries and soldiers sought to convert Indians on the West Coast and exploit their labor; French alliances with Indian tribes posed a formidable barrier to westward expansion of the British empire.

Yet despite their attempts to tame their New World holdings, Spanish and French colonists did not develop societies that began to rival the European empires that sponsored and supported them. They did not participate in the cultural, economic, social, and religious changes experienced by their counterparts in British North America, nor did they share in the emerging political identity of the British colonists.

Identifiably colonial products from New England, the middle colonies, and the southern colonies flowed to the West Indies and across the Atlantic. Back came unquestionably British consumer goods along with fashions in ideas, faith, and politics. The bonds of the British empire required colonists to think of themselves as British subjects and, at the same time, encouraged them to consider their status as colonists. By 1750, British colonists in North America could not imagine that their distinctively dual identity—as British and as colonists—would soon become a source of intense conflict.

| What spurred the growth of the middle colonies? | Why did slavery become the defining feature of the southern colonies? | What experiences tended to unify colonists in British North America? | **Conclusion: What was the dual identity of British North American colonists?** | ✓ **LearningCurve** Check what you know. bedfordstmartins.com /roarkunderstanding |

137

CHAPTER 5 STUDY GUIDE

STEP 1

GET STARTED ONLINE

✓ **LearningCurve** ▪ bedfordstmartins.com/roarkunderstanding

Now that you've read the chapter, make it stick by completing the LearningCurve activity.

STEP 2

EXPLAIN WHY IT MATTERS

Put your reading into practice. Identify each term below, and then explain why it matters in U.S. history.

TERM	WHO OR WHAT & WHEN	WHY IT MATTERS
natural increase (p. 112)		
partible inheritance (p. 115)		
Pennsylvania Dutch (p. 118)		
Scots-Irish (p. 119)		
redemptioners (p. 119)		
Middle Passage (p. 125)		
new Negroes (p. 126)		
Stono Rebellion (p. 127)		
task system (p. 127)		
Enlightenment (p. 133)		
Great Awakening (p. 133)		
presidios (p. 135)		

STEP 3

MOVE BEYOND THE BASICS

To demonstrate a more advanced understanding, consider the economy, society, culture, and politics of the major regions of British North America in 1700 and 1770. What accounts for regional divergence?

Region	Economy (imports and exports, jobs, wealth)	Population (ethnicity, race, class)	Culture — ways of life, values (including religious beliefs)	Colonial Politics
New England in 1700				
New England in 1770				
Middle Colonies in 1700				
Middle Colonies in 1770				
Southern Colonies in 1700				
Southern Colonies in 1770				

PUT IT ALL TOGETHER

Now, take a step back and try to explain the big picture. Remember to use specific examples from the chapter in your answers.

NEW ENGLAND

▶ How did the economy of New England differ from that of other regions?

▶ Why did New England not attract as many immigrants as other areas did? How did that affect the social structure of the region?

THE MIDDLE COLONIES

▶ How did immigration shape the religious and ethnic diversity of the middle colonies? What factors led immigrants to settle in the middle colonies?

▶ How did Atlantic commerce, particularly colonial consumption, affect the middle colonies?

THE SOUTHERN COLONIES AND SPANISH CALIFORNIA

▶ What role did slavery play in the social and economic development of the South?

▶ How did slaves attempt to maintain their own culture and gain some control within the limits of slavery?

▶ Why did New Spain establish presidios and missions, and what were their consequences for Native Americans?

LOOKING BACKWARD, LOOKING AHEAD

▶ How did the relationship between the colonies and Britain in the eighteenth century differ from that of the seventeenth century?

▶ What were the most pressing sources of potential conflict between the colonies and Britain in 1770? What were the most important sources of cooperation and mutual dependence?

> **IN YOUR OWN WORDS**

Imagine that you must give an oral report to the class answering the following question: **What were the most important changes in colonial North America between 1701 and 1770?** What would be the most important points to include and why?

 Do it online at the Student Site ▪ bedfordstmartins.com/roarkunderstanding

6

THE BRITISH EMPIRE AND THE COLONIAL CRISIS

1754–1775

> **What were the most significant factors contributing to deteriorating relations between Britain and its North American colonies?** Chapter 6 explores the efforts of the British government to tax and control the colonies in the aftermath of the Seven Years' War and traces the escalating colonial responses to these efforts, from political protest, to open resistance, and—ultimately—to war.

LearningCurve
bedfordstmartins.com/roarkunderstanding
After reading the chapter, use LearningCurve to
retain what you've read.

Resistance to the Stamp Act. This contemporary engraving (ca. 1765) depicts an angry Boston crowd burning a pile of stamps in protest of the **Stamp Act.** Picture Research Consultants & Archives.

> How did the Seven Years' War lay the groundwork for colonial crisis?

> Why did the Sugar Act and the Stamp Act draw fierce opposition from colonists?

> Why did British authorities send troops to occupy Boston in the fall of 1768?

> Why did Parliament pass the Coercive Acts in 1774?

> How did enslaved people in the colonies react to the stirrings of revolution?

> Conclusion: What changes did the American colonists want in 1775?

How did the Seven Years' War lay the groundwork for colonial crisis?

FOR THE FIRST HALF OF THE EIGHTEENTH CENTURY, Britain was at war intermittently with France or Spain. Often the colonists in America experienced reverberations from these conflicts, most acutely along the frontier of New France in northern New England. In 1754, international tensions returned, this time sparked by events in America's Ohio Valley. The land — variously claimed by Virginians, Pennsylvanians, and the French — was actually inhabited by more than a dozen Indian tribes. The result was the costly **Seven Years' War** (its British name — Americans called it the French and Indian War), which spread in 1756 to encompass much of Europe, the Caribbean, and even India. The British and their colonial allies won the war, but the immense costs of the conflict — in money, death, and desire for revenge by losers and even winners — laid the groundwork for the imperial crisis of the 1760s between the British and Americans.

Seven Years' War

▶ War (1754–1762) between Britain and France that ended with British domination of North America; known in America as the French and Indian War. Its high expense laid the foundation for conflict that would lead to the American Revolution.

French-British Rivalry in the Ohio Country

For several decades, French traders had cultivated alliances with the Indian tribes in the Ohio Country, a frontier region they regarded as part of New France, establishing a profitable exchange of manufactured goods for beaver furs (**Map 6.1**). But in the 1740s, aggressive Pennsylvania traders began to infringe on the territory. Adding to the tensions, a group of enterprising Virginians, including the brothers Lawrence and Augustine Washington, formed the Ohio Company in 1747 and advanced on the same land. Their hope for profit lay not in the fur trade but in land speculation, fueled by American population expansion.

CHAPTER LOCATOR | How did the Seven Years' War lay the groundwork for colonial crisis? | Why did the Sugar Act and the Stamp Act draw fierce opposition from colonists?

142 CHAPTER 6
THE BRITISH EMPIRE AND THE COLONIAL CRISIS

MAP 6.1 ■ **European Areas of Influence and the Seven Years' War, 1754–1763**

In 1750, the French and Spanish empires had relatively few people on the ground in North America, compared with the exploding population of the Anglo-American colonies. The disputed lands shown here, contested by the imperial powers, were inhabited by a variety of Native American tribes.

Map labels: Hudson Bay; GRANT TO HUDSON'S BAY COMPANY; NEWFOUNDLAND; Wolfe to Quebec; Fort Louisbourg besieged June 8–July 26, 1758; Wolfe from Great Britain; NEW FRANCE; ALGONQUIAN; Quebec; Fort Beausejour; NOVA SCOTIA; Port Royal; Amherst; Montreal; St. Lawrence; L. Superior; L. Champlain; Fort Ticonderoga July 8, 1758; Fort William Henry Aug. 9, 1757; Fort Frontenac Aug. 27, 1758; Fort Stanwix; N.H.; L. Ontario; Boston; Fort Niagara July 25, 1759; Fort Oswego; Albany; MASS.; R.I.; CONN.; L. Huron; L. Michigan; Mississippi R.; IROQUOIS; L. Erie; N.Y.; Detroit; PA.; New York; ATLANTIC OCEAN; Fort Duquesne (became Fort Pitt, 1758); Fort Cumberland; Philadelphia; N.J.; Braddock's defeat July 9, 1755; MD.; DEL.; Fort Necessity July 3, 1754; Ohio Company of Virginia; VA.; APPALACHIAN MOUNTAINS; St. Louis; Williamsburg; LOUISIANA; BRITISH COLONIES; Ohio R.; NORTH CAROLINA; SOUTH CAROLINA; Charleston; GEORGIA; Savannah; Natchez; SPANISH FLORIDA; St. Augustine; New Orleans; Gulf of Mexico

Legend:
French claims
British claims
Spanish claims
Disputed British-French claims
Disputed British-Spanish claims
British forces
British victory
French victory
Fort

Why did British authorities send troops to occupy Boston in the fall of 1768?

Why did Parliament pass the Coercive Acts in 1774?

How did enslaved people in the colonies react to the stirrings of revolution?

Conclusion: What changes did the American colonists want in 1775?

✓ **LearningCurve**
Check what you know.
bedfordstmartins.com
/roarkunderstanding

In response to these incursions, the French sent soldiers to build a series of military forts to secure their trade routes and to create a western barrier to American expansion. In 1753, the royal governor of Virginia, Robert Dinwiddie, himself a shareholder in the Ohio Company, dispatched a messenger to warn the French that they were trespassing on Virginia land. That messenger was twenty-one-year-old George Washington, half-brother of the Ohio Company leaders, who did not disappoint. Washington returned with crucial intelligence confirming French military intentions. Impressed, Dinwiddie appointed the youth to lead a small military expedition west to assert Virginia's claim and chase the French away — but without attacking them.

Ohio River Valley, 1753

In the spring of 1754, Washington set out with 160 Virginians and a small contingent of Mingo Indians equally concerned about the French military presence in the Ohio Country. Early one morning, the Mingo chief Tanaghrisson led a detachment of Washington's soldiers to a small French encampment in the woods. Who fired first was in dispute, but fourteen Frenchmen (and no Virginians) were wounded. While Washington, lacking a translator, struggled to communicate with the injured French commander, Tanaghrisson and his men intervened to kill and then scalp the wounded soldiers, including the commander, probably with the aim of inflaming hostilities between the French and the colonists.

This sudden massacre violated Dinwiddie's instructions to Washington and raised the stakes considerably. Fearing retaliation, Washington ordered his men to throw together a makeshift "Fort Necessity." Several hundred Virginia reinforcements arrived, but the Mingos, sensing disaster and displeased by Washington's style of command, fled. (Tanaghrisson later said, "The Colonel was a good-natured man, but had no experience; he took upon him to command the Indians as his slaves, [and] would by no means take advice from the Indians.") Retaliation arrived in the form of six hundred French soldiers aided by one hundred Shawnee and Delaware warriors, who attacked Fort Necessity, killing or wounding a third of Washington's men. The message was clear: The French would not depart from the disputed territory.

The Albany Congress

British imperial leaders hoped to prevent the conflict in the Ohio Country from leading to a larger war. One obvious strategy was to strengthen an old partnership with the Mohawks of New York's Iroquois Confederacy, who since 1692 had joined with New York fur merchants in an alliance called the Covenant Chain. Yet unsavory land speculators caused the Mohawks to doubt British friendship. Authorities in London directed New York's royal governor to convene a colonial conference to repair trade relations and secure the Indians' help — or at least their neutrality — against the looming French threat. The

CHAPTER LOCATOR | **How did the Seven Years' War lay the groundwork for colonial crisis?** | Why did the Sugar Act and the Stamp Act draw fierce opposition from colonists?

144 CHAPTER 6 THE BRITISH EMPIRE AND THE COLONIAL CRISIS

Chief Hendrick and John Caldwell These two images convey versions of cross-cultural dressing. The aged Mohawk Chief Hendrick (left) appears in fine British clothing, while John Caldwell, a titled Irishman who served with the British army, sports colorful elements of Indian dress.

Hendrick: Courtesy of the John Carter Brown Library at Brown University; Caldwell: © Walker Art Gallery, National Museums Liverpool/The Bridgeman Art Library.

conference convened at Albany, in June and July 1754. All six tribes of the Iroquois Confederacy attended, along with twenty-four delegates from seven colonies, making this an unprecedented pan-colony gathering. The elderly Mohawk chief Hendrick gave a powerful and widely reprinted speech, asserting that recent British neglect would inevitably reorient Indian trade relations to the French. "Look at the French, they are men; they are fortifying every where; but we are ashamed to say it; you are like women, bare and open, without any fortifications." Hendrick urged the assembled colonists to prepare for defense against the French.

Delegates Benjamin Franklin of Pennsylvania and Thomas Hutchinson of Massachusetts had their own ambitious plan. They coauthored the Albany Plan of Union, a proposal for a unified colonial government to exercise sole authority over questions of war, peace, and trade with the Indians. Delegates at the Albany Congress, alarmed by news of the defeat of the Virginians at Fort Necessity, agreed to present the plan to their respective assemblies.

To Franklin's surprise, not a single colony approved the Albany Plan. The Massachusetts assembly feared it was "a Design of gaining power over the Colonies," especially the power of taxation. Others objected that it would be impossible to agree on unified policies toward scores of quite different Indian tribes. The British government never backed the Albany Plan either; instead, it appointed two superintendents of Indian affairs, one for the northern and another for the southern colonies, each with exclusive powers to negotiate treaties, trade, and land sales with all tribes.

| Why did British authorities send troops to occupy Boston in the fall of 1768? | Why did Parliament pass the Coercive Acts in 1774? | How did enslaved people in the colonies react to the stirrings of revolution? | Conclusion: What changes did the American colonists want in 1775? | ✓ **LearningCurve** Check what you know. bedfordstmartins.com /roarkunderstanding |

The Indians at the Albany Congress were not impressed with the Albany Plan either. The Covenant Chain alliance with the Mohawk tribe was reaffirmed, but the other Indian nations left without pledging to help the British battle the French. Some of the Iroquois figured that the French military presence around the Great Lakes would discourage the westward push of American colonists and therefore better serve their interests.

The War and Its Consequences

By 1755, George Washington's frontier skirmish had turned into a major war. The British expected quick victories on three fronts. General Edward Braddock, recently arrived from England, marched his army toward Fort Duquesne in western Pennsylvania. Farther north, British troops moved toward Fort Niagara, critically located between Lakes Erie and Ontario. And William Johnson, a New Yorker recently appointed superintendent of northern Indian affairs, led forces north toward Lake Champlain, intending to defend the border against the French in Canada (see Map 6.1).

Unfortunately for the British, the French were prepared to fight and had enlisted many Indian tribes in their cause. When Braddock's army of 2,000 British soldiers marched west toward Fort Duquesne, a mere 8 Oneida warriors came as guides. They were ambushed by 250 French soldiers joined by 640 Indian warriors. In the bloody battle, nearly a thousand on the British side were killed (including General Braddock) or wounded.

For the next two years, British leaders stumbled badly, deploying inadequate numbers of undersupplied troops. What finally turned the war around was the rise to power in 1757 of William Pitt, Britain's prime minister, a man ready to commit massive resources to fight France and Spain worldwide. In America, British troops aided by American provincial soldiers finally captured Forts Duquesne, Niagara, and Ticonderoga, followed by the French cities of Quebec and finally Montreal, all from 1758 to 1760. By 1761, the war subsided in America but expanded globally, with battles in the Caribbean, Austria, Prussia, and India. The British captured the French sugar islands Martinique and Guadeloupe and then invaded Spanish Cuba with an army of some four thousand provincial soldiers from New York and New England. By the end of 1762, France and Spain capitulated, and the Treaty of Paris was signed in 1763.

In the complex peace negotiations that followed, Britain gained control of Canada, eliminating the French threat from the north. British and American title to the eastern half of North America was confirmed. But French territory west of the Mississippi River, including New Orleans, was transferred to Spain as compensation for Spain's assistance during the war. Strangely, Cuba was returned to Spain, and Martinique and Guadeloupe were returned to France (**Map 6.2**).

The British credited their army for their victory and criticized the colonists for inadequate support. William Pitt was convinced that colonial smuggling — beaver pelts from French fur traders and illegal molasses in the French Caribbean — "principally, if not alone, enabled France to sustain and protract this long and expensive war."

Colonists read the lessons of the war differently. American soldiers had turned out in force, they claimed, but had been relegated to grunt work by British commanders and subjected to harsh military discipline, including floggings and

CHAPTER LOCATOR | **How did the Seven Years' War lay the groundwork for colonial crisis?** | Why did the Sugar Act and the Stamp Act draw fierce opposition from colonists?

146 CHAPTER 6 THE BRITISH EMPIRE AND THE COLONIAL CRISIS

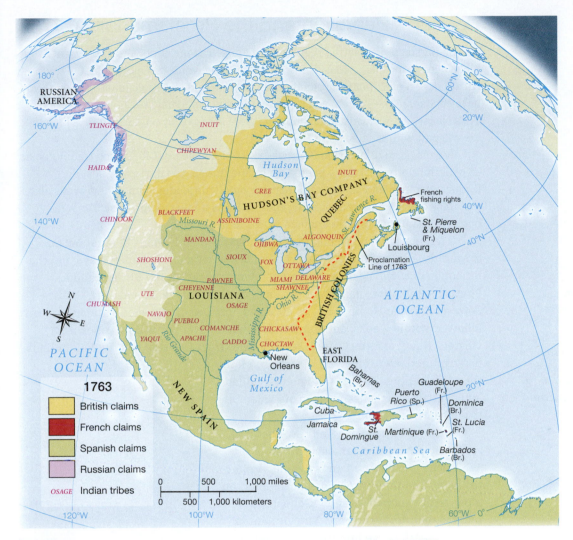

MAP 6.2 ■ Europe Redraws the Map of North America, 1763

In 1763, France ceded to Britain its interior territory from Quebec to New Orleans, retaining fishing rights in the north and sugar islands in the Caribbean. France transferred to Spain its claim to extensive territory west of the Mississippi River.

> MAP ACTIVITY

READING THE MAP: Who actually lived on and controlled the lands ceded by France? In what sense, if any, did Britain or Spain own these large territories?

CONNECTIONS: What was the goal of the Proclamation of 1763? (See page 148.) Could it ever have worked?

executions. They bristled at British arrogance, as when Benjamin Franklin heard General Braddock brag that "these savages may, indeed, be a formidable enemy to your raw American militia, but upon the king's regular and disciplined troops, sir, it is impossible they should make any impression." Braddock's crushing defeat "gave us Americans," Franklin wrote, "the first suspicion that our exalted ideas of the prowess of British regulars had not been well founded."

Perhaps most important, the enormous expense of the war cast a huge shadow over the victory. By 1763, Britain's national debt, double what it had been when Pitt took office, posed a formidable challenge to the next decade of leadership in Britain.

| Why did British authorities send troops to occupy Boston in the fall of 1768? | Why did Parliament pass the Coercive Acts in 1774? | How did enslaved people in the colonies react to the stirrings of revolution? | Conclusion: What changes did the American colonists want in 1775? | ✓ LearningCurve Check what you know. bedfordstmartins.com /roarkunderstanding |

Pontiac's Rebellion and the Proclamation of 1763

One glaring omission marred the Treaty of Paris: The major powers at the treaty table failed to include or consult the Indians. Minavavana, an Ojibwa chief of the Great Lakes region, put it succinctly to an English trader: "Englishman, although you have conquered the French, you have not yet conquered us! We are not your slaves. These lakes, these woods and mountains were left to us by our ancestors . . . ; and we will part with them to none."

Indians north of the Ohio River had cause for concern. Old French trading posts all over the Northwest were beefed up by the British into military bases. Fort Duquesne, renamed Fort Pitt to honor the victorious leader, gained new walls sixty feet thick at their base, announcing that this was no fur trading post. Tensions between the British and the Indians in this area ran high.

A religious revival among the Indians magnified feelings of antagonism toward the British. In 1763, the renewal of commitment to Indian ways and the formation of tribal alliances led to open warfare, which the British called **Pontiac's Rebellion**, named for the chief of the Ottawas. In mid-May, Ottawa, Potawatomi, and Huron warriors attacked Fort Detroit. Six more attacks on forts followed within weeks, and frontier settlements were raided by tribes from western New York, the Ohio Valley, and the Great Lakes region. By fall, Indians had captured every fort west of Detroit. More than four hundred British soldiers were dead and another two thousand colonists killed or taken captive.

Some Americans exacted revenge. The worst violent aggression occurred in late 1763, when some fifty Pennsylvania vigilantes known as the Paxton Boys descended on a peaceful village of friendly Conestoga Indians, murdering twenty. The vigilantes, now numbering five hundred, marched on Philadelphia to try to capture and murder some Christian Indians held in protective custody there. British troops prevented

Pontiac's Rebellion

▶ A coordinated uprising of Native American tribes in 1763 in the Northwest after the end of the Seven Years' War. The rebellion heightened Britain's determination to create a boundary between Americans and Indians, embodied in the Proclamation of 1763.

Pontiac's Rebellion, 1763

> The Proclamation of 1763

- Colonists were forbidden to settle west of the Appalachian Mountains.
- The Proclamation offered assurances that Indian territory would be respected. It limited trade with Indians to traders licensed by colonial governors, and it forbade private sales of Indian land.
- Western lands were referred to not as the Indians' land, but as lands that "are reserved to [Indians], as their Hunting Grounds."
- American and French colonists in Canada were British subjects entitled to English rights and privileges.
- Indians were not British subjects and were instead referred to as "Tribes of Indians with whom We are connected."

CHAPTER LOCATOR | **How did the Seven Years' War lay the groundwork for colonial crisis?** | Why did the Sugar Act and the Stamp Act draw fierce opposition from colonists?

that, but the Paxton Boys escaped punishment for their murderous attack on the Conestoga village. To minimize violence, the British government issued the Proclamation of 1763, which chiefly aimed to separate Indians and settlers, with added restrictions on trade and land sales.

The Indian uprising had faded by early 1764, but the 1763 boundary was a further provocation to American settlers and also to land speculators who had already staked claims to huge tracts of western lands in hopes of profitable resale. Yet the boundary proved impossible to enforce. Surging population growth had already sent many hundreds of settlers, many of them squatters, west of the Appalachians. Periodic bloodshed continued and left the settlers fearful, uncertain about their future, and increasingly wary of British claims to be a protective mother country.

QUICK REVIEW

How did the Seven Years' War erode relations between colonists and British authorities?

| Why did British authorities send troops to occupy Boston in the fall of 1768? | Why did Parliament pass the Coercive Acts in 1774? | How did enslaved people in the colonies react to the stirrings of revolution? | Conclusion: What changes did the American colonists want in 1775? | ✓ LearningCurve Check what you know. bedfordstmartins.com /roarkunderstanding |

Why did the Sugar Act and the Stamp Act draw fierce opposition from colonists?

George Grenville, Prime Minister, 1763–1765

George Grenville became prime minister in 1763, but King George III found him irksome: "When he has wearied me for two hours, he looks at his watch, to see if he may not tire me for an hour more," the king said, and sacked him in July 1765 for being insolent, not for his controversial colonial policies. The Earl of Halifax, Garrowby, Yorkshire.

IN 1760, GEORGE III, twenty-two years old, became king of England. Timid and insecure, George struggled to gain his footing in his new job. He rotated through a succession of leaders, searching for a prime minister he could trust. A half dozen ministers in seven years took turns dealing with one basic, underlying British reality: A huge war debt needed to be serviced, and the colonists, as British subjects, should help pay it off. To many Americans, however, that proposition seemed in deep violation of what they perceived to be their rights and liberties as British subjects, and it created resentment that eventually erupted in large-scale street protests. The first provocative revenue acts were the work of Sir George Grenville, prime minister from 1763 to 1765.

Grenville's Sugar Act

To find revenue, George Grenville scrutinized the customs service, which monitored the shipping trade and collected all import and export duties. Grenville found that the salaries of customs officers cost the government four times what was collected in revenue. The shortfall was due in part to bribery and smuggling, so Grenville began to insist on rigorous attention to paperwork and a strict accounting of collected duties. The hardest duty to enforce was the one imposed by the Molasses Act of 1733 — a stiff tax of six pence per gallon on any molasses (a key ingredient in rum) imported to British colonies from non-British sources. Rum-loving Americans, however, were eager to buy molasses from French Caribbean islands, and they had ignored the tax law for decades.

Grenville's inspired solution was the **Revenue Act** of 1764, popularly dubbed the **Sugar Act**. It lowered the duty on French molasses to three pence, making it more attractive for shippers to obey the law, and at the same time raised penalties for smuggling. The act appeared to be in the tradition of navigation acts meant to regulate trade (see chapter 4), but Grenville's actual intent was to raise revenue. The Sugar Act toughened enforcement policies. From now on, all British naval crews could act as impromptu customs officers, boarding suspicious ships and seizing cargoes found to be in violation. Smugglers caught without proper paperwork would be prosecuted, not in a local court with a friendly jury but in a vice-admiralty court located in Nova Scotia, where a crown judge presided. The implication was that justice would be sure and severe. Grenville's hopes for the Sugar Act did not materialize. The small decrease in duty did not offset the attractions of smuggling, while the increased vigilance in enforcement led to several ugly confrontations in port cities. Reaction to the Sugar Act foreshadowed questions about Britain's right to tax Americans, but in 1764 objections to the act came principally from the small number of Americans engaged in the shipping trades. From the British point of view, the Proclamation of 1763 and the Sugar Act seemed to be reasonable efforts to administer the colonies. To Americans, however, the British supervision appeared to be a disturbing intrusion into colonial practices of self-taxation by elected colonial assemblies. Benjamin Franklin, Pennsylvania's lobbyist in London, warned that "two distinct Jurisdictions or Powers of Taxing cannot well subsist together in the same country."

Sugar (Revenue) Act
▶ 1764 British law that decreased the duty on French molasses, making it more attractive for shippers to obey the law, and at the same time raised penalties for smuggling. The Sugar Act regulated trade, but its primary purpose was to raise revenue.

The Stamp Act

In February 1765, Grenville escalated his revenue program with the **Stamp Act**, precipitating a major conflict between Britain and the colonies over Parliament's right to tax. The Stamp Act imposed a tax on all paper used for official documents — newspapers, pamphlets, court documents, licenses, wills, ships' cargo lists — and required an affixed stamp as proof that the tax had been paid. Unlike the Sugar Act, which regulated trade, the Stamp Act was designed plainly and simply to raise money. It affected nearly everyone who used any taxed paper but, most of all, users of official documents in the business and legal communities. Anticipating that the stamp tax would be unpopular — Thomas Hutchinson had forewarned him — Grenville delegated the administration of the act to Americans to avoid taxpayer hostility toward British enforcers. In each colony, local stamp distributors would be hired at a handsome salary of 8 percent of the revenue collected. English tradition held that taxes were a gift of the people to their monarch, granted by the people's representatives. This view of taxes as a freely given gift preserved an essential concept of English political theory: the idea that citizens have the liberty to enjoy and use their property without fear of confiscation. The king could not demand money; only the House of Commons could grant it. Grenville agreed with the notion of taxation by consent, but he argued that the colonists were already "virtually" represented in Parliament. The House of Commons, he insisted, represented all British subjects, wherever they were. Colonial leaders emphatically rejected this view, arguing that

Stamp Act
▶ 1765 British law imposing a tax on all paper used for official documents, for the purpose of raising revenue. Widespread resistance to the Stamp Act led to its repeal in 1766.

Why did British authorities send troops to occupy Boston in the fall of 1768?

Why did Parliament pass the Coercive Acts in 1774?

How did enslaved people in the colonies react to the stirrings of revolution?

Conclusion: What changes did the American colonists want in 1775?

☑ **LearningCurve**
Check what you know.
bedfordstmartins.com
/roarkunderstanding

virtual representation

► The theory that all British subjects were represented in Parliament, whether they had elected representatives in that body or not. American colonists rejected the theory of virtual representation, arguing that only direct representatives had the right to tax the colonists.

virtual representation could not withstand the stretch across the Atlantic. Colonists willingly paid local and provincial taxes, levied by their town, county, or colonial assemblies, to fund government administrative expenses and shared necessities like local roads, schools, and poor relief. By contrast, the stamp tax was a clear departure as a fee-per-document tax, levied by a distant Parliament on unwilling colonies.

Resistance Strategies and Crowd Politics

News of the Stamp Act arrived in the colonies in April 1765, seven months before it was to take effect. There was time, therefore, to object. Governors were unlikely to challenge the law, for most of them owed their office to the king. Instead, the colonial assemblies took the lead; eight of them held discussions on the Stamp Act.

Virginia's assembly, the House of Burgesses, was the first. At the end of its May session, after two-thirds of the members had left, Patrick Henry, a young political newcomer, presented a series of resolutions on the Stamp Act that were debated and passed, one by one. They became known as the Virginia Resolves. Henry's resolutions inched the assembly toward radical opposition to the Stamp Act.

> ### > The Virginia Resolves

1. Virginians were British citizens.
2. Virginians enjoyed the same rights and privileges as Britons.
3. As British citizens, Virginians had the right to tax themselves.
4. Virginians had always taxed themselves, through their representatives in the House of Burgesses.
5. The Virginia assembly alone had the right to tax Virginians.
6. Any tax law originating from outside Virginia was not legitimate.
7. Anyone who disagreed with these propositions was an enemy of Virginia.

The final two propositions were too much for the majority of the representatives in the assembly. They voted down resolutions six and seven and later rescinded their vote on number five as well. Their caution hardly mattered, however, because newspapers in other colonies printed all seven Virginia Resolves, creating the impression that a daring first challenge to the Stamp Act had occurred. Consequently, other assemblies were willing to consider even more radical questions, such as this: By what authority could Parliament legislate for the colonies without also taxing them? No one disagreed, in 1765, that Parliament had legislative power over the colonists, who were, after all, British subjects. Several assemblies advanced the argument that there was a distinction between *external* taxes, imposed to regulate trade, and *internal* taxes, such as a stamp tax or a property tax, which could only be self-imposed.

Reaction to the Stamp Act ran far deeper than political debate in assemblies. Every person whose livelihood required official paper had to decide whether to comply with the act. The first organized resistance to the Stamp Act began in Boston in August 1765 under the direction of town leaders, chief among them Samuel Adams, John Hancock, and Ebenezer Mackintosh. Many other artisans,

CHAPTER LOCATOR | How did the Seven Years' War lay the groundwork for colonial crisis? | **Why did the Sugar Act and the Stamp Act draw fierce opposition from colonists?**

152 **CHAPTER 6** THE BRITISH EMPIRE AND THE COLONIAL CRISIS

tradesmen, printers, tavern keepers, dockworkers, and sailors — the middling and lower orders — mobilized to oppose the Stamp Act, taking the name "Sons of Liberty."

The plan hatched in Boston called for a large street demonstration highlighting a mock execution designed to convince Andrew Oliver, the designated stamp distributor, to resign. On August 14, 1765, a crowd of two thousand to three thousand demonstrators, led by the young shoemaker Mackintosh, hung an effigy of Oliver in a tree and then paraded it around town before finally beheading and burning it. In hopes of calming tensions, the royal governor Francis Bernard took no action. The next day Oliver resigned his office in a well-publicized announcement.

The demonstration provided lessons for everyone. Oliver learned that stamp distributors would be very unpopular people. Governor Bernard, with no police force to call on, learned the limitations of his power to govern. The demonstration's leaders learned that street action was effective. And hundreds of ordinary men not only learned what the Stamp Act was all about but also gained pride in their ability to have a decisive impact on politics. Twelve days later, a second crowd action showed how well these lessons had been learned. On August 26, a crowd visited the houses of three detested customs and court officials, breaking windows and raiding wine cellars. A fourth target was the finest dwelling in Massachusetts, owned by Thomas Hutchinson, lieutenant governor of Massachusetts and the chief justice of the colony's highest court. Rumors abounded that Hutchinson had urged Grenville to adopt the Stamp Act. Although he had actually done the opposite, Hutchinson refused to set the record straight, saying curtly, "I am not obliged to give an answer to all the questions that may be put me by every lawless person." The crowd attacked his house, and by daybreak only the exterior walls were standing. Governor Bernard gave orders to call out the militia, but he was told that many militiamen were among the crowd.

The destruction of Hutchinson's house brought a temporary halt to protest activities in Boston. The town meeting issued a statement of sympathy for Hutchinson, but a large reward for the arrest and conviction of rioters failed to produce a single lead. Essentially, the opponents of the Stamp Act in Boston had triumphed; no one replaced Oliver as distributor. When the act took effect on

Why did British authorities send troops to occupy Boston in the fall of 1768?

Why did Parliament pass the Coercive Acts in 1774?

How did enslaved people in the colonies react to the stirrings of revolution?

Conclusion: What changes did the American colonists want in 1775?

☑ **LearningCurve**
Check what you know.
bedfordstmartins.com/roarkunderstanding

November 1, ships without stamped permits continued to clear the harbor. Since he could not bring the lawbreakers to court, Hutchinson, ever principled, felt obliged to resign his office as chief justice. He remained lieutenant governor, however, and within five years he became the royal governor.

Liberty and Property

Boston's crowd actions of August sparked similar eruptions by groups calling themselves Sons of Liberty in nearly fifty towns throughout the colonies, and stamp distributors everywhere hastened to resign. A crowd forced one Connecticut distributor to throw his hat and powdered wig in the air while shouting a cheer for "Liberty and property!" This man fared better than another Connecticut stamp agent who was nearly buried alive by Sons of Liberty. Only when the thuds of dirt sounded on his coffin did he have a sudden change of heart, shouting out his resignation to the crowd above. Luckily, he was heard. In Charleston, South Carolina, the stamp distributor resigned after crowds burned effigies and chanted "Liberty! Liberty!"

Some colonial leaders, disturbed by the riots, sought a more moderate challenge to parliamentary authority. In October 1765, twenty-seven delegates representing nine colonial assemblies met in New York City as the Stamp Act Congress. For two weeks, the men hammered out a petition about taxation addressed to the king and Parliament. Their statement closely resembled the first five Virginia Resolves, claiming that taxes were "free gifts of the people," which only the people's representatives could give. They dismissed virtual representation: "The people of these colonies are not, and from their local circumstances, cannot be represented in the House of Commons." At the same time, the delegates carefully affirmed their subordination to Parliament and monarch in deferential language.

Nevertheless, the Stamp Act Congress, by the mere fact of its meeting, advanced a radical potential — the notion of intercolonial political action. The rallying cry of "Liberty and property" made perfect sense to many white Americans of all social ranks, who feared that the Stamp Act threatened their traditional right to liberty as British subjects. The liberty in question was the right to be taxed only by representative government. "Liberty and property" came from a trinity of concepts — "life, liberty, property" — that had come to be regarded as the birthright of freeborn British subjects since at least the seventeenth century. A powerful tradition of British political thought invested representative government with the duty to protect individual lives, liberties, and property against potential abuse by royal authority. Up to 1765, Americans had consented to accept Parliament as a body that represented them. But now, in this matter of taxation via stamps, Parliament seemed a distant body that had failed to protect Americans' liberty and property against royal authority.

Alarmed, some Americans began to speak and write about a plot by British leaders to enslave them. A Maryland writer warned that if the colonies lost "the right of exemption from all taxes without their consent," that loss would "deprive them of every privilege distinguishing freemen from slaves." In Virginia, a group of planters headed by Richard Henry Lee issued a document called the Westmoreland Resolves, claiming that the Stamp Act was an attempt

CHAPTER LOCATOR | How did the Seven Years' War lay the groundwork for colonial crisis? | **Why did the Sugar Act and the Stamp Act draw fierce opposition from colonists?**

CHAPTER 6
154 THE BRITISH EMPIRE AND THE COLONIAL CRISIS

"to reduce the people of this country to a state of abject and detestable slavery."
The opposite meanings of *liberty* and *slavery* were utterly clear to white
Americans, but they stopped short of applying similar logic to the half million
black Americans they held in bondage. Many blacks, however, could see the con-
tradiction. When a crowd of Charleston blacks paraded with shouts of "Liberty!"
just a few months after white Sons of Liberty had done the same, the town militia turned out to break up the demonstration.

Politicians and merchants in Britain reacted with distress to the American
demonstrations and petitions. Merchants particularly feared trade disruptions and
pressured Parliament to repeal the Stamp Act. By late 1765, yet another new minister, the Marquess of Rockingham, headed the king's cabinet and sought a way
to repeal the act without losing face. The solution came in March 1766: The Stamp
Act was repealed, but with the repeal came the **Declaratory Act**, which asserted
Parliament's right to legislate for the colonies "in all cases whatsoever." Perhaps
the stamp tax had been inexpedient, but the power to tax — one prime case of a
legislative power — was stoutly upheld.

Declaratory Act
▶ 1766 law issued by Parliament
to assert Parliament's
unassailable right to legislate
for British colonies "in all cases
whatsoever," putting Americans
on notice that the simultaneous
repeal of the Stamp Act changed
nothing in the imperial powers of
Britain.

QUICK REVIEW

What rights did many Americans feel were challenged
by the Sugar Act and the Stamp Act? How did they
express their disapproval of the acts?

Why did British
authorities send troops
to occupy Boston in the
fall of 1768?

Why did Parliament pass
the Coercive Acts in
1774?

How did enslaved
people in the colonies
react to the stirrings of
revolution?

Conclusion: What
changes did the
American colonists want
in 1775?

☑ LearningCurve
Check what you know.
bedfordstmartins.com
/roarkunderstanding

Why did British authorities send troops to occupy Boston in the fall of 1768?

Edenton Tea Ladies

Patriotic women in Edenton, North Carolina, pledged to renounce British tea and were satirized in this British cartoon, which shows brazen women shedding traditional notions of femininity. Neglected babies, urinating dogs, wanton sexuality, and mean-looking women were the consequences of meddling in politics, according to the artist. The cartoon was humorous to the British because of the gender reversals it predicts and because of the insult it directs at American men. Library of Congress.

ROCKINGHAM DID NOT LAST LONG as prime minister. By the summer of 1766, George III had persuaded William Pitt to resume that position. Pitt appointed Charles Townshend to be chancellor of the exchequer, the chief financial minister. Facing both the old war debt and the cost of the British troops in America, Townshend turned again to taxation, but his plan to raise revenue touched off coordinated boycotts of British goods in 1768 and 1769. Even women were politicized as self-styled "Daughters of Liberty." Boston led the uproar, causing the British to send peacekeeping soldiers to assist the royal governor. The stage was thus set for the first fatalities in the brewing revolution.

CHAPTER LOCATOR | How did the Seven Years' War lay the groundwork for colonial crisis? | Why did the Sugar Act and the Stamp Act draw fierce opposition from colonists?

The Townshend Duties

Townshend proposed new taxes in the old form of a navigation act. Officially called the Revenue Act of 1767, it established new duties on tea, glass, lead, paper, and painters' colors imported into the colonies, to be paid by the importer but passed on to consumers in the retail price. A recent further reduction in the duty on French molasses had persuaded some American shippers to quit smuggling, and finally Britain was deriving a moderate revenue stream from its colonies. Townshend naively concluded that Americans accepted external taxes. The **Townshend duties** were not especially burdensome, but the principle they embodied — taxation through trade duties — looked different to the colonists in the wake of the Stamp Act crisis. Although Americans once distinguished between external and internal taxes, accepting external duties as a means to direct the flow of trade, that distinction was wiped out by an external tax meant only to raise money. John Dickinson, a Philadelphia lawyer, articulated this view in an essay titled *Letters from a Farmer in Pennsylvania*, widely circulated in late 1767. "We are taxed without our consent. . . . We are therefore — SLAVES," Dickinson wrote, calling for "a total denial of the power of Parliament to lay upon these colonies any 'tax' whatever." A controversial provision of the Townshend duties directed that some of the revenue generated would pay the salaries of royal governors. Before 1767, local assemblies set the salaries of their own officials, giving them significant influence over crown-appointed officeholders. Through his new provision, Townshend aimed to strengthen the governors' position as well as to curb what he perceived to be the growing independence of the assemblies. Massachusetts again took the lead in protesting the Townshend duties. Samuel Adams, now an elected member of the provincial assembly, argued that any form of parliamentary taxation was unjust because Americans were not represented in Parliament. Further, he argued that the new way to pay governors' salaries subverted the proper relationship between the people and their rulers. The assembly circulated a letter with Adams's arguments to other colonial assemblies for their endorsement. As with the Stamp Act Congress of 1765, colonial assemblies were starting to coordinate their protests.

In response to Adams's letter, Lord Hillsborough, the new man in charge of colonial affairs in Britain, instructed Massachusetts governor Francis Bernard to dissolve the assembly if it refused to repudiate the letter. The assembly refused, by a vote of 92 to 17, and Bernard carried out his instruction. In the summer of 1768, Boston was in an uproar.

Nonconsumption and the Daughters of Liberty

The Boston town meeting led the way with nonconsumption agreements, calling for a boycott of all British-made goods. Dozens of other towns passed similar resolutions in 1767 and 1768. For example, prohibited purchases in the town of New Haven, Connecticut, included carriages, furniture, hats, clothing, lace, clocks, and textiles. The idea was to encourage home manufacture and to hurt trade, causing London merchants to pressure Parliament for repeal of the Townshend duties. Nonconsumption agreements were very hard to enforce.

Townshend duties

▶ New duties (established by the Revenue Act of 1767) on tea, glass, lead, paper, and painters' colors imported into the colonies. The Townshend duties led to boycotts and heightened tensions between Britain and the American colonies.

> CHRONOLOGY

1767
– Parliament enacts Townshend duties.

1768
– British station troops in Boston.

1768–1769
– Merchants sign nonimportation agreements.

1770
– Boston Massacre.

Why did British authorities send troops to occupy Boston in the fall of 1768?

Why did Parliament pass the Coercive Acts in 1774?

How did enslaved people in the colonies react to the stirrings of revolution?

Conclusion: What changes did the American colonists want in 1775?

☑ LearningCurve
Check what you know.
bedfordstmartins.com /roarkunderstanding

With the Stamp Act, there was one hated item, a stamp, and a limited number of official distributors. By contrast, an agreement to boycott all British goods required serious personal sacrifice, which not everyone was prepared to make. A more direct blow to trade came from nonimportation agreements, but getting merchants to agree to these proved more difficult, because of fears that merchants in other colonies might continue to import goods and make handsome profits. Not until late 1768 could Boston merchants agree to suspend trade through a nonimportation agreement lasting one year starting January 1, 1769. Sixty signed the agreement. New York merchants soon followed suit, as did Philadelphia and Charleston merchants in 1769.

Many of the British products specified in nonconsumption agreements were household goods traditionally under the control of the "ladies." By 1769, male leaders in the patriot cause clearly understood that women's cooperation in nonconsumption and home manufacture was beneficial to their cause. The Townshend duties thus provided an unparalleled opportunity for encouraging female patriotism. During the Stamp Act crisis, Sons of Liberty took to the streets in protest. During the difficulties of 1768 and 1769, the concept of Daughters of Liberty emerged to give shape to a new idea — that women might play a role in public affairs. Any woman could express affiliation with the colonial protest through conspicuous boycotts of British-made goods. In Boston, more than three hundred women signed a petition to abstain from tea, "sickness excepted," in order to "save this abused Country from Ruin and Slavery."

Homespun cloth became a prominent symbol of patriotism. A young Boston girl learning to spin called herself "a daughter of liberty," noting that "I chuse to wear as much of our own manufactory as pocible." In the boycott period of 1768 to 1770, newspapers reported on spinning matches, or bees, in some sixty New England towns, in which women came together in public to make yarn. Newspaper accounts variously called the spinners "Daughters of Liberty" or "Daughters of Industry."

This surge of public spinning was related to the politics of the boycott, which infused traditional women's work with new political purpose. But the women spinners were not equivalents of the Sons of Liberty. The Sons marched in streets, burned effigies, threatened hated officials, and celebrated anniversaries of their successes with raucous drinking in taverns. The Daughters manifested their patriotism quietly, in ways marked by piety, industry, and charity. The difference was due in part to cultural ideals of gender, which prized masculine self-assertion and feminine selflessness. It also was due to class. The Sons were a cross-class alliance, with leaders from the middling orders reliant on men and boys of the lower ranks to fuel their crowds. The Daughters were genteel ladies accustomed to buying British goods. The difference between the Sons and the Daughters also speaks to two views of how best to challenge authority: violent threats and street actions, or the self-disciplined, self-sacrificing boycott of goods?

On the whole, the anti-British boycotts were a success. Imports fell by more than 40 percent; British merchants felt the pinch and let Parliament know it. In Boston, the extended Hutchinson family — whose fortune rested on British trade — also endured losses, but even more alarming to the lieutenant governor, Boston

CHAPTER LOCATOR | How did the Seven Years' War lay the groundwork for colonial crisis? | Why did the Sugar Act and the Stamp Act draw fierce opposition from colonists?

158 CHAPTER 6 THE BRITISH EMPIRE AND THE COLONIAL CRISIS

seemed overrun with anti-British sentiment. The Sons of Liberty staged rollicking annual celebrations of the Stamp Act riot, and both Hutchinson and Governor Bernard concluded that British troops were necessary to restore order.

Military Occupation and "Massacre" in Boston

In the fall of 1768, three thousand uniformed troops arrived to occupy Boston. Although the situation was frequently tense, no major troubles occurred that winter and through most of 1769. But as January 1, 1770, approached, marking the end of the nonimportation agreement, it was clear that some merchants — such as Thomas Hutchinson's two sons, both importers — were ready to break the boycott.

Trouble began in January, when a crowd smeared the door of the Hutchinson brothers' shop with excrement. In February, a crowd surrounded the house of a confrontational customs official who panicked and fired a musket,

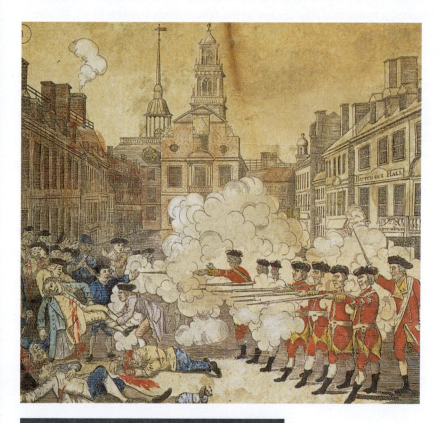

The Bloody Massacre Perpetrated in King Street, Boston, on March 5, 1770

Paul Revere's mass-produced engraving shows the patriot version of events. Soldiers appear as a firing squad, shooting simultaneously at an unarmed and bewigged crowd; more likely the shooting was chaotic, and the fatalities were from lower classes who rarely wore wigs. Crispus Attucks, an African-Indian dockworker, was killed, but Revere depicts only whites among the injured. Anne S. K. Brown Military Collection, Providence, Rhode Island.

> **VISUAL ACTIVITY**

READING THE IMAGE: How does this picture attempt to enlist its viewers' sympathies?
CONNECTIONS: Does this picture accurately represent the events of the Boston Massacre? What might account for its biases?

Why did British authorities send troops to occupy Boston in the fall of 1768?

Why did Parliament pass the Coercive Acts in 1774?

How did enslaved people in the colonies react to the stirrings of revolution?

Conclusion: What changes did the American colonists want in 1775?

☑ LearningCurve
Check what you know.
bedfordstmartins.com
/roarkunderstanding

accidentally killing a young boy passing on the street. The Sons of Liberty mounted a massive funeral procession to mark this first instance of violent death in the struggle with Britain.

For the next week, tension gripped Boston. The climax came on Monday evening, March 5, 1770, when a crowd taunted eight British soldiers guarding the customs house. Onlookers threw snowballs and rocks and dared the soldiers to fire; finally one did. After a short pause, someone yelled "Fire!" and the other soldiers shot into the crowd, hitting eleven men, killing five of them.

The **Boston Massacre**, as the event was quickly labeled, was over in minutes. Hutchinson, now acting governor of the colony, immediately removed the regiments to an island in the harbor to prevent further bloodshed, and he jailed Captain Thomas Preston and his eight soldiers for their own protection, promising they would be held for trial.

The Sons of Liberty staged elaborate martyrs' funerals for the five victims. Significantly, the one nonwhite victim shared equally in the public's veneration. Crispus Attucks, a sailor and rope maker in his forties, was the son of an African man and a Natick Indian woman. A slave in his youth, he was at the time of his death a free laborer at the Boston docks. Attucks was one of the first American partisans to die in the revolutionary struggle with Britain, and certainly the first African American.

At trial in the fall of 1770, the eight soldiers were ably defended by two Boston attorneys, John Adams and Josiah Quincy. While both had direct ties to the leadership of the Sons of Liberty, Adams was deeply committed to the principle that even unpopular defendants deserved a fair trial. The five-day trial resulted in acquittal for Preston and for all but two of the soldiers, who were convicted of manslaughter, branded on the thumbs, and released.

Boston Massacre

▶ March 1770 incident in Boston in which British soldiers fired on an American crowd, killing five. The Boston Massacre became a rallying point for colonists who increasingly saw the British government as tyrannical and illegitimate.

> **QUICK REVIEW**

Why were Boston's resistance to British policies and British reaction to the resistance so pronounced?

CHAPTER LOCATOR | How did the Seven Years' War lay the groundwork for colonial crisis? | Why did the Sugar Act and the Stamp Act draw fierce opposition from colonists?

CHAPTER 6

160   THE BRITISH EMPIRE AND THE COLONIAL CRISIS

Tossing the Tea This colored engraving appeared in an English book published in 1789 recounting the history of North America from its earliest settlement to "becoming united, free, and independent states." This event was not dubbed the "Tea Party" until the 1830s, when a later generation celebrated the illegal destruction of the tea and made heroes out of the few surviving participants, by then in their eighties and nineties. Library of Congress.

Why did Parliament pass the Coercive Acts in 1774?

IN THE SAME WEEK as the Boston Massacre, yet another new British prime minister, Frederick North, acknowledged the harmful impact of the boycott on trade and recommended repeal of the Townshend duties. Seeking peace with the colonies and prosperity for British merchants, Lord North persuaded Parliament to remove all the duties except the tax on tea, kept as a symbol of Parliament's power. For nearly two years following repeal of the Townshend duties, peace seemed possible, but tense incidents in 1772, followed by a renewed struggle over the tea tax in 1773, precipitated a full-scale crisis in the summer and fall of 1774. In response, men from nearly all the colonies came together in a special "Continental Congress" to debate the crisis.

The Calm before the Storm

Repeal of the Townshend duties brought an end to nonimportation. Trade boomed in 1770 and 1771, driven by pent-up demand. Moreover, the leaders of the popular movement seemed to be losing their power. Samuel Adams, for example, ran for a minor local office and lost to a conservative merchant. Then in 1772, several incidents again brought the conflict with Britain into sharp focus. One was the burning of the *Gaspée*, a Royal Navy ship pursuing suspected smugglers near Rhode Island. A British investigating commission failed to arrest anyone but announced that it would send suspects, if any were found, to Britain for trial on charges of high treason. This ruling seemed to fly in the face of the traditional English right to trial by a jury of one's peers.

> **CHRONOLOGY**

1770
– Parliament repeals Townshend duties.

1772
– British navy ship *Gaspée* is burned.
– Committees of correspondence begin forming.

1773
– Parliament passes Tea Act.
– Tea is dumped in Boston harbor.

1774
– Parliament passes Coercive Acts.
– Powder Alarm shows colonists' readiness.
– First Continental Congress meets.

Why did British authorities send troops to occupy Boston in the fall of 1768?

Why did Parliament pass the Coercive Acts in 1774?

How did enslaved people in the colonies react to the stirrings of revolution?

Conclusion: What changes did the American colonists want in 1775?

☑ **LearningCurve** Check what you know. bedfordstmartins.com /roarkunderstanding

161

When news of the *Gaspée* investigation spread, it was greeted with disbelief in other colonies. Patrick Henry, Thomas Jefferson, and Richard Henry Lee in the Virginia House of Burgesses proposed that a network of standing committees be established to link the colonies and pass along alarming news. By mid-1773, all but one colonial assembly had set up a "committee of correspondence."

Massachusetts, the continuing hotspot of the conflict, developed its own rapid communications network, with urgency provided by a new proposal by Lord North to pay the salaries of county court justices out of the tea revenue, reminiscent of Townshend's plan for paying royal governors. By the spring of 1773, more than half the towns in Massachusetts had set up **committees of correspondence** to receive, discuss, distribute, and act on political news. The first message to circulate came from Boston. It framed North's salary plan for judges as the latest proof of a British conspiracy to undermine traditional liberties: first taxation without consent, then military occupation and a massacre, and now a plot to subvert the justice system. Express riders swiftly distributed the message, which sparked ordinary townspeople to embrace a revolutionary language of rights and constitutional duties. Eventually the committees of correspondence would foster rapid mobilization to defend a countryside feeling under literal attack.

The paramount incident shattering the relative calm of the early 1770s was the **Tea Act of 1773**. Americans had resumed buying the taxed British tea, but they were also smuggling large quantities of Dutch tea, cutting into the sales of Britain's East India Company. So Lord North proposed legislation giving favored status to the East India Company, allowing it to sell tea directly to a few selected merchants in four colonial cities, cutting out British middlemen. The hope was to lower the price of the East India tea, including the duty, below that of smuggled Dutch tea, thus motivating Americans to obey the law.

Tea in Boston Harbor

In the fall of 1773, news of the Tea Act reached the colonies. Parliamentary legislation to make tea inexpensive struck many colonists as an insidious plot to trick Americans into buying the dutied tea. The real goal, some argued, was the increased revenue that would pay the salaries of royal governors and judges.

But how to resist the Tea Act? Nonimportation was not viable, because the tea trade was too lucrative to expect merchants to give it up willingly. Consumer boycotts seemed ineffective, because it was impossible to distinguish between dutied tea and smuggled tea once it was in the teapot. The appointment of official tea agents, parallel to the Stamp Act distributors, suggested one solution. In every port city, revived Sons of Liberty pressured tea agents to resign. Without agents, governors yielded, and tea cargoes either landed duty-free or were sent home.

Governor Hutchinson, however, would not bend any rules. Three ships bearing tea arrived in Boston in November 1773. The ships cleared customs, and the crews, sensing the town's extreme tension, unloaded all cargo except the tea. Picking up on the tension in Boston, the captains wished to return to England, but Hutchinson would not grant them clearance to leave without paying the tea duty. He gave them twenty days to pay, after which time the tea would be confiscated.

committees of correspondence
▶ A communications network established among towns in Massachusetts and also among colonial capital towns in 1772–1773 to provide for rapid dissemination of news about important political developments. These committees politicized ordinary townspeople, sparking a revolutionary language of rights and duties.

Tea Act of 1773
▶ British act that lowered the existing tax on tea to entice boycotting Americans to buy it. Resistance to the Tea Act led to the passage of the Coercive Acts and imposition of military rule in Massachusetts.

CHAPTER LOCATOR

How did the Seven Years' War lay the groundwork for colonial crisis?

Why did the Sugar Act and the Stamp Act draw fierce opposition from colonists?

162   CHAPTER 6
THE BRITISH EMPIRE AND THE COLONIAL CRISIS

TABLE 6.1 ■ The Coercive (Intolerable) Acts

1. Boston Port Act	Closed Boston harbor to all shipping as of June 1, 1774, until the destroyed tea was paid for. Britain's objective was to halt the commercial life of the city.
2. Massachusetts Government Act	Augmented the royal governor's powers. The governor could appoint the Massachusetts council, which before was elected. He could appoint and remove all judges, sheriffs, and officers of the court. Going forward, town meetings could be held only with the governor's approval.
3. Impartial Administration of Justice Act	Stipulated that any royal official accused of a capital crime would be tried in Britain. The act implied that there would be further violent confrontations between British soldiers and colonists.
4. Quartering Act	Permitted military commanders to lodge soldiers wherever necessary, even in private households, a step toward military rule in Massachusetts.
5. Quebec Act	Not directly related to the Coercive Acts, it gave control of disputed land throughout the Ohio Valley to Quebec.

For the full twenty days, crowds swelled by concerned people from surrounding towns kept the pressure high. On the final day, December 16, a large crowd gathered at Old South Church to debate a course of action. No solution emerged at that meeting, but immediately after, 100 to 150 men disguised as Indians boarded the three ships and dumped thousands of pounds of tea into the harbor while a crowd of 2,000 watched. In admiration, John Adams wrote: "This Destruction of the Tea is so bold, so daring, so firm, intrepid and inflexible, and it must have so important Consequences."

The Coercive Acts

Lord North's response was swift and stern: In 1774, he persuaded Parliament to issue the **Coercive Acts**, four laws meant to punish Massachusetts. In America, those laws, along with a fifth one, the Quebec Act, were soon known as the **Intolerable Acts** (**Table 6.1**). In a related move, Lord North appointed General Thomas Gage, commander of the Royal Army in New York, governor of Massachusetts, replacing Thomas Hutchinson.

These five acts spread alarm in all the colonies. If Britain could squelch Massachusetts — change its charter, suspend local government, inaugurate military rule, and on top of that give Ohio to Catholic Quebec — what liberties were secure? Fearful royal governors in a half dozen colonies dismissed the sitting assemblies, adding to the sense of urgency. A few of the assemblies defiantly continued to meet in new locations. Via the committees of correspondence, colonial leaders arranged to convene in Philadelphia in September 1774 to respond to the crisis.

Beyond Boston: Rural New England

The Coercive Acts fired up all of New England to open insubordination. With a British general occupying the Massachusetts governorship and some three

Coercive (Intolerable) Acts
▶ Four British acts of 1774 meant to punish Massachusetts for the destruction of three shiploads of tea. Known in America as the Intolerable Acts, they led to open rebellion in the northern colonies.

| Why did British authorities send troops to occupy Boston in the fall of 1768? | **Why did Parliament pass the Coercive Acts in 1774?** | How did enslaved people in the colonies react to the stirrings of revolution? | Conclusion: What changes did the American colonists want in 1775? | ✓ LearningCurve Check what you know. bedfordstmartins.com /roarkunderstanding |

163

thousand troops controlling Boston, the revolutionary momentum shifted from urban radicals to rural farmers who protested in dozens of spontaneous, dramatic showdowns. Some towns found creative ways to get around the prohibition on new town meetings, and others just ignored the law. Governor Gage's call for elections for a new provincial assembly under his control sparked the formation of a competing unauthorized assembly that met in defiance of his orders. In all Massachusetts counties outside Boston, crowds of thousands of armed men converged to prevent the opening of county courts run by crown-appointed jurists. By August 1774, farmers and artisans all over Massachusetts had effectively taken full control of their local institutions.

Gage was especially distressed by the military preparations of citizen militias, drilling on village greens to gain proficiency with muskets. The governor wrote London begging for troop reinforcements, and he beefed up fortifications around Boston. But without more soldiers, his options were limited. Seizing stockpiles of gunpowder was his best move.

The Powder Alarm of September 1 showed just how ready the defiant Americans were to take up arms against Britain. Gage sent troops to a town just outside Boston reported to have a hidden powder storehouse, and in the surprise and scramble of the attack, false news spread that the troops had fired on men defending the powder, killing six. Within twenty-four hours, several thousand armed men from Massachusetts, New Hampshire, and Connecticut streamed on foot to Boston to avenge the first blood spilled. At this moment, ordinary men became insurgents, willing to kill or be killed in the face of the British clampdown. Once the error was corrected and the crisis defused, the men returned home peaceably. But Gage could no longer doubt the speed and determination of the rebellious subjects.

All this had occurred without orchestration by Boston radicals, Gage reported. But British leaders found it hard to believe, as one put it, that "a tumultuous Rabble, without any Appearance of general Concert, or without any Head to advise, or Leader to conduct" could pull off such effective resistance. Repeatedly in the years to come, the British would seriously underestimate their opponents.

The First Continental Congress

First Continental Congress
▶ September 1774 gathering of colonial delegates in Philadelphia to discuss the crisis precipitated by the Coercive Acts. The congress produced a declaration of rights and an agreement to impose a limited boycott of trade with Britain.

Every colony except Georgia sent delegates to Philadelphia in September 1774 to discuss the looming crisis at the **First Continental Congress**. Delegates sought to articulate their liberties as British subjects and the powers Parliament held over them, and they debated possible responses to the Coercive Acts. Some wanted a total ban on trade with Britain to force repeal, while others, especially southerners dependent on tobacco and rice exports, opposed halting trade. Samuel Adams and Patrick Henry were eager for a ringing denunciation of all parliamentary control. The conservative Joseph Galloway of Pennsylvania proposed a plan (quickly defeated) to create a secondary parliament in America to assist the British Parliament in ruling the colonies.

The congress met for seven weeks and produced a declaration of rights couched in traditional language: "We ask only for peace, liberty and security. We wish no diminution of royal prerogatives, we demand no new rights." But from Britain's point of view, the rights assumed already to exist were radical. Chief

CHAPTER LOCATOR | How did the Seven Years' War lay the groundwork for colonial crisis? | Why did the Sugar Act and the Stamp Act draw fierce opposition from colonists?

164 CHAPTER 6 THE BRITISH EMPIRE AND THE COLONIAL CRISIS

among them was the claim that because Americans were not represented in Parliament, each colonial government had the sole right to govern and tax its own people. To put pressure on Britain, the delegates agreed to a staggered and limited boycott of trade: imports prohibited this year, exports the following, and rice totally exempted (to keep South Carolinians happy). To enforce the boycott, they called for a Continental Association, with chapters in each town variously called committees of public safety or of inspection, to monitor all commerce and punish suspected violators of the boycott. Its work done in a month, the congress disbanded with an agreement to reconvene in May.

The committees of public safety, the committees of correspondence, the regrouped colonial assemblies, and the Continental Congress were all political bodies functioning defiantly without any constitutional authority. British officials did not recognize them as legitimate, but many Americans who supported the patriot cause instantly accepted them. A key reason for the stability of such unauthorized governing bodies was that they were composed of many of the same men who had held elective office before.

Britain's severe reaction to Boston's destruction of the tea finally succeeded in making many colonists from New Hampshire to Georgia realize that the problems of British rule went far beyond questions of nonconsensual taxation. The Coercive Acts infringed on liberty and denied self-government; they could not be ignored. With one colony already subordinated to military rule and a British army camped in Boston, the threat of a general war was very real.

QUICK REVIEW

In what ways did colonial responses to British actions change after 1772?

Why did British authorities send troops to occupy Boston in the fall of 1768?

Why did Parliament pass the Coercive Acts in 1774?

How did enslaved people in the colonies react to the stirrings of revolution?

Conclusion: What changes did the American colonists want in 1775?

✓ LearningCurve
Check what you know.
bedfordstmartins.com
/roarkunderstanding

165

How did enslaved people in the colonies react to the stirrings of revolution?

Phillis Wheatley's Title Page Phillis, born in Africa, was sold into slavery to John Wheatley of Boston at age seven. She published her first poem at age twelve, in 1766. In 1773, her master took her to London, where *Poems on Various Subjects, Religious and Moral* was published, gaining her great literary notice. Library of Congress.

BEFORE THE SECOND CONTINENTAL CONGRESS could meet, violence and bloodshed came to Massachusetts in the towns of Lexington and Concord. Fearing domestic insurrection, General Thomas Gage sent his soldiers there to capture an ammunition depot, but New England farmers mobilized against an intrusive power they feared would enslave them. To the south, a different and inverted version of the same story began to unfold, as thousands of enslaved black men and women seized an unprecedented opportunity to mount a different kind of insurrection — against planter-patriots who looked over their shoulders uneasily whenever they called out for liberty from the British.

Lexington and Concord

During the winter of 1774–75, Americans pressed on with boycotts. Optimists hoped to effect a repeal of the Coercive Acts; pessimists stockpiled arms and ammunition. In Massachusetts, militia units known as minutemen prepared to respond at a minute's notice to any threat from the British troops in Boston.

Thomas Gage realized how desperate the British position was. The people, Gage wrote Lord North, were "numerous, worked up to a fury, and not a Boston rabble but the freeholders and farmers of the country." Gage requested twenty thousand reinforcements. He also strongly advised repeal of the Coercive Acts, but leaders in Britain could not admit failure. Instead, in mid-April 1775, they ordered Gage to arrest the troublemakers.

CHAPTER LOCATOR | How did the Seven Years' War lay the groundwork for colonial crisis? | Why did the Sugar Act and the Stamp Act draw fierce opposition from colonists?

CHAPTER 6
166 THE BRITISH EMPIRE AND THE COLONIAL CRISIS

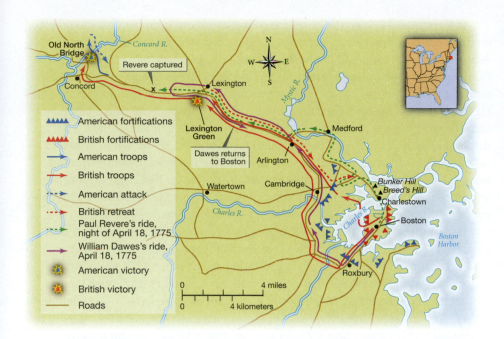

Two Americans slipped out of Boston to warn of a surprise British attack on Concord. Paul Revere went by boat to Charlestown and then by horse to Lexington, while William Dawes casually rode past British sentries and then galloped at full speed through Lexington to Concord.

> **MAP ACTIVITY**

READING THE MAP: How did Dawes's route differ from Revere's? What kinds of terrain and potential dangers did each man face during his ride, according to the map?
CONNECTIONS: Why send two men on the same mission? Why not send four or more?

Gage quickly planned a surprise attack on a suspected ammunition storage site at Concord, a village eighteen miles west of Boston (**Map 6.3**). Near midnight on April 18, British soldiers moved west across the Charles River. Paul Revere and William Dawes raced ahead to alert the minutemen. When the British soldiers got to Lexington, five miles east of Concord, they were met by some seventy armed men. The British commander barked out, "Lay down your arms, you damned rebels, and disperse." The militiamen hesitated and began to comply, but then someone — nobody knows who — fired. Within two minutes, eight Americans were dead and ten were wounded.

The British units continued their march to Concord, any pretense of surprise gone. Three companies of minutemen nervously occupied the town center but offered no challenge to the British as they searched in vain for the ammunition. Finally, at Old North Bridge in Concord, British troops and minutemen exchanged shots, killing two Americans and three British soldiers. As the British returned to Boston, militia units ambushed them, bringing the bloodiest fighting of the day. In the end, 273 British soldiers were wounded or dead; the toll for the Americans stood at about 95. It was April 19, 1775, and the war had begun.

Rebelling against Slavery

News of the battles of Lexington and Concord spread within days. In Virginia, Thomas Jefferson observed that "a phrenzy of revenge seems to have seized all ranks of people," causing the royal governor of Virginia, Lord Dunmore, to remove all gunpowder from the Williamsburg powder house to a ship, out of reach of angry Virginians. Dunmore also threatened to arm slaves, if necessary, to ward off attacks by colonists. This proved effective for several months.

Why did British authorities send troops to occupy Boston in the fall of 1768? | Why did Parliament pass the Coercive Acts in 1774? | **How did enslaved people in the colonies react to the stirrings of revolution?** | Conclusion: What changes did the American colonists want in 1775? | ✓ LearningCurve Check what you know. bedfordstmartins.com /roarkunderstanding

In November 1775, as the crisis deepened, Dunmore issued an official proclamation promising freedom to defecting able-bodied slaves who would fight for the British. He had no intention of liberating all slaves, and astute blacks noticed that Dunmore neglected to free his own slaves. A Virginia barber named Caesar declared that "he did not know any one foolish enough to believe him [Dunmore], for if he intended to do so, he ought first to set his own free." Within a month, some fifteen hundred slaves had joined Dunmore's "Ethiopian Regiment." Camp diseases quickly set in: dysentery, typhoid fever, and smallpox. When Dunmore sailed for England in mid-1776, he took three hundred black survivors with him. But the association of freedom with the British authorities had been established, and throughout the war thousands more southern slaves fled their masters whenever the British army was close enough to offer safe refuge.

In the northern colonies as well, slaves clearly recognized the evolving political struggle with Britain as an ideal moment to bid for freedom. A twenty-one-year-old Boston domestic slave employed biting sarcasm in a 1774 newspaper essay to call attention to the hypocrisy of local slave owners: "How well the Cry for Liberty, and the reverse Disposition for exercise of oppressive Power over others agree, — I humbly think it does not require the Penetration of a Philosopher to Determine." This extraordinary young woman, Phillis Wheatley, had already gained international recognition through a book of poems published in London in 1773. Wheatley's poems spoke of "Fair Freedom" as the "Goddess long desir'd" by Africans enslaved in America. Wheatley's master freed the young poet in 1775.

From north to south, groups of slaves pressed their case. Several Boston blacks offered to fight for the British in exchange for freedom, but General Gage turned them down. In Maryland, a planter complained that blacks impatient for freedom had to be disarmed of about eighty guns along with some swords. In North Carolina, white suspicions about a planned slave uprising led to the arrest of scores of African Americans who were ordered to be whipped by the revolutionary committee of public safety.

By 1783, when the Revolutionary War ended, as many as twenty thousand blacks had voted against slavery with their feet by seeking refuge with the British army. About half failed to achieve the liberation they were seeking, instead succumbing to disease, especially smallpox, in refuge camps. But some eight thousand to ten thousand persisted through the war and later, under the protection of the British army, left America to start new lives of freedom in Canada's Nova Scotia or Africa's Sierra Leone.

> QUICK REVIEW

What was the connection between rebelling against slavery and rebelling against the British?

CHAPTER LOCATOR | How did the Seven Years' War lay the groundwork for colonial crisis? | Why did the Sugar Act and the Stamp Act draw fierce opposition from colonists?

Conclusion: What changes did the American colonists want in 1775?

IN THE AFTERMATH of the Seven Years' War, neither losers nor victors came away satisfied. France lost vast amounts of North American land claims, and Indian land rights were increasingly violated or ignored. Britain's huge war debt and subsequent revenue-generating policies distressed Americans and set the stage for the imperial crisis of the 1760s and 1770s. The years 1763 to 1775 brought repeated attempts by the British government to subordinate the colonies into contributing partners in the larger scheme of empire.

American resistance to British policies grew slowly but steadily. In 1765, both loyalist Thomas Hutchinson and patriot Samuel Adams agreed that it was unwise for Britain to assert a right to taxation because Parliament did not adequately represent Americans. As a royal official, Hutchinson was obliged to uphold policy, while Adams protested and made political activists out of thousands in the process.

By 1775, events propelled many Americans to the conclusion that a concerted effort was afoot to deprive them of all their liberties, the most important of which were the right to self-rule and the right to live free of an occupying army. Prepared to die for those liberties, hundreds of minutemen converged on Concord. April 19 marked the start of their rebellion. Another rebellion under way in 1775 was doomed to be short-circuited. Black Americans who had experienced actual slavery listened to shouts of "Liberty!" from white crowds and appropriated the language of revolution to their own circumstances. Defiance of authority was indeed contagious.

Despite the military conflict at the battles of Lexington and Concord, a war with Britain seemed far from inevitable to colonists outside New England. In the months ahead, American colonial leaders pursued peaceful as well as military solutions to the question of who actually had authority over them. By the end of 1775, however, reconciliation with the crown would be unattainable.

Why did British authorities send troops to occupy Boston in the fall of 1768?

Why did Parliament pass the Coercive Acts in 1774?

How did enslaved people in the colonies react to the stirrings of revolution?

Conclusion: What changes did the American colonists want in 1775?

LearningCurve Check what you know. bedfordstmartins.com /roarkunderstanding

CHAPTER 6 STUDY GUIDE

STEP 1

GET STARTED ONLINE

LearningCurve ■ bedfordstmartins.com/roarkunderstanding

Now that you've read the chapter, make it stick by completing the LearningCurve activity.

STEP 2

EXPLAIN WHY IT MATTERS

Put your reading into practice. Identify each term below, and then explain why it matters in U.S. history.

TERM	WHO OR WHAT & WHEN	WHY IT MATTERS
Seven Years' War (p. 142)		
Pontiac's Rebellion (p. 148)		
Sugar (Revenue) Act (p. 151)		
Stamp Act (p. 151)		
virtual representation (p. 152)		
Declaratory Act (p. 155)		
Townshend duties (p. 157)		
Boston Massacre (p. 160)		
committees of correspondence (p. 162)		
Tea Act of 1773 (p. 162)		
Coercive (Intolerable) Acts (p. 163)		
First Continental Congress (p. 164)		

STEP 3

MOVE BEYOND THE BASICS

To demonstrate a more advanced understanding, describe the key pieces of British legislation aimed at the colonies between 1763 and 1774, the British rationale, and the colonial response.

Legislation	Provisions	British rationale	Colonial response
Proclamation of 1763			
Sugar (Revenue) Act			
Stamp Act			
Townshend duties			
Tea Act of 1773			
Coercive (Intolerable) Acts			

PUT IT ALL TOGETHER

Now, take a step back and try to explain the big picture. Remember to use specific examples from the chapter in your answers.

THE SEVEN YEARS' WAR

▶ How did the outcome of the Seven Years' War change the European balance of power in North America?

▶ How did British and colonial views of the war and its consequences differ?

TAXING THE COLONIES

▶ Why did some colonists see British efforts to tax the colonies as illegitimate? How did the British justify their efforts to raise revenue?

▶ What different groups, both in the colonies and in Great Britain, encouraged Parliament to repeal various taxes? What were their motives?

THE ESCALATION OF THE CONFLICT

▶ Why was the Tea Act so provocative? How did some colonists protest its passage?

▶ How did the British response to these protests, and the colonial reaction, help put Britain and the colonies on the path toward war?

LOOKING BACKWARD, LOOKING AHEAD

▶ How did the relationship between Britain and its North American colonies before 1763 differ from the relationship after 1763?

▶ Was war between Britain and the colonies inevitable after 1774? Why or why not?

> ## IN YOUR OWN WORDS

Imagine that you must give an oral report to the class answering the following question: **What were the most significant factors contributing to deteriorating relations between Britain and its North American colonies?** What would be the most important points to include and why?

 Do it online at the Student Site ■ bedfordstmartins.com/roarkunderstanding

7

FIGHTING THE AMERICAN REVOLUTION

1775–1783

> **How were the North American colonists able to successfully gain their independence from Great Britain in 1783?** Chapter 7 follows the course of the American Revolution from the Declaration of Independence in 1776 to the Treaty of Paris in 1783. It examines the events leading up to the signing of the Declaration of Independence, the military strategies of both sides, the experience of war on the home front, the role of Native Americans and the French, and the ultimate defeat of the British against seemingly improbable odds.

LearningCurve
bedfordstmartins.com/roarkunderstanding
After reading the chapter, use LearningCurve to retain what you've read.

Grosvenor and Salem, 1775. Lieutenant Thomas Grosvenor (1744–1825) and his servant Peter Salem at the Battle of Bunker Hill, 17 June 1775. Detail of an oil painting on canvas, 1786, by John Trumbull. The Granger Collection.

> Why did Americans wait so long before they declared their independence?

> What initial challenges did the opposing armies face?

> What role did the home front play in the war?

> How were Native Americans and the French involved in the war?

> Why did the British southern strategy ultimately fail?

> Conclusion: Why did the British lose the American Revolution?

Why did Americans wait so long before they declared their independence?

Second Continental Congress

▶ Legislative body that governed the United States from May 1775 through the war's duration. It established an army, created its own money, and declared independence once all hope for a peaceful reconciliation with Britain was gone.

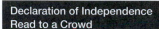N MAY 10, 1775, nearly one month after the fighting at Lexington and Concord, the **Second Continental Congress** assembled in Philadelphia. The congress immediately set to work on two crucial but contradictory tasks: to raise and supply an army and to explore reconciliation with Britain. To raise an army, they needed soldiers and a commander, they needed money, and they needed to work out a declaration of war. To reconcile with Britain, they needed diplomacy to approach the king. But King George III was not receptive, and by 1776, as the war progressed and hopes of reconciliation faded, delegates at the congress began to ponder the treasonous act of declaring independence.

Assuming Political and Military Authority

The delegates to the Second Continental Congress were prominent figures at home, but they now had to learn to know and trust one another. Moreover, they did not always agree. The Adams cousins John and Samuel defined the radical end of the spectrum, favoring independence. John Dickinson of Pennsylvania,

CHAPTER LOCATOR | **Why did Americans wait so long before they declared their independence?** | What initial challenges did the opposing armies face?

174   **CHAPTER 7**   FIGHTING THE AMERICAN REVOLUTION

who in 1767 critiqued British tax policy in *Letters from a Farmer*, was now a moderate, seeking reconciliation with Britain. Benjamin Franklin, fresh off a ship from an eleven-year residence in London, was feared by some to be a British spy. Mutual suspicions flourished easily when the undertaking was so dangerous, opinions were so varied, and a misstep could spell disaster.

Most of the delegates were not yet prepared to break with Britain. Some felt that government without a king was unworkable, while others feared it might be suicidal to lose Britain's protection against its traditional enemies, France and Spain. Colonies that traded actively with Britain feared undermining their economies. Probably the vast majority of ordinary Americans were unable to envision complete independence from the monarchy.

The few men at the Continental Congress who did think that independence was desirable were, not surprisingly, from Massachusetts, the target of the Coercive Acts. Even so, those men knew that it was premature to push for a break with Britain. John Adams wrote his wife, Abigail, in June 1775: "America is a great, unwieldy body. Its progress must be slow. It is like a large fleet sailing under convoy. The fleetest sailors must wait for the dullest and slowest."

Yet swift action was needed, for the Massachusetts countryside was under threat of further attack. Even the hesitant moderates in the congress agreed that a military buildup was necessary. Around the country, militia units from New York to Georgia collected arms and trained on village greens in anticipation. On June 14, the congress voted to create the **Continental army**, choosing a Virginian, George Washington, as commander in chief. This sent the clear message that there was widespread commitment to war beyond New England.

Next the congress drew up a document titled "A Declaration on the Causes and Necessity of Taking Up Arms," which rehearsed familiar arguments about the tyranny of Parliament and the need to defend English liberties. This declaration was first drafted by a young Virginia planter, Thomas Jefferson, a radical on the question of independence. The moderate John Dickinson, fearing that the declaration would offend Britain, was allowed to rewrite it. However, he left intact much of Jefferson's highly charged language about choosing "to die freemen rather than to live slaves."

To pay for the military buildup, the congress authorized a currency issue of $2 million. The Continental dollars were merely paper; they were not backed by gold or silver. The delegates somewhat naively expected that the currency would be accepted as valuable on trust as it spread in the population through the hands of soldiers, farmers, munitions suppliers, and beyond.

In just two months, the Second Continental Congress had created an army, declared war, and issued its own currency. It had taken on the major functions of a legitimate government, both military and financial, without any legal basis for its authority, for it had not yet declared independence from the king.

Pursuing Both War and Peace

The second battle of the Revolution occurred on June 16, 1775, in Boston. New England militia units had fortified the hilly terrain of the peninsula of Charlestown, which faced the city, and Thomas Gage, still commander in Boston, prepared to attack, aided by the arrival of new troops and three talented generals, William Howe, John Burgoyne, and Henry Clinton.

> **CHRONOLOGY**

1775
– Second Continental Congress convenes.
– Battle of Bunker Hill.
– Olive Branch Petition.

1776
– *Common Sense* is published.
– British evacuate Boston.
– Declaration of Independence.

Continental army

▶ The army created in June 1775 by the Second Continental Congress to oppose the British. Virginian George Washington, commander in chief, had the task of turning local militias and untrained volunteers into a disciplined army.

Battle of Bunker Hill, 1775

What role did the home front play in the war?

How were Native Americans and the French involved in the war?

Why did the British southern strategy ultimately fail?

Conclusion: Why did the British lose the American Revolution?

☑ LearningCurve
Check what you know.
bedfordstmartins.com
/roarkunderstanding

175

General William Howe insisted on a bold frontal assault, sending 2,500 soldiers across the water and up Bunker Hill in an intimidating but potentially costly attack. Three bloody assaults were needed before the British took the hill, the third succeeding mainly because the American ammunition supply gave out, and the defenders quickly retreated. The **battle of Bunker Hill** was thus a British victory, but an expensive one. The dead numbered 226 on the British side, with more than 800 wounded; the Americans suffered 140 dead, 271 wounded, and 30 captured.

Instead of pursuing the fleeing Americans, Howe retreated to Boston, unwilling to risk more raids into the countryside. If the British had had any grasp of the basic instability of the American units around Boston, they might have decisively defeated the Continental army in its infancy. Instead, they lingered in Boston, abandoning it without a fight nine months later.

Howe used the time in Boston to inoculate his army against smallpox because a new epidemic of the deadly disease was spreading in port cities along the Atlantic. Inoculation worked by producing a mild but real (and therefore risky) case of smallpox, followed by lifelong immunity. Howe's instinct was right: During the American Revolution, some 130,000 people on the American continent, most of them Indians, died of smallpox.

A week after Bunker Hill, when General Washington arrived to take charge of the new Continental army, he found enthusiastic but undisciplined troops. Sanitation was an unknown concept, with inadequate latrines fouling the campground. Washington attributed the disarray to the New England custom of letting militia units elect their own officers, which he felt undermined deference. Washington spotted a militia captain, a barber in civilian life, shaving an ordinary soldier, and he moved quickly to impose more hierarchy and authority. "Be easy," he advised his newly appointed officers, "but not too familiar, lest you subject yourself to a want of that respect, which is necessary to support a proper command."

While military plans moved forward, the Second Continental Congress pursued its contradictory objective: reconciliation with Britain. Delegates from the middle colonies (Pennsylvania, Delaware, and New York), whose merchants depended on trade with Britain, urged that channels for negotiation remain open. In July 1775, congressional moderates led by John Dickinson engineered an appeal to the king called the Olive Branch Petition, affirming loyalty to the monarchy and blaming all the troubles on the king's ministers and on Parliament. It proposed that the American colonial assemblies be recognized as individual parliaments under the umbrella of the monarchy. King George III rejected the Olive Branch Petition and heatedly condemned the Americans as traitors.

battle of Bunker Hill
▶ Second battle of the war, on June 16, 1775, involving a massive British attack on New England militia units on a hill facing Boston. The militiamen finally yielded the hill, but not before inflicting heavy casualties on the British.

Thomas Paine, Abigail Adams, and the Case for Independence

Pressure for independence started to mount in January 1776, when a pamphlet titled *Common Sense* appeared in Philadelphia. Thomas Paine, its author, was an English artisan and coffeehouse intellectual who had come to America in the fall of 1774. With the encouragement of members of the Second Continental Congress, he wrote *Common Sense* to justify independence.

Common Sense
▶ A pamphlet written by Thomas Paine in 1776 that laid out the case for independence. In it, Paine rejected monarchy, advocating its replacement with republican government based on the consent of the people. The pamphlet influenced public opinion throughout the colonies.

CHAPTER LOCATOR | Why did Americans wait so long before they declared their independence? | What initial challenges did the opposing armies face?

176   CHAPTER 7   FIGHTING THE AMERICAN REVOLUTION

An Exact View of the Late Battle at Charlestown, June 17th 1775

This engraving was for sale within weeks of the battle of Bunker Hill. British and American soldiers in fixed formation fire muskets at each other, while Charlestown is in flames in the background. Who would buy this picture? Technically, the British won the battle by taking the hill. Is that the story being told here? Colonial Williamsburg Foundation.

In simple yet forceful language, Paine elaborated on the absurdities of the British monarchy. Why should one man, by accident of birth, claim extensive power over others? he asked. A king might be foolish or wicked. "One of the strongest natural proofs of the folly of hereditary right in kings," Paine wrote, "is that nature disapproves it; otherwise she would not so frequently turn it into ridicule by giving mankind *an ass for a lion*." To replace monarchy, Paine advocated republican government based on the consent of the people. Rulers, according to Paine, were only representatives of the people, and the best form of government relied on frequent elections to achieve the most direct democracy possible.

Paine's pamphlet sold more than 150,000 copies in a matter of weeks. Newspapers reprinted it; men read it aloud in taverns and coffeehouses; John Adams sent a copy to his wife, Abigail, who passed it around to neighbors in Braintree, Massachusetts. New Englanders desired independence, but other colonies, under no immediate threat of violence, remained cautious.

Abigail Adams was impatient not only for independence but also for other legal changes that would revolutionize the new country. In a series of astute letters to her husband, she outlined obstacles and gave advice. She worried that southern slave owners might shrink from a war in the name of liberty: "I have

| What role did the home front play in the war? | How were Native Americans and the French involved in the war? | Why did the British southern strategy ultimately fail? | Conclusion: Why did the British lose the American Revolution? | ☑ **LearningCurve** Check what you know. bedfordstmartins.com /roarkunderstanding |

sometimes been ready to think that the passion for Liberty cannot be Equally strong in the Breasts of those who have been accustomed to deprive their fellow Creatures of theirs." And in March 1776, she expressed her hope that women's legal status would improve under the new government: "In the new Code of Laws which I suppose it will be necessary for you to make I desire you would Remember the Ladies, and be more generous and favourable to them than your ancestors." John Adams dismissed his wife's concerns. But to a male politician, John privately rehearsed the reasons why women (and men who were free blacks, or young, or propertyless) should remain excluded from political participation. Even though he concluded that nothing should change, at least Abigail's letter had forced him to ponder the exclusion, something few men — or women — did in 1776. Urgent talk of political independence was as radical as most could imagine.

The Declaration of Independence

In addition to Paine's *Common Sense*, another factor hastening independence was the prospect of an alliance with France, Britain's archrival. France was willing to provide military supplies and naval power only if assured that the Americans would separate from Britain. News that the British were negotiating to hire German mercenary soldiers further solidified support for independence. By May 1776, all but four colonies were agitating for a declaration. The holdouts were Pennsylvania, Maryland, New York, and South Carolina, the latter two containing large loyalist populations. An exasperated Virginian wrote to his friend in the congress, "For God's sake, why do you dawdle in the Congress so strangely? Why do you not at once declare yourself a separate independent state?"

In early June, the Virginia delegation introduced a resolution calling for independence. The moderates still commanded enough support to postpone a vote on the measure until July. In the meantime, the congress appointed a committee,

CHAPTER LOCATOR | **Why did Americans wait so long before they declared their independence?** | What initial challenges did the opposing armies face?

178 CHAPTER 7 FIGHTING THE AMERICAN REVOLUTION

with Thomas Jefferson and others, to draft a longer document setting out the case for independence.

On July 2, after intense politicking, all but one state voted for independence; New York abstained. The congress then turned to the document drafted by Jefferson and his committee. Jefferson began with a preamble that articulated philosophical principles about natural rights, equality, the right of revolution, and the consent of the governed as the only true basis for government. He then listed more than two dozen specific grievances against King George. The congress passed over the preamble with little comment, and instead wrangled over the list of grievances, especially the issue of slavery. Jefferson had included an impassioned statement blaming the king for slavery, which delegates from Georgia and South Carolina struck out, not wishing to denounce their labor system. But the congress let stand another of Jefferson's grievances, blaming the king for mobilizing "the merciless Indian Savages" into bloody frontier warfare, a reference to Pontiac's Rebellion (see chapter 6).

On July 4, the amendments to Jefferson's text were complete, and the congress formally adopted the **Declaration of Independence**. A month later, the delegates gathered to sign the official parchment copy. Four men, including John Dickinson, declined to sign; several others "signed with regret . . . and with many doubts," according to John Adams. The document was then printed, widely distributed, and read aloud in celebrations everywhere. (Printed copies did not include the signers' names, for they had committed treason, a crime punishable by death.) On July 15, the New York delegation came on board, making the vote on independence unanimous.

Declaration of Independence
▶ A document containing philosophical principles and a list of grievances that declared separation from Britain. The Second Continental Congress adopted the Declaration on July 4, 1776, ending a period of intense debate with moderates still hoping to reconcile with Britain.

QUICK REVIEW

Why were many Americans initially reluctant to pursue independence from Britain?

What role did the home front play in the war?

How were Native Americans and the French involved in the war?

Why did the British southern strategy ultimately fail?

Conclusion: Why did the British lose the American Revolution?

☑ **LearningCurve**
Check what you know.
bedfordstmartins.com
/roarkunderstanding

What initial challenges did the opposing armies face?

Backcountry Riflemen

A German officer with the British army drew this sketch of two American riflemen, dressed in rustic hunting shirts and leggings. One wears moccasins; the other is barefoot. Their celebrated ability to hit small targets at great distances and their willingness to snipe from behind trees and aim particularly at officers made them a terror to the British. Ten companies of riflemen were recruited in 1775 from western Pennsylvania and Virginia. General Washington worried that they were too undisciplined to make good soldiers, but others suggested that the trademark hunting shirt should become the Continental army uniform for all soldiers, just for the fear it provoked in the enemy. Anne S. K. Brown Military College, Brown University Library.

BOTH SIDES APPROACHED the war for America with uneasiness. The Americans, with inexperienced militias, were opposing the mightiest military power in the world. Also, their country was not unified; many people remained loyal to Britain. The British faced serious obstacles as well. Their disdain for the fighting abilities of the Americans required reassessment in light of the Bunker Hill battle. The logistics of supplying an army with food across three thousand miles of water were daunting. And since the British goal was to regain allegiance, not to destroy and conquer, the army was often constrained in its actions.

The American Military Forces

Americans claimed that the initial months of the war were purely defensive, triggered by the British invasion. But the war also quickly became a rebellion, an overthrowing of long-established authority. As both defenders and rebels, many Americans were highly motivated to fight, and the potential manpower that could be mobilized was, in theory, very great.

CHAPTER LOCATOR | Why did Americans wait so long before they declared their independence? | **What initial challenges did the opposing armies face?**

180 **CHAPTER 7**
FIGHTING THE AMERICAN REVOLUTION

Local defense in the colonies had long rested with a militia composed of all able-bodied men over age sixteen. Militias, however, were best suited for local and limited engagements, responding to conflict with Indians or slave rebellions. In forming the Continental army, the congress set enlistment at one year, which proved inadequate as the war progressed. Incentives produced longer commitments: a $20 bonus for three years of service, a hundred acres of land for enlistment for the duration of the war. Over the course of the war, some 230,000 men enlisted, about one-quarter of the white male adult population.

Women also served in the Continental army, cooking, washing, and nursing the wounded. Close to 20,000 "camp followers," as they were called, served during the war, many of them wives of men in service. Some 12,000 children also tagged along, and babies were born in the camps. Some women helped during battles, supplying drinking water or ammunition to soldiers.

Black Americans at first were excluded from the Continental army. But as manpower needs increased, northern states welcomed free blacks into service; slaves in some states could serve with their masters' permission. About 5,000 black men served in the Revolutionary War on the rebel side, nearly all from the northern states. Black soldiers sometimes were segregated into separate units, and while some of these men were draftees, others were clearly inspired by ideals of freedom in a war against tyranny. For example, twenty-three blacks gave "Liberty," "Freedom," and "Freeman" as their surnames at the time of enlistment.

The American army was at times raw and inexperienced, and often woefully undermanned. It never had the precision and discipline of European professional armies. But it was never as bad as the British continually assumed. The British would learn that it was a serious mistake to underrate the enemy.

Flute-Playing African American

This musician is thought to be Barzillai Lew of Groton, Massachusetts. As a boy, Lew served as a fifer in the Seven Years' War, and in 1775 he again was a fifer in the Revolution through three enlistments, seeing action at Bunker Hill and Fort Ticonderoga. Fife and drum music supplied rhythm and mood for military marches, so fifing was an essential job. Courtesy of Mae Theresa Bonitto; photograph courtesy of the *Boston Globe*.

The British Strategy

The American strategy was straightforward — to repulse and defeat an invading army. The British strategy was not as clear. Britain wanted to put down a rebellion and restore monarchical power in the colonies, but the question was how to accomplish this. A decisive defeat of the Continental army was essential but not sufficient to end the rebellion, for the British would still have to contend with an armed and motivated insurgent population. Furthermore, there was no single political nerve center whose capture would spell certain victory. The Continental Congress moved from place to place, staying just out of reach of the British. During the course of the war, the British captured and occupied every major port city, but that brought no serious loss to the Americans, 95 percent of whom lived in the countryside.

> **> CHRONOLOGY**

1775
– Battle of Quebec.

1776
– Battle of Long Island.
– Washington captures German troops along the Delaware River.

What role did the home front play in the war? | How were Native Americans and the French involved in the war? | Why did the British southern strategy ultimately fail? | Conclusion: Why did the British lose the American Revolution? | ✓ LearningCurve Check what you know. bedfordstmartins.com /roarkunderstanding

181

Britain's delicate task was to restore the old governments, not to destroy an enemy country. British generals were at first reluctant to ravage the countryside, confiscate food, or burn villages. There were thirteen distinct political entities to capture, pacify, and then restore to the crown, and they stretched in a long line from New Hampshire to Georgia. Clearly, a large land army was required for the job. Without the willingness to seize food from the locals, the British needed hundreds of supply ships — hence their desire to capture the ports. The British strategy also assumed that many Americans remained loyal to the king and would come to their aid.

The overall British plan was a divide-and-conquer approach, focusing first on New York, the state judged to have the greatest number of loyal subjects. New York offered a geographic advantage as well: Control of the Hudson River would allow the British to isolate New England. British armies could descend from Canada and move north from New York City along the Hudson River. Squeezed between a naval blockade on the eastern coast and army raids in the west, Massachusetts could be driven to surrender. New Jersey and Pennsylvania would fall in line, the British thought, because of loyalist strength. Virginia was a problem, like Massachusetts, but the British were confident that the Carolinas would help them isolate and subdue Virginia.

Quebec, New York, and New Jersey

In late 1775, an American expedition was launched to capture the cities of Montreal and Quebec before British reinforcements could arrive (**Map 7.1**). This offensive was a clear sign that the war was not purely a reaction to the invasion of Massachusetts. A force of New York Continentals commanded by General Richard Montgomery took Montreal easily in September 1775 and then advanced on Quebec. Meanwhile, a second contingent of Continentals led by Colonel Benedict Arnold moved north through Maine to Quebec, a punishing trek through freezing rain with woefully inadequate supplies. Arnold and Montgomery jointly attacked Quebec in December but failed to take the city. Worse yet, they encountered smallpox, which killed more men than had the battle for Quebec.

The main action of the first year of the war came not in Canada, however, but in New York. In August 1776, some 45,000 British troops (including 8,000 German mercenaries, called Hessians) under the command of General Howe landed south of New York City. General Washington had anticipated this move and had relocated his army of 20,000 south from Massachusetts. The **battle of Long Island** in late August pitted the well-trained British "redcoats" (slang referring to their red uniforms) against a very green Continental army. Howe attacked, inflicting many casualties and taking a thousand prisoners. A British general crowed, "If a good bleeding can bring those Bible-faced Yankees to their senses, the fever of independency should soon abate." Howe failed to press forward, however, perhaps remembering the costly victory of Bunker Hill, and Washington evacuated his troops to Manhattan Island.

Washington knew it would be hard to hold Manhattan, so he withdrew farther north to two forts on either side of the Hudson River. For two months, the armies engaged in limited skirmishing, but in November Howe finally captured

battle of Long Island

▶ First major engagement of the new Continental army, defending against 45,000 British troops newly arrived on western Long Island (today Brooklyn). The Continentals retreated, with high casualties and many taken prisoner.

CHAPTER LOCATOR | Why did Americans wait so long before they declared their independence?

What initial challenges did the opposing armies face?

182   CHAPTER 7
FIGHTING THE AMERICAN REVOLUTION

MAP 7.1 ■ **The War in the North, 1775–1778**

After battles in Massachusetts in 1775, rebel forces invaded Canada but failed to capture Quebec. The British army landed in New York in 1776, causing turmoil in New Jersey in 1777 and 1778. Burgoyne attempted to isolate New England, but he was stopped at Saratoga in 1777 in the decisive battle of the early war.

> MAP ACTIVITY

READING THE MAP: Which general's troops traveled the farthest in each of these years: 1775, 1776, and 1777? How did the availability of water routes affect British and American strategy?
CONNECTIONS: Why did the French wait until early 1778 to join American forces against the British? What did France hope to gain from participating in the war?

Map labels:

BRITISH NORTH AMERICA

Battle of Quebec
Dec. 31, 1775
Siege of Quebec
Nov. 1775–Mar. 1776
Trois Rivières
June 7, 1776
Arnold 1776
Montgomery 1775

MAINE
(part of MASS.)

45°N

Montreal

St. Leger 1777
St. Lawrence R.
Burgoyne 1777
Lake Champlain

Fort Ticonderoga
Captured by British
July 1777

Fort Stanwix
Held by Americans
under Benedict Arnold
Aug. 1777

Lake George

VERMONT
(Claimed by N.Y. & N.H.)

NEW HAMPSHIRE

Kennebec R.

Lake Ontario

Fort Oswego

Oriskany
Aug. 6, 1777

Mohawk R.

Saratoga
Burgoyne surrenders
Oct. 17, 1777

Bemis Heights
Oct. 7, 1777

Gates 1777

Albany

Bennington
Aug. 16, 1777

NEW YORK

Concord
April 19, 1775

Lexington
April 19, 1775

Newburyport
Bunker Hill
June 17, 1775

Arnold 1775

Howe 1776

British leave Boston
March 17, 1776

Siege of Boston
July 1775–March 1776

MASSACHUSETTS

R.I.

CONNECTICUT

Hudson R.

Morristown
American winter quarters
1776–1777

Fort Washington

Fort Lee

PENNSYLVANIA

Delaware R.

Germantown
Oct. 4, 1777

Princeton
Jan. 3, 1777

Brooklyn
Aug. 27, 1776

Manhattan

Long Island

Howe 1776

40°N

Staten Island

Valley Forge
American winter quarters
1777–1778

Washington 1776

Clinton 1778

Brandywine Creek
Sept. 11, 1777

Trenton
Dec. 26, 1776

Monmouth Court House
June 28, 1778

Philadelphia
Captured by British
under Howe
Sept. 26, 1777

MARYLAND

DEL.

Chesapeake Bay

VIRGINIA

Howe 1777

ATLANTIC OCEAN

N W E S

0 25 50 75 100 miles
0 50 100 kilometers

75°W   70°W

→ American forces
→ British forces
✶ American victory
✶ British victory

What role did the home front play in the war?

How were Native Americans and the French involved in the war?

Why did the British southern strategy ultimately fail?

Conclusion: Why did the British lose the American Revolution?

Fort Washington and Fort Lee, taking another 3,000 prisoners. Washington retreated quickly across New Jersey into Pennsylvania. Again Howe unaccountably failed to press his advantage. Instead, he parked his German troops in winter quarters along the Delaware River. Perhaps he knew that many of the Continental soldiers' enlistment periods ended on December 31, making him confident that the Americans would not attack him. He was wrong.

On December 25, in an icy rain, Washington stealthily moved his army across the Delaware River and at dawn made a quick capture of the unsuspecting German soldiers. This impressive victory lifted the sagging morale of the patriot side. For the next two weeks, Washington remained on the offensive, capturing supplies in a clever attack on British units at Princeton. Soon he was safe in Morristown, in northern New Jersey, where he settled his army for the winter. Washington finally had time to administer mass smallpox inoculations and see his men through the abbreviated course of the disease.

All in all, in the first year of declared war, the rebellious Americans had a few proud moments but also many worries. The inexperienced Continental army had barely hung on in the New York campaign. Washington had shown exceptional daring and admirable restraint, but what really saved the Americans was the repeated reluctance of the British to follow through militarily when they had the advantage.

> **QUICK REVIEW**

Why did the British initially exercise restraint in their efforts to defeat the rebellious colonies?

CHAPTER LOCATOR | Why did Americans wait so long before they declared their independence? | What initial challenges did the opposing armies face?

184 CHAPTER 7 FIGHTING THE AMERICAN REVOLUTION

What role did the home front play in the war?

Rivington's New York Loyal Gazette
Not all newspaper editors supported the Revolution. James Rivington of New York City heaped abuse on Washington and others and earned a reputation for mean-spirited polemics. When New York City became British headquarters, Rivington curried favor with the British command. Yet it appears now that long-standing rumors about his duplicity are likely true. Evidence suggests that by 1781 he was passing codes to George Washington about British military plans. Courtesy, American Antiquarian Society.

BATTLEFIELDS ALONE DID not determine the outcome of the war. Struggles on the home front were equally important. Men who joined the army often left wives to manage on their own. Some men did not join because they were loyal to Britain and did not welcome war, and many others were undecided about independence. In many communities, both persuasion and force were used to gain the allegiance of the many neutrals. A major factor pushing neutrals to side with the Revolution was the harsh treatment of prisoners of war by the British. Adding to the turbulence of the times was a very shaky wartime economy. The creative financing of the fledgling government brought hardships as well as opportunities, forcing Americans to confront new manifestations of virtue and corruption.

Patriotism at the Local Level

Committees of correspondence, of public safety, and of inspection dominated the political landscape in patriot communities. These committees took on more than customary local governance; they enforced boycotts, picked army draftees, and policed suspected traitors. They sometimes invaded homes to search for contraband goods such as British tea or textiles.

Loyalists were dismayed by the increasing show of power by patriots. A man in Westchester, New York, described his response to intrusions by committees: "Choose your committee or suffer it to be chosen by a half dozen fools in your neighborhood — open your doors to them — let them examine your tea-cannisters and molasses-jugs, and your wives' and daughters' petty coats — bow and cringe and tremble and quake — fall down and worship our sovereign lord the mob. . . .

> **CHRONOLOGY**

1775
- **June.** The Second Continental Congress declares all loyalists traitors.
- Mohawk leader Joseph Brant travels to England to pledge support for the British side.

1776
- In New York City, loyalists sign "A Declaration of Dependence."

1777
- British Parliament suspends habeas corpus.

1778
- Colonial committees of public safety fix prices on essential commodities.

1780
- Philadelphia Ladies Association raises money for soldiers.

What role did the home front play in the war? | How were Native Americans and the French involved in the war? | Why did the British southern strategy ultimately fail? | Conclusion: Why did the British lose the American Revolution? | ✓ LearningCurve Check what you know. bedfordstmartins.com /roarkunderstanding

185

Should any pragmatical committee-gentleman come to my house and give himself airs, I shall show him the door." Oppressive or not, the local committees were rarely challenged. Their persuasive powers convinced many middle-of-the-road citizens that neutrality was not a comfortable option.

Another group new to political life — white women — increasingly demonstrated a capacity for patriotism as wartime hardships dramatically altered their work routines. Many wives whose husbands were away on military or political service took on masculine duties. Their competence to manage farms and make business decisions encouraged some to assert interest in politics as well, as Abigail Adams did while John Adams served in the Continental Congress in Philadelphia. Eliza Wilkinson managed a South Carolina plantation and talked revolutionary politics with women friends. "None were greater politicians than the several knots of ladies who met together," she remarked, alert to the unusual turn female conversations had taken.

Women from prominent Philadelphia families took more direct action, forming the **Ladies Association** in 1780 to collect money for Continental soldiers. A published broadside, "The Sentiments of an American Woman," defended their female patriotism: "The time is arrived to display the same sentiments which animated us at the beginning of the Revolution, when we renounced the use of teas [and] when our republican and laborious hands spun the flax."

The Loyalists

Around one-fifth of the American population remained loyal to the crown in 1776, and another two-fifths tried to stay neutral, providing a strong base for the British. In general, **loyalists** believed that social stability depended on a government anchored by monarchy and aristocracy. They feared that democratic tyranny was emergent among the self-styled patriots who appeared to be unscrupulous, violent men grabbing power for themselves. Pockets of loyalism thus existed everywhere (**Map 7.2**).

> ### > Who Were the Loyalists?

- Royal officials, such as governors, local judges, and customs officers
- Wealthy merchants
- Conservative urban lawyers
- People who already disliked pro-Revolution citizens, such as many backcountry Carolina farmers who resented the power of the pro-Revolution gentry
- Southern slaves who looked to Britain in hope of freedom
- Many Indian tribes

Even New England towns at the heart of the turmoil, such as Concord, Massachusetts, had a small and increasingly silenced core of loyalists. On occasion, husbands and wives, fathers and sons disagreed completely on the war.

Many Indian tribes chose neutrality at the war's start, seeing the conflict as a civil war between the English and the Americans. Eventually, however, they were drawn in, most taking the British side. One young Mohawk leader, Thayendanegea (known also by his English name, Joseph Brant), traveled to England in 1775 to

Ladies Association

▶ A women's organization in Philadelphia that collected substantial money donations in 1780 to give to the Continental troops as a token of the citizens' appreciation. A woman leader authored a declaration, "The Sentiments of an American Woman," to justify women's unexpected entry into political life.

loyalists

▶ Colonists who remained loyal to Britain during the Revolutionary War, probably numbering around one-fifth of the population in 1776. Colonists remained loyal to Britain for many reasons, and loyalists could be found in every region of the country.

CHAPTER LOCATOR | Why did Americans wait so long before they declared their independence? | What initial challenges did the opposing armies face?

186 CHAPTER 7 FIGHTING THE AMERICAN REVOLUTION

complain to King George about land-hungry New York settlers. "It is very hard when we have let the King's subjects have so much of our lands for so little value," he wrote; "they should want to cheat us in this manner of the small spots we have left for our women and children to live on." Brant pledged Indian support for the king in exchange for protection from encroaching settlers. In the Ohio Country, parts of the Shawnee and Delaware tribes started out pro-American but shifted to the British side by 1779 in the face of repeated betrayals by American settlers and soldiers.

Loyalists were most vocal between 1774 and 1776, when the possibility of a full-scale rebellion against Britain was still uncertain. They challenged the emerging patriot side in pamphlets and newspapers. In 1776 in New York City, 547 loyalists signed and circulated a broadside titled "A Declaration of Dependence" in rebuttal to the congress's July 4 declaration, denouncing the "most unnatural, unprovoked Rebellion that ever disgraced the annals of Time."

Who Is a Traitor?

In June 1775, the Second Continental Congress declared all loyalists to be traitors. Over the next year, state laws defined as treason acts such as provisioning the British army, saying anything that undermined patriot morale, and discouraging men from enlisting in the Continental army. Punishments ranged from house arrest and suspension of voting privileges to confiscation of property and deportation. Sometimes self-appointed committees of Tory-hunters bypassed the judicial niceties and terrorized loyalists, raiding their houses or tarring and feathering them.

Were wives of loyalists also traitors? When loyalist families fled the country, their property was typically confiscated. But if the wife stayed, courts usually allowed her to keep one-third of the property, the amount due her if widowed, and confiscated the rest. Yet a wife who fled with her husband might have little choice in the matter. After the Revolution, descendants of refugee loyalists filed several lawsuits to regain property that had entered the family through the mother's inheritance. In 1805, the American son of loyalist refugee

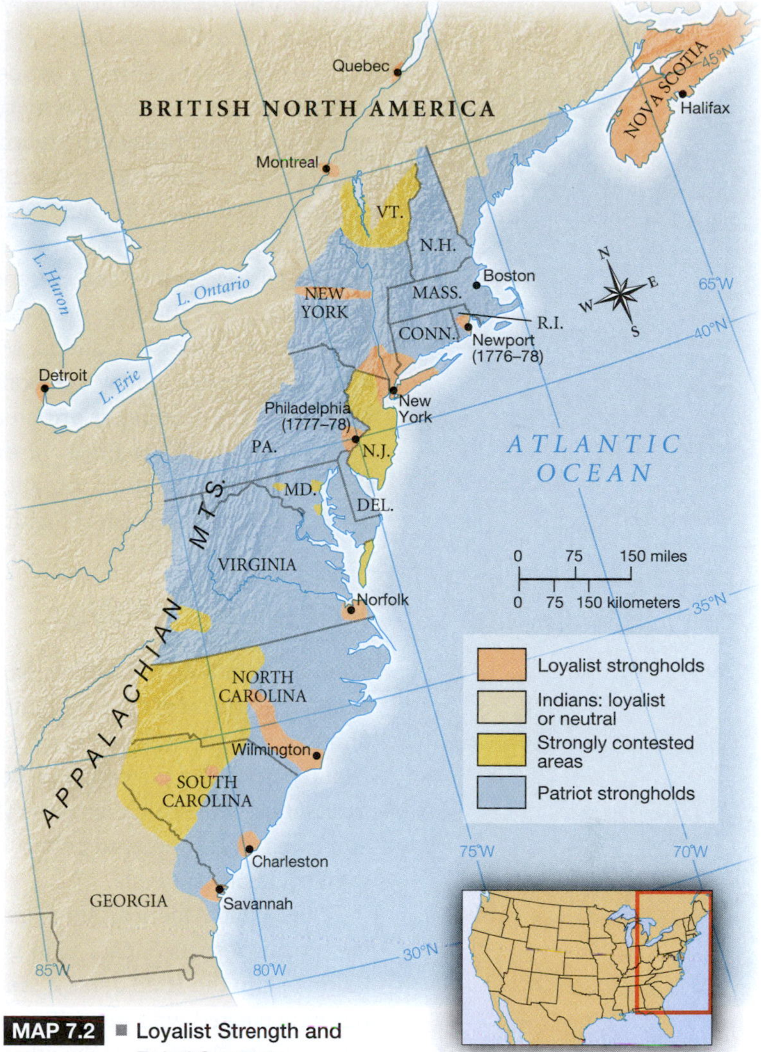

MAP 7.2 ■ Loyalist Strength and Rebel Support

Legend:
- Loyalist strongholds
- Indians: loyalist or neutral
- Strongly contested areas
- Patriot strongholds

The exact number of loyalists can never be known. No one could have made an accurate count at the time, and political allegiance often shifted with the wind. This map shows the regions of loyalist strength on which the British relied — most significantly, the lower Hudson valley and the Carolina Piedmont.

> **MAP ACTIVITY**

READING THE MAP: Which forces were stronger, those loyal to Britain or those rebelling? (Consider the size of their respective areas, centers of population, and vital port locations.) What areas were contested? If the contested areas ultimately had sided with the British, how would the balance of power have changed?

CONNECTIONS: Who was more likely to be a loyalist and why? How many loyalists left the United States? Where did they go?

What role did the home front play in the war?   How were Native Americans and the French involved in the war?   Why did the British southern strategy ultimately fail?   Conclusion: Why did the British lose the American Revolution?   ✓ LearningCurve Check what you know. bedfordstmartins.com /roarkunderstanding

187

Anna Martin recovered her dowry property on the grounds that she had no independent will to be a loyalist.

Tarring and feathering, property confiscation, deportation, terrorism — to the loyalists, such denials of liberty of conscience and of freedom to own private property proved that democratic tyranny was more to be feared than the monarchical variety. A Boston loyalist named Mather Byles aptly expressed this point: "They call me a brainless Tory, but tell me . . . which is better — to be ruled by one tyrant three thousand miles away, or by three thousand tyrants not a mile away?" Byles was soon sentenced to deportation.

Throughout the war, probably 7,000 to 8,000 loyalists fled to England, and 28,000 found haven in Canada. Many stayed put while the war's outcome was unknown. In New Jersey, for example, 3,000 Jerseyites felt protected (or scared) enough by the occupying British army in 1776 to swear an oath of allegiance to the king. But then the British drew back to New York City, leaving the loyalists at the mercy of local patriot committees. Despite the staunch backing of loyalists in 1776, the British found it difficult to build a winning strategy on their support.

Prisoners of War

The poor handling of loyalists as traitors paled in comparison to the handling of American prisoners of war by the British. Among European military powers, humane treatment of captured soldiers was the custom, including adequate provisions (paid for by the captives' own government) and the possibility of prisoner exchanges. But British leaders refused to see American captives as foot soldiers employed by a sovereign nation. Instead, they were traitors, to be treated worse than common criminals.

The 4,000 American prisoners taken in the fall of 1776 were crowded onto two dozen vessels anchored in the river between Manhattan and Brooklyn. The largest ship, the HMS *Jersey*, was a broken-down hull built to house a crew of 400 but now packed with more than 1,100 prisoners. Survivors described the dark, stinking space below decks where more than half a dozen men died daily. A twenty-year-old captive seaman described his first view of the hold: "Here was a motley crew, covered with rags and filth; visages pallid with disease, emaciated with hunger and anxiety, . . . and surrounded with the horrors of sickness and death." The Continental Congress sent food to the prisoners, but most was diverted to British use, leaving General Washington fuming.

Treating the captives as criminals potentially triggered the Anglo-American right of habeas corpus, a thirteenth-century British liberty that guaranteed every prisoner the right to challenge his detention before a judge and to learn the charges against him. To remove that possibility, Parliament voted in early 1777 to suspend habeas corpus specifically for "persons taken in the act of high treason" in any of the colonies.

Despite the prison-ship horrors, Washington insisted that captured British soldiers be treated humanely. From the initial group of Hessians taken on Christmas of 1776 to the several thousand more soldiers captured in American victories by 1778, America's prisoners of war were gathered in rural encampments. Guarded by local townsmen, the captives typically could cultivate small gardens, move about freely during the day, and even hire themselves out to farmers suffering

CHAPTER LOCATOR | Why did Americans wait so long before they declared their independence? | What initial challenges did the opposing armies face?

188 CHAPTER 7 FIGHTING THE AMERICAN REVOLUTION

wartime labor shortages. Officers with money could purchase lodging with local families and mix socially with Americans. Many officers were even allowed to keep their guns as they waited for prisoner exchanges to release them.

Such exchanges were negotiated when the British became desperate to regain valued officers and thus freed American officers. Death was the most common fate of ordinary American soldiers and seamen. More than 15,000 men endured captivity in the prison ships, and two-thirds of them died, a larger number than those who died in battle (estimated to be around 5,000). News of the horrors of the British death ships increased the revolutionaries' resolve and convinced some neutrals of the necessity of the war.

Financial Instability and Corruption

Wars cost money — for arms and ammunition, for food and uniforms, for soldiers' pay, for provisions for prisoners. The Continental Congress printed money, but its value quickly deteriorated because the congress held no precious metals to back the currency. The dollar eventually bottomed out at one-fortieth of its face value. States, too, were printing paper money to pay for wartime expenses, further complicating the economy.

As the currency depreciated, the congress turned to other means to procure supplies and labor. One method was to borrow hard money (gold or silver coins) from wealthy men in exchange for certificates of debt (public securities) promising repayment with interest. The certificates of debt were similar to present-day government bonds. To pay soldiers, the congress issued land grant certificates, written promises of acreage usually located in frontier areas such as central Maine or eastern Ohio. Both the public securities and the land grant certificates quickly became forms of negotiable currency, but they too soon depreciated.

Depreciating currency inevitably led to rising prices, as sellers compensated for the falling value of the money. The wartime economy of the late 1770s, with its unreliable currency and price inflation, was extremely demoralizing to Americans everywhere. In 1778, in an effort to impose stability, local committees of public safety began to fix prices on essential goods such as flour. Inevitably, some turned this unstable situation to their advantage. Money that fell fast in value needed to be spent quickly; being in debt was suddenly advantageous because the debt could be repaid in devalued currency. A brisk black market sprang up in prohibited luxury imports, such as tea, sugar, textiles, and wines, even though these items came from Britain. A New Hampshire delegate to the Continental Congress denounced the trade: "We are a crooked and perverse generation, longing for the fineries and follies of those Egyptian task masters from whom we have so lately freed ourselves."

QUICK REVIEW

How did the patriots promote support
for their cause in the colonies?

What role did the home front play in the war?

How were Native Americans and the French involved in the war?

Why did the British southern strategy ultimately fail?

Conclusion: Why did the British lose the American Revolution?

LearningCurve
Check what you know.
bedfordstmartins.com
/roarkunderstanding

How were Native Americans and the French involved in the war?

Death of Jane McCrea

Jane McCrea, a patriot's daughter in love with a loyalist in Burgoyne's army, gained fame as a martyr in 1777. She met death on her way to join her fiancé — either shot in the crossfire of battle (the British claim) or murdered by Indians (the patriots' version). American leaders used the story of the vulnerable young woman as propaganda to inspire the American drive for victory at Saratoga. Wadsworth Athenaeum Museum of Art, Hartford/Art Resource, NY.

IN EARLY 1777, the Continental army faced bleak choices. General Washington had skillfully avoided defeat, but the minor victories in New Jersey lent only faint optimism to the American side. Meanwhile, British troops moved south from Quebec, aiming to isolate New England by taking control of the Hudson River. Their presence drew the Continental army up into central New York, polarizing tribes of the Iroquois Nation and turning the Mohawk Valley into a bloody war zone. By 1779, tribes in western New York and in Indian country in the Ohio Valley were fully involved in the Revolutionary War. Despite an important patriot victory at Saratoga, the involvement of Indians and the continuing strength of the British forced the American government to look to France for help.

Burgoyne's Army and the Battle of Saratoga

In 1777, British general John Burgoyne, commanding a considerable army, began the northern squeeze on the Hudson River valley. Coming from Canada, he marched south hoping to capture Albany, near the intersection of the Hudson and Mohawk rivers. Accompanied by 1,000 "camp followers" (cooks, laundresses, musicians) and some 400 Indian warriors, Burgoyne's army of 7,800 men did not travel light. Food had to be packed in, not only for people but also for 400 horses hauling heavy artillery. Primitive roads through dense forests slowed their progress to a crawl.

CHAPTER LOCATOR | Why did Americans wait so long before they declared their independence? | What initial challenges did the opposing armies face?

190 CHAPTER 7 FIGHTING THE AMERICAN REVOLUTION

Battle of Saratoga, 1777

The logical second step in isolating New England should have been to advance troops up the Hudson from New York City to meet Burgoyne. American surveillance indicated that General Howe in Manhattan was readying his men for a major move in August 1777. But Howe surprised everyone by sailing south to attack Philadelphia.

To reinforce Burgoyne, British and Hessian troops from Montreal came from the east along the Mohawk River, aided by Mohawks and Senecas of the Iroquois Confederacy. The British were counting on loyalism among the numerous German colonists living in the Mohawk Valley. A hundred miles west of Albany, they encountered American Continental soldiers at Fort Stanwix and laid siege, causing local German militiamen and a small number of Oneida Indians to rush to the Continentals' support. Mohawk chief Joseph Brant led the Senecas and Mohawks in an ambush on the German Americans and the Oneidas in a narrow ravine called Oriskany, killing nearly 500 out of 840 of them. On Brant's side, some 90 warriors were killed. The defenders of Fort Stanwix ultimately repelled their attackers. These deadly battles of **Oriskany** and Fort Stanwix were also complexly multiethnic, pitting Indians against Indians, German Americans against German mercenaries, New York patriots against New York loyalists, and English Americans against British soldiers.

The British retreat at Fort Stanwix deprived General Burgoyne of the additional troops he expected. Camped at a small village called Saratoga, he was isolated, with food supplies dwindling and men deserting. His adversary at Albany, General Horatio Gates, began moving his army toward Saratoga. Burgoyne decided to attack first, and the British prevailed, but at the great cost of 600 dead or wounded. Three weeks later, an American attack on Burgoyne's forces in the second stage of the **battle of Saratoga** cost the British another 600 men and most of their cannons. General Burgoyne finally surrendered to the American forces on October 17, 1777.

General Howe, meanwhile, had succeeded in occupying Philadelphia in September 1777. Figuring that the Saratoga loss was balanced by the capture of Philadelphia, the British government proposed a negotiated settlement — not including independence — to end the war. The American side refused.

But supplies of arms and food ran precariously low. Washington moved his troops into winter quarters at Valley Forge, just west of Philadelphia. Quartered in drafty huts, the men lacked blankets, boots, stockings, and food. Some 2,000 men at Valley Forge died of disease; another 2,000 deserted over the bitter six-month encampment.

Washington blamed the citizenry for lack of support; indeed, evidence of corruption and profiteering was abundant. Army suppliers too often provided defective food, clothing, and gunpowder. One shipment of bedding arrived with

> **CHRONOLOGY**

1777
– Ambush at Oriskany; Americans hold Fort Stanwix.
– British occupy Philadelphia.
– British surrender at Saratoga.

1777–1778
– Continental army winters at Valley Forge.

1778
– France signs treaty with America.

1779
– Americans destroy Iroquois villages in New York.
– Militias attack Cherokee settlements in North Carolina.
– Americans take Forts Kaskaskia and Vincennes.

battle of Oriskany
▶ A punishing defeat for Americans in a ravine named Oriskany near Fort Stanwix in New York in August 1777. Mohawk and Seneca Indians ambushed German American militiamen aided by allied Oneida warriors, and 500 on the Revolutionary side were killed.

battle of Saratoga
▶ A two-stage battle in New York ending with the decisive defeat and surrender of British general John Burgoyne on October 17, 1777. This victory convinced France to throw its official support to the American side in the war.

What role did the home front play in the war? | **How were Native Americans and the French involved in the war?** | Why did the British southern strategy ultimately fail? | Conclusion: Why did the British lose the American Revolution? | ☑ **LearningCurve** Check what you know. bedfordstmartins.com /roarkunderstanding

191

blankets one-quarter their customary size. Food supplies arrived rotten. As one Continental officer said, "The people at home are destroying the Army by their conduct much faster than Howe and all his army can possibly do by fighting us."

The War in the West: Indian Country

Between the fall of 1777 and the summer of 1778, the fighting on the Atlantic coast slowed. But in the interior western areas — the Mohawk Valley, the Ohio Valley, and Kentucky — the war of Indians against the American rebels heated up.

The ambush and slaughter at Oriskany in August 1777 marked the beginning of three years of terror for the inhabitants of the Mohawk Valley. Loyalists and Indians engaged in many raids throughout 1778, capturing or killing inhabitants. In retaliation, American militiamen destroyed Joseph Brant's village, killing several children. A month later, Brant's warriors attacked the town of Cherry Valley, killing 16 soldiers and 32 civilians.

The following summer, General Washington authorized a campaign to wreak "total destruction and devastation" on all the Iroquois villages of central New York. Some 4,500 troops commanded by General John Sullivan implemented a campaign of terror in the fall of 1779. Forty Indian towns met with total obliteration; the soldiers torched dwellings, cornfields, and orchards. In a few towns, women and children were slaughtered, but in most, the inhabitants managed to escape, fleeing to the British at Fort Niagara. Thousands of Indian refugees, sick and starving, camped around the fort in one of the most miserable winters on record.

Much farther to the west, beyond Fort Pitt, another complex story of alliances and betrayals between American militiamen and Indians unfolded. Some 150,000 native people lived between the Appalachian Mountains and the Mississippi River. Most sided with the British, but a portion of the Shawnee and Delaware at first sought peace with the Americans. In mid-1778, the Delaware chief White Eyes negotiated a treaty at Fort Pitt, pledging Indian support for the Americans in exchange for supplies and trade goods. But escalating violence undermined the agreement. That fall, when American soldiers killed two friendly Shawnee chiefs, Cornstalk and Red Hawk, the Continental Congress hastened to apologize, as did the governors of Pennsylvania and Virginia, but the soldiers who stood trial for the murders were acquitted. Two months later, White Eyes died under mysterious circumstances, almost certainly murdered by militiamen, who repeatedly had trouble honoring distinctions between allied and enemy Indians.

West of North Carolina (today's Tennessee), militias attacked Cherokee settlements in 1779, destroying thirty-six villages, while Indian raiders repeatedly attacked white settlements such as Boonesborough (in present-day Kentucky) (**Map 7.3**). In retaliation, a young Virginian, George Rogers Clark, led Kentucky militiamen into what is now Illinois, attacking and taking the British fort at Kaskaskia. Clark's men wore native clothing — hunting shirts and breechcloths — but their dress was not a sign of solidarity with the Indians. When they attacked British-held Fort Vincennes in 1779, Clark's troops tomahawked Indian captives and threw their still-live bodies into the river in a gory spectacle witnessed by the redcoats. "To excel them in barbarity is the only way to make war upon Indians," Clark announced.

By 1780, very few Indians remained neutral. Violent raids by Americans drove Indians into the arms of the British at Forts Detroit and Niagara, or into the arms of

CHAPTER LOCATOR | Why did Americans wait so long before they declared their independence? | What initial challenges did the opposing armies face?

192 CHAPTER 7
FIGHTING THE AMERICAN REVOLUTION

MAP 7.3 ■ The Indian War in the West, 1777–1782

Most Indian tribes supported the British. Iroquois Indians attacked New York's Mohawk Valley throughout 1778, causing the Continental army to destroy Iroquois villages throughout central New York. Shawnee and Delaware Indians in western Pennsylvania tangled with American militiamen in 1779, while tribes near Fort Detroit conducted raids on Kentucky settlers. Sporadic frontier fighting continued through 1782.

the Spaniards, west of the Mississippi River. Said one officer on the Sullivan campaign, "Their nests are destroyed but the birds are still on the wing." For those who stayed near their native lands, chaos and confusion prevailed. Rare as it was, Indian support for the American side occasionally emerged out of a strategic sense that the Americans were unstoppable in their westward pressure and that it was better to work out an alliance than to lose in a war. But American treatment of even friendly Indians showed that there was no winning strategy for them.

The French Alliance

On their own, the Americans could not have defeated Britain, especially as pressure from hostile Indians increased. Essential help arrived as a result of the victory at Saratoga, which convinced the French to enter the war; a formal alliance was signed in February 1778. France recognized the United States as an independent nation and promised full military and commercial support. Most crucial was the French navy, which could challenge British supplies and troops at sea and aid the Americans in taking and holding prisoners of war.

| What role did the home front play in the war? | **How were Native Americans and the French involved in the war?** | Why did the British southern strategy ultimately fail? | Conclusion: Why did the British lose the American Revolution? | ✓ LearningCurve Check what you know. bedfordstmartins.com /roarkunderstanding |

193

"The Ballance of Power," 1780

This English cartoon mocks the alliance of Spain and the Netherlands with France in support of the American war. On the left, the female figure Britannia cannot be moved by all the lightweights on the right. France and Spain embrace while a Dutch boy hops on, saying, "I'll do anything for Money." The forlorn Indian woman, representing America, wails, "My Ingratitude is Justly punished." Print Collection, Miriam and Ira D. Wallach Division of Art, Prints, and Photographs, The New York Public Library. Astor, Lenox, and Tilden Foundations.

> **VISUAL ACTIVITY**

READING THE IMAGE: What does this cartoon reveal about British perceptions of the American Revolution?
CONNECTIONS: How did British attitudes toward the colonies contribute to the British defeat in the war?

Well before 1778, however, the French had been covertly providing cannons, muskets, gunpowder, and highly trained military advisers to the Americans. From the French perspective, the main attraction of an alliance was the opportunity it provided to defeat archrival Britain. A victory would also open pathways to trade and perhaps result in France's acquiring the coveted British West Indies. Even an American defeat would not be a disaster for France if the war lasted many years and drained Britain of men and money.

French support would prove indispensable to the American cause in 1780 and 1781, but the alliance's first months brought no dramatic changes, and some Americans grumbled that the partnership would prove worthless.

> **QUICK REVIEW**

Why did the Americans need assistance from the French to ensure victory?

CHAPTER LOCATOR | Why did Americans wait so long before they declared their independence? | What initial challenges did the opposing armies face?

194 CHAPTER 7 FIGHTING THE AMERICAN REVOLUTION

Why did the British southern strategy ultimately fail?

Lafayette at Yorktown

An enthusiast for American liberty, the young French nobleman Lafayette came to the United States in 1777 at age twenty to volunteer his services to General Washington. After proving his leadership in several northern campaigns, he went to Virginia in 1781 to fight Cornwallis. Near Richmond, he met James, a slave belonging to William Armistead, who loaned him to Lafayette. At the siege of Yorktown, James, pretending to be an escaped slave, infiltrated the British command, giving them misinformation and bringing crucial intelligence back to Lafayette. James obtained his freedom in 1786 after Lafayette wrote a letter on his behalf to the Virginia assembly. Art Gallery, Williams Center, Lafayette College.

WHEN FRANCE JOINED the war, some British officials favored abandoning the war. As one troop commander shrewdly observed, "We are far from an anticipated peace, because the bitterness of the rebels is too widespread, and in regions where we are masters the rebellious spirit is still in them. The land is too large, and there are too many people. The more land we win, the weaker our army gets in the field." The commander of the British navy agreed, as did Lord North, the prime minister. But the king was determined to crush the rebellion, and he encouraged a new strategy for victory focusing on the southern colonies, thought to be more persuadably loyalist. It was a brilliant but desperate plan, and ultimately unsuccessful.

Georgia and South Carolina

The new strategy called for British forces to abandon New England and focus on the South, with its valuable crops and its large slave population, a destabilizing factor that might keep rebellious white southerners in line. Georgia and the Carolinas appeared to hold large numbers of loyalists, providing a base for the British to recapture the southern colonies one by one, before moving north to the more problematic middle colonies and New England.

| What role did the home front play in the war? | How were Native Americans and the French involved in the war? | **Why did the British southern strategy ultimately fail?** | Conclusion: Why did the British lose the American Revolution? | ✔ **LearningCurve** Check what you know. bedfordstmartins.com /roarkunderstanding |

MAP 7.4 ■ **The War in the South, 1780–1781**

After taking Charleston in May 1780, the British advanced into South and North Carolina, touching off a bloody civil war. An American loss at Camden was followed by victories at King's Mountain and Cowpens. The British next invaded Virginia but were ultimately trapped and overpowered at Yorktown in the fall of 1781.

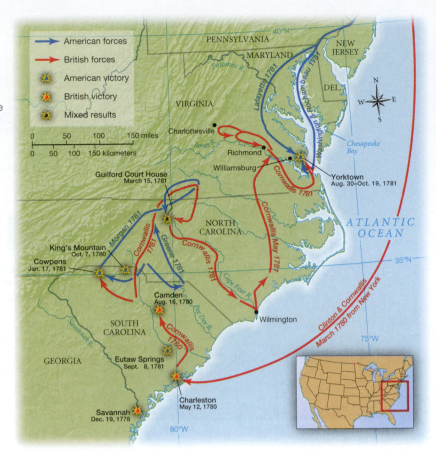

Georgia, the first target, fell at the end of December 1778 (**Map 7.4**). A small army of British soldiers occupied Savannah and Augusta, and a new royal governor and loyalist assembly were quickly installed. The British quickly organized twenty loyal militia units, and 1,400 Georgians swore an oath of allegiance to the king. So far, the southern strategy looked as if it might work.

Next came South Carolina. The Continental army put ten regiments into the port city of Charleston to defend it from attack by British troops shipped south from New York under the command of General Henry Clinton, Howe's replacement as commander in chief. For five weeks in early 1780, the British laid siege to the city and took it in May 1780, capturing 3,300 American soldiers.

Clinton next announced that slaves owned by rebel masters were welcome to seek refuge with his army, and several thousand escaped to the coastal city. Untrained in formal warfare, they were of use to the British as knowledgeable guides to the countryside and as laborers building defensive fortifications. Escaped slaves with boat-piloting skills were particularly valuable for crucial aid in navigating the inland rivers of the southern colonies.

Clinton returned to New York, leaving the task of pacifying the rest of South Carolina to General Charles Cornwallis and 4,000 troops. A bold commander, Lord Cornwallis quickly chased out the remaining Continentals and established military rule of South Carolina by midsummer. He purged rebels from government

CHAPTER LOCATOR | Why did Americans wait so long before they declared their independence? | What initial challenges did the opposing armies face?

office and disarmed rebel militias. Exports of rice, South Carolina's main crop, resumed, and pardons were offered to Carolinians willing to prove their loyalty by taking up arms for the British.

By August, American troops arrived from the North to strike back at Cornwallis. General Gates, the hero of Saratoga, led 3,000 troops, many of them newly recruited militiamen, into battle against Cornwallis at Camden, South Carolina, on August 16 (see Map 7.4). The militiamen panicked at the sight of the approaching British cavalry, however, and fled. When regiment leaders tried to regroup the next day, only 700 soldiers showed up. The battle of Camden was a devastating defeat, the worst of the entire war, and prospects seemed very grim for the Americans.

Treason and Guerrilla Warfare

Britain's southern strategy succeeded in 1780 in part because of information about American troop movements secretly conveyed by an American officer, Benedict Arnold. The hero of several American battles, Arnold was a deeply insecure man who never felt he got his due. Sometime in 1779, he opened secret negotiations with General Clinton in New York, trading information for money and hinting that he could deliver far more of value. When General Washington made him commander of West Point, a new fort on the Hudson River sixty miles north of New York City, Arnold's plan crystallized. West Point controlled the Hudson; its capture might well have meant victory in the war.

Arnold's plot to sell a West Point victory to the British was foiled in the fall of 1780 when Americans captured the man carrying plans of the fort's defense from Arnold to Clinton. News of Arnold's treason created shock waves. Arnold

A Shaming Ritual Targeting the Great Traitor

In late 1780, Philadelphians staged a ritual humiliation of Benedict Arnold, represented by a two-faced effigy. Behind him stands the devil, prodding him with a pitchfork and shaking a bag of coins near his ear, reminding all that Arnold sold out for money. Library of Congress.

| What role did the home front play in the war? | How were Native Americans and the French involved in the war? | **Why did the British southern strategy ultimately fail?** | Conclusion: Why did the British lose the American Revolution? | LearningCurve Check what you know. bedfordstmartins.com /roarkunderstanding |

represented all of the patriots' worst fears about themselves: greedy self-interest, like that of the war profiteers; the unprincipled abandonment of war aims, like that of turncoat southern Tories; panic, like that of the terrified soldiers at Camden. But instead of demoralizing the Americans, Arnold's treachery revived their commitment to the patriot cause. Vilifying Arnold allowed Americans to stake out a wide distance between themselves and dastardly conduct. It inspired a renewal of patriotism at a particularly low moment.

Shock over Gates's defeat at Camden and Arnold's treason revitalized rebel support in western South Carolina, an area that Cornwallis thought was pacified and loyal. The backcountry of the South soon became the site of guerrilla warfare. In hit-and-run attacks, both sides burned and ravaged not only opponents' property but also the property of anyone claiming to be neutral. Loyalist militia units organized by the British were met by fierce rebel militia units. In South Carolina, some 6,000 rebels met loyalist units in engagements. Guerrilla warfare soon spread to Georgia and North Carolina. Both sides committed atrocities and plundered property, clear deviations from standard military practice.

The British southern strategy depended on sufficient loyalist strength to hold reconquered territory as Cornwallis's army moved north. The backcountry civil war proved this assumption false. The Americans won few major battles in the South, but they ultimately succeeded by harassing the British forces and preventing them from foraging for food. Cornwallis moved the war into North Carolina in the fall of 1780 because the North Carolinians were supplying the South Carolina rebels with arms and men (see Map 7.4). Then news of a massacre of loyalist units by 1,400 frontier riflemen at the battle of King's Mountain, in western South Carolina, sent him hurrying back. The British were stretched too thin to hold even two colonies.

Surrender at Yorktown

By early 1781, the war was going very badly for the British. Their defeat at King's Mountain was quickly followed by a second major defeat at the battle of Cowpens in South Carolina in January 1781. Cornwallis retreated to North Carolina and thence to Virginia, where he captured Williamsburg in June. A raiding party proceeded to Charlottesville, the seat of government, capturing members of the Virginia assembly but not Governor Thomas Jefferson, who escaped the soldiers by a mere ten minutes. These minor victories allowed Cornwallis to imagine he was succeeding in Virginia. His army, now swelled by some 4,000 escaped slaves, marched to Yorktown, near the Chesapeake Bay area. As the general waited for backup troops by ship from British headquarters in New York City, smallpox and typhus began to set in among the black recruits.

At this juncture, the French-American alliance came into play. French regiments commanded by the Comte de Rochambeau had joined General Washington in Newport, Rhode Island, in mid-1780, and in early 1781 warships under the Comte de Grasse had sailed from France to the West Indies. Washington, Rochambeau, and de Grasse now fixed their attention on Chesapeake Bay. The French fleet got there ahead of the British troop ships from New York; a five-day naval battle left the French navy in clear control of the Virginia coast. This proved

CHAPTER LOCATOR | Why did Americans wait so long before they declared their independence? | What initial challenges did the opposing armies face?

198   CHAPTER 7
FIGHTING THE AMERICAN REVOLUTION

Siege of Yorktown, 1781

to be the decisive factor in ending the war, because the French ships prevented any rescue of Cornwallis's army.

On land, General Cornwallis and his 7,500 troops faced a combined French and American army of 16,000. For twelve days, the Americans and French bombarded the British fortifications at Yorktown; Cornwallis ran low on food and ammunition. He also began to expel the black recruits, some of them sick and dying. A Hessian officer serving under Cornwallis later criticized this British action as disgraceful: "We had used them to good advantage, and set them free, and now, with fear and trembling, they had to face the reward of their cruel masters." The twelve-day siege brought Cornwallis to the realization that neither victory nor escape was possible. He surrendered on October 19, 1781.

What began as a promising southern strategy in 1778 had turned into a discouraging defeat. British attacks in the South had energized American resistance, as did the timely exposure of Benedict Arnold's treason. The arrival of the French fleet sealed the fate of Cornwallis at the **battle of Yorktown**, and major military operations came to a halt.

The Losers and the Winners

The surrender at Yorktown spelled the end for the British, but two more years of skirmishes ensued. Frontier areas in Kentucky, Ohio, and Illinois blazed with battles pitting Americans against various Indian tribes. The British army still occupied three coastal cities, including New York, and in response, an augmented Continental army stayed at the ready, north of New York City.

The **Treaty of Paris**, also called the **Peace of Paris**, was two years in the making. Commissioners from America and Britain worked out the ten articles of peace, while a side treaty signed by Britain, France, Spain, and the Netherlands sealed related deals. The first article went to the heart of the matter: "His Britannic Majesty acknowledges the said United States to be free Sovereign and independent States." Other articles set the western boundary at the Mississippi River and guaranteed that creditors on both sides would be paid in sterling money, a provision important to British merchants. Britain agreed to withdraw its troops quickly, but more than a decade later this promise still had not been fully kept. Another agreement prohibited the British from "carrying away any Negroes or other property of the American inhabitants." The treaty was signed on September 3, 1783.

News of the treaty signing was cause for celebration among most Americans, but not among the thousands of self-liberated blacks who had joined the British under the promise of freedom. South Carolinian Boston King, a refugee in New York City, recalled that the provision prohibiting evacuation of black refugees "filled us with inexpressible anguish and terror." King and others pressed the

battle of Yorktown
▶ October 1781 battle that sealed American victory in the Revolutionary War. American troops and a French fleet trapped the British army under the command of General Charles Cornwallis at Yorktown, Virginia.

Treaty (Peace) of Paris, 1783
▶ September 3, 1783, treaty that ended the Revolutionary War. The treaty acknowledged America's independence, set its boundaries, and promised the quick withdrawal of British troops from American soil. It failed to recognize Indians as players in the conflict.

What role did the home front play in the war?

How were Native Americans and the French involved in the war?

Why did the British southern strategy ultimately fail?

Conclusion: Why did the British lose the American Revolution?

✓ LearningCurve
Check what you know.
bedfordstmartins.com
/roarkunderstanding

199

British commander in New York, Sir Guy Carleton, to honor pre-treaty British promises. Carleton obliged: For all refugees under British protection for more than a year, he issued certificates of freedom — making them no longer "property" to be returned. More than 4,000 blacks sailed out of New York for Nova Scotia, Boston King and his family among them. As Carleton coolly explained to a protesting George Washington, "The Negroes in question . . . I found free when I arrived at New York, I had therefore no right, as I thought, to prevent their going to any part of the world they thought proper." British commanders in Savannah and Charleston followed Carleton's lead and aided the exit of perhaps 10,000 blacks from the United States.

The Treaty of Paris had nothing to say about the Indian participants in the Revolutionary War. As one American told the Shawnee people, "Your Fathers the English have made Peace with us for themselves, but forgot you their Children, who Fought with them, and neglected you like Bastards." Indian lands were assigned to the victors as though they were uninhabited. Some Indian refugees fled west into present-day Missouri and Arkansas, and others, such as Joseph Brant's Mohawks, relocated to Canada. But significant numbers remained within the new United States, occupying their traditional homelands in areas west and north of the Ohio River. For them, the Treaty of Paris brought no peace at all; their longer war against the Americans would extend at least until 1795 and for some until 1813. Their ally, Britain, conceded defeat, but the Indians did not.

With the treaty finally signed, the British began their evacuation of New York, Charleston, and Savannah, a process complicated by the sheer numbers involved — soldiers, fearful loyalists, and refugees from slavery by the thousands. In New York City, more than 27,000 soldiers and 30,000 loyalists sailed on hundreds of ships for England in the late fall of 1783. In a final act of mischief, on the November day when the last ships left, the losing side raised the British flag at the southern tip of Manhattan, cut away the ropes used to hoist it, and greased the flagpole.

> ## QUICK REVIEW

What missteps led to the failure of British strategy in the South?

CHAPTER LOCATOR | Why did Americans wait so long before they declared their independence? | What initial challenges did the opposing armies face?

200   CHAPTER 7   FIGHTING THE AMERICAN REVOLUTION

Conclusion: Why did the British lose the American Revolution?

THE BRITISH BEGAN the war for America convinced that they could not lose. They had the best-trained army and navy in the world, they were familiar with the landscape from the Seven Years' War, they had the willing warrior-power of most of the native tribes of the backcountry, and they easily captured every port city of consequence in America. A majority of colonists were either neutral or loyal to the crown. Why, then, did the British lose?

One continuing problem the British faced was the uncertainty of supplies. The army depended on a steady stream of supply ships from home, and insecurity about food helps explain their reluctance to pursue the Continental army aggressively. A further obstacle was their continual misuse of loyalist energies. Any plan to repacify the colonies required the cooperation of the loyalists, but the British repeatedly left them to the mercy of vengeful rebels. French aid also helps explain the British defeat. Even before the formal alliance, French artillery and ammunition proved vital to the Continental army. After 1780, the French army fought alongside the Americans, and the French navy made the Yorktown victory possible. Finally, the British abdicated civil power in the colonies in 1775 and 1776, when royal officials fled to safety, and they never really regained it. The basic British goal — to turn back the clock to imperial rule — receded into impossibility as the war dragged on.

The Revolution profoundly disrupted the lives of Americans everywhere. It was a war for independence from Britain, but it was more. It was a war that required men and women to think about politics and the legitimacy of authority. The rhetoric employed to justify the revolution against Britain put the words *liberty*, *tyranny*, *slavery*, *independence*, and *equality* into common usage. These words carried far deeper meanings than a mere complaint over taxation without representation. The Revolution unleashed a dynamic of equality and liberty that was largely unintended and unwanted by many of the political leaders of 1776. But that dynamic emerged as a potent force in American life in the decades to come.

What role did the home front play in the war? | How were Native Americans and the French involved in the war? | Why did the British southern strategy ultimately fail? | **Conclusion: Why did the British lose the American Revolution?** | ✔ **LearningCurve** Check what you know. bedfordstmartins.com /roarkunderstanding

201

CHAPTER 7 STUDY GUIDE

STEP 1

GET STARTED ONLINE

✓ **LearningCurve** ▪ bedfordstmartins.com/roarkunderstanding

Now that you've read the chapter, make it stick by completing the LearningCurve activity.

STEP 2

EXPLAIN WHY IT MATTERS

Put your reading into practice. Identify each term below, and then explain why it matters in U.S. history.

TERM	WHO OR WHAT & WHEN	WHY IT MATTERS
Second Continental Congress (p. 174)		
Continental army (p. 175)		
battle of Bunker Hill (p. 176)		
Common Sense (p. 176)		
Declaration of Independence (p. 179)		
battle of Long Island (p. 182)		
Ladies Association (p. 186)		
loyalists (p. 186)		
battle of Oriskany (p. 191)		
battle of Saratoga (p. 191)		
battle of Yorktown (p. 199)		
Treaty (Peace) of Paris, 1783 (p. 199)		

STEP 3

MOVE BEYOND THE BASICS

To demonstrate a more advanced understanding, provide the detail of the American strategy, the British strategy, key events, and major battles. Why were the Americans ultimately victorious?

Period	American strategy	British strategy	Key events	Major battles/victor
June 1775– December 1776				
January 1777– February 1778				
March 1778– September 1783				

STEP **4** **PUT IT ALL TOGETHER** Now, take a step back and try to explain the big picture. Remember to use specific examples from the chapter in your answers.

DECLARING INDEPENDENCE

▶ Why were so many Americans divided about the question of independence from Britain?

▶ What factors contributed to the decision by the Continental Congress to declare independence in July 1776?

THE FIRST TWO YEARS OF WAR

▶ What challenges did the Americans face in the first year of the war? How successful were they in meeting them?

▶ What impact did other European powers and Indian peoples have on the course of the war?

AMERICAN VICTORY

▶ Why did the British switch to the southern strategy? Why did it fail?

▶ Is it more accurate to say that the Americans won the Revolutionary War or that the British lost it? Why?

LOOKING BACKWARD, LOOKING AHEAD

▶ When did the chain of events that culminated in the establishment of an independent United States begin? In 1763? In 1776? In 1783? At another date? Present evidence to support your answer.

▶ What challenges did the United States face as it emerged victorious from the Revolutionary War?

> **IN YOUR OWN WORDS**

Imagine that you must give an oral report to the class answering the following question: **How were the North American colonists able to successfully gain their independence from Great Britain in 1783?** What would be the most important points to include and why?

> **Do it online at the Student Site** ■ **bedfordstmartins.com/roarkunderstanding**

8

BUILDING A REPUBLIC

1775–1789

> **What were the most significant events that led to the formulation and ratification of the U.S. Constitution?** Chapter 8 examines the challenges America faced in the 1780s, the efforts of the states to define freedom and citizenship, and the process that led to the abandonment of the Articles of Confederation and the adoption of the Constitution.

LearningCurve

bedfordstmartins.com/roarkunderstanding

After reading the chapter, use LearningCurve to retain what you've read.

George Washington presides over the constitutional convention. Philadelphia, 1787. The Granger Collection, New York.

> What kind of government did the Articles of Confederation create?

> How did the states define citizenship and freedom?

> Why did the Articles of Confederation fail?

> How did the Constitution change how the nation was governed?

> What were the objections to ratification of the Constitution?

> Conclusion: What was the "republican remedy"?

What kind of government did the Articles of Confederation create?

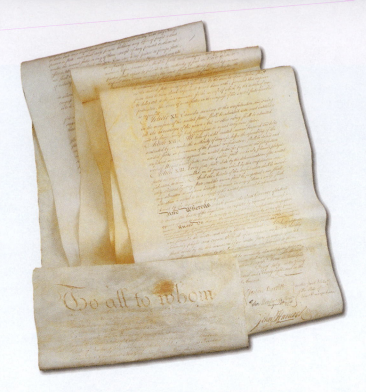

Articles of Confederation Delegates to the Second Continental Congress hammered out the Articles of Confederation over many months in 1776 and 1777. Once the congress agreed on it, the plan was printed and distributed to state legislatures for ratification, a process that took nearly five years because it required the assent of thirteen states. National Archives.

Articles of Confederation

▶ The written document defining the structure of the government from 1781 to 1788. Under the Articles, the Union was a confederation of equal states, with no executive (president) and with limited powers, existing mainly to foster a common defense.

CREATING AND APPROVING A WRITTEN plan of government for the new confederation took five years, as delegates and states sought agreement on fundamental principles. With monarchy gone, where would sovereignty lie? What would be the nature of representation? Who would hold the power of taxation? The resulting plan, called the **Articles of Confederation**, proved to be surprisingly difficult to implement, mainly because the thirteen states disagreed over boundaries in the land to the west of the states. Once the Articles were ratified and the active phase of the war had drawn to a close, the Continental Congress faded in importance compared with politics in the individual states.

Confederation and Taxation

Only after declaring independence did the Continental Congress turn its attention to creating a written document that would specify what powers the congress had and by what authority it existed. There was widespread agreement on key government powers: pursuing war and peace, conducting foreign relations, regulating trade, and running a postal service. By late 1777, congressmen reached agreement on the Articles of Confederation, defining the Union as a loose confederation of states existing mainly to foster a common defense. Much like the existing Continental Congress, there was no national executive (that is, no president) and no judiciary.

CHAPTER LOCATOR | **What kind of government did the Articles of Confederation create?** | How did the states define citizenship and freedom?

Anywhere from two to seven delegates could represent each state, with each delegation casting a single vote. Routine decisions required a simple majority of seven states, whereas momentous decisions, such as declaring war, required nine. To approve or amend the Articles required the unanimous consent both of the thirteen state delegations and of the thirteen state legislatures—giving any state a crippling veto power. Most crucially, the Articles gave the national government no power of direct taxation.

Yet taxation was a necessity, since all governments require money. To finance the Revolutionary War, the confederation congress issued interest-bearing bonds purchased by French and Dutch bankers as well as middling to wealthy Americans, and revenue was necessary to repay these loans. Other routine government functions required money: Trade regulation required salaried customs officers; a postal system required postmen, horses and wagons, and well-maintained postal roads; the western lands required surveyors; and Indian diplomacy (or war) added further large costs. Article 8 of the confederation document declared that taxes were needed to support "the common defence or general welfare" of the country, yet the congress also had to be sensitive to the rhetoric of the Revolution, which denounced taxation by a nonrepresentative power.

The Articles of Confederation posed a delicate two-step solution. The congress would requisition (that is, request) money to be paid into the common treasury, and each state legislature would then levy taxes within its borders to pay the requisition. The Articles called for state contributions assessed in proportion to the improved property value of the state's land, so that populous states paid more than did sparsely populated states. Requiring that the actual tax bill be passed by the state legislatures preserved the Revolution's principle of taxation only by direct representation. However, no mechanism compelled states to pay.

The lack of authority in the confederation government was exactly what many state leaders wanted in the late 1770s. A league of states with rotating personnel, no executive branch, no power of direct taxation, and a requirement of unanimity for any major change seemed to be a good way to keep government in check. The catch was that ratification of the Articles required unanimous agreement, and that proved difficult to secure.

The Problem of Western Lands

The most serious disagreement delaying ratification of the Articles concerned the absence of any plan for the lands to the west of the thirteen original states. This absence was deliberate: Virginia and Connecticut had old colonial charters that located their western boundaries at the Mississippi River, and six other states also claimed parts of that land. But five states without extensive land claims insisted on redrawing those colonial boundaries to create a national domain to be sold to settlers (**Map 8.1**). As one Rhode Island delegate put it, "The western world opens an amazing prospect as a national fund; it is equal to our debt."

The eight land-claiming states were ready to sign the Articles of Confederation in 1777, since it protected their interests. Three states without claims—Rhode Island, Pennsylvania, and New Jersey—eventually capitulated and signed, "not from a Conviction of the Equality and Justness of it," said a New Jersey

> CHRONOLOGY

1777
– Articles of Confederation are sent to states.

1781
– Articles of Confederation are ratified.
– Creation of executive departments.

Why did the Articles of Confederation fail?

How did the Constitution change how the nation was governed?

What were the objections to ratification of the Constitution?

Conclusion: What was the "republican remedy"?

LearningCurve
Check what you know.
bedfordstmartins.com /roarkunderstanding

delegate, "but merely from an absolute Necessity there was of complying to save the Continent." But Delaware and Maryland continued to hold out, insisting on a national domain policy. In 1779, the disputants finally compromised: Any land a state volunteered to relinquish would become the national domain. When Virginia representatives James Madison and Thomas Jefferson ceded Virginia's huge land claim in 1781, the Articles of Confederation were at last unanimously approved.

MAP 8.1 ■ Cession of Western Lands, 1782–1802

The thirteen new states found it hard to ratify the Articles of Confederation without settling their conflicting land claims in the West, a vast area occupied by Indian tribes. The five states objecting to the Articles' silence over western land policy were Maryland, Delaware, New Jersey, Rhode Island, and Pennsylvania.

> MAP ACTIVITY

READING THE MAP: Which state had the largest claims on western territory?

CONNECTIONS: In what context did the first dispute regarding western lands arise? How was it resolved? Does the map suggest a reason why Pennsylvania, a large state, joined the four much smaller states on this issue?

CHAPTER LOCATOR | What kind of government did the Articles of Confederation create? | How did the states define citizenship and freedom?

208
CHAPTER 8
BUILDING A REPUBLIC

The western land issue demonstrated that powerful interests divided the thirteen new states. The apparent unity of purpose inspired by fighting the war against Britain papered over sizable cracks in the new confederation.

Running the New Government

No fanfare greeted the long-awaited inauguration of the new government in 1781. The congress continued to sputter along, its problems far from solved by the signing of the Articles. Lack of a quorum, defined as two men from seven states, often hampered day-to-day activities. State legislatures were slow to select delegates, and many politicians preferred to devote their energies to state governments, especially when the congress seemed deadlocked or, worse, irrelevant.

It did not help that the congress had no permanent home. During the war, when the British army threatened Philadelphia, the congress relocated to small Pennsylvania towns such as Lancaster and York and then to Baltimore. After hostilities ceased, the congress moved from Trenton to Princeton to Annapolis to New York City. Many delegates were reluctant to travel far from home, especially if they had wives and children. Consequently, some of the most committed delegates were young bachelors, such as James Madison, and men in their fifties and sixties whose families were grown, such as Samuel Adams.

To address the difficulties of an inefficient congress, executive departments of war, finance, and foreign affairs were created in 1781 to handle purely administrative functions. When the department heads were ambitious—as was Robert Morris, a wealthy Philadelphia merchant who served as superintendent of finance—they could exercise considerable executive power. The Articles of Confederation had deliberately refrained from setting up an executive branch, but a modest one was being invented by necessity.

QUICK REVIEW

Why was the confederation government's authority so limited?

| Why did the Articles of Confederation fail? | How did the Constitution change how the nation was governed? | What were the objections to ratification of the Constitution? | Conclusion: What was the "republican remedy"? | ☑ LearningCurve Check what you know. bedfordstmartins.com /roarkunderstanding |

How did the states define citizenship and freedom?

Widow from Essex County

Mrs. Elizabeth Alexander Stevens was married to John Stevens, a New Jersey delegate to the Continental Congress in 1783. Widowed in 1792, she would have then been eligible to vote in state elections according to New Jersey's unique enfranchisement of property-holding women. The widow Stevens died in 1799, before suffrage was redefined to be the exclusive right of males. *New Jersey Historical Society.*

I**N THE FIRST DECADE OF INDEPENDENCE,** the states were sovereign and all-powerful. Only a few functions, such as declaring war and peace, had been transferred to the confederation government. Familiar and close to home, state governments claimed the allegiance of citizens and became the arena in which the Revolution's innovations would first be tried. Each state implemented a constitution and determined voter qualifications, and many states grappled with the issue of squaring slavery with Revolutionary ideals, with varying outcomes.

The State Constitutions

republicanism

▶ A social philosophy that embraced representative institutions (as opposed to monarchy), a citizenry attuned to civic values above private interests, and a virtuous community in which individuals work to promote the public good.

In May 1776, the congress recommended that all states draw up constitutions based on "the authority of the people." By 1778, ten states had done so, and three more (Connecticut, Massachusetts, and Rhode Island) had adopted and updated their original colonial charters. A shared feature of all the state constitutions was the conviction that government ultimately rests on the consent of the governed. Political writers in the late 1770s embraced the concept of **republicanism** as the underpinning of the new governments. Republicanism meant more than popular

CHAPTER LOCATOR | What kind of government did the Articles of Confederation create? | **How did the states define citizenship and freedom?**

210
CHAPTER 8
BUILDING A REPUBLIC

elections and representative institutions. For some, republicanism stood for leaders who were autonomous, virtuous citizens putting civic values above private interests. For others, it suggested direct democracy, with nothing standing in the way of the will of the people. For all, it meant government that promoted the people's welfare.

Widespread agreement about the virtues of republicanism went hand in hand with the idea that republics could succeed only in relatively small units, where people could make sure their interests were being served. Eleven states continued the colonial practice of a two-chamber assembly but greatly augmented the powers of the lower house. Pennsylvania and Georgia abolished the more elite upper house altogether, and most states severely limited the powers of the governor. Real power thus resided with the lower houses, responsive to popular majorities due to annual elections and guaranteed rotation in office (term limits).

Six of the state constitutions included bills of rights—lists of individual liberties that government could not abridge. Virginia's bill was the first. Passed in June 1776, it asserted "That all men are by nature equally free and independent, and have certain inherent rights, of which, when they enter into a state of society, they cannot by any compact deprive or divest their posterity; namely, the enjoyment of life and liberty, with the means of acquiring and possessing property, and pursuing and obtaining happiness and safety." Along with these inherent rights went more specific rights to freedom of speech, freedom of the press, and trial by jury.

Who Are "the People"?

When the Continental Congress called for state constitutions based on "the authority of the people," and when the Virginia bill of rights granted "all men" certain rights, who was meant by "the people"? Who exactly were the citizens of this new country, and how far would the principle of democratic government extend? Different people answered these questions differently, but in the 1770s certain limits to political participation were widely agreed upon.

One limit was defined by property. In nearly every state, voters and political candidates had to meet varying property qualifications. Only property owners were presumed to possess the necessary independence of mind to make wise political choices. Are not propertyless men, asked John Adams, "too little acquainted with public affairs to form a right judgment, and too dependent upon other men to have a will of their own?" Property qualifications probably disfranchised from one-quarter to one-half of adult white males in all the states. Not all of them took their nonvoter status quietly. One Maryland man wondered what was so special about being worth £30, his state's threshold for voting: "Every poor man has a life, a personal liberty, and a right to his earnings; and is in danger of being injured by government in a variety of ways." Others noted that propertyless men were fighting and dying in the Revolutionary War; surely they had legitimate political concerns. A few radical voices challenged the notion that wealth was correlated with good citizenship; maybe the opposite was true. But ideas like this were outside the mainstream. The writers of the new constitutions, themselves men of property, viewed the right to own and preserve property as a central principle of the Revolution.

1776
- Declaration of Independence is adopted.
- Virginia adopts state bill of rights.

1778
- State constitutions are completed.

1780
- Pennsylvania institutes gradual emancipation.

1781
- Several Massachusetts slaves sue for freedom.

1783
- Massachusetts enfranchises taxpaying free blacks.

1784
- Gradual emancipation laws are passed in Rhode Island and Connecticut.

1799
- Gradual emancipation law is passed in New York.

1804
- Gradual emancipation law is passed in New Jersey.

Why did the Articles of Confederation fail? | How did the Constitution change how the nation was governed? | What were the objections to ratification of the Constitution? | Conclusion: What was the "republican remedy"? | ☑ LearningCurve Check what you know. bedfordstmartins.com /roarkunderstanding

Another exclusion from voting—women—was so ingrained that few stopped to question it. Yet the logic of allowing propertied females to vote did occur to a handful of well-placed women. Abigail Adams wrote to her husband, John, in 1782, "Even in the freest countrys our property is subject to the controul and disposal of our partners, to whom the Laws have given a sovereign Authority. Deprived of a voice in Legislation, obliged to submit to those Laws which are imposed upon us, is it not sufficient to make us indifferent to the publick Welfare?"

Only three states specified that voters had to be male, so powerful was the unspoken assumption that only men could vote. Yet in New Jersey, small numbers of women began to go to the polls in the 1780s. The state's constitution of 1776 enfranchised all free inhabitants worth more than £50, language that in theory opened the door to free blacks and unmarried women who met the property requirement. (Married women owned no property, for by law their husbands held title to everything.)

In 1790, only about 1,000 free black adults of both sexes lived in New Jersey, a state with a population of 184,000. The number of unmarried adult white women was probably also small and comprised mainly widows. In view of the property requirement, the voter blocs enfranchised under this law were minuscule. Still, this highly unusual situation lasted until 1807, when a new state law specifically disfranchised both blacks and women. Henceforth, independence of mind, held to be essential for voting, was redefined to be sex- and race-specific.

In the 1780s, voting everywhere was class-specific because of property restrictions. John Adams urged the framers of the Massachusetts constitution to stick with traditional property qualifications. If suffrage is brought up for debate, he warned, "there will be no end of it. New claims will arise; women will demand a vote; lads from twelve to twenty-one will think their rights not enough attended to; and every man who has not a farthing, will demand an equal voice with any other."

Equality and Slavery

Restrictions on political participation did not mean that propertyless people enjoyed no civil rights and liberties. The various state bills of rights applied to all individuals who were free; unfree people were another matter.

The author of the Virginia bill of rights was George Mason, a planter who owned 118 slaves. When he wrote that "all men are by nature equally free and independent," Mason did not have slaves in mind; he instead was asserting that white Americans were the equals of the British and entitled to equal liberties. Other Virginia legislators, worried about misinterpretations, added a qualifying clause: that all men "when they enter into a state of society" have inherent rights. As one legislator wrote, with relief, "Slaves, not being constituent members of our society, could never pretend to any benefit from such a maxim."

One month later, the Declaration of Independence used essentially the same phrase about equality, this time without the modifying clause about entering society. Two state constitutions, Pennsylvania and Massachusetts, also picked it up. In Massachusetts, one town suggested rewording the draft constitution to

CHAPTER LOCATOR | What kind of government did the Articles of Confederation create? | How did the states define citizenship and freedom?

CHAPTER 8
212   BUILDING A REPUBLIC

read "All men, whites and blacks, are born free and equal." The suggestion was not implemented.

Nevertheless, after 1776, the ideals of the Revolution about natural equality and liberty began to erode the institution of slavery. Often, enslaved blacks led the challenge. In 1777, several Massachusetts slaves petitioned for their "natural & unalienable right to that freedom which the great Parent of the Universe hath bestowed equally on all mankind." They modestly asked for freedom for their children at age twenty-one and were turned down. In 1779, similar petitions in Connecticut and New Hampshire met with no success. Seven Massachusetts free men, including the mariner brothers Paul and John Cuffe, refused to pay taxes on the grounds that they could not vote and so were not represented. The Cuffe brothers landed in jail in 1780 for tax evasion, but their petition to the Massachusetts legislature spurred the extension of suffrage to taxpaying free blacks in 1783.

Another way to bring the issue before lawmakers was to sue in court. In 1781, a woman called Elizabeth Freeman (Mum Bett) was the first to win freedom in a Massachusetts court, basing her case on the just-passed state constitution that declared "all men are born free and equal." Another Massachusetts slave, Quok Walker, charged his master with assault and battery, arguing that he was a freeman under that same constitutional phrase. Walker won and was set free, a decision confirmed in an appeal to the state's superior court in 1783. Several similar cases followed, and by 1789 slavery had been effectively abolished by a series of judicial decisions in Massachusetts.

State legislatures acted more slowly. Pennsylvania enacted a **gradual emancipation** law in 1780, providing that infants born to a slave mother on or after March 1, 1780, would be freed at age twenty-eight. Not until 1847 did Pennsylvania fully abolish slavery, but slaves did not wait for such slow implementation. Untold numbers in Pennsylvania simply ran away and asserted their freedom. One estimate holds that more than half of young slave men in Philadelphia joined the ranks of free blacks, and by 1790, free blacks outnumbered slaves in Pennsylvania two to one.

Rhode Island and Connecticut adopted gradual emancipation laws in 1784; New York waited until 1799 and New Jersey until 1804 to enact theirs. These last were the two northern states with the largest number of slaves—New York with 20,000 in 1800, New Jersey with more than 12,000—whereas Pennsylvania had just 1,700. Gradual emancipation illustrates the tension between radical and conservative implications of republican ideology. Republican government protected people's liberties and property, yet slaves were both people and property. Gradual emancipation balanced the civil rights of blacks and the property rights of their owners by promising delayed freedom.

South of Pennsylvania, in Delaware, Maryland, and Virginia, where slavery was critical to the economy, emancipation bills were rejected. All three states,

Elizabeth Freeman in 1811

After suing for her freedom in court, Elizabeth Freeman ("Mum Bett") found secure employment with the family of her lawyer, Theodore Sedgwick. A Sedgwick son later wrote: "If there could be a practical refutation of the imagined superiority of our race to hers, the life and character of this woman would afford that refutation. . . . She had, when occasion required it, an air of command which conferred a degree of dignity." Massachusetts Historical Society.

gradual emancipation
▶ Laws passed in five northern states that balanced slaves' civil rights against slaveholders' property rights by providing a multistage process for freeing slaves, distinguishing persons already alive from those not yet born and providing benchmark dates when freedom would arrive for each group.

Why did the Articles of Confederation fail? | How did the Constitution change how the nation was governed? | What were the objections to ratification of the Constitution? | Conclusion: What was the "republican remedy"? | ✓ LearningCurve Check what you know. bedfordstmartins.com /roarkunderstanding

213

Legal Changes to Slavery, 1777–1804

however, eased legal restrictions and allowed individual acts of emancipation for adult slaves below the age of forty-five under new manumission laws. By 1790, close to 10,000 newly freed Virginia slaves had formed local free black communities complete with schools and churches.

In the deep South—the Carolinas and Georgia—freedom for slaves was unthinkable among whites. Yet several thousand slaves had defected to the British during the war, and between 3,000 and 4,000 left with the British at the war's conclusion. Adding northern blacks evacuated from New York City in 1783, the probable total of emancipated blacks who left the United States was between 8,000 and 10,000. Some went to Canada, some to England, and some to Sierra Leone on the west coast of Africa. Many hundreds took refuge with the Seminole and Creek Indians, becoming permanent members of their communities in Spanish Florida and western Georgia.

Although all these instances of emancipation were gradual, small, and certainly incomplete, their symbolic importance was enormous. Every state from Pennsylvania north acknowledged that slavery was fundamentally inconsistent with Revolutionary ideology; "all men are created equal" was beginning to acquire real force as a basic principle.

> **QUICK REVIEW**

What were the limits of citizenship, rights, and freedom within the various states?

CHAPTER LOCATOR | What kind of government did the Articles of Confederation create? | How did the states define citizenship and freedom?

214 CHAPTER 8 BUILDING A REPUBLIC

Why did the Articles of Confederation fail?

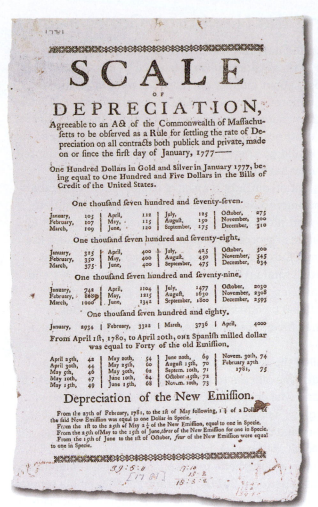

IN 1783, THE CONFEDERATION government faced three interrelated concerns: paying down the large war debt, making formal peace with the Indians, and dealing with western settlement. Lacking the power to enforce its tax requisitions, the congress faced added debt pressures when army officers suddenly demanded secure pensions. Revenue from sales of western lands seemed to be a promising solution, but Indian inhabitants of those lands had different ideas.

From 1784 to 1786, the congress struggled mightily with these three issues. Some leaders were gripped by a sense of crisis, fearing that the Articles of Confederation were too weak. Others defended the Articles as the best guarantee of liberty because real governance occurred at the state level, closer to the people. A major outbreak of civil disorder in western Massachusetts quickly crystallized the debate and propelled the critics of the Articles into decisive and far-reaching action.

| Why did the Articles of Confederation fail? | How did the Constitution change how the nation was governed? | What were the objections to ratification of the Constitution? | Conclusion: What was the "republican remedy"? | ☑ LearningCurve Check what you know. bedfordstmartins.com /roarkunderstanding |

Newburgh Conspiracy

▶ A bogus threatened coup staged by Continental army officers and leaders in the Continental Congress in 1782–1783. They hoped that a forceful demand for military back pay and pensions would create pressure for stronger taxation powers. General Washington defused the threat.

The War Debt and the Newburgh Conspiracy

For nearly two years, the Continental army camped at Newburgh, north of the British-occupied city of New York, awaiting news of a peace treaty. The soldiers were bored, restless, and upset about military payrolls that were far in arrears. An earlier promise to officers of generous pensions (half pay for life), made in 1780 in a desperate effort to retain them, seemed unlikely to be honored. In December 1782, officers petitioned the congress for immediate back pay for their men so that when peace arrived, no one would go home penniless. The petition darkly hinted that failure to pay the men "may have fatal effects."

Instead of rejecting the petition outright for lack of money, several members of the congress saw an opportunity to pressure the states to approve taxation powers. One of these was Robert Morris, a Philadelphia merchant with a gift for financial dealings. As the congress's superintendent of finance, Morris kept the books and wheedled loans from European bankers using his own substantial fortune as collateral. To forestall total insolvency, Morris led efforts in 1781 and again in 1786 to amend the Articles to allow collection of a 5 percent impost (an import tax). Each time it failed by one vote, illustrating the difficulties of achieving unanimity. Now the officers' petition offered new prospects to make the case for taxation.

The result was a plot called the **Newburgh Conspiracy**. Morris and several other congressmen encouraged the officers to march the army on the congress to demand its pay. No actual coup was envisioned; both sides shared the goal of wanting to augment the congress's power of taxation. Yet the risks were great, for not everyone would understand that this was a ruse. What if the soldiers, incited by their grievances, could not be held in check?

General George Washington, sympathetic to the plight of unpaid soldiers and officers, had approved the initial petition. But the plotters, knowing of his reputation for integrity, did not inform him of their collusion with congressional leaders. In March 1783, when the general learned of these developments, he delivered an emotional speech to a meeting of five hundred officers, reminding them in stirring language of honor, heroism, and sacrifice. He urged them to put their faith in the congress, and he denounced the plotters as "subversive of all order and discipline." His audience was left speechless and tearful, and the plot was immediately defused.

Morris continued to work to find money to pay the soldiers, but in the end, a trickle of money from a few states was too little and too late, coming after the army had begun to disband. For its part, the congress voted to endorse a plan to commute, or transform, the lifetime pension promised the officers into a lump-sum payment of full pay for five years. But no lump sum of money was available. Instead, the officers were issued "commutation certificates," promising future payment with interest, which quickly depreciated in value.

In 1783, the soldiers' pay and officers' pensions added some $5 million to the rising public debt, forcing the congress to press for larger requisitions from the states. The confederation, however, had one new source of enormous untapped wealth: the extensive western territories, attractive to the fast-growing white population but currently inhabited by Indians.

CHAPTER LOCATOR | What kind of government did the Articles of Confederation create? | How did the states define citizenship and freedom?

The Treaty of Fort Stanwix

Since the Indians had not participated in the Treaty of Paris of 1783, the confederation government hoped to formalize treaties ending ongoing hostilities between Indians and settlers and securing land cessions. The most pressing problem was the land inhabited by the Iroquois Confederacy, a league of six tribes, now claimed by the states of New York and Massachusetts based on their colonial charters (see Map 8.1).

Treaty of Fort Stanwix, 1784

At issue was the revenue stream that land sales would generate: Which government would get it? The congress summoned the Iroquois to a meeting in October 1784 at Fort Stanwix, on the upper Mohawk River. The Articles of Confederation gave the congress (as opposed to individual states) the right to manage diplomacy, war, and "all affairs with the Indians, not members of any of the States." But New York's governor seized on that ambiguous language, claiming that the Iroquois were in fact "members" of his state, and called his own meeting at Fort Stanwix in September. Suspecting that New York's claim to authority might be superseded by the congress, the most important chiefs declined to come and instead sent deputies without authority to negotiate. The Mohawk leader Joseph Brant shrewdly identified the problem of divided authority that afflicted the confederation government: "Here lies some Difficulty in our Minds, that there should be two separate bodies to manage these Affairs." No deal was struck with New York.

Three weeks later, U.S. commissioners opened proceedings at Fort Stanwix with the Seneca chief Cornplanter and Captain Aaron Hill, a Mohawk leader, accompanied by six hundred Iroquois. The Americans demanded a return of prisoners of war; recognition of the confederation's (and not states') authority to negotiate; and an all-important cession of a strip of land from Fort Niagara due south, which established U.S.-held territory adjacent to the border with Canada. This cession of territory would enclose the Iroquois land within the United States and would make it impossible for the Indians to claim to be between the United States and Canada. When the tribal leaders balked, one of the commissioners sternly replied, "You are mistaken in supposing that, having been excluded from the treaty between the United States and the King of England, you are become a free and independent nation and may make what terms you please. It is not so. You are a subdued people."

In the end, the treaty was signed, gifts were given, and six high-level Indian hostages were kept at the fort awaiting the release of the American prisoners taken during the Revolutionary War, mostly women and children. In addition, a significant side deal sealed the release of much of the Seneca tribe's claim to the Ohio Valley to the United States. This move was a major surprise to the Delaware, Mingo, and Shawnee Indians who lived there. In the months to come, tribes not at the meeting tried to disavow the **Treaty of Fort Stanwix** as a document signed under coercion by virtual hostages. But the confederation government ignored those complaints and made plans to survey and develop the Ohio Territory.

New York's governor astutely figured that the congress's power to implement the treaty terms was limited. So New York quietly began surveying and then selling the very land it had failed to secure by treaty with the Iroquois. As that fact became generally known, it pointed up the weakness of the confederation government. One Connecticut leader wondered, "What is to defend us from the ambition and rapacity of New York, when she has spread over that vast territory, which she claims and holds?"

Treaty of Fort Stanwix
▶1784 treaty with the Iroquois Confederacy that established the primacy of the American confederation (and not states) to negotiate with Indians and that resulted in large land cessions in the Ohio Country (northwestern Pennsylvania). Tribes not present at Fort Stanwix disavowed the treaty.

Why did the Articles of Confederation fail? | How did the Constitution change how the nation was governed? | What were the objections to ratification of the Constitution? | Conclusion: What was the "republican remedy"? | ☑ LearningCurve Check what you know. bedfordstmartins.com /roarkunderstanding

217

Land Ordinances and the Northwest Territory

The congress ignored western New York and turned instead to the Ohio Valley to make good on the promise of western expansion. Congressman Thomas Jefferson, charged with drafting a policy, proposed dividing the territory north of the Ohio River and east of the Mississippi—the Northwest Territory—into nine new states with evenly spaced east-west boundaries and townships ten miles square. He even advocated giving, not selling, the land to settlers, because future property taxes on the improved land would be payment enough. Jefferson's aim was to encourage rapid and democratic settlement and to discourage land speculation. Jefferson projected representative governments in the new states; they would not become colonies of the older states. Finally, Jefferson's draft prohibited slavery in the nine new states.

The congress adopted parts of Jefferson's plan in the Ordinance of 1784: the rectangular grid, the nine states, and the guarantee of self-government and eventual statehood. What the congress found too radical was the proposal to give away the land; it badly needed immediate revenue. The slavery prohibition also failed, by a vote of seven to six states.

Jefferson's Map of the Northwest Territory

Thomas Jefferson proposed nine states in his initial plan for the Northwest Territory in 1784. Straight lines and right angles held a strong appeal for him. But such regularity ignored inconvenient geographic features such as rivers and even more inconvenient political facts such as Indian territorial claims. William L. Clements Library.

> **VISUAL ACTIVITY**

READING THE IMAGE: What does this map indicate about Jefferson's vision of the Northwest Territory?

CONNECTIONS: What were the problems with Jefferson's design for the division of the territory? Why did the congress alter it in the land ordinances of 1784, 1785, and 1787?

CHAPTER LOCATOR | What kind of government did the Articles of Confederation create? | How did the states define citizenship and freedom?

218 CHAPTER 8 BUILDING A REPUBLIC

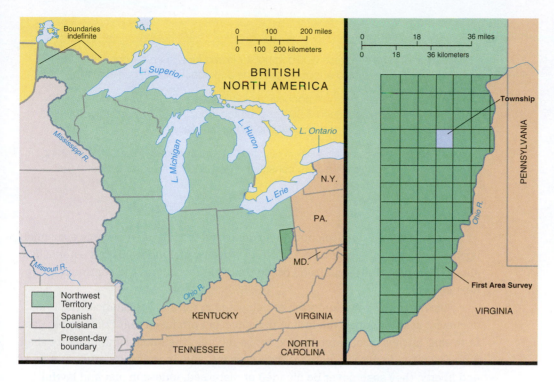

MAP 8.2 ■ The Northwest Ordinance and the Ordinance of 1785

Surveyors mapping the Northwest Territory followed the Ordinance of 1785, using the stars as well as poles and chains (standard surveying equipment) to run boundary lines. The result was a blanket of six-mile-square townships, subdivided into one-mile squares each containing sixteen 40-acre farms.

A year later, the congress revised the legislation with procedures for mapping and selling the land. The Ordinance of 1785 called for three to five states, divided into townships six miles square, further divided into thirty-six sections of 640 acres, each section enough for four family farms. Reduced to easily mappable squares, the land would be sold at public auction for a minimum of one dollar an acre, with highly desirable land bid up for more (**Map 8.2**). Two further restrictions applied: The minimum purchase was 640 acres, and payment had to be in hard money or in certificates of debt from Revolutionary days. This effectively meant that the land's first owners would be prosperous speculators, many of whom never set foot on the acreage. The commodification of land had been taken to a new level.

Speculators who held the land for resale avoided direct contact with the most serious obstacle to settlement: the dozens of Indian tribes that claimed the land as their own. The treaty signed at Fort Stanwix in 1784 was followed in 1785 by the Treaty of Fort McIntosh, which similarly coerced partial cessions of land from the Delaware, Wyandot, Chippewa, and Ottawa tribes. Finally, in 1786, a united Indian meeting near Detroit issued an ultimatum: No cession would be valid without the unanimous consent of the tribes. For two more decades, violent Indian wars in Ohio and Indiana would continue to impede white settlement (as discussed in chapter 9).

A third land act, called the **Northwest Ordinance** of 1787, set forth a three-stage process by which settled territories would advance to statehood. At all three territorial stages, the inhabitants were subject to taxation to support the Union, in the same manner as were the original states.

The Northwest Ordinance of 1787 was perhaps the most important legislation passed by the confederation government. It ensured that the new United States,

Northwest Ordinance

▶ Land act of 1787 that established a three-stage process by which settled territories would become states. It also banned slavery in the Northwest Territory. The ordinance guaranteed that western lands with white populations would not become colonial dependencies.

Why did the Articles of Confederation fail? | How did the Constitution change how the nation was governed? | What were the objections to ratification of the Constitution? | Conclusion: What was the "republican remedy"? | ✓ LearningCurve Check what you know. bedfordstmartins.com /roarkunderstanding

219

> The Northwest Ordinance of 1787 and the Path to Statehood	
Phase One	The congress would appoint officials for a sparsely populated territory who would adopt a legal code and appoint local magistrates.
Phase Two	When the male population of voting age and landowning status (fifty acres) reached 5,000, the territory could elect its own legislature and send a nonvoting delegate to the congress.
Phase Three	When the population of voting citizens reached 60,000, the territory could write a state constitution and apply for full admission to the Union.

so recently released from colonial dependency, would not itself become a colonial power—at least not with respect to white citizens. The mechanism it established allowed for the orderly expansion of the United States across the continent in the next century.

Nonwhites were not forgotten or neglected in the 1787 ordinance. The brief document acknowledged the Indian presence and promised that "the utmost good faith shall always be observed towards the Indians; their lands and property shall never be taken from them without their consent; and, in their property, rights, and liberty, they shall never be invaded or disturbed, unless in just and lawful wars authorized by Congress." The 1787 ordinance further pledged that "laws founded in justice and humanity, shall from time to time be made for preventing wrongs being done to them." Such promises indicated noble intentions, but they were not generally honored in the decades to come.

Jefferson's original and remarkable suggestion to prohibit slavery in the North-west Territory resurfaced in the 1787 ordinance, passing this time without any debate. Probably the addition of a fugitive slave provision in the act set southern congressmen at ease: Escaped slaves caught north of the Ohio River would be returned south. Also, abundant territory south of the Ohio remained available for the spread of slavery. The ordinance thus acknowledged and supported slavery even as it barred it from one region. Still, the prohibition of slavery in the Northwest Territory perpetuated the dynamic of gradual emancipation in the North. North-South sectionalism based on slavery was slowly taking shape.

The Requisition of 1785 and Shays's Rebellion, 1786–1787

Without an impost amendment and with public land sales projected but not yet realized, the confederation again requisitioned the states to contribute revenue. In 1785, the amount requested was $3 million, four times larger than the previous year's levy. Of this sum, 30 percent was needed for the government's operating costs, and another 30 percent was earmarked to pay debts owed to foreign lenders. The remaining 40 percent was to go to Americans who owned government bonds, the IOUs of the Revolutionary years. A significant slice of that 40 percent represented the interest owed to army officers for their recently issued "commutation certificates." This was a tax that, if collected, was going to hurt.

CHAPTER LOCATOR | What kind of government did the Articles of Confederation create? | How did the states define citizenship and freedom?

CHAPTER 8
220   BUILDING A REPUBLIC

At this time, states were struggling under state tax levies. Several states without major ports (and the import duties that ports generated) were already pressing their farmer citizens in order to retire state debts from the Revolution. New Jersey and Connecticut fit this profile, and both state legislatures voted to ignore the confederation's requisition. In New Hampshire, town meetings voted to refuse to pay, because they could not. In 1786, two hundred armed insurgents surrounded the New Hampshire capitol to protest the taxes but were driven off by an armed militia. The shocked assemblymen backed off from an earlier order to haul delinquent taxpayers into courts. Rhode Island, North Carolina, and Georgia responded to their constituents' protests by issuing abundant amounts of paper money and allowing taxes to be paid in greatly depreciated currency.

Nowhere were the tensions so extreme as in Massachusetts. For four years in a row, a fiscally conservative legislature, dominated by the coastal commercial centers, had passed tough tax laws to pay state creditors who required payment in hard money, not cheap paper. Then in March 1786, the legislature in Boston loaded the federal requisition onto the bill. In June, farmers in southeastern Massachusetts marched on a courthouse in an effort to close it down, and petitions of complaint about oppressive taxation poured in from the western two-thirds of the state. In July 1786, when the legislature adjourned, having yet again ignored their complaints, dissidents held a series of conventions and called for revisions to the state constitution to promote democracy, eliminate the elite upper house, and move the capital farther west in the state.

Still unheard in Boston, the dissidents targeted the county courts, the local symbol of state authority. In the fall of 1786, several thousand armed men shut down courthouses in six counties; sympathetic local militias did not intervene. The insurgents were not predominantly poor or debt-ridden farmers; they

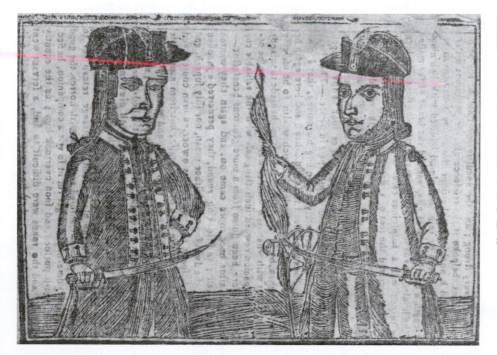

Daniel Shays and Job Shattuck

A Boston almanac of 1787 yields the only rough depiction of Daniel Shays in existence. Shays is standing with another rebel leader, Job Shattuck, from the town of Groton. This particular almanac series was quite pro-Constitution in 1788, so very likely this picture was intended to mock the rebels by showing them in fancy uniforms and armed with swords, trappings beyond their presumed lowly means. National Portrait Gallery, Smithsonian Institution/Art Resource, NY.

Why did the Articles of Confederation fail? | How did the Constitution change how the nation was governed? | What were the objections to ratification of the Constitution? | Conclusion: What was the "republican remedy"? | ✓ **LearningCurve** Check what you know. bedfordstmartins.com /roarkunderstanding

221

included veteran soldiers and officers in the Continental army as well as town leaders. One was a farmer and onetime army captain, Daniel Shays.

The governor of Massachusetts, James Bowdoin, once a protester against British taxes, now characterized the western dissidents as illegal rebels. He vilified Shays as the chief leader, and a Boston newspaper claimed that Shays planned to burn Boston to the ground and overthrow the government. Another former radical, Samuel Adams, took the extreme position that "the man who dares rebel against the laws of a republic ought to suffer death." The dissidents challenged the aging revolutionaries' assumption that popularly elected governments would always be fair and just.

Members of the Continental Congress had much to worry about. In nearly every state, the requisition of 1785 spawned some combination of crowd protests, demands for inflationary paper money, and anger at state authorities and alleged money speculators. The Massachusetts insurgency was the worst episode, and it seemed to be spinning out of control. In October, the congress attempted to triple the size of the federal army, but fewer than 100 men enlisted. So Governor Bowdoin raised a private army, gaining the services of some 3,000 men with pay provided by wealthy and fearful Boston merchants.

In January 1787, the insurgents learned of the private army marching west from Boston, and 1,500 of them moved swiftly to capture a federal armory in Springfield to obtain weapons. But a militia band loyal to the state government beat them to the weapons facility and met their attack with gunfire; 4 rebels were killed and another 20 wounded. The final and bloodless encounter came at Petersham, where Bowdoin's army surprised the rebels and took several hundred of them prisoner. In the end, 2 men were executed for rebellion; 16 more who were sentenced to hang were reprieved at the last moment on the gallows. Some 4,000 men obtained leniency by confessing their misconduct and swearing an oath of allegiance to the state.

Shays's Rebellion caused leaders throughout the country to worry about the confederation's ability to handle civil disorder. Inflammatory Massachusetts newspapers wrote about bloody mob rule spreading to other states. New York lawyer John Jay wrote to George Washington, "Our affairs seem to lead to some crisis, some revolution—something I cannot foresee or conjecture. I am uneasy and apprehensive; more so than during the war." Benjamin Franklin, in his eighties, shrewdly observed that in 1776 Americans had feared "an excess of power in the rulers" but now the problem was perhaps "a defect of obedience" in the subjects. Among such leaders, the sense of crisis in the confederation had greatly deepened.

Shays's Rebellion, 1786–1787

★ Attack by Shays's followers

★ Encounter between Shays's and government forces

Shays's Rebellion

▶ Uprising (1786–1787) led by farmers centered in western Massachusetts. Dissidents protested taxation policies of the eastern elites who controlled the state's government. Shays's Rebellion caused leaders throughout the country to worry about the confederation's ability to handle civil disorder.

> **QUICK REVIEW**

What were the most important factors in the failure of the Articles of Confederation?

CHAPTER LOCATOR | What kind of government did the Articles of Confederation create? | How did the states define citizenship and freedom?

The constitutional convention assembled at the Pennsylvania statehouse in the summer of 1787. Despite the heat, the delegates nailed the windows shut to eliminate the chance of being heard by eavesdroppers, so intent were they on secrecy. The building is now called Independence Hall in honor of the signing of the Declaration of Independence there in 1776. Historical Society of Pennsylvania.

How did the Constitution change how the nation was governed?

SHAYS'S REBELLION PROVOKED an odd mixture of fear and hope that the government under the Articles of Confederation was losing its grip on power. A small circle of Virginians decided to try one last time to augment the powers granted to the government by the Articles. Their innocuous call for a meeting to discuss trade regulation led within a year to a total reworking of the national government, one with extensive powers and multiple branches based on differing constituencies.

From Annapolis to Philadelphia

The Virginians, led by James Madison, convinced the confederation congress to allow a September 1786 meeting of delegates at Annapolis, Maryland, to try again to revise the trade regulation powers of the Articles. Only five states participated, and the delegates planned a second meeting for Philadelphia in May 1787. The congress reluctantly endorsed the Philadelphia meeting and limited its scope to "the sole and express purpose of revising the Articles of Confederation." But a few leaders, such as Alexander Hamilton of New York, had far more ambitious plans.

The fifty-five men who assembled at Philadelphia in May 1787 for the constitutional convention were generally those who had already concluded that there

Why did the Articles of Confederation fail?

How did the Constitution change how the nation was governed?

What were the objections to ratification of the Constitution?

Conclusion: What was the "republican remedy"?

☑ LearningCurve
Check what you know.
bedfordstmartins.com
/roarkunderstanding

223

The Constitutional Convention of 1787

- Rhode Island refused to send a single representative.
- Most delegates were from the wealthier classes.
- Convention established the three-fifths clause in counting slaves for the apportionment of representation.
- All but three delegates signed the Constitution produced by the convention.

Virginia Plan

▶ Plan drafted by James Madison and presented at the opening of the Philadelphia constitutional convention. Proposing a powerful three-branch government, with representation in both houses of the congress tied to population, this plan eclipsed the voice of small states in national government.

New Jersey Plan

▶ Alternative plan drafted by delegates from small states, retaining the confederation's single-house congress with one vote per state. But like the Virginia Plan, it proposed enhanced congressional powers, including the right to tax, regulate trade, and use force on unruly state governments.

were weaknesses in the Articles of Confederation. Patrick Henry, author of the Virginia Resolves in 1765 and more recently state governor, refused to go to the convention, saying he "smelled a rat." Rhode Island declined to send delegates. Two men sent by New York's legislature to check the influence of fellow delegate Alexander Hamilton left in dismay in the middle of the convention, leaving Hamilton as the sole representative of the state.

This gathering of white men included no artisans, day laborers, or ordinary farmers. Two-thirds of the delegates were lawyers. Half had been officers in the Continental army. The majority had served in the confederation congress and knew its strengths and weaknesses. Seven men had been governors of their states and knew firsthand the frustrations of thwarted executive power. A few elder statesmen attended, such as Benjamin Franklin and George Washington, but on the whole the delegates were young, like Madison and Hamilton.

The Virginia and New Jersey Plans

The convention worked in secrecy, which enabled the men to freely explore alternatives without fear that their honest opinions would come back to haunt them. The Virginia delegation first laid out a fifteen-point plan, known as the **Virginia Plan**, that repudiated the principle of a confederation of states. Largely the work of Madison, the Virginia Plan set out a three-branch government composed of a two-chamber legislature, a powerful executive, and a judiciary. It practically eliminated the voices of the smaller states by pegging representation in both houses of the congress to population. The theory was that government operated directly on people, not on states. Among the breathtaking powers assigned to the congress were the rights to veto state legislation and to coerce states militarily to obey national laws. To prevent the congress from having absolute power, the executive and judiciary could jointly veto its actions.

In mid-June, delegates from New Jersey, Connecticut, Delaware, and New Hampshire — all small states — unveiled an alternative proposal called the **New Jersey Plan**. The New Jersey Plan retained the existing single-house congress of the Articles of Confederation in which each state had one vote. Acknowledging the need for an executive, the plan created a plural presidency to be shared by three men elected by the congress from among its membership. Where it sharply departed from the existing government was in the sweeping powers it gave to the new congress: the right to tax, regulate trade, and use force on unruly state governments. In favoring national power over states' rights, it aligned itself with the Virginia Plan. But the New Jersey Plan retained the confederation principle that the national government was to be an assembly of states, not of people. For two weeks, delegates debated the two plans, focusing on the key issue of representation. The small-state delegates conceded that one house in a two-house legislature could be apportioned by population, but they would never agree that both houses could be. Madison was equally vehement about bypassing representation by state, which he viewed as the fundamental flaw in the Articles.

The debate seemed deadlocked, and for a while the convention was "on the verge of dissolution, scarce held together by the strength of a hair," according to one delegate. Only in mid-July did the so-called Great Compromise break the

CHAPTER LOCATOR | What kind of government did the Articles of Confederation create? | How did the states define citizenship and freedom?

stalemate and produce the basic structural features of the emerging United States Constitution. Proponents of the competing plans agreed on a bicameral legislature. Representation in the lower house, the House of Representatives, would be apportioned by population, and representation in the upper house, the Senate, would come from all the states equally, with each state represented by two independently voting senators.

Representation by population turned out to be an ambiguous concept once it was subjected to rigorous discussion. Who counted? Were slaves, for example, people or property? As people, they would add weight to the southern delegations in the House of Representatives, but as property they would add to the tax burdens of those states. What emerged was the compromise known as the **three-fifths clause**: All free persons plus "three-fifths of all other Persons" constituted the numerical base for the apportionment of representatives.

Using "all other Persons" as a substitute for "slaves" indicates the discomfort delegates felt in acknowledging in the Constitution the existence of slavery. But though slavery was nowhere named, nonetheless it was recognized, protected, and thereby perpetuated by the U.S. Constitution.

three-fifths clause
▶ A clause in the Constitution stipulating that all free persons plus "three-fifths of all other Persons" would constitute the numerical base for apportioning both representation and taxation. The clause tacitly acknowledged the existence of slavery in the United States.

Democracy versus Republicanism

The delegates in Philadelphia made a distinction between democracy and republicanism new to the American political vocabulary. Pure democracy was now taken to be a dangerous thing. As a Massachusetts delegate put it, "The evils we experience flow from the excess of democracy." The delegates still favored republican institutions, but they created a government that gave direct voice to the people only in the House and that granted a check on that voice to the Senate, a body of men elected not by direct popular vote but by the state legislatures. Senators served for six years, with no limit on reelection; they were protected from the whims of democratic majorities, and their long terms fostered experience and maturity in office.

Similarly, the presidency evolved into a powerful office out of the reach of direct democracy. The delegates devised an electoral college whose only function was to elect the president and vice president. Each state's legislature would choose the electors, whose number was the sum of representatives and senators for the state, an interesting blending of the two principles of representation. The president thus would owe his office not to the Congress, the states, or the people, but to a temporary assemblage of distinguished citizens who could vote their own judgment on the candidates. His term of office was four years, but he could be reelected without limitation.

The framers had developed a far more complex form of federal government than that provided by the Articles of Confederation. To curb the excesses of democracy, they devised a government with limits and checks on all three of its branches. They set forth a powerful president who could veto legislation passed in Congress, but they gave Congress the power to override presidential vetoes. They set up a national judiciary to settle disputes between states and citizens of different states. The framers separated the branches of government not only by functions and reciprocal checks but also by deliberately basing the election of

Why did the Articles of Confederation fail?

How did the Constitution change how the nation was governed?

What were the objections to ratification of the Constitution?

Conclusion: What was the "republican remedy"?

✓ LearningCurve
Check what you know.
bedfordstmartins.com
/roarkunderstanding

225

the legislative and executive branches on different universes of voters—voting citizens (the House), state legislators (the Senate), and the electoral college (the presidency).

The convention carefully listed the powers of the president and of Congress. The president could initiate policy, propose legislation, and veto acts of Congress; he could command the military and direct foreign policy; and he could appoint the entire judiciary, subject to Senate approval. Congress held the purse strings: the power to levy taxes, to regulate trade, and to coin money and control the currency. States were expressly forbidden to issue paper money. Two more powers of Congress—to "provide for the common defence and general Welfare" of the country and "to make all laws which shall be necessary and proper" for carrying out its powers—provided elastic language that came closest to Madison's wish to grant sweeping powers to the new government.

While no one was entirely satisfied with every line of the Constitution, only three dissenters refused to sign the document. The Constitution specified a mechanism for ratification that avoided the dilemma faced earlier by the confederation government: Nine states, not all thirteen, had to ratify it, and special ratifying conventions elected only for that purpose, not state legislatures, would make the crucial decision.

> **QUICK REVIEW**

Why did the Constitution proposed by the Philadelphia convention devise multiple checks on the branches of the government?

CHAPTER LOCATOR | What kind of government did the Articles of Confederation create? | How did the states define citizenship and freedom?

CHAPTER 8
226 BUILDING A REPUBLIC

The Looking Glass for 1787

This pro-Federalist cartoon depicts the debate over the ratification of the Constitution. On the left, Federalists pull a stuck cart toward the shining sun. To the right, Antifederalists pull it toward stormy skies. Library of Congress.

THE PROCESS OF RATIFYING the Constitution was highly contentious. In the three most populous states—Virginia, Massachusetts, and New York—substantial majorities opposed a powerful new national government. North Carolina and Rhode Island refused to call ratifying conventions. Seven of the eight remaining states were easy victories for the Constitution, but securing the approval of the ninth proved difficult. Pro-Constitution forces, called Federalists, had to strategize very shrewdly to defeat anti-Constitution forces, called Antifederalists.

The Federalists

Proponents of the Constitution moved swiftly into action. They first secured agreement from an uneasy confederation congress to defer a vote and instead send the Constitution to the states for their consideration. The pro-Constitution forces next called themselves **Federalists**, a word that implied endorsement of a confederated government. Their opponents thus became known as Antifederalists, a label that made them sound defensive and negative, lacking a program of their own.

To gain momentum, the Federalists targeted the states most likely to ratify quickly. Delaware ratified in early December, before the Antifederalists had even begun to campaign. Pennsylvania, New Jersey, and Georgia followed within a month (**Map 8.3**). Delaware and New Jersey were small states surrounded by more powerful neighbors; a government that would regulate trade and set taxes according to population was an attractive proposition. Georgia sought the

Federalists

▶ Originally the term for the supporters of the ratification of the U.S. Constitution in 1787–1788. In the 1790s, it became the name for one of the two dominant political groups that emerged during that decade. Federalist leaders of the 1790s supported Britain in foreign policy and commercial interests at home. Prominent Federalists included George Washington, Alexander Hamilton, and John Adams.

Why did the Articles of Confederation fail? | How did the Constitution change how the nation was governed? | **What were the objections to ratification of the Constitution?** | Conclusion: What was the "republican remedy"? | ✓ LearningCurve Check what you know. bedfordstmartins.com /roarkunderstanding

227

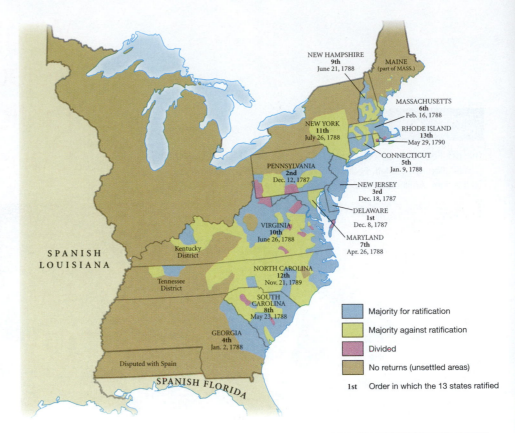

MAP 8.3 ■ Ratification of the Constitution, 1788–1790

Populated areas cast votes for delegates to state ratification conventions. This map shows Antifederalist strength generally concentrated in backcountry, noncoastal, and non-urban areas, but with significant exceptions (for example, Rhode Island).

> MAP ACTIVITY

READING THE MAP: Where was Federalist strength concentrated? How did the distribution of Federalist and Antifederalist sentiment affect the order of state ratifications of the Constitution?

CONNECTIONS: What objections did Antifederalists have to the new U.S. Constitution? How did their locations affect their view of the Federalist argument?

Map labels:

NEW HAMPSHIRE
9th
June 21, 1788

MAINE
(part of MASS.)

MASSACHUSETTS
6th
Feb. 16, 1788

RHODE ISLAND
13th
May 29, 1790

NEW YORK
11th
July 26, 1788

CONNECTICUT
5th
Jan. 9, 1788

PENNSYLVANIA
2nd
Dec. 12, 1787

NEW JERSEY
3rd
Dec. 18, 1787

DELAWARE
1st
Dec. 8, 1787

VIRGINIA
10th
June 26, 1788

MARYLAND
7th
Apr. 26, 1788

SPANISH LOUISIANA

Kentucky District

NORTH CAROLINA
12th
Nov. 21, 1789

Tennessee District

SOUTH CAROLINA
8th
May 23, 1788

GEORGIA
4th
Jan. 2, 1788

Disputed with Spain

SPANISH FLORIDA

Legend:
- Majority for ratification
- Majority against ratification
- Divided
- No returns (unsettled areas)
- **1st** Order in which the 13 states ratified

> CHRONOLOGY

1787
– Pro-Constitution essays called *The Federalist Papers* begin to be published.

1788
– U.S. Constitution is ratified.

protection that a stronger national government would afford against hostile Indians and Spanish Florida to the south.

Another three easy victories came in Connecticut, Maryland, and South Carolina. Again, merchants, lawyers, and urban artisans in general favored the new Constitution, as did large landowners and slaveholders. Antifederalists in these states tended to be rural, western, and noncommercial, men whose access to news was limited and whose participation in state government was tenuous.

Massachusetts was the first state to give the Federalists serious difficulty. The vote to select the ratification delegates decidedly favored the Antifederalists, whose strength lay in the western areas of the state, home to Shays's Rebellion. One rural delegate from Worcester County voiced widely shared suspicions: "These lawyers and men of learning and money men that talk so finely, and gloss over matters so smoothly, to make us poor illiterate people swallow down the pill, expect to get into Congress themselves; they expect to be the managers of the Constitution and get all the power and all the money into their own hands, and then they will swallow up all us little folks." Nevertheless, the Antifederalists' lead was slowly eroded by a vigorous newspaper campaign. In the end, the Federalists won in Massachusetts by a very slim margin and only with promises that amendments to the Constitution would be taken up in the first Congress.

By May 1788, eight states had ratified; only one more was needed. North Carolina and Rhode Island were hopeless for the Federalist cause, and New

CHAPTER LOCATOR | What kind of government did the Articles of Confederation create? | How did the states define citizenship and freedom?

228 CHAPTER 8
BUILDING A REPUBLIC

Hampshire seemed nearly as bleak. More worrisome was the failure to win over the largest and most economically critical states, Virginia and New York.

The Antifederalists

The **Antifederalists** were a composite group, united mainly in their desire to block the Constitution. Although much of their strength came from backcountry areas long suspicious of eastern elites, many Antifederalist leaders came from the same social background as Federalist leaders. The Antifederalists also drew strength in states that were already on sure economic footing, such as New York, which could afford to remain independent. Probably the biggest appeal of the Antifederalists' position lay in the long-nurtured fear that distant power might infringe on people's liberties.

But by the time eight states had ratified the Constitution, the Antifederalists faced a difficult task. First, they were no longer defending the status quo now that the momentum lay with the Federalists. Second, it was difficult to defend the confederation government with its admitted flaws. Even so, the Antifederalists remained genuinely fearful that the new government would be too distant from the people and could thus become corrupt or tyrannical. "The difficulty, if not impracticability, of exercising the equal and equitable powers of government by a single legislature over an extent of territory that reaches from the Mississippi to the western lakes, and from them to the Atlantic ocean, is an insuperable objection to the adoption of the new system," wrote Mercy Otis Warren, an Antifederalist woman writing under the name "A Columbia Patriot."

The new government was indeed distant. In the proposed House of Representatives, the only directly democratic element of the Constitution, one member represented some 30,000 people. How could that member really know or communicate with his whole constituency, Antifederalists worried. They also worried that representatives would always be elites and thus "ignorant of the sentiments of the middling and much more of the lower class of citizens, strangers to their ability, unacquainted with their wants, difficulties, and distress," as one Maryland man fretted.

The Federalists generally agreed that the elite would be favored for national elections. Indeed, Federalists wanted power to reside with intelligent, virtuous leaders like themselves. They did not envision a government constituted of every class of people. "Fools and knaves have voice enough in government already," quipped one Federalist, without being guaranteed representation in proportion to their total population. Alexander Hamilton claimed that mechanics and laborers preferred to have their social betters represent them. Antifederalists disagreed: "In reality, there will be no part of the people represented, but the rich. . . . It will literally be a government in the hands of the few to oppress and plunder the many."

Antifederalists fretted over many specific features of the Constitution, such as the prohibition on state-issued paper money, or the federal power to control the time and place of elections. The most widespread objection was the Constitution's glaring omission of any guarantees of individual liberties in a bill of rights like those contained in many state constitutions.

Antifederalists
▶ Opponents of the ratification of the Constitution. Antifederalists feared that a powerful and distant central government would be out of touch with the needs of citizens. They also complained that the Constitution failed to guarantee individual liberties in a bill of rights.

Why did the Articles of Confederation fail?

How did the Constitution change how the nation was governed?

What were the objections to ratification of the Constitution?

Conclusion: What was the "republican remedy"?

☑ LearningCurve
Check what you know.
bedfordstmartins.com
/roarkunderstanding

229

In the end, a small state—New Hampshire—provided the decisive ninth vote for ratification on June 21, 1788, following an intensive and successful lobbying effort by Federalists.

The Big Holdouts: Virginia and New York

Four states still remained outside the new Union, and a glance at a map demonstrated the necessity of pressing the Federalist case in the two largest, Virginia and New York (see Map 8.3). In Virginia, an influential Antifederalist group led by Patrick Henry and George Mason made the outcome uncertain. The Federalists finally but barely won ratification by proposing twenty specific amendments that the new government would promise to consider.

New York voters tilted toward the Antifederalists out of a sense that a state so large and powerful need not relinquish so much authority to the new federal government. But New York was also home to some of the most persuasive Federalists. Starting in October 1787, Alexander Hamilton collaborated with James Madison and New York lawyer John Jay on a series of eighty-five essays on the political philosophy of the new Constitution. Published in New York newspapers and later republished as *The Federalist Papers*, the essays set out the failures of the Articles of Confederation and offered an analysis of the complex nature of the Federalist position. In one of the most compelling essays, number 10, Madison challenged the Antifederalists' conviction that republican government had to be small-scale. Madison argued that a large and diverse population was itself a guarantee of liberty. In a national government, no single faction could ever be large enough to subvert the freedom of other groups. "Extend the sphere, and you take in a greater variety of parties and interests; you make it less probable that a majority of the whole will have a common motive to invade the rights of other citizens," Madison asserted. He called it "a republican remedy for the diseases most incident to republican government."

At New York's ratifying convention, Antifederalists predominated, but impassioned debate and lobbying—plus the dramatic news of Virginia's ratification—finally tipped the balance to the Federalists. Even so, the Antifederalists' approval of the document was accompanied by a list of twenty-four individual rights and thirty-three structural changes they hoped to see in the Constitution. New York's ratification ensured the legitimacy of the new government, yet it took another year and a half for Antifederalists in North Carolina to come around. Fiercely independent Rhode Island held out until May 1790, and even then it ratified by only a two-vote margin.

In less than twelve months, the U.S. Constitution was both written and ratified. (See appendix I, page A-3.) The Federalists had faced a formidable task, but by building momentum and ensuring consideration of a bill of rights, they did indeed carry the day.

> QUICK REVIEW

Why did Antifederalists oppose the Constitution?

CHAPTER LOCATOR | What kind of government did the Articles of Confederation create? | How did the states define citizenship and freedom?

230 CHAPTER 8 BUILDING A REPUBLIC

THUS ENDED ONE OF THE MOST intellectually tumultuous and creative periods in American history.

The period began in 1775 with a confederation government that could barely be ratified because of its requirement of unanimity, but there was no reaching unanimity on the western lands, an impost, and the proper way to respond to unfair taxation in a republican state. The new Constitution offered a different approach to these problems by loosening the grip of impossible unanimity and by embracing the ideas of a heterogeneous public life and a carefully balanced government that together would prevent any one part of the public from tyrannizing another. The genius of James Madison was to anticipate that diversity of opinion was not only an unavoidable reality but also a hidden strength of the new society beginning to take shape. This is what he meant in Federalist essay number 10 when he spoke of the "republican remedy" for the troubles most likely to befall a government in which the people are the source of authority.

Despite Madison's optimism, political differences remained keen and worrisome to many. The Federalists still hoped for a society in which leaders of exceptional wisdom would discern the best path for public policy. They looked backward to a society of hierarchy, rank, and benevolent rule by an aristocracy of talent, but they created a government with forward-looking checks and balances as a guard against corruption, which they figured would most likely emanate from the people. The Antifederalists also looked backward, but to an old order of small-scale direct democracy and local control, in which virtuous people kept a close eye on potentially corruptible rulers. The Antifederalists feared a national government led by distant, self-interested leaders who needed to be held in check. In the 1790s, these two conceptions of republicanism and of leadership would be tested in real life.

| Why did the Articles of Confederation fail? | How did the Constitution change how the nation was governed? | What were the objections to ratification of the Constitution? | Conclusion: What was the "republican remedy"? | ✓ LearningCurve Check what you know. bedfordstmartins.com /roarkunderstanding |

231

CHAPTER 8 STUDY GUIDE

STEP 1

GET STARTED ONLINE

✓ **LearningCurve** ■ bedfordstmartins.com/roarkunderstanding

Now that you've read the chapter, make it stick by completing the LearningCurve activity.

STEP 2

EXPLAIN WHY IT MATTERS

Put your reading into practice. Identify each term below, and then explain why it matters in U.S. history.

TERM	WHO OR WHAT & WHEN	WHY IT MATTERS
Articles of Confederation (p. 206)		
republicanism (p. 210)		
gradual emancipation (p. 213)		
Newburgh Conspiracy (p. 216)		
Treaty of Fort Stanwix (p. 217)		
Northwest Ordinance (p. 219)		
Shays's Rebellion (p. 222)		
Virginia Plan (p. 224)		
New Jersey Plan (p. 224)		
three-fifths clause (p. 225)		
Federalists (p. 227)		
Antifederalists (p. 229)		

STEP 3

MOVE BEYOND THE BASICS

To demonstrate a more advanced understanding, fill in the chart below with the powers and responsibilities of the various branches of government under the Articles of Confederation and under the Constitution. What were the important differences between the two?

	Powers and responsibilities under Articles of Confederation	Powers and responsibilities under U.S. Constitution
Congress		
Executive branch		
Federal judiciary		
States		

STEP 4 — PUT IT ALL TOGETHER

Now, take a step back and try to explain the big picture. Remember to use specific examples from the chapter in your answers.

THE ARTICLES OF CONFEDERATION

▶ How did the confederation government deal with the problem of western lands?

▶ What do the state constitutions drawn up during the confederation period tell us about the range of political opinion during the Revolutionary War and the years immediately following?

THE CREATION OF A NEW CONSTITUTION

▶ What forces and events combined to produce momentum for the creation of a new constitution?

▶ What political compromises were embodied in the Constitution?

THE FIGHT FOR RATIFICATION

▶ Where was support for the Constitution strongest? Where was it weakest? Why?

▶ Why did the Federalists ultimately prevail over the Antifederalists? What were the Federalists' most important weapons in the debate over the Constitution?

LOOKING BACKWARD, LOOKING AHEAD

▶ How did pre-revolutionary experiences with colonial legislatures and the British government shape the Articles of Confederation? The United States Constitution?

▶ What issues were left unresolved by the framers of the Constitution? Why?

> IN YOUR OWN WORDS

Imagine that you must give an oral report to the class answering the following question: **What were the most significant events that led to the formulation and ratification of the U.S. Constitution?** What would be the most important points to include and why?

 Do it online at the Student Site ▪ **bedfordstmartins.com/roarkunderstanding**

9

FORMING THE NEW NATION

1789–1800

> **What were the developments that led to the establishment of political parties with distinctive agendas by the end of the 1790s?**

Chapter 9 examines the efforts to achieve political stability in the decade following the ratification of the Constitution. It explores Alexander Hamilton's plans to bring economic stability to the federal government and the external threats and internal arguments the new United States faced.

LearningCurve
bedfordstmartins.com/roarkunderstanding
After reading the chapter, use LearningCurve to retain what you've read.

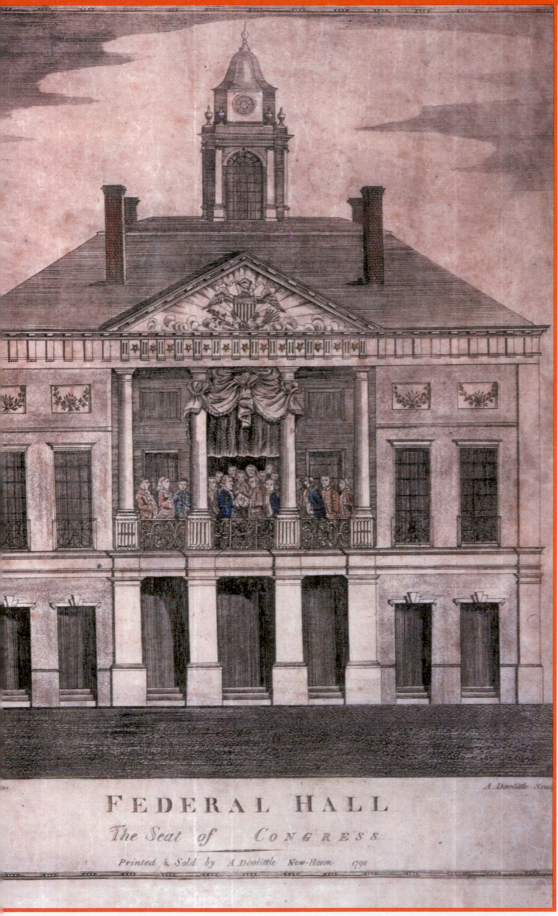

FEDERAL HALL

The Seat of Congress

Printed & Sold by A. Doolittle New-Haven 1790

A. Doolittle Scu

> What were the sources of political stability in the 1790s?

> What were Hamilton's economic policies?

> What external threats did the United States face in the 1790s?

> How did partisan rivalries shape the politics of the late 1790s?

> Conclusion: Why did the new nation ultimately form political parties?

George Washington takes the oath of office. Federal Hall, Philadelphia, April 30, 1789. Courtesy, The Henry Francis du Pont Winterthur Museum.

> What were the sources of political stability in the 1790s?

AFTER THE STRUGGLES of the 1780s, the most urgent task in establishing the new government was to secure stability. Leaders sought ways to heal old divisions, and the first presidential election offered the means to do that in the person of George Washington, who enjoyed widespread veneration. People trusted him to exercise the untested and perhaps elastic powers of the presidency.

Congress had important work as well in initiating the new government. Congress quickly agreed on the Bill of Rights, which answered the concerns of many Antifederalists. Beyond politics, cultural change in the area of gender also enhanced political stability. The private virtue of women was mobilized to bolster the public virtue of male citizens and to enhance political stability. Republicanism was forcing a rethinking of women's relation to the state.

Washington Inaugurates the Government

George Washington was elected president in February 1789 by a unanimous vote of the electoral college. (John Adams got just half as many votes; he became vice president, but his pride was wounded.) Washington perfectly embodied the republican ideal of disinterested, public-spirited leadership. Indeed, he cultivated that image through astute ceremonies such as the dramatic surrender of his sword to the Continental Congress at the end of the war, symbolizing the subservience of military power to the law.

Once in office, Washington calculated his moves, knowing that every step set a precedent and that any misstep could be dangerous for the fragile government. Congress debated a title for Washington, ranging from "His Highness" to "His Majesty, the President"; Washington favored "His High Mightiness." But in the end, republican simplicity prevailed. The final title was simply "President of the United States of America," and the established form of address became "Mr. President," a subdued yet dignified title reserved for property-owning white males.

Washington's genius in establishing the presidency lay in his capacity for implanting his own reputation for integrity into the office itself. In the political language of the day, he was "virtuous," meaning that he took pains to elevate the public good over private interest and projected honesty and honor over ambition. He remained aloof, resolute, and dignified, to the point of appearing wooden at times. He encouraged pomp and ceremony to create respect for the office, traveling with six horses to pull his coach, hosting formal balls, and surrounding himself with uniformed servants. He even held weekly "levees," as European monarchs did, hour-long audiences granted to distinguished visitors (including women), at which Washington appeared attired in black velvet, with a feathered hat and a polished sword. The president and his guests bowed, avoiding the egalitarian familiarity of a handshake. But he always managed, perhaps just barely, to avoid the extreme of royal splendor.

Washington chose talented and experienced men to preside over the newly created Departments of War, Treasury, and State.

> Washington's Cabinet	
Secretary of war	General Henry Knox
Secretary of the treasury	Alexander Hamilton
Secretary of state	Thomas Jefferson
Attorney general	Edmund Randolph
Chief justice of the Supreme Court	John Jay

Soon Washington began to hold regular meetings with these men, thereby establishing the precedent of a presidential cabinet. No one anticipated that two decades of party turbulence would emerge from the brilliant but explosive mix of Washington's first cabinet.

The Bill of Rights

An important piece of business for the First Congress, meeting in 1789, was the passage of the **Bill of Rights**. Seven states had ratified the Constitution on the condition that guarantees of individual liberties and limitations to federal power be swiftly incorporated. The Federalists of 1787 had thought an enumeration of rights unnecessary, but in 1789 Congressman James Madison of Virginia understood that healing the divisions of the 1780s was of prime importance: "It will be

> **CHRONOLOGY**

1789
– George Washington is inaugurated as the first president.
– First Congress meets.

1790
– Judith Sargent Murray publishes "On the Equality of the Sexes."

1791
– States ratify Bill of Rights.

Bill of Rights
▶ The first ten amendments to the Constitution, officially ratified by 1791. The First through Eighth Amendments dealt with individual liberties, and the Ninth and Tenth concerned the boundary between federal and state authority.

What were Hamilton's economic policies?

What external threats did the United States face in the 1790s?

How did partisan rivalries shape the politics of the late 1790s?

Conclusion: Why did the new nation ultimately form political parties?

☑ LearningCurve
Check what you know.
bedfordstmartins.com
/roarkunderstanding

a desirable thing to extinguish from the bosom of every member of the community, any apprehensions that there are those among his countrymen who wish to deprive them of the liberty for which they valiantly fought and honorably bled."

Drawing on existing state constitutions with bills of rights, Madison enumerated guarantees of freedom of speech, the press, and religion; the right to petition and assemble; and the right to be free from unwarranted searches and seizures. One amendment asserted the right to keep and bear arms in support of a "well-regulated militia," to which Madison added, "but no person religiously scrupulous of bearing arms, shall be compelled to render military service in person." That provision for what a later century would call "conscientious objector" status failed to gain acceptance in Congress.

In September 1789, Congress approved a set of twelve amendments and sent them to the states for approval; by 1791, ten were eventually ratified. The First through Eighth Amendments dealt with individual liberties, and the Ninth and Tenth concerned the boundary between federal and state authority.

Still, not everyone was entirely satisfied. State ratifying conventions had submitted some eighty proposed amendments. Congress never considered proposals to change structural features of the new government, and Madison had no intention of reopening debates about the length of the president's term or the power to levy excise taxes.

Significantly, no one complained about one striking omission in the Bill of Rights: the right to vote. Only much later was voting seen as a fundamental liberty requiring protection by constitutional amendment—indeed, by four amendments. The Constitution deliberately left the definition of eligible voters to the states because of the existing wide variation in local voting practices. Most of these practices were based on property qualifications, but some touched on religion and, in one unusual case (New Jersey), on sex and race (see chapter 8).

The Republican Wife and Mother

The exclusion of women from political activity did not mean they had no civic role or responsibility. A flood of periodical articles in the 1790s by both male and female writers reevaluated courtship, marriage, and motherhood in light of republican ideals. Tyrannical power in the ruler, whether king or husband, was declared a thing of the past. Affection, not duty, bound wives to their husbands and citizens to their government. In republican marriages, the writers claimed, women had the capacity to reform the morals and manners of men. One male author promised women that "the solidity and stability of the liberties of your country rest with you; since Liberty is never sure, 'till Virtue reigns triumphant. . . . While you thus keep our country virtuous, you maintain its independence."

Until the 1790s, public virtue was strictly a masculine quality. But another sort of virtue enlarged in importance: sexual chastity, a private asset prized as a feminine quality. Essayists of the 1790s explicitly advised young women to use sexual virtue to increase public virtue in men. "Love and courtship . . . invest a lady with more authority than in any other situation that falls to the lot of human beings," one male essayist proclaimed.

Republican ideals also cast motherhood in a new light. Throughout the 1790s, advocates for female education, still a controversial proposition, argued that education would produce better mothers, who in turn would produce better citizens,

The young woman in this 1772 portrait became known in the 1790s as America's foremost spokeswoman for woman's equality. Judith Sargent Murray published essays under the pen name "Constantia." She argued that women had "natural powers" of mind fully the equal of men's. George Washington and John Adams each bought a copy of her collected essays published in 1798. John Singleton Copley, Terra Foundation for America, Chicago/Art Resource, NY.

a concept historians call republican motherhood. Benjamin Rush, a Pennsylvania physician and educator, called for female education because "our ladies should be qualified . . . in instructing their sons in the principles of liberty and government." A series of essays by Judith Sargent Murray of Massachusetts favored education that would remake women into self-confident, rational beings. Her first essay, published in 1790, was boldly titled "On the Equality of the Sexes." In a subsequent essay on education, Murray asserted that educated women would retain their "characteristic trait" of sweetness, thus reassuring readers that education would not undermine women's compliant nature.

Although women's obligations as wives and mothers were now infused with political meaning, traditional gender relations remained unaltered. The analogy between marriage and civil society worked precisely because of the self-subordination inherent in the term *virtue*. Men should put the public good first, before selfish desires, just as women must put their husbands and families first, before themselves. Women might gain literacy and knowledge, but only in the service of improved domestic duty. In Federalist America, wives and citizens alike should feel affection for and trust in their rulers; neither should ever rebel.

QUICK REVIEW

How did political leaders in the 1790s attempt to overcome the divisions of the 1780s?

| What were Hamilton's economic policies? | What external threats did the United States face in the 1790s? | How did partisan rivalries shape the politics of the late 1790s? | Conclusion: Why did the new nation ultimately form political parties? | **LearningCurve** Check what you know. bedfordstmartins.com /roarkunderstanding |

> What were Hamilton's economic policies?

Alexander Hamilton, by John Trumbull

Hamilton was confident, handsome, audacious, brilliant, and very hardworking. Ever slender, in marked contrast to the more corpulent leaders of his day, he posed for this portrait in 1792, at the age of thirty-seven and at the height of his power. CSFB Collection of Americana, NYC.

> CHRONOLOGY

1790
– Congress approves Hamilton's debt plan.
– National capital is moved to Philadelphia.

1791
– Bank of the United States is chartered.
– Congress passes whiskey tax.
– Hamilton issues *Report on Manufactures.*

1793
– Eli Whitney invents cotton gin.

1794
– Whiskey Rebellion.

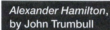OMPARED WITH THE severe financial instability of the 1780s, the 1790s brimmed with opportunity, as seen in improved trade, in transportation, and in banking. In 1790, the federal government moved from New York City to Philadelphia, a more central location with a substantial mercantile class. There, Alexander Hamilton, secretary of the treasury, embarked on multiple plans to solidify the government's economic base. But controversy ensued. His ambitious plans to fund the national debt, set up a national bank, promote manufacturing through trade laws, and raise revenue through a tax on whiskey mobilized severe opposition.

Agriculture, Transportation, and Banking

Dramatic increases in international grain prices, caused by underproduction in war-stricken Europe, motivated American farmers to boost agricultural production for the export trade. From the Connecticut River valley to the Chesapeake, farmers planted more wheat, generating new jobs for millers, coopers, dockworkers, and shipbuilders.

CHAPTER LOCATOR | What were the sources of political stability in the 1790s?

Cotton production also boomed, spurred by market demand from British textile manufacturers and a mechanical invention. Limited amounts of smooth-seed cotton had long been grown in the coastal areas of the South, but this variety of cotton did not thrive in the drier inland regions. Greenseed cotton grew well inland, but its rough seeds stuck to the cotton fibers and were labor-intensive to remove. In 1793, Yale graduate Eli Whitney devised a machine called a gin that easily separated out the seeds; cotton production soared.

A surge of road building further stimulated the economy. Before 1790, one road connected Maine to Georgia, but with the establishment of the U.S. Post Office in 1792, road mileage increased sixfold. Private companies also built toll roads, such as the Lancaster Turnpike west of Philadelphia, the Boston-to-Albany turnpike, and a third road from Virginia to Tennessee. By 1800, a dense network of dirt, gravel, and plank roadways connected towns in southern New England and the Middle Atlantic states, spurring the establishment of commercial stage companies. A trip from New York to Boston took four days; from New York to Philadelphia, less than two (**Map 9.1**). In 1790, Boston had only three stagecoach companies; by 1800, there were twenty-four.

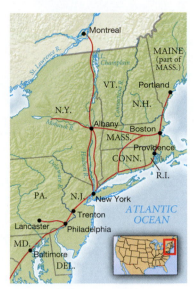

Major Roads in the 1790s

MAP 9.1 ■ Travel Times from New York City in 1800

Notice that travel out of New York extends over a much greater distance in the first week than in subsequent weeks. River corridors in the West and East speeded up travel — but only going downriver. Also notice that travel by sea (along the coast) was much faster than land travel.

> **MAP ACTIVITY**

READING THE MAP: Compare this map to the map "Major Roads in the 1790s" (above) and to Map 9.2 (page 249). What physical and cultural factors account for the slower travel times west of Pittsburgh?

CONNECTIONS: Why did Americans in the 1790s become so interested in traveling long distances? How did travel times affect the U.S. economy?

| What were Hamilton's economic policies? | What external threats did the United States face in the 1790s? | How did partisan rivalries shape the politics of the late 1790s? | Conclusion: Why did the new nation ultimately form political parties? | ✓ LearningCurve Check what you know. bedfordstmartins.com /roarkunderstanding |

A third development signaling economic resurgence was the growth of commercial banking. During the 1790s, the number of banks nationwide multiplied tenfold, from three to twenty-nine in 1800. Banks drew in money chiefly through the sale of stock. They then made loans in the form of banknotes, paper currency backed by the gold and silver from stock sales. By issuing two or three times as much money in banknotes as they held in hard money, they were creating new money for the economy.

The U.S. population expanded along with economic development, propelled by large average family size and better than adequate food and land resources. As measured by the first two federal censuses in 1790 and 1800, the population grew from 3.9 million to 5.3 million, an increase of 35 percent.

The Public Debt and Taxes

The upturn in the economy, plus the new taxation powers of the government, suggested that the government might soon repay its wartime debt, amounting to more than $52 million owed to foreign and domestic creditors. But Hamilton had a different plan. He issued a *Report on Public Credit* in January 1790, recommending that the debt be funded—but not repaid immediately—at full value. This meant that old certificates of debt would be rolled over into new bonds, which would earn interest until they were retired several years later. There would still be a public debt, but it would be secure, giving its holders a direct financial stake in the new government. The bonds would circulate, injecting millions of dollars of new money into the economy. "A national debt if not excessive will be to us a national blessing; it will be a powerful cement of our union," Hamilton wrote to a financier. Hamilton's goal was to make the new country creditworthy, not debt-free.

Funding the debt in full was controversial because speculators had already bought up debt certificates cheaply, and Hamilton's report touched off further speculation. Hamilton compounded controversy with his proposal to add to the federal debt another $25 million that some state governments still owed to individuals. During the war, states had obtained supplies by issuing IOUs to farmers, merchants, and money-lenders. Some states, such as Virginia and New York, had paid off these debts entirely. Others, such as Massachusetts, had partially paid them off through heavy taxation of the people. About half the states had made little headway. Hamilton called for the federal government to assume these state debts and combine them with the federal debt, in effect consolidating federal power over the states.

Congressman James Madison strenuously objected to putting windfall profits in the pockets of speculators. He instead proposed a complex scheme to pay both the original holders of the federal debt and the speculators, each at fair fractions of the face value. He also strongly objected to assumption of all the states' debts. A large debt was dangerous, Madison warned, especially because it would lead to high taxation. Secretary of State Thomas Jefferson was also fearful of Hamilton's proposals: "No man is more ardently intent to see the public debt soon and sacredly paid off than I am. This exactly marks the difference between Colonel Hamilton's views and mine, that I would wish the debt paid tomorrow; he wishes it never to be paid, but always to be a thing where with to corrupt and manage the legislature."

Report on Public Credit

▶ Hamilton's January 1790 report recommending that the national debt be funded — but not repaid immediately — at full value. Hamilton's goal was to make the new country creditworthy, not debt-free. Critics of his plan complained that it would benefit speculators.

CHAPTER LOCATOR | What were the sources of political stability in the 1790s?

242 CHAPTER 9
FORMING THE NEW NATION

The Return for SOUTH CAROLINA having been made since the foregoing Schedule was originally printed, the whole Enumeration is here given complete, except for the N. Western Territory, of which no Return has yet been published.

DISTICTS	Free white Males of 16 years and upwards, including heads of families	Free white Males under sixteen years	Free white Females, including heads of families	All other free persons	Slaves	Total
Vermont	22435	22328	40505	255	16	85539
N. Hampshire	36086	34851	70160	630	158	141885
Maine	24384	24748	46870	538	NONE	96540
Massachusetts	95453	87289	190582	5463	NONE	378787
Rhode Island	16019	15799	32652	3407	948	68825
Connecticut	60523	54403	117448	2808	2764	237946
New York	83700	78122	152320	4654	21324	340120
New Jersey	45251	41416	83287	2762	11423	184139
Pennsylvania	110788	106948	206363	6537	3737	434373
Delaware	11783	12143	22384	3899	8887	59094
Maryland	55915	51339	101395	8043	103036	319728
Virginia	110936	116135	215046	12866	292627	747610
Kentucky	15154	17057	28922	114	12430	73677
N. Carolina	69988	77506	140710	4975	100572	393751
S. Carolina	35576	37722	66880	1801	107094	249073
Georgia	13103	14044	25739	398	29264	82548
	807094	791850	1541263	59150	694280	3893635

Total number of Inhabitants of the United States exclusive of S. Western and N. Territory.	Free white Males of 21 years and upwards	Free Males under 21 years of age	Free white Females	All other Persons	Slaves	Total
S. W. territory N. Ditto	6271	10277	15365	361	3417	35691

1790 Census Page

This page summarizes the tally of the first federal census, data that determined representation in Congress and proportional taxation of the states. Notice the five classifications: free white males sixteen or older, the same under sixteen, free white females, "all other free persons," and slaves. Separating white males at sixteen provided a rough measure of military strength. U.S. Census Bureau.

> VISUAL ACTIVITY

READING THE IMAGE: Which northern states still had slaves? Which state had the largest population? Which had the largest white population?

CONNECTIONS: Why did the census separate males from females? Free from enslaved? Who might "all other free persons" include? Since women, children, and "all other free persons" counted for purposes of apportionment, could it be said that those groups were represented in the new government?

A solution to this impasse arrived when Jefferson invited Hamilton and Madison to dinner. Over good food and wine, Hamilton secured the reluctant Madison's promise to restrain his opposition. In return, Hamilton pledged to back efforts to locate the nation's new capital city in the South, along the Potomac River, an outcome that was sure to please Virginians. In early July 1790, Congress voted for the Potomac site, and in late July Congress passed the debt package, assumption and all.

The First Bank of the United States and the *Report on Manufactures*

The second and third major elements of Hamilton's economic plan were his proposal to create a national Bank of the United States and his program to encourage domestic manufacturing. Arguing that banks were the "nurseries of national wealth," Hamilton modeled his bank plan on European central banks that used their government's money to invigorate the economy. According to Hamilton's plan,

What were Hamilton's economic policies?

What external threats did the United States face in the 1790s?

How did partisan rivalries shape the politics of the late 1790s?

Conclusion: Why did the new nation ultimately form political parties?

LearningCurve
Check what you know.
bedfordstmartins.com
/roarkunderstanding

the central bank was to be capitalized at $10 million, a sum larger than all the hard money in the entire nation. The federal government would hold 20 percent of the bank's stock, making the bank in effect the government's fiscal agent, holding its revenues derived from import duties, land sales, and various other taxes. The other 80 percent of the bank's capital would come from private investors, who could buy stock in the bank with either hard money (silver or gold) or the recently funded and thus sound federal securities. Because of its size and the privilege of being the only national bank, the central bank would help stabilize the economy by exerting prudent control over credit, interest rates, and the value of the currency.

Concerned that a few rich bankers might have undue influence over the economy, Madison tried but failed to stop the plan in Congress. Jefferson advised President Washington that the Constitution did not permit Congress to charter banks. Hamilton countered that Congress had explicit powers to regulate commerce and a broad mandate "to make all laws which shall be necessary and proper for carrying into execution the foregoing powers." Washington sided with Hamilton and signed the Bank of the United States into law in February 1791, giving it a twenty-year charter.

When the bank's privately held stock went on sale in Philadelphia, Boston, and New York City in July, it sold out in a few hours, touching off a lively period of speculative trading by hundreds of urban merchants and artisans. A discouraged Madison reported that in New York "the Coffee House is an eternal buzz with the gamblers," and wide swings in the stock's price pained Jefferson: "The spirit of gaming, once it has seized a subject, is incurable. The tailor who has made thousands in one day, tho' he has lost them the next, can never again be content with the slow and moderate earnings of his needle."

The third component of Hamilton's plan was issued in December 1791 in the *Report on Manufactures*, a proposal to encourage the production of American-made goods. Domestic manufacturing was in its infancy, and Hamilton aimed to mobilize the new powers of the federal government to grant subsidies to manufacturers and to impose moderate tariffs on those same products from overseas. Hamilton's plan targeted manufacturing of iron goods, arms and ammunition, coal, textiles, wood products, and glass. The *Report on Manufactures*, however, was never approved by Congress, and indeed never even voted on. Many confirmed agriculturalists in Congress feared that manufacturing was a curse rather than a blessing. Madison and Jefferson in particular were alarmed by stretching the "general welfare" clause of the Constitution to include public subsidies to private businesses.

The Whiskey Rebellion

Hamilton's plan to restore public credit required new taxation to pay the interest on the large national debt. In deference to the merchant class, Hamilton did not propose a general increase in import duties, nor did he propose land taxes, which would have fallen hardest on the nation's wealthiest landowners. Instead, he convinced Congress in 1791 to pass a 25 percent excise tax on whiskey, to be paid by farmers bringing grain to the distillery and then passed on to whiskey consumers in higher prices. Even Madison approved, in the hope that the tax might promote "sobriety and thereby prevent disease and untimely deaths."

Report on Manufactures
▶ A proposal by Treasury Secretary Alexander Hamilton in 1791 calling for the federal government to encourage domestic manufacturers with subsidies while imposing tariffs on foreign imports. Congress initially rejected the measure.

Not surprisingly, the new excise tax proved unpopular. In 1791, farmers in Kentucky and the western parts of Pennsylvania, Virginia, Maryland, and the Carolinas forcefully conveyed their resentment to Congress. One farmer complained that he had already paid half his grain to the local distillery for distilling his rye, and now the distiller was taking the new whiskey tax out of the farmer's remaining half. "If this is not an oppressive tax, I am at a loss to describe what is so," the farmer wrote. Congress responded with modest modifications to the tax in 1792, but even so, discontent — along with tax evasion — was rampant. In some places, crowds threatened to tar and feather tax collectors. Four counties in Pennsylvania established committees of correspondence and held rallies. Hamilton admitted to Congress that the revenue was far less than anticipated. But rather than abandon the law, he tightened up the prosecution of tax evaders.

In western Pennsylvania, Hamilton had one ally, a stubborn tax collector named John Neville who refused to quit even after a group of spirited farmers burned him in effigy. In May 1794, Neville filed charges against seventy-five farmers and distillers for tax evasion. His action touched off the **Whiskey Rebellion**. In July, a group of forty men ambushed him and a federal marshal in Allegheny County. Then a crowd of five hundred burned down Neville's house. At the end of July, seven thousand Pennsylvania farmers planned a march — or perhaps an attack, some thought — on Pittsburgh to protest the tax.

In response, President Washington nationalized the Pennsylvania militia and set out, with Hamilton at his side, at the head of thirteen thousand soldiers. A worried Philadelphia newspaper criticized the show of force: "Shall torrents of blood be spilled to support an odious excise system?" But in the end, no blood was spilled. By the time the army arrived in late September, the demonstrators had dispersed. No battles were fought, and no shots were exchanged. Twenty men were rounded up and charged with high treason, but only two were convicted, and Washington soon pardoned both.

Had the federal government overreacted? Thomas Jefferson thought so; he saw the event as a replay of Shays's Rebellion of 1786, when tax protesters had been met with military force (see chapter 8). The rebel farmers agreed; they felt entitled to protest oppressive taxation. Hamilton and Washington, however, thought that laws passed by a republican government must be obeyed. To them, the Whiskey Rebellion presented an opportunity for the new federal government to flex its muscles and stand up to civil disorder.

Whiskey Rebellion
▶ July 1794 uprising by farmers in western Pennsylvania in response to enforcement of an unpopular excise tax on whiskey. The federal government responded with a military presence that caused dissidents to disperse before blood was shed.

QUICK REVIEW

Why were Hamilton's economic policies controversial?

| **What were Hamilton's economic policies?** | What external threats did the United States face in the 1790s? | How did partisan rivalries shape the politics of the late 1790s? | Conclusion: Why did the new nation ultimately form political parties? | ☑ LearningCurve Check what you know. bedfordstmartins.com /roarkunderstanding |

> What external threats did the United States face in the 1790s?

WHILE THE WHISKEY REBELS challenged federal leadership from within the country, disorder threatened the United States from external sources as well. From 1789 onward, serious trouble brewed in four directions. To the southwest, Creek Indians pushed back against the westward-moving white southern population, giving George Washington an opportunity to test diplomacy. To the northwest, a powerful confederation of Indian tribes in the Ohio Country resisted white encroachment, resulting in a brutal war. At the same time, conflicts between the major European powers forced Americans to take sides and nearly pulled the country into another war. And to the south, a Caribbean slave rebellion raised fears that racial war might be imported to the United States. Despite these grave prospects, Washington won reelection to the presidency unanimously in the fall of 1792.

CHAPTER LOCATOR | What were the sources of political stability in the 1790s?

Creeks in the Southwest

An urgent task of the new government was to take charge of Indian affairs while avoiding the costs of warfare. Some twenty thousand Indians affiliated with the Creeks occupied lands extending from Georgia into what is now Mississippi, and border skirmishes with land-hungry Georgians were becoming a frequent occurrence. Washington and his secretary of war, Henry Knox, singled out one Creek chief, Alexander McGillivray, and sent a delegation to Georgia for preliminary treaty negotiations.

McGillivray had a mixed-race heritage that prepared him to be a major cultural broker. His French-Creek mother conferred a legitimate claim to Creek leadership, while his Scottish fur-trading father provided exposure to literacy and numeracy. Fluent in English and near fluent in Spanish, McGillivray spoke several Creek languages and had even studied Greek and Latin. In the 1770s, he worked for the British distributing gifts to various southern tribes; in the 1780s, he gained renown for brokering negotiations with the Spanish in Florida.

The chief reluctantly met with Knox's delegates and spurned the substantial concessions the American negotiators offered, chief among them a guarantee of the Creeks' extensive tribal lands. McGillivray sent the negotiators away, enjoying, as he wrote to a Spanish trader, the spectacle of the self-styled "masters of the new world" having "to bend and supplicate for peace at the feet of a people whom shortly before they despised."

A year later, Secretary Knox reopened diplomatic relations. To coax McGillivray to the treaty table, Knox invited him to New York City to meet with the president. McGillivray arrived in a triumphal procession of various lesser Creek chiefs and was accorded the honors of a head of state.

The negotiations stretched out for a month, resulting in the 1790 Treaty of New York that looked much like Knox's original plan.

> **> Treaty of New York**

- Creek tribal lands were guaranteed. Federal troops were to provide boundary protection against land-seeking settlers.
- The Creeks were assured of annual payments in money and trade goods.
- The Creeks promised to accept the United States as its only trading partner, thus excluding Spain.

Actually, both sides had made promises they could not keep. McGillivray figured that the Creeks' interests were best served by maintaining creative tension between the American and Spanish authorities, and by 1792 he had signed an agreement with the Spanish governor of New Orleans, in which each side offered mutual pledges to protect against encroachments by Georgia settlers. By the time Alexander McGillivray died in 1793, his purported leadership of the Creeks was in serious question, and the Treaty of New York joined the list of treaties never implemented. Its promise of federal protection of Creek boundaries was unrealistic from the start, and its pledge of full respect for Creek sovereignty also was only a promise on paper.

> **CHRONOLOGY**

1789
– French Revolution begins.
– Fort Washington is erected in western Ohio.

1790
– Indians in Ohio defeat General Josiah Harmar.
– Treaty of New York.

1791
– Ohio Indians defeat General Arthur St. Clair.
– Haitian Revolution begins.

1793
– War between Great Britain and France begins in Europe.
– Washington issues Neutrality Proclamation.

1794
– Battle of Fallen Timbers.

1795
– Treaty of Greenville.
– Jay Treaty.

What were Hamilton's economic policies?

What external threats did the United States face in the 1790s?

How did partisan rivalries shape the politics of the late 1790s?

Conclusion: Why did the new nation ultimately form political parties?

☑ LearningCurve Check what you know. bedfordstmartins.com /roarkunderstanding

247

At the very start of the new government, in dealing with the Creeks, Washington and Knox tried to find a different way to approach Indian affairs, one rooted more in British than in American experience. But in the end, the demographic imperative of explosive white population growth and westward-moving, land-seeking settlers, together with the economic imperative of land speculation, meant that confrontation with the native population was nearly inevitable. As Washington wrote in 1796, "I believe scarcely any thing short of a Chinese Wall, or line of Troops will restrain Land Jobbers, and the encroachment of Settlers, upon Indian Territory."

Ohio Indians in the Northwest

Tribes of the Ohio Valley were even less willing to negotiate with the new federal government. Left vulnerable by the 1784 Treaty of Fort Stanwix (see chapter 8)— in which Iroquois tribes in New York had relinquished Ohio lands to the Americans—the Shawnee, Delaware, Miami, and other tribes in Ohio stood their ground. To confuse matters further, British troops still occupied half a dozen forts in the Northwest, protecting an ongoing fur trade between British traders and Indians and thereby sustaining Indians' claims to that land.

Under the terms of the Northwest Ordinance (see chapter 8), the federal government started to survey and map eastern Ohio, and settlers were eager to buy. So Washington sent units of the U.S. Army into Ohio's western half to subdue the various tribes. Fort Washington, built on the Ohio River in 1789 at the site of present-day Cincinnati, became the command post for three major invasions of Indian country (**Map 9.2**). The first occurred in the fall of 1790, when General Josiah Harmar marched with 1,400 men into Ohio's northwest region, burning Indian villages. His inexperienced troops were ambushed by Miami and Shawnee Indians led by their chiefs, Little Turtle and Blue Jacket. Harmar lost one-eighth of his soldiers and retreated.

Harmar's defeat spurred enhanced efforts to clear Ohio for permanent American settlement. General Arthur St. Clair, the military governor of the Northwest Territory, had pursued peaceful tactics in the 1780s, signing questionable treaties with Indians for land in eastern Ohio. In the wake of Harmar's bungled operation, St. Clair geared up for military action, and in the fall of 1791 he led two thousand men (accompanied by two hundred women camp followers) north from Fort Washington along Harmar's route. A surprise attack at the headwaters of the Wabash River left 55 percent of the Americans dead or wounded; only three of the women escaped alive. The Indians captured valuable weaponry and scalped and dismembered the dying on the field of battle. With more than nine hundred lives lost, this was the most stunning American loss in the history of the U.S. Indian wars.

Washington doubled the U.S. military presence in Ohio and appointed a new commander, General Anthony Wayne of Pennsylvania. About the Ohio natives, Wayne wrote, "I have always been of the opinion that we never should have a permanent peace with those Indians until they were made to experience our superiority." Throughout 1794, Wayne's army engaged in skirmishes with various tribes. Chief Little Turtle of the Miami tribe advised negotiation; in his view, Wayne's large army looked overpowering. But Blue Jacket of the Shawnees counseled continued warfare, and his view prevailed.

CHAPTER LOCATOR | What were the sources of political stability in the 1790s?

248 CHAPTER 9
FORMING THE NEW NATION

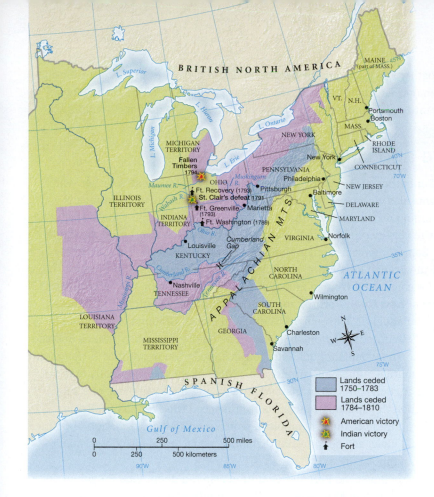

The decisive action came in August 1794 at the battle of Fallen Timbers, near the Maumee River. The confederated Indians—mainly Ottawas, Potawatomis, Shawnees, and Delawares numbering around eight hundred—ambushed the Americans but were underarmed, and Wayne's troops made effective use of their guns and bayonets. The Indians withdrew and sought refuge at nearby Fort Miami, still held by the British, but their former allies locked the gate and refused protection. The surviving Indians fled to the woods, their ranks decimated.

Fallen Timbers was a major defeat for the Indians. The Americans had destroyed cornfields and villages on the march north, and with winter approaching, the Indians' confidence was sapped. They reentered negotiations in a much less powerful bargaining position. In 1795, about a thousand Indians representing nearly a dozen tribes met with Wayne and other American emissaries to work out the **Treaty of Greenville**. The Americans offered treaty goods (calico shirts, axes, knives, blankets, kettles, mirrors, ribbons, thimbles, and abundant wine and liquor casks) worth $25,000 and promised additional shipments every year. The government's idea was to create a dependency on American goods to keep the Indians friendly. In exchange, the Indians ceded most of Ohio to the Americans; only the northwest part of the territory was reserved solely for the Indians.

The treaty brought temporary peace to the region, but it did not restore a peaceful life to the Indians. The annual allowance from the United States too often came in the form of liquor. "More of us have died since the Treaty of Greenville

Treaty of Greenville

▶ 1795 treaty between the United States and various Indian tribes in Ohio. The United States gave the tribes treaty goods valued at $25,000. In exchange, the Indians ceded most of Ohio to the Americans. The treaty brought only temporary peace to the region.

What were Hamilton's economic policies?

What external threats did the United States face in the 1790s?

How did partisan rivalries shape the politics of the late 1790s?

Conclusion: Why did the new nation ultimately form political parties?

✓ LearningCurve
Check what you know.
bedfordstmartins.com /roarkunderstanding

249

than we lost by the years of war before, and it is all owing to the introduction of liquor among us," said Chief Little Turtle in 1800. "This liquor that they introduce into our country is more to be feared than the gun and tomahawk."

France and Britain

While Indian battles engaged the American military in the west, another war overseas was also closely watched. In 1789, monarchy came under attack in France, bringing on a revolution that inspired Americans in many states to celebrate the victory of the French people. Even fashions expressed symbolic solidarity: Some American women donned sashes and cockades made with ribbons of the French Revolution's red, white, and blue colors. Pro-French headgear for committed women included an elaborate turban, leading one horrified Federalist newspaper editor to chastise the "fiery frenchified dames" thronging Philadelphia's streets. In Charleston, South Carolina, a pro-French pageant in 1793 united two women as partners, one representing France and the other America. The women repudiated their husbands "on account of ill treatment" and pledged mutual "union and friendship." Most likely, this ceremony was not the country's first civil union but instead a richly metaphorical piece of street theater in which the spurned husbands represented the French and British monarchs. In addition to these symbolic actions, the growing exchange of political and intellectual ideas across the Atlantic helped plant the seeds of a woman's rights movement in America.

Sentiments against the French Revolution also ran deep. Vice President John Adams, who had lived in France in the 1780s, trembled to think of radicals in France or America. "Too many Frenchmen, after the example of too many Americans, pant for the equality of persons and property," Adams said. "The impracticability of this, God Almighty has decreed, and the advocates for liberty, who attempt it, will surely suffer for it."

French Dress Style: Woman with Cockade

In the early 1790s, some Americans showed enthusiasm for the French Revolution by wearing a tricolor cockade — a distinctive bow made from red, white, and blue ribbons. Bibliothèque Nationale de France.

CHAPTER LOCATOR | What were the sources of political stability in the 1790s?

CHAPTER 9
250 FORMING THE NEW NATION

Support for the French Revolution remained a matter of personal conviction until 1793, when Britain and France went to war and divided loyalties now framed critical foreign policy debates. Pro-French Americans remembered France's critical help during the American Revolution and wanted to offer aid now. But those shaken by the report of the guillotining of thousands of French people—including the king—as well as those with strong commercial ties to Britain sought ways to stay neutral.

In May 1793, President Washington issued the Neutrality Proclamation, which contained friendly assurances to both sides, in an effort to stay out of European wars. Yet American ships continued to trade between the French West Indies and France. In early 1794, the British expressed their displeasure by capturing more than three hundred of these vessels near the West Indies. Clearly, the president thought, something had to be done to assert American power.

Washington tapped John Jay, the chief justice of the Supreme Court and a man of strong pro-British sentiments, to negotiate commercial relations in the British West Indies and secure compensation for the seized American ships. Jay was also told to resolve southern demands for reimbursement for the slaves evacuated by the British during the war along with western settlers' desires to end the British occupation of frontier forts. Jay returned from his diplomatic mission with the **Jay Treaty**, a treaty that no one could love. First, the Jay Treaty failed to address the captured cargoes or the lost property in slaves. Second, it granted the British a lenient eighteen months to withdraw from the frontier forts, as well as continued rights in the fur trade. (This provision disheartened the Indians just then negotiating the Treaty of Greenville in Ohio. It was a significant factor in their decision to make peace.) Finally, the treaty called for repayment with interest of the debts that some American planters still owed to British firms dating from the Revolutionary War. In exchange for such generous terms, Jay secured limited trading rights in the West Indies and agreement that some issues—boundary disputes with Canada and the damage and loss claims of shipowners—would be decided later by arbitration commissions.

When newspapers published the terms of the treaty, powerful opposition quickly emerged. In Massachusetts, disrespectful anti-Jay graffiti appeared on walls, and effigies of Jay along with copies of the treaty were ceremoniously burned. Nevertheless, the treaty passed the Senate in 1795 by a vote of 20 to 10. The corresponding vote in the House, on funding the implementation of the treaty, passed by only 3 votes. The bitter votes in Congress divided along the same lines as the Hamilton-Jefferson split on economic policy.

The Haitian Revolution

In addition to the Indian troubles and the European war across the Atlantic, another bloody conflict to the south polarized and even terrorized many Americans in the 1790s. The French colony of Saint Domingue, in the western third of the large Caribbean island of Hispaniola, became engulfed in revolution starting in 1791. Bloody war raged for more than a decade, resulting in 1804 in the birth of the Republic of Haiti, the first and only independent black state to arise out of a successful slave revolution.

Jay Treaty
▶ 1795 treaty between the United States and Britain, negotiated by John Jay. It secured limited trading rights in the West Indies but failed to ensure timely removal of British forces from western forts and reimbursement for slaves removed by the British after the Revolution.

What were Hamilton's economic policies?

What external threats did the United States face in the 1790s?

How did partisan rivalries shape the politics of the late 1790s?

Conclusion: Why did the new nation ultimately form political parties?

☑ LearningCurve
Check what you know.
bedfordstmartins.com
/roarkunderstanding

251

Haitian Revolution

▶ The 1791–1804 conflict involving diverse Haitian participants and armies from three European countries. At its end, Haiti became a free, independent, black-run country. The Haitian Revolution fueled fears of slave insurrections in the United States.

Haitian Revolution, 1791–1804

The **Haitian Revolution** was a complex event involving many participants, including the diverse local population and, eventually, three European countries. Some 30,000 whites dominated the island in 1790, running sugar and coffee plantations with close to half a million blacks, two-thirds of them of African birth. The white French colonists were not the only plantation owners, however. About 28,000 free mixed-race people (*gens de couleur*) owned one-third of the island's plantations and nearly a quarter of the slave labor force. Despite their economic status, these mixed-race planters were barred from political power, but they aspired to it.

The French Revolution of 1789 was the immediate catalyst for rebellion in this already tense society. First, white colonists challenged the white royalist government in an effort to link Saint Domingue with the new revolutionary government in France. Next, the mixed-race planters rebelled in 1791, demanding equal civil rights with the whites. No sooner was this revolt viciously suppressed than another part of the island's population rose up; thousands of slaves armed with machetes and torches wreaked devastation. In 1793, the civil war escalated to include French, Spanish, and British troops fighting the inhabitants and also one another. Led by former slave Toussaint L'Ouverture, slaves and free blacks in alliance with Spain occupied the northern regions of the island, leaving a thousand plantations in ruins and tens of thousands of people dead. Thousands of white and mixed-race planters, along with some of their slaves, fled to Spanish Louisiana and southern cities in the United States.

White Americans followed the revolution in horror through newspapers and refugees' accounts. A few sympathized with the impulse for liberty, but many more feared that violent black insurrection might spread to the United States. Many black American slaves also followed the revolution, for the news of the success of a first-ever massive revolution by slaves traveled quickly in this oral culture.

The Haitian Revolution provoked naked fear of a race war in white southerners. Thomas Jefferson, agonizing over the contagion of liberty in 1797, wrote another Virginia slaveholder that "if something is not done, and soon done, we shall be the murderers of our own children . . . ; the revolutionary storm, now sweeping the globe, will be upon us, and happy if we make timely provision to give it an easy passage over our land. From the present state of things in Europe and America, the day which brings our combustion must be near at hand; and only a single spark is wanting to make that day to-morrow."

> ## QUICK REVIEW

Why did the United States feel vulnerable to international threats in the 1790s?

CHAPTER LOCATOR | What were the sources of political stability in the 1790s?

252 CHAPTER 9 FORMING THE NEW NATION

How did partisan rivalries shape the politics of the late 1790s?

Cartoon of the Lyon-Griswold Fight in Congress

Political tensions ran high in 1798. On the floor of Congress, Federalist Roger Griswold called Republican Matthew Lyon a coward. Lyon responded with some well-aimed spit, the first departure from the gentleman's code of honor. Griswold raised his cane to strike Lyon, whereupon Lyon grabbed fire tongs to defend himself. James Madison later commented that the two should have dueled, the honorable way to avenge insults. Library of Congress.

BY THE MID-1790s, polarization over the French Revolution, Haiti, the Jay Treaty, and Hamilton's economic plans had led to two distinct and consistent rival political groups: **Federalists** and **Republicans**. Federalist leaders supported Britain in foreign policy and commercial interests at home, while Republicans rooted for liberty in France and worried about monarchical Federalists at home. The labels did not yet describe full-fledged political parties; such division was still thought to be a sign of failure of the experiment in government. Washington's decision not to seek a third term led to serious partisan electioneering in the presidential and congressional elections of 1796. Federalist John Adams won the presidency, but party strife accelerated over failed diplomacy in France, bringing the country to the brink of war. Pro-war and antiwar antagonism created a major crisis over political free speech, militarism, and fears of sedition and treason.

The Election of 1796

Washington struggled to appear to be above party politics, and in his farewell address he stressed the need to maintain a "unity of government" reflecting a unified body politic. He also urged the country to "steer clear of permanent alliances with any portion of the foreign world." The leading contenders for his position, John Adams of Massachusetts and Thomas Jefferson of Virginia, in theory agreed with him, but around them raged a party contest split along pro-British versus pro-French lines.

Federalists

▶ Originally the term for the supporters of the ratification of the U.S. Constitution in 1787–1788. In the 1790s, it became the name for one of the two dominant political groups that emerged during that decade. Federalist leaders of the 1790s supported Britain in foreign policy and commercial interests at home. Prominent Federalists included George Washington, Alexander Hamilton, and John Adams.

Republicans

▶ One of the two dominant political groups that emerged in the 1790s. Republicans supported the revolutionaries in France and worried about monarchical Federalists at home. Prominent Republicans included Thomas Jefferson and James Madison.

What were Hamilton's economic policies?

What external threats did the United States face in the 1790s?

How did partisan rivalries shape the politics of the late 1790s?

Conclusion: Why did the new nation ultimately form political parties?

✓ **LearningCurve**
Check what you know.
bedfordstmartins.com
/roarkunderstanding

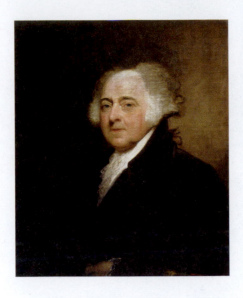

John Adams

The artist Gilbert Stuart began painting this portrait in 1800 when Adams was sixty-five. A friend once described Adams's shortcoming as a politician: "He can't dance, drink, game, flatter, promise, dress, swear with gentlemen, and small talk and flirt with the ladies." National Gallery of Art, Washington, D.C.

The leading Federalists informally caucused and chose Adams as their candidate, with Thomas Pinckney of South Carolina to run with him. The Republicans settled on Aaron Burr of New York to pair with Jefferson. The Constitution did not anticipate parties and tickets. Instead, each electoral college voter could cast two votes for any two candidates, but on only one ballot. The top vote-getter became president, and the next-highest assumed the vice presidency. (This procedural flaw was corrected by the Twelfth Amendment, adopted in 1804.) With only one ballot, careful maneuvering was required to make sure that the chief rivals for the presidency did not land in the top two spots.

A failed effort by Alexander Hamilton to influence the outcome of the election landed the country in just such a position. Hamilton did not trust Adams; he preferred Pinckney, and he tried to influence southern electors to throw their support to the South Carolinian. But his plan backfired: Adams was elected president with 71 electoral votes; Jefferson came in second with 68 and thus became vice president. Pinckney got 59 votes, while Burr trailed with 30.

Adams's inaugural speech pledged neutrality in foreign affairs and respect for the French people, which made Republicans hopeful. To please Federalists, Adams retained three cabinet members from Washington's administration—the secretaries of state, treasury, and war. But the three were Hamilton loyalists, passing off Hamilton's judgments and advice as their own to the unwitting Adams. Vice President Jefferson extended a conciliatory hand to Adams, but the Hamiltonian cabinet ruined the honeymoon. Jefferson's advice was spurned, and he withdrew from active counsel of the president.

The XYZ Affair

From the start, Adams's presidency was in crisis. France retaliated for the British-friendly Jay Treaty by abandoning its 1778 alliance with the United States. French privateers—armed private vessels—started detaining American ships carrying British goods; by March 1797, more than three hundred American vessels had been seized. To avenge these insults, Federalists started murmuring openly about

CHAPTER LOCATOR | What were the sources of political stability in the 1790s?

war with France. Adams preferred negotiations and dispatched a three-man commission to France in the fall of 1797. But at the same time, he asked Congress to approve expenditures on increased naval defense.

When the three American commissioners arrived in Paris, French officials would not receive them. Finally, the French minister of foreign affairs, Talleyrand, sent three French agents—unnamed and later known to the American public as X, Y, and Z—to the American commissioners with the information that $250,000 might grease the wheels of diplomacy and that a $12 million loan to the French government would be the price of a peace treaty. Incensed, the commissioners brought news of the bribery attempt to the president.

Americans reacted to the **XYZ affair** with shock and anger. Even staunch pro-French Republicans began to reevaluate their allegiance. The Federalist-dominated Congress appropriated money for an army of ten thousand soldiers and repealed all prior treaties with France. In 1798, twenty naval warships launched the United States into its first undeclared war, called the Quasi-War by historians to underscore its uncertain legal status. The main scene of action was the Caribbean, where more than one hundred French ships were captured.

There was no home-front unity in this time of undeclared war; antagonism only intensified between Federalists and Republicans. Republican newspapers heaped abuse on Adams. One denounced him as "a person without patriotism, without philosophy, and a mock monarch." Pro-French mobs roamed the streets of Philadelphia, the capital, and Adams, fearing for his personal safety, stocked weapons in his presidential quarters. Federalists, too, went on the offensive. In Newburyport, Massachusetts, they lit a huge bonfire and burned issues of the state's Republican newspapers. Officers in a New York militia unit drank a menacing toast on July 4, 1798: "One and but one party in the United States." A Federalist editor ominously declared that "he who is not for us is against us."

XYZ affair
▶ A 1797 incident in which American negotiators in France were rebuffed for refusing to pay a substantial bribe. The incident led the United States into an undeclared war with France, known as the Quasi-War, which intensified antagonism between Federalists and Republicans.

The Alien and Sedition Acts

With tempers so dangerously high and fears that political dissent was akin to treason, Federalist leaders moved to muffle the opposition. In mid-1798, Congress passed the Sedition Act, which not only made conspiracy and revolt illegal but also criminalized any speech or words that defamed the president or Congress. One Federalist warned of the threat that existed "to overturn and ruin the government by publishing the most shameless falsehoods against the representatives of the people." In all, twenty-five men, almost all Republican newspaper editors, were charged with sedition; twelve were convicted.

Congress also passed two Alien Acts. The first extended the waiting period for an alien to achieve citizenship from five to fourteen years and required all aliens to register with the federal government. The second empowered the president in time of war to deport or imprison without trial any foreigner suspected of being a danger to the United States. The clear intent of these laws was to harass French immigrants already in the United States and to discourage others from coming.

Republicans strongly opposed the **Alien and Sedition Acts** on the grounds that they were in conflict with the Bill of Rights, but they did not have the votes to revoke the acts in Congress, nor could the federal judiciary, dominated by Federalist judges, be counted on to challenge the acts. Jefferson and Madison

Alien and Sedition Acts
▶ 1798 laws passed to suppress political dissent. The Sedition Act criminalized conspiracy and criticism of government leaders. The two Alien Acts extended the waiting period for citizenship and empowered the president to deport or imprison without trial any foreigner deemed a danger.

What were Hamilton's economic policies?

What external threats did the United States face in the 1790s?

How did partisan rivalries shape the politics of the late 1790s?

Conclusion: Why did the new nation ultimately form political parties?

✓ LearningCurve
Check what you know.
bedfordstmartins.com
/roarkunderstanding

255

Virginia and Kentucky Resolutions

▶ 1798 resolutions condemning the Alien and Sedition Acts submitted to the federal government by the Virginia and Kentucky state legislatures. The resolutions tested the idea that state legislatures could judge the constitutionality of federal laws and nullify them.

turned to the state legislatures, the only other competing political arena, to press their opposition. Each man anonymously drafted a set of resolutions condemning the acts and convinced the legislatures of Virginia and Kentucky to present them to the federal government in late fall 1798. The **Virginia and Kentucky Resolutions** tested the novel argument that state legislatures have the right to judge and even nullify the constitutionality of federal laws, bold claims that held the risk that one or both men could be accused of sedition. The resolutions in fact made little dent in the Alien and Sedition Acts, but the idea of a state's right to nullify federal law did not disappear. It would resurface several times in decades to come, most notably in a major tariff dispute in 1832 and in the sectional arguments that led to the Civil War.

Amid all the war hysteria and sedition fears in 1798, President Adams regained his balance. He was uncharacteristically restrained in pursuing opponents under the Sedition Act, and he finally refused to declare war on France, as extreme Federalists wished. No doubt he was beginning to realize how much he had been the dupe of Hamilton. He also shrewdly realized that France was not eager for war and that a peaceful settlement might be close at hand. In January 1799, a peace initiative from France arrived in the form of a letter assuring Adams that diplomatic channels were open again and that new peace commissioners would be welcomed in France.

Adams accepted this overture and appointed new negotiators. By late 1799, the Quasi-War with France had subsided, and in 1800 the negotiations resulted in a treaty declaring "a true and sincere friendship" between the United States and France. But Federalists were not pleased; Adams lost the support of a significant part of his own party and sealed his fate as the first one-term president of the United States.

The election of 1800 was openly organized along party lines. The self-designated national leaders of each group met to handpick their candidates for president and vice president. Adams's chief opponent was Thomas Jefferson. When the election was finally over, President Jefferson mounted the inaugural platform to announce, "We are all republicans, we are all federalists," an appealing rhetoric of harmony appropriate to an inaugural address. But his formulation perpetuated a denial of the validity of party politics, a denial that ran deep in the founding generation of political leaders.

> ## QUICK REVIEW

How did war between Britain and France intensify the political divisions in the United States?

CHAPTER LOCATOR | What were the sources of political stability in the 1790s?

256 CHAPTER 9 FORMING THE NEW NATION

Conclusion: Why did the new nation ultimately form political parties?

AMERICAN POLITICAL LEADERS began operating the new government in 1789 with great hopes of unifying the country and overcoming selfish factionalism. The enormous trust in President Washington was the central foundation for those hopes, and Washington did not disappoint, becoming a model Mr. President with a blend of integrity and authority. Stability was further aided by easy passage of the Bill of Rights (to appease Antifederalists) and by attention to cultivating a virtuous citizenry of upright men supported and rewarded by republican womanhood. Yet the hopes of the honeymoon period soon turned to worries and then fears as major political disagreements flared up.

At the core of the conflict was a group of talented men—Hamilton, Madison, Jefferson, and Adams—so recently allies but now opponents. They diverged over Hamilton's economic program, over relations with the British and the Jay Treaty, over the French and Haitian revolutions, and over preparedness for war abroad and free speech at home. Hamilton was perhaps the driving force in these conflicts, but the antagonism was not about mere personality. Parties were taking shape not around individuals, but around principles, such as ideas about what constituted enlightened leadership, how powerful the federal government should be, who was the best ally in Europe, and when oppositional political speech turned into treason.

In his inaugural address of 1801, Jefferson offered his conciliatory assurance that Americans were at the same time "all republicans" and "all federalists," suggesting that both groups shared two basic ideas—the value of republican government, in which power derived from the people, and the value of the unique federal system of shared governance structured by the Constitution. But by 1800, Federalist and Republican defined competing philosophies of government. To at least some of his listeners, Jefferson's assertion of harmony across budding party lines could only have seemed bizarre. For the next two decades, these two groups would battle each other, each fearing that the success of the other might bring about the demise of the country.

What were Hamilton's economic policies?

What external threats did the United States face in the 1790s?

How did partisan rivalries shape the politics of the late 1790s?

Conclusion: Why did the new nation ultimately form political parties?

☑ **LearningCurve**
Check what you know.
bedfordstmartins.com
/roarkunderstanding

257

CHAPTER 9 STUDY GUIDE

STEP 1 **GET STARTED ONLINE**

 LearningCurve ■ bedfordstmartins.com/roarkunderstanding

Now that you've read the chapter, make it stick by completing the LearningCurve activity.

STEP 2 **EXPLAIN WHY IT MATTERS**

Put your reading into practice. Identify each term below, and then explain why it matters in U.S. history.

TERM	WHO OR WHAT & WHEN	WHY IT MATTERS
Bill of Rights (p. 237)		
Report on Public Credit (p. 242)		
Report on Manufactures (p. 244)		
Whiskey Rebellion (p. 245)		
Treaty of Greenville (p. 249)		
Jay Treaty (p. 251)		
Haitian Revolution (p. 252)		
Federalists (p. 253)		
Republicans (p. 253)		
XYZ affair (p. 255)		
Alien and Sedition Acts (p. 255)		
Virginia and Kentucky Resolutions (p. 256)		

STEP 3 **MOVE BEYOND THE BASICS**

To demonstrate a more advanced understanding, assess the positions and policies of the Federalists and the Republicans. Is it accurate to describe them as political parties? Why or why not?

	Federalists	Republicans
States' rights		
Government influence on economy		
Social and political hierarchy		
Relations with Britain		
Relations with France		

PUT IT ALL TOGETHER

Now, take a step back and try to explain the big picture. Remember to use specific examples from the chapter in your answers.

DOMESTIC AFFAIRS

▶ What important precedents did George Washington set? How did he use the presidency to bring political stability to the country?

▶ How did Hamilton imagine the future of the United States? How did his vision conflict with that of Jefferson?

NATIONAL SECURITY

▶ What were the most important threats to America's national security in the 1790s? How did the Washington and Adams administrations respond to those threats?

▶ How did the French Revolution contribute to the split between Federalists and Republicans in the United States?

FEDERALISTS AND REPUBLICANS

▶ What led to the factionalizing of American politics in the 1790s?

▶ How did the development of political factions affect the country domestically? In its external affairs?

LOOKING BACKWARD, LOOKING AHEAD

▶ How did the government Washington headed differ from the government created by the Articles of Confederation?

▶ What steps had been taken toward the creation of national political parties by 1800? What steps were still required before a true party system was in place?

> ## IN YOUR OWN WORDS

Imagine that you must give an oral report to the class answering the following question: **What were the developments that led to the establishment of political parties with distinctive agendas by the end of the 1790s?** What would be the most important points to include and why?

 Do it online at the Student Site ■ bedfordstmartins.com/roarkunderstanding

10

A MATURING REPUBLIC

1800–1824

> **What were the most important political, social, cultural, and diplomatic changes in the early decades of the nineteenth century?** Chapter 10 explores the changing political landscape of the nation from the election of Thomas Jefferson in 1800 to the election of John Quincy Adams in 1824. It examines the foreign and domestic challenges and opportunities that shaped American politics, as well as the shifting political culture that resulted in the expansion of voting rights for white men, the disfranchisement of most black men, and new educational opportunities for white women.

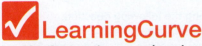 **LearningCurve**

bedfordstmartins.com/roarkunderstanding
After reading the chapter, use LearningCurve to
retain what you've read.

The Artist in His Museum, a self-portrait by American painter, inventor, and museum founder Charles Willson Peale, 1822. The Granger Collection, New York.

> How did Jefferson attempt to undo the Federalist innovations of earlier administrations?

> What was the significance of the Louisiana Purchase for the United States?

> Why did Congress declare war on Great Britain in 1812?

> How did the civil status of American women and men differ in the early Republic?

> Why did partisan conflict increase during the administrations of Monroe and Adams?

> Conclusion: How did republican simplicity become complex?

How did Jefferson attempt to undo the Federalist innovations of earlier administrations?

Thomas Jefferson, by John Trumbull This portrait of Jefferson was made in the late 1780s, when he was a young widower and lived in Paris as a diplomat with his daughters and slave Sally Hemings. In 1802, a scandal erupted when a journalist charged that Jefferson had fathered several children by Hemings. DNA evidence and historical evidence of Jefferson's whereabouts during the start of Hemings's pregnancies make a powerful case that he did father at least some of the children. Monticello/Thomas Jefferson Memorial Foundation, Inc.

CHRONOLOGY

1800
– Thomas Jefferson and Aaron Burr tie in electoral college.
– Gabriel's rebellion is reported.

1801
– House of Representatives elects Jefferson president.
– Barbary War with Tripoli begins.

1803
– *Marbury v. Madison.*

1805
– United States defeats Tripoli.

THE FIRST PRESIDENTIAL election of the new century was an all-out partisan battle. A panicky Federalist newspaper in Connecticut predicted that a victory by Thomas Jefferson would produce a bloody civil war and usher in an immoral reign of "murder, robbery, rape, adultery and incest." Apocalyptic fears gripped parts of the South, where a frightful slave uprising seemed a possible consequence of Jefferson's victory. But nothing nearly so dramatic occurred. Jefferson later called his election the "revolution of 1800," referring to his repudiation of Federalist practices and his cutbacks in military spending and taxes. While he cherished a republican simplicity in governance, he inevitably encountered events that required decisive and sometimes expensive government action, including military action overseas to protect American shipping.

Turbulent Times: Election and Rebellion

The election of 1800 was historic for procedural reasons: It was the first election to be decided by the House of Representatives. Probably by mistake, Republican

CHAPTER LOCATOR | **How did Jefferson attempt to undo the Federalist innovations of earlier administrations?** | What was the significance of the Louisiana Purchase for the United States?

CHAPTER 10
262 A MATURING REPUBLIC

voters in the electoral college gave Jefferson and his running mate, Senator Aaron Burr of New York, an equal number of votes, an outcome possible because of the single balloting to choose both president and vice president (**Map 10.1**). (To fix this problem, the Twelfth Amendment to the Constitution, adopted in 1804, provided for distinct ballots for the two offices.) The tie meant that the House had to choose between those two men, leaving the Federalist candidate, John Adams, out of the race. The vain and ambitious Burr declined to concede, so the sitting Federalist-dominated House of Representatives, in its waning days in early 1801, got to choose the president.

Some Federalists preferred Burr, believing that his character flaws made him susceptible to Federalist pressure. But the influential Alexander Hamilton, though no friend of Jefferson, recognized that the high-strung Burr would be more danger-ous in the presidency. Jefferson was a "contemptible hypocrite" in Hamilton's opin-ion, but at least he was not corrupt. Thirty-six ballots and six days later, Jefferson got the votes he needed to win the presidency. This election demonstrated a remarkable feature of the new government: No matter how hard fought the cam-paign, the leadership of the nation could shift from one group to its rivals in a peaceful transfer of power.

As the country struggled over its white leadership crisis, a twenty-four-year-old blacksmith named Gabriel, the slave of Thomas Prossor, plotted rebel-lion in Virginia. Inspired by the Haitian Revolution (see chapter 9), Gabriel was said to be organizing a thousand slaves to march on the state capital of Richmond and take the governor, James Monroe, hostage. On the appointed day, however, a few nervous slaves went to the authorities with news of Gabriel's rebellion, and within days scores of implicated conspirators were jailed and brought to trial.

One of the jailed rebels compared himself to the most venerated icon of the early Republic: "I have nothing more to offer than what General Washington would have had to offer, had he been taken by the British and put to trial by them." Such talk worried white Virginians, and in the fall of 1800 twenty-seven black men were hanged for allegedly contemplating rebellion. Finally, Jefferson advised Governor Monroe to halt the hangings. "The world at large will forever condemn us if we indulge a principle of revenge," Jefferson wrote.

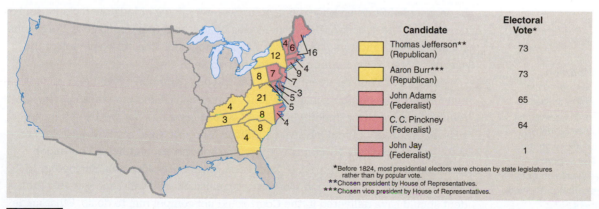

Candidate	Electoral Vote*
Thomas Jefferson** (Republican)	73
Aaron Burr*** (Republican)	73
John Adams (Federalist)	65
C. C. Pinckney (Federalist)	64
John Jay (Federalist)	1

*Before 1824, most presidential electors were chosen by state legislatures rather than by popular vote.
**Chosen president by House of Representatives.
***Chosen vice president by House of Representatives.

MAP 10.1 ■ The Election of 1800

Why did Congress declare war on Great Britain in 1812?

How did the civil status of American women and men differ in the early Republic?

Why did partisan conflict increase during the administrations of Monroe and Adams?

Conclusion: How did republican simplicity become complex?

☑ LearningCurve
Check what you know.
bedfordstmartins.com
/roarkunderstanding

The Jeffersonian Vision
of Republican Simplicity

Once elected, Thomas Jefferson turned his attention to establishing his administration in clear contrast to the Federalists. For his inauguration, he dressed in everyday clothing to strike a tone of republican simplicity, and he walked to the Capitol for the modest swearing-in ceremony. As president, he scaled back Federalist building plans for Washington City and cut the government budget.

Martha Washington and Abigail Adams had received the wives of government officials at weekly teas, thereby cementing social relations in the governing class. But Jefferson, a longtime widower, disdained female gatherings and avoided the women of Washington City. He abandoned George Washington's practice of holding weekly formal receptions. He preferred small dinner parties with carefully chosen politicos, either all Republicans or all Federalists (and all male). At these intimate dinners, the president exercised influence and strengthened informal relationships that would help him govern.

Jefferson was no Antifederalist; he had supported the Constitution in 1788. But events of the 1790s had caused him to worry about the stretching of powers in the executive branch. Jefferson had watched with distrust as Hamiltonian policies refinanced the public debt, established a national bank, and secured commercial ties with Britain (see chapter 9). To him, these policies seemed to promote the interests of greedy speculators and profiteers at the expense of the rest of the country. In Jefferson's vision, the source of true liberty in America was the independent farmer, someone who owned and worked his land both for himself and for the market.

Jefferson set out to dismantle Federalist innovations. He reduced the size of the army by a third, preferring a militia-based defense, and he cut back the navy to six ships. With the consent of Congress, he abolished all federal taxes based on population or whiskey. Government revenue would now derive solely from customs duties and the sale of western land. This strategy benefited the South, where three-fifths of the slaves counted for representation but not for taxation now. By the end of his first term, Jefferson had deeply reduced Hamilton's cherished national debt.

A limited federal government, according to Jefferson, maintained a postal system, federal courts, and coastal lighthouses; it collected customs duties and conducted the census. The president had one private secretary, a young man named Meriwether Lewis, and Jefferson paid him out of his own pocket. The Department of State employed 8 people: Secretary James Madison, 6 clerks, and a messenger. The Treasury Department was by far the largest unit, with 73 revenue commissioners, auditors, and clerks, plus 2 watchmen. The entire payroll of the executive branch amounted to a mere 130 people in 1801.

However, 217 government workers lay beyond Jefferson's command, all judicial and military appointments made by John Adams as his last act in office. Jefferson refused to honor those "midnight judges" whose hires had not yet been fully processed. One disappointed job seeker, William Marbury, sued the new secretary of state, James Madison, for failure to make good on the appointment. This action gave rise to a landmark Supreme Court case, **Marbury v. Madison**, decided in 1803. The Court ruled that although Marbury's commission was valid and the new president should have delivered it, the Court could not compel him to do so. What made

Marbury v. Madison
▶ 1803 Supreme Court case that established the concept of judicial review in finding that parts of the Judiciary Act of 1789 were in conflict with the Constitution. The Supreme Court assumed legal authority to overrule acts of other branches of the government.

CHAPTER LOCATOR | How did Jefferson attempt to undo the Federalist innovations of earlier administrations? | What was the significance of the Louisiana Purchase for the United States?

CHAPTER 10
264 A MATURING REPUBLIC

the case significant was little noted at the time: The Court found that the grounds of Marbury's suit, resting in the Judiciary Act of 1789, were in conflict with the Constitution. For the first time, the Supreme Court disallowed a federal law on the grounds that it was unconstitutional.

Dangers Overseas: The Barbary Wars

Jefferson's desire to keep government and the military small met a severe test in the western Mediterranean Sea, where U.S. trading interests ran afoul of several states on the northern coast of Africa. For well over a century, Morocco, Algiers, Tunis, and Tripoli, called the Barbary States by Americans, controlled all Mediterranean shipping traffic by demanding large annual payments (called "tribute") for safe passage. Countries electing not to pay found their ships and crews at risk for seizure. After several years in which about a hundred American crew members were taken captive, the United States agreed to pay $50,000 a year in tribute.

In May 1801, when the monarch of Tripoli failed to secure a large increase in his tribute, he declared war on the United States. Jefferson considered such payments extortion, and he sent four warships to the Mediterranean to protect U.S. shipping. From 1801 to 1803, U.S. frigates engaged in skirmishes with Barbary privateers.

Then, in late 1803, the USS *Philadelphia* ran aground near Tripoli's harbor and was captured along with its 300-man crew. In early 1804, a U.S. naval ship commanded by Lieutenant Stephen Decatur sailed into the harbor after dark and set the *Philadelphia* on fire, rendering it useless to the Tripolitan monarch. Later that year, a small force of U.S. ships attacked the harbor and damaged or destroyed nineteen Tripolitan ships and bombarded the city, winning high praise

The Burning of the Frigate *Philadelphia* in Tripoli Harbor, 1804

After the capture of the warship *Philadelphia* in 1803, Commander Stephen Decatur engineered a daring nighttime raid to destroy the vessel. With his men concealed, Decatur sailed into the harbor using an Arabic-speaking pilot to fool harbor sentries. The Americans quickly boarded the *Philadelphia* and set it ablaze, forcing the Tripolitan guards to swim to shore. Decatur departed with only one injured man. The Mariners Museum, Newport News, Virginia.

Why did Congress declare war on Great Britain in 1812?

How did the civil status of American women and men differ in the early Republic?

Why did partisan conflict increase during the administrations of Monroe and Adams?

Conclusion: How did republican simplicity become complex?

☑ LearningCurve
Check what you know.
bedfordstmartins.com
/roarkunderstanding

and respect from European governments. Yet the sailors from the *Philadelphia* remained in captivity.

In 1805, William Eaton, an American officer stationed in Tunis, requested a thousand Marines to invade Tripoli, but Secretary of State James Madison rejected the plan. On his own, Eaton assembled a force of four hundred men (mostly Greek and Egyptian mercenaries plus eight Marines) and marched them over five hundred miles of desert for a surprise attack on Tripoli's second-largest city. Amazingly, he succeeded. The monarch of Tripoli yielded, released the prisoners taken from the *Philadelphia*, and negotiated a treaty in 1805 with the United States.

Periodic attacks by Algiers and Tunis continued to plague American ships during Jefferson's second term of office and into his successor's presidency. This Second Barbary War ended in 1815 when the hero of 1804, Stephen Decatur, now a captain, arrived on the northern coast of Africa with a fleet of twenty-seven ships. By show of force, he engineered three treaties that put an end to the tribute system and provided reparations for damages to U.S. ships. Decatur was widely hailed for restoring honor to the United States.

> **QUICK REVIEW**

How did Jefferson's views of the role of the federal government differ from those of his predecessors?

CHAPTER LOCATOR | How did Jefferson attempt to undo the Federalist innovations of earlier administrations?

What was the significance of the Louisiana Purchase for the United States?

266 CHAPTER 10 A MATURING REPUBLIC

What was the significance of the Louisiana Purchase for the United States?

Comanche Feats of Horsemanship, 1834

Pennsylvania artist George Catlin toured the Great Plains and captured Comanche equestrian warfare in training. "Every young man," Catlin wrote, learned "to drop his body upon the side of his horse at the instant he is passing, effectually screened from his enemies' weapons. . . . [H]e will hang whilst his horse is at fullest speed, carrying with him his bow and his shield, and also his long lance . . . which he will wield upon his enemy as he passes; rising and throwing his arrows over the horse's back, or with equal ease and equal success under the horse's neck." Smithsonian American Art Museum, Washington, DC/Art Resource, NY.

JEFFERSON SET ASIDE his cautious exercise of federal power to take advantage of an unexpected offer from France to buy the Louisiana Territory. The president sent four expeditions into the prairie and mountains to explore this huge acquisition of land. The powerful Osage of the Arkansas River valley responded to overtures for an alliance and were soon lavishly welcomed by Jefferson in Washington City, but the even more powerful Comanche of the southern Great Plains stood their ground against all invaders. Meanwhile, the expedition by Lewis and Clark, the longest and northernmost trek of the four launched by Jefferson, mapped U.S. terrain all the way to the Pacific Ocean, giving a boost to expansionist aspirations.

> **CHRONOLOGY**

1803
– Louisiana Purchase.

1804
– Jefferson meets with Osage Indians.

1804–1806
– Lewis and Clark expedition.

1807
– United States establishes trade with Comanche Indians.

Why did Congress declare war on Great Britain in 1812?

How did the civil status of American women and men differ in the early Republic?

Why did partisan conflict increase during the administrations of Monroe and Adams?

Conclusion: How did republican simplicity become complex?

☑ **LearningCurve** Check what you know. bedfordstmartins.com /roarkunderstanding

The Louisiana Purchase

In 1763, at the end of the Seven Years' War, a large area west of the United States shifted from France to Spain, but Spain never effectively controlled it (see chapter 6). Centered on the Great Plains, it was home to Indian tribes, most notably the powerful and expansionist Comanche nation. New Orleans was Spain's principal stronghold, a city strategically sited on the Mississippi River near its outlet to the Gulf of Mexico. Spain profited modestly from trade taxes it imposed on the small flow of agricultural products shipped down the river from American farms in the western parts of Kentucky and Tennessee.

Spanish officials in New Orleans and St. Louis worried that their sparse population could not withstand an anticipated westward movement of Americans. At first, they hoped for a Spanish-Indian alliance to halt the expected demographic wave, but defending many hundreds of miles along the Mississippi River against Americans on the move was a daunting prospect. Thus, in 1800 Spain struck a secret deal to return this trans-Mississippi territory to France, in the hopes that a French Louisiana would provide a buffer zone between Spain's more valuable holdings in northern Mexico and the land-hungry Americans. The French emperor Napoleon accepted the transfer and agreed to Spain's condition that France could not sell Louisiana to anyone without Spain's permission.

From the U.S. perspective, Spain had proved a weak western neighbor, but France was another story. Jefferson was so alarmed by the rumored transfer that he instructed Robert R. Livingston, America's minister in France, to try to buy New Orleans. When Livingston hinted that the United States might seize it if buying was not an option, the French negotiator asked him to name his price for the entire Louisiana Territory from the Gulf of Mexico north to Canada. Livingston shrewdly stalled and within days accepted the bargain price of $15 million (**Map 10.2**).

On the verge of war with Britain, France needed both money and friendly neutrality from the United States, and it got both from the quick sale of the Louisiana Territory. In addition, the recent and costly loss of Haiti as a colony made a French presence in New Orleans less feasible as well. But in selling Louisiana to the United States, France had broken its agreement with Spain, which protested that the sale was illegal.

Moreover, there was no clarity on the western border of this land transfer. Spain claimed that the border was about one hundred miles west of the Mississippi River, while in Jefferson's eyes it was some eight hundred miles farther west, defined by the crest of the Rocky Mountains. When Livingston pressured the French negotiator to clarify his country's understanding of the boundary, the negotiator replied, "I can give you no direction. You have made a noble bargain for yourself, and I suppose you will make the most of it."

Jefferson gained congressional approval for the **Louisiana Purchase**, but without the votes of Federalist New England, which was anxious about the geographic balance of power under threat by such a large acquisition of land. In late 1803, the American army took formal control of the Louisiana Territory, and the United States nearly doubled in size — at least on paper.

Louisiana Purchase

▶ 1803 purchase of French territory west of the Mississippi River that stretched from the Gulf of Mexico to Canada. The Louisiana Purchase nearly doubled the size of the United States and opened the way for future American expansion west.

CHAPTER LOCATOR | How did Jefferson attempt to undo the Federalist innovations of earlier administrations?

What was the significance of the Louisiana Purchase for the United States?

268 CHAPTER 10 A MATURING REPUBLIC

MAP 10.2 ■ Jefferson's Expeditions in the West, 1804–1806

The Louisiana Purchase of 1803 brought the United States a large territory without clear boundaries. Jefferson sent off four scientific expeditions to take stock of the land's possibilities and to assess the degree of potential antagonism from Indian and Spanish inhabitants.

> MAP ACTIVITY

READING THE MAP: How did the size of the newly acquired territory compare to the land area of the existing American states and territories? What natural features of the land might have suggested boundaries for the Louisiana Purchase? Did those natural features coincide with actual patterns of human habitation already in place?

CONNECTIONS: What political events in Europe created the opportunity for the Jefferson administration to purchase Louisiana? How did the acquisition of Louisiana affect Spain's hold on North America?

The Lewis and Clark Expedition

Jefferson quickly launched four government-financed expeditions up the river valleys of the new territory to establish relationships with Indian tribes and to determine Spanish influence and presence. The first set out in 1804 to explore the upper reaches of the Missouri River. Jefferson appointed twenty-eight-year-old Meriwether Lewis, his secretary, to head the expedition and instructed him to investigate Indian cultures, to collect plant and animal specimens, and to chart the geography of the West. Congress wanted the expedition to scout locations for military posts, negotiate fur trade agreements, and identify river routes to the West (see Map 10.2).

For his co-leader, Lewis chose Kentuckian William Clark, a veteran of the 1790s Indian wars. With a crew of forty-five, the explorers left St. Louis in the spring of 1804, working their way northwest up the Missouri River. They camped for the winter at a Mandan village in what is now central North Dakota.

Why did Congress declare war on Great Britain in 1812?	How did the civil status of American women and men differ in the early Republic?	Why did partisan conflict increase during the administrations of Monroe and Adams?	Conclusion: How did republican simplicity become complex?	✓ **LearningCurve** Check what you know. bedfordstmartins.com /roarkunderstanding

The following spring, the explorers headed west, accompanied by a sixteen-year-old Shoshoni woman named Sacajawea. Kidnapped by Mandans at about age ten, she had been sold to a French trapper as a slave/wife. Hers was not a unique story among Indian women; such women knew several languages, making them valuable translators and mediators. Further, Sacajawea and her new baby allowed the American expedition to appear peaceful to suspicious tribes. As Lewis wrote in his journal, "No woman ever accompanies a war party of Indians in this quarter."

The **Lewis and Clark expedition** reached the Pacific Ocean at the mouth of the Columbia River in November 1805. When the two leaders returned home the following year, they were greeted as national heroes. They had established favorable relations with dozens of Indian tribes; they had collected invaluable information on the peoples, soils, plants, animals, and geography of the West; and they had inspired a nation of restless explorers and solitary imitators.

Lewis and Clark expedition

▶ 1804–1806 expedition led by Meriwether Lewis and William Clark that explored the trans-Mississippi West for the U.S. government. The expedition's mission was scientific, political, and geographic.

Osage and Comanche Indians

The three additional expeditions set forth between 1804 and 1806 to probe the contested southwestern border of the Louisiana Purchase. The first exploring party ascended the Red River to the Ouachita River, ending at a hot springs in present-day Arkansas. Two years later, the second group followed the Red River west into eastern Texas, and the third embarked from St. Louis and traveled west, deep into the Rockies. This third group, led by Zebulon Pike, had gone too far, in the view of the Spaniards: Pike and his men were arrested, taken to northern Mexico, and soon released.

Of the scores of Indian tribes in this lower Great Plains region, two enjoyed reputations for territorial dominance. The Osage ruled the land between the Missouri and the lower Arkansas rivers, while the trading and raiding grounds of the Comanche stretched from the upper Arkansas River to the Rockies and south into Texas, a vast area called Comanchería. Both were formidable tribes that proved equal to the Spaniards. The Osage accomplished this through careful diplomacy and periodic shows of strength, the Comanche by expert horsemanship, a brisk trade in guns and captives, and a readiness to employ deadly force.

In 1804, Jefferson invited Osage tribal leaders to Washington City and greeted them with ceremonies and gifts. He positioned the Osage as equals of the Americans: "The great spirit has given you strength & has given us strength, not that we might hurt one another, but to do each other all the good in our power." Jefferson wanted a trade agreement that would introduce new agricultural tools to the Osage: hoes and ploughs for the men; spinning wheels and looms for the women. These gendered tools signified a departure from the native gender system in which women tended crops while men hunted game. With an agricultural civilization, men would give up the hunt and thus need far less land to sustain their communities. In exchange, the Osage asked for protection against Indian refugees displaced by American settlers east of the Mississippi. Jefferson's Osage alliance soon proved to be quite expensive, driven up by the costs of providing defense, brokering treaties, and giving gifts all around. In 1806, a second ceremonial visit to Washington and other eastern cities by a dozen Osage leaders cost the federal government $10,000.

CHAPTER LOCATOR | How did Jefferson attempt to undo the Federalist innovations of earlier administrations?

What was the significance of the Louisiana Purchase for the United States?

270 CHAPTER 10 A MATURING REPUBLIC

These promising peace initiatives were short-lived. By 1808, intertribal warfare was on the rise, and the governor of the Louisiana Territory declared that the U.S. government no longer had an obligation to protect the Osage. Jefferson's presidency was waning, and soon the practice of whittling away Indian lands through coercive treaties reasserted itself. Four treaties between 1808 and 1839 shrank the Osage lands, and by the 1860s they had been relocated to present-day Oklahoma.

By contrast, the Comanche resisted attempts to dominate them. European maps marking Spanish ownership of vast North American lands simply did not correspond to the reality on the ground, and for decades after the Louisiana Purchase of 1803, nothing much changed. In 1807, a newly appointed U.S. Indian agent invited Comanche leaders to Natchitoches in Louisiana, where he proclaimed an improbable solidarity with the Comanche: "It is now so long since our Ancestors came from beyond the great Water that we have no remembrance of it. We ourselves are Natives of the Same land that you are, in other words white Indians, we therefore Should feel & live together like brothers & Good Neighbours." Trade relations flourished, with American traders allowed to enter Comanchería to attend local market fairs, selling weapons, cloth, and household metal goods in exchange for horses, bison, and furs. No matter what the map of the United States looked like, on the ground Comanchería remained under the control of the Comanches and thus off-limits to settlement by white Americans until the late nineteenth century (see Map 10.2).

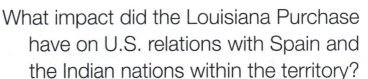

QUICK REVIEW

What impact did the Louisiana Purchase have on U.S. relations with Spain and the Indian nations within the territory?

Why did Congress declare war on Great Britain in 1812?

How did the civil status of American women and men differ in the early Republic?

Why did partisan conflict increase during the administrations of Monroe and Adams?

Conclusion: How did republican simplicity become complex?

☑ LearningCurve
Check what you know.
bedfordstmartins.com
/roarkunderstanding

> Why did Congress declare war on Great Britain in 1812?

The Burning of Washington City

This British engraving celebrates the British army's attack on Washington, D.C., in 1814. Disciplined troops control the street in front of the burning White House; the dome of the blazing Capitol is on the right. Anne S. K. Brown Military Collection, Brown University Library.

JEFFERSON EASILY RETAINED the presidency in the election of 1804, trouncing Federalist Charles Cotesworth Pinckney of South Carolina. A more difficult problem was the threat of war with both France and Britain, which led Jefferson to try a novel tactic, an embargo. His successor, James Madison, continued with a modified embargo, but his much narrower margin of victory over Pinckney in the election of 1808 indicated growing dissatisfaction with the Jefferson-Madison handling of foreign policy.

Madison broke with Jefferson on one very domestic matter: He allowed his gregarious wife, Dolley Madison, to participate in serious politics. Under James Madison's leadership, the country declared war in 1812 on Britain and on a confederacy of Indians in the old Northwest. The two-year war cost the young nation its White House and its Capitol, but victory was proclaimed at the end nonetheless.

Impressment and Embargo

In 1803, France and Britain went to war, and both repeatedly warned the United States not to ship arms to the other. Britain acted on these threats in 1806, stopping U.S. ships to inspect cargoes for military aid to France and seizing suspected deserters from the British navy, along with many Americans. Ultimately, 2,500 U.S. sailors were "impressed" (taken by force) by the British, who needed them for

CHAPTER LOCATOR | How did Jefferson attempt to undo the Federalist innovations of earlier administrations? | What was the significance of the Louisiana Purchase for the United States?

The *Chesapeake* Incident,
June 22, 1807

their war with France. In retaliation against the **impressment** of American sailors, Jefferson convinced Congress to pass a nonimportation law banning certain British-made goods.

Jefferson found one event particularly provoking. In June 1807, the American ship *Chesapeake*, harboring some British deserters, was ordered to stop by the British frigate *Leopard*. The *Chesapeake* refused, and the *Leopard* opened fire, killing three Americans — right at the mouth of Chesapeake Bay, well within U.S. territory. In response, Congress passed the **Embargo Act of 1807**, prohibiting U.S. ships from traveling to all foreign ports, a measure that brought a swift halt to all overseas trade carried in American vessels. Though a drastic measure, the embargo was meant to forestall war by forcing concessions from the British through economic pressure.

The Embargo Act of 1807 was a disaster. From 1790 to 1807, U.S. exports had increased fivefold, but the embargo brought commerce to a standstill. In New England, the heart of the shipping industry, unemployment rose. Grain plummeted in value, river traffic halted, tobacco rotted in the South, and cotton went unpicked. Protest petitions flooded Washington. The federal government suffered, too, for import duties were a significant source of revenue. The Federalist Party, in danger of fading away after its weak showing in the election of 1804, began to revive.

As the presidential election of 1808 approached, Republican caucuses — informal political groups that orchestrated the selection of candidates — chose Secretary of State James Madison as their nominee. The Federalist caucuses again chose Charles Cotesworth Pinckney. Madison won, but Pinckney secured 47 electoral votes, nearly half of Madison's total. Support for the Federalists remained centered in New England, and Republicans still held the balance of power nationwide.

Dolley Madison and Social Politics

Although women could not vote and supposedly left politics to men, the female relatives of Washington politicians took on several overtly political functions that greased the wheels of the affairs of state. They networked through dinners, balls, receptions, and the intricate custom of "calling," in which men and women paid brief visits at each other's homes. Webs of friendship and influence in turn facilitated female political lobbying. It was not uncommon for women in this social set to write letters of recommendation for men seeking government work.

When James Madison became president, Dolley Madison, called by some the "presidentress," struck a balance between queenliness and republican openness. She dressed the part in resplendent clothes, and she opened three elegant rooms in the executive mansion for a weekly open-house party called "Mrs. Madison's crush" or "squeeze." In contrast to George and Martha Washington's stiff, brief

impressment
▶ A British naval practice of seizing sailors on American ships under the claim that they were deserters from the British navy. Some 2,500 American men were taken by force into service, a grievance that helped propel the United States to declare war on Britain.

Embargo Act of 1807
▶ Act of Congress that prohibited U.S. ships from traveling to foreign ports and effectively banned overseas trade in an attempt to deter Britain from halting U.S. ships at sea. The embargo caused grave hardships for Americans engaged in overseas commerce.

Why did Congress declare war on Great Britain in 1812?

How did the civil status of American women and men differ in the early Republic?

Why did partisan conflict increase during the administrations of Monroe and Adams?

Conclusion: How did republican simplicity become complex?

☑ **LearningCurve**
Check what you know.
bedfordstmartins.com
/roarkunderstanding

Dolley Madison, by Gilbert Stuart

The "presidentress" of the Madison administration sat for this official portrait in 1804. She wears a high-fashion empire-style dress, a style worn by many women at the coronation of the emperor Napoleon in Paris. The style featured a light fabric (muslin or chiffon) that dropped from a high waistline straight to the ground, with short sleeves and a daringly low neckline, as shown here. © White House Historical Association.

receptions, the Madisons' parties went on for hours, with scores or even hundreds of guests milling about, talking, and eating. Members of Congress, cabinet officers, distinguished guests, envoys from foreign countries, and their womenfolk attended with regularity. Mrs. Madison's weekly squeeze was an essential event for gaining political access, trading information, and establishing informal channels that would smooth the governing process.

In 1810–1811, the Madisons' house acquired its present name, the White House. The many guests simultaneously experienced both the splendor of the executive mansion and the atmosphere of republicanism that made it accessible to so many. Dolley Madison, ever an enormous political asset to her rather shy husband, understood well the symbolic function of the White House to enhance the power and legitimacy of the presidency.

Tecumseh and Tippecanoe

While the Madisons cemented alliances at home, difficulties with Britain and France overseas and with Indians in the old Northwest continued to increase. The Shawnee chief Tecumseh was, by all accounts, a charismatic leader. The Ohio Country, where Tecumseh was born in 1768, was home to some dozen Indian tribes. During the Revolutionary War, the region became a battleground, and Tecumseh lost his father and two brothers to American fighters. The Revolution's end in 1783 brought no peace to Indian country. The youthful Tecumseh fought at the battle of Fallen Timbers (see chapter 9), a major Indian defeat, and stood by as eight treaties ceded much of Ohio to the Americans between 1795 and 1805. Some resigned Indians looked for ways to accommodate, taking up farming, trade, and intermarriage with white settlers. Others spent their treaty payments on alcohol. Tecumseh's younger brother Tenskwatawa led an embittered life of idleness and

CHAPTER LOCATOR | How did Jefferson attempt to undo the Federalist innovations of earlier administrations? | What was the significance of the Louisiana Purchase for the United States?

274 CHAPTER 10 A MATURING REPUBLIC

Tecumseh

This 1848 engraving was adapted from an earlier drawing of Tecumseh made in a live sitting by a French fur trader in 1808. The engraver has given Tecumseh a British army officer's uniform, showing that he fought on the British side in the War of 1812. Notice the head covering and the medallion around Tecumseh's neck, marking his Indian identity. Library of Congress.

drink. But Tecumseh rejected accommodation and instead campaigned for a return to ancient ways. Donning traditional animal-skin clothing, he traveled around the Great Lakes region persuading tribes to join his pan-Indian confederacy. The territorial governor of Indiana, William Henry Harrison, both admired and feared Tecumseh, calling him "one of those uncommon geniuses which spring up occasionally to produce revolutions."

Even Tecumseh's dissolute brother was born anew. After a near-death experience in 1805, Tenskwatawa revived and recounted a startling vision of meeting the Master of Life. Renaming himself the Prophet, he urged his many Indian followers to regard whites as children of the Evil Spirit, destined to be destroyed.

In the years after 1805, Tecumseh actively solidified his confederacy, while the more northern tribes renewed their ties with supportive British agents in Canada, a potential source of food and weapons. If the United States went to war with Britain, there would clearly be serious repercussions on the frontier.

Shifting demographics put the Indians under pressure. The 1810 census counted some 230,000 Americans in Ohio, while another 40,000 inhabited the territories of Indiana, Illinois, and Michigan. The Indian population of the same area was much smaller, probably about 70,000.

Up to 1805, Indiana's territorial governor, William Henry Harrison, had negotiated a series of treaties in a divide-and-conquer strategy aimed at extracting Indian lands for paltry payments. But with the rise to power of Tecumseh and his brother Tenskwatawa, the Prophet, Harrison's strategy faltered. A fundamental part of Tecumseh's message was the assertion that all Indian lands were held in common by all the tribes. "No tribe has the right to sell [these lands], even to each other, much less to strangers . . . ," Tecumseh said. "Sell a country! Why not sell

Why did Congress declare war on Great Britain in 1812?

How did the civil status of American women and men differ in the early Republic?

Why did partisan conflict increase during the administrations of Monroe and Adams?

Conclusion: How did republican simplicity become complex?

✓ **LearningCurve**
Check what you know.
bedfordstmartins.com
/roarkunderstanding

275

Battle of Tippecanoe, 1811

the air, the great sea, as well as the earth? Didn't the Great Spirit make them all for the use of his children?" In 1809, while Tecumseh was away on a recruiting trip, Harrison assembled the leaders of the Potawatomi, Miami, and Delaware tribes to negotiate the Treaty of Fort Wayne. After promising (falsely) that this was the last cession of land the United States would seek, Harrison secured three million acres at about two cents per acre.

When he returned, Tecumseh was furious with both Harrison and the tribal leaders. Leaving his brother in charge at Prophetstown on the Tippecanoe River, the Shawnee chief left to seek alliances with tribes in the South. In November 1811, Harrison decided to attack Prophetstown with a thousand men. The two-hour battle resulted in the deaths of sixty-two Americans and forty Indians before the Prophet's forces fled. The Americans won the **battle of Tippecanoe**, but Tecumseh was now more ready than ever to make war on the United States.

The War of 1812

The Indian conflicts in the old Northwest soon merged into the wider conflict with Britain, now known as the War of 1812. Between 1809 and 1812, Madison teetered between declaring either Britain or France America's primary enemy, as attacks by both countries on U.S. ships continued. In 1809, Congress replaced Jefferson's embargo with the Non-Intercourse Act, which prohibited trade only with Britain and France and their colonies, thus opening up other trade routes to alleviate the economic distress of American shippers, farmers, and planters. By 1811, the country was seriously divided and on the verge of war.

The new Congress seated in March 1811 contained several dozen young Republicans from the West and South who would come to be known as the **War Hawks**. Led by thirty-four-year-old Henry Clay from Kentucky and twenty-nine-year-old John C. Calhoun from South Carolina, they welcomed a war with Britain both to justify attacks on the Indians and to bring an end to impressment. Many were also expansionists, looking to occupy Florida and threaten Canada. Clay was elected Speaker of the House, and Calhoun won a seat on the Foreign Relations Committee. The War Hawks approved major defense expenditures, and the army soon quadrupled in size.

In June 1812, Congress declared war on Great Britain in a vote divided along sectional lines: New England and some Middle Atlantic states opposed the war, fearing its effect on commerce, while the South and West were strongly for it. Ironically, Britain had just announced that it would stop the search and seizure of American ships, but the war momentum would not be slowed. The Foreign Relations Committee issued an elaborate justification titled *Report on the Causes and Reasons for War*, written mainly by Calhoun and containing extravagant language about Britain's "lust for power," "unbounded tyranny," and "mad ambition."

battle of Tippecanoe
▶ An attack on Shawnee Indians at Prophetstown on the Tippecanoe River in 1811 by American forces headed by William Henry Harrison, Indiana's territorial governor. Tenskwatawa, the Prophet, fled with his followers. Tecumseh, his brother, deepened his resolve to make war on the United States.

War Hawks
▶ Young men newly elected to the Congress of 1811 who were eager for war against Britain in order to end impressments, fight Indians, and expand into neighboring British territory. Leaders included Henry Clay of Kentucky and John C. Calhoun of South Carolina.

CHAPTER LOCATOR | How did Jefferson attempt to undo the Federalist innovations of earlier administrations? | What was the significance of the Louisiana Purchase for the United States?

276 CHAPTER 10 A MATURING REPUBLIC

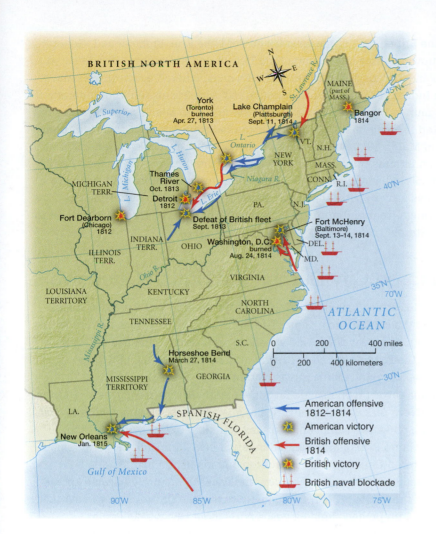

MAP 10.3 ■ **The War of 1812**

During the War of 1812, battles were fought along the Canadian border and in the Chesapeake region. The most important American victory came in New Orleans two weeks after a peace agreement had been signed in England.

These were fighting words in a war that was in large measure about insult and honor.

The War Hawks proposed an invasion of Canada, confidently predicting victory in four weeks. Instead, the war lasted two and a half years, and Canada never fell. The northern invasion turned out to be a series of blunders that revealed America's grave unpreparedness for war against the unexpectedly powerful British and Indian forces (**Map 10.3**). By the fall of 1812, the outlook was grim.

Worse, the New England states were slow to raise troops, and some New England merchants carried on illegal trade with Britain. The fall presidential election pitted Madison against DeWitt Clinton of New York, nominally a Republican but able to attract the Federalist vote. Clinton picked up all of New England's electoral votes, with the exception of Vermont's, and also took New York, New Jersey, and part of Maryland. Madison won in the electoral college, 128 to 89, but his margin of victory was considerably smaller than in 1808.

In late 1812 and early 1813, the tide began to turn in the Americans' favor. First came some victories at sea. Then the Americans attacked York (now Toronto) and burned it in April 1813. A few months later, Commodore Oliver Hazard Perry

Why did Congress declare war on Great Britain in 1812?

How did the civil status of American women and men differ in the early Republic?

Why did partisan conflict increase during the administrations of Monroe and Adams?

Conclusion: How did republican simplicity become complex?

✓ **LearningCurve**
Check what you know.
bedfordstmartins.com
/roarkunderstanding

277

defeated the British fleet at the western end of Lake Erie. Emboldened, General Harrison drove an army into Canada from Detroit and in October 1813 defeated the British and Indians at the battle of the Thames, where Tecumseh was killed.

Creek Indians in the South who had allied with Tecumseh's confederacy were also plunged into war. Some 10,000 living in the Mississippi Territory put up a spirited fight against U.S. forces for ten months. But the **Creek War** ended suddenly in March 1814 when a general named Andrew Jackson led 2,500 Tennessee militiamen in a bloody attack called the Battle of Horseshoe Bend. More than 550 Indians were killed, and several hundred more died trying to escape across a river. Later that year, General Jackson extracted from the defeated tribe a treaty relinquishing thousands of square miles of their land to the United States.

Washington City Burns: The British Offensive

In August 1814, British ships sailed into Chesapeake Bay, landing 5,000 troops and throwing the capital into a panic. The British troops burned the White House, the Capitol, a newspaper office, and a well-stocked arsenal. Instead of trying to hold the city, the British headed north and attacked Baltimore, but a fierce defense by the Maryland militia thwarted that effort.

In another powerful offensive that same month, British troops marched from Canada into New York State, but a series of mistakes cost them a naval skirmish at Plattsburgh on Lake Champlain, and they retreated to Canada. Five months later, another large British army landed in lower Louisiana and, in early January 1815, encountered General Andrew Jackson and his militia just outside New Orleans. Jackson's forces carried the day, and Jackson instantly became known as the hero of the **battle of New Orleans**. No one in the United States knew that negotiators in Europe had signed a peace agreement two weeks earlier.

The Treaty of Ghent, signed in December 1814, settled few of the surface issues that had led to war. Neither country could claim victory, and no land changed hands. Instead, the treaty reflected a mutual agreement to give up certain goals. The Americans dropped their plea for an end to impressments, which in any case subsided as soon as Britain and France ended their war in 1815. They also gave up any claim to Canada. The British agreed to stop all aid to the Indians. Nothing was said about shipping rights.

Antiwar Federalists in New England could not gloat over the war's ambiguous conclusion because of an ill-timed and seemingly unpatriotic move on their part. The region's leaders had convened a secret meeting in Hartford, Connecticut, in December 1814 to discuss a series of proposals aimed at reducing the South's power and breaking Virginia's lock on the presidency.

> **> Proposals Supported at the Hartford Convention**

- Abolition of the Constitution's three-fifths clause as a basis of representation.
- Requirement of a two-thirds vote instead of a simple majority for imposing embargoes, admitting states, or declaring war.
- Limit of one term for presidents.
- Prohibition of the election of successive presidents from the same state.

Creek War
▶ Part of the War of 1812 involving the Creek nation in the Mississippi Territory and Tennessee militiamen. General Andrew Jackson's forces defeated the Creeks at the Battle of Horseshoe Bend in 1814, forcing them to sign away much of their land.

battle of New Orleans
▶ The final battle in the War of 1812, fought and won by General Andrew Jackson and his militiamen against the much larger British army in New Orleans. The celebrated battle made no difference since the peace had already been negotiated.

CHAPTER LOCATOR | How did Jefferson attempt to undo the Federalist innovations of earlier administrations? | What was the significance of the Louisiana Purchase for the United States?

278 CHAPTER 10 A MATURING REPUBLIC

They even discussed secession from the Union but rejected that path. Coming just as peace was achieved, however, the **Hartford Convention** looked very unpatriotic. The Federalist Party never recovered, and within a few years it was reduced to a shadow of its former self, even in New England.

No one really won the War of 1812. The war did, however, give rise to a new spirit of nationalism. The paranoia over British tyranny evident in the 1812 declaration of war was laid to rest, replaced by pride in a more equal relationship with the old mother country. Indeed, in 1817 the two countries signed the Rush-Bagot disarmament treaty (named after its two negotiators), which limited each country to a total of four naval vessels, each with just a single cannon, to patrol the vast watery border between them. It was the most successful disarmament treaty for a century to come.

The biggest winners in the War of 1812 were the young men, once called War Hawks, who took up the banner of the Republican Party and carried it in new, expansive directions. These young politicians favored trade, western expansion, internal improvements, and the energetic development of new economic markets. The biggest losers of the war were the Indians. Tecumseh was dead, his brother the Prophet was discredited, the prospects of an Indian confederacy were dashed, the Creeks' large homeland was seized, and the British protectors were gone.

Hartford Convention

▶ A secret meeting of New England Federalist politicians held in late 1814 to discuss constitutional changes to reduce the South's political power and thus help block policies that injured northern commercial interests.

QUICK REVIEW

Was the War of 1812 inevitable?
Why or why not?

Why did Congress declare war on Great Britain in 1812?

How did the civil status of American women and men differ in the early Republic?

Why did partisan conflict increase during the administrations of Monroe and Adams?

Conclusion: How did republican simplicity become complex?

☑ LearningCurve
Check what you know.
bedfordstmartins.com
/roarkunderstanding

How did the civil status of American women and men differ in the early Republic?

Portrait of Emma Willard

Emma Willard, founder of the famed and rigorous Troy Female Seminary, was an exemplary role model to her students. Elizabeth Cady, a student in the 1830s and later an important figure in the woman's rights movement, recalled that Willard had a "profound self respect (a rare quality in a woman) which gave her a dignity truly regal." Her confidence shines through in this portrait. Emma Willard School.

DOLLEY MADISON'S PIONEERING role as "presidentress" showed that elite women could assume an active presence in civic affairs. But, as with the 1790s cultural compromise that endorsed female education to make women better wives and mothers (see chapter 9), Mrs. Madison and her female circle practiced politics to further their husbands' careers. There was little talk of the "rights of woman." Indeed, from 1800 to 1825, key institutions central to the shaping of women's lives — the legal system, marriage, and religion — proved fairly resistant to change. Nonetheless, the trend toward increased commitment to female education that began in the 1780s and 1790s continued in the first decades of the nineteenth century.

Women and the Law

In English common law, wives had no independent legal or political personhood. The legal doctrine of ***feme covert*** (covered woman) held that a wife's civic life was completely subsumed by her husband's. A wife was obligated to obey her

feme covert
▶ Legal doctrine grounded in British common law that held that a wife's civic life was subsumed by her husband's. Married women lacked independence to own property, make contracts, or keep wages earned. The doctrine shaped women's status in the early Republic.

CHAPTER LOCATOR | How did Jefferson attempt to undo the Federalist innovations of earlier administrations? | What was the significance of the Louisiana Purchase for the United States?

280 CHAPTER 10
A MATURING REPUBLIC

husband; her property was his, her domestic and sexual services were his, and even their children were legally his. Women had no right to keep their wages, to make contracts, or to sue or be sued. American state legislatures generally passed up the opportunity to rewrite the laws of domestic relations even though they redrafted other British laws in light of republican principles. Lawyers never paused to defend, much less to challenge, the assumption that unequal power relations lay at the heart of marriage.

The one aspect of family law that changed in the early Republic was divorce. Before the Revolution, only New England jurisdictions recognized a limited right to divorce; by 1820, every state except South Carolina did so. However, divorce was uncommon and in many states could be obtained only by petition to the state's legislature, a daunting obstacle for many ordinary people. A mutual wish to terminate a marriage was never sufficient grounds for a legal divorce. A New York judge affirmed that "it would be aiming a deadly blow at public morals to decree a dissolution of the marriage contract merely because the parties requested it. Divorces should never be allowed, except for the protection of the innocent party, and for the punishment of the guilty." States upheld the institution of marriage both to protect persons they thought of as naturally dependent (women and children) and to regulate the use and inheritance of property. (Unofficial self-divorce, desertion, and bigamy were remedies that ordinary people sometimes chose to get around the law, but all of these practices were socially unacceptable.) Legal enforcement of marriage as an unequal relationship played a major role in maintaining gender inequality in the nineteenth century.

Single adult women could own and convey property, make contracts, initiate lawsuits, and pay taxes. They could not vote (except in New Jersey before 1807), serve on juries, or practice law, so their civil status was limited. Single women's economic status was often limited as well, as much by custom as by law. Job prospects were few and low-paying. Unless they had inherited adequate property or could live with married siblings, single adult women in the early Republic very often were poor.

None of the legal institutions that structured white gender relations applied to black slaves. As property themselves, under the jurisdiction of slave owners, they could not freely consent to any contractual obligations, including marriage. The protective features of state-sponsored unions were thus denied to black men and women in slavery. But this also meant that slave unions did not establish unequal power relations between partners backed by the force of law, as did marriages among the free.

Women and Church Governance

In most Protestant denominations around 1800, white women made up the majority of congregants. Yet church leadership of most denominations rested in men's hands. There were some exceptions, however. In Baptist congregations in New England, women served along with men on church governance committees, deciding on the admission of new members, voting on hiring ministers, and even debating doctrinal points. Quakers, too, had a history of recognizing women's spiritual talents. Some were accorded the status of minister, capable of leading and speaking in Quaker meetings.

> CHRONOLOGY

1790–1820
– In an era of religious ferment, a small number of women openly engage in preaching.

1821
– Emma Willard founds Troy Female Seminary in New York.

1822
– Catharine Beecher founds Hartford Seminary in Connecticut.

Why did Congress declare war on Great Britain in 1812?

How did the civil status of American women and men differ in the early Republic?

Why did partisan conflict increase during the administrations of Monroe and Adams?

Conclusion: How did republican simplicity become complex?

☑ LearningCurve
Check what you know.
bedfordstmartins.com
/roarkunderstanding

281

In this early woodcut, Jemima Wilkinson, "the Publick Universal Friend," wears a clerical collar and body-obscuring robe, in keeping with the claim that the former Jemima was now a person without gender. With hair pulled back tight on the head and curled at the neck in a masculine style of the 1790s, was Wilkinson masculinized, or did the "Universal Friend" truly transcend gender? Rhode Island Historical Society.

Between 1790 and 1820, a small and highly unusual set of women openly engaged in preaching. Most were from Freewill Baptist groups centered in New England and upstate New York. Others came from small Methodist sects, and yet others rejected any formal religious affiliation. Probably fewer than a hundred such women existed, but several dozen traveled beyond their local communities, creating converts and controversy.

The best-known exhorting woman was Jemima Wilkinson, who called herself "the Publick Universal Friend." After a near-death experience from a high fever, Wilkinson proclaimed her body no longer female or male but the incarnation of the "Spirit of Light." She dressed in men's clothes, wore her hair in a masculine style, shunned gender-specific pronouns, and preached openly in Rhode Island and Philadelphia. In the early nineteenth century, Wilkinson established a town called New Jerusalem in western New York with some 250 followers.

The decades from 1790 to the 1820s marked a period of unusual confusion, ferment, and creativity in American religion. New denominations blossomed, new styles of religiosity gripped adherents, and an extensive periodical press devoted to religion popularized all manner of theological and institutional innovations. In such a climate, the age-old tradition of gender subordination came into question here and there among the most radically democratic of the churches. But the presumption of male authority over women was deeply entrenched in American culture. Even denominations that had allowed women to participate in church governance began to pull back, and most churches reinstated patterns of hierarchy along gender lines.

Female Education

First in the North and then in the South, states and localities began investing in public schools to foster an educated citizenry deemed essential in a republic. Young girls attended district schools along with boys, and by 1830, girls had made rapid gains, in many places approaching male literacy rates.

More advanced female education came from a growing number of private academies. Some dozen were established in the 1790s, and by 1830 that number had grown to nearly two hundred. Students came from elite families as well as those of middling families with intellectual aspirations, such as ministers' daughters.

CHAPTER LOCATOR | How did Jefferson attempt to undo the Federalist innovations of earlier administrations? | What was the significance of the Louisiana Purchase for the United States?

282   CHAPTER 10
A MATURING REPUBLIC

The three-year curriculum included both ornamental arts and solid academics. The former strengthened female gentility: drawing, needlework, music, and French conversation. The academic subjects included English grammar, literature, history, the natural sciences, geography, and elocution (the art of effective public speaking). The most ambitious female academies equaled the training offered at male colleges such as Harvard, Yale, Dartmouth, and Princeton, with classes in Latin, rhetoric, theology, moral philosophy, algebra, geometry, and even chemistry and physics.

Two of the best-known female academies were the Troy Female Seminary in New York, founded by Emma Willard in 1821, and the Hartford Seminary in Connecticut, founded by Catharine Beecher in 1822. Both prepared their female students to teach, on the grounds that women made better teachers than did men. Author Harriet Beecher Stowe, educated at her sister's school and then a teacher there, agreed: "If men have more knowledge they have less talent at communicating it. Nor have they the patience, the long-suffering, and gentleness necessary to superintend the formation of character."

The most immediate value of advanced female education lay in the self-cultivation and confidence it provided. Female graduation exercises showcased speeches and recitations performed in front of a mixed-sex audience of family, friends, and local notables. Academies also took care to promote a pleasing female modesty. Female pedantry or intellectual immodesty triggered the stereotype of the "bluestocking," a British term of hostility for a too-learned woman doomed to fail in the marriage market.

By the mid-1820s, the total annual enrollment at the female academies equaled enrollment at the nearly six dozen male colleges in the United States. Both groups accounted for only about 1 percent of their age cohorts in the country at large, indicating that advanced education was clearly limited to a privileged few. Most female graduates in time married and raised families, but first many of them became teachers at academies and district schools. A large number also became authors, contributing essays and poetry to newspapers, editing periodicals, and publishing novels. The new attention to the training of female minds laid the foundation for major changes in the gender system as girl students of the 1810s matured into adult women of the 1830s.

QUICK REVIEW <

In what ways did women influence society in the early Republic?

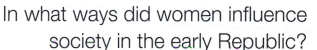

Why did Congress declare war on Great Britain in 1812?

How did the civil status of American women and men differ in the early Republic?

Why did partisan conflict increase during the administrations of Monroe and Adams?

Conclusion: How did republican simplicity become complex?

☑ LearningCurve
Check what you know.
bedfordstmartins.com
/roarkunderstanding

> Why did partisan conflict increase during the administrations of Monroe and Adams?

> VISUAL ACTIVITY

READING THE IMAGE: What might the chain at the sailor's feet indicate? What do you think the slogan on the banner means? What do you see in the picture that would help date it? (Hint: Examine the flag. And for the truly curious, consider the history of styles for men's facial hair.)

CONNECTIONS: How and why does the painting reference the War of 1812? Regardless of the painting's date, what message do you think Woodside is trying to convey here?

VIRGINIANS CONTINUED THEIR hold on the presidency with the election of James Monroe in 1816 and again in 1820, when Monroe garnered all but one electoral vote. The collapse of the Federalist Party ushered in an apparent period of one-party rule, but politics remained highly partisan. At the state level, increasing political engagement sparked a drive for universal white male suffrage. At the national level, ill feelings were stirred by a sectional crisis in 1820 over the admission of Missouri to the Union, and foreign policy questions involving European claims to Latin America animated sharp disagreements as well. Four candidates vied for the presidency in 1824 in an election decided by the House of Representatives. One-party rule was far from harmonious.

CHAPTER LOCATOR | How did Jefferson attempt to undo the Federalist innovations of earlier administrations? | What was the significance of the Louisiana Purchase for the United States?

From Property to Democracy

Up to 1820, presidential elections occurred in the electoral college, at a remove from ordinary voters. The excitement generated by state elections, however, created an insistent pressure for greater democratization of presidential elections.

In the 1780s, twelve of the original thirteen states enacted property qualifications based on the theory that only male freeholders — landowners, as distinct from tenants or servants — had sufficient independence of mind to be entrusted with the vote. Of course, not everyone accepted that restricted idea of the people's role in government (see chapter 8). In the 1790s, Vermont became the first state to enfranchise all adult males, and four other states soon broadened suffrage considerably by allowing all male taxpayers to vote. As new states joined the Union, most opted for suffrage for all free white men, which added pressure for eastern states to consider broadening their suffrage laws. Between 1800 and 1830, greater democratization became a contentious issue.

Not everyone favored expanded suffrage; propertied elites tended to defend the status quo. But others managed to get legislatures to call new constitutional conventions in which questions of suffrage, balloting procedures, apportionment, and representation were debated. By 1820, half a dozen states passed suffrage reform, some choosing universal manhood suffrage while others tied the vote to tax status or militia service. In the remainder of the states, the defenders of landed property qualifications managed to delay expanded suffrage for two more decades. But it was increasingly hard to persuade the disfranchised that landowners alone had a stake in government. Proponents of the status quo began to argue instead that the "industry and good habits" necessary to achieve a propertied status in life were what gave landowners the right character to vote. Opponents fired back blistering attacks. One delegate to New York's constitutional convention said, "More integrity and more patriotism are generally found in the labouring class of the community than in the higher orders." Owning land was no more predictive of wisdom and good character than it was of a person's height or strength, said another observer.

Both sides of the debate generally agreed that character mattered, and many ideas for ensuring an electorate of proper wisdom came up for discussion. The exclusion of paupers and felons convicted of "infamous crimes" found favor in legislation in many states. Literacy tests and raising the voting age to a figure in the thirties were debated but ultimately discarded. In one exceptional moment, at the Virginia constitutional convention in 1829, a delegate wondered aloud why unmarried women over the age of twenty-one could not vote; he was quickly silenced with the argument that all women lacked the "free agency and intelligence" necessary for wise voting.

Free black men's enfranchisement was another story, generating much discussion at all the conventions. Under existing freehold qualifications, a small number of propertied black men could vote; universal or taxpayer suffrage would inevitably enfranchise many more. Many delegates at the various state conventions spoke against that extension, claiming that blacks as a race lacked prudence, independence, and knowledge. With the exception of New York, which retained the existing property qualification for black voters as it removed it for whites, the general pattern was one of expanded suffrage for whites and a total eclipse of suffrage for blacks.

> CHRONOLOGY

1816
– James Monroe is elected president.

1819
– Adams-Onís Treaty.

1820
– Missouri Compromise.

1823
– Monroe Doctrine is asserted.

1825
– John Quincy Adams is elected president by House of Representatives.

Why did Congress declare war on Great Britain in 1812?

How did the civil status of American women and men differ in the early Republic?

Why did partisan conflict increase during the administrations of Monroe and Adams?

Conclusion: How did republican simplicity become complex?

☑ LearningCurve
Check what you know.
bedfordstmartins.com
/roarkunderstanding

285

The Missouri Compromise

The politics of race produced the most divisive issue during Monroe's term. In February 1819, Missouri — so recently the territory of the powerful Osage Indians — applied for statehood. Since 1815, four other states (Indiana, Mississippi, Illinois, and Alabama) had joined the Union, following the blueprint laid out by the Northwest Ordinance of 1787. But Missouri posed a problem. Although much of its area was on the same latitude as the free state of Illinois, its territorial population included ten thousand slaves brought there by southern planters.

The problem led a New York congressman, James Tallmadge Jr., to propose two amendments to the statehood bill. The first stipulated that slaves born in Missouri after statehood would be free at age twenty-five, and the second declared that no new slaves could be imported into the state. Tallmadge's model was New York's gradual emancipation law of 1799 (see chapter 8). It did not strip slave owners of their current property, and it allowed them full use of the labor of newborn slaves well into their prime productive years. Still, southern congressmen objected because in the long run the amendments would make Missouri a free state, presumably no longer allied with southern economic and political interests. Just as southern economic power rested on slave labor, southern political power drew extra strength from the slave population because of the three-fifths rule. In 1820, the South owed seventeen of its seats in the House of Representatives to its slave population.

Tallmadge's amendments passed in the House by a close and sharply sectional vote of North against South. The ferocious debate led a Georgia representative to observe that the question had started "a fire which all the waters of the ocean could not extinguish. It can be extinguished only in blood." The Senate, with an even number of slave and free states, voted down the amendments, and Missouri statehood was postponed until the next congressional term.

In 1820, a compromise emerged. Maine, once part of Massachusetts, applied for statehood as a free state, balancing against Missouri as a slave state. The Senate further agreed that the southern boundary of Missouri — latitude 36°30' — extended west, would become the permanent line dividing slave from free states, guaranteeing the North a large area where slavery was banned (**Map 10.4**). The House also approved the **Missouri Compromise**, thanks to expert deal brokering by Kentucky's Henry Clay. The whole package passed because seventeen northern congressmen decided that minimizing sectional conflict was the best course and voted with the South.

President Monroe and former president Jefferson at first worried that the Missouri crisis would reinvigorate the Federalist Party as the party of the North. But even ex-Federalists agreed that the split between free and slave states was too dangerous a fault line to be permitted to become a shaper of national politics. When new parties did develop in the 1830s, they took pains to bridge geography, each party developing a presence in both the North and the South. Monroe and Jefferson also worried about the future of slavery. Both understood slavery to be deeply problematic, but, as Jefferson said, "We have the wolf by the ears, and we can neither hold him, nor safely let him go. Justice is in one scale, and self-preservation in the other."

Missouri Compromise

▶ 1820 congressional compromise engineered by Henry Clay that paired Missouri's entrance into the Union as a slave state with Maine's entrance as a free state. The compromise also established Missouri's southern border as the permanent line dividing slave from free states.

CHAPTER LOCATOR | How did Jefferson attempt to undo the Federalist innovations of earlier administrations? | What was the significance of the Louisiana Purchase for the United States?

286 CHAPTER 10 A MATURING REPUBLIC

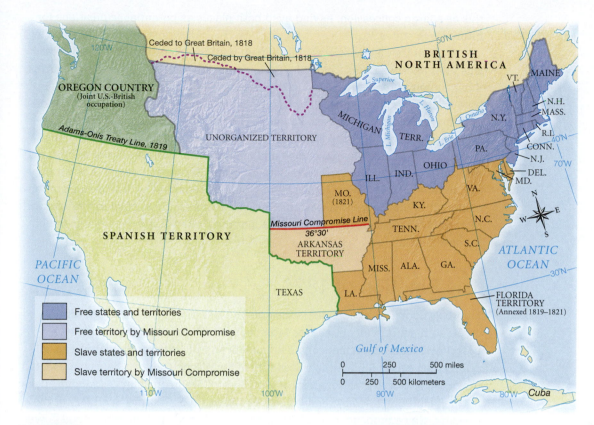

MAP 10.4 ■ The Missouri Compromise, 1820

After a difficult battle in Congress, Missouri entered the Union in 1821 as part of a package of compromises. Maine was admitted as a free state to balance slavery in Missouri, and a line drawn at latitude 36°30' put most of the rest of the Louisiana Territory off-limits to slavery in the future.

> MAP ACTIVITY

READING THE MAP: How many free and how many slave states were there before the Missouri Compromise? What did the admission of Missouri as a slave state threaten to do?

CONNECTIONS: Who precipitated the crisis over Missouri, what did he propose, and where did the idea come from? Who proposed the Missouri Compromise, and who benefited from it?

The Monroe Doctrine

New foreign policy challenges arose even as Congress struggled with the slavery issue. In 1816, U.S. troops led by General Andrew Jackson invaded Spanish Florida in search of Seminole Indians harboring escaped slaves. Once there, Jackson declared himself the commander of northern Florida, demonstrating his power in 1818 by executing two British men who he claimed were dangerous enemies. In asserting rule over the territory, and surely in executing the two British subjects on Spanish land, Jackson had gone too far. Privately, President Monroe was distressed and pondered court-martialing Jackson, prevented only by Jackson's immense popularity as the hero of the battle of New Orleans. Instead, John Quincy Adams, the secretary of state, negotiated with Spain the Adams-Onís Treaty, which delivered Florida to the United States in 1819. In exchange, the Americans agreed to abandon any claim to Texas or Cuba. Southerners viewed

| Why did Congress declare war on Great Britain in 1812? | How did the civil status of American women and men differ in the early Republic? | **Why did partisan conflict increase during the administrations of Monroe and Adams?** | Conclusion: How did republican simplicity become complex? | ✓ LearningCurve Check what you know. bedfordstmartins.com /roarkunderstanding |

this as a large concession, having eyed both places as potential acquisitions for future slave states.

Spain at that moment was preoccupied with its colonies in South America. One after another, Chile, Colombia, Peru, and finally Mexico declared themselves independent in the early 1820s. To discourage Spain and other European countries from reconquering these colonies, Monroe in 1823 formulated a declaration of principles on South America, known in later years as the Monroe Doctrine. The president warned that "the American Continents, by the free and independent condition which they have assumed and maintain, are henceforth not to be considered as subjects for future colonization by any European power." Any attempt to interfere in the Western Hemisphere would be regarded as "the manifestation of an unfriendly disposition towards the United States." In exchange for noninterference by Europeans, Monroe pledged that the United States would stay out of European struggles.

The Election of 1824

Monroe's nonpartisan administration was the last of its kind, a throwback to eighteenth-century ideals, as was Monroe, with his powdered wig and knee breeches. Monroe's cabinet contained men of sharply different philosophies, all calling themselves Republicans. Secretary of State John Quincy Adams represented the urban Northeast; as secretary of war, South Carolinian John C. Calhoun spoke for the planter aristocracy; and William H. Crawford of Georgia, secretary of the treasury, was a proponent of Jeffersonian states' rights and limited federal power. Even before the end of Monroe's first term, these men and others began to maneuver for the election of 1824.

Crucially helping them to maneuver were their wives, who accomplished some of the work of modern campaign managers by courting men — and women — of influence. Louisa Catherine Adams had a weekly party for guests numbering in the hundreds. The somber Adams lacked charm — "I am a man of reserved, cold, austere, and forbidding manners," he once wrote — but his abundantly charming (and hardworking) wife made up for that. She attended to the etiquette of social calls, sometimes making two dozen in a morning, and counted sixty-eight members of Congress as her regular guests.

John Quincy Adams (and Louisa Catherine) were ambitious for the presidency, but so were others. Candidate Henry Clay, Speaker of the House and negotiator of the Treaty of Ghent with Britain in 1814, promoted a new "American System," a package of protective tariffs to encourage manufacturing and federal expenditures for internal improvements such as roads and canals. Treasury Secretary William Crawford was a favorite of Republicans from Virginia and New York, even after he suffered an incapacitating stroke in mid-1824. John C. Calhoun was another serious contender, having served in Congress and in several cabinets. A southern planter, he attracted northern support for his backing of internal improvements and protective tariffs.

The final candidate was an outsider and a latecomer: General Andrew Jackson of Tennessee. Jackson had far less national political experience than the others, but he enjoyed great celebrity from his military career. When Jackson's supporters put his name forward for the presidency and voters in the West and South reacted with

CHAPTER LOCATOR | How did Jefferson attempt to undo the Federalist innovations of earlier administrations? | What was the significance of the Louisiana Purchase for the United States?

288 CHAPTER 10 A MATURING REPUBLIC

enthusiasm, Adams was dismayed, and Calhoun dropped out of the race and shifted his attention to winning the vice presidency.

Along with democratizing the vote, eighteen states (out of the full twenty-four) had put the power to choose members of the electoral college directly in the hands of voters, making the 1824 election the first one to have a popular vote tally for the presidency. Jackson proved by far to be the most popular candidate, winning 153,544 votes. Adams was second with 108,740, Clay won 47,136 votes, and the debilitated Crawford garnered 46,618.

In the electoral college, Jackson received 99 votes, Adams 84, Crawford 41, and Clay 37 (**Map 10.5**). Jackson lacked a majority, so the House of Representatives stepped in for the second time in U.S. history. Each congressional delegation had one vote; according to the Constitution's Twelfth Amendment, passed in 1804, only the top three candidates joined the runoff. Thus, Henry Clay was out of the race and in a position to bestow his support on another candidate.

Jackson's supporters later characterized the election of 1824 as the "corrupt bargain." Clay backed Adams, and Adams won by one vote in the House in February 1825. Clay's support made sense on several levels. Despite strong mutual dislike, he and Adams agreed on issues such as federal support to build roads and canals. Moreover, Clay was uneasy with Jackson's volatile temperament and unstated political views and with Crawford's diminished capacity. What made Clay's decision look "corrupt" was that immediately after the election Adams offered to appoint Clay secretary of state — and Clay accepted.

In fact, there probably was no concrete bargain; Adams's subsequent cabinet appointments demonstrated his lack of political astuteness. But Andrew Jackson felt that the election had been stolen from him, and he wrote bitterly that "the Judas of the West [Clay] has closed the contract and will receive the thirty pieces of silver."

MAP 10.5 ■ The Election of 1824

Candidate*	Electoral Vote	Popular Vote	Percent of Popular Vote
John Q. Adams	84	108,740	30.5
Andrew Jackson	99	153,544	43.1
Henry Clay	37	47,136	13.2
W. H. Crawford	41	46,618	13.1

*No distinct political parties

Note: Because no candidate garnered a majority in the electoral college, the election was decided in the House of Representatives. Although Clay was eliminated from the running, as Speaker of the House he influenced the final decision in favor of Adams.

Why did Congress declare war on Great Britain in 1812?

How did the civil status of American women and men differ in the early Republic?

Why did partisan conflict increase during the administrations of Monroe and Adams?

Conclusion: How did republican simplicity become complex?

LearningCurve
Check what you know.
bedfordstmartins.com
/roarkunderstanding

The Adams Administration

John Quincy Adams, like his father, was a one-term president. His career had been built on diplomacy, not electoral politics, and despite his wife's deftness in the art of political influence, his own political horse sense was not well developed. With his cabinet choices, he welcomed his opposition into his inner circle. He asked Crawford to stay on in the Treasury. He retained an openly pro-Jackson postmaster general even though that position controlled thousands of nationwide patronage appointments. He even asked Jackson to become secretary of war. With Calhoun as vice president (elected without opposition by the electoral college) and Clay at the State Department, the whole argumentative crew would have been thrust into the executive branch. Crawford and Jackson had the good sense to decline the appointments.

Adams had lofty ideas for federal action during his presidency, and the plan he put before Congress was sweeping. Adams called for federally built roads, canals, and harbors. He proposed a national university in Washington as well as government-sponsored scientific research. He wanted to build observatories to advance astronomical knowledge and to promote precision in timekeeping, and he backed a decimal-based system of weights and measures. In all these endeavors, Adams believed he was continuing the legacy of Jefferson and Madison, using the powers of government to advance knowledge. But his opponents feared he was too Hamiltonian, using federal power inappropriately to advance commercial interests.

Whether he was more truly Federalist or Republican was a moot point. Lacking the give-and-take political skills required to gain congressional support, Adams was unable to implement much of his program. He scorned the idea of courting voters to gain support and using the patronage system to enhance his power. He often made appointments to placate enemies rather than to reward friends. A story of a toast offered to the president may well have been mythical, but it came to summarize Adams's precarious hold on leadership. A dignitary raised a glass and said, "May he strike confusion to his foes," to which another voice scornfully chimed in, "as he has already done to his friends."

> **QUICK REVIEW**

How did the collapse of the Federalist Party influence the administrations of James Monroe and John Quincy Adams?

CHAPTER LOCATOR | How did Jefferson attempt to undo the Federalist innovations of earlier administrations? | What was the significance of the Louisiana Purchase for the United States?

290 CHAPTER 10 A MATURING REPUBLIC

Conclusion: How did republican simplicity become complex?

THE JEFFERSONIAN REPUBLICANS at first tried to undo much of what the Federalists had created in the 1790s, but their promise of a simpler government gave way to the complexities of domestic and foreign issues. The Louisiana Purchase and the Barbary Wars required a powerful government response, and the challenges posed by Britain on the seas finally drew America into declaring war on the onetime mother country. The War of 1812, joined by restive Indian nations allied with the British, was longer and more costly than anticipated, and it ended inconclusively.

The war elevated to national prominence General Andrew Jackson, whose popularity with voters in the 1824 election surprised traditional politicians and threw the one-party rule of Republicans into a tailspin. John Quincy Adams had barely assumed office in 1825 before the election campaign of 1828 was off and running. Reformed suffrage laws ensured that appeals to the mass of white male voters would be the hallmark of all nineteenth-century elections after 1824. In such a system, Adams and men like him were at a great disadvantage.

Ordinary American women, whether white or free black, had no place in government. All-male legislatures maintained women's *feme covert* status, keeping wives dependent on husbands. A few women found a pathway to greater personal autonomy through religion, while many others benefited from expanded female education in schools and academies. These substantial gains in education would blossom into a major transformation of gender in the 1830s and 1840s.

Two other developments would prove momentous in later decades. The bitter debate over slavery that surrounded the Missouri Compromise accentuated the serious divisions between northern and southern states — divisions that would only widen in the decades to come. And Jefferson's long embargo and Madison's wartime trade stoppage gave a big boost to American manufacturing by removing competition with British factories. When peace returned in 1815, the years of independent development burst forth into a period of sustained economic growth that continued nearly unabated into the mid-nineteenth century.

| Why did Congress declare war on Great Britain in 1812? | How did the civil status of American women and men differ in the early Republic? | Why did partisan conflict increase during the administrations of Monroe and Adams? | **Conclusion: How did republican simplicity become complex?** | ✓ **LearningCurve** Check what you know. bedfordstmartins.com /roarkunderstanding |

291

CHAPTER 10 STUDY GUIDE

STEP 1 GET STARTED ONLINE

✓ **LearningCurve** ■ bedfordstmartins.com/roarkunderstanding

Now that you've read the chapter, make it stick by completing the LearningCurve activity.

STEP 2 EXPLAIN WHY IT MATTERS

Put your reading into practice. Identify each term below, and then explain why it matters in U.S. history.

TERM	WHO OR WHAT & WHEN	WHY IT MATTERS
Marbury v. Madison (p. 264)		
Louisiana Purchase (p. 268)		
Lewis and Clark expedition (p. 270)		
impressment (p. 273)		
Embargo Act of 1807 (p. 273)		
battle of Tippecanoe (p. 276)		
War Hawks (p. 276)		
Creek War (p. 278)		
battle of New Orleans (p. 278)		
Hartford Convention (p. 279)		
feme covert (p. 280)		
Missouri Compromise (p. 286)		

STEP 3 MOVE BEYOND THE BASICS

To demonstrate a more advanced understanding, assess the positions and policies of the early-nineteenth-century presidents. What core assumptions and beliefs informed each president's policies and positions? How did each successive president change the presidency?

Aspects and developments	Jefferson	Madison	Monroe	J. Q. Adams
Power of the presidency				
Expansion of the nation				
Domestic affairs				
Foreign affairs				
Difficulties				
Successes				

STEP 4

PUT IT ALL TOGETHER

Now, take a step back and try to explain the big picture. Remember to use specific examples from the chapter in your answers.

JEFFERSON AND REPUBLICANISM

▶ What steps did Jefferson take in the aftermath of the Louisiana Purchase to help facilitate western expansion of the United States?

▶ How did foreign policy issues shape the Jefferson presidency?

MADISON AND THE WAR OF 1812

▶ Where was support for the War of 1812 strongest? Where was it weakest? Why?

▶ How did the status of women change in the early decades of the nineteenth century? In what ways did some women exert political influence?

MONROE, ADAMS, AND PARTISANSHIP

▶ What forces led to the expansion of the voting rights in the early nineteenth century?

▶ In what ways did the election of 1824 mark a turning point in American politics?

LOOKING BACKWARD, LOOKING AHEAD

▶ How did the partisanship of the 1820s differ from the partisanship of the 1790s? What explains the changes you note?

▶ What problems were solved by the Missouri Compromise? What tensions and conflicts were left unresolved?

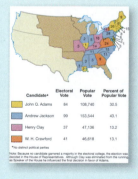

Candidate*	Electoral Vote	Popular Vote	Percent of Popular Vote
John Q. Adams	84	108,740	30.5
Andrew Jackson	99	153,544	43.1
Henry Clay	37	47,136	13.2
W. H. Crawford	41	46,618	13.1

*No distinct political parties

Note: Because no candidate garnered a majority in the electoral college, the election was decided in the House of Representatives. Although Clay was eliminated from the running, as Speaker of the House he influenced the final decision in favor of Adams.

> **IN YOUR OWN WORDS**

Imagine that you must give an oral report to the class answering the following question: **What were the most important political, social, and cultural changes in the early decades of the nineteenth century?** What would be the most important points to include and why?

> **Do it online at the Student Site** ■ bedfordstmartins.com/roarkunderstanding

11

THE EXPANDING REPUBLIC

1815–1840

> **What were the most important causes and consequences of the market revolution from 1815 to 1840?** Chapter 11 explores the impact of the economic expansion known as the market revolution on American life. It also traces political developments and Indian policy under the presidency of Andrew Jackson as well as the contemporaneous appearance of reform movements.

LearningCurve

bedfordstmartins.com/roarkunderstanding
After reading the chapter, use LearningCurve to retain what you've read.

The *Clermont*. Robert Fulton's steamboat travels up the Hudson River from New York City. The Granger Collection, New York.

> Why did the United States experience a market revolution after 1815?

> Why did Andrew Jackson defeat John Quincy Adams so dramatically in the 1828 election?

> What was Andrew Jackson's impact on the presidency?

> How did social and cultural life change in the 1830s?

> Why was Martin Van Buren a one-term president?

> Conclusion: The Age of Jackson or the era of reform?

> Why did the United States experience a market revolution after 1815?

The Erie Canal at Lockport

The Erie Canal, completed in 1825, was impressive not only for its length of 350 miles but also for its elevation, requiring the construction of eighty-three locks. The biggest engineering challenge came at Lockport, twenty miles northeast of Buffalo, where the canal traversed a steep slate escarpment. Work crews — mostly immigrant Irishmen — used gunpowder and grueling physical labor to blast the deep artificial gorge shown here. Department of Rare Books and Special Collections, Rush Rhees Library, University of Rochester.

THE RETURN OF PEACE IN 1815 unleashed powerful forces that revolutionized the organization of the economy. Spectacular changes in transportation facilitated the movement of commodities, information, and people, while textile mills and other factories created many new jobs, especially for young unmarried women. Innovations in banking, legal practices, and tariff policies promoted swift economic growth.

This was not yet an industrial revolution, as was beginning in Britain, but rather a market revolution fueled by traditional sources — water, wood, beasts of burden, and human muscle. What was new was the accelerated pace of economic activity and the scale of the distribution of goods. The new nature and scale of production and consumption changed Americans' economic behavior, attitudes, and expectations.

CHAPTER LOCATOR | **Why did the United States experience a market revolution after 1815?** | Why did Andrew Jackson defeat John Quincy Adams so dramatically in the 1828 election?

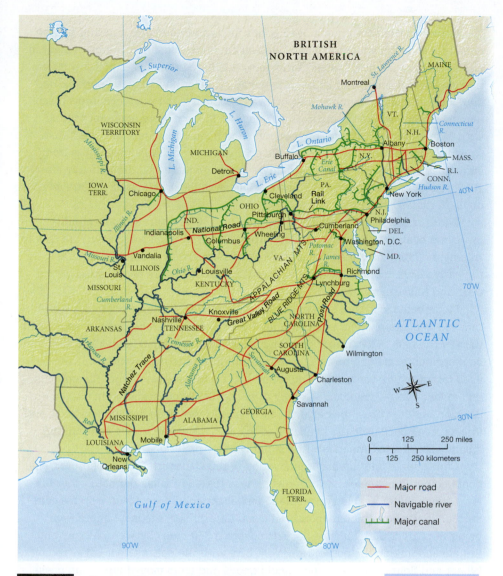

MAP 11.1 ■ Routes of Transportation in 1840

Transportation advances cut travel times significantly. On the Erie Canal, goods and people could move from New York City to Buffalo in four days, a two-week trip by road. Steamboats cut travel time from New York to New Orleans from four weeks by road to less than two weeks by river.

> MAP ACTIVITY

READING THE MAP: In what parts of the country were canals built most extensively? Were most of them within a single state's borders, or did they encourage interstate travel and shipping?

CONNECTIONS: What impact did the Erie Canal have on the development of New York City? How did improvements in transportation affect urbanization in other parts of the country?

Improvements in Transportation

Before 1815, transportation in the United States was slow and expensive; it cost as much to ship a crate over thirty miles of domestic roads as it did to send it across the Atlantic Ocean. A stagecoach trip from Boston to New York City took four days. But between 1815 and 1840, networks of roads, canals, steamboats, and finally railroads dramatically raised the speed and lowered the cost of travel (**Map 11.1**).

What was Andrew Jackson's impact on the presidency?	How did social and cultural life change in the 1830s?	Why was Martin Van Buren a one-term president?	Conclusion: The Age of Jackson or the era of reform?	✔️ LearningCurve Check what you know. bedfordstmartins.com /roarkunderstanding

> CHRONOLOGY

1807
– Robert Fulton sets off steamboat craze.

1816
– Second Bank of the United States is chartered.

1819
– Economic panic.

1825
– Erie Canal is completed in New York.

1829
– Baltimore and Ohio railroad is begun.

1834
– Female mill workers strike in Lowell, Massachusetts, and again in 1836.

Erie Canal
▶ Canal finished in 1825, covering 350 miles between Albany and Buffalo and linking the port of New York City with the entire Great Lakes region. The canal turned New York City into the country's premier commercial city.

Improved transportation moved goods into wider markets. It moved passengers, too, allowing young people as well as adults to take up new employment in cities or factory towns. Transportation also facilitated the flow of political information via the U.S. mail, with its bargain postal rates for newspapers, periodicals, and books. Enhanced public transport was expensive and produced uneven economic benefits, so presidents from Jefferson to Monroe were reluctant to fund it with federal dollars. Instead, private investors pooled resources and chartered transport companies, receiving significant subsidies and monopoly rights from state governments. Turnpike and roadway mileage increased dramatically after 1815, reducing shipping costs. Stagecoach companies proliferated, and travel time on main routes was cut in half.

Water travel was similarly transformed. In 1807, Robert Fulton's steam-propelled boat, the *Clermont*, churned up the Hudson River from New York City to Albany, touching off a steamboat craze on eastern rivers and the Great Lakes. By the early 1830s, more than seven hundred steamboats were in operation on the Ohio and Mississippi rivers.

Steamboats were not benign advances, however. The urgency to cut travel time led to overstoked furnaces, sudden boiler explosions, and terrible mass fatalities. By the mid-1830s, nearly three thousand Americans had been killed in steamboat accidents, leading to the first federal attempt to regulate safety on vessels used for interstate commerce. Environmental costs were also large: Steamboats had to load fuel—"wood up"—every twenty miles or so, resulting in mass deforestation. By the 1830s, the banks of many main rivers were denuded of trees, and forests miles back from the rivers fell to the ax. The smoke from wood-burning steamboats created America's first significant air pollution.

Canals were another major innovation of the transportation revolution. Canal boats powered by mules moved slowly—less than five miles per hour—but the low-friction water enabled one mule to pull a fifty-ton barge. Several states commenced major government-sponsored canal enterprises, the most impressive being the **Erie Canal**, finished in 1825, covering 350 miles between Albany and Buffalo and linking the port of New York City with the entire Great Lakes region. Wheat and flour moved east, household goods and tools moved west, and passengers went in both directions. By the 1830s, the cost of shipping by canal fell to less than one-tenth of the cost of overland transport, and New York City quickly blossomed into the premier commercial city in the United States.

In the 1830s, private railroad companies heavily subsidized by state legislatures began to give canals competition. The nation's first railroad, the Baltimore and Ohio, laid thirteen miles of track in 1829, and by 1840 three thousand more miles of track materialized nationwide. Rail lines in the 1830s were generally short, on the order of twenty to one hundred miles. They did not yet provide an efficient distribution system for goods, but passengers flocked to experience the marvelous speeds of fifteen to twenty miles per hour. Railroads and other advances in transportation served to unify the country culturally and economically.

CHAPTER LOCATOR | **Why did the United States experience a market revolution after 1815?** | Why did Andrew Jackson defeat John Quincy Adams so dramatically in the 1828 election?

298 CHAPTER 11 THE EXPANDING REPUBLIC

This daguerreotype (the earliest form of photograph) shows a young woman tending a power loom in a textile mill. In the 1830s, women weavers generally tended two machines at a time. In the 1840s, some companies increased the workload to four. American Textile History Museum.

Factories, Workingwomen, and Wage Labor

Transportation advances accelerated manufacturing after 1815, creating an ever-expanding market for goods. The two leading industries, textiles and shoes, altered methods of production and labor relations. Textile production was greatly spurred by the development of water-driven machinery built near fast-coursing rivers. Shoe manufacturing, still using the power and skill of human hands, involved only a reorganization of production. Both industries pulled young women into wage-earning labor for the first time.

Cotton Textile Industry, ca. 1840

Largest circle represents 8,000 employees

The earliest American textile factory was built in the 1790s by an English immigrant in Pawtucket, Rhode Island. By 1815, nearly 170 spinning mills stood along New England rivers. While British manufacturers hired entire families for mill work, American factory owners innovated by hiring young women, assumed to be cheap to hire because of their limited employment options and their short-term prospects, since most left to get married.

In 1821, a group of Boston entrepreneurs founded the town of Lowell on the Merrimack River, centralizing all aspects of cloth production: combing, shrinking, spinning, weaving, and dyeing. By 1836, the eight **Lowell mills** employed more than five thousand young women, who lived in carefully managed company-owned boardinghouses. A typical

Lowell mills

▶ Water-powered textile mills constructed along the Merrimack River in Lowell, Massachusetts, that pioneered the extensive use of female laborers. By 1836, the eight mills there employed more than five thousand young women, who lived in boardinghouses under close supervision.

What was Andrew Jackson's impact on the presidency?

How did social and cultural life change in the 1830s?

Why was Martin Van Buren a one-term president?

Conclusion: The Age of Jackson or the era of reform?

✓ LearningCurve
Check what you know.
bedfordstmartins.com
/roarkunderstanding

299

mill worker earned $2 to $3 for a seventy-hour week, more than a seamstress or domestic servant could earn but less than a young man's wages.

Despite the long hours, young women embraced factory work as a means to earn spending money and build savings before marriage; several banks in town held the nest eggs of thousands of workers. Also welcome was the unprecedented, though still limited, personal freedom of living in an all-female social space, away from parents and domestic tasks. In the evening, the women could engage in self-improvement activities, such as attending lectures. In 1837, 1,500 mill girls crowded Lowell's city hall to hear the sisters Angelina and Sarah Grimké speak about the evils of slavery.

In the mid-1830s, worldwide growth and competition in the cotton market impelled mill owners to speed up work and decrease wages. The workers protested, emboldened by their communal living arrangement and by their relative independence as temporary employees. In 1834 and again in 1836, hundreds of women at the Lowell mills went out on strike. Such strikes spread; in 1834, mill workers in Dover, New Hampshire, denounced their owners for trying to turn them into "slaves." Their assertiveness surprised many, but ultimately the ease of replacing them undermined their bargaining power, and owners in the 1840s began to shift to immigrant families as their primary labor source.

The shoe manufacturing industry centered in eastern New England reorganized production and hired women, including wives, as shoebinders. Male shoemakers still cut the leather and made the soles in shops, but female shoebinders working from home now stitched the upper parts of the shoes. Working from home meant that wives could contribute to family income—unusual for most wives in that period—and still perform their domestic chores.

In the economically turbulent 1830s, shoebinder wages fell. Unlike mill workers, female shoebinders worked in isolation, a serious hindrance to organized protest. In Lynn, Massachusetts, a major shoemaking center, women used female church networks to organize resistance, communicating via religious newspapers. The Lynn shoebinders who demanded higher wages in 1834 built on a collective sense of themselves as women. "Equal rights should be extended to all—to the weaker sex as well as the stronger," they proclaimed.

In the end, the Lynn shoebinders' protests failed to achieve wage increases. At-home workers all over New England continued to accept low wages, and even in Lynn many women shied away from organized protest, preferring to situate their work in the context of family duty (helping their husbands finish the shoes) instead of market relations.

Bankers and Lawyers

Entrepreneurs like the Lowell factory owners relied on innovations in the banking system to finance their ventures. Between 1814 and 1816, the number of state-chartered banks in the United States more than doubled, from fewer than 90 to 208. By 1830, there were 330, and by 1840 hundreds more. Banks stimulated the economy by making loans to merchants and manufacturers and by enlarging the money supply. Borrowers were issued loans in the form of banknotes—certificates

CHAPTER LOCATOR | **Why did the United States experience a market revolution after 1815?** | Why did Andrew Jackson defeat John Quincy Adams so dramatically in the 1828 election?

300 CHAPTER 11
THE EXPANDING REPUBLIC

unique to each bank—that were used as money for all transactions. Neither federal nor state governments issued paper money, so banknotes became the country's currency.

Bankers exercised great power over the economy, deciding who would get loans and what the discount rates would be. The most powerful bankers sat on the board of directors for the **second Bank of the United States**, headquartered in Philadelphia and featuring eighteen branches throughout the country. The twenty-year charter of the first Bank of the United States had expired in 1811, and the second Bank of the United States opened for business in 1816 under another twenty-year charter. The rechartering of this bank would become a major issue in the 1832 presidential campaign.

Lawyer-politicians too exercised economic power, by refashioning commercial law to enhance the prospects of private investment. In 1811, states started to rewrite their laws of incorporation (allowing the chartering of businesses by states), and the number of corporations expanded rapidly, from about twenty in 1800 to eighteen hundred by 1817. Incorporation protected individual investors from being held liable for corporate debts. State lawmakers also wrote laws of eminent domain, empowering states to buy land for roads and canals even from unwilling sellers. In such ways, entrepreneurial lawyers created the legal foundation for an economy that favored ambitious individuals interested in maximizing their own wealth.

Not everyone applauded these developments. Andrew Jackson, himself a skillful lawyer turned politician, spoke for a large and mistrustful segment of the population when he warned about the potential abuses of power "which the moneyed interest derives from a paper currency which they are able to control [and] from the multitude of corporations with exclusive privileges which they have succeeded in obtaining in the different states." Jacksonians believed that ending government-granted privileges was the way to maximize individual liberty and economic opportunity.

second Bank of the United States
▶ National bank with multiple branches chartered in 1816 for twenty years. Intended to help regulate the economy, the bank became a major issue in Andrew Jackson's reelection campaign in 1832, framed in political rhetoric about aristocracy versus democracy.

Booms and Busts

One aspect of the economy that the lawyer-politicians could not control was the threat of financial collapse. The boom years from 1815 to 1818 exhibited a volatility that resulted in the first sharp, large-scale economic downturn in U.S. history. Americans called this downturn a "panic," and the pattern was repeated in the 1830s. Some blamed the panic of 1819 on the second Bank of the United States for failing to control an economic bubble and then contracting the money supply, sending tremors throughout the economy. The crunch was made worse by a financial crisis in Europe in the spring of 1819. Overseas, prices for American cotton, tobacco, and wheat plummeted by more than 50 percent. Thus, when the banks began to call in their outstanding loans, American debtors involved in the commodities trade could not come up with the money. Business and personal bankruptcies skyrocketed. The intricate web of credit and debt relationships meant that almost everyone with even a toehold in the new commercial economy was affected by the panic. Thousands of Americans lost their savings and property, and unemployment estimates suggest that half a million people lost their jobs.

What was Andrew Jackson's impact on the presidency? | How did social and cultural life change in the 1830s? | Why was Martin Van Buren a one-term president? | Conclusion: The Age of Jackson or the era of reform? | ✓ LearningCurve Check what you know. bedfordstmartins.com /roarkunderstanding

301

Recovery took several years. Unemployment declined, but bitterness lingered, ready to be stirred up by politicians in the decades to come. The dangers of a system dependent on extensive credit were now clear. In one folksy formulation that circulated around 1820, a farmer compared credit to "a man pissing in his breeches on a cold day to keep his arse warm — very comfortable at first but I dare say . . . you know how it feels afterwards."

By the mid-1820s, the economy was back on track, driven by increases in productivity, consumer demand for goods, and international trade. Despite the panic of 1819, credit financing continued to fuel the system. A network of credit and debt relations grew dense by the 1830s in a system that encouraged speculation and risk taking. A pervasive optimism about continued growth supported the elaborate system, but a single business failure could produce many innocent victims. Well after the panic of 1819, an undercurrent of anxiety about rapid economic change continued to shape the political views of many Americans.

> **QUICK REVIEW**

What role did state governments and private businesses play in the market revolution?

CHAPTER LOCATOR | Why did the United States experience a market revolution after 1815?

Why did Andrew Jackson defeat John Quincy Adams so dramatically in the 1828 election?

302 CHAPTER 11 THE EXPANDING REPUBLIC

Jackson Forever!
The Hero of Two Wars and of Orleans!
The Man of the People!
HE WHO COULD NOT BARTER NOR BARGAIN FOR THE
PRESIDENCY!

Who, although "*A Military Chieftain*," valued the purity of Elections and of the Electors, MORE than the Office of PRESIDENT itself! Although the greatest in the gift of his countrymen, and the highest in point of dignity of any in the world,

BECAUSE
It should be derived from the
PEOPLE!

No Gag Laws! No Black Cockades! No Reign of Terror! No Standing Army or Navy Officers, when under the pay of Government, to browbeat, or

KNOCK DOWN

Old Revolutionary Characters, or our Representatives while in the discharge of their duty. To the Polls then, and vote for those who will support

OLD HICKORY
AND THE ELECTORAL LAW.

Campaign Poster for the 1828 Election This poster praises Andrew Jackson as a war hero and a "man of the people" and reminds its readers that Jackson, who won the largest popular vote in 1824, did not stoop to "bargain for the presidency," as John Quincy Adams presumably had in his dealing with Henry Clay. © Collection of the New-York Historical Society.

Why did Andrew Jackson defeat John Quincy Adams so dramatically in the 1828 election?

JUST AS THE MARKET REVOLUTION held out the promise, if not the reality, of economic opportunity for all who worked, the political transformation of the 1830s held out the promise of political opportunity for hundreds of thousands of new voters. During Andrew Jackson's presidency (1829–1837), the second American party system took shape, defined by Jackson's charismatic personality expressed in his efforts to dominate Congress. Not until 1836, however, would the parties have distinct names and consistent programs transcending the particular personalities running for office. Over those years, more men could and did vote, responding to new methods of arousing voter interest.

Popular Politics and Partisan Identity

The election of 1828, pitting Andrew Jackson against John Quincy Adams, was the first presidential contest in which the popular vote determined the outcome. In twenty-two out of twenty-four states, voters—not state legislatures—designated

| What was Andrew Jackson's impact on the presidency? | How did social and cultural life change in the 1830s? | Why was Martin Van Buren a one-term president? | Conclusion: The Age of Jackson or the era of reform? | ✓ LearningCurve Check what you know. bedfordstmartins.com /roarkunderstanding |

the number of electors committed to a particular candidate. More than a million voters participated, three times the number in 1824 and nearly half the free male population, reflecting the high stakes that voters perceived in the Adams-Jackson rematch. Throughout the 1830s, voter turnout continued to rise and reached 70 percent in some localities, partly because of the disappearance of property qualifications in all but three states and partly because of heightened political interest.

The 1828 election inaugurated new campaign styles. State-level candidates routinely gave speeches at rallies, picnics, and banquets. Adams and Jackson still declined such appearances as undignified, but Henry Clay of Kentucky, campaigning for Adams, earned the nickname "the Barbecue Orator." Campaign rhetoric became more informal and even blunt. The Jackson camp established many Hickory Clubs, trading on Jackson's popular nickname, "Old Hickory," from a common Tennessee tree suggesting resilience and toughness.

Partisan newspapers in ever-larger numbers defined issues and publicized political personalities as never before. Improved printing technology and rising literacy rates fueled a great expansion of newspapers of all kinds (**Table 11.1**). Party leaders dispensed subsidies and other favors to secure the support of papers, even in remote towns and villages. Political news stories traveled swiftly in the mail, gaining coverage by reprintings in sympathetic newspapers. Presidential campaigns were now coordinated in a national arena.

TABLE 11.1 ■ The Growth of Newspapers, 1820–1840

	1820	1830	1835	1840
U.S. population (in millions)	9.6	12.8	15.0	17.1
Number of newspapers published	500	800	1,200	1,400
Daily newspapers	42	65	—	138

Whigs

▶ Political party that evolved out of the National Republicans after 1834. With a Northeast power base, the Whigs supported federal action to promote commercial development and generally looked favorably on the reform movements associated with the Second Great Awakening.

Democrats

▶ Political party that evolved out of the Democratic Republicans after 1834. Strongest in the South and West, the Democrats embraced Andrew Jackson's vision of limited government, expanded political participation for white men, and the promotion of an ethic of individualism.

Politicians at first identified themselves as Jackson or Adams men, honoring the fiction of Republican Party unity. By 1832, however, the terminology had evolved to National Republicans, who favored federal action to promote commercial development, and Democratic Republicans, who promised to be responsive to the will of the majority. Between 1834 and 1836, National Republicans came to be called **Whigs**, while Jackson's party became simply the **Democrats**.

The Election of 1828 and the Character Issue

The campaign of 1828 was the first national election dominated by scandal and character questions. Claims about morality, honor, and discipline became central because voters used them to comprehend the kind of public official each man would make. Jackson and Adams presented two radically different styles of manhood.

John Quincy Adams was vilified by his opponents as an elitist, a bookish academic, and even a monarchist. They attacked his "corrupt bargain" of 1824—the alleged election deal between Adams and Henry Clay (see chapter 10). Adams's

CHAPTER LOCATOR | Why did the United States experience a market revolution after 1815?

Why did Andrew Jackson defeat John Quincy Adams so dramatically in the 1828 election?

304 CHAPTER 11 THE EXPANDING REPUBLIC

supporters countered by playing on Jackson's fatherless childhood to portray him as the bastard son of a prostitute. Worse, the cloudy circumstances around his marriage to Rachel Donelson Robards in 1791 gave rise to the story that Jackson was a seducer and an adulterer, having married a woman whose divorce from her first husband was not entirely legal. Pro-Adams newspapers howled that Jackson was sinful and impulsive, while portraying Adams as pious, learned, and virtuous.

Editors in favor of Adams played up Jackson's violent temper, as evidenced by his participation in many duels, brawls, and canings. Jackson's supporters used the same stories to project Old Hickory as a tough frontier hero who knew how to command obedience. As for learning, Jackson's rough frontier education gave him a "natural sense," wrote a Boston editor, that "can never be acquired by reading books — it can only be acquired, in perfection, by reading men."

Jackson won a sweeping victory, with 56 percent of the popular vote and 178 electoral votes to Adams's 83 (**Map 11.2**). Old Hickory took most of the South and West and carried Pennsylvania and New York as well; Adams carried the remainder of the East. Jackson's vice president was John C. Calhoun, who had just served as vice president under Adams but had broken with Adams's policies.

After 1828, national politicians no longer deplored the existence of political parties. They were coming to see that parties mobilized and delivered voters, sharpened candidates' differences, and created party loyalty that surpassed loyalty to individual candidates and elections. Adams and Jackson clearly symbolized the competing ideas of the emerging parties: a moralistic, top-down party (the Whigs) ready to make major decisions to promote economic growth competing against a contentious, energetic party (the Democrats) ready to embrace liberty-loving individualism.

Candidate	Electoral Vote	Popular Vote	Percent of Popular Vote
Andrew Jackson (Democratic Republican)	178	647,286	56
John Q. Adams (National Republican)	83	508,064	44

MAP 11.2 ■ The Election of 1828

Jackson's Democratic Agenda

Jackson's supporters went wild at his March 1829 inauguration. Thousands cheered his ten-minute inaugural address, the shortest in history. An open reception at the White House turned into a near riot as well-wishers jammed the premises, used windows as doors, stood on furniture for a better view of the great man, and broke thousands of dollars' worth of china and glasses. During his presidency, Jackson continued to offer unprecedented hospitality to the public. The courteous Jackson, committed to his image as president of the "common man," held audiences with unannounced visitors throughout his two terms.

Past presidents had tried to lessen party conflict by including men of different factions in their cabinets, but Jackson would have only loyalists, a political tactic followed by most later presidents. For secretary of state, the key job, he tapped New Yorker Martin Van Buren, one of the shrewdest politicians of the day. Throughout the federal government, from postal clerks to ambassadors,

What was Andrew Jackson's impact on the presidency?

How did social and cultural life change in the 1830s?

Why was Martin Van Buren a one-term president?

Conclusion: The Age of Jackson or the era of reform?

✓ LearningCurve
Check what you know.
bedfordstmartins.com
/roarkunderstanding

305

Jackson replaced competent civil servants with party loyalists. Jackson's appointment practices were termed a "spoils system" by his opponents, after a Democratic politician coined the affirmative slogan "to the victor belong the spoils."

Jackson's agenda quickly emerged. Fearing that intervention in the economy inevitably favored some groups at the expense of others, Jackson favored a Jeffersonian limited federal government. He therefore opposed federal support of transportation and grants of monopolies and charters that benefited wealthy investors. Like Jefferson, he anticipated the rapid settlement of the country's interior, where land sales would spread economic democracy to settlers. Thus, establishing a federal policy to remove the Indians from this area had high priority. Jackson was freer than previous presidents with the use of the presidential veto power over Congress. In 1830, he vetoed a highway project in Maysville, Kentucky, Henry Clay's home state. The Maysville Road veto articulated Jackson's principled stand that citizens' tax dollars could be spent only on projects of a "general, not local" character.

> **QUICK REVIEW**

Why role did character play in the 1828 election?

CHAPTER LOCATOR | Why did the United States experience a market revolution after 1815? | Why did Andrew Jackson defeat John Quincy Adams so dramatically in the 1828 election?

306 CHAPTER 11
THE EXPANDING REPUBLIC

What was Andrew Jackson's impact on the presidency?

Andrew Jackson as "the Great Father"

In 1828, a new process of commercial lithography brought political cartooning to new prominence. Out of some sixty satirical cartoons lampooning Jackson, only one featured his controversial Indian policy. This cropped cartoon lacks the cartoonist's caption, important for understanding the artist's intent. Still, the visual humor of Jackson cradling Indians packs an immediate punch. William L. Clements Library.

> VISUAL ACTIVITY

READING THE IMAGE: Examine the body language conveyed in the various characters' poses. Are the Indians depicted as children or as powerless, miniature adults? What is going on in the picture on the wall?

CONNECTIONS: Does the cartoon suggest that Jackson offers protection to Indians? What does the picture on the wall contribute to our understanding of the artist's opinion of Jackson's Indian removal policy?

IN HIS TWO TERMS AS PRESIDENT, Andrew Jackson worked to implement his vision of a politics of opportunity for all white men. To open land for white settlement, he favored the relocation of all eastern Indian tribes. He dramatically confronted John C. Calhoun and South Carolina when that state tried to nullify the tariff of 1828. Disapproving of all government-granted privilege, Jackson challenged and defeated the Bank of the United States. In all this, he greatly enhanced the power of the presidency.

Indian Removal Act of 1830
▶ Act that directed the mandatory relocation of eastern tribes to territory west of the Mississippi. Jackson insisted that his goal was to save the Indians. Indians resisted the controversial act, but in the end most were forced to comply.

Indian Policy and the Trail of Tears

Probably nothing defined Jackson's presidency more than his efforts to solve what he saw as the Indian problem. Thousands of Indians lived in the South and the old Northwest, and many remained in New England and New York. In his first message to Congress in 1829, Jackson declared that removing the Indians to territory west of the Mississippi was the only way to save them. White civilization destroyed Indian resources and thus doomed the Indians, he claimed: "That this fate surely awaits them if they remain within the limits of the states does not admit of a doubt. Humanity and national honor demand that every effort should be made to avert so great a calamity." Jackson never publicly wavered from this seemingly noble theme, returning to it in his next seven annual messages.

Prior administrations had experimented with different Indian policies. Starting in 1819, Congress funded missionary associations eager to "civilize" native peoples by converting them to Christianity and to whites' agricultural practices. The federal government had also pursued aggressive treaty making with many tribes, dealing with the Indians as foreign nations (see chapters 9 and 10). By contrast, Jackson saw Indians as subjects of the United States (neither foreigners nor citizens) who needed to be relocated to assure their survival. Congress agreed and passed the **Indian Removal Act of 1830.** About 100 million acres of eastern land would be vacated for eventual white settlement under this act authorizing ethnic expulsion (**Map 11.3**).

The Indian Removal Act generated widespread controversy. Newspapers, public lecturers, and local clubs debated the expulsion law, and public opinion, especially in the North, was heated. "One would think that the guilt of African slavery was enough for the nation to bear, without the additional crime of injustice to the aborigines," one writer declared in 1829. In an unprecedented move, thousands of northern white women signed anti-removal petitions. Between 1830 and 1832, women's petitions rolled into Washington, arguing that sovereign peoples on the road to Christianity were entitled to stay on their land. Jackson ignored the petitions.

For many northern tribes, diminished by years of war, removal was already under way. But not all went quietly. In 1832 in western Illinois, Black Hawk, a leader of the Sauk and Fox Indians who had fought in alliance with Tecumseh in the War of 1812 (see chapter 10), resisted removal. Volunteer militias attacked and chased the Indians into southern Wisconsin, where, after several skirmishes and a deadly battle (later called the Black Hawk War), Black Hawk was captured and some four hundred of his people were massacred.

The large southern tribes—the Creek, Chickasaw, Choctaw, Seminole, and Cherokee—proved even more resistant to removal. Georgia Cherokees had already taken several assimilationist steps. They had adopted written laws, including, in 1827, a constitution modeled on the U.S. Constitution. Two hundred of the wealthiest Cherokee men had intermarried with whites, adopting white styles of housing, dress, and cotton agriculture, including the ownership of slaves. They developed a written alphabet and published a newspaper and Christian prayer books in their language. These features helped make their cause attractive to the northern white women who petitioned the government on their behalf. Yet most of the seventeen thousand Cherokees maintained cultural continuity with past traditions.

CHAPTER LOCATOR | Why did the United States experience a market revolution after 1815? | Why did Andrew Jackson defeat John Quincy Adams so dramatically in the 1828 election?

MAP 11.3 ■ Indian Removal and the Trail of Tears

The federal government under President Andrew Jackson pursued a vigorous policy of Indian removal in the 1830s, forcibly moving tribes west to land known as Indian Territory (present-day Oklahoma). In 1838, as many as a quarter of the Cherokee Indians died on the route known as the Trail of Tears.

> MAP ACTIVITY

READING THE MAP: From which states were most of the Native Americans removed? Through which states did the Trail of Tears go?
CONNECTIONS: Before Jackson's presidency, how did the federal government view Native Americans, and what policy initiatives were undertaken by the government and private groups? How did Jackson change the government's policy toward Native Americans?

In 1831, when Georgia announced its plans to seize all Cherokee property, the tribal leadership took their case to the U.S. Supreme Court. In *Worcester v. Georgia* (1832), the Court upheld the territorial sovereignty of the Cherokee people, recognizing their existence as "a distinct community, occupying its own territory, in which the laws of Georgia can have no force." An angry President Jackson ignored the Court and pressed the Cherokee tribe to move west: "If they now refuse to accept the liberal terms offered, they can only be liable for whatever evils and difficulties may arise. I feel conscious of having done my duty to my red children."

| **What was Andrew Jackson's impact on the presidency?** | How did social and cultural life change in the 1830s? | Why was Martin Van Buren a one-term president? | Conclusion: The Age of Jackson or the era of reform? | ✓ LearningCurve Check what you know. bedfordstmartins.com /roarkunderstanding |

The Cherokee tribe remained in Georgia for two more years without significant violence. Then, in 1835, a small, unauthorized faction of the acculturated leaders signed a treaty selling all the tribal lands to the state, which rapidly resold the land to whites. Chief John Ross, backed by several thousand Cherokees, petitioned the U.S. Congress to ignore the bogus treaty, but to no avail. Most Cherokees refused to move, so in May 1838, the deadline for voluntary removal, federal troops arrived to remove them. Under armed guard, the Cherokees embarked on a 1,200-mile journey west that came to be called the **Trail of Tears.** Nearly a quarter of the Cherokees died en route from the hardship. Survivors joined the fifteen thousand Creek, twelve thousand Choctaw, five thousand Chickasaw, and several thousand Seminole Indians also forcibly relocated to Indian Territory (which became the state of Oklahoma in 1907).

In his farewell address to the nation in 1837, Jackson professed his belief in the humanitarian benefits of Indian removal: "This unhappy race . . . are now placed in a situation where we may well hope that they will share in the blessings of civilization and be saved from the degradation and destruction to which they were rapidly hastening while they remained in the states." Perhaps Jackson genuinely believed that removal was necessary, but for the forcibly removed tribes, the costs of relocation were high.

The Tariff of Abominations and Nullification

Just as Indian removal in Georgia had pitted a state against a federal power, in the form of a Supreme Court ruling, a second explosive issue also pitted a state against federal regulation. This was the issue of federal tariff policy, strongly opposed by South Carolina.

Federal tariffs as high as 33 percent on imports such as textiles and iron goods had been passed in 1816 and again in 1824 in an effort to shelter new American manufacturers from foreign competition. Some southern congressmen opposed the steep tariffs, fearing they would reduce overseas shipping and thereby hurt cotton exports. In 1828, Congress passed a revised tariff that came to be known as the Tariff of Abominations. A bundle of conflicting duties, some as high as 50 percent, the legislation contained provisions that either pleased or angered every economic and sectional interest.

South Carolina in particular suffered from the Tariff of Abominations. Worldwide prices for cotton had declined in the late 1820s, and the falloff in shipping caused by the high tariffs further hurt the South. In 1828, a group of South Carolina politicians headed by John C. Calhoun advanced a doctrine called **nullification.** They argued that when Congress overstepped its powers, states had the right to nullify Congress's acts. As precedents, they pointed to the Virginia and Kentucky Resolutions of 1798, intended to invalidate the Alien and Sedition Acts (see chapter 9). Congress had erred in using tariff policy to benefit specific industries, they claimed; tariffs should be used only to raise revenue.

On assuming the presidency in 1829, Jackson ignored the South Carolina statement of nullification and shut out Calhoun, his new vice president, from influence or power. Tariff revisions in early 1832 brought little relief to the South. Calhoun resigned the vice presidency and became a senator to better serve his state. Finally, strained to their limit, South Carolina leaders took the radical step

Trail of Tears
▶ Forced westward journey of Cherokees from their lands in Georgia to present-day Oklahoma in 1838. Despite favorable legal action, the Cherokees endured a grueling 1,200-mile march overseen by federal troops. Nearly a quarter of the Cherokees died en route.

nullification
▶ Theory asserting that states could nullify acts of Congress that exceeded congressional powers. South Carolina advanced the theory of nullification in 1828 in response to an unfavorable federal tariff. A show of force by Andrew Jackson, combined with tariff revisions, ended the crisis.

CHAPTER LOCATOR | Why did the United States experience a market revolution after 1815? | Why did Andrew Jackson defeat John Quincy Adams so dramatically in the 1828 election?

310 CHAPTER 11 THE EXPANDING REPUBLIC

of declaring federal tariffs null and void in their state as of February 1, 1833. The constitutional crisis was out in the open.

In response, Jackson sent armed ships to Charleston harbor and threatened to invade the state. He pushed through Congress the Force Bill, defining South Carolina's stance as treason and authorizing military action to collect federal tariffs. At the same time, Congress moved quickly to pass a revised tariff that was more acceptable to the South, reducing tariffs to their 1816 level. On March 1, 1833, Congress passed both the new tariff and the Force Bill. South Carolina withdrew its nullification of the old tariff—and then nullified the Force Bill. It was a symbolic gesture, since Jackson's show of muscle was no longer necessary.

Yet the question of federal power versus states' rights was far from settled. The implied threat behind nullification was secession, a position articulated in 1832 by some South Carolinians whose concerns went beyond tariff policy. In the 1830s, the political moratorium on discussions of slavery agreed on at the time of the Missouri Compromise (see chapter 10) was coming unglued, and new northern voices opposed to slavery gained increasing attention. If and when a northern-dominated federal government decided to end slavery, the South Carolinians thought, the South should nullify such laws or else remove itself from the Union.

The Bank War and Economic Boom

Along with the tariff and nullification, President Jackson fought another political battle, over the Bank of the United States. With twenty-nine branches, the bank handled the federal government's deposits, extended credit and loans, and issued banknotes—by 1830, the most stable currency in the country. Jackson, however, thought the bank concentrated undue economic power in the hands of a few.

National Republican (Whig) senators Daniel Webster and Henry Clay decided to force the issue. They convinced the bank to apply for charter renewal in 1832, well before the fall election, even though the existing charter ran until 1836. They fully expected that Congress's renewal would force Jackson to follow through on his rhetoric with a veto, that the unpopular veto would cause Jackson to lose the election, and that the bank would survive on an override vote by a new Congress swept into power on the anti-Jackson tide.

At first, the plan seemed to work. The bank applied for rechartering, Congress voted to renew, and Jackson, angry over being manipulated, issued his veto. But it was a brilliantly written veto, positioning Jackson as the champion of the democratic masses. "Many of our rich men have not been content with equal protection and equal benefits, but have besought us to make them richer by act of Congress," Jackson wrote.

Jackson's translation of the bank controversy into a language of class antagonism and egalitarian ideals resonated with many Americans. Jackson won the election easily, gaining 55 percent of the popular vote and 219 electoral votes to Clay's 49. Jackson's party still controlled Congress, so no override was possible. The second Bank of the United States would cease to exist after 1836.

Jackson wanted to destroy the bank sooner. Calling it a "monster," he ordered the sizable federal deposits to be removed from its vaults and redeposited into Democratic-inclined state banks. In retaliation, the Bank of the United States raised interest rates and called in loans. This action caused a brief decline in the

What was Andrew Jackson's impact on the presidency? | How did social and cultural life change in the 1830s? | Why was Martin Van Buren a one-term president? | Conclusion: The Age of Jackson or the era of reform? | ✓ LearningCurve Check what you know. bedfordstmartins.com /roarkunderstanding

311

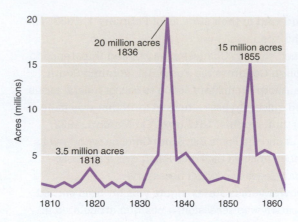

FIGURE 11.1 ■ Western Land Sales, 1810–1860

Land sales peaked in the 1810s, 1830s, and 1850s as Americans rushed to speculate in western land sold by the federal government. The surges in 1818 and 1836 demonstrate the volatile, speculative economy that suddenly collapsed in the panics of 1819 and 1837.

economy in 1833 and actually enhanced Jackson's claim that the bank was too powerful for the good of the country.

Unleashed and unregulated, the economy went into high gear in 1834. Just at this moment, an excess of silver from Mexican mines made its way into American banks, giving bankers license to print ever more banknotes. From 1834 to 1837, inflation soared; prices of basic goods rose more than 50 percent. States quickly chartered hundreds of new private banks, each issuing its own banknotes. Entrepreneurs borrowed and invested money, and the webs of credit and debt relationships that were the hallmark of the American economy grew denser yet. The market in western land sales also heated up. In 1834, about 4.5 million acres of the public domain had been sold, the highest annual volume since 1818. By 1836, the total reached an astonishing 20 million acres (**Figure 11.1**).

In one respect, the economy attained an admirable goal: The national debt disappeared, and from 1835 to 1837, for the only time in American history, the government had a monetary surplus. But much of that surplus consisted of questionable bank currencies — "bloated, diseased" currencies, in Jackson's vivid terminology. While the boom was on, however, few stopped to worry about the consequences if and when the bubble burst.

> ## QUICK REVIEW

What were the most significant policies of Andrew Jackson's presidency?

CHAPTER LOCATOR | Why did the United States experience a market revolution after 1815? | Why did Andrew Jackson defeat John Quincy Adams so dramatically in the 1828 election?

How did social and cultural life change in the 1830s?

Images of the Family at Home

Hundreds of itinerant amateur artists journeyed the back roads and small villages of antebellum America, earning a modest living painting individuals and families. This picture from the 1830s exhibits a common convention — the arrangement of family members by age and by sex, as if to emphasize the ideal of separate spheres. Museum of Fine Arts, Boston, Gift of Maxim Karolik for the M. and M. Karolik Collection of American Watercolors and Drawings, 1800–1875.

THE GROWING ECONOMY, booming by the mid-1830s, transformed social and cultural life. For many families, especially in the commercialized Northeast, standards of living rose, consumption patterns changed, and the nature and location of work were altered. All this had a direct impact on the duties of men and women and on the training of youths for the economy of the future.

Along with economic change came an unprecedented revival of evangelical religion known as the Second Great Awakening. Among the most serious adherents of evangelical Protestantism were men and women of the new merchant classes. Not content with individual perfection, many of these people sought to perfect society as well, by defining excessive alcohol consumption, nonmarital sex, and slavery as three major evils of modern life in need of correction. Three social movements championing temperance, moral reform, and abolition gained strength from evangelistic Christianity.

The Family and Separate Spheres

The centerpiece of new ideas about gender relations was the notion that husbands found their status and authority in the new world of work, leaving wives to tend the hearth and home. Sermons, advice books, periodicals, and novels reinforced the idea that men and women inhabited separate spheres and had separate duties. "To woman it belongs . . . to elevate the intellectual character of her household [and] to kindle the fires of mental activity in childhood," wrote Mrs. A. J. Graves in a popular book titled *Advice to American Women*. For men, by contrast, "the absorbing passion for gain, and the pressing demands of business, engross their whole attention."

What was Andrew Jackson's impact on the presidency?

How did social and cultural life change in the 1830s?

Why was Martin Van Buren a one-term president?

Conclusion: The Age of Jackson or the era of reform?

☑ **LearningCurve** Check what you know. bedfordstmartins.com /roarkunderstanding

313

In particular, the home, now said to be the exclusive domain of women, was sentimentalized as the source of intimacy, love, and safety, a refuge from the cruel and competitive world of market relations.

Some new aspects of society gave substance to this formulation of separate spheres. Men's work was undergoing profound change after 1815 and increasingly brought cash to the household, especially in the manufacturing and urban Northeast. Farmers and tradesmen sold products in a market, and bankers, bookkeepers, shoemakers, and canal diggers earned regular salaries or wages. Furthermore, many men now worked away from the home, at an office or a store.

A woman's domestic role was more complicated than the cultural prescriptions indicated. Although the vast majority of married white women did not hold paying jobs, their homes required time-consuming labor. But the advice books treated housework as a loving familial duty, thus rendering it invisible in an economy that evaluated work by how much cash it generated. In reality, many wives contributed to family income by taking in boarders or sewing for pay. Wives in the poorest classes, including most free black wives, did not have the luxury of husbands earning adequate wages; for them, work as servants or laundresses helped augment family income.

Idealized notions about the feminine home and the masculine workplace gained acceptance in the 1830s because of the cultural ascendancy of the commercialized Northeast, with its domination of book and periodical publishing. Beyond white families of the middle and upper classes, however, these new gender ideals had limited applicability. Despite their apparent authority in printed material of the period, these gender ideals were never all-pervasive.

The Education and Training of Youths

The market economy required expanded opportunities for training youths of both sexes. By the 1830s, in both the North and the South, state-supported public school systems were the norm, designed to produce pupils of both sexes able, by age twelve to fourteen, to read, write, and participate in marketplace calculations. Literacy rates for white females climbed dramatically, rivaling the rates for white males for the first time. The fact that taxpayers paid for children's education created an incentive to seek an inexpensive teaching force. By the 1830s, school districts replaced male teachers with young females, for, as a Massachusetts report on education put it, "females can be educated cheaper, quicker, and better, and will teach cheaper after they are qualified."

Advanced education continued to expand in the 1830s, with an additional two dozen colleges for men and several more female seminaries offering education on a par with the male colleges. Still, only a very small percentage of young people attended institutions of higher learning. The vast majority of male youths left public school at age fourteen to apprentice in specific trades or to embark on business careers by seeking entry-level clerkships, abundant in the growing urban centers. Young women headed for mill towns or cities in unprecedented numbers, seeking work in the expanding service sector as seamstresses and domestic servants. Changes in patterns of youth employment meant that large numbers of youngsters escaped the watchful eyes of their parents, a cause of great concern for moralists of the era. Advice books published by the hundreds instructed youths in the virtues of hard work and delayed gratification.

CHAPTER LOCATOR | Why did the United States experience a market revolution after 1815? | Why did Andrew Jackson defeat John Quincy Adams so dramatically in the 1828 election?

314 CHAPTER 11 THE EXPANDING REPUBLIC

The Second Great Awakening

A newly invigorated version of Protestantism gained momentum in the 1820s and 1830s as the economy reshaped gender and age relations. The earliest manifestations of this fervent piety, which historians call the **Second Great Awakening**, appeared in 1801 in Kentucky, when a crowd of ten thousand people camped out on a hillside at Cane Ridge for a revival meeting that lasted several weeks. By the 1810s and 1820s, "camp meetings" had spread to the Atlantic seaboard states, accelerating and intensifying the emotional impact of the revival.

The gatherings attracted women and men hungry for a more immediate access to spiritual peace, one not requiring years of soul-searching. One eyewitness reported that "some of the people were singing, others praying, some crying for mercy. . . . At one time I saw at least five hundred swept down in a moment as if a battery of a thousand guns had been opened upon them, and then immediately followed shrieks and shouts that rent the very heavens."

From 1800 to 1820, church membership doubled in the United States, much of it among the evangelical groups. Methodists, Baptists, and Presbyterians formed the core of the new movement, which attracted women more than men; wives and mothers typically recruited husbands and sons to join them.

A central leader of the Second Great Awakening was a lawyer turned minister named Charles Grandison Finney. Finney lived in western New York, where the completion of the Erie Canal in 1825 fundamentally altered the social and economic landscape overnight. Growth and prosperity came with other, less admirable side effects, such as prostitution, drinking, and gaming. Finney saw New York canal towns as ripe for evangelical awakening. In Rochester, he sustained a six-month revival through the winter of 1830–31, generating thousands of converts.

Finney's message, directed primarily at the business classes, argued for a public-spirited outreach to the less-than-perfect to foster their salvation. Evangelicals promoted Sunday schools to bring piety to children; they battled to honor the Sabbath by ending mail delivery, stopping public transport, and closing shops on

Second Great Awakening

▶ Unprecedented religious revival in the 1820s and 1830s that promised access to salvation. The Second Great Awakening proved to be a major impetus for reform movements of the era, inspiring efforts to combat drinking, sexual sin, and slavery.

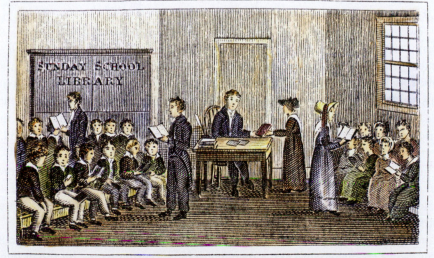

SUNDAY SCHOOL.

Sunday School

In the 1820s, free Sunday Schools for indigent children became a popular national movement, and by 1832 the American Sunday School Union formed to generate curriculum materials and provide volunteer teachers, both male and female, mainly from the newly awakened Protestant churches. Students, both white and free black, often worked six days a week, leaving only the Sabbath free for schooling. The Granger Collection, NYC.

What was Andrew Jackson's impact on the presidency?

How did social and cultural life change in the 1830s?

Why was Martin Van Buren a one-term president?

Conclusion: The Age of Jackson or the era of reform?

☑ LearningCurve Check what you know. bedfordstmartins.com /roarkunderstanding

315

Sundays. Many women formed missionary societies that distributed millions of Bibles and religious tracts. Through such avenues, evangelical religion offered women expanded spheres of influence. Finney adopted the tactics of Jacksonian-era politicians—publicity, argumentation, rallies, and speeches—to sell his cause. His object, he said, was to get Americans to "vote in the Lord Jesus Christ as the governor of the Universe."

The Temperance Movement and the Campaign for Moral Reform

The evangelical fervor animated vigorous campaigns to eliminate alcohol abuse and eradicate sexual sin. Millions of Americans took the temperance pledge to abstain from strong drink, and thousands became involved in efforts to end prostitution.

Alcohol consumption had risen steadily in the decades up to 1830. All classes imbibed. A lively saloon culture fostered masculine camaraderie along with extensive alcohol consumption among laborers, while in elite homes the after-dinner whiskey or sherry was commonplace. Colleges before 1820 routinely served students a pint of ale with meals, and the military included rum in the daily ration.

Organized opposition to drinking first surfaced in the 1810s among health and religious reformers. In 1826, Lyman Beecher, a Connecticut minister of an "awakened" church, founded the **American Temperance Society**, which warned that drinking led to poverty, idleness, crime, and family violence. Temperance lecturers spread the word, and middle-class drinking began a steep decline. One powerful tool of persuasion was the temperance pledge, which many business owners began to require of employees.

In 1836, leaders of the temperance movement regrouped into a new society, the American Temperance Union, which demanded total abstinence from its adherents. The intensified war against alcohol moved beyond individual moral suasion into the realm of politics as reformers sought to deny taverns liquor licenses. By 1845, temperance advocates had put an impressive dent in alcohol consumption, which diminished to one-quarter of the per capita consumption of 1830.

More controversial than temperance was a social movement called "moral reform," which first aimed at public morals in general but quickly narrowed to a campaign to eradicate sexual sin. In 1833, a group of Finneyite women started the **New York Female Moral Reform Society**. Its members insisted that uncontrolled male sexual expression, manifested in seduction and prostitution, posed a serious threat to society in general and to women in particular. Within five years, more than four thousand auxiliary groups of women had sprung up, mostly in New England, New York, Pennsylvania, and Ohio.

In its analysis of the causes of licentiousness and its conviction that women had a duty to speak out about unspeakable things, the Moral Reform Society pushed the limits of what even the men in the evangelical movement could tolerate. Yet these women did not regard themselves as radicals. They were simply pursuing the logic of a gender system that defined home protection and morality as women's special sphere and a religious conviction that called for the eradication of sin.

American Temperance Society

▶ Organization founded in 1826 by Lyman Beecher that linked drinking with poverty, idleness, ill health, and violence. Temperance lecturers traveled the country gaining converts to the cause. The temperance movement had considerable success, contributing to a sharp drop in American alcohol consumption.

New York Female Moral Reform Society

▶ An organization of religious women inspired by the Second Great Awakening to eradicate sexual sin and male licentiousness. Formed in 1833, it spread to hundreds of auxiliaries and worked to curb male licentiousness, prostitution, and seduction.

CHAPTER LOCATOR | Why did the United States experience a market revolution after 1815? | Why did Andrew Jackson defeat John Quincy Adams so dramatically in the 1828 election?

Organizing against Slavery

More radical still was the movement in the 1830s to abolish the sin of slavery. Previously, the American Colonization Society, founded in 1817 by Maryland and Virginia planters, promoted gradual individual emancipation of slaves followed by colonization in Africa. By the early 1820s, several thousand ex-slaves had been transported to Liberia on the West African coast. But not surprisingly, newly freed men and women often were not eager to emigrate; their African roots were three or more generations in the past. Colonization was too gradual (and too expensive) to have much impact on American slavery.

Around 1830, northern challenges to slavery intensified, beginning in free black communities. In 1829, a Boston printer named David Walker published *An Appeal . . . to the Coloured Citizens of the World,* which condemned racism, invoked the egalitarian language of the Declaration of Independence, and hinted at racial violence if whites did not change their prejudiced ways. In 1830, at the inaugural National Negro Convention meeting in Philadelphia, forty blacks from nine states discussed the racism of American society and proposed emigration to Canada. In 1832 and 1833, a twenty-eight-year-old black woman named Maria Stewart delivered public lectures on slavery and racial prejudice to black audiences in Boston. Her lectures gained wider circulation when they were published in a national publication called the *Liberator.*

The *Liberator,* founded in 1831 in Boston, took antislavery agitation to new heights. Its founder and editor, William Lloyd Garrison, advocated immediate abolition: "On this subject, I do not wish to think, or speak, or write, with moderation. No! No! Tell a man whose house is on fire to give a moderate alarm; tell him to moderately rescue his wife from the hands of the ravisher; tell the mother to gradually extricate her babe from the fire into which it has fallen . . . — but urge me not to use moderation in a cause like the present." In 1832, Garrison's supporters started the New England Anti-Slavery Society.

Similar groups were organized in Philadelphia and New York in 1833. Soon a dozen antislavery newspapers and scores of antislavery lecturers were spreading

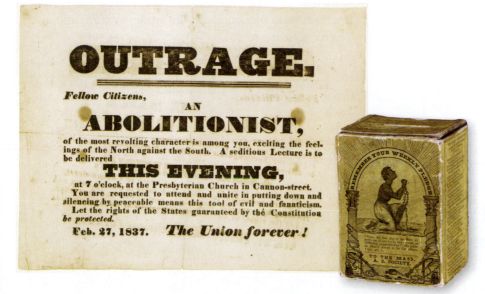

Controversy over Abolitionism

Mob violence erupted in northern cities with regularity when abolitionist speakers came to town. This 1837 poster from Poughkeepsie, New York, exemplifies the extremely inflammatory language that kindled riots. Antislavery societies raised money to support these lecture tours, one way being the weekly pledge. This contribution box is inscribed with biblical passages and the symbolic yet disturbing image of the slave in chains. Poster: Library of Congress; box: Boston Public Library/Rare Books Department—Courtesy of the Trustees.

What was Andrew Jackson's impact on the presidency?

How did social and cultural life change in the 1830s?

Why was Martin Van Buren a one-term president?

Conclusion: The Age of Jackson or the era of reform?

✓ LearningCurve
Check what you know.
bedfordstmartins.com
/roarkunderstanding

the word and inspiring the formation of new local societies, which numbered 1,300 by 1837. Confined entirely to the North, their membership totaled a quarter of a million men and women.

Many white northerners, even those who opposed slavery, were not prepared to embrace the abolitionist call for emancipation. From 1834 to 1838, there were more than a hundred eruptions of serious mob violence against abolitionists and free blacks. In one incident, Illinois abolitionist editor Elijah Lovejoy was killed by a rioting crowd attempting to destroy his printing press. When Angelina and Sarah Grimké, sisters from South Carolina who opposed slavery, lectured in 1837, some authorities tried to intimidate them and deny them meeting space. The following year, rocks shattered windows when Angelina Grimké gave a speech at a female antislavery convention in Philadelphia. After the women vacated the building, a mob burned the building to the ground.

Despite these dangers, large numbers of northern women played a prominent role in abolition. They formed women's auxiliaries and held fairs to sell handmade crafts to support male lecturers in the field. They circulated antislavery petitions, presented to the U.S. Congress with tens of thousands of signatures. At first, women's petitions were framed as respectful memorials to Congress about the evils of slavery, but soon they demanded political action to end slavery in the District of Columbia, under Congress's jurisdiction.

By the late 1830s, the cause of abolition divided the nation as no other issue did. Even among abolitionists, significant divisions emerged. The Grimké sisters, radicalized by the public reaction to their speaking tour, began to write and speak about woman's rights. Angelina Grimké compared the silencing of women to the silencing of slaves: "The denial of our duty to act, is a bold denial of our right to act; and if we have no right to act, then may we well be termed 'the white slaves of the North'—for, like our brethren in bonds, we must seal our lips in silence and despair." The Grimkés were opposed by moderate abolitionists who were unwilling to mix the new and controversial issue of woman's rights with their first cause, the rights of blacks.

The many men and women active in reform movements in the 1830s found their initial inspiration in evangelical Protestantism's dual message: Salvation was open to all, and society needed to be perfected. Their activist mentality squared well with the interventionist tendencies of the Whig Party forming in opposition to Andrew Jackson's Democrats.

> **QUICK REVIEW**

How did evangelical Protestantism contribute to the reform movements of the 1830s?

CHAPTER LOCATOR | Why did the United States experience a market revolution after 1815? | Why did Andrew Jackson defeat John Quincy Adams so dramatically in the 1828 election?

318 CHAPTER 11 THE EXPANDING REPUBLIC

Why was Martin Van Buren a one-term president?

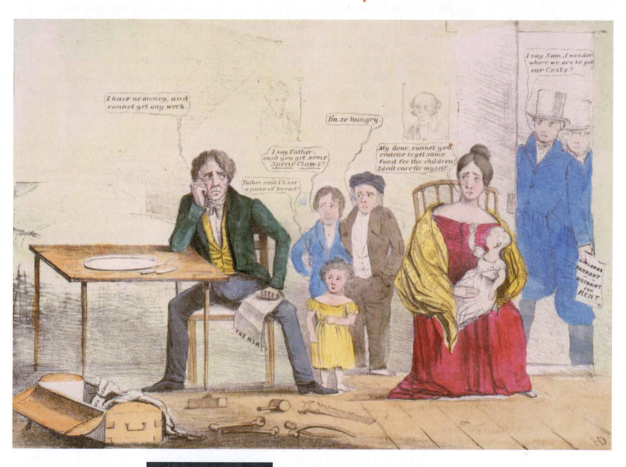

Panic of 1837 Cartoon A sad family with an unemployed father faces sudden hardship in this cartoon showing the consequences of the panic of 1837. The wife and children complain of hunger, the house is stripped nearly bare, and rent collectors loom in the doorway. Faint pictures on the wall show Andrew Jackson and Martin Van Buren presiding over the economic devastation of the family. Library of Congress.

BY THE MID-1830s, a vibrant and tumultuous political culture occupied center stage in American life. Andrew Jackson, too ill to stand for a third term, made way for Martin Van Buren, who faced tough opposition from an array of opposing Whigs and even from slave-owning Jacksonians. Van Buren was a skilled politician, but soon after his inauguration the country faced economic collapse. A shattering panic in 1837, followed by another in 1839, brought the country its worst economic depression yet.

The Politics of Slavery

Sophisticated party organization was the specialty of Martin Van Buren, nicknamed "the Little Magician" for his consummate political skills. First a senator and then a governor, the New Yorker became Jackson's secretary of state and then his running mate in 1832, replacing John C. Calhoun. His eight years in the volatile Jackson administration required the full measure of his political deftness as he sought repeatedly to save Jackson from both his enemies and his own obstinacy.

Jackson clearly favored Van Buren for the nomination in 1836, but starting in 1832, the major political parties had developed nominating conventions to choose their candidates. In 1835, Van Buren got the convention nod unanimously, to the dismay of his archrival, Calhoun, who then worked to discredit Van Buren among southern proslavery Democrats. Van Buren spent months assuring them that he was a "northern man with southern principles." This was a credible line, since his Dutch family hailed from the Hudson River counties where New York slavery had once flourished, and his own family had owned slaves as late as the 1810s, permitted under New York's gradual emancipation law.

Calhoun was able to stir up trouble for Van Buren because southerners were becoming increasingly alarmed by the rise of northern antislavery sentiment. When, in late 1835, abolitionists prepared to circulate in the South a million pamphlets condemning slavery, a mailbag of their literature was hijacked at the post office in Charleston, South Carolina, and ceremoniously burned along with effigies of leading abolitionists. President Jackson condemned the theft but issued approval for individual postmasters to exercise their own judgment about whether to allow incendiary materials to reach their destination. Abolitionists saw this as censorship of the mail.

The petitioning tactics of abolitionists escalated sectional tensions. When hundreds of antislavery petitions inundated Congress, proslavery congressmen responded by passing a "gag rule" in 1836. The gag rule prohibited entering the documents into the public record on the grounds that what the abolitionists prayed for was unconstitutional and, further, an assault on the rights of white southerners, as one South Carolina representative put it. Abolitionists like the Grimké sisters considered the gag rule to be an abridgment of free speech. They also argued that, tabled or not, the petitions were effective. "The South already turns pale at the number sent," Angelina Grimké said in a speech exhorting more petitions to be circulated.

Van Buren shrewdly seized on both mail censorship and the gag rule to express his prosouthern sympathies. Abolitionists were "fanatics," he repeatedly claimed, possibly under the influence of "foreign agents" (British abolitionists). He dismissed the issue of abolition in the District of Columbia as "inexpedient" and promised that if he was elected president, he would not allow any interference in southern "domestic institutions."

Elections and Panics

Although the elections of 1824, 1828, and 1832 clearly bore the stamp of Jackson's personality, by 1836 the party apparatus was sufficiently developed to give Van Buren, a backroom politician, a shot at the presidency. Local and state committees

CHAPTER LOCATOR | Why did the United States experience a market revolution after 1815? | Why did Andrew Jackson defeat John Quincy Adams so dramatically in the 1828 election?

existed throughout the country, and more than four hundred newspapers were Democratic partisans.

The Whigs had also built state-level organizations and newspaper loyalty. They had no top contender with nationwide support, so three regional candidates opposed Van Buren. Senator Daniel Webster of Massachusetts could deliver New England, home to reformers, merchants, and manufacturers; Senator Hugh Lawson White of Tennessee attracted proslavery voters still suspicious of the northern Magician; and the aging General William Henry Harrison, now residing in Ohio and remembered for his Indian war heroics in 1811, pulled in the western anti-Indian vote. Not one of the three candidates had the ability to win the presidency, but together they came close to denying Van Buren a majority vote. Van Burenites called the three-Whig strategy a deliberate plot to derail the election and move it to the House of Representatives.

In the end, Van Buren won with 170 electoral votes, while the other three received a total of 113. But Van Buren's victories came from narrow majorities, far below those Jackson had commanded. Although Van Buren had pulled together a national Democratic Party with wins in both the North and the South, he had done it at the cost of committing northern Democrats to the proslavery agenda. And running three candidates had maximized the Whigs' success by drawing Whigs into office at the state level.

When Van Buren took office in March 1837, the financial markets were already quaking; by April, the country was plunged into crisis. The causes of the **panic of 1837** were multiple and far-ranging.

panic of 1837

▶ Major economic crisis that led to several years of hard times in the United States from 1837 to 1841. Sudden bankruptcies, contraction of credit, and runs on banks worked hardships nationwide. The causes were multiple and global and not well understood.

> ## > Causes of the Panic of 1837

- Bad harvests in Europe and a large trade imbalance between Britain and the United States caused the Bank of England to start calling in loans to American merchants.
- Failures in various crop markets and a 30 percent downturn in international cotton prices contributed to the growing disaster.
- Cotton merchants in the South could no longer meet their obligations to New York creditors, whose firms began to fail.
- Frightened citizens quickly tried to withdraw their money from the banks.
- Businesses rushed to liquefy their remaining assets to pay off debts.

The prices of stocks, bonds, and real estate fell 30 to 40 percent. The familiar events of the panic of 1819 unfolded again, with terrifying rapidity, and the credit market tumbled like a house of cards. Newspapers describing the economic free fall generally used the language of emotional states—excitement, anxiety, terror, panic. Such words focused on human reactions to the crisis rather than on the structural features of the economy that had interacted to amplify the downturn. The vocabulary for understanding the wider economy was still quite limited, making it hard to track the bigger picture of the workings of capitalism.

Instead, many observers looked to politics, religion, and character flaws to explain the crisis. Some Whig leaders were certain that Jackson's antibank and hard-money policies were responsible for the ruin. New Yorker Philip Hone, a wealthy Whig, called the Jackson administration "the most disastrous in the

What was Andrew Jackson's impact on the presidency?

How did social and cultural life change in the 1830s?

Why was Martin Van Buren a one-term president?

Conclusion: The Age of Jackson or the era of reform?

☑ LearningCurve
Check what you know.
bedfordstmartins.com/roarkunderstanding

321

annals of the country" for its "wicked interference" in banking and monetary matters. Others framed the devastation as retribution for the frenzy of speculation that had gripped the nation. A religious periodical in Boston hoped that Americans would now moderate their greed: "We were getting to think that there was no end to the wealth, and could be no check to the progress of our country; that economy was not needed, that prudence was weakness." In this view, the panic was a wakeup call, a blessing in disguise. Others identified the competitive, profit-maximizing capitalist system as the cause and looked to Britain and France for new socialist ideas calling for the common ownership of the means of production. American socialists, though few in number, were vocal and imaginative, and in the early 1840s several thousand developed utopian alternative communities (as discussed in chapter 12).

The panic of 1837 subsided by 1838, but in 1839 another run on the banks and ripples of business failures deflated the economy, creating a second panic. President Van Buren called a special session of Congress to consider creating an independent treasury system to perform some of the functions of the defunct Bank of the United States. Such a system, funded by government deposits, would deal only in hard money and would exert a powerful moderating influence on inflation and the credit market. But Van Buren encountered strong resistance in Congress, even among Democrats. The treasury system finally won approval in 1840, but by then Van Buren's chances of winning a second term in office were virtually nil.

In 1840, the Whigs settled on William Henry Harrison to oppose Van Buren. The campaign drew on voter involvement as no other presidential campaign ever had. The Whigs borrowed tricks from the Democrats: Harrison was touted as a common man born in a log cabin (in reality, he was born on a Virginia plantation), and campaign parades featured toy log cabins held aloft. His Indian-fighting days, now thirty years behind him, were played up to give him a Jacksonian aura. Whigs staged festive rallies around the country, drumming up mass appeal with candlelight parades and song shows, and women participated in rallies as never before. Some 78 percent of eligible voters cast ballots—the highest percentage ever in American history.

Harrison took 53 percent of the popular vote and won a resounding 234 electoral college votes to Van Buren's 60. A Democratic editor lamented, "We have taught them how to conquer us!"

> ## QUICK REVIEW

What were the most significant issues of Martin Van Buren's presidency?

CHAPTER LOCATOR | Why did the United States experience a market revolution after 1815? | Why did Andrew Jackson defeat John Quincy Adams so dramatically in the 1828 election?

322 CHAPTER 11 THE EXPANDING REPUBLIC

Conclusion: The Age of Jackson or the era of reform?

ECONOMIC TRANSFORMATIONS LOOM large in explaining the fast-paced changes of the 1830s. Transportation advances put goods and people in circulation, augmenting urban growth and helping to create a national culture, and water-powered manufacturing began to change the face of wage labor. Trade and banking mushroomed, and western land once occupied by Indians was auctioned off in a landslide of sales. Two periods of economic downturn—including the panic of 1819 and the panics of 1837 and 1839—offered sobering lessons about speculative fever.

Andrew Jackson symbolized this age of opportunity for many. His fame as an aggressive general, an Indian fighter, a champion of the common man, and a defender of slavery attracted growing numbers of voters to the emergent Democratic Party, which championed personal liberty, free competition, and egalitarian opportunity for all white men.

Jackson's constituency was challenged by a small but vocal segment of the population troubled by serious moral problems that Jacksonians preferred to ignore. Inspired by the Second Great Awakening, reformers targeted personal vices (illicit sex and intemperance) and social problems (prostitution, poverty, and slavery) and joined forces with evangelicals and wealthy lawyers and merchants (in both the North and the South) who appreciated a national bank and protective tariffs. The Whig Party was the party of activist moralism and state-sponsored entrepreneurship. Whig voters were, of course, male, but thousands of reform-minded women broke new ground by signing political petitions on the issues of Indian removal and slavery. A few exceptional women, like Sarah and Angelina Grimké, captured the national limelight by offering powerful testimony against slavery and in the process pioneering new pathways for women to contribute a moral voice to politics.

National politics in the 1830s were more divisive than at any time since the 1790s. The new party system of Democrats and Whigs reached far deeper into the electorate than had the Federalists and Republicans. Stagecoaches and steamboats carried newspapers from the cities to the backwoods, politicizing voters and creating party loyalty. Politics acquired immediacy and excitement, causing nearly four out of five white men to cast ballots in 1840.

High rates of voter participation would continue into the 1840s and 1850s. Unprecedented urban growth, westward expansion, and early industrialism marked those decades, sustaining the Democrat-Whig split in the electorate. But critiques of slavery, concerns for free labor, and an emerging protest against women's second-class citizenship complicated the political scene of the 1840s, leading to third-party political movements. One of these third parties, called the Republican Party, would achieve dominance in 1860 with the election of an Illinois lawyer, Abraham Lincoln, to the presidency.

What was Andrew Jackson's impact on the presidency?

How did social and cultural life change in the 1830s?

Why was Martin Van Buren a one-term president?

Conclusion: The Age of Jackson or the era of reform?

LearningCurve
Check what you know.
bedfordstmartins.com
/roarkunderstanding

CHAPTER 11 STUDY GUIDE

STEP 1

GET STARTED ONLINE

 LearningCurve ■ bedfordstmartins.com/roarkunderstanding

Now that you've read the chapter, make it stick by completing the LearningCurve activity.

STEP 2

EXPLAIN WHY IT MATTERS

Put your reading into practice. Identify each term below, and then explain why it matters in U.S. history.

TERM	WHO OR WHAT & WHEN	WHY IT MATTERS
Erie Canal (p. 298)		
Lowell mills (p. 299)		
second Bank of the United States (p. 301)		
Whigs (p. 304)		
Democrats (p. 304)		
Indian Removal Act of 1830 (p. 308)		
Trail of Tears (p. 310)		
nullification (p. 310)		
Second Great Awakening (p. 315)		
American Temperance Society (p. 316)		
New York Female Moral Reform Society (p. 316)		
panic of 1837 (p. 321)		

STEP 3

MOVE BEYOND THE BASICS

To demonstrate a more advanced understanding, consider change over time as it affected the American economy, politics, society, and culture. What was the relationship between each of the developments?

	1815	1830–1840
Transportation		
Industry and labor		
Economy		
Politics		
Social reform and cultural developments		

STEP 4 PUT IT ALL TOGETHER

Now, take a step back and try to explain the big picture. Remember to use specific examples from the chapter in your answers.

THE MARKET REVOLUTION

▶ Why were improvements in transportation so crucial to America's economic growth and development in the early nineteenth century?

▶ What changes in workers' lives and status accompanied industrialization?

THE AGE OF JACKSON

▶ What does Andrew Jackson's rise to the presidency tell us about popular politics in the 1820s?

▶ How did Andrew Jackson change the presidency? How did he see and manipulate the relationship among the president, Congress, and the courts?

THE ERA OF REFORM

▶ How did the Second Great Awakening lead to a variety of social reform movements? What impact did these various reform movements have on politics and society in the 1830s?

▶ What role did women play in the reform movements of the early nineteenth century?

LOOKING BACKWARD, LOOKING AHEAD

▶ How did the second American party system differ from the first party system? How did it differ from the partisanship of the 1790s?

▶ How do the reform movements of the 1820s and 1830s shed light on the causes of the sectional tensions that would dominate the 1840s and 1850s?

> **IN YOUR OWN WORDS**

Imagine that you must give an oral report to the class answering the following question: **What were the most important causes and consequences of the market revolution from 1815 to 1840?** What would be the most important points to include and why?

 Do it online at the Student Site ■ bedfordstmartins.com/roarkunderstanding

12

THE NEW WEST AND THE FREE NORTH

1840–1860

> ## How was freedom defined in the North and West in the mid-nineteenth century?

Chapter 12 focuses on how the concept of freedom helped shape economics, politics, and social reform. It explores the factors that propelled American economic growth, territorial expansion, political debate, and social reform. It also examines the growing tensions between the ideology of free labor and slavery.

 **LearningCurve**

bedfordstmartins.com/roarkunderstanding
After reading the chapter, use LearningCurve to
retain what you've read.

Westward the Star of Empire Takes Its Way. Artist Andrew Melrose depicted a mid-nineteenth-century landscape of agricultural and technological progress. Museum of the American West, Autry National Center, 92.147.1.

> What factors contributed to the United States' "industrial evolution"?

> How did the free-labor ideal account for economic inequality?

> What factors spurred westward expansion?

> Why did the United States go to war with Mexico?

> How did reform movements change after 1840?

> Conclusion: How was white freedom in the West and North defined?

> What factors contributed to the United States' "industrial evolution"?

Harvesting Grain with Cradles

This late-nineteenth-century painting shows a grain harvest during the mid-nineteenth century at Bishop Hill, Illinois, a Swedish community where the artist, Olof Krans, and his parents settled in 1850. The men swing cradles, slowly cutting a swath through the grain; the women gather the cut grain into sheaves to be hauled away later for threshing. Although most Bishop Hill farmers had only a few family members and a hired hand or two, they could call upon the labor of the many men and women from the community at harvest time. Notice that all the work is done by hand; there is no machine in sight. Private Collection/Art Resource, NY.

DURING THE 1840S AND 1850S, Americans experienced a profound economic transformation. Since 1800, the total output of the U.S. economy had multiplied twelvefold. Four fundamental changes in American society fueled this remarkable economic growth.

> Changes That Led to Economic Growth

- Millions of Americans moved from farms to towns and cities.
- Factory workers (primarily in towns and cities) increased to about 20 percent of the labor force by 1860.
- A shift from water power to steam as a source of energy raised productivity, especially in factories and transportation. Railroads in particular harnessed steam power, speeding transport and cutting costs.
- Agricultural productivity nearly doubled between 1800 and 1860, spurring the nation's economic growth more than any other factor.

Historians often refer to this cascade of changes as an industrial revolution. However, these changes did not cause an abrupt discontinuity in America's economy or society, which remained overwhelmingly agricultural. Old methods of production continued alongside the new. The changes in the American economy during the 1840s and 1850s might better be termed "industrial evolution."

CHAPTER LOCATOR | **What factors contributed to the United States' "industrial evolution"?** | How did the free-labor ideal account for economic inequality?

Agriculture and Land Policy

The foundation of the United States' economic growth lay in agriculture. As farmers pushed westward in a quest for cheap land, they encountered the Midwest's comparatively treeless prairie, where they could spend less time clearing land and more time with a plow and hoe. Rich prairie soils yielded bumper crops, enticing farmers to migrate to the Midwest by the tens of thousands between 1830 and 1860.

Laborsaving improvements in farm implements also boosted agricultural productivity. Inventors tinkered to craft stronger, more efficient plows. In 1837, John Deere made a strong, smooth steel plow that sliced through prairie soil so cleanly that farmers called it the "singing plow." Deere's company produced more than ten thousand plows a year by the late 1850s. Human and animal muscles provided the energy for plowing, but Deere's plows permitted farmers to break more ground and plant more crops.

Improvements in wheat harvesting also increased farmers' productivity. In 1850, most farmers harvested wheat by hand, cutting two or three acres a day. In the 1840s, Cyrus McCormick and others experimented with designs for **mechanical reapers**, and by the 1850s a McCormick reaper that cost between $100 and $150 allowed a farmer to harvest twelve acres a day. Improved reapers and plows allowed farmers to cultivate more land, doubling the corn and wheat harvests between 1840 and 1860.

Federal land policy made possible the leap in agricultural productivity. Up to 1860, the United States continued to be land-rich and labor-poor. Territorial acquisitions made the nation a great deal richer in land, adding more than a billion acres with the Louisiana Purchase (see chapter 10) and vast territories following the Mexican-American War. The federal government made most of this land available for purchase to attract settlers and to generate revenue. Millions of ordinary farmers bought federal land for just $1.25 an acre, or $50 for a forty-acre farm that could support a family. Millions of other farmers squatted on unclaimed federal land and carved out farms. By making land available on relatively easy terms, federal land policy boosted the increase in agricultural productivity that fueled the nation's impressive economic growth.

Manufacturing and Mechanization

Changes in manufacturing arose from the nation's land-rich, labor-poor economy. Western expansion and government land policies buoyed agriculture, keeping millions of people on the farm — 80 percent of the nation's 31 million people lived in rural areas in 1860 — and thereby limiting the supply of workers for manufacturing and elevating wages. Because of this relative shortage of workers, American manufacturers searched constantly for ways to save labor.

Mechanization allowed manufacturers to produce more with less labor. In general, factory workers produced twice as much (per unit of labor) as agricultural workers. The practice of manufacturing and then assembling interchangeable parts spread from gun making to other industries and became known as the **American system**. Using standardized parts produced by machine allowed manufacturers to employ unskilled workers, whose wages were much lower than those of highly trained craftsmen.

Manufacturing and agriculture meshed into a dynamic national economy. New England led the nation in manufacturing, shipping goods such as guns, clocks, plows, and axes west and south, while southern and western states sent

> **CHRONOLOGY**

1837
– Steel plow is patented.

1840s
– Practical mechanical reapers are created.

1844
– Samuel F. B. Morse demonstrates telegraph.

1850
– Railroads are granted six square miles of land for every mile of track.

1861
– California is connected to the nation by telegraph.

mechanical reapers
▶ Tools usually powered by horses or oxen that enabled farmers to harvest twelve acres of wheat a day, compared with the two or three acres a day possible with manual harvesting methods.

American system
▶ The practice of manufacturing and then assembling interchangeable parts. A system that spread quickly across American industries, the use of standardized parts allowed American manufacturers to employ unskilled workers at low wages.

What factors spurred westward expansion? | Why did the United States go to war with Mexico? | How did reform movements change after 1840? | Conclusion: How was white freedom in the West and North defined? | ✓ LearningCurve Check what you know. bedfordstmartins.com /roarkunderstanding

329

commodities such as wheat, pork, whiskey, tobacco, and cotton north and east. Between 1840 and 1860, coal production in Pennsylvania, Ohio, and elsewhere multiplied eightfold, cutting prices in half and powering innumerable coal-fired steam engines. Nonetheless, by 1860 coal accounted for less than a fifth of the nation's energy consumption, and even in manufacturing, muscles provided thirty times more energy than steam did.

American manufacturers specialized in producing for the gigantic domestic market rather than for export. British goods dominated the international market and usually were cheaper and better than American-made products. U.S. manufacturers supported tariffs to minimize British competition, but their best protection from British competitors was to please their American customers, most of them farmers. The burgeoning national economy was accelerated by the growth of railroads, which linked farmers and factories in new ways.

Railroads: Breaking the Bonds of Nature

Railroads captured Americans' imagination because they seemed to break the bonds of nature. When canals and rivers froze in winter or became impassable during summer droughts, trains steamed ahead, averaging more than twenty miles an hour during the 1850s. Above all, railroads gave cities not blessed with canals or navigable rivers a way to compete for rural trade.

In 1850, trains steamed along 9,000 miles of track, almost two-thirds of it in New England and the Middle Atlantic states. By 1860, several railroads spanned the Mississippi River, connecting frontier farmers to the nation's 30,000 miles of track, approximately as much as in all of the rest of the world combined (**Map 12.1**).

In addition to speeding transportation, railroads propelled the growth of other industries, such as iron and communications. Iron production grew five times faster than the population during the decades up to 1860, in part to meet railroads' demand. Railroads also stimulated the fledgling telegraph industry. In 1844, Samuel F. B. Morse demonstrated the potential of his telegraph by transmitting an electronic message between Washington, D.C., and Baltimore. By 1861, more than fifty thousand miles of telegraph wire stretched across the continent to the Pacific Ocean, often alongside railroad tracks, accelerating communications of all sorts.

In contrast to the government ownership of railroads common in other industrial nations, private corporations built and owned almost all American railroads. But the railroads received massive government aid, especially federal land grants. Up to 1850, the federal government had granted a total of seven million acres of federal land to various turnpike, highway, and canal projects. In 1850, Congress approved a precedent-setting grant to railroads of six square miles of federal land for each mile of track laid. By 1860, Congress had granted railroads more than twenty million acres of federal land, thereby underwriting construction costs and promoting the expansion of the rail network, the settlement of federal land, and the integration of the domestic market.

The railroad boom of the 1850s signaled the growing industrial might of the American economy. Like other industries, railroads succeeded because they served both farms and cities. But transportation was not revolutionized overnight. Most Americans in 1860 were still far more familiar with horses than with locomotives.

The economy of the 1840s and 1850s linked an expanding, westward-moving population in farms and cities with muscles, animals, machines, steam, and

The Telegraph

Samuel F. B. Morse is credited with inventing the telegraph because of his patent in June 1840, but, as one contemporary observed, Morse's talent consisted of "combining and applying the discoveries of others in the invention of a particular instrument and process for telegraphic purposes." Morse sent the first message in 1844 on this telegraph using a code he devised that represented each letter and number with dots and dashes.
Division of Political History, Smithsonian Institution, Washington, D.C.

CHAPTER LOCATOR | **What factors contributed to the United States' "industrial evolution"?** | How did the free-labor ideal account for economic inequality?

330   CHAPTER 12
THE NEW WEST AND THE FREE NORTH

MAP 12.1 ■ Railroads in 1860

Railroads were a crucial component of the revolutions in transportation and communications that transformed nineteenth-century America. The railroad system reflected the differences in the economies of the North and South.

> MAP ACTIVITY

READING THE MAP: In which sections of the country was most of the railroad track laid by the middle of the nineteenth century? What cities served as the busiest railroad hubs?
CONNECTIONS: How did the expansion of railroad networks affect the American economy? Why was the U.S. government willing to grant more than twenty million acres of public land to the private corporations that ran the railroads?

railroads. Abraham Lincoln planted corn and split fence rails as a young man before he moved to Springfield, Illinois, and became a successful attorney who defended, among others, railroad corporations. His mobility — westward, from farm to city, from manual to mental labor, and upward — illustrated the direction of economic change and the opportunities that beckoned enterprising individuals.

QUICK REVIEW

Why did the United States become a leading industrial power in the nineteenth century?

What factors spurred westward expansion?	Why did the United States go to war with Mexico?	How did reform movements change after 1840?	Conclusion: How was white freedom in the West and North defined?	☑ **LearningCurve** Check what you know. bedfordstmartins.com /roarkunderstanding

> How did the free-labor ideal account for economic inequality?

A German Immigrant in New York

This 1855 painting depicts a German immigrant in New York City asking directions from an African American man who is cutting firewood. Like many other German immigrants, the man shown here appears relatively well off. Compare his clothing with that of the sawyer and the white laborer on the right. The German appears to be speaking respectfully to the black sawyer, suggesting that he did not fully share assumptions of white supremacy common among native-born white working men. North Carolina Museum of Art, Raleigh, purchased with funds from the State of North Carolina (52.9.2).

> KEY FACTORS

1840s–1850s

- Free-labor ideal developed to describe the economic and social successes and shortcomings in the North and West.
- Almost 4.5 million immigrants arrived in the United States, three-fourths of them from Ireland and Germany.

THE NATION'S IMPRESSIVE economic performance did not reward all Americans equally. Native-born white men tended to do better than immigrants. With few exceptions, women were excluded from opportunities open to men. Tens of thousands of women worked as seamstresses, laundresses, domestic servants, factory hands, and teachers but had little opportunity to aspire to higher-paying jobs. In the North and West, slavery was slowly eliminated in the half century after the American Revolution, but most free African Americans were relegated to dead-end jobs as laborers and servants. Discrimination against immigrants, women, and free blacks did not trouble most white men. With certain notable exceptions, they considered it proper and just, the outcome of the free-labor system that rewarded hard work and, ideally, education.

CHAPTER LOCATOR | What factors contributed to the United States' "industrial evolution"? | **How did the free-labor ideal account for economic inequality?**

332   CHAPTER 12
THE NEW WEST AND THE FREE NORTH

The Free-Labor Ideal

During the 1840s and 1850s, leaders throughout the North and West emphasized a set of ideas that seemed to explain why the changes under way in their society benefited some people more than others. They referred again and again to the advantages of what they termed *free labor*. (The word *free* referred to laborers who were not slaves. It did not mean laborers who worked for nothing.) By the 1850s, free-labor ideas described a social and economic ideal that accounted for both the successes and the shortcomings of the economy and society taking shape in the North and West.

> ## > The Free-Labor Ideology
>
> - Hard work, self-reliance, and independence were highly valued.
> - Self-made men had a chance at success.
> - Free labor benefited farmers and artisans as well as wageworkers.
> - The free-labor ideal affirmed an egalitarian vision of human potential.
> - This ideology inspired calls for universal public education for young children throughout the North and West.

In rural areas, where the labor of children was more difficult to spare, schools typically enrolled no more than half the school-age children. Textbooks and teachers — most of whom were young women — drummed into students the valued traits of the free-labor system: self-reliance, discipline, and, above all else, hard work. "Remember that all the ignorance, degradation, and misery in the world is the result of indolence and vice," one textbook intoned. Both in and outside school, free-labor ideology emphasized labor as much as freedom.

Economic Inequality

The free-labor ideal made sense to many Americans, especially in the North and West, because it seemed to describe their own experiences. Abraham Lincoln frequently referred to his humble beginnings as a hired laborer and implicitly invited his listeners to consider how far he had come. In 1860, his assets of $17,000 easily placed him in the wealthiest 5 percent of the population. A few men became much richer. Most Americans, however, measured success in more modest terms. The average wealth of adult white men in the North in 1860 barely topped $2,000. Nearly half of American men had no wealth at all; about 60 percent owned no land. Because property possessed by married women was normally considered to belong to their husbands, women typically had less wealth than men. Free African Americans had still less; 90 percent of them were propertyless.

Free-labor spokesmen considered these economic inequalities a natural outgrowth of freedom — the inevitable result of some individuals being both luckier and more able and willing to work. These inequalities also demonstrate the gap between the promise and the performance of the free-labor ideal. Economic growth permitted many men to move from being landless squatters to landowning farmers and from being hired laborers to independent, self-employed producers. But many more Americans remained behind, landless and working for wages.

What factors spurred westward expansion?

Why did the United States go to war with Mexico?

How did reform movements change after 1840?

Conclusion: How was white freedom in the West and North defined?

✓ **LearningCurve**
Check what you know.
bedfordstmartins.com
/roarkunderstanding

Even those who realized their aspirations often had a precarious hold on their independence. Bad debts, market volatility, crop failure, sickness, or death could quickly eliminate a family's gains.

Seeking out new opportunities in pursuit of free-labor ideals created restless social and geographic mobility. While fortunate people such as Abraham Lincoln rose far beyond their social origins, others shared the misfortune of a merchant who, an observer noted, "has been on the sinking list all his life." In search of better prospects, roughly two-thirds of the rural population moved every decade, and population turnover in cities was even greater.

Immigrants and the Free-Labor Ladder

The risks and uncertainties of free labor did not deter millions of immigrants from entering the United States during the 1840s and 1850s. Almost 4.5 million immigrants arrived between 1840 and 1860, six times more than had come during the previous two decades (**Figure 12.1**). Nearly three-fourths of the immigrants who arrived in the United States between 1840 and 1860 came from either Germany or Ireland.

In America's labor-poor economy, Irish laborers could earn more in one day than they could in several weeks in Ireland. In America, one immigrant explained in 1853, there was "plenty of work and plenty of wages plenty to eat and no land lords thats enough what more does a man want." But many immigrants also craved respect and decent working conditions.

FIGURE 12.1 ■ Antebellum Immigration, 1840–1860

After increasing gradually for several decades, immigration shot up in the mid-1840s. Between 1848 and 1860, nearly 3.5 million immigrants entered the United States.

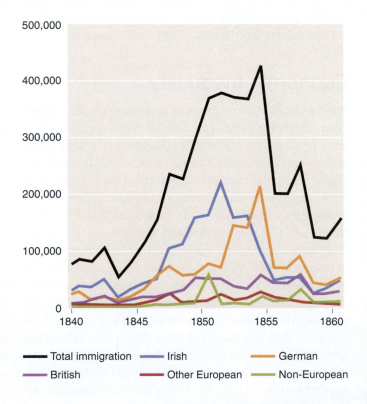

CHAPTER LOCATOR | What factors contributed to the United States' "industrial evolution"?

How did the free-labor ideal account for economic inequality?

334 CHAPTER 12
THE NEW WEST AND THE FREE NORTH

Amid the opportunities for some immigrants and native-born laborers, the free-labor system often did not live up to its promise. Many wage laborers could not realistically aspire to become independent, self-sufficient property holders, despite the claims of free-labor proponents.

> German and Irish Immigrants

Germans	Irish
1.4 million German immigrants entered the United States between 1840 and 1860.	Nearly 1.7 million Irish immigrants arrived between 1840 and 1860.
Majority were skilled tradesmen and their families.	Nearly all were poor and often weakened by hunger and disease.
Roughly one-quarter were farmers.	Potato blight caused a catastrophic famine in Ireland in 1845 and returned repeatedly in subsequent years.
Many were Protestants.	Almost all were Catholics.
Relatively few worked as wage laborers or domestic servants.	Roughly three-quarters worked as laborers or domestic servants.

QUICK REVIEW

What values or assumptions underlay free-labor ideology?

| What factors spurred westward expansion? | Why did the United States go to war with Mexico? | How did reform movements change after 1840? | Conclusion: How was white freedom in the West and North defined? | ✔ LearningCurve Check what you know. bedfordstmartins.com /roarkunderstanding |

What factors spurred westward expansion?

Pioneer Family on the Trail West

In 1860, W. G. Chamberlain photographed these unidentified travelers momentarily at rest by the upper Arkansas River in Colorado. We do not know their fates, but we can only hope that they fared better than the Sager family. In 1844, Henry and Naomi Sager and their children set out from Missouri to Oregon. Still far from Oregon, Henry Sager died of fever. Twenty-six days later, Naomi died, leaving seven children. The Sager children, under the care of other families in the wagon train, pressed on. After traveling two thousand miles, they arrived in Oregon, where Marcus and Narcissa Whitman, whose own daughter had drowned, adopted all seven of the Sager children. Denver Public Library, Western History Division # F3226.

> **VISUAL ACTIVITY**

READING THE IMAGE: Based on this photograph, what were some of the difficulties faced by pioneers traveling west?
CONNECTIONS: How did wagon trains change the western United States?

BEGINNING IN THE 1840S, the nation's swelling population, booming economy, and boundless confidence propelled a new era of rapid westward migration. Under the banner of manifest destiny, American migrants encountered Native Americans who inhabited the plains, deserts, and rugged coasts of the West; the British, who claimed the Oregon Country; and Mexicans, whose flag flew over the vast expanse of the Southwest. Nevertheless, by 1850 the United States stretched to the Pacific, and the nation had more than doubled its size.

The human cost of aggressive expansionism was high. The young Mexican nation lost a war and half of its territory. Two centuries of Indian wars, which ended east of the Mississippi during the 1830s, continued for another half century in the West.

Manifest Destiny

Most Americans believed that the superiority of their institutions and white culture bestowed on them a God-given right to spread across the continent. They imagined the West as a howling wilderness, empty and undeveloped. If they recognized Indians and Mexicans at all, they dismissed them as primitives who would have to be redeemed, shoved aside, or exterminated. The West provided

CHAPTER LOCATOR | What factors contributed to the United States' "industrial evolution"? | How did the free-labor ideal account for economic inequality?

336   CHAPTER 12
THE NEW WEST AND THE FREE NORTH

young men especially an arena in which to "show their manhood." Most Americans believed that the West needed the civilizing power of the hammer and the plow, the ballot box and the pulpit, which had transformed the East.

In 1845, a New York political journal edited by John L. O'Sullivan coined the term **manifest destiny** to justify white settlers taking the land they coveted. O'Sullivan called on Americans to resist any effort to thwart "the fulfillment of our manifest destiny to overspread the continent allotted by Providence for the free development of our yearly multiplying millions . . . [and] for the development of the great experiment of liberty and federative self-government entrusted to us." Almost overnight, the magic phrase *manifest destiny* swept the nation, providing an ideological shield for conquering the West.

As important as national pride and racial arrogance were to manifest destiny, economic gain made up its core. Land hunger drew hundreds of thousands of Americans westward. Some politicians, moreover, had become convinced that national prosperity depended on capturing the rich trade of the Far East. To trade with Asia, the United States needed the Pacific coast ports that stretched from San Diego to Puget Sound. The United States and Asia must "talk together, and trade together," Missouri senator Thomas Hart Benton declared. "Commerce is a great civilizer." In the 1840s, American economic expansion came wrapped in the rhetoric of uplift and civilization.

Oregon and the Overland Trail

American expansionists and the British competed for the Oregon Country — a vast region bounded on the west by the Pacific Ocean, on the east by the Rocky Mountains, on the south by the forty-second parallel, and on the north by Russian Alaska. In 1818, the United States and Great Britain decided on "joint occupation" that would leave Oregon "free and open" to settlement by both countries. By the 1820s, a handful of American fur traders and "mountain men" roamed the region.

In the late 1830s, settlers began to trickle along the **Oregon Trail**, following a path blazed by the mountain men (**Map 12.2**). The first wagon trains headed west in 1841, and by 1843 about 1,000 emigrants a year set out from Independence, Missouri. By 1869, when the first transcontinental railroad was completed, approximately 350,000 migrants had traveled west in wagon trains.

Emigrants encountered the Plains Indians, a quarter of a million Native Americans scattered over the area between the Mississippi River and the Rocky Mountains. Some were farmers who lived peaceful, sedentary lives, but a majority — the Sioux, Cheyenne, Shoshoni, and Arapaho of the central plains and the Kiowa, Wichita, and Comanche of the southern plains — were horse-mounted, nomadic, nonagricultural peoples whose warriors symbolized the "savage Indian" in the minds of whites.

Horses, which had been brought to North America by Spaniards in the sixteenth century, permitted the Plains tribes to become highly mobile hunters of buffalo. They came to depend on buffalo for nearly everything — food, clothing, shelter, and fuel. Competition for buffalo led to war between the tribes. Young men were introduced to warfare early, learning to ride ponies at breakneck speed while firing off arrows and, later, rifles with astounding accuracy. "A Comanche on his feet is out of his element," observed western artist George Catlin, "but the moment he lays his hands upon his horse, his *face* even becomes handsome, and he gracefully flies away like a different being."

> **CHRONOLOGY**

1836
– Battle of the Alamo.
– Texas declares independence from Mexico.

1841
– First wagon trains head west on Oregon Trail.

1845
– Term *manifest destiny* is coined.

1846
– Bear Flag Revolt.

1847
– Mormons settle in Utah.

1850
– Utah Territory is annexed.

1851
– Fort Laramie conference marks the beginning of Indian concentration.

1857
– Mormon War.

manifest destiny
▶ Term coined in 1845 by journalist John L. O'Sullivan to justify American expansion. O'Sullivan claimed that it was the nation's "manifest destiny" to transport its values and civilization westward. Manifest destiny framed the American conquest of the West as part of a divine plan.

Oregon Trail
▶ Route from Independence, Missouri, to Oregon traveled by American settlers starting in the late 1830s. Disease and accidents caused many more deaths along the trail than did Indian attacks, which migrants feared.

What factors spurred westward expansion? | Why did the United States go to war with Mexico? | How did reform movements change after 1840? | Conclusion: How was white freedom in the West and North defined? | ✔ LearningCurve Check what you know. bedfordstmartins.com /roarkunderstanding

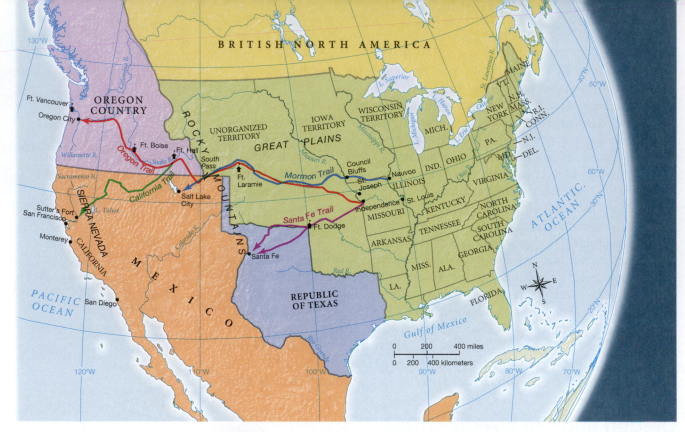

MAP 12.2 ■ Major Trails West

In the 1830s, wagon trains began snaking their way to the Southwest and the Pacific coast. Deep ruts, some of which can still be seen today, soon marked the most popular routes.

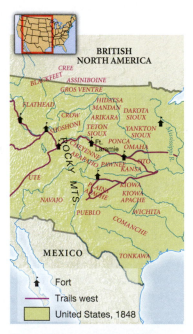

Plains Indians and Trails West in the 1840s and 1850s

The Plains Indians struck fear in the hearts of whites on the wagon trains. But Native Americans had far more to fear from whites. Indians killed fewer than four hundred emigrants on the Oregon Trail between 1840 and 1860, while whites brought alcohol and deadly epidemics. Moreover, white hunters slaughtered buffalo for the international hide market and sometimes just for sport.

The government constructed a chain of forts along the Oregon Trail (see Map 12.2) and adopted a new Indian policy: "concentration." In 1851, government negotiators at the Fort Laramie conference persuaded the Plains Indians to sign agreements that cleared a wide corridor for wagon trains by restricting Native Americans to specific areas that whites promised they would never violate. This policy of concentration became the seedbed for the subsequent policy of reservations. But whites would not keep out of Indian territory, and Indians would not easily give up their traditional ways of life. Struggle for control of the West meant warfare for decades to come.

Still, Indians threatened emigrants less than life on the trail did. Emigrants could count on at least six months of grueling travel. With nearly two thousand miles to go and traveling no more than fifteen miles a day, the pioneers endured parching heat, drought, treacherous rivers, disease, physical and emotional exhaustion, and, if the snows closed the mountain passes before they got through, freezing and starvation. It was said that a person could walk from Missouri to the Pacific stepping only on the graves of those who had died heading west.

CHAPTER LOCATOR | What factors contributed to the United States' "industrial evolution"? | How did the free-labor ideal account for economic inequality?

Men usually found Oregon "one of the greatest countries in the world." From "the Cascade mountains to the Pacific, the whole country can be cultivated," exclaimed one eager settler. When women reached Oregon, they found that neighbors were scarce and things were in a "primitive state." Work seemed unending. "I am a very old woman," declared twenty-nine-year-old Sarah Everett. "My face is thin sunken and wrinkled, my hands bony withered and hard." Another settler observed, "A woman that can not endure almost as much as a horse has no business here." Yet despite the ordeal of the trail and the difficulties of starting from scratch, emigrants kept coming.

The Mormon Exodus

Not every wagon train heading west was bound for the Pacific Slope. One remarkable group of religious emigrants halted near the Great Salt Lake in what was then Mexican territory. After years of persecution in the East, the **Mormons** fled west to find religious freedom and communal security.

In the 1820s, an upstate New York farm boy named Joseph Smith Jr. said that he was visited by an angel who led him to golden tablets buried near his home. With the aid of magic stones, he translated the mysterious language on the tablets to produce *The Book of Mormon,* which he published in 1830. It told the story of an ancient Hebrew civilization in the New World and predicted the appearance of an American prophet who would reestablish Jesus Christ's undefiled kingdom in America. Converts, attracted to the promise of a pure faith in the midst of antebellum America's social turmoil and rampant materialism, flocked to the new Church of Jesus Christ of Latter-Day Saints (the Mormons).

Neighbors branded Mormons heretics and drove Smith and his followers from New York to Ohio, then to Missouri, and finally in 1839 to Nauvoo, Illinois, where they built a prosperous community. But after Smith sanctioned "plural marriage" (polygamy), non-Mormons arrested Smith and his brother. On June 27, 1844, a mob stormed the jail and shot both men dead.

The embattled church turned to an extraordinary new leader, Brigham Young, who in 1847 oversaw a great exodus to a new home beside the Great Salt Lake. Young described the region as a barren waste, "the paradise of the lizard, the cricket and the rattlesnake." Within ten years, however, the Mormons developed an irrigation system that made the desert bloom. Under Young's stern leadership, the Mormons built a thriving community.

In 1850, the Mormon kingdom was annexed to the United States as the Utah Territory. Shortly afterward, Brigham Young announced that many Mormons practiced polygamy. Although only one Mormon man in five had more than one wife (Young had twenty-three), Young's statement forced the U.S. government to establish its authority in Utah. In 1857, 2,500 U.S. troops invaded Salt Lake City in what was known as the Mormon War. The bloodless occupation illustrated that most Americans viewed the Mormons as a threat to American morality and institutions.

The Mexican Borderlands

In the Mexican Southwest, westward-moving Anglo-American pioneers confronted northern-moving Spanish-speaking frontiersmen. On this frontier as elsewhere, national cultures, interests, and aspirations collided. Mexico won its

Mormons
▶ Members of the Church of Jesus Christ of Latter-Day Saints, founded by Joseph Smith in 1830. Most Americans deemed the Mormons heretics. After Smith's death at the hands of an angry mob in 1844, Brigham Young led the Mormons to Utah in 1846.

What factors spurred westward expansion?

Why did the United States go to war with Mexico?

How did reform movements change after 1840?

Conclusion: How was white freedom in the West and North defined?

✔ LearningCurve
Check what you know.
bedfordstmartins.com /roarkunderstanding

339

MAP 12.3 ■ Texas and Mexico in the 1830s

As Americans spilled into lightly populated and loosely governed northern Mexico, Texas and then other Mexican provinces became contested territory.

independence from Spain in 1821 (**Map 12.3**), but the young nation was plagued by civil wars, economic crises, quarrels with the Roman Catholic Church, and devastating raids by the Comanche, Apache, and Kiowa. Mexico found it increasingly difficult to defend its northern provinces, especially when faced with a neighbor convinced of its superiority and bent on territorial acquisition.

The American assault began quietly. In the 1820s, Anglo-American traders drifted into Santa Fe, a remote outpost in the northern province of New Mexico. The traders made the long trek southwest along the Santa Fe Trail (see Map 12.2) with wagons crammed with inexpensive American manufactured goods and returned home with Mexican silver, furs, and mules.

The Mexican province of Texas attracted a flood of Americans who had settlement, not long-distance trade, on their minds (see Map 12.3). Wanting to populate and develop its northern territory, the Mexican government granted the American Stephen F. Austin a huge tract of land along the Brazos River. In the 1820s, Austin offered land at only ten cents an acre, and thousands of Americans poured across the border. Most were Southerners who brought cotton and slaves with them.

By the 1830s, the settlers had established a thriving plantation economy in Texas. Americans numbered 35,000, while the *Tejano* (Spanish-speaking) population was fewer than 8,000. Few Anglo-American settlers were Roman Catholic,

CHAPTER LOCATOR | What factors contributed to the United States' "industrial evolution"? | How did the free-labor ideal account for economic inequality?

CHAPTER 12

340 THE NEW WEST AND THE FREE NORTH

spoke Spanish, or cared about assimilating into Mexican culture. The Mexican government in 1830 banned further immigration to Texas from the United States and outlawed the introduction of additional slaves. The Anglo-Americans made it clear that they wanted to be rid of the "despotism of the sword and the priest-hood" and to govern themselves.

When the Texan settlers rebelled, General Antonio López de Santa Anna ordered the Mexican army northward. In February 1836, the army arrived at the outskirts of San Antonio. Commanded by Colonel William B. Travis from Alabama, the rebels included the Tennessee frontiersman Davy Crockett and the Louisiana adventurer James Bowie, as well as a handful of Tejanos. They took refuge in a former Franciscan mission known as the Alamo. Santa Anna sent wave after wave of his 2,000-man army crashing against the walls until the attackers finally broke through and killed all 187 rebels. A few weeks later, outside the small town of Goliad, Mexican forces captured and executed almost 400 Texans as "pirates and outlaws." In April 1836, at San Jacinto, General Sam Houston's army adopted the massacre of Goliad as a battle cry and crushed Santa Anna's troops in a surprise attack. The Texans had succeeded in establishing the **Lone Star Republic**, and the following year the United States recognized the independence of Texas from Mexico.

Earlier, in 1824, in an effort to increase Mexican migration to the province of California, the Mexican government granted *ranchos* — huge estates devoted to cattle raising — to new settlers. *Rancheros* ruled over near-feudal empires worked by Indians whose condition sometimes approached that of slaves. In 1834, *rancheros* persuaded the Mexican government to confiscate the Franciscan missions and make their lands available to new settlement, a development that accelerated the decline of the California Indians. Devastated by disease, the Indians, who had numbered approximately 300,000 when the Spanish arrived in 1769, had declined to half that number by 1846.

Despite the efforts of the Mexican government, California in 1840 had a population of only 7,000 Mexican settlers. Non-Mexican settlers numbered only 380, but among them were Americans who championed manifest destiny. They sought to convince American emigrants who were traveling the Oregon Trail to head southwest on the California Trail (see Map 12.2). As a New York newspaper put it in 1845, "Let the tide of emigration flow toward California and the American population will soon be sufficiently numerous to play the Texas game." Few Americans in California wanted a war, but many dreamed of living again under the U.S. flag.

In 1846, American settlers in the Sacramento Valley took matters into their own hands. Prodded by John C. Frémont, a former army captain and an explorer who had arrived with a party of sixty buckskin-clad frontiersmen spoiling for a fight, the Californians raised an independence movement known as the Bear Flag Revolt. By then, James K. Polk, a champion of aggressive expansion, sat in the White House.

Lone Star Republic
▶ Independent republic, also known as the Republic of Texas, that was established by a rebellion of Texans against Mexican rule. The victory at San Jacinto in April 1836 helped ensure the region's independence and recognition by the United States.

QUICK REVIEW

Why did westward migration expand dramatically in the mid-nineteenth century?

What factors spurred westward expansion?

Why did the United States go to war with Mexico?

How did reform movements change after 1840?

Conclusion: How was white freedom in the West and North defined?

☑ LearningCurve
Check what you know.
bedfordstmartins.com
/roarkunderstanding

Why did the United States go to war with Mexico?

Polk and Dallas Banner, 1844

In 1844, Democratic presidential nominee James K. Polk and vice presidential nominee George M. Dallas campaigned under this cotton banner. The extra star spilling over into the red and white stripes symbolizes Polk's vigorous support for annexing the huge slave republic of Texas, which had declared its independence from Mexico eight years earlier. Collection of Janice L. and David J. Frent.

ALTHOUGH EMIGRANTS ACTED as the advance guard of American empire, there was nothing automatic about the U.S. annexation of territory in the West. Acquiring territory required political action. In the 1840s, the politics of expansion became entangled with sectionalism and the slavery question. Texas, Oregon, and the Mexican borderlands also thrust the United States into dangerous diplomatic crises with Great Britain and Mexico.

Aggravation between Mexico and the United States escalated to open antagonism in 1845 when the United States annexed Texas. Absorbing territory still claimed by Mexico set the stage for war. But it was President James K. Polk's insistence on having Mexico's other northern provinces that made war certain. The war was not as easy as Polk anticipated, but it ended in American victory and the acquisition of a new American West. The discovery of gold in one of the nation's new territories, California, prompted a massive wave of emigration that nearly destroyed Native American and Californio society.

The Politics of Expansion

Texans had sought admission to the Union almost since winning their independence from Mexico in 1836. Almost constant border warfare between Mexico and the Republic of Texas in the decade following the revolution underscored the precarious nature of independence. But any suggestion of adding another slave state to the Union outraged most Northerners, who applauded westward expansion but imagined the expansion of liberty, not slavery.

John Tyler, who became president in April 1841 when William Henry Harrison died one month after taking office, understood that Texas was a dangerous issue. Adding to the danger, Great Britain began sniffing around Texas, apparently contemplating adding the young republic to its growing empire. In

CHAPTER LOCATOR | What factors contributed to the United States' "industrial evolution"? | How did the free-labor ideal account for economic inequality?

342   CHAPTER 12
THE NEW WEST AND THE FREE NORTH

1844, Tyler, an ardent expansionist, decided to risk annexing the Lone Star Republic. However, howls of protest erupted across the North. Future Massachusetts senator Charles Sumner deplored the "insidious" plan to annex Texas and carve from it "great slaveholding states." The Senate soundly rejected the annexation treaty.

During the election of 1844, the Whig nominee for president, Henry Clay, in an effort to woo northern voters, came out against annexation of Texas. "Annexation and war with Mexico are identical," he declared. The Democratic nominee, Tennessean James K. Polk, vigorously backed annexation. To make annexation palatable to Northerners, the Democrats shrewdly yoked the annexation of Texas to the annexation of Oregon, thus tapping the desire for expansion in the free states of the North as well as in the slave states of the South.

When Clay finally recognized the popularity of expansion, he waffled, hinting that he might accept the annexation of Texas after all. His retreat succeeded only in alienating antislavery opinion in the North. In the November election, Polk won a narrow victory.

In his inaugural address on March 4, 1845, Polk underscored his faith in America's manifest destiny. "This heaven-favored land," he proclaimed, enjoyed the "most admirable and wisest system of well-regulated self-government . . . ever devised by human minds." He asked, "Who shall assign limits to the achievements of free minds and free hands under the protection of this glorious Union?"

The nation did not have to wait for Polk's inauguration to see results from his victory. One month after the election, President Tyler announced that the triumph of the Democratic Party provided a mandate for the annexation of Texas "promptly and immediately." In February 1845, after a fierce debate between antislavery and proslavery forces, Congress approved a joint resolution offering the Republic of Texas admission to the United States. Texas entered as the fifteenth slave state.

While Tyler delivered Texas, Polk had promised Oregon, too. But Polk was close to war with Mexico and could not afford a war with Britain over U.S. claims in Canada. He renewed an old offer to divide Oregon along the forty-ninth parallel. When Britain accepted the compromise, the nation gained an enormous territory peacefully. When the Senate approved the treaty in June 1846, the United States and Mexico were already at war.

The Mexican-American War, 1846–1848

From the day he entered the White House, Polk craved Mexico's remaining northern provinces: California and New Mexico, land that today makes up California, Nevada, Utah, most of New Mexico and Arizona, and parts of Wyoming and Colorado. Since the 1830s, Comanches, Kiowas, Apaches, and others had attacked Mexican ranches and towns, killing thousands, and the Polk administration invoked Mexico's inability to control its northern provinces to denigrate its claims to them. Polk hoped to buy the territory, but when the Mexicans refused to sell, he concluded that military force would be needed to realize the United States' manifest destiny.

Polk ordered General Zachary Taylor to march his 4,000-man army 150 miles south from its position on the Nueces River, the southern boundary of Texas according to the Mexicans, to the banks of the Rio Grande, the boundary claimed

> CHRONOLOGY

1841
- Vice President John Tyler becomes president when William Henry Harrison dies.

1844
- James K. Polk is elected president.

1845
- Texas enters Union as slave state.

1846
- Congress declares war on Mexico.
- United States and Great Britain divide Oregon Country.

1848
- Treaty of Guadalupe Hidalgo.

1849
- California gold rush begins.

What factors spurred westward expansion?

Why did the United States go to war with Mexico?

How did reform movements change after 1840?

Conclusion: How was white freedom in the West and North defined?

✓ LearningCurve Check what you know. bedfordstmartins.com /roarkunderstanding

343

MAP 12.4 ■ The Mexican-American War, 1846–1848

American and Mexican soldiers skirmished across much of northern Mexico, but the major battles took place between the Rio Grande and Mexico City.

by Texans (**Map 12.4**). Viewing the American advance as aggression, Mexican cavalry on April 25, 1846, attacked a party of American soldiers, killing or wounding sixteen and capturing the rest.

On May 11, the president told Congress, "Mexico has passed the boundary of the United States, has invaded our territory, and shed American blood upon American soil." Thus "war exists, and, notwithstanding all our efforts to avoid it, exists by the act of Mexico herself." Congress passed a declaration of war and began raising an army. The U.S. Army was pitifully small, only 8,600 soldiers. Faced with the nation's first foreign war, against a Mexican army that numbered more than 30,000, Polk called for volunteers. Eventually, more than 112,000 white Americans (40 percent of whom were immigrants; blacks were banned) joined the army to fight in Mexico.

Despite the flood of volunteers, the war divided the nation. Northern Whigs in particular condemned the war. The Massachusetts legislature claimed that the war was being fought for the "triple object of extending slavery, of strengthening the slave power, and of obtaining control of the free states." On January 12, 1848,

CHAPTER LOCATOR | What factors contributed to the United States' "industrial evolution"? | How did the free-labor ideal account for economic inequality?

CHAPTER 12

344 THE NEW WEST AND THE FREE NORTH

Mexican Family

This family had its portrait taken in 1847, in the middle of the war. Mexican civilians were vulnerable to atrocities committed by the invading army. Volunteers, who made up a large part of U.S. troops, received little training and resisted discipline. The "lawless Volunteers stop at no outrage," Brigadier General William Worth declared. "Innocent blood has been basely, cowardly, and barbarously shed in cold blood." Unknown photographer. Daguerreotype, ca. 1847, $2\frac{7}{8} \times \frac{3}{16}$ inches, Amon Carter Museum, Fort Worth, Texas, P1981.65.18.

a gangly freshman Whig representative from Illinois rose in the House of Representatives. Before Abraham Lincoln sat down, he had questioned Polk's intelligence, honesty, and sanity. The president ignored the upstart representative, but antislavery, antiwar Whigs kept up the attack throughout the conflict.

President Polk expected a short war in which U.S. armies would occupy Mexico's northern provinces and defeat the Mexican army in a decisive battle or two, after which Mexico would sue for peace and the United States would keep the territory its armies occupied. At first, Polk's strategy seemed to work. In May 1846, Zachary Taylor's troops drove south from the Rio Grande and routed the Mexican army, first at Palo Alto, then at Resaca de la Palma (see Map 12.4). "Old Rough and Ready," as Taylor was affectionately known among his adoring troops, became an instant war hero. Polk rewarded Taylor for his victories by making him commander of the Mexican campaign.

A second prong of the campaign centered on Colonel Stephen Watts Kearny, who led a 1,700-man army from Missouri into New Mexico. Without firing a shot, U.S. forces took Santa Fe in August 1846. Kearny then marched to San Diego, where he encountered a major Mexican rebellion against American rule. In January 1847, after several clashes and severe losses, U.S. forces occupied Los Angeles. California and New Mexico were in American hands.

By then, Taylor had driven deep into the interior of Mexico. In September 1846, he had taken the city of Monterrey. Taylor then pushed his 5,000 troops southwest, where the Mexican hero of the Alamo, General Antonio López de Santa Anna, was concentrating an army of 21,000. On February 23, 1847, Santa Anna's troops attacked Taylor at Buena Vista. The Americans won the day but suffered heavy casualties. The Mexicans suffered even greater losses (some 3,400 dead, wounded, and missing, compared with 650 Americans). During the night, Santa Anna withdrew his battered army.

The series of uninterrupted victories in northern Mexico fed the American troops' sense of invincibility. "No American force has ever thought of being defeated by any

| What factors spurred westward expansion? | **Why did the United States go to war with Mexico?** | How did reform movements change after 1840? | Conclusion: How was white freedom in the West and North defined? | ☑ **LearningCurve** Check what you know. bedfordstmartins.com /roarkunderstanding |

345

amount of Mexican troops," one soldier declared. The Americans worried about other hazards, however. "I can assure you that fighting is the least dangerous & arduous part of a soldier's life," one young man declared. Letters home told of torturous marches across arid wastes alive with tarantulas, scorpions, and rattlesnakes. Others recounted dysentery, malaria, smallpox, cholera, and yellow fever. Of the 13,000 American soldiers who died (some 50,000 Mexicans perished), fewer than 2,000 fell to Mexican bullets and shells. Disease killed most of the others. Medicine was so primitive that, as one Tennessee man observed, "nearly all who take sick die."

Victory in Mexico

Despite heavy losses on the battlefield, Mexico refused to trade land for peace. One American soldier captured the Mexican mood: "They cannot submit to be deprived of California after the loss of Texas, and nothing but the conquest of their Capital will force them to such a humiliation." Polk had arrived at the same conclusion. While Taylor occupied the north, General Winfield Scott would land an army on the Gulf coast of Mexico and march 250 miles inland to the capital. Polk's plan entailed enormous risk because Scott would have to cut himself off from supplies and lead his men deep into enemy country against a much larger army.

An amphibious landing on March 9, 1847, near Veracruz put some 10,000 American troops ashore. After furious shelling, Veracruz surrendered. In April 1847, Scott's forces moved westward, following the path blazed more than three centuries earlier by Hernán Cortés to "the halls of Montezuma" (see chapter 2).

After the defeat at Buena Vista, Santa Anna had returned to Mexico City, where he rallied his ragged troops and marched them east to set a trap for Scott in the mountain pass at Cerro Gordo. Knifing through Mexican lines, the Americans almost captured Santa Anna, who fled the field on foot. So complete was the victory that Scott gloated to Taylor, "Mexico no longer has an army." But Santa Anna, ever resilient, again rallied the Mexican army. Some 30,000 troops took up defensive positions on the outskirts of Mexico City and began melting down church bells to cast new cannons.

In August 1847, Scott began his assault on the Mexican capital. The fighting proved the most brutal of the war. Santa Anna backed his army into the city, fighting each step of the way. At the battle of Churubusco, the Mexicans took 4,000 casualties in a single day and the Americans more than 1,000. At the castle of Chapultepec, American troops scaled the walls and fought the Mexican defenders hand to hand. After Chapultepec, Mexico City officials persuaded Santa Anna to evacuate the city to save it from destruction, and on September 14, 1847, Scott rode in triumphantly.

On February 2, 1848, American and Mexican officials signed the **Treaty of Guadalupe Hidalgo** in Mexico City.

Treaty of Guadalupe Hidalgo

▶ February 1848 treaty that ended the Mexican-American War. Mexico gave up all claims to Texas north of the Rio Grande and ceded New Mexico and California to the United States. The United States agreed to pay Mexico $15 million and to assume American claims against Mexico.

> **> Terms of the Treaty of Guadalupe Hidalgo**

- Mexico agreed to give up all claims to Texas north of the Rio Grande and to cede the provinces of New Mexico and California to the United States.
- The United States agreed to pay Mexico $15 million and to assume $3.25 million in claims that American citizens had against Mexico.

CHAPTER LOCATOR | What factors contributed to the United States' "industrial evolution"? | How did the free-labor ideal account for economic inequality?

346 CHAPTER 12 THE NEW WEST AND THE FREE NORTH

MAP 12.5 ■ Territorial Expansion by 1860

Less than a century after its founding, the United States spread from the Atlantic seaboard to the Pacific coast. War, purchase, and diplomacy had gained a continent.

> MAP ACTIVITY

READING THE MAP: List the countries from which the United States acquired land. Which nation lost the most land because of U.S. expansion?
CONNECTIONS: Who coined the term *manifest destiny*? When? What does it mean? What areas targeted for expansion were the subjects of debate during the presidential campaign of 1844?

The American triumph had enormous consequences. Less than three-quarters of a century after its founding, the United States had achieved its self-proclaimed manifest destiny to stretch from the Atlantic to the Pacific (**Map 12.5**). It would enter the industrial age with vast new natural resources and a two-ocean economy, while Mexico faced a sharply diminished economic future.

Golden California

Another consequence of the Mexican defeat was that California gold poured into American, not Mexican, pockets. In January 1848, James Marshall discovered gold in the American River in the foothills of the Sierra Nevada. His discovery set off the **California gold rush**, one of the wildest mining stampedes in the world's history. Between 1849 and 1852, more than 250,000 "forty-niners," as the would-be miners were known, descended on the Golden State. In less than two years, Marshall's discovery transformed California from foreign territory to statehood.

California gold rush

▶ Mining rush initiated by James Marshall's discovery of gold in the foothills of the Sierra Nevada in 1848. The hope of striking it rich drew more than 250,000 aspiring miners to California between 1849 and 1852, an influx that accelerated the push for statehood.

What factors spurred westward expansion?

Why did the United States go to war with Mexico?

How did reform movements change after 1840?

Conclusion: How was white freedom in the West and North defined?

✓ LearningCurve
Check what you know.
bedfordstmartins.com
/roarkunderstanding

347

This young man exhibits the spirit of individual effort that was the foundation of free-labor ideals. Posing with a pick and shovel to loosen gold-bearing deposits and a pan to wash away debris, the man appears determined to succeed as a miner by his own muscles and sweat. Hard work with these tools, the picture suggests, promised rewards and maybe riches. Collection of Matthew Isenburg.

Gold fever quickly spread around the world. A stream of men of various races and nationalities poured into California. Only a few struck it rich, and life in the goldfields was nasty, brutish, and often short. The prospectors faced cholera and scurvy, exorbitant prices for food (eggs cost a dollar apiece), deadly encounters with claim jumpers, and endless backbreaking labor.

Violent crime was an everyday occurrence, and establishing civic order was made more difficult by California's diversity. The Chinese attracted special scrutiny from Anglos. By 1851, 25,000 Chinese lived in California, and their religion, language, dress, queues (long pigtails), eating habits, and use of opium convinced many Anglos that they were not fit citizens of the Golden State. In 1850, the California legislature passed the Foreign Miners' Tax Law, which levied high taxes on non-Americans to drive them from the goldfields, except as hired laborers working on claims owned by Americans. The Chinese were segregated residentially and occupationally and, along with blacks and Indians, were denied public education and the right to testify in court.

Opponents demanded a halt to Chinese immigration, but Chinese leaders in San Francisco fought back. Admitting deep cultural differences, they insisted that "in the important matters we are good men. We honor our parents; we take care of our children; we are industrious and peaceable; we trade much; we are trusted

CHAPTER LOCATOR | What factors contributed to the United States' "industrial evolution"? | How did the free-labor ideal account for economic inequality?

348 CHAPTER 12 THE NEW WEST AND THE FREE NORTH

for small and large sums; we pay our debts; and are honest, and of course must tell the truth." Their protestations offered little protection, however, and racial violence grew.

Anglo-American prospectors asserted their dominance over other groups, especially Native Americans and the Californios, Spanish and Mexican settlers who had lived in California for decades. Despite the U.S. government's pledge to protect Mexican and Spanish land titles, Americans took the land of the *rancheros* and through discriminatory legislation pushed Hispanic professionals, merchants, and artisans into the ranks of unskilled labor. Mariano Vallejo, a leading Californio, said of the forty-niners, "The good ones were few and the wicked many."

For Indians, the gold rush was catastrophic. Numbering about 150,000 in 1848, the Indian population of California fell to 25,000 by 1854. Starvation, disease, and a declining birthrate took a heavy toll. Indians also fell victim to wholesale murder. The nineteenth-century historian Hubert Howe Bancroft described white behavior toward Indians during the gold rush as "one of the last human hunts of civilization, and the basest and most brutal of them all."

The forty-niners created dazzling wealth: In 1852, 81 million ounces of gold, nearly half of the world's production, came from California. However, most miners eventually took up farming, opened small businesses, or worked for wages for the corporations that took over the mining industry. Others Americans traded furs, hides, and lumber and engaged in whaling and the China trade in tea, silk, and porcelain. Still, as one Californian observed, the state was separated "by thousands of miles of plains, deserts, and almost impossible mountains" from the rest of the Union. Some dreamers imagined a railroad that would someday connect the Golden State with the thriving agriculture and industry of the East. Others imagined a country transformed not by transportation but by progressive individual and institutional reform.

Chinese Man

This daguerreotype of an unidentified Chinese man was made by Isaac Wallace Baker, a photographer who traveled through California's mining camps in his wagon studio. One of the earliest known portraits of an Asian in California, the portrait shows a proud man boldly displaying his queue (long braid). This was almost certainly an act of defiance, for Anglos ridiculed Chinese cultural traditions, and vigilantes chased down men who wore queues. Copyright the Dorothea Lange Collection, Oakland Museum of California, City of Oakland. Gift of Paul S. Taylor.

QUICK REVIEW

What were the most significant consequences of the U.S. war with Mexico?

What factors spurred westward expansion?

Why did the United States go to war with Mexico?

How did reform movements change after 1840?

Conclusion: How was white freedom in the West and North defined?

☑ LearningCurve Check what you know. bedfordstmartins.com /roarkunderstanding

349

How did reform movements change after 1840?

Abolitionist Meeting This rare daguerreotype portrays an abolitionist meeting in New York in 1850. Frederick Douglass, who had escaped from slavery in Maryland, is seated on the platform next to the woman at the table. One of the nation's most eloquent abolitionists, Douglass also supported equal rights for women. The man behind Douglass is Gerrit Smith, a wealthy and militant abolitionist whose funds supported many reform activities. Collection of the J. Paul Getty Museum, Malibu, CA.

WHILE MANIFEST DESTINY, the Mexican-American War, and the California gold rush transformed the nation's boundaries, many Americans sought personal and social reform. The emphasis on self-discipline and individual effort at the core of the free-labor ideal led Americans to believe that insufficient self-control caused the major social problems of the era. Evangelical Protestants struggled to control individuals' propensity to sin. Temperance advocates exhorted drinkers to control their taste for alcohol. Only about one-third of Americans belonged to a church in 1850, but the influence of evangelical religion reached far beyond church members.

The evangelical temperament — a conviction of righteousness coupled with energy, self-discipline, and faith that the world could be improved — animated

CHAPTER LOCATOR | What factors contributed to the United States' "industrial evolution"? | How did the free-labor ideal account for economic inequality?

most reformers. However, a few activists pointed out that certain fundamental injustices lay beyond the reach of individual self-control. Transcendentalists and utopians believed that perfection required rejecting the competitive, individualistic values of mainstream society. Woman's rights activists and abolitionists sought to reverse the subordination of women and to eliminate the enslavement of blacks by changing laws, social institutions, attitudes, and customs. These reformers confronted the daunting challenge of repudiating widespread beliefs in male supremacy and white supremacy and somehow challenging the entrenched institutions that reinforced those views: the family and slavery.

The Pursuit of Perfection: Transcendentalists and Utopians

A group of New England writers who came to be known as transcendentalists believed that individuals should conform neither to the dictates of the materialistic world nor to the dogma of formal religion. Instead, people should look within themselves for truth and guidance. The leading transcendentalist, Ralph Waldo Emerson — an essayist, poet, and lecturer — proclaimed that the power of the solitary individual was nearly limitless. But the inward gaze and confident egoism of transcendentalism represented less an alternative to mainstream values than an extreme form of the rampant individualism of the age.

Unlike transcendentalists who sought to turn inward, a few reformers tried to change the world by organizing utopian communities as alternatives to prevailing social arrangements. Although these communities never attracted more than a few thousand people, the activities of their members demonstrated dissatisfaction with the larger society and efforts to realize their visions of perfection.

Some communities set out to become models of perfection whose success would point the way toward a better life for everyone. During the 1840s, more than two dozen communities organized themselves around the ideas of Charles Fourier. Members of Fourierist phalanxes, as these communities were called, believed that individualism and competition were evils that denied the basic truth that "men . . . are brothers and not competitors." Phalanxes aspired to replace competition with harmonious cooperation based on communal ownership of property. But Fourierist communities failed to realize their lofty goals, and few survived more than two or three years.

The **Oneida community** went beyond the Fourierist notion of communalism. John Humphrey Noyes, the charismatic leader of Oneida, believed that American society's commitment to private property made people greedy and selfish. Noyes claimed that the root of private property lay in marriage, in men's conviction that their wives were their exclusive property. Drawing from a substantial inheritance, Noyes organized the Oneida community in New York in 1848 to abolish marital property rights by permitting sexual intercourse between any consenting man and woman in the community. Noyes also required all members to relinquish their economic property to the community. Most of their neighbors considered Oneidans adulterers and blasphemers. Yet the practices that set Oneida apart from its mainstream neighbors strengthened the community, and it survived long after the Civil War.

> **CHRONOLOGY**

1840s
– Fourierist communities are founded.

1848
– Oneida community is organized.
– Seneca Falls convention.

1849
– Harriet Tubman escapes from slavery and becomes a leader of the underground railroad.

Oneida community
▶ Utopian community organized by John Humphrey Noyes in New York in 1848. Noyes's opposition to private property led him to denounce marriage as the root of the problem. The community embraced sexual and economic communalism, to the dismay of its mainstream neighbors.

What factors spurred westward expansion?

Why did the United States go to war with Mexico?

How did reform movements change after 1840?

Conclusion: How was white freedom in the West and North defined?

☑ LearningCurve
Check what you know.
bedfordstmartins.com
/roarkunderstanding

351

Woman's Rights Activists

Women participated in the many reform activities that grew out of evangelical churches. Women church members outnumbered men two to one and worked to put their religious ideas into practice by joining peace, temperance, antislavery, and other societies. Involvement in reform organizations gave a few women activists practical experience in such political arts as speaking in public, running a meeting, drafting resolutions, and circulating petitions.

In 1848, about three hundred reformers led by Elizabeth Cady Stanton and Lucretia Mott gathered at Seneca Falls, New York, for the first national woman's rights convention in the United States. As Stanton recalled, "The general discontent I felt with women's portion as wife, mother, housekeeper, physician, and spiritual guide, [and] the wearied anxious look of the majority of women impressed me with a strong feeling that some active measure should be taken to right the wrongs of society in general, and of women in particular." The **Seneca Falls Declaration of Sentiments** set an ambitious agenda to demand civil liberties for women and to right the wrongs of society. The declaration proclaimed that "the history of mankind is a history of repeated injuries and usurpations on the part of man toward woman, having in direct object the establishment of an absolute tyranny over her." In the style of the Declaration of Independence (see appendix I, page A-1), the Seneca Falls declaration demanded that women "have immediate admission to all the rights and privileges which belong to them as citizens of the United States," particularly the "inalienable right to the elective franchise."

Nearly two dozen other woman's rights conventions assembled before 1860, repeatedly calling for suffrage and an end to discrimination against women. But women had difficulty receiving a respectful hearing, much less achieving legislative action. Even so, the Seneca Falls declaration served as a pathbreaking

Seneca Falls Declaration of Sentiments

▶ Declaration issued in 1848 at the first national woman's rights convention in the United States, which was held in Seneca Falls, New York. The document adopted the style of the Declaration of Independence and demanded equal rights for women, including the franchise.

Bloomers and Woman's Emancipation

This 1851 British cartoon lampoons bloomers, the trouserlike garment worn beneath shortened skirts by two cigar-smoking American women. Bloomers were invented in the United States as an alternative to the uncomfortable, confining, and awkward dresses worn by the "respectable" women on the right. In the 1850s, Elizabeth Cady Stanton and other woman's rights activists wore bloomers and urged all American women to do likewise. Miriam and Ira D. Wallach Division of Art, Prints, and Photographs, The New York Public Library. Astor, Lenox, and Tilden Foundations.

BLOOMERISM—AN AMERICAN CUSTOM.

CHAPTER LOCATOR | What factors contributed to the United States' "industrial evolution"? | How did the free-labor ideal account for economic inequality?

352 CHAPTER 12 THE NEW WEST AND THE FREE NORTH

manifesto of dissent against male supremacy and of support for woman suffrage, and it inspired many women to challenge the barriers that limited their opportunities.

Stanton and other activists sought fair pay and expanded employment opportunities for women by appealing to free-labor ideology. Woman's rights advocate Paula Wright Davis urged Americans to stop discriminating against able and enterprising women: "Let [women] . . . open a Store, . . . learn any of the lighter mechanical Trades, . . . study for a Profession, . . . be called to the lecture-room, [and] . . . the Temperance rostrum . . . [and] let her be appointed [to serve in the Post Office]." Some women pioneered in these and many other occupations during the 1840s and 1850s. Woman's rights activists also succeeded in protecting married women's rights to their own wages and property in New York in 1860. But discrimination against women persisted, as most men believed that free-labor ideology required no compromise of male supremacy.

Abolitionists and the American Ideal

During the 1840s and 1850s, abolitionists continued to struggle to draw the nation's attention to the plight of slaves and the need for emancipation. Former slaves Frederick Douglass, Henry Bibb, and Sojourner Truth lectured to reform audiences throughout the North about the cruelties of slavery. Abolitionists published newspapers, held conventions, and petitioned Congress, but they never attracted a mass following among white Americans. Many white Northerners became convinced that slavery was wrong, but they still believed that blacks were inferior. Many other white Northerners shared the common view of white Southerners that slavery was necessary and even desirable. The westward extension of the nation during the 1840s offered abolitionists an opportunity to link their unpopular ideal to a goal that many white Northerners found much more attractive — limiting the geographic expansion of slavery, an issue that moved to the center of national politics during the 1850s (as discussed in chapter 14).

Black leaders rose to prominence in the abolitionist movement during the 1840s and 1850s. African Americans had actively opposed slavery for decades, but a new generation of leaders came to the forefront in these years. Frederick Douglass, Henry Highland Garnet, William Wells Brown, Martin R. Delany, and others became impatient with white abolitionists' appeals to the conscience of the white majority. To express their own uncompromising ideas, black abolitionists founded their own newspapers and held their own antislavery conventions, although they still cooperated with sympathetic whites.

The commitment of black abolitionists to battling slavery grew out of their own experiences with white supremacy. The 250,000 free African Americans in the North and West constituted less than 2 percent of the total population in 1860. They confronted the humiliations of racial discrimination in nearly every arena of daily life. Only Maine, Massachusetts, New Hampshire, and Vermont permitted black men to vote; New York imposed a special property-holding requirement on black — but not white — voters, effectively excluding most black men from the franchise. The pervasive racial discrimination both handicapped and energized black abolitionists. Some cooperated with the efforts of the **American Colonization Society** to send freed slaves and other black Americans to Liberia in West Africa. Others sought to move to Canada, Haiti, or elsewhere. Most black

American Colonization Society

▶ An organization dedicated to sending freed slaves and other black Americans to Liberia in West Africa. Although some African Americans cooperated with the movement, others campaigned against segregation and discrimination.

What factors spurred westward expansion? | Why did the United States go to war with Mexico? | **How did reform movements change after 1840?** | Conclusion: How was white freedom in the West and North defined? | ✓ LearningCurve Check what you know. bedfordstmartins.com /roarkunderstanding

353

American leaders refused to embrace emigration and worked against racial prejudice in their own communities, organizing campaigns against segregation, particularly in transportation and education. Their most notable success came in 1855 when Massachusetts integrated its public schools. Elsewhere, white supremacy continued unabated.

Outside the public spotlight, free African Americans in the North and West contributed to the antislavery cause by quietly aiding fugitive slaves. Harriet Tubman escaped from slavery in Maryland in 1849 and repeatedly risked her freedom and her life to return to the South to escort slaves to freedom. When the opportunity arose, free blacks in the North provided fugitive slaves with food, a safe place to rest, and a helping hand. An outgrowth of the antislavery sentiment and opposition to white supremacy that unified nearly all African Americans in the North, this **underground railroad** ran mainly through black neighborhoods, black churches, and black homes.

underground railroad
► Network consisting mainly of black homes, black churches, and black neighborhoods that helped slaves escape to the North by supplying shelter, food, and general assistance.

> ## QUICK REVIEW

Why were women especially prominent in many nineteenth-century reform efforts?

CHAPTER LOCATOR | What factors contributed to the United States' "industrial evolution"? | How did the free-labor ideal account for economic inequality?

354 CHAPTER 12 THE NEW WEST AND THE FREE NORTH

Conclusion: How was white freedom in the West and North defined?

DURING THE 1840S AND 1850S, a cluster of interrelated developments — population growth, steam power, railroads, and the growing mechanization of agriculture and manufacturing — meant greater economic productivity, a burst of output from farms and factories, and prosperity for many. Diplomacy with Great Britain and war with Mexico handed the United States 1.2 million square miles and more than 1,000 miles of Pacific coastline. One prize of manifest destiny, California, almost immediately rewarded its new owners with tons of gold. Most Americans believed that the new territory and vast riches were appropriate rewards for the nation's stunning economic progress and superior institutions.

To Northerners, industrial evolution confirmed the choice they had made to eliminate slavery and promote free labor as the key to independence, equality, and prosperity. Like Abraham Lincoln, millions of Americans could point to their personal experiences as evidence of the practical truth of the free-labor ideal. But millions of others knew that in the free-labor system, poverty and wealth continued to rub shoulders. Free-labor enthusiasts denied that the problems were inherent in the country's social and economic systems. Instead, they argued, most social ills — including poverty and dependency — sprang from individual deficiencies. Consequently, many reformers focused on personal self-control and discipline, on avoiding sin and alcohol. Other reformers focused on woman's rights and the abolition of slavery. They challenged widespread conceptions of male supremacy and black inferiority, but neither group managed to overcome the prevailing free-labor ideology based on individualism, racial prejudice, and notions of male superiority.

By midcentury, half of the nation had prohibited slavery, and half permitted it. The North and the South were animated by different economic interests, cultural values, and political aims. Each celebrated its regional identity and increasingly disparaged that of the other. Not even the victory over Mexico could bridge the deepening divide between North and South.

| What factors spurred westward expansion? | Why did the United States go to war with Mexico? | How did reform movements change after 1840? | **Conclusion: How was white freedom in the West and North defined?** | ✔ **LearningCurve** Check what you know. bedfordstmartins.com /roarkunderstanding |

355

CHAPTER 12 STUDY GUIDE

STEP 1 **GET STARTED ONLINE**

✓ **LearningCurve** ■ bedfordstmartins.com/roarkunderstanding

Now that you've read the chapter, make it stick by completing the LearningCurve activity.

STEP 2 **EXPLAIN WHY IT MATTERS**

Put your reading into practice. Identify each term below, and then explain why it matters in U.S. history.

TERM	WHO OR WHAT & WHEN	WHY IT MATTERS
mechanical reapers (p. 329)		
American system (p. 329)		
manifest destiny (p. 337)		
Oregon Trail (p. 337)		
Mormons (p. 339)		
Lone Star Republic (p. 341)		
Treaty of Guadalupe Hidalgo (p. 346)		
California gold rush (p. 347)		
Oneida community (p. 351)		
Seneca Falls Declaration of Sentiments (p. 352)		
American Colonization Society (p. 353)		
underground railroad (p. 354)		

STEP 3 **MOVE BEYOND THE BASICS**

To demonstrate a more advanced understanding, assess the key economic developments described in the chapter and their contributions to industrialization. How did agriculture and manufacturing benefit and complement each other?

	Key developments	Consequences/who benefited
Agricultural technology		
Federal land policy		
Mechanization and energy sources		
Railroads		

PUT IT ALL TOGETHER

Now, take a step back and try to explain the big picture. Remember to use specific examples from the chapter in your answers.

INDUSTRIAL DEVELOPMENT AND WESTWARD EXPANSION

▶ What were the social consequences of American industrial development in the first half of the nineteenth century?

▶ What role did American nationalism and economic opportunity play in promoting westward expansion?

THE MEXICAN-AMERICAN WAR

▶ Where was support for war with Mexico strongest? Where was there the least support? Why?

▶ How did victory in the Mexican-American War contribute to rising tensions over slavery?

REFORM

▶ What common concerns linked the reform movements of the 1840s and 1850s?

▶ What role did women play in reform movements in the decades before the Civil War?

LOOKING BACKWARD, LOOKING AHEAD

▶ How had America's economy and society changed between 1800 and 1860?

▶ How did American expansion and industrial development contribute to the sectional conflicts that culminated in the Civil War?

> ## IN YOUR OWN WORDS

Imagine that you must give an oral report to the class answering the following question: **How was freedom defined in the North and West in the mid-nineteenth century?** What would be the most important points to include and why?

 Do it online at the Student Site ■ bedforstmartins.com/roarkunderstanding

13

UNDERSTANDING THE SLAVE SOUTH

1820–1860

> **How did slavery shape the institutions and values of the antebellum South?** Chapter 13 explores the emergence and development of a distinctive slave society in the American South. It examines the causes and consequences of the divergence of North and South, the social world of the plantation, and the lives of nonslaveholding whites and free blacks. Finally, it assesses the impact of slavery on southern politics.

LearningCurve
bedfordstmartins.com/roarkunderstanding
After reading the chapter, use LearningCurve to retain what you've read.

Slave quarter. This early photograph depicts a slave family in Savannah, Georgia, ca. 1860. Collection of the New-York Historical Society.

> Why did the South become so distinctly different from the North?

> What was plantation life like for masters and mistresses?

> What was plantation life like for slaves?

> How did nonslaveholding southern whites work and live?

> What place did free blacks occupy in the South?

> How did slavery shape southern politics?

> Conclusion: How did slavery come to define the South?

> Why did the South become so distinctly different from the North?

Steamboats and Cotton in New Orleans, circa 1858

Smokestacks of dozens of steamboats overlook hundreds of bales of cotton at the foot of Canal Street. This photograph by Jay Dearborn Edwards captures something of the magnitude of the cotton trade in the South's largest city and major port. Few Southerners doubted that cotton was king. Historic New Orleans Collection.

FROM THE EARLIEST SETTLEMENTS, inhabitants of the southern colonies had shared a great deal with northern colonists. Most whites in both sections were British and Protestant, spoke a common language, and celebrated their victorious revolution against British rule. The creation of the new nation under the Constitution in 1789 forged political ties that bound all Americans. The beginnings of a national economy fostered economic interdependence and communication across regional boundaries. White Americans everywhere praised the prosperous young nation, and they looked forward to its seemingly boundless future.

Despite these national similarities, Southerners and Northerners grew increasingly different. The French political observer Alexis de Tocqueville believed he knew why. "I could easily prove," he asserted in 1831, "that almost all the differences which may be noticed between the character of the Americans in the Southern and Northern states have originated in slavery." Slavery made the South different, and it was the differences between the North and South, not the similarities, that increasingly shaped antebellum American history.

CHAPTER LOCATOR | **Why did the South become so distinctly different from the North?** | What was plantation life like for masters and mistresses?

Cotton Kingdom, Slave Empire

In the first half of the nineteenth century, millions of Americans migrated west. In the South, hard-driving slaveholders seeking virgin acreage for new plantations, ambitious farmers looking for patches of cheap land for small farms, striving herders and drovers pushing their hogs and cattle toward fresh pastures — everyone felt the pull of western land.

But more than anything it was cotton that propelled Southerners westward. South of the **Mason-Dixon line**, climate and geography were ideally suited for the cultivation of cotton. By the 1830s, cotton fields stretched from the Atlantic seaboard to central Texas. Heavy migration led to statehood for Arkansas in 1836 and for

Mason-Dixon line

▶ A surveyors' mark that had established the boundary between Maryland and Pennsylvania in colonial times. By the 1830s, the boundary divided the free North and the slave South.

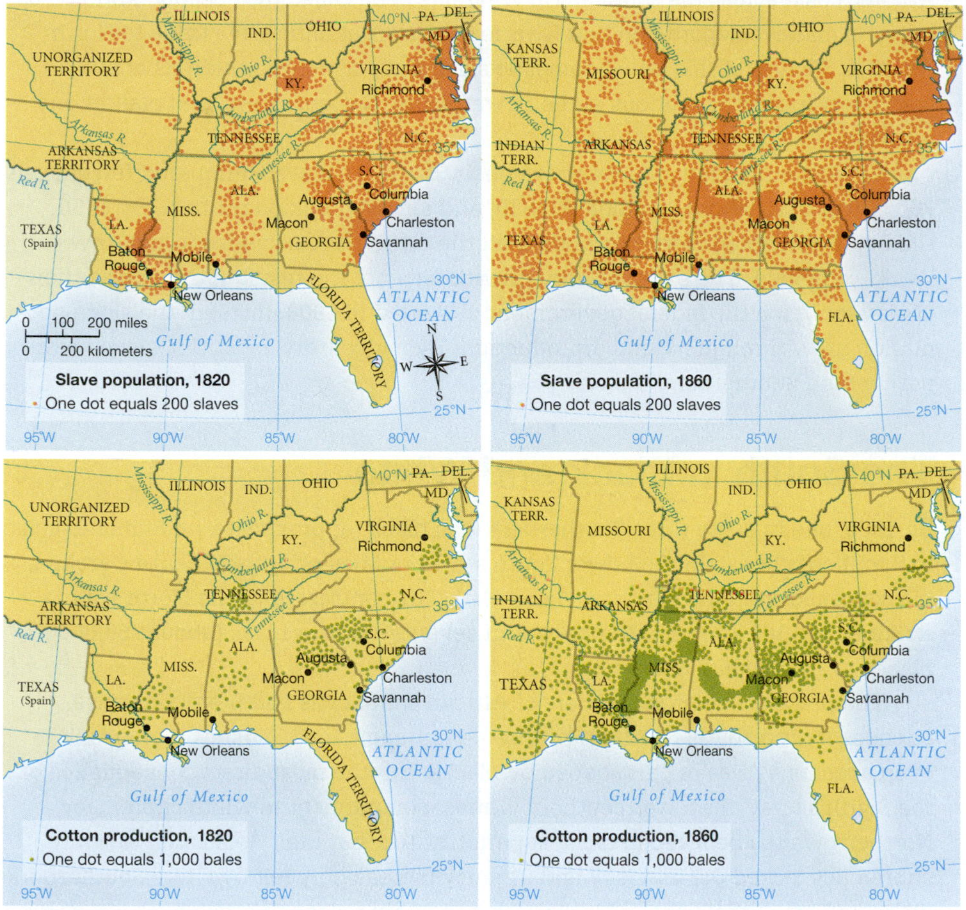

MAP 13.1 ■ Cotton Kingdom, Slave Empire: 1820 and 1860

As the production of cotton soared, the slave population increased dramatically. Slaves continued to toil in tobacco and rice fields, but in Alabama, Mississippi, and Texas, they increasingly worked on cotton plantations.

> MAP ACTIVITY

READING THE MAP: Where was slavery most prevalent in 1820? In 1860? How did the spread of slavery compare with the spread of cotton?

CONNECTIONS: How much of the world's cotton was produced in the American South in 1860? How did the number of slaves in the American South compare with that in the rest of the world? What does this suggest about the South's cotton kingdom?

| What was plantation life like for slaves? | How did nonslaveholding southern whites work and live? | What place did free blacks occupy in the South? | How did slavery shape southern politics? | Conclusion: How did slavery come to define the South? | ✔ **LearningCurve** Check what you know. bedfordstmartins.com /roarkunderstanding |

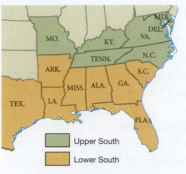

Upper South

Lower South

The Upper and Lower South

(**Map 13.1**, page 361).

Texas and Florida in 1845. Cotton production soared to nearly 5 million bales in 1860, when the South produced three-fourths of the world's supply. The South — especially that tier of states from South Carolina west to Texas called the Lower South — had become the **cotton kingdom** (**Map 13.1**, page 361).

The cotton kingdom was also a slave empire. The South's cotton boom rested on the backs of slaves. As cotton agriculture expanded westward, whites shipped more than a million enslaved men, women, and children from the Atlantic coast across the continent in what has been called the "Second Middle Passage," a massive deportation that dwarfed the transatlantic slave trade to North America. Victims of this brutal domestic slave trade marched hundreds of miles southwest to new plantations in the Lower South. Cotton, slaves, and plantations moved west together.

The slave population grew enormously. Southern slaves numbered fewer than 700,000 in 1790, about 2 million in 1830, and almost 4 million by 1860. By 1860, the South contained more slaves than all the other slave societies in the New World combined. The extraordinary growth was not the result of the importation of slaves, which the federal government outlawed in 1808. Instead, the slave population grew through natural reproduction; by midcentury, most U.S. slaves were native-born Southerners.

cotton kingdom

▶ Term for the South that reflected the dominance of cotton in the southern economy. Cotton was particularly important in the tier of states from South Carolina west to Texas. Cotton cultivation was the key factor in the growth of slavery.

The South in Black and White

By 1860, one in every three Southerners was black (approximately 4 million blacks to 8 million whites). In the Lower South states of Mississippi and South Carolina, blacks constituted the majority (**Figure 13.1**). The contrast with the North was striking: In 1860, only one Northerner in seventy-six was black (about 250,000 blacks to 19 million whites).

The presence of large numbers of African Americans had profound consequences for the South. Southern culture — language, food, music, religion, and even accents — was in part shaped by blacks. But the most direct consequence of the South's biracialism was southern whites' commitment to white supremacy. Northern whites believed in racial superiority, too, but their dedication to white supremacy lacked the intensity and urgency increasingly felt by white Southerners who lived among millions of blacks who had every reason to strike back.

After 1820, attacks on slavery — from slaves and from northern abolitionists — caused white Southerners to make extraordinary efforts to strengthen slavery. State legislatures constructed **slave codes** (laws) that required the total submission of slaves. As the Louisiana code stated, a slave "owes his master . . . a respect without bounds, and an absolute obedience." The laws also underlined the authority of all whites, not just masters. Any white could "correct" slaves who did not stay "in their place."

Intellectuals joined legislators in the campaign to strengthen slavery. The South's academics, writers, and clergy employed every imaginable defense. They

slave codes

▶ Laws enacted in southern states in the 1820s and 1830s that required the total submission of slaves. Attacks by antislavery activists and by slaves convinced southern legislators that they had to do everything in their power to strengthen the institution of slavery.

CHAPTER LOCATOR | **Why did the South become so distinctly different from the North?** | What was plantation life like for masters and mistresses?

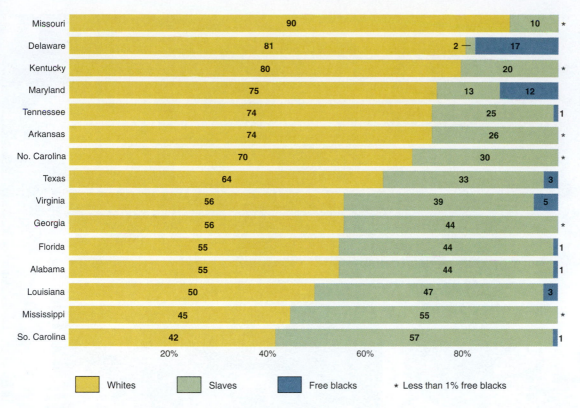

Missouri	90		10	*
Delaware	81		2 —	17
Kentucky	80		20	*
Maryland	75		13	12
Tennessee	74		25	1
Arkansas	74		26	*
No. Carolina	70		30	*
Texas	64		33	3
Virginia	56		39	5
Georgia	56		44	*
Florida	55		44	1
Alabama	55		44	1
Louisiana	50		47	3
Mississippi	45		55	*
So. Carolina	42		57	1

20%   40%   60%   80%

☐ Whites   ☐ Slaves   ☐ Free blacks   * Less than 1% free blacks

FIGURE 13.1 ■ Black and White Populations in the South, 1860

Blacks represented a much larger fraction of the population in the South than in the North, but considerable variation existed from state to state. Only one Missourian in ten, for example, was black, while Mississippi and South Carolina had black majorities. States in the Upper South were "whiter" than states in the Lower South, despite the Upper South's greater number of free blacks.

argued that slaves were legal property, and wasn't the protection of property the bedrock of American liberty? History also endorsed slavery, they claimed. Weren't the great civilizations — such as those of the Hebrews, Greeks, and Romans — slave societies? They argued that the Bible, properly interpreted, also sanctioned slavery. Old Testament patriarchs owned slaves, they observed, and in the New Testament, Paul returned the runaway slave Onesimus to his master. Proslavery spokesmen claimed that the freeing of slaves would lead to the sexual mixing of the races, or **miscegenation**.

George Fitzhugh of Virginia defended slavery by attacking the North's free-labor economy and society. Gouging capitalists exploited wageworkers unmercifully, Fitzhugh declared, and he contrasted the North's vicious free-labor system with the humane relations that he said prevailed between masters and slaves because slaves were valuable capital that masters sought to protect. John C. Calhoun, an influential southern politician, declared that in the states where slavery had been abolished, "the condition of the African, instead of being improved, has become worse," while in the slave states, the Africans "have improved greatly in every respect."

But at the heart of the defense of slavery lay the claim of black inferiority. Black enslavement was both necessary and proper, slavery's defenders argued, because Africans were lesser beings. Rather than exploitative, slavery was a mass civilizing

miscegenation

▶ Interracial sex. Proslavery spokesmen played on the fears of whites when they suggested that giving blacks equal rights would lead to miscegenation. In reality, slavery led to considerable sexual abuse of black women by their white masters.

What was plantation life like for slaves?	How did nonslaveholding southern whites work and live?	What place did free blacks occupy in the South?	How did slavery shape southern politics?	Conclusion: How did slavery come to define the South?	☑ LearningCurve Check what you know. bedfordstmartins.com /roarkunderstanding

THE FRUITS OF AMALGAMATION.

The Fruits of Amalgamation

In this lithograph from 1839, Edward W. Clay of Philadelphia attacked abolitionists by imagining the miscegenation (also known as "amalgamation") that would come from emancipation. He drew a beautiful white woman, her two biracial children, and her dark-skinned, ridiculously overdressed husband, resting his feet in his wife's lap. Courtesy, American Antiquarian Society.

effort that lifted lowly blacks from barbarism and savagery, taught them disciplined work, and converted them to soul-saving Christianity. According to Virginian Thomas R. Dew, most slaves were grateful. He declared that "the slaves of a good master are his warmest, most constant, and most devoted friends."

African slavery encouraged southern whites to unify around race rather than to divide by class. The grubbiest, most tobacco-stained white man could proudly proclaim his superiority to all blacks and his equality with the most refined southern planter. Georgia attorney Thomas R. R. Cobb observed that every white Southerner "feels that he belongs to an elevated class. It matters not that he is no slaveholder; he is not of the inferior race; he is a freeborn citizen." Consequently, the "poorest meets the richest as an equal; sits at his table with him; salutes him as a neighbor; meets him in every public assembly, and stands on the same social platform." In the South, Cobb boasted, "there is no war of classes." By providing every white Southerner membership in the ruling race, slavery helped whites bridge differences in wealth, education, and culture.

CHAPTER LOCATOR | **Why did the South become so distinctly different from the North?** | What was plantation life like for masters and mistresses?

The Plantation Economy

As important as slavery was in unifying white Southerners, only about a quarter of the white population lived in slaveholding families. Most slaveholders owned fewer than five slaves. Only about 12 percent of slaveholders owned twenty or more, the number of slaves that historians consider necessary to distinguish a **planter** from a farmer. Despite their small numbers, planters dominated the southern economy. In 1860, 52 percent of the South's slaves lived and worked on **plantations**. Plantation slaves produced more than 75 percent of the South's export crops, the backbone of the region's economy.

The South's major cash crops — tobacco, sugar, rice, and cotton — grew on plantations (**Map 13.2**). Tobacco, the original plantation crop in North America, had

planter

▶ A substantial landowner who tilled his estate with twenty or more slaves. Planters dominated the social and political world of the South. Their values and ideology influenced the values of all southern whites.

plantation

▶ A large farm worked by twenty or more slaves. Although small farms were more numerous, plantations produced more than 75 percent of the South's export crops.

MAP 13.2 ■ The Agricultural Economy of the South, 1860

Cotton dominated the South's agricultural economy, but the region grew a variety of crops and was largely self-sufficient in foodstuffs.

> MAP ACTIVITY

READING THE MAP: In what type of geographic areas were rice and sugar grown? After cotton, what crop commanded the greatest agricultural area in the South? In which region of the South was this crop predominantly found?

CONNECTIONS: What role did the South play in the U.S. economy in 1860? How did the economy of the South differ from that of the North?

| What was plantation life like for slaves? | How did nonslaveholding southern whites work and live? | What place did free blacks occupy in the South? | How did slavery shape southern politics? | Conclusion: How did slavery come to define the South? | ✓ LearningCurve Check what you know. bedfordstmartins.com /roarkunderstanding |

shifted westward in the nineteenth century from the Chesapeake to Tennessee and Kentucky. Large-scale sugar production began in 1795, when Étienne de Boré built a modern sugar mill in what is today New Orleans, and sugar plantations were confined almost entirely to Louisiana. Commercial rice production began in the seventeenth century, and like sugar, rice was confined to a small geographic area, a narrow strip of coast stretching from the Carolinas into Georgia.

But by the nineteenth century, cotton reigned as king of the South's plantation crops. Cotton became commercially significant in the 1790s after the invention of a new cotton gin by Eli Whitney (see chapter 9). Cotton was relatively easy to grow and took little capital to get started — just enough for land, seed, and simple tools. Thus, small farmers as well as planters grew cotton. But planters, whose extensive fields were worked by gangs of slaves, produced three-quarters of the South's cotton, and cotton made planters rich.

Plantation slavery also enriched the nation. By 1840, cotton accounted for more than 60 percent of American exports. Most of the cotton was shipped to Great Britain, the world's largest manufacturer of cotton textiles. Much of the profit from the sale of cotton overseas returned to planters, but some went to northern middlemen who bought, sold, insured, warehoused, and shipped cotton to the mills in Great Britain. As one New York merchant observed, "Cotton has enriched all through whose hands it has passed." As middlemen invested their profits in the booming northern economy, industrial development received a burst of much-needed capital. Furthermore, southern plantations benefited northern industry by providing an important market for textiles, agricultural tools, and other manufactured goods.

The Cotton Gin

Machines for separating cotton fibers from seeds that clung to the fiber — cotton gins (the word *gin* is short for *engine*) — had been around for centuries, but none cleaned cotton quickly and efficiently. In 1793, Eli Whitney, a young New Englander living on a Georgia plantation, built a simple little device that was crude but effective. Smithsonian Institution, National Museum of American History, Behring Center.

The economies of the North and South steadily diverged. While the North developed a mixed economy — agriculture, commerce, and manufacturing — the South remained overwhelmingly agricultural. Year after year, planters funneled the profits they earned from land and slaves back into more land and more slaves. With its capital flowing into agriculture, the South did not develop many factories. By 1860, only 10 percent of the nation's industrial workers lived in the South. Some cotton mills sprang up, but the region that produced 100 percent of the nation's cotton manufactured less than 7 percent of its cotton textiles.

Without significant economic diversification, the South developed fewer cities than did the North and West. In 1860, it was the least urban region in the country. Whereas nearly

37 percent of New England's population lived in cities, less than 12 percent of Southerners were urban dwellers. Because the South had so few cities and industrial jobs, it attracted small numbers of European immigrants. Seeking economic opportunity, not competition with slaves (whose labor would keep wages low), immigrants steered northward. In 1860, 13 percent of all Americans were born abroad. But in nine of the fifteen slave states, only 2 percent or less of the population was foreign-born.

Northerners claimed that slavery was a backward labor system, and compared with Northerners, Southerners invested less of their capital in industry, transportation, and public education. But planters' pockets were never fuller than in the 1850s. Planters' decisions to reinvest in agriculture ensured the momentum of the plantation economy and the political and social relationships rooted in it.

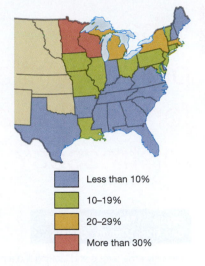

Less than 10%

10–19%

20–29%

More than 30%

Immigrants as a Percentage of State Populations, 1860

QUICK REVIEW

Why did the nineteenth-century southern economy remain primarily agricultural?

| What was plantation life like for slaves? | How did nonslaveholding southern whites work and live? | What place did free blacks occupy in the South? | How did slavery shape southern politics? | Conclusion: How did slavery come to define the South? | ✓ **LearningCurve** Check what you know. bedfordstmartins.com /roarkunderstanding |

What was plantation life like for masters and mistresses?

Southern Man with Children and Their Mammy

Obviously prosperous and looking like a man accustomed to giving orders and being obeyed, this patriarch poses around 1848 with his young daughters and their nurse. The absent mother may be dead, and her death might account for the inclusion of the African American domestic servant in the family circle. Collection of the J. Paul Getty Museum, Malibu, CA.

NOWHERE WAS THE CONTRAST between northern and southern life more vivid than on the plantations of the South. A plantation typically included a "big house," where the plantation owner and his family lived, and a slave quarter. Near the big house were the kitchen, storehouse, smokehouse (for curing and preserving meat), and hen coop. More distant were the barns, toolsheds, artisans' workshops, and overseer's house. Large plantations sometimes had an infirmary and a chapel for slaves. Depending on the crop, there was also a tobacco shed, a rice mill, a sugar refinery, or a cotton gin house. Lavish or plain, plantations everywhere had an underlying similarity (**Figure 13.2**).

The plantation was the home of masters, mistresses, and slaves. A hierarchy of rigid roles and duties governed their relationships. Presiding was the master, who by law ruled his wife, children, and slaves as dependents under his dominion and protection.

Paternalism and Male Honor

Whereas smaller planters supervised the labor of their slaves themselves, larger planters hired overseers who went to the fields with the slaves, leaving the planters free to concentrate on marketing, finance, and the general affairs of the plantation. Planters also found time to escape to town to discuss cotton prices, to the courthouse and legislature to debate politics, and to the woods to hunt and fish.

Increasingly, planters characterized their mastery in terms of what they called "Christian guardianship" and what historians have called **paternalism**. The concept of paternalism denied that the form of slavery practiced in the South was brutal and exploitative. Instead, paternalism claimed that plantations benefited all. In exchange for the slaves' work and obedience, masters provided basic care and necessary guidance for a childlike, dependent people. In 1814, Thomas Jefferson captured the essence of the advancing ideal: "We should endeavor, with those whom fortune has thrown on our

paternalism

▶ The theory of slavery that emphasized reciprocal duties and obligations between masters and their slaves, with slaves providing labor and obedience and masters providing basic care and direction. Whites employed the concept of paternalism to deny that the slave system was brutal and exploitative.

CHAPTER LOCATOR | Why did the South become so distinctly different from the North? | **What was plantation life like for masters and mistresses?**

hands, to feed & clothe them well, protect them from ill usage, require such reasonable labor only as is performed voluntarily by freemen, and be led by no repugnancies to abdicate them, and our duties to them." A South Carolina rice planter insisted, "I manage them as my children."

Paternalism was part propaganda and part self-delusion. But it was also economically shrewd. Masters increasingly recognized slaves as valuable assets, particularly after the nation closed its external slave trade in 1808 and the cotton boom stimulated the demand for slaves. The expansion of the slave labor force could come only from natural reproduction. As one slave owner declared in 1849, "It behooves those who own them to make them last as long as possible."

One consequence of paternalism and economic self-interest was a small improvement in slaves' welfare. Diet improved, although nineteenth-century slaves still ate mainly fatty pork and cornmeal. Housing improved, although the cabins still had cracks large enough, slaves said, for cats to slip through. Clothing improved, although slaves seldom received much more than two crude outfits a year and perhaps a pair of cheap shoes. Workdays remained sunup to sundown, but most planters ceased the colonial practice of punishing slaves by branding and mutilation.

Paternalism should not be mistaken for "Ol' Massa's" kindness and goodwill. It encouraged better treatment because it made economic sense to provide at least minimal care for valuable slaves. Nor did paternalism require that planters put aside their whips. State laws gave masters nearly "uncontrolled authority over the body" of the slave, according to one North Carolina judge, and whipping remained planters' basic form of coercion.

Paternalism never won universal acceptance among planters, but by the nineteenth century it had become a kind of communal standard. With its notion that slavery imposed on masters a burden and a duty, paternalism provided slaveholders with a means of rationalizing their rule. But it also provided some slaves with leverage in controlling the conditions of their lives. Slaves learned to manipulate the slaveholder's need to see himself as a good master. To avoid a reputation as a cruel tyrant, planters sometimes negotiated with slaves, rather than just resorting to the whip. Masters sometimes granted slaves small garden plots in which they could work for themselves after working all day in the fields, or they gave slaves a few days off and a dance when they had gathered the last of the cotton.

Virginia statesman Edmund Randolph argued that slavery created in white southern men a "quick and acute sense of personal liberty" and a "disdain for every abridgement of personal independence." Indeed, prickly individualism and aggressive independence became crucial features of the southern concept of honor. Social standing, political advancement, and even self-esteem rested on an honorable reputation. Defending honor became a male passion. Andrew Jackson's mother reportedly told her son, "Never tell a lie, nor take what is not your own, nor sue anybody for slander or assault and battery. *Always settle them cases yourself.*"

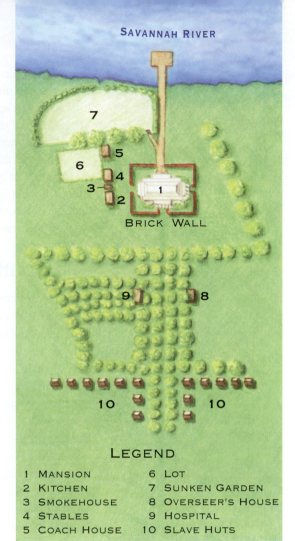

FIGURE 13.2 ■ A Southern Plantation

Slavery determined how masters laid out their plantations, where they situated their "big houses" and slave quarters, and what kinds of buildings they constructed. This model of the Hermitage, the mansion built in 1830 for Henry McAlpin, a Georgia rice planter, shows the overseer's house poised in a grove of oak trees halfway between the owner's mansion and the slave huts. The placement of the mansion at the end of an extended road leading up from the river underscored McAlpin's affluence and authority.

Adapted from *Back of the Big House: The Architecture of Plantation Slavery* by John Michael Vlach. Copyright © 1993 by the University of North Carolina Press. Reprinted with permission of the University of North Carolina Press. Original illustration property of the Historic American Buildings Survey, a division of the National Park Service.

| What was plantation life like for slaves? | How did nonslaveholding southern whites work and live? | What place did free blacks occupy in the South? | How did slavery shape southern politics? | Conclusion: How did slavery come to define the South? | ✓ LearningCurve Check what you know. bedfordstmartins.com /roarkunderstanding |

Plantation Masters
- Often characterized their roles in terms of paternalism.
- On larger plantations, hired overseers to supervise slaves in the field.
- Were increasingly interested in extending the lives of slave property.

Plantation Mistresses
- Were expected to conform to gender norms for white women.
- Lived within a system that both glorified and subordinated them.
- Lived privileged lives but also experienced disadvantages.

chivalry

▶ The South's romantic ideal of male-female relationships. Chivalry's underlying assumptions about the weakness of white women and the protective authority of men resembled the paternalistic defense of slavery.

Southerners also expected an honorable gentleman to be a proper patriarch. Nowhere in America was masculine power more accentuated. The master's absolute dominion sometimes led to miscegenation. Laws prohibited interracial sex, but as long as slavery gave white men extraordinary power, slave women were forced to submit to the sexual demands of the men who owned them.

In time, as the children of one elite family married the children of another, ties of blood and kinship, as well as ideology and economic interest, linked planters to one another. Aware of what they shared as slaveholders, planters worked together to defend their common interests. The values of the big house — slavery, honor, male domination — washed over the boundaries of plantations and flooded all of southern life.

The Southern Lady and Feminine Virtues

Like their northern counterparts, southern ladies were expected to possess the feminine virtues of piety, purity, chastity, and obedience within the context of marriage, motherhood, and domesticity. Countless toasts praised the southern lady as the perfect complement to her husband, the commanding patriarch. She was physically weak, "formed only for the less laborious occupations," and thus dependent on male protection. To gain this protection, she exhibited modesty and delicacy, possessed beauty and grace, and cultivated refinement and charm.

Chivalry — the South's romantic ideal of male-female relationships — glorified the lady while it subordinated her. Chivalry's underlying assumptions about the weakness of women and the protective authority of men resembled the paternalistic defense of slavery. Just as the slaveholder's mastery was written into law, so too were the paramount rights of husbands. Married women lost almost all their property rights to their husbands. Women throughout the nation found divorce difficult, but southern women found it almost impossible.

Daughters of planters confronted chivalry's demands at an early age. At their private boarding schools, they learned to be southern ladies, reading literature, learning languages, and studying the appropriate drawing-room arts. Elite women began courting young and married early. Kate Carney exaggerated only slightly when she despaired in her diary: "Today, I am seventeen, getting quite old, and am not married." Yet marriage meant turning their fates over to their husbands and making enormous efforts to live up to their region's lofty ideal.

Proslavery advocates claimed that slavery freed white women from drudgery. Surrounded "by her domestics," declared Thomas R. Dew, "she ceases to be a mere beast of burden" and "becomes the cheering and animating center of the family circle." In reality, however, having servants required the plantation mistress to work long hours. She managed the big house, directly supervising as many as a dozen slaves. But unlike her husband, the mistress had no overseer. All house servants answered directly to her. She assigned them tasks each morning, directed their work throughout the day, and punished them when she found fault.

Whereas masters used their status as slaveholders as a springboard into public affairs, mistresses' lives were circumscribed by the plantation. Masters left when they pleased, but mistresses needed chaperones to travel. When they could, they went to church, but women spent most days at home, where they often became lonely. In 1853, Mary Kendall wrote how much she enjoyed her sister's

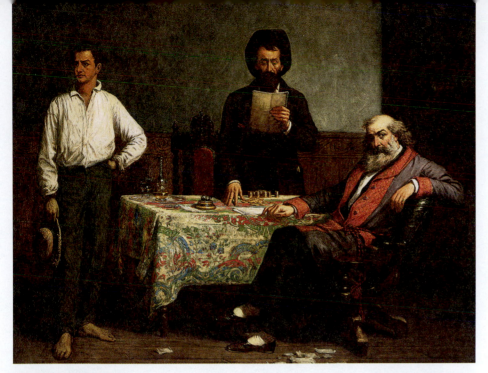

The Price of Blood This 1868 painting by T. S. Noble depicts a transaction between a slave trader and a rich planter. The trader nervously pretends to study the contract, while the planter waits impatiently for the completion of the sale. The planter's mulatto son, who is being sold, looks away. The children of white men and slave women were property and could be sold by the father/master. Morris Museum of Art, Augusta, GA.

> VISUAL ACTIVITY

READING THE IMAGE: Who is absent from the painting, and what does this suggest about the tragedy of miscegenation?
CONNECTIONS: The white male planter represented the pinnacle of southern society. How did white women, black men, and black women fit into this strict hierarchy?

letter: "For about three weeks I did not have the pleasure of seeing one white female face, there being no white family except our own upon the plantation."

No feature of plantation life generated more anguish among mistresses than miscegenation. Mary Boykin Chesnut of Camden, South Carolina, confided in her diary: "Ours is a monstrous system, a wrong and iniquity. Like the patriarchs of old, our men live all in one house with their wives and their concubines; and the mulattos one sees in every family partly resemble the white children. Any lady is ready to tell you who is the father of all the mulatto children in everybody's household but her own. Those, she seems to think drop from the clouds."

But most planters' wives, including Chesnut, accepted slavery. After all, the privileged life of a mistress rested on slave labor as much as a master's did. Mistresses enjoyed the rewards of their class and race. But these rewards came at a price. Still, the heaviest burdens of slavery fell not on those who lived in the big house, but on those who toiled to support them.

QUICK REVIEW <

Why did the ideology of paternalism gain currency among planters in the nineteenth century?

What was plantation life like for slaves?	How did nonslaveholding southern whites work and live?	What place did free blacks occupy in the South?	How did slavery shape southern politics?	Conclusion: How did slavery come to define the South?	✓ LearningCurve Check what you know. bedfordstmartins.com /roarkunderstanding

> What was plantation life like for slaves?

Slave Quarter, South Carolina

On large plantations, several score of African Americans lived in cabins that were often arranged along what slaves called "the street." The dwellings in this picture were better built than the typical rickety, one-room, dirt-floored slave cabin. During the daylight hours of the workweek, when most men and women labored in the fields, the quarter was mostly empty. At night and on Sundays, it was a busy place. Collection of the New-York Historical Society.

> KEY FACTORS

– An overwhelming majority of plantation slaves worked as field hands.
– Nine out of ten house slaves were women.
– Family and religion provided refuge for slaves.
– Slaves resisted by running away; outright rebellion was rare.

ON MOST PLANTATIONS, only a few hundred yards separated the big house and the slave quarter. But the distance was great enough to provide slaves with some privacy. Out of eyesight and earshot of the big house, slaves drew together and built lives of their own. They created families, worshipped God, and developed an African American community and culture. Individually and collectively, slaves found ways to resist their bondage.

Despite the rise of plantations, almost half of the South's slaves lived and worked elsewhere. Most labored on small farms, where they wielded a hoe alongside another slave or two and perhaps their master. But by 1860, almost half a million slaves (one in eight) did not work in agriculture at all. Some lived in towns and cities, where they worked as domestics, day laborers, bakers, barbers, tailors, and more. Other slaves, far from urban centers, toiled as fishermen, lumbermen, railroad workers, and deckhands on riverboats. Slaves could also be found in most of the South's factories. Nevertheless, a majority of slaves (52 percent) counted plantations as their workplaces and homes,

CHAPTER LOCATOR | Why did the South become so distinctly different from the North? | What was plantation life like for masters and mistresses?

Work

Whites enslaved blacks for their labor, and all slaves who were capable of productive labor worked. Former slave Carrie Hudson recalled that children who were "knee high to a duck" were sent to the fields to carry water to thirsty workers or to protect ripening crops from hungry birds. Others helped in the slave nursery, caring for children even younger than themselves, or in the big house, where they swept floors or shooed flies in the dining room. When slave boys and girls reached the age of eleven or twelve, masters sent most of them to the fields. After a lifetime of labor, old women left the fields to care for the small children and spin yarn, and old men moved on to mind livestock and clean stables.

The overwhelming majority of plantation slaves worked as field hands. Planters sometimes assigned men and women to separate gangs, the women working at lighter tasks and the men doing the heavy work of clearing and breaking the land. But women also did heavy work. "I had to work hard," Nancy Boudry remembered, and "plow and go and split wood just like a man." The backbreaking labor and the monotonous routines caused one ex-slave to observe that the "history of one day is the history of every day."

A few slaves (about one in ten) became house servants. Nearly all of those (nine out of ten) were women. They cooked, cleaned, babysat, washed clothes, and did the dozens of other tasks the master and mistress required. House servants were constantly on call, with no time that was entirely their own. Since no servant could please constantly, most bore the brunt of white frustration and rage. Ex-slave Jacob Branch of Texas remembered, "My poor mama! Every washday old Missy give her a beating."

Even rarer than house servants were skilled artisans. In the cotton South, no more than one slave in twenty (almost all men) worked in a skilled trade. Most were blacksmiths and carpenters, but slaves also worked as masons, mechanics, millers, and shoemakers. Skilled slave fathers took pride in teaching their crafts to their sons. "My pappy was one of the black smiths and worked in the shop," John Mathews remembered. "I had to help my pappy in the shop when I was a child and I learnt how to beat out the iron and make wagon tires, and make plows."

Isaac Jefferson

In this 1845 daguerreotype, seventy-year-old Isaac Jefferson proudly poses in the apron he wore while practicing his crafts as a tinsmith and nail maker. Isaac, his wife, and their two children, all slaves of Thomas Jefferson, were deeded to Jefferson's daughter Mary when she married in 1797. Isaac worked at Jefferson's home, Monticello, until 1820, when he moved to Petersburg, Virginia. When work was slow on the home plantation, slave owners often would hire out their skilled artisans to neighbors who needed a carpenter, blacksmith, mason, or tinsmith. Special Collections Department, University of Virginia Library.

What was plantation life like for slaves?

How did nonslaveholding southern whites work and live?

What place did free blacks occupy in the South?

How did slavery shape southern politics?

Conclusion: How did slavery come to define the South?

LearningCurve
Check what you know.
bedfordstmartins.com
/roarkunderstanding

Rarest of all slave occupations was that of slave driver. Probably no more than one male slave in a hundred worked in this capacity. These men were well named, for their primary task was driving other slaves to work harder in the fields. In some drivers' hands, the whip never rested. Ex-slave Jane Johnson of South Carolina called her driver the "meanest man, white or black, I ever see." But other drivers showed all the restraint they could. "Ole Gabe didn't like that whippin' business," West Turner of Virginia remembered. "When Marsa was there, he would lay it on 'cause he had to. But when old Marsa wasn't lookin', he never would beat them slaves."

Normally, slaves worked from what they called "can to can't," from "can see" in the morning to "can't see" at night. Even with a break at noon for a meal and rest, it made for a long day. For slaves, Lewis Young recalled, "work, work, work, 'twas all they do."

Family and Religion

From dawn to dusk, slaves worked for the master, but at night and all day Sunday and usually Saturday afternoon, slaves were left largely to themselves. Bone tired perhaps, they nonetheless used the time to develop and enjoy what mattered most to them.

Though severely battered, the black family survived slavery. Young men and women in the quarter fell in love, married, and set up housekeeping in cabins of their own. But no laws recognized slave marriage, and therefore no master was legally obligated to honor the bond. While plantation records show that some slave marriages were long-lasting, the massive deportation associated with the Second Middle Passage destroyed hundreds of thousands of slave families.

In 1858, a slave named Abream Scriven wrote to his wife, who lived on a neighboring plantation in South Carolina. "My dear wife," he began, "I take the pleasure of writing you . . . with much regret to inform you I am Sold to man by the name of Peterson, a Treader and Stays in New Orleans." Before he left for Louisiana, Scriven asked his wife to "give my love to my father and mother and tell them good Bye for me. And if we do not meet in this world I hope to meet in heaven. . . . My dear wife for you and my children my pen cannot express the griffe I feel to be parted from you all." He closed with words no master would have permitted in a slave's marriage vows: "I remain your truly husband until Death." The letter makes clear Scriven's love for his family; it also demonstrates slavery's massive assault on family life in the quarter.

Masters sometimes permitted slave families to work on their own, "overwork," as it was called. In the evenings and on Sundays, they tilled gardens, raised pigs and fowl, and chopped wood, selling the products in the market for a little pocket change. "Den each fam'ly have some chickens and sell dem and de eggs and maybe go huntin' and sell de hides and git some money," a former Alabama slave remembered. "Den us buy what am Sunday clothes with dat money, sech as hats and pants and shoes and dresses."

Religion also provided slaves with a refuge and a reason for living. In the nineteenth century, evangelical Baptists and Methodists had great success in converting slaves from their African beliefs. Planters promoted Christianity in the quarter because they believed that the slaves' salvation was part of the obligation of paternalism; they also hoped that religion would make slaves more obedient. South Carolina

CHAPTER LOCATOR | Why did the South become so distinctly different from the North? | What was plantation life like for masters and mistresses?

slaveholder Charles Colcock Jones, the leading missionary to the slaves, instructed them "to count their Masters 'worthy of all honour,' as those whom God has placed over them in this world." But slaves laughed up their sleeves at such messages. "That old white preacher just was telling us slaves to be good to our masters," one ex-slave said with a chuckle. "We ain't cared a bit about that stuff he was telling us 'cause we wanted to sing, pray, and serve God in our own way."

Meeting in their cabins or secretly in the woods, slaves created an African American Christianity that served their needs, not the masters'. Laws prohibited teaching slaves to read, but a few could read enough to struggle with the Bible. They interpreted the Christian message themselves. Rather than obedience, their faith emphasized justice. Slaves believed that God kept score and that the accounts of this world would be settled in the next. But the slaves' faith also spoke to their experiences in this world. In the Old Testament, they discovered Moses, who delivered his people from slavery, and in the New Testament, they found Jesus, who offered salvation to all. Jesus' message of equality provided a potent antidote to the planters' claim that blacks were an inferior people whom God condemned to slavery.

Christianity did not entirely drive out traditional African beliefs. Even slaves who were Christians sometimes continued to believe that conjurers, witches, and spirits possessed the power to injure and protect. Moreover, slaves' Christian music, preaching, and rituals reflected the influence of Africa, as did many of their secular activities, such as wood carving, quilt making, dancing, and storytelling. But by the mid-nineteenth century, black Christianity had assumed a central place in slaves' quest for freedom. In the words of one spiritual, "O my Lord delivered Daniel / O why not deliver me too?"

Resistance and Rebellion

Slaves did not suffer slavery passively. They were, as whites said, "troublesome property." Slaves understood that accommodation to what they could not change was the price of survival, but in a hundred ways they protested their bondage. Theoretically, the master was all-powerful and the slave powerless. But sustained by their families, religion, and community, slaves engaged in day-to-day resistance against their enslavers.

The spectrum of slave resistance ranged from mild to extreme. Telling a pointed story by the fireside in a slave cabin was probably the mildest form of protest. But when the weak got the better of the strong, as they did in tales of Br'er Rabbit and Br'er Fox (Br'er is a contraction of Brother), listeners could enjoy the thrill of a vicarious victory over their masters. Protest in the fields was riskier and included putting rocks in their cotton bags before having them weighed, feigning illness, and pretending to be so thickheaded that they could not understand the simplest instruction. Slaves broke so many hoes that owners outfitted the tools with oversized handles. Slaves so mistreated the work animals that masters switched from horses to mules, which could absorb more abuse. Although slaves worked hard in the master's fields, they also sabotaged his interests.

Running away was a common form of protest, but except along the borders with northern states and with Mexico, escape to freedom was almost impossible. Most runaways could hope only to escape for a few days. They sought temporary

| What was plantation life like for slaves? | How did nonslaveholding southern whites work and live? | What place did free blacks occupy in the South? | How did slavery shape southern politics? | Conclusion: How did slavery come to define the South? | ✓ LearningCurve Check what you know. bedfordstmartins.com /roarkunderstanding |

375

Horrid Massacre in Virginia

In August 1831, the slave Nat Turner led a bloody rebellion. Although the local militia quickly killed or captured all the rebels except Turner, rebelling slaves had slaughtered fifty-seven whites. When Turner was finally captured, he was tried, convicted, and executed. Although there was never another rebellion as deadly as Turner's, images of black violence continued to haunt white imaginations. Library of Congress.

respite from hard labor or avoided punishment, and their "lying out," as it was known, usually ended when the runaway, worn-out and ragged, gave up or was finally chased down by slave-hunting dogs.

Although resistance was common, outright rebellion — a violent assault on slavery by large numbers of slaves — was very rare. Conditions gave rebels almost no chance of success. By 1860, whites in the South outnumbered blacks two to one and were heavily armed. Moreover, communication between plantations was difficult, and the South provided little protective wilderness into which rebels could retreat and defend themselves.

Despite steady resistance and occasional rebellion, slaves did not have the power to end their bondage. Slavery thwarted their hopes and aspirations. It broke some and crippled others. But slavery's destructive power had to contend with the resiliency of the human spirit. Slaves fought back physically, culturally, and spiritually. Not only did they survive bondage, but they also created in the quarter a vibrant African American culture that buoyed them up during long hours in the fields and brought them joy and hope in the few hours they had to themselves.

> **QUICK REVIEW**

What types of resistance did slaves participate in, and why did slave resistance rarely take the form of rebellion?

CHAPTER LOCATOR | Why did the South become so distinctly different from the North? | What was plantation life like for masters and mistresses?

How did nonslaveholding southern whites work and live?

Gathering Corn in Virginia

In this romanticized agricultural scene, painter Felix O. C. Darley depicts members of a white farm family gathering its harvest by hand. In reality, growing corn was hard work. The artist, however, is less concerned with realism than with extolling rural family labor as virtuous and noble. Darley surrounds the southern yeomen with an aura of republican independence, dignity, and freedom. Warner Collection of Gulf States Paper Corporation.

MOST WHITES IN THE South did not own slaves, not even one. In 1860, more than six million of the South's eight million whites lived in slaveless households. Some nonslaveholding whites lived in cities and worked as artisans, mechanics, and traders. Others lived in the country and worked as storekeepers, parsons, and schoolteachers. But most "plain folk" were small farmers. Perhaps three out of four were **yeomen**, small farmers who owned their own land. As in the North, farm ownership provided a family with an economic foundation, social respectability, and political standing. Unlike their northern counterparts, however, southern yeomen lived in a region whose economy and society were increasingly dominated by unfree labor.

In an important sense, the South had more than one white yeomanry. The huge southern landscape provided space enough for two yeoman societies, separated roughly along geographic lines. Yeomen throughout the South had much in common, but the life of a small farm family in the cotton belt (the flatlands that spread from South Carolina to Texas) differed from the life of a family in the upcountry (the area of hills and mountains). And some rural slaveless whites were not yeomen; they owned no land at all and were sometimes desperately poor.

yeomen

▶ Farmers who owned and worked their own small plots of land. Yeomen living within the plantation belt were more dependent on planters than were yeomen in the upcountry, where small farmers dominated.

What was plantation life like for slaves?

How did nonslaveholding southern whites work and live?

What place did free blacks occupy in the South?

How did slavery shape southern politics?

Conclusion: How did slavery come to define the South?

☑ **LearningCurve** Check what you know. bedfordstmartins.com /roarkunderstanding

377

The Cotton Belt

plantation belt

▶ Flatlands that spread from South Carolina to east Texas and were dominated by large plantations.

Plantation-Belt Yeomen

Plantation-belt yeomen lived within the orbit of the planter class. Small farms outnumbered plantations in the **plantation belt**, but they were dwarfed in importance. Small farmers grew mainly food crops, particularly corn, and produced only a few 400-pound bales of cotton each year. Large planters measured their cotton crop in hundreds of bales. Small farmers' cotton tied them to planters. Unable to afford cotton gins or baling presses of their own, they relied on slave owners to gin and bale their cotton. With no link to merchants in the port cities, plantation-belt yeomen also turned to better-connected planters to ship and sell their cotton.

A network of relationships laced small farmers and planters together. Planters hired out surplus slaves to ambitious yeomen who wanted to expand cotton production. They sometimes chose overseers from among the sons of local farm families. Plantation mistresses occasionally nursed ailing neighbors. Family ties could span class lines, making planter and yeoman kin as well as neighbors. Yeomen helped police slaves by riding in slave patrols, which nightly scoured country roads to make certain that no slaves were moving about without permission. On Sundays, plantation dwellers and plain folk came together in church to worship.

Plantation-belt yeomen may have envied, and at times even resented, wealthy slaveholders, but small farmers learned to accommodate. Planters made accommodation easier by going out of their way to behave as good neighbors and avoid direct exploitation of slaveless whites in their community. As a consequence, rather than raging at the oppression of the planter regime, the typical plantation-belt yeoman sought entry into it. He dreamed of adding acreage to his farm, buying a few slaves of his own, and retiring from exhausting field work.

upcountry

▶ The hills and mountains of the South whose higher elevation, colder climate, rugged terrain, and poor transportation made the region less hospitable than the flatlands to slavery and large plantations.

Upcountry Yeomen

By contrast, the hills and mountains of the South resisted the spread of slavery and plantations. In the western parts of Virginia, North Carolina, and South Carolina; in northern Georgia and Alabama; and in eastern Tennessee and Kentucky, the higher elevation, colder climate, rugged terrain, and poor transportation made it difficult for commercial agriculture to make headway. As a result, yeomen dominated, and planters and slaves were scarce.

All members of the **upcountry** farm family worked, their tasks depending on their sex and age. Husbands labored in the fields, and with their sons they cleared, plowed, planted, and cultivated primarily food crops — corn, wheat, beans, sweet potatoes, and perhaps some fruit. Women and their daughters labored in and about the cabin. One upcountry farmer remembered that his mother "worked in the house cooking, spinning, weaving [and doing] patchwork." Women also tended the vegetable garden, kept a cow and some chickens, preserved food, cleaned their homes, fed their families, and cared for their children. Male and female tasks were equally crucial to the farm's success, but as in other white southern households, the male patriarch ruled the domestic sphere.

The typical upcountry yeoman also grew a little cotton or tobacco, but food production was more important than cash crops. Not much currency changed hands in the upcountry. Barter was common. A yeoman might trade his small

Upcountry of the South

CHAPTER LOCATOR | Why did the South become so distinctly different from the North? | What was plantation life like for masters and mistresses?

cotton or tobacco crop to a country store owner for a little salt, bullets, needles, and nails, or swap extra sweet potatoes for a plow from a blacksmith or for leather from a tanner. Networks of exchange and mutual assistance tied individual homesteads to the larger community. Farm families joined together in logrolling, house and barn raising, and cornhusking.

Even the hills had some plantations and slaves, but the few upcountry folks who owned slaves usually had only two or three. As a result, slaveholders had much less social and economic power, and yeomen had more. But the upcountry did not oppose slavery. As long as plain folk there were free to lead their own lives, they defended slavery and white supremacy just as staunchly as other white Southerners.

Poor Whites

The majority of nonslaveholding white Southerners were hardworking, landholding small farmers, but Northerners held a different image of this group. They believed that slavery had condemned most whites to poverty and backwardness. One antislavery advocate charged that the South harbored three classes: "the slaves on whom devolves all the regular industry, the slaveholders who reap all the fruits, and an idle and lawless rabble who live dispersed over vast plains little removed from absolute barbarism." Critics called this third class a variety of derogatory names: hillbillies, crackers, rednecks, and poor white trash. According to critics, poor whites were not just whites who were poor. They were also supposedly ignorant, diseased, and degenerate.

Contrary to northern opinion, only about one in four nonslaveholding rural white men was landless and very poor. Some worked as tenants, renting land and struggling to make a go of it. Others survived by herding pigs and cattle. And still others worked for meager wages, ditching, mining, logging, and laying track for railroads.

Some poor white men earned reputations for mayhem and violence. One visitor claimed that a "bowie-knife was a universal, and a pistol a not at all unusual companion." Edward Isham, an illiterate roustabout, spent about as much time fighting as he did working. When he wasn't engaged in ear-biting, eye-gouging free-for-alls, he gambled, drank, stole, had run-ins with the law, and in 1860 murdered a respected slaveholder, for which he was hanged.

Unlike Isham, most poor white men worked hard and dreamed of becoming yeomen. The Lipscomb family illustrates the possibility of upward mobility. In 1845, Smith and Sally Lipscomb and their children abandoned their worn-out land in South Carolina for Benton County, Alabama. "Benton is a mountainous country but ther is a heep of good levil land to tend in it," Smith wrote back to his brother. Alabama, Smith said, "will be better for the rising generation if not for ourselves but I think it will be the best for us all that live any length of time."

Because they had no money to buy land, they squatted on seven unoccupied acres. With the help of neighbors, they built a 22-by-24-foot cabin, a detached kitchen, and two stables. In the first year, Smith and his sons produced several bales of cotton and enough food for the table. The women worked just as hard in the cabin, and Sally contributed to the family's income by selling homemade shirts

What was plantation life like for slaves? | **How did nonslaveholding southern whites work and live?** | What place did free blacks occupy in the South? | How did slavery shape southern politics? | Conclusion: How did slavery come to define the South? | ✓ LearningCurve Check what you know. bedfordstmartins.com /roarkunderstanding

379

and socks. In time, the Lipscombs bought land and joined the Baptist church, completing their transformation to respectable yeomen.

Many poor whites succeeded in climbing the economic ladder, but in the 1850s upward mobility slowed. The cotton boom of that decade caused planters to expand their operations, driving the price of land beyond the reach of poor families. Whether they gained their own land or not, however, poor whites shared common cultural traits with yeoman farmers.

The Culture of the Plain Folk

The lives of most plain folk revolved around farms, family, a handful of neighbors, the local church, and perhaps a country store. Work occupied most hours, but plain folk still found time for pleasure. "Dancing they are all fond of," a visitor to North Carolina discovered, "especially when they can get a fiddle, or bagpipe." But the most popular pastimes of men and boys were fishing and hunting. A traveler in Mississippi recalled that his host sent "two of his sons, little fellows that looked almost too small to shoulder a gun," for food. "One went off towards the river and the other struck into the forest, and in a few hours we were feasting on delicious venison, trout and turtle."

Plain folk did not have much "book learning." Private academies charged fees that yeomen could not afford, and public schools were scarce. Although most people managed to pick up the "three R's," approximately one southern white man in five was illiterate in 1860, and the rate for white women was even higher. "People here prefer talking to reading," a Virginian remarked. Telling stories, reciting ballads, and singing hymns were important activities in yeoman culture.

Plain folk spent more hours in revival tents than in classrooms. Preachers spoke day and night to save souls. Baptists and Methodists adopted revivalism most readily and by midcentury had become the South's largest religious groups. By emphasizing free choice and individual worth, the plain folk's religion was hopeful and affirming. Hymns and spirituals provided guides to right and wrong — praising humility and steadfastness, condemning drunkenness and profanity. Above all, hymns spoke of the eventual release from worldly sorrows and the assurance of eternal salvation.

> **QUICK REVIEW**

Why did the lives of plantation-belt yeomen and upcountry yeomen diverge?

CHAPTER LOCATOR | Why did the South become so distinctly different from the North? | What was plantation life like for masters and mistresses?

CHAPTER 13

380 UNDERSTANDING THE SLAVE SOUTH

What place did free blacks occupy in the South?

Freedom Paper This legal document attests to the free status of the Reverend John F. Cook of Washington, D.C., his daughter Mary, and his son George. Cook was a free black man who kept his "freedom paper" in this watertight tin, which he probably carried with him at all times. Moorland-Spingarn Research Center, Howard University, Washington, D.C.

ALL WHITE SOUTHERNERS — slaveholders and slaveless alike — considered themselves superior to all blacks. But not every black Southerner was a slave. In 1860, some 260,000 (approximately 6 percent) of the region's 4.1 million African Americans were free. What is surprising is not that their numbers were small but that they existed at all. According to proslavery thinking, blacks were supposed to be slaves; only whites were supposed to be free. Blacks who were free stood out, and whites made them targets of oppression. But a few found success despite the restrictions placed on them by white Southerners.

Precarious Freedom

The population of **free blacks** swelled after the Revolutionary War, when the natural rights philosophy of the Declaration of Independence, the egalitarian message of evangelical Protestantism, and a depression in the tobacco economy led to a brief flurry of emancipation — the act of freeing a person from slavery. The soaring numbers of free blacks worried white Southerners, who, because of the cotton boom, wanted more slaves, not more blacks who were free.

free blacks

▶ African Americans who were not enslaved. Southern whites worried about the increasing numbers of free blacks. In the 1820s and 1830s, state legislatures stemmed the growth of the free black population and shrank the liberty of free blacks.

> CHRONOLOGY

1822
– Denmark Vesey is executed.

1820s–1830s
– Southern legislatures restrict free blacks.

1860
– Some 260,000 free blacks live in the South.

In the 1820s and 1830s, state legislatures stemmed the growth of the free black population and shrank the liberty of those blacks who had gained their freedom. New laws denied masters the right to free their slaves. Increasingly, whites subjected free blacks to the same laws as slaves. Free blacks could not testify under oath in a court of law or serve on juries. "Free negroes belong to a degraded caste of society," a South Carolina judge said in 1848. "They are in no respect on a perfect equality with the white man. . . . They ought, by law, to be compelled to demean themselves as inferiors."

> **Limits on Free Blacks**

- Subjected to special taxes.
- Prohibited from interstate travel.
- Denied the right to have schools.
- Denied the right to participate in politics.
- Required to carry "freedom papers" to prove they were not slaves.

Laws confined most free African Americans to poverty and dependence. Typically, free blacks were rural, uneducated, unskilled agricultural laborers and domestic servants who had to scramble to survive. Opportunities of any kind — for work, education, or community — were slim. Planters believed that free blacks set a bad example for slaves, subverting the racial subordination that was the essence of slavery.

Whites feared that free blacks might lead slaves in rebellion. In 1822, whites in Charleston accused Denmark Vesey, a free black carpenter, of conspiring with plantation slaves to slaughter Charleston's white inhabitants. The authorities rounded up scores of suspects, who, prodded by torture and the threat of death, implicated others in a "plot to riot in blood, outrage, and rapine." Although the city fathers never found any weapons and Vesey and most of the accused steadfastly denied the charges of conspiracy, officials hanged thirty-five black men, including Vesey, and banished another thirty-seven blacks from the state.

Achievement despite Restrictions

Despite increasingly harsh laws and stepped-up persecution, free African Americans made the most of the advantages their status offered. Unlike slaves, free blacks could legally marry and pass on their heritage of freedom to their children. Freedom also meant that they could choose occupations and own property. For most, however, these economic rights proved only theoretical, for a majority of the South's free blacks remained propertyless.

Still, some free blacks escaped the poverty and degradation whites thrust on them. Particularly in the South's cities, a free black elite emerged. Consisting of light-skinned African Americans, they worked at skilled trades, as tailors, carpenters, mechanics, and the like. They operated schools for their children and traveled in and out of their states, despite laws forbidding both activities. They worshipped

CHAPTER LOCATOR | Why did the South become so distinctly different from the North? | What was plantation life like for masters and mistresses?

382 CHAPTER 13 UNDERSTANDING THE SLAVE SOUTH

with whites (in separate seating) and lived scattered about in white neighborhoods, not in ghettos. And some owned slaves. Of the 3,200 black slaveholders (barely 1 percent of the free black population), most owned only a few family members whom they could not legally free. Others owned slaves in large numbers and exploited them for labor.

One such free black slave owner was William Ellison of South Carolina. Born a slave in 1790, Ellison bought his freedom in 1816 and set up business as a cotton gin maker, a trade he had learned as a slave. By 1835, he was prosperous enough to purchase the home of a former governor of the state. By the time of his death in 1861, he had become a cotton planter, with sixty-three slaves and an 800-acre plantation.

Most free blacks neither became slaveholders nor sought to raise a slave rebellion, as whites accused Denmark Vesey of doing. Rather, most free blacks simply tried to preserve their freedom, which was under increasing attack. Unlike blacks in the North whose freedom was secure, free blacks in the South clung to a precarious freedom by seeking to impress whites with their reliability, economic contributions, and good behavior.

QUICK REVIEW

Why did many state legislatures pass laws restricting free blacks' rights in the 1820s and 1830s?

| What was plantation life like for slaves? | How did nonslaveholding southern whites work and live? | **What place did free blacks occupy in the South?** | How did slavery shape southern politics? | Conclusion: How did slavery come to define the South? | ☑ LearningCurve Check what you know. bedfordstmartins.com /roarkunderstanding |

> How did slavery shape southern politics?

James Chesnut

James Chesnut came from a family with a large number of slaves and thus represents the power of slaveholders in southern politics. He served in the South Carolina state legislature for years before becoming a U.S. senator in 1858. He resigned in 1860 and became a colonel in the Confederate army during the Civil War. Courtesy of South Carolina Library, University of South Carolina, Columbia.

Gen. James Chesnut, Jr., C.S.A.

BY THE MID-NINETEENTH CENTURY, all southern white men — planters and plain folk — and no southern black men, even those who were free, could vote. The nonslaveholding white majority wielded less political power than their numbers indicated. The slaveholding white minority wielded more. With a well-developed sense of class interest, slaveholders engaged in party politics, campaigns, and officeholding, and as a result they received significant benefits from state governments. Nonslaveholding whites were concerned mainly with preserving their liberties and keeping their taxes low. They asked government for little of an economic nature, and they received little.

Slaveholders sometimes worried about nonslaveholders' loyalty to slavery, but most whites accepted the planters' argument that the existing social order served all Southerners' interests. Slavery rewarded every white man — no matter how poor — with membership in the South's white ruling race. It also provided the means by which nonslaveholders might someday advance into the ranks of the planters. White men in the South argued furiously about many things, but they agreed that they should take land from Indians, promote agriculture, uphold white supremacy and masculine privilege, and defend slavery from its enemies.

> KEY FACTORS

- Suffrage was extended throughout the South to all adult white males by 1850.
- Slaveholding white men were most active in politics and were far more likely to hold political office than those without slaves.

CHAPTER LOCATOR | Why did the South become so distinctly different from the North? | What was plantation life like for masters and mistresses?

The Democratization of the Political Arena

In the first half of the nineteenth century, Southerners eliminated the wealth and property requirements that had once restricted political participation. Most southern states also removed the property requirements for holding state offices. To be sure, undemocratic features lingered. Plantation districts still wielded disproportionate power in several state legislatures. Nevertheless, southern politics took place within an increasingly democratic political structure, as it did elsewhere in the nation.

White male suffrage ushered in an era of vigorous electoral competition in the South. Eager voters rushed to the polls to exercise their new rights. Candidates crisscrossed their electoral districts, treating citizens to barbecues and bands, rum and races, as well as stirring oratory. In the South, it seemed, "everybody talked politics everywhere," even the "illiterate and shoeless."

As politics became aggressively democratic, it also grew fiercely partisan. From the 1830s to the 1850s, Whigs and Democrats battled for the electorate's favor. Both parties presented themselves as the plain white folk's best friend. All candidates declared their allegiance to republican equality and pledged themselves to defend the people's liberty. And each party sought to portray the other as a collection of rich, snobbish, selfish men who had antidemocratic designs up their silk sleeves.

Planter Power

Whether Whig or Democrat, southern officeholders were likely to be slave owners. By 1860, the percentage of slave owners in state legislatures ranged from 41 percent in Missouri to nearly 86 percent in North Carolina. Legislators not only tended to own slaves; they also often owned large numbers. The percentage of planters (individuals with twenty or more slaves) in southern legislatures in 1860 ranged from 5.3 percent in Missouri to 55.4 percent in South Carolina. Even in North Carolina, where only 3 percent of the state's white families belonged to the planter class, more than 36 percent of state legislators were planters. Almost everywhere nonslaveholders were in the majority, but plain folk did not throw the planters out of office.

Upper-class dominance of southern politics reflected the elite's success in persuading the yeoman majority that what was good for slaveholders was also good for plain folk. In reality, the South had, on the whole, done well by common white men. Most had farms of their own. They participated as equals in a democratic political system. They enjoyed an elevated social status, above all blacks and in theory equal to all other whites. They commanded patriarchal authority over their households. And as long as slavery existed, they could dream of joining the planter class. Slaveless white men found much to celebrate in the slave South.

Most slaveholders took pains to win the plain folk's trust and to nurture their respect. One nonslaveholder told his wealthy neighbor that he had a bright political future because he never thought himself "too good to sit down & talk to a poor man." Mary Boykin Chesnut complained about the fawning attention her husband, a U.S. senator from South Carolina, showed to poor men, including one who

| What was plantation life like for slaves? | How did nonslaveholding southern whites work and live? | What place did free blacks occupy in South? | **How did slavery shape southern politics?** | Conclusion: How did slavery come to define the South? | ☑ LearningCurve Check what you know. bedfordstmartins.com /roarkunderstanding |

385

had "mud sticking up through his toes." Smart candidates found ways to convince wary plain folk of their democratic convictions and egalitarian sentiments, whether they were genuine or not. Walter L. Steele, who ran for a seat in the North Carolina legislature in 1846, detested campaigning for votes, but he learned, he said, to speak with a "candied tongue."

In addition to politics, slaveholders defended slavery in other ways. In the 1830s, Southerners decided that slavery was too important to debate. "So interwoven is [slavery] with our interest, our manners, our climate and our very being," one man declared in 1833, "that no change can ever possibly be effected without a civil commotion from which the heart of a patriot must turn with horror." Powerful whites dismissed slavery's critics from college faculties, drove them from pulpits, and hounded them from political life. Sometimes antislavery Southerners fell victim to vigilantes and mob violence. One could defend slavery; one could even delicately suggest mild reforms. But no Southerner could any longer safely call slavery evil or advocate its destruction.

In the South, therefore, the rise of the common man occurred alongside the continuing, even growing, power of the planter class. Rather than pitting slaveholders against nonslaveholders, elections remained an effective means of binding the region's whites together. Elections affirmed the sovereignty of white men, whether planter or plain folk, and the subordination of African Americans. Those twin themes played well among white women as well. Though unable to vote, white women supported equality for whites and slavery for blacks. In the antebellum South, the politics of slavery helped knit together all of white society.

> **QUICK REVIEW**

How did planters retain political power in a democratic system?

CHAPTER LOCATOR | Why did the South become so distinctly different from the North? | What was plantation life like for masters and mistresses?

Conclusion: How did slavery come to define the South?

BY THE EARLY NINETEENTH CENTURY, northern states had either abolished slavery or put it on the road to extinction, while southern states were building the largest slave society in the New World. Regional differences increased over time, not merely because the South became more and more dominated by slavery, but also because developments in the North rapidly propelled it in a very different direction.

By 1860, one-third of the South's population was enslaved. Bondage saddled blacks with enormous physical and spiritual burdens: hard labor, harsh treatment, broken families, and, most important, the denial of freedom itself. Although degraded and exploited, they were not defeated. Out of African memories and New World realities, blacks created a life-affirming African American culture that sustained and strengthened them. Their families, religion, and community provided defenses against white racism and power. Defined as property, they refused to be reduced to things. Perceived as inferior beings, they rejected the notion that they were natural slaves.

The South was not merely a society with slaves; it had become a slave society. Slavery shaped the region's economy, culture, social structure, and politics. Whites south of the Mason-Dixon line believed that racial slavery was necessary and just. By making all blacks a pariah class, all whites gained a measure of equality and harmony.

Many features of southern life helped to confine class tensions among whites: the wide availability of land, rapid economic mobility, the democratic nature of political life, the patriarchal power among all white men, and, most of all, slavery and white supremacy. All stress along class lines did not disappear, however, and anxious slaveholders continued to worry that yeomen would defect from the proslavery consensus. But during the 1850s, white Southerners' nearly universal acceptance of slavery would increasingly unite them in political opposition to their northern neighbors.

| What was plantation life like for slaves? | How did nonslaveholding southern whites work and live? | What place did free blacks occupy in the South? | How did slavery shape southern politics? | **Conclusion: How did slavery come to define the South?** | ✓ **LearningCurve** Check what you know. bedfordstmartins.com /roarkunderstanding |

CHAPTER 13 STUDY GUIDE

STEP 1 **GET STARTED ONLINE**

 LearningCurve ■ bedfordstmartins.com/roarkunderstanding

Now that you've read the chapter, make it stick by completing the LearningCurve activity.

STEP 2 **EXPLAIN WHY IT MATTERS**

Put your reading into practice. Identify each term below, and then explain why it matters in U.S. history.

TERM	WHO OR WHAT & WHEN	WHY IT MATTERS
Mason-Dixon line (p. 361)		
cotton kingdom (p. 362)		
slave codes (p. 362)		
miscegenation (p. 363)		
planter (p. 365)		
plantation (p. 365)		
paternalism (p. 368)		
chivalry (p. 370)		
yeomen (p. 377)		
plantation belt (p. 378)		
upcountry (p. 378)		
free blacks (p. 381)		

STEP 3 **MOVE BEYOND THE BASICS**

To demonstrate a more advanced understanding, assess the key characteristics and trends in the North (see chapter 12) and the South in the nineteenth century. How did slavery shape white racial attitudes in both the North and the South?

Key characteristics and trends	North	South
Agriculture		
Urbanization/industrialization		
White racial attitudes		
Economic diversity/labor		
Population/immigration		

STEP 4 **PUT IT ALL TOGETHER**

Now, take a step back and try to explain the big picture. Remember to use specific examples from the chapter in your answers.

REGIONAL DIVERGENCE

▶ How and why did the economies of the North and South steadily diverge over the course of the first half of the nineteenth century?

▶ How did the presence of large numbers of African Americans shape southern culture?

PLANTATION LIFE

▶ How did plantation owners see the relationship between master and slave? How did slavery shape other social relationships in the antebellum South?

▶ In what ways did slaves create communities for themselves and develop methods to resist their bondage?

SOUTHERN SOCIETY AND POLITICS

▶ How did southern yeomen see themselves and their place in southern society? How was slavery a part of that place?

▶ How did slavery shape southern politics?

LOOKING BACKWARD, LOOKING AHEAD

▶ How did southern slave society change from the eighteenth to nineteenth centuries?

▶ Why did many white Southerners come to believe that slavery had to be preserved at any cost? How might that have influenced national politics?

> **IN YOUR OWN WORDS**

Imagine that you must give an oral report to the class answering the following question: **How did slavery shape the institutions and values of the antebellum South?** What would be the most important points to include and why?

 Do it online at the Student Site ■ bedfordstmartins.com/roarkunderstanding

14

THE HOUSE DIVIDED

1846–1861

> **How did the issue of slavery drive the United States toward Civil War in the mid-nineteenth century?** Chapter 14 explores the politics of slavery in the years leading up to the Civil War. It examines how the recurring issue of the expansion of slavery into newly acquired territories deepened sectional divisions, undermined existing political parties, and helped create new ones. Finally, it looks at the events that ultimately led to secession and civil war.

LearningCurve
bedfordstmartins.com/roarkunderstanding
After reading the chapter, use LearningCurve to retain what you've read.

Henry Clay offers his "California compromise" to the U.S. Senate, February 5, 1860. The Granger Collection, New York.

> Why did the acquisition of land from Mexico contribute to sectional tensions?

> What factors helped unravel the balance between slave and free states?

> How did the party system change in the 1850s?

> Why did northern fear of the "Slave Power" intensify in the 1850s?

> Why did some southern states secede immediately after Lincoln's election?

> Conclusion: Why did political compromise fail?

> Why did the acquisition of land from Mexico contribute to sectional tensions?

Oak Home Farm, San Joaquin County, California

The discovery of gold in California initiated a stampede west, but not everyone wanted to be a prospector. In 1860, an unknown artist painted this idyllic view of the farm of W. I. Overhiser in California's fertile San Joaquin Valley. Thousands of miles away, farmers compared farmsteads like Overhiser's with their own. Many judged life more bountiful in the West and trekked across the country to try to strike it rich in western agriculture. University of California at Berkeley, Bancroft Library.

VICTORY IN THE MEXICAN-AMERICAN WAR brought vast new territories in the West into the United States. The gold rush of 1849 transformed the sleepy frontier of California into a booming economy (see chapter 12). The 1850s witnessed new "rushes," for gold in Colorado and silver in Nevada's Comstock Lode. The phenomenal economic growth of the West demanded the attention of the federal government, but it quickly became clear that Northerners and Southerners had very different visions of the West, particularly the place of slavery in its future. From 1846, when it first appeared that the war with Mexico might mean new territory for the United States, politicians battled over whether to ban slavery from former Mexican land or permit it to expand to the Pacific. In 1850, Congress patched together a plan that Americans hoped would last.

The Wilmot Proviso and the Expansion of Slavery

Most Americans agreed that the Constitution left the issue of slavery to the individual states to decide. Northern states had done away with slavery, while southern states had retained it. But what about slavery in the nation's territories? The Constitution states that "Congress shall have power to . . . make all needful rules

CHAPTER LOCATOR | **Why did the acquisition of land from Mexico contribute to sectional tensions?** | What factors helped unravel the balance between slave and free states?

392 CHAPTER 14
THE HOUSE DIVIDED

and regulations respecting the territory . . . belonging to the United States." The debate about slavery, then, turned toward Congress.

> Slavery in the Territories: Contradictory Precedents

- 1787: Northwest Ordinance bans slavery north of the Ohio River.
- 1803: Congress allows slavery to remain in the newly acquired Louisiana Territory.
- 1820: The Missouri Compromise prohibits slavery in part of the Louisiana Territory but allows it in the rest.

The spark for the national debate appeared in August 1846 when a Democratic representative from Pennsylvania, David Wilmot, proposed that Congress bar slavery from all lands acquired in the war with Mexico. The Mexicans had abolished slavery in their country, and Wilmot declared, "God forbid that we should be the means of planting this institution upon it."

Regardless of party affiliation, Northerners lined up behind the **Wilmot Proviso**. Many supported free soil, by which they meant territory in which slavery would be prohibited, because they wanted to preserve the West for **free labor**, for hard-working, self-reliant free men, not for slaveholders and slaves. But support also came from those who were simply anti-South. New slave territories would eventually mean new slave states. Wilmot himself said his proposal would blunt "the power of slaveholders" in the national government.

Additional support for free soil came from Northerners who were hostile to blacks and wanted to reserve new land for whites. Wilmot himself blatantly encouraged racist support when he declared, "I would preserve for free white labor a fair country, a rich inheritance, where the sons of toil, of my own race and own color, can live without the disgrace which association with negro slavery brings upon free labor." It is no wonder that some called the Wilmot Proviso the "White Man's Proviso."

The thought that slavery might be excluded in the territories outraged white Southerners. Like Northerners, they regarded the West as a ladder for economic and social opportunity. They also believed that the exclusion of slavery was a slap in the face to southern veterans of the Mexican-American War. "When the war-worn soldier returns home," one Alabaman asked, "is he to be told that he cannot carry his property to the country won by his blood?" In addition, southern leaders also sought to maintain political parity with the North to protect the South's interests, especially slavery. The need seemed especially urgent in the 1840s, when the North's population and wealth were booming. James Henry Hammond of South Carolina predicted that ten new states would be carved from the acquired Mexican land. If free soil won, the North would "ride over us roughshod" in Congress, he claimed. "Our only safety is in *equality* of power."

Mexican Cession, 1848

> CHRONOLOGY

1846
- Wilmot Proviso is introduced.

1847
- Wilmot Proviso is defeated in Senate.
- "Popular sovereignty" compromise is offered.

1848
- Free-Soil Party is founded.
- Zachary Taylor is elected president.

1849
- California gold rush.

1850
- Taylor dies; Vice President Millard Fillmore becomes president.
- Compromise of 1850 becomes law.

Wilmot Proviso
► Proposal put forward by Representative David Wilmot of Pennsylvania in August 1846 to ban slavery in territory acquired from the Mexican-American War. The Proviso enjoyed widespread support in the North, but Southerners saw it as an attack on their interests.

free labor
► Term referring to work conducted free from constraint and according to the laborer's own inclinations and will. The ideal of free labor lay at the heart of the North's argument that slavery should not be extended into the western territories.

How did the party system change in the 1850s?

Why did northern fear of the "Slave Power" intensify in the 1850s?

Why did some southern states secede immediately after Lincoln's election?

Conclusion: Why did political compromise fail?

✓ **LearningCurve**
Check what you know.
bedfordstmartins.com /roarkunderstanding

Because Northerners had a majority in the House, they easily passed the Wilmot Proviso. In the Senate, however, where slave states outnumbered free states fifteen to fourteen, Southerners defeated it in 1847. Senator John C. Calhoun of South Carolina denied that Congress had the constitutional authority to exclude slavery from the nation's territories. He argued that because the territories were the "joint and common property" of all the states, Congress could not bar citizens of one state from migrating with their property (including slaves) to the territories. Whereas Wilmot demanded that Congress slam shut the door to slavery, Calhoun called on Congress to hold the door wide open.

In 1847, Senator Lewis Cass of Michigan offered a compromise through the doctrine of **popular sovereignty**, by which the people who settled the territories would decide for themselves slavery's fate. This solution, Cass argued, sat squarely in the American tradition of democracy and local self-government. Popular sovereignty's most attractive feature was its ambiguity about the precise moment when settlers could determine slavery's fate. Northern advocates believed that the decision on slavery could be made as soon as the first territorial legislature assembled. With free-soil majorities likely because of the North's greater population, they would shut the door to slavery immediately. Southern supporters believed that popular sovereignty guaranteed that slavery would be unrestricted throughout the entire territorial period. Only when settlers in a territory drew up a constitution and applied for statehood could they decide the issue of slavery. By then, slavery would have sunk deep roots. As long as the matter of timing remained vague, popular sovereignty gave hope to both sides.

When Congress ended its session in 1848, no plan had won a majority in both houses. Northerners who demanded no new slave territory anywhere, ever, and Southerners who demanded entry for their slave property into all territories, or else, staked out their extreme positions. Unresolved in Congress, the territorial question naturally became an issue in the presidential election of 1848.

popular sovereignty

▶ The idea that government is subject to the will of the people. Applied to the territories, popular sovereignty meant that the residents of a territory should determine, through their legislatures, whether to allow slavery.

General Taylor Cigar Case

This papier-mâché cigar case portrays General Zachary Taylor, Whig presidential candidate in 1848, in a colorful scene from the Mexican-American War. Shown here as a dashing, elegant officer, Taylor was in fact a short, thickset, and roughly dressed Indian fighter who had spent his career commanding small frontier garrisons. The inscription reminds voters that Taylor was a victor in the first four battles fought in the war and directs attention away from the fact that in politics, he was a rank amateur. *Collection of Janice L. and David J. Frent.*

CHAPTER LOCATOR | Why did the acquisition of land from Mexico contribute to sectional tensions? | What factors helped unravel the balance between slave and free states?

394 CHAPTER 14 THE HOUSE DIVIDED

The Election of 1848

When President James Polk chose not to seek reelection, the Democratic convention nominated Lewis Cass of Michigan, the man most closely associated with popular sovereignty. The Whigs nominated a Mexican-American War hero, General Zachary Taylor. The Whigs declined to adopt a party platform, betting that the combination of a military hero and total silence on the slavery issue would unite their divided party. Taylor, who owned more than one hundred slaves on plantations in Mississippi and Louisiana, was hailed by Georgia politician Robert Toombs as a "Southern man, a slaveholder, a cotton planter."

Antislavery Whigs balked. Senator Charles Sumner called for a major political realignment, "one grand Northern party of Freedom." In the summer of 1848, antislavery Whigs and anti-slavery Democrats founded the Free-Soil Party, nominating a Democrat, Martin Van Buren, for president and a Whig, Charles Francis Adams, for vice president. The platform boldly proclaimed, "Free soil, free speech, free labor, and free men."

The November election dashed the hopes of the Free-Soilers. They did not carry a single state. Taylor won the all-important electoral vote 163 to 127, carrying eight of the fifteen slave states and seven of the fifteen free states (**Map 14.1**). (Wisconsin had entered the Union earlier in 1848 as the fifteenth free state.) Northern voters were not yet ready for Sumner's "one grand Northern party of Freedom," but the struggle over slavery in the territories had shaken the major parties badly.

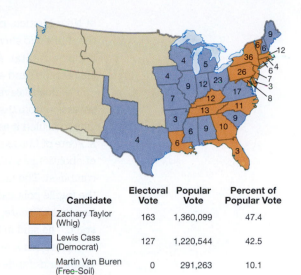

Candidate	Electoral Vote	Popular Vote	Percent of Popular Vote
Zachary Taylor (Whig)	163	1,360,099	47.4
Lewis Cass (Democrat)	127	1,220,544	42.5
Martin Van Buren (Free-Soil)	0	291,263	10.1

MAP 14.1 ■ The Election of 1848

Debate and Compromise

Believing that he could avoid further sectional strife if California and New Mexico skipped the territorial stage, new president Zachary Taylor encouraged the set-tlers to apply for admission to the Union as states. Predominantly antislavery, the settlers began writing free-state constitutions. "For the first time," Mississippian Jefferson Davis lamented, "we are about permanently to destroy the balance of power between the sections."

Congress convened in December 1849, beginning one of the most contentious and most significant sessions in its history. President Taylor urged Congress to admit California as a free state immediately and to admit New Mexico, which lagged behind a few months, as soon as it applied. Southerners exploded. A North Carolinian declared that Southerners who would "consent to be thus degraded and enslaved, ought to be whipped through their fields by their own negroes."

Into this rancorous scene stepped Senator Henry Clay of Kentucky, who offered a series of resolutions meant to answer and balance "all questions in controversy between the free and slave states, growing out of the subject of slavery." Admit California as a free state, he proposed, but organize the rest of the South-west without restrictions on slavery. Require Texas to abandon its claim to parts

How did the party system change in the 1850s? | Why did northern fear of the "Slave Power" intensify in the 1850s? | Why did some southern states secede immediately after Lincoln's election? | Conclusion: Why did political compromise fail? | ✔ **LearningCurve** Check what you know. bedfordstmartins.com /roarkunderstanding

395

of New Mexico, but compensate it by assuming its preannexation debt. Abolish the domestic slave trade in Washington, D.C., but confirm slavery itself in the nation's capital. Affirm Congress's lack of authority to interfere with the interstate slave trade, and enact a more effective fugitive slave law.

Both antislavery advocates and "fire-eaters" (as radical Southerners who urged secession from the Union were called) savaged Clay's plan. Senator Salmon P. Chase of Ohio ridiculed it as "sentiment for the North, substance for the South." Senator Henry S. Foote of Mississippi denounced it as more offensive to the South than the speeches of abolitionists William Lloyd Garrison, Wendell Phillips, and Frederick Douglass combined. The most ominous response came from John C. Calhoun, who argued that the fragile political unity of North and South depended on continued equal representation in the Senate, which Clay's plan for a free California destroyed. "As things now stand," he said in February 1850, the South "cannot with safety remain in the Union."

Massachusetts senator Daniel Webster then addressed the Senate. Like Clay, Webster defended compromise. He told Northerners that the South had legitimate complaints, but he told Southerners that secession from the Union would mean civil war. He argued that the Wilmot Proviso's ban on slavery in the territories was unnecessary because the harsh climate effectively prohibited the expansion of cotton and slaves into the new American Southwest. "I would not take pains uselessly to reaffirm an ordinance of nature, nor to reenact the will of God," Webster declared.

Free-soil forces recoiled from what they saw as Webster's desertion. Senator William H. Seward of New York responded that Webster's and Clay's compromise with slavery was "radically wrong and essentially vicious." He rejected Calhoun's argument that Congress lacked the constitutional authority to exclude slavery from the territories. In any case, Seward said, there was a "higher law than the

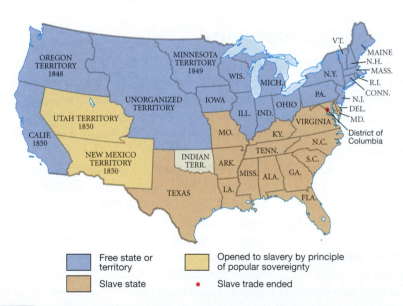

Free state or territory
Slave state
Opened to slavery by principle of popular sovereignty
Slave trade ended

MAP 14.2 ■ The Compromise of 1850

The patched-together sectional agreement was both clumsy and unstable. Few Americans — in either the North or the South — supported all five parts of the Compromise.

CHAPTER LOCATOR | **Why did the acquisition of land from Mexico contribute to sectional tensions?** | What factors helped unravel the balance between slave and free states?

396 CHAPTER 14 THE HOUSE DIVIDED

Constitution" — the law of God — to ensure freedom in all the public domain. Claiming that God was a Free-Soiler did nothing to cool the superheated political atmosphere.

In May 1850, the Senate considered a bill that joined Clay's resolutions into a single comprehensive package. Clay bet that a majority of Congress wanted compromise and that the members would vote for the package. But the omnibus strategy backfired. Free-Soilers and proslavery Southerners voted down the comprehensive plan.

Fortunately for those who favored a settlement, Senator Stephen A. Douglas, a rising Democratic star from Illinois, broke the bill into its parts and skillfully ushered each through Congress. The agreement Douglas won in September 1850 was very much the one Clay had proposed in January. Millard Fillmore, who had become president when Zachary Taylor died in July, signed into law each bill, collectively known as the **Compromise of 1850** (**Map 14.2**). The nation breathed a sigh of relief, for the Compromise preserved the Union and peace for the moment.

Compromise of 1850
▶ Laws passed in 1850 meant to resolve the dispute over the spread of slavery in the territories. Key elements included the admission of California as a free state and the Fugitive Slave Act. The compromise soon unraveled.

> **> Compromise of 1850**

- California entered the Union as a free state.

- New Mexico and Utah became territories where slavery would be decided by popular sovereignty.

- Texas accepted its boundary with New Mexico and received $10 million from the federal government.

- Congress ended the slave trade in the District of Columbia but enacted a more stringent fugitive slave law that stipulated that all citizens were expected to assist officials in apprehending runaway slaves.

QUICK REVIEW <

How might the Compromise of 1850 have eased sectional tensions?

How did the party system change in the 1850s? | Why did northern fear of the "Slave Power" intensify in the 1850s? | Why did some southern states secede immediately after Lincoln's election? | Conclusion: Why did political compromise fail? | **LearningCurve** Check what you know. bedfordstmartins.com /roarkunderstanding

What factors helped unravel the balance between slave and free states?

135,000 SETS, 270,000 VOLUMES SOLD.

UNCLE TOM'S CABIN

FOR SALE HERE.

AN EDITION FOR THE MILLION, COMPLETE IN 1 Vol., PRICE 37 1-2 CENTS.
" " IN GERMAN, IN 1 Vol., PRICE 50 CENTS.
" " IN 2 Vols., CLOTH, 6 PLATES, PRICE $1.50.
SUPERB ILLUSTRATED EDITION, IN 1 Vol., WITH 153 ENGRAVINGS,
PRICES FROM $2.50 TO $5.00.

The Greatest Book of the Age.

Uncle Tom's Cabin Poster After Congress passed the Fugitive Slave Act in 1850, Harriet Beecher Stowe's outraged sister-in-law told her, "Now Hattie, if I could use a pen as you can, I would write something that will make this whole nation feel what an accursed thing slavery is." This poster advertising the novel Stowe wrote calls it "The Greatest Book of the Age." The novel fueled the growing antislavery crusade. The Granger Collection, NY.

Uncle Tom's Cabin
▶ Enormously popular antislavery novel written by Harriet Beecher Stowe and published in 1852. It helped to solidify northern sentiment against slavery and to confirm white Southerners' sense that no sympathy remained for them in the free states.

THE COMPROMISE OF 1850 began to come apart almost immediately. The implementation of the Fugitive Slave Act brought the horrors of slavery into the North. Moreover, millions of Northerners who never saw a runaway slave confronted slavery through Harriet Beecher Stowe's *Uncle Tom's Cabin*, a novel that vividly depicts the brutality of the South's "peculiar institution." Congress did its part to undo the Compromise as well. Four years after Congress stitched the sectional compromise together, it ripped the threads out. With the Kansas-Nebraska Act in 1854, it again posed the question of slavery in the territories, the deadliest of all sectional issues.

The Fugitive Slave Act

The issue of runaway slaves was as old as the Constitution, which contained a provision for the return of any "person held to service or labor in one state" who escaped to another. In 1793, a federal law gave muscle to the provision by authorizing slave owners to enter other states to recapture their slave property. Proclaiming the 1793 law a license to kidnap free blacks, northern states in the 1830s began passing "personal liberty laws" that provided fugitives with some protection.

CHAPTER LOCATOR | Why did the acquisition of land from Mexico contribute to sectional tensions? | **What factors helped unravel the balance between slave and free states?**

Some northern communities also formed vigilance committees to help runaways. Each year, a few hundred slaves escaped into free states and found friendly northern "conductors" who put them aboard the underground railroad, which was not a railroad at all but a series of secret "stations" (hideouts) on the way to Canada.

Furious about northern interference, Southerners in 1850 insisted on the stricter fugitive slave law that was part of the Compromise. According to the **Fugitive Slave Act**, to seize an alleged slave, a slaveholder simply had to appear before a commissioner and swear that the runaway was his. The commissioner earned $10 for every individual returned to slavery but only $5 for those set free. Most galling to Northerners, the law stipulated that all citizens were expected to assist officials in apprehending runaways.

In Boston in February 1851, an angry crowd overpowered federal marshals and snatched a runaway named Shadrach from a courtroom, put him on the underground railroad, and whisked him off to Canada. Three years later, when another Boston crowd rushed the courthouse in a failed attempt to rescue runaway Anthony Burns, a guard was shot dead. To white Southerners, it seemed that fanatics of the "higher law" creed had whipped Northerners into a frenzy of massive resistance.

Actually, the overwhelming majority of fugitives claimed by slaveholders were reenslaved peacefully. But brutal enforcement of the unpopular law had a radicalizing effect in the North, particularly in New England. To Southerners, it seemed that Northerners had betrayed the Compromise. "The continued existence of the United States as one nation," warned the *Southern Literary Messenger*, "depends upon the full and faithful execution of the Fugitive Slave Bill."

Fugitive Slave Act
▶ A law included in the Compromise of 1850 to help attract southern support for the legislative package. Its strict provisions for capturing runaway slaves provoked outrage in the North and intensified antislavery sentiment in the region.

Uncle Tom's Cabin

The spectacle of shackled African Americans being herded south seared the conscience of every Northerner who witnessed such a scene. But even more Northerners were turned against slavery by a novel. Harriet Beecher Stowe, a white Northerner who had never set foot on a plantation, made the South's slaves into flesh-and-blood human beings almost more real than life.

A member of a famous clan of preachers, teachers, and reformers, Stowe despised the slave catchers and wrote to expose the sin of slavery. Published as a book in 1852, *Uncle Tom's Cabin, or Life among the Lowly* became a blockbuster hit, selling 300,000 copies in its first year and more than 2 million copies within ten years. Stowe's characters leaped from the page. Here was the gentle slave Uncle Tom, a Christian saint who forgave those who beat him to death; the courageous slave Eliza, who fled with her child across the frozen Ohio River; and the fiendish overseer Simon Legree, whose Louisiana plantation was a nightmare of torture and death.

Stowe aimed her most powerful blows at slavery's destructive impact on the family. Her character Eliza succeeds in keeping her son from being sold away, but other mothers are not so fortunate. When told that her infant has been sold, Lucy drowns herself. Driven half mad by the sale of a son and a daughter, Cassy decides "never again [to] let a child live to grow up!" She gives her third child an opiate and

| How did the party system change in the 1850s? | Why did northern fear of the "Slave Power" intensify in the 1850s? | Why did some southern states secede immediately after Lincoln's election? | Conclusion: Why did political compromise fail? | ☑ **LearningCurve** Check what you know. bedfordstmartins.com /roarkunderstanding |

399

watches as "he slept to death." Northerners shed tears and sang praises to *Uncle Tom's Cabin*.

What Northerners accepted as truth, Southerners denounced as slander. The Virginian George F. Holmes proclaimed Stowe a member of the "Woman's Rights" and "Higher Law" schools and dismissed the novel as a work of "intense fanaticism." Although it is impossible to measure precisely the impact of a novel on public opinion, *Uncle Tom's Cabin* clearly helped to crystallize northern sentiment against slavery and to confirm white Southerners' suspicion that they no longer received any sympathy in the free states.

Other writers — ex-slaves who knew life in slave cabins firsthand — also produced stinging indictments of slavery. Solomon Northup's compelling *Twelve Years a Slave* (1853) sold 27,000 copies in two years, and the powerful *Narrative of the Life of Frederick Douglass, as Told by Himself* (1845) eventually sold more than 30,000 copies. But no work touched the North's conscience as did the novel by a free white woman. A decade after its publication, when Stowe visited Abraham Lincoln at the White House, he reportedly said, "So you are the little woman who wrote the book that made this great war."

The Kansas-Nebraska Act

As the 1852 election approached, the Democrats and Whigs sought to close the sectional rifts that had opened within their parties. For their presidential nominee, the Democrats turned to Franklin Pierce of New Hampshire. Pierce's well-known sympathy with southern views on public issues caused his northern critics to include him among the "doughfaces," northern men malleable enough to champion southern causes. The Whigs chose another Mexican-American War hero, General Winfield Scott of Virginia. But the Whigs' northern and southern factions were hopelessly divided, and the Democrat Pierce carried twenty-seven states to Scott's four and won the electoral college vote 254 to 42 (see Map 14.4, page 404). The Free-Soil Party lost almost half of the voters who had turned to it in the tumultuous political atmosphere of 1848.

Eager to leave the sectional controversy behind, the new president turned swiftly to foreign expansion. Manifest destiny remained robust. Pierce's major objective was Cuba, but when antislavery Northerners blocked Cuba's acquisition to keep more slave territory from entering the Union, he turned to Mexico. In 1853, diplomat James Gadsden negotiated a $10 million purchase of some 30,000 square miles of land in present-day Arizona and New Mexico. The Gadsden Purchase furthered the dream of a transcontinental railroad to California and Pierce's desire for a southern route through Mexican territory. Talk of a railroad ignited rivalries in cities from New Orleans to Chicago as they maneuvered to become the eastern terminus. Inevitably in the 1850s, the contest for a transcontinental railroad became a sectional struggle over slavery.

Gadsden Purchase, 1853

CHAPTER LOCATOR | Why did the acquisition of land from Mexico contribute to sectional tensions? | **What factors helped unravel the balance between slave and free states?**

400 CHAPTER 14 THE HOUSE DIVIDED

Illinois's Democratic senator Stephen A. Douglas badly wanted the transcontinental railroad for Chicago. Any railroad that ran west from Chicago would pass through a region that Congress in 1830 had designated a "permanent" Indian reserve (see chapter 11). Douglas proposed giving this vast area between the Missouri River and the Rocky Mountains an Indian name, Nebraska, and then throwing the Indians out. Once the region achieved territorial status, whites could survey and sell the land, establish a civil government, and build a railroad.

Nebraska lay within the Louisiana Purchase and, according to the Missouri Compromise of 1820, was closed to slavery (see chapter 10). Douglas needed southern votes to pass his Nebraska legislation, but Southerners had no incentive to create another free territory or to help a northern city win the transcontinental railroad. Southerners, however, agreed to help if Congress organized Nebraska according to popular sovereignty. That meant giving slavery a chance in Nebraska Territory and reopening the dangerous issue of slavery expansion.

In January 1854, Douglas introduced his bill to organize Nebraska Territory, leaving to the settlers themselves the decision about slavery. At southern insistence, Douglas added an explicit repeal of the Missouri Compromise. Free-Soilers branded Douglas's plan "a gross violation of a sacred pledge" and an "atrocious plot" to transform free land into a "dreary region of despotism, inhabited by masters and slaves."

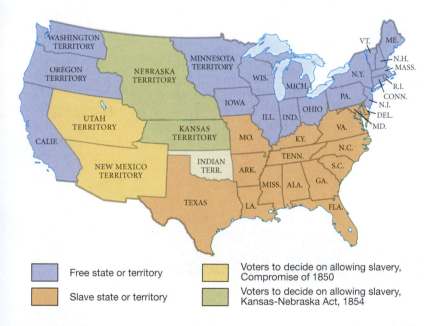

Free state or territory

Slave state or territory

Voters to decide on allowing slavery, Compromise of 1850

Voters to decide on allowing slavery, Kansas-Nebraska Act, 1854

MAP 14.3 ■ The Kansas-Nebraska Act, 1854

Americans hardly thought twice about dispossessing the Indians of land guaranteed them by treaty, but many worried about the outcome of repealing the Missouri Compromise and opening up the region to slavery.

> MAP ACTIVITY

READING THE MAP: How many slave states and how many free states does the map show? Estimate the percentage of new territory likely to be settled by slaveholders.

CONNECTIONS: Who would be more likely to support changes in government legislation to discontinue the Missouri Compromise — slaveholders or free-soil advocates? Why?

How did the party system change in the 1850s?

Why did northern fear of the "Slave Power" intensify in the 1850s?

Why did some southern states secede immediately after Lincoln's election?

Conclusion: Why did political compromise fail?

✔ LearningCurve
Check what you know.
bedfordstmartins.com
/roarkunderstanding

Kansas-Nebraska Act

▶ 1854 law that divided Indian territory into Kansas and Nebraska, repealed the Missouri Compromise, and left the new territories to decide the issue of slavery on the basis of popular sovereignty. The measure led to bloody fighting in Kansas.

Undaunted, Douglas skillfully shepherded the explosive bill through Congress in May 1854. Nine-tenths of the southern members (Whigs and Democrats) and half of the northern Democrats cast votes in favor of the bill. Like Douglas, most northern supporters believed that popular sovereignty would make Nebraska free territory. The **Kansas-Nebraska Act** divided the huge territory in two: Nebraska and Kansas (**Map 14.3**, page 401). With this act, the government pushed the Plains Indians farther west, making way for farmers and railroads.

> **QUICK REVIEW**

Why did the Compromise of 1850 fail to achieve sectional peace?

CHAPTER LOCATOR | Why did the acquisition of land from Mexico contribute to sectional tensions? | What factors helped unravel the balance between slave and free states?

CHAPTER 14
402   THE HOUSE DIVIDED

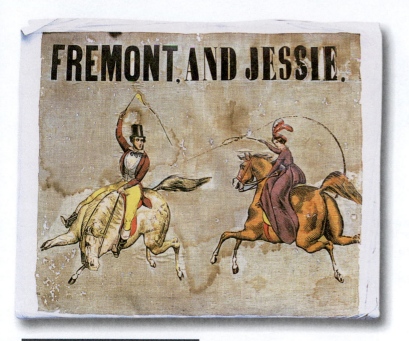

John and Jessie Frémont Poster

The election of 1856 marked the first time a candidate's wife appeared on campaign items. Jessie Benton Frémont helped plan her husband's campaign, coauthored his election biography, and drew northern women into political activity as never before. "What a shame that women can't vote!" declared abolitionist Lydia Maria Child. "We'd carry 'our Jessie' into the White House on our shoulders, wouldn't we." Museum of American Political Life.

SINCE THE EARLY 1830s, Whigs and Democrats had organized and channeled political conflict in the nation. This party system dampened sectionalism and strengthened the Union. To achieve national political power, the Whigs and Democrats had to retain their strength in both the North and the South. Strong northern and southern wings required that each party compromise and find positions acceptable to both sections.

The Kansas-Nebraska controversy shattered this stabilizing political system. In place of two national parties with bisectional strength, the mid-1850s witnessed the development of one party heavily dominated by one section and another party entirely limited to the other section. Rather than "national" parties, the country had what one critic disdainfully called "geographic" parties, a development that thwarted political compromise between the sections.

The Old Parties: Whigs and Democrats

As early as the Mexican-American War, members of the Whig Party had clashed over the future of slavery in annexed Mexican lands. By 1852, the Whig Party could please its proslavery southern wing or its antislavery northern wing, but not both. The Whigs' miserable showing in the election of 1852 made it clear that they were no longer a strong national party. By 1856, after more than two decades of contesting the Democrats, they were hardly a party at all (**Map 14.4**).

| How did the party system change in the 1850s? | Why did northern fear of the "Slave Power" intensify in the 1850s? | Why did some southern states secede immediately after Lincoln's election? | Conclusion: Why did political compromise fail? | ✓ **LearningCurve** Check what you know. bedfordstmartins.com /roarkunderstanding |

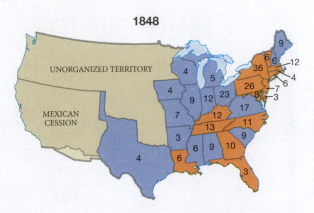

1848

Candidate	Electoral Vote	Popular Vote	Percent of Popular Vote
Zachary Taylor (Whig)	163	1,360,099	47.4
Lewis Cass (Democrat)	127	1,220,544	42.5
Martin Van Buren (Free-Soil)	0	291,263	10.1

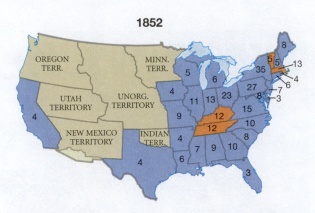

1852

Candidate	Electoral Vote	Popular Vote	Percent of Popular Vote
Franklin Pierce (Democrat)	254	1,601,274	50.9
Winfield Scott (Whig)	42	1,386,580	44.1
John P. Hale (Free-Soil)	5	155,825	5.0

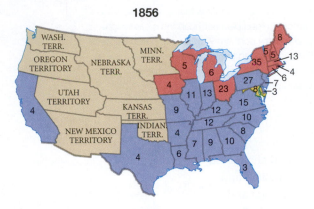

1856

Candidate	Electoral Vote	Popular Vote	Percent of Popular Vote
James Buchanan (Democrat)	174	1,838,169	45.3
John C. Frémont (Republican)	114	1,341,264	33.1
Millard Fillmore (American)	8	874,534	21.6

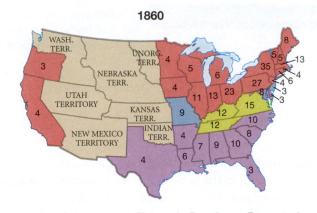

1860

Candidate	Electoral Vote	Popular Vote	Percent of Popular Vote
Abraham Lincoln (Republican)	180	1,866,452	39.9
John C. Breckinridge (Southern Democrat)	72	847,953	18.1
Stephen A. Douglas (Northern Democrat)	12	1,375,157	29.4
John Bell (Constitutional Union)	39	590,631	12.6

MAP 14.4 ■ Political Realignment, 1848–1860

In 1848, slavery and sectionalism began taking their toll on the country's party system. The Whig Party was an early casualty. By 1860, national parties — those that contended for votes in both the North and the South — had been replaced by regional parties.

> MAP ACTIVITY

READING THE MAP: Which states did the Democrats pick up in 1852 compared with 1848? Which of these states did the Democrats lose in 1856? Compare the general geographic location of the states won by the Republicans in 1856 with those won in 1860.

CONNECTIONS: In the 1860 election, which party benefited the most from the western and midwestern states added to the Union since 1848? Why do you think these states chose to back this party?

CHAPTER LOCATOR | Why did the acquisition of land from Mexico contribute to sectional tensions? | What factors helped unravel the balance between slave and free states?

The collapse of the Whig Party left the Democrats as the country's only national party. Popular sovereignty provided a doctrine that many Democrats could support. Even so, popular sovereignty very nearly undid the party. When Stephen Douglas applied the doctrine to the part of the Louisiana Purchase where slavery had been barred, he divided northern Democrats and destroyed the dominance of the Democratic Party in the free states. After 1854, the Democrats were a southern-dominated party. Still, gains in the South more than balanced Democratic losses in the North, and during the 1850s Democrats elected two presidents and won majorities in Congress in almost every election.

The breakup of the Whigs and the disaffection of many northern Democrats set millions of Americans politically adrift. As they searched for new political harbors, Americans found that the death of the old party system created a multitude of fresh political alternatives.

The New Parties: Know-Nothings and Republicans

Dozens of new political organizations vied for voters' attention. Out of the confusion, two emerged as true contenders. One grew out of the slavery controversy, a coalition of indignant antislavery Northerners. The other arose from an entirely different split in American society, between native Protestants and Roman Catholic immigrants.

The wave of immigrants that arrived in America from 1845 to 1855 produced a nasty backlash among Protestant Americans, who feared that the Republic was about to drown in a sea of Roman Catholics from Ireland and Germany (see Figure 12.1, page 334). Nativists (individuals who were anti-immigrant) began to organize, first into secret fraternal societies and then in 1854 into a political party. Recruits swore never to vote for either foreign-born or Roman Catholic candidates and not to reveal any information about the organization. When questioned, they said, "I know nothing." Officially, they were the American Party, but most Americans called them Know-Nothings.

The Know-Nothings enjoyed dazzling success in 1854 and 1855. They captured state legislatures throughout the nation and claimed dozens of seats in Congress. Democrats and Whigs described the Know-Nothings' phenomenal record as a

> CHRONOLOGY

1854
– American (Know-Nothing) Party emerges.
– Republican Party is founded.

1856
– James Buchanan is elected president.

Campaign Flag of the Know-Nothing Party

Convinced that the incendiary issue of slavery had blinded Americans to the greater dangers of uncontrolled immigration and foreign influence, the Know-Nothings nominated Millard Fillmore for president in 1856. Milwaukee County Historical Society.

| How did the party system change in the 1850s? | Why did northern fear of the "Slave Power" intensify in the 1850s? | Why did some southern states secede immediately after Lincoln's election? | Conclusion: Why did political compromise fail? | ☑ LearningCurve Check what you know. bedfordstmartins.com /roarkunderstanding |

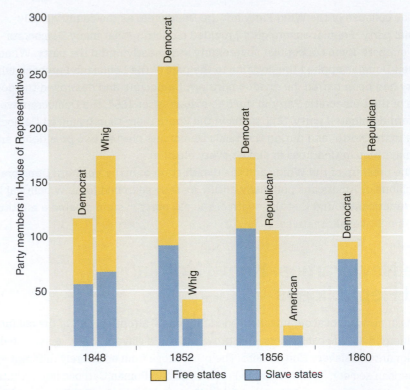

FIGURE 14.1 ■ Changing Political Landscape, 1848–1860

The polarization of American politics between free states and slave states occurred in little more than a decade.

"tornado," a "hurricane," and "a freak of political insanity." But by 1855, an observer might reasonably have concluded that the Know-Nothings had emerged as the successor to the Whigs.

The Know-Nothings were not the only new party making noise, however. One of the new antislavery organizations provoked by the Kansas-Nebraska Act called itself the **Republican Party**. The Republicans attempted to unite all those who opposed the extension of slavery into any territory of the United States (**Figure 14.1**).

The Republican creed tapped into the basic beliefs and values of Northerners. Slavery, Republicans believed, degraded the dignity of white labor by associating work with blacks and servility. As evidence, they pointed to the South, where, one Republican claimed, nonslaveholding whites "retire to the outskirts of civilization, where they live a semi-savage life, sinking deeper and more hopelessly into barbarism with every succeeding generation." Republicans warned that the insatiable slaveholders of the South, whom antislavery Northerners called the "Slave Power," were conspiring through their control of the Democratic Party to expand slavery, subvert liberty, and undermine the Constitution.

Only by restricting slavery to the South, Republicans believed, could free labor flourish elsewhere. In the North, one Republican declared in 1854, "every man holds his fortune in his own right arm; and his position in society, in life, is to be tested by his own individual character." Without slavery, western territories would provide vast economic opportunity for free men. Powerful images of liberty and opportunity attracted a wide range of Northerners to the Republican cause.

Republican Party

▶ Antislavery party formed in 1854 following passage of the Kansas-Nebraska Act. The Republicans attempted to unite all those who opposed the extension of slavery into any territory of the United States.

Women as well as men rushed to the new Republican Party. Indeed, three women helped found the party in Ripon, Wisconsin, in 1854. Although they could not vote and suffered from other legal handicaps, women nevertheless participated in partisan politics by writing campaign literature, marching in parades, giving speeches, and lobbying voters. Women's antislavery fervor attracted them to the Republican Party, and participation in party politics in turn nurtured the woman's rights movement. Susan B. Anthony, who attended Republican meetings throughout the 1850s, found that her political activity made her disfranchisement all the more galling. She and other women in the North worked on behalf of antislavery and woman suffrage and the right of married women to control their own property.

The Election of 1856

The election of 1856 revealed that the Republicans had become the Democrats' main challenger, and slavery in the territories, not nativism, was the election's principal issue. When the Know-Nothings insisted on a platform that endorsed the Kansas-Nebraska Act, most of the Northerners walked out, and the party came apart. The few Know-Nothings who remained nominated ex-president Millard Fillmore.

The Republican platform focused mostly on "making every territory free." When Republicans labeled slavery a "relic of barbarism," they signaled that they had written off the South. For president, they nominated the soldier and California adventurer John C. Frémont. Frémont lacked political credentials, but his wife, Jessie Frémont, the daughter of Senator Thomas Hart Benton of Missouri, knew the political map well. Though careful to maintain a proper public image, the vivacious young mother and antislavery zealot helped attract voters and draw women into politics.

The Democrats, successful in 1852 in bridging sectional differences by nominating a northern man with southern principles, chose another "doughface," James Buchanan of Pennsylvania. They portrayed the Republicans as extremists ("Black Republican Abolitionists") whose support for the Wilmot Proviso risked pushing the South out of the Union.

The Democratic strategy carried the day for Buchanan, who won 174 electoral votes against Frémont's 114 and Fillmore's 8 (see Map 14.4, page 404). But the big news was that the Republicans, despite being a brand-new party, carried all but five of the states north of the Mason-Dixon line. Sectionalism had fashioned a new party system, one that spelled danger for the Democrats and the Republic. Indeed, war had already broken out between proslavery and antislavery forces in distant Kansas Territory.

QUICK REVIEW

Why did the Whig Party disintegrate in the 1850s?

How did the party system change in the 1850s?	Why did northern fear of the "Slave Power" intensify in the 1850s?	Why did some southern states secede immediately after Lincoln's election?	Conclusion: Why did political compromise fail?	☑ **LearningCurve** Check what you know. bedfordstmartins.com /roarkunderstanding

> Why did northern fear of the "Slave Power" intensify in the 1850s?

Armed Settlers Near Lawrence, Kansas Armed with rifles, knives, swords, and pistols, these tough antislavery men gathered for a photograph near the free-soil town of Lawrence in 1856. Equally well-armed proslavery men attacked and briefly occupied Lawrence that same year. Kansas State Historical Society.

EVENTS IN KANSAS TERRITORY in the mid-1850s underscored the Republicans' contention that the slaveholding South presented a profound threat to "free soil, free labor, and free men." Kansas reeled with violence that Republicans argued was southern in origin. Republicans also pointed to the brutal beating by a Southerner of a respected northern senator on the floor of Congress. Even the Supreme Court, in the Republicans' view, reflected the South's drive toward minority rule and tyranny. Then, in 1858, the issues dividing North and South received an extraordinary hearing in a senatorial contest in Illinois, when the nation's foremost Democrat debated a resourceful Republican.

"Bleeding Kansas"

Three days after the House of Representatives approved the Kansas-Nebraska Act in 1854, Senator William H. Seward of New York boldly challenged the South. "Come on then, Gentlemen of the Slave States," he cried, "since there is no escaping your challenge, I accept it in behalf of the cause of freedom. We will engage in competition for the virgin soil of Kansas, and God give the victory to the side which is stronger in numbers as it is in right." Because of Stephen Douglas, popular sovereignty would determine whether Kansas became slave or free.

Emigrant aid societies sprang up to promote settlement from free states or slave states. Missourians, already bordered on the east by the free state of Illinois and on the north by the free state of Iowa, especially thought it important to secure Kansas for slavery. Thousands of rough frontiersmen, egged on by Missouri senator David Rice Atchison, invaded Kansas. "There are eleven hundred coming over from Platte County to vote," Atchison reported, "and if that ain't

CHAPTER LOCATOR | Why did the acquisition of land from Mexico contribute to sectional tensions? | What factors helped unravel the balance between slave and free states?

enough we can send five thousand — enough to kill every God-damned abolitionist in the Territory." Not surprisingly, proslavery candidates swept the territorial elections in November 1854. When Kansas's first territorial legislature met, it enacted a raft of proslavery laws. Ever-pliant President Pierce endorsed the work of the fraudulently elected legislature. Free-soil Kansans did not. They elected their own legislature, which promptly banned both slaves and free blacks from the territory. Organized into two rival governments and armed to the teeth, Kansans verged on civil war.

Fighting broke out on the morning of May 21, 1856, when several hundred proslavery men raided the town of Lawrence, the center of free-state settlement. The "Sack of Lawrence," as free-soil forces called it, inflamed northern opinion. Elsewhere in Kansas, news of events in Lawrence provoked John Brown, a free-soil settler, to announce that "it was better that a score of bad men should die than that one man who came here to make Kansas a Free State should be driven out" and to lead the posse that massacred five allegedly proslavery settlers along Pottawatomie Creek. After that, guerrilla war engulfed the territory.

Just as **"Bleeding Kansas"** gave the fledgling Republican Party fresh ammunition for its battle against the Slave Power, so too did an event that occurred in the nation's capital. In May 1856, Senator Charles Sumner of Massachusetts delivered a speech titled "The Crime against Kansas," which included a scalding personal attack on South Carolina senator Andrew P. Butler. Preston Brooks, a young South Carolina member of the House and a kinsman of Butler's, felt compelled to defend the honor of his aged relative. On May 22, Brooks entered the Senate, where he found Sumner working at his desk. He beat Sumner over the head with his cane until Sumner lay bleeding and unconscious on the floor. Brooks resigned his seat in the House, only to be promptly reelected. In the North, the southern hero became an arch-villain. Like "Bleeding Kansas," "Bleeding Sumner" provided the Republican Party with a potent symbol of the South's "twisted and violent civilization."

The *Dred Scott* Decision

Political debate over slavery in the territories became so heated in part because the Constitution lacked precision on the issue. In 1857, in the case of *Dred Scott v. Sandford*, the Supreme Court announced its understanding of the meaning of the Constitution regarding slavery in the territories. The Court's decision demonstrated that it enjoyed no special immunity from the sectional and partisan passions that were convulsing the land.

In 1833, an army doctor bought the slave Dred Scott in St. Louis, Missouri, and took him as his personal servant to Fort Armstrong, Illinois, and then to Fort Snelling in Wisconsin Territory. Back in St. Louis in 1846, Scott, with the help of white friends,

"Bleeding Kansas," 1850s

> CHRONOLOGY

1856
– "Bleeding Kansas."
– "Sack of Lawrence."
– Pottawatomie massacre.

1857
– *Dred Scott* decision.
– Congress rejects Lecompton constitution.
– Panic of 1857.

1858
– Lincoln-Douglas debates; Douglas wins Senate seat.

"Bleeding Kansas"
▶ Term for the bloody struggle between proslavery and antislavery factions in Kansas in the fall of 1854 following its organization as a territory. Corrupt election tactics led to a proslavery victory, but free-soil Kansans established a rival territorial government, and violence quickly ensued.

How did the party system change in the 1850s? | **Why did northern fear of the "Slave Power" intensify in the 1850s?** | Why did some southern states secede immediately after Lincoln's election? | Conclusion: Why did political compromise fail? | ✔ LearningCurve Check what you know. bedfordstmartins.com /roarkunderstanding

409

Dred Scott

This portrait of Dred Scott was painted in 1857, the year of the Supreme Court's decision. African Americans in the North were particularly alarmed by the Court's ruling. Although the Court rejected his suit, he gained his freedom in May 1857 when a white man purchased and freed Scott and his family. Collection of the New-York Historical Society.

Dred Scott decision

▶ 1857 Supreme Court decision that ruled the Missouri Compromise unconstitutional. The Court ruled against the slave Dred Scott, who claimed that travels with his master into free states made him and his family free. The decision also denied the federal government the right to exclude slavery in the territories and declared that African Americans were not citizens.

sued to prove that he and his family were legally entitled to their freedom. Scott argued that living in Illinois, a free state, and Wisconsin, a free territory, had made his family free and that they remained free even after returning to Missouri, a slave state.

In 1857, Chief Justice Roger B. Taney, who hated Republicans and detested racial equality, wrote the Court's **Dred Scott decision**. The Court explicitly declared the Missouri Compromise unconstitutional, even though it had already been voided by the Kansas-Nebraska Act.

> **Dred Scott Decision**

- Scott could not legally claim violation of his constitutional rights because he was not a citizen of the United States.
- The laws of Dred Scott's home state, Missouri, determined his status, and thus his travels in free areas did not make him free.
- Congress did not have the power to prohibit slavery in the territories.

The Taney Court's extreme proslavery decision outraged Republicans. By denying the federal government the right to exclude slavery in the territories, it cut the legs out from under the Republican Party. Moreover, as the *New York Tribune* lamented, the decision cleared the way for "all our Territories . . . to be ripened into Slave States." Particularly frightening to African Americans in the North was the Court's declaration that free blacks were not citizens and had no rights.

In a seven-to-two decision, the Court validated an extreme statement of the South's territorial rights. John C. Calhoun's claim that Congress had no authority to exclude slavery became the law of the land. White Southerners cheered, but the *Dred Scott* decision actually strengthened the young Republican Party. Indeed,

CHAPTER LOCATOR | Why did the acquisition of land from Mexico contribute to sectional tensions? | What factors helped unravel the balance between slave and free states?

410   CHAPTER 14
THE HOUSE DIVIDED

that "outrageous" decision, one Republican argued, was "the best thing that could have happened," for it provided powerful evidence of the Republicans' claim that a hostile Slave Power conspired against northern liberties.

Prairie Republican: Abraham Lincoln

By reigniting the sectional flames, the *Dred Scott* case provided Republican politicians with fresh challenges and fresh opportunities. Abraham Lincoln had long since put behind him his hardscrabble log-cabin beginnings in Kentucky and Indiana. Now living in Springfield, Illinois, he earned good money as a lawyer, but politics was his life. "His ambition was a little engine that knew no rest," observed his law partner William Herndon. Lincoln had served as a Whig in the Illinois state legislature and in the House of Representatives, but he had not held public office since 1849.

Convinced that slavery was a "monstrous injustice," a "great moral wrong," and an "unqualified evil to the negro, the white man, and the State," Lincoln condemned the Kansas-Nebraska Act of 1854 for giving slavery a new life and in 1856 joined the Republican Party. He accepted that the Constitution permitted slavery in those states where it existed, but he believed that Congress could contain its spread. Penned in, Lincoln believed, plantation slavery would wither, and in time Southerners would end slavery themselves.

Lincoln held what were, for his times, moderate racial views. Although he denounced slavery and defended black humanity, he also viewed black equality as impractical and unachievable. "Negroes have natural rights . . . as other men have," he said, "although they cannot enjoy them here." Insurmountable white prejudice made it impossible to extend full citizenship to blacks in America, he believed. In Lincoln's mind, social stability and black progress required that slavery end and that blacks leave the country.

Lincoln envisioned the western territories as "places for poor people to go to, and better their conditions." But slavery's expansion threatened free men's basic right to succeed. The Kansas-Nebraska Act and the *Dred Scott* decision persuaded him that slaveholders were engaged in a dangerous conspiracy to nationalize slavery. The next step, Lincoln warned, would be "another Supreme Court decision, declaring that the Constitution of the United States does not permit a State to exclude slavery from its limits." Unless the citizens of Illinois woke up, he warned, the Supreme Court would make "Illinois a slave State."

In Lincoln's view, the nation could not "endure, permanently half slave and half free." Either opponents of slavery would arrest its spread and place it on the "course of ultimate extinction," or its advocates would see that it became legal in "*all* the States, *old* as well as *new — North* as well as *South.*" Lincoln's convictions that slavery was wrong and that Congress must stop its spread formed the core of the Republican ideology. In 1858, Republicans in Illinois chose him to challenge the nation's premier Democrat, who was seeking reelection to the U.S. Senate.

The Lincoln-Douglas Debates

When Stephen Douglas learned that the Republican Abraham Lincoln would be his opponent for the Senate, he observed: "He is the strong man of the party—full of wit, facts, dates—and the best stump speaker, with his droll ways and dry jokes, in the West. He is as honest as he is shrewd, and if I beat him my victory will be hardly won."

How did the party system change in the 1850s?

Why did northern fear of the "Slave Power" intensify in the 1850s?

Why did some southern states secede immediately after Lincoln's election?

Conclusion: Why did political compromise fail?

☑ LearningCurve
Check what you know.
bedfordstmartins.com
/roarkunderstanding

Not only did Douglas have to contend with a formidable foe, but the previous year the nation's economy had experienced a sharp downturn. Prices had plummeted, thousands of businesses had failed, and many were unemployed. As a Democrat, Douglas had to go before the voters as a member of the party whose policies stood accused of causing the panic of 1857.

Douglas's response to another crisis in 1857, however, helped shore up his standing in Illinois. Proslavery forces in Kansas met in the town of Lecompton, drafted a proslavery constitution, and applied for statehood. Everyone knew that free-soilers outnumbered proslavery settlers, but President Buchanan instructed Congress to admit Kansas as the sixteenth slave state. Senator Douglas broke with the Democratic administration and denounced the Lecompton constitution; Congress killed the Lecompton bill. (When Kansans reconsidered the Lecompton constitution in an honest election, they rejected it six to one. Kansas entered the Union in 1861 as a free state.) By denouncing the fraudulent proslavery constitution, Douglas declared his independence from the South and, he hoped, made himself acceptable at home.

A relative unknown and a decided underdog in the Illinois election, Lincoln challenged Douglas to debate him face-to-face. The two met in seven communities for what would become a legendary series of debates. Thousands stood straining to hear the two men debate the crucial issues of the age — slavery and freedom.

Lincoln badgered Douglas with the question of whether he favored the spread of slavery. He tried to force Douglas into the damaging admission that the Supreme Court had repudiated Douglas's own territorial solution, popular sovereignty. At Freeport, Illinois, Douglas admitted that settlers could not now pass legislation barring slavery, but he argued that they could ban slavery just as effectively by not passing protective laws, such as those found in slave states. Southerners condemned Douglas's "Freeport Doctrine" and charged him with trying to steal the victory they had gained with the *Dred Scott* decision. Lincoln chastised his opponent for his "don't care" attitude about slavery, for "blowing out the moral lights around us."

Douglas worked the racial issue. He called Lincoln an abolitionist and an egalitarian enamored of "our colored brethren." Put on the defensive, Lincoln reaffirmed his faith in white rule: "I will say, then, that I am not, nor ever have been, in favor of bringing about in any way the social and political equality of the white and black race." But unlike Douglas, Lincoln was no negrophobe. He tried to steer the debate back to what he considered the true issue: the morality and future of slavery. "Slavery is wrong," Lincoln repeated, because "a man has the right to the fruits of his own labor."

As Douglas predicted, the election was hard-fought and closely contested. Until the adoption of the Seventeenth Amendment in 1913, citizens voted for state legislators, who in turn selected U.S. senators. Since Democrats won a slight majority in the Illinois legislature, the members returned Douglas to the Senate. But the **Lincoln-Douglas debates** thrust Lincoln, the prairie Republican, into the national spotlight.

Lincoln-Douglas debates
▶ Series of debates on the issue of slavery and freedom between Democrat Stephen Douglas and Republican Abraham Lincoln, held as part of the 1858 U.S. senatorial race in Illinois. Douglas became senator, but the debates helped catapult Lincoln to national prominence.

> ## QUICK REVIEW

Why did the *Dred Scott* decision strengthen northern suspicions of a Slave Power conspiracy?

CHAPTER LOCATOR | Why did the acquisition of land from Mexico contribute to sectional tensions? | What factors helped unravel the balance between slave and free states?

412 CHAPTER 14
THE HOUSE DIVIDED

Why did some southern states secede immediately after Lincoln's election?

Abraham Lincoln

While in New York City to give a political address, Lincoln had this dignified photograph taken by Mathew Brady. "While I was there I was taken to one of the places where they get up such things," Lincoln explained, sounding more innocent than he was, "and I suppose they got my shadow, and can multiply copies indefinitely." Multiply they did. From the Lincoln Financial Foundation Collection, courtesy of the Indiana State Museum and Allen County Public Library.

FROM THE REPUBLICAN PERSPECTIVE, the Kansas-Nebraska Act, the Brooks-Sumner affair, the *Dred Scott* decision, and the Lecompton constitution amounted to irrefutable evidence of the South's aggressive promotion of slavery. White Southerners, of course, saw things differently. They were the ones who were under siege, they declared. They believed that Northerners were itching to use their numerical advantage to attack slavery, and not just in the territories. Republicans had made it clear that they were unwilling to accept the *Dred Scott* ruling as the last word on the issue of slavery expansion. And John Brown's attempt to incite a slave insurrection in Virginia in 1859 proved that Northerners would do anything to end slavery.

Talk of leaving the Union had been heard for years, but until the final crisis, Southerners had used secession as a ploy to gain concessions within the Union, not to destroy it. Then the 1850s delivered powerful blows to Southerners' confidence that they could remain in the Union and protect slavery. When the Republican Party won the White House in 1860, many Southerners concluded that they would have to leave.

> **CHRONOLOGY**

1859
– John Brown raids Harpers Ferry.

1860
– Abraham Lincoln is elected president.
– South Carolina secedes from Union.

1861
– Six other Lower South states secede.
– Confederate States of America is formed.

How did the party system change in the 1850s?

Why did northern fear of the "Slave Power" intensify in the 1850s?

Why did some southern states secede immediately after Lincoln's election?

Conclusion: Why did political compromise fail?

 LearningCurve
Check what you know.
bedfordstmartins.com
/roarkunderstanding

John Brown's Raid

John Brown, an ardent abolitionist and the man who instigated the massacre at Pottawatomie, Kansas, in 1856, took his war against slavery into the South. On October 16, 1859, he and twenty-one men, including five African Americans, invaded Harpers Ferry, Virginia. His band quickly seized the town's army and rifle works, but the invaders were immediately surrounded, first by local militia and then by Colonel Robert E. Lee, who commanded the U.S. troops in the area. When Brown refused to surrender, federal soldiers charged with bayonets. Seventeen men, two of whom were slaves, lost their lives. Although a few of Brown's raiders escaped, federal forces killed ten and captured seven, among them Brown.

For his attack on Harpers Ferry, John Brown stood trial for treason, murder, and incitement of slave insurrection. "To hang a fanatic is to make a martyr of him and fledge another brood of the same sort," cautioned one newspaper, but on December 2, 1859, Virginia executed Brown. In life, he was a ne'er-do-well, but, as the poet Stephen Vincent Benét observed, "he knew how to die." Brown told his wife that he was "determined to make the utmost possible out of a defeat." He told the court: "If it is deemed necessary that I should forfeit my life for the furtherance of the ends of justice, and mingle my blood further with the blood of . . . millions in this slave country whose rights are disregarded by wicked, cruel, and unjust enactments, I say, let it be done."

After Brown's execution, Americans across the land contemplated the meaning of his life and death. Some Northerners celebrated his "splendid martyrdom." Ralph Waldo Emerson likened Brown to Christ when he declared that Brown made "the gallows as glorious as the cross." Most Northerners did not advocate bloody rebellion, however. Like Lincoln, they concluded that Brown's noble antislavery ideals could not "excuse violence, bloodshed, and treason."

Still, when northern churches marked John Brown's hanging with tolling bells, hymns, and prayer vigils, white Southerners contemplated what they had in common with people who "regard John Brown as a martyr and a Christian hero, rather than a murderer and robber." Georgia senator Robert Toombs announced solemnly that Southerners must "never permit this Federal government to pass into the traitorous hands of the black Republican party."

Republican Victory in 1860

When the Democrats converged on Charleston, South Carolina, for their convention in April 1860, fire-eating Southerners denounced Stephen Douglas and demanded a platform that included federal protection of slavery in the territories. When the delegates approved a platform with popular sovereignty, representatives from the entire Lower South and Arkansas stomped out of the convention. The remaining Democrats adjourned to meet a few weeks later in Baltimore, where they nominated Douglas for president.

When bolting southern Democrats reconvened, they approved a platform with a federal slave code and nominated Vice President John C. Breckinridge of Kentucky. Southern moderates, however, refused to support Breckinridge. They formed the Constitutional Union Party to provide voters with a Unionist choice. Instead of adopting a platform and confronting the slavery question, the

CHAPTER LOCATOR | Why did the acquisition of land from Mexico contribute to sectional tensions? | What factors helped unravel the balance between slave and free states?

414 CHAPTER 14 THE HOUSE DIVIDED

John Brown Going to His Hanging, by Horace Pippin, 1942

The grandparents of Horace Pippin, a Pennsylvania artist, were slaves. His grandmother witnessed the hanging of John Brown, and this painting recalls the scene she so often described to him. Pippin used a muted palette to establish the bleak setting, but he also managed to convey its striking intensity. Historically accurate, the painting depicts Brown tied and sitting erect on his coffin, passing resolutely before the silent, staring white men. The black woman in the lower right corner presumably is Pippin's grandmother. Romare Bearden, another African American artist, recalled the central place of John Brown in black memory: "Lincoln and John Brown were as much a part of the actuality of the Afro-American experience, as were the domino games and the hoe cakes for Sunday morning breakfast. I vividly recall the yearly commemorations for John Brown." Pennsylvania Academy of Fine Arts, Philadelphia. John Lambert Fund.

> **VISUAL ACTIVITY**

READING THE IMAGE: What was the artist trying to convey about the tone of John Brown's execution? According to the painting, what were the feelings of those gathered to witness the event?

CONNECTIONS: How did Brown's trial and execution contribute to the growing split between North and South?

Constitutional Union Party merely approved a vague resolution pledging "to recognize no political principle other than *the Constitution . . . the Union . . . and the Enforcement of the Laws.*" For president, they nominated former senator John Bell of Tennessee.

The Republicans smelled victory, but they needed to carry nearly all the free states to win. To make their party more appealing, they expanded their platform

How did the party system change in the 1850s?	Why did northern fear of the "Slave Power" intensify in the 1850s?	**Why did some southern states secede immediately after Lincoln's election?**	Conclusion: Why did political compromise fail?	☑ LearningCurve Check what you know. bedfordstmartins.com /roarkunderstanding

beyond antislavery. They hoped that free homesteads, a protective tariff, a transcontinental railroad, and a guarantee of immigrant political rights would provide an agenda broad enough to unify the North. While reasserting their commitment to stop the spread of slavery, they also denounced John Brown's raid as "among the gravest of crimes" and confirmed the security of slavery in the South.

The foremost Republican, William H. Seward, had made enemies with his radical "higher law" doctrine, which claimed that there was a higher moral law than the Constitution, and with his "irrepressible conflict" speech, in which he declared that North and South were fated to collide. Lincoln, however, since bursting onto the national scene in 1858, had demonstrated his clear purpose, good judgment, and solid Republican credentials. That, and his residence in Illinois, a crucial state, made him attractive to the party. On the third ballot, the delegates chose Lincoln. Defeated by Douglas in a state contest less than two years earlier, Lincoln now stood ready to take him on for the presidency.

The election of 1860 was like none other in American politics. It took place in the midst of the nation's severest crisis. Four major candidates crowded the presidential field. Rather than a four-cornered contest, however, the election broke into two contests, each with two candidates. In the North, Lincoln faced Douglas; in the South, Breckinridge confronted Bell. So outrageous did Southerners consider the Republican Party that they did not even permit Lincoln's name to appear on the ballot in ten of the fifteen slave states.

On November 6, 1860, Lincoln swept all of the eighteen free states except New Jersey, which split its electoral votes between him and Douglas. Although Lincoln received only 39 percent of the popular vote, he won easily in the electoral college with 180 votes, 28 more than he needed for victory (**Map 14.5**). Lincoln did not win because his opposition was splintered. Even if the votes of his three opponents had been combined, Lincoln still would have won. He won

Candidate	Electoral Vote	Popular Vote	Percent of Popular Vote
Abraham Lincoln (Republican)	180	1,866,452	39.9
John C. Breckinridge (Southern Democrat)	72	847,953	18.1
Stephen A. Douglas (Northern Democrat)	12	1,375,157	29.4
John Bell (Constitutional Union)	39	590,631	12.6

MAP 14.5 ■ The Election of 1860

CHAPTER LOCATOR | Why did the acquisition of land from Mexico contribute to sectional tensions? | What factors helped unravel the balance between slave and free states?

CHAPTER 14
THE HOUSE DIVIDED

416

because his votes were concentrated in the free states, which contained a majority of electoral votes. Ominously, however, Breckinridge, running on a southern-rights platform, won the entire Lower South, plus Delaware, Maryland, and North Carolina.

Secession Winter

Anxious Southerners immediately began debating what to do. Although Breckinridge had carried the South, a vote for "southern rights" was not necessarily a vote for secession. Besides, slightly more than half of the Southerners who had voted had cast ballots for Douglas and Bell, two stout defenders of the Union.

Southern Unionists tried to calm the fears that Lincoln's election triggered. Former congressman Alexander Stephens of Georgia asked what Lincoln had done to justify something as extreme as secession. Had he not promised to respect slavery where it existed? In Stephens's judgment, secession might lead to war, which would loosen the hinges of southern society and possibly even open the door to slave insurrection. "Revolutions are much easier started than controlled," he warned. "I consider slavery much more secure in the Union than out of it."

Secessionists emphasized the dangers of delay. "Mr. Lincoln and his party assert that this doctrine of equality applies to the negro," former Georgia governor Howell Cobb declared, "and necessarily there can exist no such thing as property in our equals." Lincoln's election without a single electoral vote from the South meant that Southerners were no longer able to defend themselves within the Union, Cobb argued. Why wait, he asked, for abolitionists to attack? As for war, there would be none. The Union was a voluntary compact, and Lincoln would not coerce patriotism. If Northerners did resist with force, secessionists argued, one southern woodsman could whip five of Lincoln's greasy mechanics.

For all their differences, southern whites agreed that they had to defend slavery. John Smith Preston of South Carolina spoke for the overwhelming majority when he declared, "The South cannot exist without slavery." They disagreed about whether the mere presence of a Republican in the White House made it necessary to exercise what they considered a legitimate right to secede.

South Carolina seceded from the Union on December 20, 1860. By February 1861, the six other Lower South states followed in South Carolina's footsteps. In general, slaveholders spearheaded secession, while nonslaveholders in the Piedmont and mountain counties, where slaves were relatively few, displayed the greatest attachment to the Union. In February, representatives from South Carolina, Georgia, Florida, Alabama, Mississippi, Louisiana, and Texas met in Montgomery, Alabama, where they created the **Confederate States of America**. Mississippi senator Jefferson Davis became president, and Alexander Stephens of Georgia, who had spoken so eloquently about the dangers of revolution, became vice president. In March 1861, Stephens declared that the Confederacy's "cornerstone" was "the great truth that the negro is not equal to the white man; that slavery, subordination to the superior race, is his natural and moral condition."

Lincoln's election had split the Union. Now secession split the South. Seven slave states seceded during the winter, but the eight slave states of the Upper South rejected secession, at least for the moment. The Upper South had a smaller

Confederate States of America

▶ Government formed by Lower South states on February 7, 1861, following their secession from the Union. Secessionists argued that the election of a Republican to the presidency imperiled slavery and that the South no longer had political protection within the Union.

How did the party system change in the 1850s? | Why did northern fear of the "Slave Power" intensify in the 1850s? | **Why did some southern states secede immediately after Lincoln's election?** | Conclusion: Why did political compromise fail?

☑ LearningCurve
Check what you know.
bedfordstmartins.com
/roarkunderstanding

Secession of the Lower South,
December 1860–February 1861

stake in slavery. Barely half as many white families in the Upper South held slaves (21 percent) as in the Lower South (37 percent). Slaves represented twice as large a percentage of the population in the Lower South (48 percent) as in the Upper South (23 percent). Consequently, whites in the Upper South had fewer fears that Republican ascendancy meant economic catastrophe, social chaos, and racial war. Lincoln would need to do more than just be elected to provoke them into secession.

The nation had to wait until March 4, 1861, when Lincoln took office, to see what he would do. He chose to stay in Springfield after his election and to say nothing. "Lame-duck" president James Buchanan sat in Washington and did nothing. Congress's efforts at cobbling together a peace-saving compromise came to nothing.

Lincoln began his inaugural address with reassurances to the South. He had "no lawful right" to interfere with slavery where it existed, he declared again, adding for emphasis that he had "no inclination to do so." Conciliatory about slavery, Lincoln proved inflexible about the Union. The Union, he declared, was "perpetual." Secession was "anarchy" and "legally void." The Constitution required him to execute the law "in all the States."

The decision for war or peace rested in the South's hands, Lincoln said. "You can have no conflict, without being yourselves the aggressors. You have no oath registered in Heaven to destroy the government, while I shall have the most solemn one to 'preserve, protect, and defend' it."

> **QUICK REVIEW**

Why were the states of the Lower and Upper South divided on the question of secession during the winter of 1860–1861?

CHAPTER LOCATOR | Why did the acquisition of land from Mexico contribute to sectional tensions? | What factors helped unravel the balance between slave and free states?

418   CHAPTER 14
THE HOUSE DIVIDED

AS THEIR ECONOMIES, societies, and cultures diverged in the nineteenth century, Northerners and Southerners expressed different concepts of the American promise and the place of slavery within it. Their differences crystallized into political form in 1846 when David Wilmot proposed banning slavery in any territory won in the Mexican-American War. "As if by magic," a Boston newspaper observed, "it brought to a head the great question that is about to divide the American people." Discovery of gold and other precious metals in the West added urgency to the controversy over slavery in the territories. Congress attempted to address the issue with the Compromise of 1850, but the Fugitive Slave Act and the publication of *Uncle Tom's Cabin* hardened northern sentiments against slavery and confirmed southern suspicions of northern ill will. The bloody violence that erupted in Kansas in 1856 and the incendiary *Dred Scott* decision in 1857 further eroded hope for a solution to this momentous question.

During the extended crisis of the Union that stretched from 1846 to 1861, the slavery question intertwined with national politics. The traditional Whig and Democratic parties struggled to hold together as new parties, most notably the Republican Party, emerged. Politicians fixed their attention on the expansion of slavery, but from the beginning Americans recognized that the controversy had less to do with slavery in the territories than with the future of slavery in the nation.

For more than seventy years, statesmen had found compromises that accepted slavery and preserved the Union. But as each section grew increasingly committed to its labor system, Americans discovered that accommodation had limits. In 1859, John Brown's militant antislavery pushed white Southerners to the edge. In 1860, Lincoln's election convinced whites in the Lower South that slavery and the society they had built on it were at risk in the Union, and they seceded. But it remained to be seen whether disunion would mean war.

| How did the party system change in the 1850s? | Why did northern fear of the "Slave Power" intensify in the 1850s? | Why did some southern states secede immediately after Lincoln's election? | **Conclusion: Why did political compromise fail?** | ✔ **LearningCurve** Check what you know. bedfordstmartins.com /roarkunderstanding |

CHAPTER 14 STUDY GUIDE

STEP 1

GET STARTED ONLINE

✓ **LearningCurve** ■ bedfordstmartins.com/roarkunderstanding
Now that you've read the chapter, make it stick by completing the LearningCurve activity.

STEP 2

EXPLAIN WHY IT MATTERS

Put your reading into practice. Identify each term below, and then explain why it matters in U.S. history.

TERM	WHO OR WHAT & WHEN	WHY IT MATTERS
Wilmot Proviso (p. 393)		
free labor (p. 393)		
popular sovereignty (p. 394)		
Compromise of 1850 (p. 397)		
Uncle Tom's Cabin (p. 398)		
Fugitive Slave Act (p. 399)		
Kansas-Nebraska Act (p. 402)		
Republican Party (p. 406)		
"Bleeding Kansas" (p. 409)		
Dred Scott decision (p. 410)		
Lincoln-Douglas debates (p. 412)		
Confederate States of America (p. 417)		

STEP 3

MOVE BEYOND THE BASICS

To demonstrate a more advanced understanding, use the table below to sketch the political landscape of the 1850s. How did slavery help transform the American political landscape?

Party	Who supported this party?	Position on slavery	Views on expansion	Perspectives on immigration
Democratic Party				
Whig Party				
Republican Party				
American (Know-Nothing) Party				

STEP 4

PUT IT ALL TOGETHER

Now, take a step back and try to explain the big picture. Remember to use specific examples from the chapter in your answers.

EXPANSION AND SECTIONALISM

▶ Why was the Wilmot Proviso so controversial? What did the response to the Proviso reveal about the diverging visions of America in the North and in the South?

▶ Why was the expansion of slavery not only a moral issue for abolitionists but also an economic concern to both Northerners and Southerners?

POLITICAL INSTABILITY

▶ Why did the Compromise of 1850 ultimately fail?

▶ What were the consequences of the events of the 1840s and 1850s for America's political parties? How did the party system change under the pressure of the sectional divide?

THE ROAD TO SECESSION

▶ If most Northerners and Southerners wanted to avoid war, why did war come?

▶ Why did so many Southerners see the election of Abraham Lincoln as a threat to their way of life? Why did more than half of the southern electorate vote for pro-Union candidates?

LOOKING BACKWARD, LOOKING AHEAD

▶ Why, in the early nineteenth century, was compromise on the issue of slavery possible? Why did so many reject compromise in the 1840s and 1850s?

▶ What consequences might Southerners have imagined would follow from secession? What might have led them to underestimate Lincoln's determination to fight for the Union?

> IN YOUR OWN WORDS

Imagine that you must give an oral report to the class answering the following question: **How did the issue of slavery drive the United States toward Civil War in the mid-nineteenth century?** What would be the most important points to include and why?

 **Do it online at the Student Site** ■ bedfordstmartins.com/roarkunderstanding

15

THE CRUCIBLE OF WAR

1861–1865

> How did the Civil War change the nation, North and South? Chapter 15 traces the course of the Civil War, exploring the connections between events on the battlefield and the political, social, and economic divisions on the home fronts. It explains how the war became a fight for black freedom and examines why the North ultimately won the war.

LearningCurve
bedfordstmartins.com/roarkunderstanding
After reading the chapter, use LearningCurve to
retain what you've read.

"Price Raid," October 1874. This 1865 illustration by Samuel J. Reader shows a regiment of Kansas militia captured by Confederate soldiers in Texas. Reader was one of the captives. Kansas State Historical Society.

> Why did both the Union and the Confederacy consider control of the border states crucial?

> Why did each side expect to win?

> How did each side fare in the early years of the war?

> How did the war for union become a fight for black freedom?

> What problems did the Confederacy face at home?

> How did the war affect the economy and politics of the North?

> How did the Union finally win the war?

> Conclusion: In what ways was the Civil War a "Second American Revolution"?

> Why did both the Union and the Confederacy consider control of the border states crucial?

Fort Sumter Bombardment Located on an artificial island inside the entrance to Charleston harbor, Fort Sumter had walls eight to twelve feet thick. The fort was so undermanned that when Confederate shells began raining down on April 12, U.S. troops could answer back with only a few of the fort's forty-eight guns. Minnesota Historical Society.

ABRAHAM LINCOLN faced the worst crisis in the history of the nation: disunion. He revealed his strategy to save the Union in his inaugural address on March 4, 1861. He was firm yet conciliatory. First, he denied the right of secession and sought to stop its spread by avoiding any act that would push the skittish Upper South (North Carolina, Virginia, Maryland, Delaware, Kentucky, Tennessee, Missouri, and Arkansas) out of the Union. Second, he sought to reassure the seceding Lower South (South Carolina, Georgia, Florida, Alabama, Mississippi, Louisiana, and Texas) that the Republicans would not abolish slavery. Lincoln believed that Unionists there would assert themselves and overturn the secession decision.

His counterpart, Jefferson Davis, fully intended to establish the Confederate States of America as an independent republic. To achieve permanence, Davis had to sustain the secession fever that had carried the Lower South out of the Union. Even if the Lower South held firm, however, the Confederacy would remain weak without additional states. Davis watched for opportunities to add new stars to the Confederate flag.

CHAPTER LOCATOR | **Why did both the Union and the Confederacy consider control of the border states crucial?** | Why did each side expect to win? | How did each side fare in the early years of the war?

Both men wanted to achieve their objectives peacefully. As Lincoln later observed, "Both parties deprecated war, but one of them would *make* war rather than let the nation survive, and the other would *accept* war rather than let it perish. And the war came."

Attack on Fort Sumter

Major Robert Anderson and some eighty U.S. soldiers occupied **Fort Sumter**, which was perched on a tiny island at the entrance to Charleston harbor in South Carolina. Lincoln decided to hold the fort, but Anderson and his men were running dangerously short of food. In early April 1861, Lincoln authorized a peaceful expedition to bring supplies, but not military reinforcements, to the fort. The president understood that he risked war, but his plan honored his inaugural promises to defend federal property and to avoid using military force unless first attacked. Masterfully, Lincoln had shifted the fateful decision of war or peace to Jefferson Davis.

On April 9, Davis and his cabinet met to consider the situation in Charleston harbor. Davis argued for military action, but his secretary of state, Robert Toombs of Georgia, replied: "Mr. President, at this time it is suicide, murder, and will lose us every friend at the North. You will wantonly strike a hornet's nest which extends from mountain to ocean, and legions now quiet will swarm out and sting us to death." But Davis ordered Confederate troops in Charleston to take the fort before the relief expedition arrived. Thirty-three hours of bombardment on April 12 and 13 reduced the fort to rubble. On April 14, Major Anderson offered his surrender and lowered the U.S. flag. The Confederates had Fort Sumter, but they also had war.

On April 15, when Lincoln called for 75,000 militiamen to serve for ninety days to put down the rebellion, several times that number rushed to defend the flag. Stephen A. Douglas, the recently defeated Democratic candidate for president, pledged his support and noted, "There can be no neutrals in this war, *only patriots — or traitors.*"

The Upper South Chooses Sides

The Upper South faced a horrendous choice: either to fight against the Lower South or to fight against the Union. Many who only months earlier had rejected secession now embraced the Confederacy. Thousands felt betrayed, believing that Lincoln had promised to achieve a peaceful reunion by waiting patiently for Unionists to retake power in the seceding states. It was a "politician's war," one man declared, but he conceded that "this is no time now to discuss the causes, but it is the duty of all who regard Southern institutions of value to side with the South, make common cause with the Confederate States and sink or swim with them."

Virginia, Arkansas, Tennessee, and North Carolina joined the Confederacy (**Map 15.1**). But in the border states of Delaware, Maryland, Kentucky, and Missouri, Unionism triumphed. Only in Delaware, where slaves accounted for less than 2 percent of the population, was the victory easy. In Maryland, Lincoln suspended the writ of habeas corpus, essentially setting aside constitutional

> CHRONOLOGY

1861
– Attack on Fort Sumter.
– Four Upper South states join Confederacy.

Fort Sumter
▶ Union fort on an island at the entrance to Charleston harbor in South Carolina. After Confederate leaders learned that President Lincoln intended to resupply Fort Sumter, Confederate forces attacked the fort on April 12, 1861, thus marking the start of the Civil War.

How did the war for union become a fight for black freedom? | What problems did the Confederacy face at home? | How did the war affect the economy and politics of the North? | How did the Union finally win the war? | Conclusion: In what ways was the Civil War a "Second American Revolution"? | ☑ LearningCurve Check what you know. bedfordstmartins.com /roarkunderstanding

425

MAP 15.1 ■ Secession, 1860–1861

After Lincoln's election, the fifteen slave states debated what to do. Seven states quickly left the Union, four left after the firing on Fort Sumter, and four remained loyal to the Union.

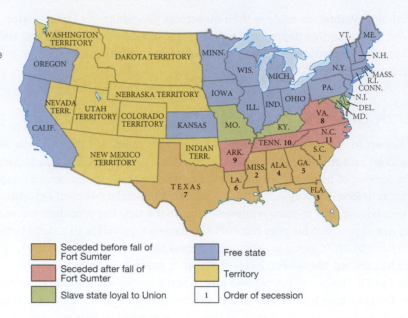

Seceded before fall of Fort Sumter

Seceded after fall of Fort Sumter

Slave state loyal to Union

Free state

Territory

1 Order of secession

guarantees that protect citizens from arbitrary arrest and detention, and he ordered U.S. troops into Baltimore. Maryland's legislature rejected secession.

The struggle turned violent in the West. In Missouri, Unionists won a narrow victory, but southern-sympathizing guerrilla bands roamed the state for the duration of the war, terrorizing civilians and soldiers alike. In Kentucky, Unionists also narrowly defeated secession, but the prosouthern minority claimed otherwise.

Lincoln understood that the border states — particularly Kentucky — contained indispensable resources, population, and wealth and also controlled major rivers and railroads. "I think to lose Kentucky is nearly the same as to lose the whole game," Lincoln said. "Kentucky gone, we can not hold Missouri, nor, as I think, Maryland. These all against us, . . . we would as well consent to separation at once."

In the end, only eleven of the fifteen slave states joined the Confederate States of America. Moreover, the four seceding Upper South states contained significant numbers of people who felt little affection for the Confederacy. Dissatisfaction was so rife in the western counties of Virginia that in 1863 citizens there voted to create the separate state of West Virginia, loyal to the Union. Still, the acquisition of four new states greatly strengthened the Confederacy's drive for national independence.

> ## QUICK REVIEW

Why did the attack on Fort Sumter force the Upper South to choose sides?

CHAPTER LOCATOR | Why did both the Union and the Confederacy consider control of the border states crucial? | Why did each side expect to win? | How did each side fare in the early years of the war?

426 CHAPTER 15
THE CRUCIBLE OF WAR

Union Ordnance, Yorktown, Virginia

As the North successfully harnessed its enormous industrial capacity to meet the needs of the war, cannons, mortars, and shells poured out of its factories. A fraction of that abundance is seen here at Yorktown in 1862, ready for transportation to Union troops in the field. Library of Congress.

ONLY SLAVEHOLDERS had a direct economic stake in preserving slavery, but most whites in the Confederacy defended the institution, the way of life built on it, and the Confederate nation. The degraded and subjugated status of blacks elevated the status of the poorest whites. "It is enough that one simply belongs to the superior and ruling race, to secure consideration and respect." Moreover, Yankee "aggression" was no longer a mere threat; it was real and at the South's door.

For Northerners, the South's failure to accept the democratic election of a president and its firing on the nation's flag challenged the rule of law, the authority of the Constitution, and the ability of the people to govern themselves. As an Indiana soldier told his wife, a "good government is the best thing on earth. Property is nothing without it, because it is not protected; a family is nothing without it, because they cannot be educated."

Northerners and Southerners rallied behind their separate flags, fully convinced that they were in the right and that God was on their side. Yankees took heart from their superior power, but the rebels believed they had advantages that nullified every northern strength. Both sides mobilized swiftly in 1861, and each devised what it believed would be a winning military and diplomatic strategy.

How They Expected to Win

The balance sheet of northern and southern resources reveals enormous advantages for the Union (**Figure 15.1**). The twenty-three states remaining in the Union had a population of 22.3 million; the eleven Confederate states had a population of only 9.1 million, of whom 3.67 million (40 percent) were slaves. The North's economic advantages were even more overwhelming. Yet Southerners expected to win — for some good reasons — and they came very close to doing so.

How did the war for union become a fight for black freedom?	What problems did the Confederacy face at home?	How did the war affect the economy and politics of the North?	How did the Union finally win the war?	Conclusion: In what ways was the Civil War a "Second American Revolution"?	✔ **LearningCurve** Check what you know. bedfordstmartins.com /roarkunderstanding

Confederate Expectations

- "King Cotton" could help create alliances based on Europe's (especially Britain's) reliance on cotton imports.
- Defensive war strategy meant the South could win simply by outlasting the Union.
- President Jefferson Davis was an experienced military commander.

Union Expectations

- Superior navy could blockade trade between the Confederacy and Europe.
- Superior numbers meant a larger army.
- Greater industrial capacity meant a stronger army.
- President Abraham Lincoln appointed well-qualified men to key positions in government.

Southerners knew they bucked the military odds, but hadn't the liberty-loving colonists in 1776 also done so? "Britain could not conquer three million," a Louisianan proclaimed, and "the world cannot conquer the South." How could anyone doubt the outcome of a contest between lean, hard, country-born rebel warriors defending family, property, and liberty, and soft, flabby, citified Yankee mechanics waging an unconstitutional war?

The South's confidence also rested on its belief that northern prosperity depended on the South's cotton. Without cotton, New England textile mills would stand idle. Without planters purchasing northern manufactured goods, northern factories would drown in their own unsold surpluses. And without the foreign exchange earned by the overseas sales of cotton, the financial structure of the entire Yankee nation would collapse.

Cotton would also make Europe a powerful ally of the Confederacy, Southerners reasoned. Of the 900 million pounds of cotton Britain imported annually, more than 700 million pounds came from the American South. If the supply was interrupted, sheer economic need would make Britain (and perhaps France) a Confederate ally. And because the British navy ruled the seas, the North would find Britain a formidable foe.

The Confederacy devised a military strategy to exploit its advantages and minimize its limitations. It recognized that a Union victory required the North to defeat and subjugate the South, but a Confederate victory required only that the

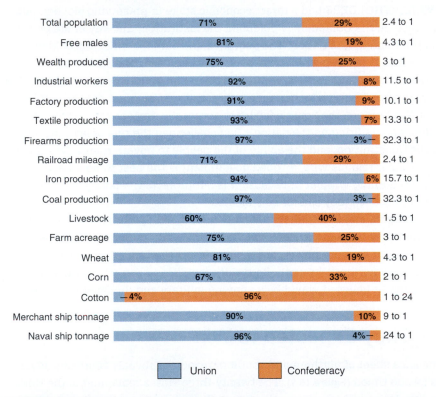

FIGURE 15.1 ■ Resources of the Union and Confederacy

The Union's enormous statistical advantages failed to convince Confederates that their cause was doomed.

CHAPTER LOCATOR | Why did both the Union and the Confederacy consider control of the border states crucial? | **Why did each side expect to win?** | How did each side fare in the early years of the war?

South stay at home, blunt invasions, avoid battles that risked annihilating its army, and outlast the North's will to fight. When an opportunity presented itself, the South would strike the invaders. Like the American colonists, the South could win independence by not losing the war.

The Lincoln administration countered with a strategy designed to take advantage of its superior resources. Lincoln declared a naval blockade of the Confederacy to deny it the ability to sell cotton abroad, giving the South far fewer dollars to pay for war goods. Lincoln also ordered the Union army into Virginia, at the same time planning a march through the Mississippi valley that would cut the Confederacy in two.

Lincoln and Davis Mobilize

Mobilization required effective political leadership, and at first glance the South appeared to have the advantage. Jefferson Davis brought to the Confederate presidency a distinguished political career, including experience in the U.S. Senate. He was also a West Point graduate, a combat veteran and authentic hero of the Mexican-American War, and a former secretary of war. Dignified and ramrod straight, with "a jaw sawed in steel," Davis appeared to be everything a nation could want in a wartime leader.

By contrast, Abraham Lincoln brought to the White House one lackluster term in the House of Representatives and almost no administrative experience. His sole brush with anything military was as a captain in the militia in the Black Hawk War, a brief struggle in Illinois in 1832 in which whites expelled the last Indians from the state. The lanky, disheveled Illinois lawyer-politician looked anything but military or presidential in his bearing.

Davis, however, proved to be less than he appeared. Although he worked hard, he had no gift for military strategy yet intervened often in military affairs. He was an even less able political leader. Quarrelsome and proud, he had an acid tongue that made enemies the Confederacy could ill afford.

With Lincoln the North got far more than met the eye. He proved himself a master politician and a superb leader. When forming his cabinet, Lincoln appointed the ablest men, no matter that they were often his chief rivals and critics. He appointed Salmon P. Chase secretary of the treasury, knowing that Chase had presidential ambitions. As secretary of state, he chose his chief opponent for the Republican nomination in 1860, William H. Seward. Despite his civilian background, Lincoln displayed an innate understanding of military strategy. No one was more crucial in mapping the Union war plan.

Lincoln and Davis began gathering their armies. Confederates had to build almost everything from scratch, and Northerners had to channel their superior numbers and industrial resources to war. On the eve of the war, the federal army numbered only 16,000 men. One-third of the officers followed the example of the Virginian Robert E. Lee, resigning their commissions and heading south. The U.S. Navy was in better shape. Forty-two ships were in service, and a large merchant marine would in time provide more ships and sailors for the Union cause.

The Confederacy made prodigious efforts to supply its armies, but even when factories produced what soldiers needed, southern railroads often could not

| How did the war for union become a fight for black freedom? | What problems did the Confederacy face at home? | How did the war affect the economy and politics of the North? | How did the Union finally win the war? | Conclusion: In what ways was the Civil War a "Second American Revolution"? | ✓ LearningCurve Check what you know. bedfordstmartins.com /roarkunderstanding |

429

deliver the goods. And each year, more railroads were captured, destroyed, or left in disrepair. Food production proved less of a problem, but food sometimes rotted before it reached the soldiers. The one bright spot was the Confederacy's Ordnance Bureau, headed by Josiah Gorgas. In April 1864, Gorgas proudly observed: "Where three years ago we were not making a gun, a pistol nor a sabre, no shot nor shell . . . we now make all these in quantities to meet the demands of our large armies."

Recruiting and supplying huge armies required enormous new revenues. At first, the Union and the Confederacy sold war bonds, which essentially were loans from patriotic citizens. In addition, both sides turned to taxes. Eventually, both began printing paper money. Inflation soared, but the Confederacy suffered more because it financed a greater part of its wartime costs through the printing press. Prices in the Union rose by about 80 percent during the war, while inflation in the Confederacy topped 9,000 percent.

Within months of the bombardment of Fort Sumter, both sides found men to fight and ways to supply them. But the underlying strength of the northern economy gave the Union the decided advantage. With their military and industrial muscles beginning to ripple, Northerners became itchy for action that would smash the rebellion. Horace Greeley's *New York Tribune* began to chant: "Forward to Richmond! Forward to Richmond!"

> **QUICK REVIEW**

Why did the South believe it could win the war despite its numerical disadvantages?

CHAPTER LOCATOR | Why did both the Union and the Confederacy consider control of the border states crucial? | Why did each side expect to win? | **How did each side fare in the early years of the war?**

430 CHAPTER 15 THE CRUCIBLE OF WAR

How did each side fare in the early years of the war?

The Dead of Antietam In October 1862, photographer Mathew Brady opened an exhibition that presented the battle of Antietam as the soldiers saw it. A *New York Times* reporter observed: "Mr. Brady has done something to bring to us the terrible reality and earnestness of the war. If he has not brought bodies and laid them in our door-yards and along [our] streets, he had done something very like it." Library of Congress.

DURING THE FIRST YEAR and a half of the war, armies fought major campaigns in both the East and the West. While the eastern campaign was more dramatic, Lincoln had trouble finding a capable general, and the fighting ended in a stalemate. Battles in the West proved more decisive. Union general Ulysses S. Grant won important victories in Kentucky and Tennessee. As Yankee and rebel armies pounded each other on land, the navies fought on the seas and on the rivers of the South. In Europe, Confederate and U.S. diplomats competed for advantage in the corridors of power. All the while, casualty lists on both sides reached appalling lengths.

Stalemate in the Eastern Theater

In the summer of 1861, Lincoln ordered the 35,000 Union troops assembling outside Washington to attack the 20,000 Confederates defending Manassas, a railroad junction in Virginia about thirty miles southwest of Washington. On July 21, the army forded Bull Run, a branch of the Potomac River, and engaged the southern forces (**Map 15.2**). But fast-moving southern reinforcements blunted the Union attack and then counterattacked. What began as an orderly Union retreat turned into a panicky stampede.

By Civil War standards, the casualties (wounded and dead) at the **battle of Bull Run** (or **Manassas**, as Southerners called the battle) were light, about 2,000

battle of Bull Run (Manassas)

▶ First major battle of the Civil War, fought at a railroad junction in northern Virginia on July 21, 1861. The Union suffered a sobering defeat, while the Confederates felt affirmed in their superiority and the inevitability of Confederate nationhood.

| How did the war for union become a fight for black freedom? | What problems did the Confederacy face at home? | How did the war affect the economy and politics of the North? | How did the Union finally win the war? | Conclusion: In what ways was the Civil War a "Second American Revolution"? | ✓ LearningCurve Check what you know. bedfordstmartins.com /roarkunderstanding |

MAP 15.2 ■ The Civil War, 1861–1862

While most eyes were focused on the eastern theater, especially the ninety-mile stretch of land between Washington, D.C., and the Confederate capital of Richmond, Virginia, Union troops were winning strategic victories in the West.

> MAP ACTIVITY

READING THE MAP: In which states did the Confederacy and the Union each win the most battles during this period? Which side used or followed water routes most for troop movements and attacks?

CONNECTIONS: Which major cities in the South and West fell to Union troops in 1862? Which strategic area did those Confederate losses place in Union hands? How did this outcome affect the later movement of troops and supplies?

Confederates and 1,600 Federals. The significance of the battle lay in the lessons Northerners and Southerners drew from it. For Southerners, it confirmed the superiority of rebel fighting men and the inevitability of Confederate nationhood. While victory fed southern pride, defeat sobered Northerners. It was a major setback, admitted the *New York Tribune*, but "let us go to work, then, with a will." Within four days of the disaster, the president authorized the enlistment of 1 million men for three years.

CHAPTER LOCATOR | Why did both the Union and the Confederacy consider control of the border states crucial? | Why did each side expect to win? | **How did each side fare in the early years of the war?**

CHAPTER 15
THE CRUCIBLE OF WAR

432

Lincoln also appointed the young George B. McClellan commander of the newly named Army of the Potomac. Having graduated from West Point second in his class, the thirty-four-year-old McClellan believed that he was a great soldier and that Lincoln was a dunce, the "original Gorilla." A superb administrator and organizer, McClellan energetically whipped his dispirited soldiers into shape, but for all his energy, McClellan lacked decisiveness. Lincoln wanted a general who would advance, take risks, and fight, but McClellan went into winter quarters. "If General McClellan does not want to use the army I would like to *borrow* it," Lincoln declared in frustration.

Finally, in May 1862, McClellan launched his long-awaited offensive. He transported his highly polished army, now 130,000 strong, to the mouth of the James River and began slowly moving up the Yorktown peninsula toward Richmond. When he was within six miles of the Confederate capital, General Joseph Johnston hit him like a hammer. In the assault, Johnston was wounded and was replaced by Robert E. Lee, who would become the South's most celebrated general. Lee named his command the Army of Northern Virginia.

The contrast between Lee and McClellan could hardly have been greater. McClellan brimmed with conceit; Lee was courteous and reserved. On the battlefield, McClellan grew timid and irresolute, and Lee became audaciously, even recklessly, aggressive. And Lee had at his side in the peninsula campaign military men of real talent: Thomas J. Jackson, nicknamed "Stonewall" for holding the line at Manassas, and James E. B. ("Jeb") Stuart, a dashing twenty-nine-year-old cavalry commander who rode circles around Yankee troops.

Lee's assault initiated the Seven Days Battle (June 25–July 1) and began McClellan's march back down the peninsula. By the time McClellan reached safety, 30,000 men from both sides had died or been wounded. Although Southerners suffered twice the casualties of Northerners, Lee had saved Richmond. Lincoln fired McClellan and replaced him with General John Pope.

In August, north of Richmond, at the second battle of Bull Run, Lee's smaller army battered Pope's forces and sent them scurrying back to Washington. Lincoln ordered Pope to Minnesota to pacify the Indians and restored McClellan to command.

Believing that he had the enemy on the run, Lee pushed his army across the Potomac and invaded Maryland. A victory on northern soil would dislodge Maryland from the Union, Lee reasoned, and might even cause Lincoln to sue for peace. On September 17, 1862, McClellan's forces engaged Lee's army at Antietam Creek (see Map 15.2). With "solid shot . . . cracking skulls like eggshells," according to one observer, the armies went after each other. At Miller's Cornfield, the firing was so intense that "every stalk of corn in the . . . field was cut as closely as could have been done with a knife." By nightfall, 6,000 men lay dead or dying on the battlefield, and 17,000 more had been wounded. The **battle of Antietam** would be the bloodiest day of the war and sent the battered Army of Northern Virginia limping back home. McClellan claimed to have saved the North, but Lincoln again removed him from command of the Army of the Potomac and appointed General Ambrose Burnside.

Though bloodied, Lee found an opportunity in December to punish the enemy at Fredericksburg, Virginia, where Burnside's 122,000 Union troops faced 78,500 Confederates dug in behind a stone wall on the heights above the

Peninsula Campaign, 1862

battle of Antietam
► Battle fought in Maryland on September 17, 1862, between the Union forces of George McClellan and Confederate troops of Robert E. Lee. The battle, a Union victory that left 6,000 dead and 17,000 wounded, was the bloodiest day of the war.

| How did the war for union become a fight for black freedom? | What problems did the Confederacy face at home? | How did the war affect the economy and politics of the North? | How did the Union finally win the war? | Conclusion: In what ways was the Civil War a "Second American Revolution"? | ☑ LearningCurve Check what you know. bedfordstmartins.com /roarkunderstanding |

433

Rappahannock River. Half a mile of open ground separated the armies. "A chicken could not live on that field when we open on it," a Confederate artillery officer predicted. Yet Burnside ordered a frontal assault. When the shooting ceased, the Federals counted nearly 13,000 casualties, the Confederates fewer than 5,000. The battle of Fredericksburg was one of the Union's worst defeats. As 1862 ended, the North seemed no nearer to ending the rebellion than it had been when the war began. Rather than checkmate, military struggle in the East had reached stalemate.

Union Victories in the Western Theater

While most eyes focused on events in the East, the decisive early encounters of the war were taking place between the Appalachian Mountains and the Ozarks (see Map 15.2). Confederates wanted Missouri and Kentucky, states they claimed but did not control. Federals wanted to split Arkansas, Louisiana, and Texas from the Confederacy by taking control of the Mississippi River and to occupy Tennessee, one of the Confederacy's main producers of food, mules, and iron — all vital resources.

Before Union forces could march on Tennessee, they needed to secure Missouri to the west. Union troops swept across Missouri to the border of Arkansas, where in March 1862 they encountered a 16,000-man Confederate army, which included three regiments of Indians from the so-called Five Civilized Tribes — the Choctaw, Chickasaw, Creek, Seminole, and Cherokee. The Union victory at the battle of Pea Ridge left Missouri free of Confederate troops, but guerrilla bands led by the notorious William Clarke Quantrill and "Bloody Bill"

Battle of Glorieta Pass, 1862

Anderson burned, tortured, scalped, and murdered Union civilians and soldiers until the final year of the war.

Even farther west, Confederate armies sought to fulfill Jefferson Davis's vision of a slaveholding empire stretching all the way to the Pacific. Both sides recognized the immense value of the gold and silver mines of California, Nevada, and Colorado. And both sides bolstered their armies in the Southwest with Mexican Americans. A quick strike by Texas troops took Santa Fe, New Mexico, in the winter of 1861–62. Then in March 1862, a band of Colorado miners ambushed and crushed southern forces at Glorieta Pass, outside Santa Fe, effectively ending dreams of a Confederate empire beyond Texas.

The principal western battles took place in Tennessee, where General Ulysses S. Grant emerged as the key northern commander. Grant, a West Point graduate who had served in Mexico, was a thirty-nine-year-old dry-goods clerk in Galena, Illinois, when the war began. Gentle at home, he became pugnacious on the battlefield. "The art of war is simple," he said. "Find out where your enemy is, get at him as soon as you can and strike him as hard as you can, and keep moving on." Grant's philosophy of war as attrition would take a huge toll in

CHAPTER LOCATOR | Why did both the Union and the Confederacy consider control of the border states crucial? | Why did each side expect to win? | **How did each side fare in the early years of the war?**

434 CHAPTER 15 THE CRUCIBLE OF WAR

human life, but it played to the North's superiority in manpower. Later, to critics who wanted the president to sack Grant because of his drinking, Lincoln would say, "*I can't spare this man. He fights.*"

In February 1862, operating in tandem with U.S. Navy gunboats, Grant captured Fort Henry on the Tennessee River and Fort Donelson on the Cumberland (see Map 15.2). Defeat forced the Confederates to withdraw from all of Kentucky and most of Tennessee, but Grant followed.

On April 6, General Albert Sidney Johnston's army surprised Grant at Shiloh Church in Tennessee. Union troops were badly mauled the first day, but Grant remained cool and brought up reinforcements throughout the night. The next morning, the Union army counterattacked, driving the Confederates before it. The **battle of Shiloh** was terribly costly to both sides; there were 20,000 casualties, among them General Johnston. Grant later said that after Shiloh he "gave up all idea of saving the Union except by complete conquest."

Although no one knew it at the time, Shiloh ruined the Confederacy's bid to control the theater of operations in the West. The Yankees quickly captured the strategic town of Corinth, Mississippi; the river city of Memphis; and the South's largest city, New Orleans. By the end of 1862, the far West and most—but not all—of the Mississippi valley lay in Union hands. At the same time, the outcome of the struggle in another theater of war was also becoming clearer.

battle of Shiloh

▶ Battle at Shiloh Church, Tennessee, on April 6–7, 1862, between Albert Sidney Johnston's Confederate forces and Ulysses S. Grant's Union army. The Union army ultimately prevailed, though at great cost to both sides. Shiloh ruined the Confederacy's bid to control the war in the West.

> Major Battles of the Civil War, 1861–1862

April 12–13, 1861	Attack on Fort Sumter
July 21, 1861	First battle of Bull Run (Manassas)
February 6, 1862	Battle of Fort Henry
February 16, 1862	Battle of Fort Donelson
March 6–8, 1862	Battle of Pea Ridge
March 9, 1862	Battle of the *Merrimack* (the *Virginia*) and the *Monitor*
March 26, 1862	Battle of Glorieta Pass
April 6–7, 1862	Battle of Shiloh
May–July 1862	McClellan's peninsula campaign
June 6, 1862	Fall of Memphis
June 25–July 1, 1862	Seven Days Battle
August 29–30, 1862	Second battle of Bull Run (Manassas)
September 17, 1862	Battle of Antietam
December 13, 1862	Battle of Fredericksburg

How did the war for union become a fight for black freedom?

What problems did the Confederacy face at home?

How did the war affect the economy and politics of the North?

How did the Union finally win the war?

Conclusion: In what ways was the Civil War a "Second American Revolution"?

✓ LearningCurve
Check what you know.
bedfordstmartins.com
/roarkunderstanding

The Atlantic Theater

When the war began, the U.S. Navy's blockade fleet consisted of about three dozen ships to patrol more than 3,500 miles of southern coastline, and rebel merchant ships were able to slip in and out of southern ports nearly at will. Taking on cargoes in the Caribbean, sleek Confederate blockade runners brought in vital supplies — guns and medicine. But with the U.S. Navy commissioning a new blockader almost weekly, the naval fleet eventually numbered 150 ships on duty, and the Union navy dramatically improved its score.

Unable to build a conventional navy equal to the expanding U.S. fleet, the Confederates experimented with a radical new maritime design: the ironclad warship. At Norfolk, Virginia, the wooden hull of the *Merrimack* was layered with two-inch-thick armor plate. Rechristened *Virginia*, the ship steamed out in March 1862 and sank two wooden federal ships (see Map 15.2). When the *Virginia* returned to finish off the federal blockaders the next morning, it was challenged by the *Monitor*, a Union ironclad of even more radical design, topped with a revolving turret holding two eleven-inch guns. On March 9, the two ships hurled shells at each other for two hours, but the battle ended in a draw.

The Confederacy never found a way to break the **Union blockade** despite exploring many naval innovations, including a new underwater vessel — the submarine. By 1865, the blockaders were intercepting about half of the southern ships attempting to break through. The Union navy, a southern naval officer observed, "shut the Confederacy out from the world, deprived it of supplies, weakened its military and naval strength." The Confederacy was sealed off, with devastating results.

Union blockade
▶ The United States' use of its navy to patrol the southern coastline to restrict Confederate access to supplies. Over time, the blockade became increasingly effective and succeeded in depriving the Confederacy of vital supplies.

International Diplomacy

What the Confederates could not achieve on the seas, they sought to achieve through international diplomacy. They based their hope for European intervention on King Cotton. In theory, cotton-starved European nations would have no choice but to break the Union blockade and recognize the Confederacy. Southern hopes were not unreasonable, for at the height of the "cotton famine" in 1862, when 2 million British workers were unemployed, Britain tilted toward recognition. Along with several other European nations, Britain granted the Confederacy "belligerent" status, which enabled it to buy goods and build ships in European ports. But no country challenged the Union blockade or recognized the Confederate States of America as a nation, a bold act that probably would have drawn that country into war.

King Cotton diplomacy failed for several reasons. A bumper cotton crop in 1860 meant that the warehouses of British textile manufacturers bulged with surplus cotton throughout 1861. In 1862, when a cotton shortage did occur, European manufacturers found new sources in India, Egypt, and elsewhere. In addition, the development of a brisk trade between the Union and Britain — British war materiel for American grain and flour — helped offset the decline in textiles and encouraged Britain to remain neutral (**Figure 15.2**).

King Cotton diplomacy
▶ Confederate diplomatic strategy built on the hope that European nations starving for cotton would break the Union blockade and recognize the Confederacy. This strategy failed because Europeans held stores of surplus cotton and developed new sources outside the South.

CHAPTER LOCATOR | Why did both the Union and the Confederacy consider control of the border states crucial? | Why did each side expect to win? | **How did each side fare in the early years of the war?**

436 CHAPTER 15 THE CRUCIBLE OF WAR

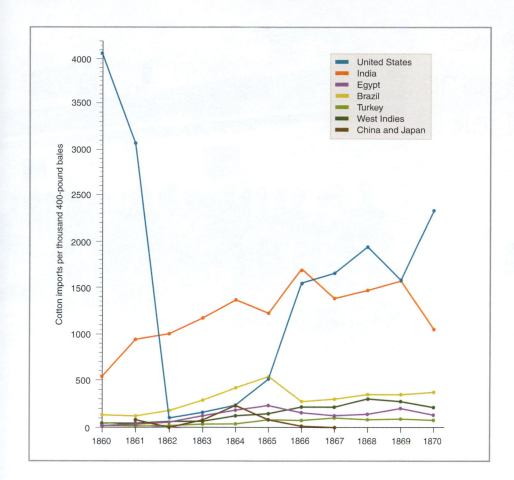

FIGURE 15.2 ■ European Cotton Imports, 1860–1870

In 1860, the South enjoyed a near monopoly in supplying cotton to Europe's textile mills, but the Civil War almost entirely halted its exports. Figures for Europe's importation of cotton for 1861 to 1865 reveal one of the reasons the Confederacy's King Cotton diplomacy failed: Europeans found other sources of cotton. Which countries were most important in filling the void? When the war ended in 1865, cotton production resumed in the South, and exports to Europe again soared. Did the South regain its near monopoly? How would you characterize the United States' competitive position five years after the war?

Europe's temptation to intervene disappeared for good in 1862. Union military successes in the West made Britain and France think twice about linking their fates to the struggling Confederacy. Moreover, in September 1862, Lincoln announced a new policy that made an alliance with the Confederacy an alliance with slavery — a commitment the French and British, who had outlawed slavery in their empires and looked forward to its eradication worldwide, were not willing to make. After 1862, the South's cause was linked irrevocably with slavery and reaction, and the Union's cause was linked with freedom and democracy. The Union, not the Confederacy, had won the diplomatic stakes.

QUICK REVIEW

Why did the Confederacy's bid for international support fail?

LearningCurve Check what you know. bedfordstmartins.com /roarkunderstanding

How did the war for union become a fight for black freedom?

Company E, Fourth U.S. Colored Infantry, Fort Lincoln, Virginia

The Lincoln administration was slow to accept black soldiers into the Union army, in part because of lingering doubts about their ability to fight. But Colonel Thomas W. Higginson, the white commander of the Union's First South Carolina Infantry, which was made up of former slaves, celebrated his men's courage: "No officer in this regiment now doubts that the key to the successful prosecution of this war lies in the unlimited employment of black troops. . . . Instead of leaving their homes and families to fight they are fighting for their homes and families." Before the war was over, ex-slaves and free blacks filled 145 Union regiments. Library of Congress.

FOR A YEAR AND A HALF, Lincoln insisted that the North fought strictly to save the Union and not to abolish slavery. Nevertheless, the war for union became a war for African American freedom. Each month the conflict dragged on, it became clearer that the Confederate war machine depended heavily on slavery. Rebel armies used slaves to build fortifications, haul materiel, tend horses, and perform camp chores. On the southern home front, slaves labored in ironworks and shipyards, and they grew the food that fed both soldiers and civilians. Slavery undergirded the Confederacy as certainly as it had the Old South. Union military commanders and politicians alike gradually realized that to defeat the Confederacy, the North would have to destroy slavery. Lincoln's Emancipation Proclamation began the work, and soon African Americans flooded into the Union army, where they fought against the Confederacy and for black freedom.

From Slaves to Contraband

Lincoln detested human bondage, but as president he felt compelled to act prudently in the interests of the Union. He doubted his right under the Constitution

CHAPTER LOCATOR | Why did both the Union and the Confederacy consider control of the border states crucial? | Why did each side expect to win? | How did each side fare in the early years of the war?

438 CHAPTER 15 THE CRUCIBLE OF WAR

to tamper with the "domestic institutions" of any state, even states in rebellion. An astute politician, Lincoln worked within the tight limits of public opinion. The issue of black freedom was particularly explosive in the loyal border states, where slaveholders threatened to jump into the arms of the Confederacy at even the hint of emancipation.

Black freedom also raised alarms in the free states. The Democratic Party gave notice that adding emancipation to the goal of union would make the war strictly a Republican affair. Moreover, many white Northerners were not about to risk their lives to satisfy what they considered abolitionist "fanaticism." "We Won't Fight to Free the Nigger," one popular banner read. They feared that emancipation would propel "two or three million semi-savages" northward, where they would crowd into white neighborhoods, compete for white jobs, and mix with white "sons and daughters."

Yet proponents of emancipation pressed Lincoln as relentlessly as did the anti-emancipation forces. Abolitionists argued that by seceding, Southerners had forfeited their right to the protection of the Constitution and that Lincoln could — as the price of their treason — legally confiscate their property in slaves. When Lincoln refused, abolitionists scalded him. Frederick Douglass labeled him "the miserable tool of traitors and rebels."

The Republican-dominated Congress declined to leave slavery policy entirely in President Lincoln's hands. In August 1861, Congress approved the Confiscation Act, which allowed the seizure of any slave employed directly by the Confederate military. It also fulfilled the free-soil dream of prohibiting slavery in the territories and abolished slavery in Washington, D.C. Democrats and border-state representatives voted against even these mild measures.

Slaves, not politicians, became the most insistent force for emancipation. By escaping their masters by the tens of thousands and running away to Union lines, they forced slavery on the North's wartime agenda. Runaways made Northerners answer a crucial question: Were the runaways now free, or were they still slaves who, according to the fugitive slave law, had to be returned to their masters? At first, Yankee military officers sent the fugitives back. But Union armies needed laborers, and at Fort Monroe, Virginia, General Benjamin F. Butler called them **contraband of war**, meaning "confiscated property," and put them to work. Congress made Butler's practice national policy in March 1862 when it forbade returning fugitive slaves to their masters. Slaves were still not legally free, but there was a tilt toward emancipation.

Lincoln's policy of noninterference with slavery gradually crumbled. To calm Northerners' racial fears, Lincoln offered colonization, the deportation of African Americans from the United States to Haiti, Panama, or elsewhere. Congress voted a small amount of money to underwrite colonization, but practical limitations and stiff black opposition sank the scheme.

While Lincoln was developing his own antislavery initiatives, he snuffed out actions that he believed would jeopardize northern unity. He was particularly alert to Union commanders who tried to dictate slavery policy from the field. In August 1861, when John C. Frémont, former Republican presidential nominee and now commander of federal troops in Missouri, freed the slaves belonging to Missouri rebels, Lincoln forced the general to revoke his edict. The following May, when General David Hunter freed the slaves in Georgia, South Carolina, and

> CHRONOLOGY

1861
– First Confiscation Act.

1862
– Second Confiscation Act.
– Militia Act.

1863
– Emancipation Proclamation is issued.

contraband of war
▶ General Benjamin F. Butler's term for runaway slaves, who were considered confiscated property of war, not fugitives, and put to work in the Union army. This policy proved to be a step on the road to emancipation.

How did the war for union become a fight for black freedom? | What problems did the Confederacy face at home? | How did the war affect the economy and politics of the North? | How did the Union finally win the war? | Conclusion: In what ways was the Civil War a "Second American Revolution"? | ☑ LearningCurve Check what you know. bedfordstmartins.com /roarkunderstanding

439

Human Contraband

These refugees from slavery crossed the Rappahannock River in Virginia in August 1862 to seek sanctuary with a federal army. Most slaves fled with little more than the clothes on their backs, but not all escaped slavery empty-handed. The oxen, horse, wagon, and goods seen here could have been purchased during slavery, "borrowed" from the former master, or gathered during flight. Library of Congress.

Florida, Lincoln countermanded his order. Events moved so rapidly, however, that Lincoln found it impossible to control federal policy on slavery.

From Contraband to Free People

On August 22, 1862, Lincoln replied to an angry abolitionist who demanded that he attack slavery. "My paramount objective in this struggle *is* to save the Union," Lincoln said, "and is *not* either to save or destroy slavery. If I could save the Union without freeing *any* slave I would do it, and if I could save it by freeing *all* the slaves I would do it; and if I could save it by freeing some and leaving others alone I would also do that." At first glance, Lincoln seemed to restate his old position that union was the North's sole objective. Instead, Lincoln announced that slavery was no longer untouchable and that he would emancipate every slave if doing so would preserve the Union.

By the summer of 1862, events were tumbling rapidly toward emancipation. On July 17, Congress adopted the second Confiscation Act. The first had confiscated slaves employed by the Confederate military; the second declared all slaves of rebel masters "forever free of their servitude." In theory, this breathtaking measure freed most Confederate slaves, for slaveholders formed the backbone of the rebellion. Congress had traveled far since the war began.

Lincoln had, too. By the summer of 1862, the president had come to believe that emancipation was "a military necessity, absolutely essential to the preservation of the Union." In September, he announced his preliminary **Emancipation Proclamation**, which promised to free *all* the slaves in the seceding states on January 1, 1863. The limitations of the proclamation — it exempted the loyal border states and the Union-occupied areas of the Confederacy — caused some to ridicule the act. The *Times* (London) observed cynically, "Where he has no power Mr. Lincoln will set the negroes free, where he retains power he will consider them as slaves." But Lincoln had no power to free slaves in loyal states, and invading Union armies would liberate slaves in the Confederacy as they advanced.

By presenting emancipation as a "military necessity," Lincoln hoped to disarm his conservative critics. Emancipation would deprive the Confederacy of valuable slave laborers, shorten the war, and thus save lives. Democrats, however, fumed

Emancipation Proclamation

▶ President Lincoln's proclamation issued on January 1, 1863, declaring all slaves in Confederate-controlled territory free. The proclamation made the Civil War a war to free slaves; however, its limitations — exemptions for loyal border states and Union-occupied areas of the Confederacy — made some ridicule the act.

CHAPTER LOCATOR | Why did both the Union and the Confederacy consider control of the border states crucial? | Why did each side expect to win? | How did each side fare in the early years of the war?

CHAPTER 15
440 THE CRUCIBLE OF WAR

that the "shrieking and howling abolitionist faction" had captured the White House and made it "a nigger war." Democrats gained thirty-four congressional seats in the November 1862 elections. House Democrats quickly proposed a resolution branding emancipation "a high crime against the Constitution." The Republicans, who maintained narrow majorities in both houses of Congress, barely beat it back.

As promised, on New Year's Day 1863, Lincoln issued the final Emancipation Proclamation. In addition to freeing the slaves in the rebel states, the Emancipation Proclamation also committed the federal government to the fullest use of African Americans to defeat the Confederate enemy.

The War of Black Liberation

Even before Lincoln proclaimed emancipation a Union war aim, African Americans in the North had volunteered to fight. But the War Department, doubtful of blacks' abilities and fearful of white reaction to serving side by side with them, refused to make black men soldiers. Instead, the army employed black men as manual laborers; black women sometimes found employment as laundresses and cooks. The navy, however, accepted blacks from the outset, including runaway slaves.

As Union casualty lists lengthened, Northerners gradually and reluctantly turned to African Americans to fill the army's blue uniforms. With the Militia Act of July 1862, Congress authorized enrolling blacks in "any military or naval service for which they may be found competent." After the Emancipation Proclamation, whites — like it or not — were fighting and dying for black freedom, and few insisted that blacks remain out of harm's way behind the lines. Indeed, whites insisted that blacks share the danger, especially after March 1863, when Congress resorted to the draft to fill the Union army.

The military was far from color-blind. The Union army established segregated black regiments, paid black soldiers $10 per month rather than the $13 it paid whites, refused blacks the opportunity to become commissioned officers, punished blacks as if they were slaves, and assigned blacks to labor battalions rather than to combat units. Still, when the war ended, 179,000 African American men had served in the Union army.

In time, whites allowed blacks to put down their shovels and to shoulder rifles. At the battles of Port Hudson and Milliken's Bend on the Mississippi River and at Fort Wagner in Charleston harbor, black courage under fire finally dispelled notions that African Americans could not fight. More than 38,000 black soldiers died in the Civil War, a mortality rate that was higher than that of white troops. Blacks played a crucial role in the triumph of the Union and the destruction of slavery in the South.

QUICK REVIEW

Why did the Union change policy in 1863 to allow black men to serve in the army?

| **How did the war for union become a fight for black freedom?** | What problems did the Confederacy face at home? | How did the war affect the economy and politics of the North? | How did the Union finally win the war? | Conclusion: In what ways was the Civil War a "Second American Revolution"? | ☑ LearningCurve Check what you know. bedfordstmartins.com /roarkunderstanding |

441

What problems did the Confederacy face at home?

Confederate Soldiers and Their Slaves

Soldiers of the Seventh Tennessee Cavalry pose with their slaves. Many slaveholders took "body servants" with them to war. These slaves cooked, washed, and cleaned for the white soldiers. In 1861, James H. Langhorne reported to his sister: "Peter . . . is charmed with being with me & 'being a soldier.' I gave him my old uniform overcoat & he says he is going to have his picture taken . . . to send to the servants." Do you think Peter was "puttin' on ol' massa" or just glad to be free of plantation labor? Daguerreotype courtesy of Tom Farish. Photographed by Michael Latil.

> **VISUAL ACTIVITY**

READING THE IMAGE: What can we glean from this image about a Confederate soldier's life in the military?
CONNECTIONS: This daguerreotype likely was not taken for any purpose other than to capture the camaraderie of four southern cavalrymen, yet the inclusion of the two slaves speaks volumes. What are the possible ramifications of slaveholders bringing "body servants" to war?

BY SECEDING, Southerners brought on themselves a firestorm of unimaginable fury. Monstrous losses on the battlefield nearly bled the Confederacy to death. Southerners on the home front also suffered, even at the hands of their own government. Efforts by the Davis administration in Richmond to centralize power in order to fight the war convinced some men and women that the Confederacy had betrayed them. They charged Richmond with tyranny when it impressed goods and slaves and drafted men into the army. War also meant severe economic deprivation. Shortages and inflation hurt everyone, some more than others. By 1863, unequal suffering meant that planters and yeomen who had stood together began to drift apart. Most disturbing of all, slaves became open participants in the destruction of slavery and the Confederacy.

Revolution from Above

As a Confederate general observed, Southerners were engaged in a total war "in which the whole population and the whole production . . . are to be put on a war

CHAPTER LOCATOR | Why did both the Union and the Confederacy consider control of the border states crucial? | Why did each side expect to win? | How did each side fare in the early years of the war?

442 CHAPTER 15
THE CRUCIBLE OF WAR

footing, where every institution is to be made auxiliary to war." Jefferson Davis faced the task of building an army and a navy from almost nothing, supplying them from factories that were scarce and anemic, and paying for it all from a treasury that did not exist. Finding eager soldiers proved easiest. Hundreds of officers defected from the U.S. Army, and hundreds of thousands of eager young rebels volunteered to follow them.

The Confederacy's economy and finances proved tougher problems. Because of the Union blockade, the government had no choice but to build an industrial sector itself. Government-owned clothing and shoe factories, mines, arsenals, and powder works sprang up. The government also harnessed private companies, such as the huge Tredegar Iron Works in Richmond, to the war effort. Paying for the war became the most difficult task. A flood of paper money caused debilitating inflation. By Christmas 1864, a Confederate soldier's monthly pay no longer bought a pair of socks. The Confederacy manufactured much more than most people imagined possible, but it never produced all that the South needed.

Richmond's war-making effort brought unprecedented government intrusion into the private lives of Confederate citizens. In April 1862, the Confederate Congress passed the first conscription (draft) law in American history. All able-bodied white males between the ages of eighteen and thirty-five (later seventeen and fifty) were liable to serve in the rebel army. The government adopted a policy of impressment, which allowed officials to confiscate food, horses, wagons, and whatever else they wanted from private citizens and to pay for them at below-market rates. After March 1863, the Confederacy legally impressed slaves, employing them as military laborers.

Richmond's centralizing efforts ran head-on into the South's traditional values of states' rights and unfettered individualism. Southerners lashed out at what Georgia governor Joseph E. Brown denounced as the "dangerous usurpation by Congress of the reserved right of the States." Richmond and the states struggled for control of money, supplies, and soldiers, with damaging consequences for the war effort.

Hardship Below

Hardships on the home front fell most heavily on the poor. The draft stripped yeoman farms of men, leaving the women and children to grow what they ate. Government agents took 10 percent of harvests as a "tax-in-kind" on agriculture. Like inflation, shortages afflicted the entire population, but the rich lost luxuries while the poor lost necessities. In the spring of 1863, bread riots broke out in a dozen cities and villages across the South. In Richmond, a mob of nearly a thousand hungry women broke into shops and took what they needed.

"Men cannot be expected to fight for the Government that permits their wives & children to starve," one Southerner observed. Although a few wealthy individuals shared their bounty and the Confederate and state governments made efforts at social welfare, every attempt fell short. When the war ended, one-third of the soldiers had already gone home. A Mississippi deserter explained, "We are poor men and are willing to defend our country but our families [come] first."

Yeomen perceived a profound inequality of sacrifice. They called it "a rich man's war and a poor man's fight." The draft law permitted a man who had

> CHRONOLOGY

1862
– Confederate Congress authorizes draft.

1863
– Bread riots break out in the South.

How did the war for union become a fight for black freedom?

What problems did the Confederacy face at home?

How did the war affect the economy and politics of the North?

How did the Union finally win the war?

Conclusion: In what ways was the Civil War a "Second American Revolution"?

☑ LearningCurve
Check what you know.
bedfordstmartins.com
/roarkunderstanding

443

money to hire a substitute to take his place. Moreover, the "twenty-Negro law" exempted one white man on every plantation with twenty or more slaves. The government intended this law to provide protection for white women and to see that slaves tended the crops, but yeomen perceived it as rich men evading military service. A Mississippian complained that stay-at-home planters sent their slaves into the fields to grow cotton while in plain view "poor soldiers' wives are plowing with their own hands to make a subsistence for themselves and children — while their husbands are suffering, bleeding and dying for their country." In fact, most slaveholders went off to war, but the extreme suffering of common folk and the relative immunity of planters increased class friction.

The Richmond government hoped that the crucible of war would mold a region into a nation. Officials actively promoted Confederate nationalism to "excite in our citizens an ardent and enduring attachment to our Government and its institutions." Clergymen assured their congregations that God had blessed slavery and the new nation. Jefferson Davis claimed that the Confederacy was part of a divine plan and asked citizens to observe national days of fasting and prayer. But these efforts failed to win over thousands of die-hard Unionists, and animosity between yeomen and planters increased. The war also threatened to rip the southern social fabric along its racial seam.

The Disintegration of Slavery

The legal destruction of slavery was the product of presidential proclamation, congressional legislation, and eventually constitutional amendment, but the practical destruction of slavery was the product of war, what Lincoln called war's "friction and abrasion." Slaves took advantage of the upheaval to reach for freedom. Some half a million of the South's 4 million slaves ran away to Union military lines. More than 100,000 runaways took up arms as federal soldiers and sailors and attacked slavery directly. Other men and women stayed in the slave quarter, where they staked their claim to more freedom.

War disrupted slavery in a dozen ways. Almost immediately, it called the master away, leaving the mistress to assume responsibility for the plantation. But mistresses could not maintain traditional standards of slave discipline in wartime, and the balance of power shifted. Slaves got to the fields late, worked indifferently, and quit early. Some slaveholders responded violently; most saw no alternative but to strike bargains — offering gifts or part of the crop — to keep slaves at home and at work. Slaveholders had believed that they "knew" their slaves, but they learned that they did not. When the war began, a North Carolina woman praised her slaves as "diligent and respectful." When it ended, she said, "As to the idea of a *faithful servant, it is all a fiction.*"

> **QUICK REVIEW**

How did wartime hardship in the South
contribute to class friction?

| Why did both the Union and the Confederacy consider control of the border states crucial? | Why did each side expect to win? | How did each side fare in the early years of the war? |

How did the war affect the economy and politics of the North?

U.S. Sanitary Commission, Brandy Station, Virginia, 1863
The burden of caring for millions of Union soldiers was more than the government could shoulder. Private initiative in the form of the U.S. Sanitary Commission brought additional medical attention to the Union wounded and boosted the comfort and morale of soldiers in the camps. National Archives.

ALTHOUGH LITTLE FIGHTING took place on northern soil, almost every family had a son, husband, father, or brother in uniform. Moreover, total war blurred the distinction between home front and battlefield. As in the South, men marched off to fight, but preserving the country was also women's work. For civilians as well as soldiers, for women as well as men, war was transforming.

The need to build and fuel the Union war machine strengthened the federal government and boosted the economy. The Union sent nearly 2 million men into the military yet managed to increase production in almost every area. But because the rewards and burdens of patriotism were distributed unevenly, the North experienced sharp, even violent, divisions. Workers confronted employers, whites confronted blacks, and Democrats confronted Republicans. Still, Northerners on the home front remained fervently attached to the Union.

The Government and the Economy

When the war began, the United States had no national banking system, no national currency, and no federal income tax. But the secession of eleven slave states cut the Democrats' strength in Congress in half and destroyed their capacity to resist Republican economic programs. Before the war ended, the Republicans had turned their economic vision into law.

> **CHRONOLOGY**

1863
– National Banking Act.
– Congress authorizes draft.
– New York City draft riots.

How did the war for union become a fight for black freedom?

What problems did the Confederacy face at home?

How did the war affect the economy and politics of the North?

How did the Union finally win the war?

Conclusion: In what ways was the Civil War a "Second American Revolution"?

✓ **LearningCurve**
Check what you know.
bedfordstmartins.com
/roarkunderstanding

- The Legal Tender Act (February 1862) creates a national currency.
- The National Banking Act (February 1863) establishes a system of national banks.
- Congress also enacts a series of sweeping tax laws, including the first income tax.

The Republicans' wartime legislation also aimed at integrating the West into the Union. In May 1862, Congress approved the Homestead Act, which offered 160 acres of public land to settlers who would live and labor on it. The Homestead Act bolstered western loyalty and in time resulted in more than a million new farms. The Pacific Railroad Act in July 1862 provided massive federal assistance for building a transcontinental railroad that ran from Omaha to San Francisco when completed in 1869. To achieve this goal, Congress also offered subsidies for the Pony Express mail service and a transcontinental telegraph.

In addition, Congress created the Department of Agriculture and passed the Land-Grant College Act (also known as the Morrill Act after its sponsor, Representative Justin Morrill of Vermont), which set aside public land to support universities that emphasized "agriculture and mechanical arts." The Lincoln administration immeasurably strengthened the North's effort to win the war, but its ideas also permanently changed the nation.

Women and Work at Home and at War

More than a million farm men were called to the military, and farm women added men's chores to their own. "I met more women driving teams on the road and saw more at work in the fields than men," a visitor to Iowa reported in the fall of 1862. Rising production testified to their success in plowing, planting, and harvesting. Rapid mechanization assisted farm women in their new roles. Cyrus McCormick sold 165,000 of his reapers during the war years. The combination of high prices for farm products and increased production ensured that war and prosperity joined hands in the rural North.

In cities, women stepped into jobs vacated by men, particularly in manufacturing, and also into essentially new occupations such as government secretaries and clerks. The number of women working for wages rose 40 percent during the war. As more and more women entered the workforce, employers cut wages. In 1864, New York seamstresses working fourteen-hour days earned only $1.54 a week. Urban workers resorted increasingly to strikes to wrench decent salaries from their employers, but their protests rarely succeeded.

Most middle-class white women stayed home and contributed to the war effort in traditional ways. They sewed, wrapped bandages, and sold homemade goods at local fairs to raise money to aid the soldiers. Other women expressed their patriotism in an untraditional way. Defying prejudices about female delicacy, thousands of women on both sides volunteered to nurse the wounded. Many northern female volunteers worked through the U.S. Sanitary Commission, a huge civilian organization that bought and distributed clothing, food, and medicine, recruited doctors and nurses, and buried the dead.

Some volunteers went on to become paid military nurses. Dorothea Dix, well known for her efforts to reform insane asylums, was named superintendent of female nurses in April 1861. By 1863, some 3,000 nurses served under her. Most

CHAPTER LOCATOR | Why did both the Union and the Confederacy consider control of the border states crucial? | Why did each side expect to win? | How did each side fare in the early years of the war?

446 CHAPTER 15 THE CRUCIBLE OF WAR

nurses worked in hospitals behind the battle lines, but some, like Clara Barton, who later founded the American Red Cross, worked in battlefield units. Women who served in the war went on to lead the postwar movement to establish training schools for female nurses.

Politics and Dissent

At first, the bustle of economic and military mobilization seemed to silence politics, but bipartisan unity did not last. Within a year, Democrats were labeling the Republican administration a "reign of terror" and denouncing as unconstitutional Republican policies expanding federal power, subsidizing private business, and emancipating the slaves. In turn, Republicans were calling Democrats the party of "Dixie, Davis, and the Devil."

When the Republican-dominated Congress enacted the draft law in March 1863, Democrats had another grievance. The law required that all men between the ages of twenty and forty-five enroll and make themselves available for a lottery that would decide who went to war. It also allowed a draftee to hire a substitute or simply to pay a $300 fee and get out of his military obligation. As in the South, common folk could be heard chanting, "A rich man's war and a poor man's fight."

Linking the draft and emancipation, Democrats argued that Republicans employed an unconstitutional means (the draft) to achieve an unconstitutional end (emancipation). In the summer of 1863, antidraft, antiblack mobs went on rampages in northern cities. In July in New York City, Democratic Irish workingmen — crowded into filthy tenements, gouged by inflation, enraged by the draft, and dead set against fighting to free blacks — erupted in four days of rioting. The **New York City draft riots** killed at least 105 people, most of them black.

Lincoln called Democratic opposition to the war "the fire in the rear" and believed that it was even more threatening to national survival than were Confederate armies. The antiwar wing of the Democratic Party, the Peace Democrats — whom some called "Copperheads," after the poisonous snake — found their chief spokesman in Ohio congressman Clement Vallandigham. Vallandigham demanded: "Stop fighting. Make an armistice. . . . Withdraw your army from the seceding States."

In September 1862, in an effort to stifle opposition to the war, Lincoln placed under military arrest any person who discouraged enlistments, resisted the draft, or engaged in "disloyal" practices. Before the war ended, his administration imprisoned nearly 14,000 individuals, most in the border states. The administration's heavy-handed tactics suppressed free speech, but the campaign fell short of a reign of terror, for the majority of the prisoners were not northern Democratic opponents but Confederates, blockade runners, and citizens of foreign countries, and most of those arrested gained quick release. Still, the administration's net captured Vallandigham, who was arrested, convicted of treason, and banished.

New York City draft riots
▶ Four days of rioting in New York City in July 1863 triggered by efforts to enforce the military draft. Democratic Irish workingmen — suffering economic hardship, infuriated by the draft, and opposed to emancipation — killed at least 105 people, most of them black.

QUICK REVIEW ◀

Why was the U.S. Congress able to pass such a bold legislative agenda during the war?

| How did the war for union become a fight for black freedom? | What problems did the Confederacy face at home? | **How did the war affect the economy and politics of the North?** | How did the Union finally win the war? | Conclusion: In what ways was the Civil War a "Second American Revolution"? | ☑ LearningCurve Check what you know. bedfordstmartins.com /roarkunderstanding |

How did the Union finally win the war?

Ruins of Richmond As the Confederate government evacuated Richmond during the evening of April 2, 1865, demolition squads set fire to everything that had military or industrial value. Huge explosions devastated the arsenal, the ruins of which are shown here. As one witness observed, "The old war-scarred city seemed to prefer annihilation to conquest." Library of Congress.

siege of Vicksburg
▶ Six-week siege by General Ulysses S. Grant intended to starve out Vicksburg, Mississippi. On July 4, 1863, the 30,000 Confederate troops holding the city surrendered. The victory gave the Union control of the Mississippi River and, together with Gettysburg, marked a major turning point of the war.

Vicksburg Campaign, 1863

IN THE EARLY MONTHS of 1863, the Union's prospects looked bleak, and the Confederate cause stood at high tide. Then, in July 1863, the tide began to turn. The military man most responsible for this shift was Ulysses S. Grant. Elevated to supreme command in 1864, Grant knit together a powerful war machine that integrated a sophisticated command structure, modern technology, and complex logistics and supply systems. Grant's plan was simple: Killing more of the enemy than he killed of you equaled "the complete over-throw of the rebellion."

The North ground out the victory battle by bloody battle. Still, Southerners were not deterred. The fighting escalated in the last two years of the war. As national elections approached in the fall of 1864, Lincoln expected a war-weary North to reject him. Instead, northern voters declared their willingness to continue the war in the defense of the ideals of union and freedom. Lincoln lived to see victory, but only days after Lee surrendered, the president died from an assassin's bullet.

Vicksburg and Gettysburg

Vicksburg, Mississippi, situated on the eastern bank of the Mississippi River, stood between Union forces and complete control of the river. In May 1863, Union forces under Grant laid siege to the city in an effort to starve out the enemy. As the **siege of Vicksburg** dragged on, civilians ate mules and rats to survive. After six weeks, on July 4, 1863, nearly 30,000 rebels marched out of Vicksburg, stacked their arms, and surrendered unconditionally. A Yankee captain wrote home to his

CHAPTER LOCATOR

| Why did both the Union and the Confederacy consider control of the border states crucial? | Why did each side expect to win? | How did each side fare in the early years of the war? |

CHAPTER 15
THE CRUCIBLE OF WAR

448

wife: "The backbone of the Rebellion is this day broken. The Confederacy is divided. . . . Vicksburg is ours. The Mississippi River is opened, and Gen. Grant is to be our next President."

On the same Fourth of July, word arrived that Union forces had crushed General Lee at Gettysburg, Pennsylvania (**Map 15.3**). Emboldened by his victory at Chancellorsville in May, Lee and his 75,000-man army had invaded Pennsylvania. On June 28, Union forces under General George G. Meade intercepted the

MAP 15.3 ■ The Civil War, 1863–1865

Ulysses S. Grant's victory at Vicksburg divided the Confederacy at the Mississippi River. William Tecumseh Sherman's march from Chattanooga to Savannah divided it again. In northern Virginia, Robert E. Lee fought fiercely, but Grant's larger, better-supplied armies prevailed.

> MAP ACTIVITY

READING THE MAP: Describe the difference between Union and Confederate naval capacity. Were the battles shown on the map fought primarily in Union-controlled or in Confederate-controlled territory? (Look at the land areas on the map.)

CONNECTIONS: Did former slaves serve in the Civil War? If so, on which side(s), and what did they do?

| How did the war for union become a fight for black freedom? | What problems did the Confederacy face at home? | How did the war affect the economy and politics of the North? | **How did the Union finally win the war?** | Conclusion: In what ways was the Civil War a "Second American Revolution"? | ✓ *LearningCurve* Check what you know. bedfordstmartins.com /roarkunderstanding |

▶ Battle fought at Gettysburg, Pennsylvania (July 1–3, 1863), between Union forces under General George G. Meade and Confederate forces under General Robert E. Lee. The Union emerged victorious, and Lee lost more than one-third of his men. Together with Vicksburg, Gettysburg marked a major turning point of the war.

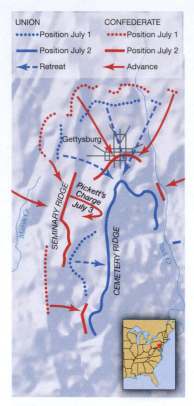

Battle of Gettysburg, July 1–3, 1863

Confederates at the small town of Gettysburg, where Union soldiers occupied the high ground. In three days of furious fighting, the Confederates failed to dislodge the Federals. The **battle of Gettysburg** cost Lee more than one-third of his army — 28,000 casualties. "It's all my fault," he lamented. On the night of July 4, 1863, he marched his battered army back to Virginia.

The twin disasters at Vicksburg and Gettysburg proved to be the turning point of the war. The Confederacy could not replace the nearly 60,000 soldiers who were captured, wounded, or killed. It is hindsight, however, that permits us to see the pair of battles as decisive. At the time, the Confederacy still controlled the heartland of the South, and Lee still had a vicious sting. War-weariness threatened to erode the North's will to win before Union armies could destroy the Confederacy's ability to go on.

Grant Takes Command

In September 1863, Union general William Rosecrans placed his army in a dangerous situation in Chattanooga, Tennessee, where he had retreated after defeat at the battle of Chickamauga (see Map 15.3). Rebels surrounded the disorganized bluecoats and threatened to starve them into submission. Grant, now commander of Union forces between the Mississippi River and the Appalachians, arrived in nearby Chattanooga in October. Within weeks, he opened an effective supply line, broke the siege, and routed the Confederate army. The victory at Chattanooga on November 25 opened the door to Georgia. In March 1864, Lincoln asked Grant to come east to become the general in chief of all Union armies.

In Washington, General Grant implemented his grand strategy for a war of attrition. He ordered a series of simultaneous assaults from Virginia all the way to Louisiana. Two actions proved particularly significant. In one, General William Tecumseh Sherman, whom Grant appointed his successor to command the western armies, plunged southeast toward Atlanta. In the other, Grant, who took control of the Army of the Potomac, went head-to-head with Lee in Virginia in May and June of 1864.

The fighting between Grant and Lee was particularly savage. At the battle of the Wilderness, where a dense tangle of forest often made it impossible to see more than ten paces, the armies pounded away at each other until approximately 18,000 Yankees and 11,000 rebels had fallen. At Spotsylvania Court House, frenzied men fought hand to hand for eighteen hours in the rain. One veteran remembered men "piled upon each other in some places four layers deep, exhibiting every ghastly phase of mutilation." Spotsylvania cost Grant another 18,000 casualties and Lee 10,000. Grant kept moving and attacked Lee again at Cold Harbor, where he suffered 13,000 additional casualties to Lee's 5,000.

Twice as many Union soldiers as rebel soldiers died in four weeks of fighting in Virginia, but because Lee had only half as many troops as Grant, his losses were equivalent to Grant's. Grant knew that the South could not replace the losses. Moreover, the campaign carried Grant to the outskirts of Petersburg, just south of Richmond, where he abandoned the costly tactic of the frontal assault and began a siege that immobilized both armies and dragged on for nine months.

Simultaneously, Sherman invaded Georgia. Skillful maneuvering, constant skirmishing, and one pitched battle, at Kennesaw Mountain, brought Sherman to

CHAPTER LOCATOR | Why did both the Union and the Confederacy consider control of the border states crucial? | Why did each side expect to win? | How did each side fare in the early years of the war?

450 CHAPTER 15 THE CRUCIBLE OF WAR

Atlanta, which fell on September 2. Intending to "make Georgia howl," Sherman marched out of Atlanta on November 15 with 62,000 battle-hardened veterans, heading for Savannah, 285 miles away on the Atlantic coast. One veteran remembered, "[We] destroyed all we could not eat, stole their niggers, burned their cotton & gins, spilled their sorghum, burned & twisted their R. Roads and raised Hell generally." **Sherman's March to the Sea** aimed at destroying the will of white Southerners to continue the war. A few weeks earlier, General Philip H. Sheridan had carried out his own scorched-earth campaign in the Shenandoah Valley. When Sherman's troops entered an undefended Savannah in mid-December, the general telegraphed Lincoln that he had "a Christmas gift" for him. A month earlier, Union voters had bestowed on the president an even greater gift.

> **CHRONOLOGY**

1863
– Vicksburg falls to Union forces.
– Lee is defeated at battle of Gettysburg.

1864
– Grant is appointed Union general in chief.
– Wilderness campaign.
– Atlanta falls to Union forces.
– Lincoln is reelected.

1865
– Richmond falls to Union forces.
– Lee surrenders at Appomattox Court House.
– Lincoln is assassinated.
– Andrew Johnson becomes president.

> Major Battles of the Civil War, 1863–1865	
May 1–4, 1863	Battle of Chancellorsville
July 1–3, 1863	Battle of Gettysburg
July 4, 1863	Fall of Vicksburg
September 16–20, 1863	Battle of Chickamauga
November 23–25, 1863	Battle of Chattanooga
May 5–7, 1864	Battle of the Wilderness
May 7–19, 1864	Battle of Spotsylvania Court House
June 3, 1864	Battle of Cold Harbor
June 27, 1864	Battle of Kennesaw Mountain
September 2, 1864	Fall of Atlanta
November–December 1864	Sheridan sacks Shenandoah Valley Sherman's March to the Sea
December 15–16, 1864	Battle of Nashville
December 22, 1864	Fall of Savannah
April 2–3, 1865	Fall of Petersburg and Richmond
April 9, 1865	Lee surrenders at Appomattox Court House

Sherman's March to the Sea

▶ Military campaign from September through December 1864 in which Union forces under General William Tecumseh Sherman marched from Atlanta, Georgia, to the coast at Savannah. Carving a path of destruction as it progressed, Sherman's army aimed at destroying white Southerners' will to continue the war.

The Election of 1864

In the summer of 1864, with Sherman temporarily checked outside Atlanta and Grant bogged down in the siege of Petersburg, the Democratic Party smelled victory in the fall elections. Lincoln himself concluded, "It seems exceedingly probable that this administration will not be re-elected."

The Democrats were badly divided, however. "Peace" Democrats insisted on an armistice, while "war" Democrats supported the conflict but opposed Republican

| How did the war for union become a fight for black freedom? | What problems did the Confederacy face at home? | How did the war affect the economy and politics of the North? | **How did the Union finally win the war?** | Conclusion: In what ways was the Civil War a "Second American Revolution"? | ✔ LearningCurve Check what you know. bedfordstmartins.com /roarkunderstanding |

means of fighting it. The party tried to paper over the chasm by nominating a war candidate, General George McClellan, but adopting a peace platform that demanded that "immediate efforts be made for a cessation of hostilities." Republicans denounced the peace plank as a cut-and-run plan that "virtually proposed to surrender the country to the rebels in arms against us."

The capture of Atlanta in September turned the political tide in favor of the Republicans. Lincoln received 55 percent of the popular vote, but his electoral margin was a whopping 212 to McClellan's 21. Lincoln's party won a resounding victory, one that gave him a mandate to continue the war until slavery and the Confederacy were dead.

The Confederacy Collapses

As 1865 dawned, military disaster littered the Confederate landscape. With the destruction of John B. Hood's army at Nashville in December 1864, the interior of the Confederacy lay in Yankee hands (see Map 15.3). Sherman's troops, resting momentarily in Savannah, eyed South Carolina hungrily. Farther north, Grant had Lee's army pinned down in Petersburg, a few miles from Richmond.

Some Confederates turned their backs on the rebellion. News from the battle-field made it difficult not to conclude that the Yankees had beaten them. Soldiers' wives begged their husbands to return home to keep their families from starving, and the stream of deserters grew dramatically. Still, white Southerners had demonstrated a remarkable endurance for their cause. Half of the 900,000 Confederate soldiers had been killed or wounded, and ragged, hungry women and children had sacrificed throughout one of the bloodiest wars then known to history.

The end came with a rush. On February 1, 1865, Sherman's troops stormed out of Savannah into South Carolina, the "cradle of the Confederacy." In Virginia, Lee abandoned Petersburg on April 2, and Richmond fell on April 3. Grant pursued Lee until he surrendered on April 9, 1865, at Appomattox Court House, Virginia. Grant offered generous peace terms. He allowed Lee's men to return home and to keep their horses to help "put in a crop to carry themselves and their families through the next winter." With Lee gone, the remaining Confederate armies lost hope and gave up within two weeks. After four years, the war was over.

No one was more relieved than Lincoln, but his celebration was restrained. He told his cabinet that his postwar burdens would weigh almost as heavily as those of wartime. Seeking a distraction, Lincoln attended Ford's Theatre on the evening of Good Friday, April 14, 1865. John Wilkes Booth, an actor with southern sympathies, slipped into the president's box and shot Lincoln, who died the next morning. Vice President Andrew Johnson became president. The man who had led the nation through the war would not lead it during the postwar search for a just peace.

> QUICK REVIEW

Why were the siege of Vicksburg and the battle of Gettysburg crucial to the outcome of the war?

CHAPTER LOCATOR | Why did both the Union and the Confederacy consider control of the border states crucial? | Why did each side expect to win? | How did each side fare in the early years of the war?

452 CHAPTER 15
THE CRUCIBLE OF WAR

Conclusion: In what ways was the Civil War a "Second American Revolution"?

A TRANSFORMED NATION EMERGED from the crucible of war. Antebellum America was decentralized politically and loosely integrated economically. To bend the resources of the country to a Union victory, Congress enacted legislation that reshaped the nation's political and economic character. It created a transcontinental railroad and miles of telegraph lines to bind the West to the rest of the nation. The massive changes brought about by the war — the creation of a national government, a national economy, and a national spirit — led one historian to call the American Civil War the "Second American Revolution."

The Civil War also had a profound effect on individual lives. Millions of men put on blue or gray uniforms and fought and suffered for what they passionately believed was right. The war disrupted families, leaving women at home with additional responsibilities and giving others wartime work in factories, offices, and hospitals. It offered blacks new and more effective ways to resist slavery and agitate for equality.

The war devastated the South. Three-fourths of southern white men of military age served in the Confederate army, and half of them were wounded or killed or died of disease. The war destroyed two-fifths of the South's livestock, wrecked half of the farm machinery, and blackened dozens of cities and towns. The struggle also cost the North a heavy price: 360,000 lives. But rather than devastating the land, the war set the countryside and cities humming with business activity. The radical shift in power from South to North signaled a new direction in American development: the long decline of agriculture and the rise of industrial capitalism.

Most revolutionary of all, the war ended slavery. Ironically, the South's war to preserve slavery destroyed it. Nearly 200,000 black men dedicated their wartime service to its eradication. Because slavery was both a labor and a racial system, the institution was entangled in almost every aspect of southern life. Slavery's uprooting inevitably meant fundamental change. But the full meaning of abolition remained unclear in 1865, and the status of ex-slaves would be the principal task of reconstruction.

How did the war for union become a fight for black freedom?

What problems did the Confederacy face at home?

How did the war affect the economy and politics of the North?

How did the Union finally win the war?

Conclusion: In what ways was the Civil War a "Second American Revolution"?

☑ **LearningCurve** Check what you know. bedfordstmartins.com /roarkunderstanding

453

CHAPTER 15 STUDY GUIDE

 STEP 1 — GET STARTED ONLINE

✓ **LearningCurve** ▪ bedfordstmartins.com/roarkunderstanding

Now that you've read the chapter, make it stick by completing the LearningCurve activity.

 STEP 2 — EXPLAIN WHY IT MATTERS

Put your reading into practice. Identify each term below, and then explain why it matters in U.S. history.

TERM	WHO OR WHAT & WHEN	WHY IT MATTERS
Fort Sumter (p. 425)		
battle of Bull Run (Manassas) (p. 431)		
battle of Antietam (p. 433)		
battle of Shiloh (p. 435)		
Union blockade (p. 436)		
King Cotton diplomacy (p. 436)		
contraband of war (p. 439)		
Emancipation Proclamation (p. 440)		
New York City draft riots (p. 447)		
siege of Vicksburg (p. 448)		
battle of Gettysburg (p. 450)		
Sherman's March to the Sea (p. 451)		

 STEP 3 — MOVE BEYOND THE BASICS

To demonstrate a more advanced understanding, assess the strengths and weaknesses of the North and South at the outset of the Civil War. Why did the war take much longer than most people imagined at the outset?

Category	South	North
Population		
Industry		
Financial resources		
Leadership		
War strategy		

STEP 4 **PUT IT ALL TOGETHER**   Now, take a step back and try to explain the big picture. Remember to use specific examples from the chapter in your answers.

THE EARLY YEARS OF THE WAR

▶ Why did the North, with all its advantages, fail to achieve a rapid victory over the South?

▶ Why did the South fail to attract international support for its cause?

THE HOME FRONT

▶ Why did Lincoln decide to issue the Emancipation Proclamation? How did Northerners respond to this decision?

▶ Why did conditions in the South deteriorate as the war went on? How did problems on the home front undermine the South's war effort?

UNION VICTORY

▶ What was Grant's strategy? How did it turn the tide of the war?

▶ Is it possible to identify a point at which Union victory became inevitable? Explain your reasoning.

LOOKING BACKWARD, LOOKING AHEAD

▶ Argue for or against the following statement: "The root cause of the Civil War was the failure of the architects of the Constitution to resolve the issue of slavery once and for all."

▶ What changes that occurred during the Civil War might have forecast what a northern victory would mean for the nation?

> **IN YOUR OWN WORDS**   Imagine that you must give an oral report to the class answering the following question: **How did the Civil War change the nation, North and South?** What would be the most important points to include and why?

> **Do it online at the Student Site** ■ **bedfordstmartins.com/roarkunderstanding**

16

RECONSTRUCTING A NATION

1863–1877

> What were the achievements and failures of reconstruction? Chapter 16 explores the era of reconstruction, in which the nation struggled to define the defeated South's status and the meaning of freedom for ex-slaves. Following the Civil War, the nation entered one of its most confused and violent periods as victorious Northerners, defeated white Southerners, and newly freed African Americans battled to shape the postwar South.

LearningCurve
bedfordstmartins.com/roarkunderstanding
After reading the chapter, use LearningCurve to retain what you've read.

Voting day, June 5, 1867. Black freedmen line up to vote in Washington, D.C. The Granger Collection, New York.

> Why did Congress object to Lincoln's wartime plan for reconstruction?

> How did the North respond to the passage of black codes in the southern states?

> How radical was congressional reconstruction?

> What brought the elements of the South's Republican coalition together?

> Why did reconstruction collapse?

> Conclusion: Was reconstruction "a revolution but half accomplished"?

Why did Congress object to Lincoln's wartime plan for reconstruction?

Military Auction of Condemned Property, Beaufort, South Carolina, 1865

During the war, thousands of acres of land in the South came into federal hands as abandoned property or as a result of seizures because of nonpayment of taxes. The government authorized the sale of some of this land at public auction. This rare photograph shows expectant blacks (and a few whites) gathered in Beaufort, South Carolina, for a sale.
The Huntington Library, San Marino, California.

RECONSTRUCTION DID NOT WAIT for the end of war. As the odds of a northern victory increased, thinking about reunification quickened. Immediately, a question arose: Who had authority to devise a plan for reconstructing the Union? President Abraham Lincoln firmly believed that reconstruction was a matter of executive responsibility. Congress just as firmly asserted its jurisdiction. Fueling the argument were significant differences about the terms of reconstruction. In their eagerness to formulate a plan for political reunification, neither Lincoln nor Congress gave much attention to the South's land and labor problem or to the aspirations of freedmen. But as the war rapidly eroded slavery and traditional plantation agriculture, Yankee military commanders in the Union-occupied areas of the Confederacy had no choice but to oversee the emergence of a new labor system.

"To Bind Up the Nation's Wounds"

As early as 1863, Lincoln began contemplating how "to bind up the nation's wounds" and achieve "a lasting peace." While deep compassion for the enemy guided his thinking about peace, his plan for reconstruction aimed primarily at shortening the war and ending slavery.

Lincoln's Proclamation of Amnesty and Reconstruction in December 1863 set out his terms. Lincoln's plan did not require ex-rebels to extend social or political rights to ex-slaves, nor did it anticipate a program of long-term federal assistance to freedmen. Clearly, the president looked forward to the rapid, forgiving restoration of the broken Union.

Lincoln's easy terms enraged abolitionists such as Wendell Phillips of Boston, who charged that the president "makes the negro's freedom a mere sham." He "is

CHAPTER LOCATOR | **Why did Congress object to Lincoln's wartime plan for reconstruction?** | How did the North respond to the passage of black codes in the southern states?

458   CHAPTER 16
RECONSTRUCTING A NATION

willing that the negro should be free but seeks nothing else for him." Phillips and other northern radicals called instead for a thorough overhaul of southern society. Their ideas proved to be too drastic for most Republicans during the war years, but Congress agreed that Lincoln's plan was inadequate.

In July 1864, Congressman Henry Winter Davis of Maryland and Senator Benjamin Wade of Ohio jointly sponsored their own less forgiving reconstruction bill. When Lincoln refused to sign the bill and let it die, Wade and Davis charged the president with usurpation of power.

Undeterred, Lincoln continued to nurture the formation of loyal state governments under his own plan. Four states — Louisiana, Arkansas, Tennessee, and Virginia — fulfilled the president's requirements, but Congress refused to seat representatives from the "Lincoln states." In his last public address in April 1865, Lincoln defended his plan but for the first time publicly expressed his endorsement of suffrage for southern blacks, at least "the very intelligent, and . . . those who serve our cause as soldiers." The announcement demonstrated that Lincoln's thinking about reconstruction was still evolving. Four days later, he was dead.

Land and Labor

Of all the problems raised by the North's victory in the war, none proved more critical than the South's transition from slavery to free labor. As federal armies invaded and occupied the Confederacy, hundreds of thousands of slaves became free workers. In addition, Union armies controlled vast territories in the South where legal title to land had become unclear. The Confiscation Acts passed during the war punished "traitors" by taking away their property. The question of what to do with federally occupied land and how to organize labor on it engaged ex-slaves, ex-slaveholders, Union military commanders, and federal government officials long before the war ended.

In the Mississippi valley, occupying federal troops announced a new labor code. It required landholders to give up whipping, to sign contracts with ex-slaves, and to

| How radical was congressional reconstruction? | What brought the elements of the South's Republican coalition together? | Why did reconstruction collapse? | Conclusion: Was reconstruction "a revolution but half accomplished"? | ✓ LearningCurve Check what you know. bedfordstmartins.com /roarkunderstanding |

459

pay wages. The code required black laborers to enter into contracts, work diligently, and remain subordinate and obedient. Military leaders clearly had no intention of promoting a social or economic revolution. The effort resulted in a hybrid system that one contemporary called "compulsory free labor," something that satisfied no one.

Planters complained because the new system fell short of slavery. Blacks could not be "transformed by proclamation," a Louisiana sugar planter declared. Without the right to whip, he argued, the new labor system did not have a chance. Either Union soldiers must "compel the negroes to work," or the planters themselves must "be authorized and sustained in using force."

African Americans found the new regime too reminiscent of slavery to be called free labor. Its chief deficiency, they believed, was the failure to provide them with land of their own. Freedmen believed they had a moral right to land because they and their ancestors had worked it without compensation for more than two centuries. "What's the use of being free if you don't own land enough to be buried in?" one man asked. Several wartime developments led freedmen to believe that the federal government planned to undergird black freedom with landownership.

In January 1865, General William Tecumseh Sherman set aside part of the coast south of Charleston for black settlement. By June 1865, some 40,000 freedmen sat on 400,000 acres of "Sherman land." In addition, in March 1865, Congress passed a bill establishing the Bureau of Refugees, Freedmen, and Abandoned Lands. The **Freedmen's Bureau**, as it was called, distributed food and clothing to destitute Southerners and eased the transition of blacks from slaves to free persons. Congress also authorized the agency to divide abandoned and confiscated land into 40-acre plots, to rent them to freedmen, and eventually to sell them "with such title as the United States can convey." By June 1865, the Bureau had situated nearly 10,000 black families on half a million acres abandoned by fleeing planters. Other ex-slaves eagerly anticipated farms of their own.

Despite the flurry of activity, wartime reconstruction failed to produce agreement about whether the president or Congress had the authority to devise policy or what proper policy should be.

The African American Quest for Autonomy

Ex-slaves never had any doubt about what they wanted from freedom. They had only to contemplate what they had been denied as slaves. Slaves had to remain on their plantations; freedom allowed blacks to see what was on the other side of the hill. Slaves had to be at work in the fields by dawn; freedom permitted blacks to sleep through a sunrise. Freedmen also tested the etiquette of racial subordination. "Lizzie's maid passed me today when I was coming from church *without speaking to me*," huffed one plantation mistress.

To whites, emancipation looked like pure anarchy. Blacks, they said, had reverted to their natural condition: lazy, irresponsible, and wild. Actually, former slaves were experimenting with freedom, but they could not long afford to roam the countryside, neglect work, and casually provoke whites. Soon, most were back at work in whites' kitchens and fields.

But they continued to dream of land and economic independence. "The way we can best take care of ourselves is to have land," one former slave declared in

Freedmen's Bureau

▶ Government organization created in March 1865 to distribute food and clothing to destitute Southerners and to ease the transition of slaves to free persons. Early efforts by the Freedmen's Bureau to distribute land to the newly freed blacks were later overturned by President Andrew Johnson.

CHAPTER LOCATOR | **Why did Congress object to Lincoln's wartime plan for reconstruction?** | How did the North respond to the passage of black codes in the southern states?

460   CHAPTER 16   RECONSTRUCTING A NATION

Harry Stephens and Family, 1866 Dressed in their Sunday best, this Virginia family sits proudly for a photograph. Many black families were not as fortunate as the Stephens family and spent years seeking missing family members. The Metropolitan Museum of Art, Gilman Collection, Purchase, The Horace W. Goldsmith Foundation Gift, 2005 (2005.100.277)/Art Resource, NY.

1865, "and turn it and till it by our own labor." Freedmen also wanted to learn to read and write. "I wishes the Childern all in School," one black veteran asserted. "It is beter for them then to be their Sureing a mistes [mistress]."

The restoration of broken families was another persistent black aspiration. Thousands of freedmen took to the roads in 1865 to look for kin who had been sold away or to free those who were being held illegally as slaves. A black soldier from Missouri wrote his daughters that he was coming for them. "I will have you if it cost me my life," he declared. "Your Miss Kitty said that I tried to steal you," he told them. "But I'll let her know that god never intended for a man to steal his own flesh and blood." And he swore that "if she meets me with ten thousand soldiers, she [will] meet her enemy."

Independent worship was another continuing aspiration. African Americans greeted freedom with a mass exodus from white churches, where they had been required to worship when slaves. Some joined the newly established southern branches of all-black northern churches, such as the African Methodist Episcopal Church. Others formed black versions of the major southern denominations, Baptists and Methodists.

QUICK REVIEW

To what extent did Lincoln's wartime plan for reconstruction reflect the concerns of newly freed slaves?

How radical was congressional reconstruction?

What brought the elements of the South's Republican coalition together?

Why did reconstruction collapse?

Conclusion: Was reconstruction "a revolution but half accomplished"?

 LearningCurve Check what you know. bedfordstmartins.com /roarkunderstanding

How did the North respond to the passage of black codes in the southern states?

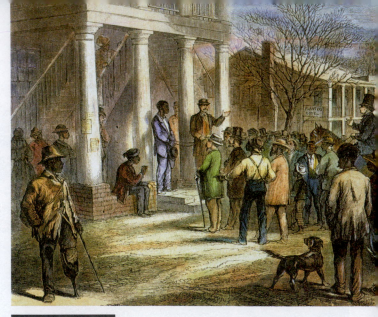

The Black Codes

Titled "Selling a Freeman to Pay His Fine at Monticello, Florida," this 1867 drawing from a northern magazine equates black codes with the institution of slavery. The ascension of Andrew Johnson to the presidency emboldened many southern states to pass laws severely restricting blacks' freedom. Granger Collection.

ABRAHAM LINCOLN DIED on April 15, 1865, just hours after John Wilkes Booth shot him at a Washington, D.C., theater. Chief Justice Salmon P. Chase immediately administered the oath of office to Vice President Andrew Johnson of Tennessee. Congress had adjourned in March and would not reconvene until December. Throughout the summer and fall, Johnson drew up and executed a plan of reconstruction without congressional advice.

Congress returned to the capital in December to find that, as far as the president and former Confederates were concerned, reconstruction was completed. Most Republicans, however, thought Johnson's plan made far too few demands of ex-rebels. They claimed that Johnson's leniency had acted as midwife to the rebirth of the Old South, that he had achieved political reunification at the cost of black freedom. Republicans in Congress then proceeded to dismantle Johnson's program and substitute a program of their own.

Johnson's Program of Reconciliation

Born in 1808 in Raleigh, North Carolina, Andrew Johnson was the son of illiterate parents. Self-educated and ambitious, Johnson moved to Tennessee, where he built a career in politics championing the South's common white people and assailing its "illegitimate, swaggering, bastard, scrub aristocracy." The only senator from a Confederate state to remain loyal to the Union, Johnson held the planter class responsible for secession.

A Democrat all his life, Johnson occupied the White House only because the Republican Party in 1864 had needed a vice presidential candidate who would

CHAPTER LOCATOR | Why did Congress object to Lincoln's wartime plan for reconstruction? | **How did the North respond to the passage of black codes in the southern states?**

appeal to loyal, Union-supporting Democrats. Johnson vigorously defended states' rights (but not secession) and opposed Republican efforts to expand the power of the federal government. A steadfast supporter of slavery, Johnson had owned slaves until 1862, when Tennessee rebels, angry at his Unionism, confiscated them. When he grudgingly accepted emancipation, it was more because he hated planters than because he sympathized with slaves. "Damn the negroes," he said. "I am fighting those traitorous aristocrats, their masters." The new president harbored unshakable racist convictions. Africans, Johnson said, were "inferior to the white man in point of intellect — better calculated in physical structure to undergo drudgery and hardship."

Like Lincoln, Johnson stressed the rapid restoration of civil government in the South. Like Lincoln, he promised to pardon most, but not all, ex-rebels. Johnson recognized the state governments created by Lincoln but set out his own requirements for restoring the other rebel states to the Union.

> **CHRONOLOGY**

1865
– Lincoln is assassinated; Andrew Johnson becomes president.
– Black codes are enacted.
– Thirteenth Amendment becomes part of Constitution.

1866
– Civil Rights Act.

> **Johnson's Plan to Restore Confederate States to the Union**

- Citizens of a state had to renounce the right of secession.
- They had to deny that the debts of the Confederacy were legal and binding.
- They had to ratify the Thirteenth Amendment abolishing slavery, which became part of the Constitution in December 1865.

Johnson also returned all confiscated and abandoned land to pardoned ex-Confederates, even if it was in the hands of freedmen. Reformers were shocked by Johnson's quick and easy plan of reconstruction. Instead of punishing treason and making planters pay as he had promised, Johnson canceled the promising beginnings made by General Sherman and the Freedmen's Bureau to settle blacks on land of their own. As one freedman observed, "Things was hurt by Mr. Lincoln getting killed."

White Southern Resistance and Black Codes

In the summer of 1865, delegates across the South gathered to draw up the new state constitutions required by Johnson's plan of reconstruction. They refused to accept even the president's mild requirements. Refusing to renounce secession, the South Carolina and Georgia conventions merely "repudiated" their secession ordinances, preserving in principle their right to secede. South Carolina and Mississippi refused to disown their Confederate war debts. Mississippi rejected the Thirteenth Amendment. Despite this defiance, Johnson did nothing. White Southerners began to think that by standing up for themselves they could shape the terms of reconstruction.

New state governments across the South adopted a series of laws known as **black codes**, which made a travesty of black freedom. The codes sought to keep ex-slaves subordinate to whites by subjecting them to every sort of discrimination. Several states made it illegal for blacks to own a gun. Mississippi made insulting gestures and language by blacks a criminal offense. The codes barred blacks from jury duty. Not a single southern state granted any black the right to vote.

black codes
▶ Laws passed by state governments in the South in 1865 that sought to keep ex-slaves subordinate to whites. At the core of the black codes lay the desire to force freedmen back to the plantations.

How radical was congressional reconstruction?

What brought the elements of the South's Republican coalition together?

Why did reconstruction collapse?

Conclusion: Was reconstruction "a revolution but half accomplished"?

☑ LearningCurve
Check what you know.
bedfordstmartins.com
/roarkunderstanding

At the core of the black codes, however, lay the matter of labor. Legislators sought to hustle freedmen back to the plantations. Whites were almost universally opposed to black landownership, and South Carolina attempted to limit blacks to either farmwork or domestic service by requiring them to pay annual taxes of $10 to $100 to work in any other occupation. Mississippi declared that blacks who did not possess written evidence of employment could be declared vagrants and be subject to involuntary plantation labor. Under so-called apprenticeship laws, courts bound thousands of black children — orphans and others whose parents were deemed unable to support them — to work for planter "guardians."

Johnson, a staunch defender of states' rights and white supremacy, refused to intervene. He also recognized that his do-nothing response offered him political advantage. A conservative Tennessee Democrat at the head of a northern Republican Party, he had begun to look southward for political allies. By pardoning powerful whites, by accepting governments even when they failed to satisfy his minimal demands, and by acquiescing in the black codes, Johnson won useful southern friends.

In the fall elections of 1865, white Southerners dramatically expressed their mood. To represent them in Congress, they chose former Confederates. Of the eighty senators and representatives they sent to Washington, fifteen had served in the Confederate army, ten of them as generals. Another sixteen had served in civil and judicial posts in the Confederacy. Nine others had served in the Confederate Congress. One — Alexander Stephens — had been vice president of the Confederacy. As one Georgian remarked, "It looked as though Richmond had moved to Washington."

Expansion of Federal Authority and Black Rights

Southerners had blundered monumentally. They had assumed that what Andrew Johnson was willing to accept, Republicans would accept as well. But southern intransigence compelled even moderates to conclude that ex-rebels were a "generation of vipers," still untrustworthy and dangerous. The black codes became a symbol of southern intentions to "restore all of slavery but its name." "We tell the white men of Mississippi," the *Chicago Tribune* roared, "that the men of the North will convert the State of Mississippi into a frog pond before they will allow such laws to disgrace one foot of the soil in which the bones of our soldiers sleep and over which the flag of freedom waves."

The moderate majority of the Republican Party wanted only assurance that slavery and treason were dead. They did not champion black equality, the confiscation of plantations, or black voting, as did the radical minority within the party. But southern obstinacy had succeeded in forging unity (at least temporarily) among Republican factions. In December 1865, Republicans refused to seat the southern representatives elected in the fall elections. Rather than accept Johnson's claim that the "work of restoration" was done, Congress challenged his executive power.

CHAPTER LOCATOR | Why did Congress object to Lincoln's wartime plan for reconstruction? | **How did the North respond to the passage of black codes in the southern states?**

464 CHAPTER 16 RECONSTRUCTING A NATION

Republican senator Lyman Trumbull of Illinois declared that the president's policy meant that an ex-slave would "be tyrannized over, abused, and virtually reenslaved without some legislation by the nation for his protection." Early in 1866, the moderates produced two bills that strengthened the federal shield. The first, the Freedmen's Bureau bill, prolonged the life of the agency established by the previous Congress. Arguing that the Constitution never contemplated a "system for the support of indigent persons," President Andrew Johnson vetoed the bill. Congress failed by a narrow margin to override the president's veto.

The moderates designed their second measure, what would become the **Civil Rights Act of 1866**, to nullify the black codes by affirming African Americans' rights to "full and equal benefit of all laws and proceedings for the security of person and property as is enjoyed by white citizens." The act required the end of racial discrimination in state laws and represented an extraordinary expansion of black rights and federal authority. The president argued that the civil rights bill amounted to "unconstitutional invasion of states' rights" and vetoed it.

In April 1866, an incensed Republican Party again pushed the civil rights bill through Congress and overrode the presidential veto. In July, it passed another Freedmen's Bureau bill and overrode Johnson's veto. For the first time in American history, Congress had overridden presidential vetoes of major legislation. As a worried South Carolinian observed, Johnson had succeeded in uniting the Republicans and probably touched off "a fight this fall such as has never been seen."

Civil Rights Act of 1866

▶ Legislation passed by Congress in 1866 that nullified the black codes and affirmed that black Americans should have equal benefit of the law. President Andrew Johnson vetoed this expansion of black rights and federal authority, but Congress later overrode his veto.

QUICK REVIEW

When the southern states passed the black codes, how did the U.S. Congress respond?

How radical was congressional reconstruction?

State Convention at Richmond, Virginia Between 1867 and 1869, every southern state except Tennessee held a convention to draft a new constitution. In Virginia, where blacks were more than 40 percent of the population, they made up about 20 percent of the convention. Richmond History Center.

BY THE SUMMER OF 1866, President Andrew Johnson and Congress had dropped their gloves and stood toe-to-toe in a bare-knuckle contest unprecedented in American history. Johnson made it clear that he would not budge on either constitutional issues or policy. Moderate Republicans responded by amending the Constitution. But the obstinacy of Johnson and white Southerners pushed Republican moderates ever closer to the radicals and to acceptance of additional federal intervention in the South. Congress also voted to impeach the president. In time, Congress debated whether to make voting rights color-blind, while women sought to make voting rights sex-blind as well.

The Fourteenth Amendment and Escalating Violence

Fourteenth Amendment
▶ Constitutional amendment passed in 1866 that made all native-born or naturalized persons U.S. citizens and prohibited states from abridging the rights of national citizens. The amendment aimed to provide a guarantee of equality before the law for black citizens.

In June 1866, Congress passed the **Fourteenth Amendment** to the Constitution, and two years later the states ratified it. The most important provisions of this complex amendment made all native-born or naturalized persons American citizens and prohibited states from abridging the "privileges and immunities" of citizens, depriving them of "life, liberty, or property without due process of law," and denying them "equal protection of the laws." By making blacks national citizens, the amendment provided a national guarantee of equality before the law. In essence, it protected blacks against violation by southern state governments.

CHAPTER LOCATOR | Why did Congress object to Lincoln's wartime plan for reconstruction? | How did the North respond to the passage of black codes in the southern states?

The Fourteenth Amendment also dealt with voting rights. It gave Congress the right to reduce the congressional representation of any state that withheld suffrage from some of its adult male population. In other words, white Southerners could either allow black men to vote or see their representation in Washington slashed.

The Fourteenth Amendment's suffrage provisions ignored the small band of women who had emerged from the war demanding "the ballot for the two disenfranchised classes, negroes and women." Founding the American Equal Rights Association in 1866, Susan B. Anthony and Elizabeth Cady Stanton lobbied for "a government by the people, and the whole people; for the people and the whole people." They felt betrayed when their old antislavery allies refused to work for their goals. "It was the Negro's hour," Frederick Douglass explained. Senator Charles Sumner suggested that woman suffrage could be "the great question of the future."

The Fourteenth Amendment provided for punishment of any state that excluded voters on the basis of race, but not on the basis of sex. The amendment also introduced the word *male* into the Constitution when it referred to a citizen's right to vote. Stanton predicted that "if that word 'male' be inserted, it will take us a century at least to get it out."

Tennessee approved the Fourteenth Amendment in July, and Congress promptly welcomed the state's representatives and senators back. Had President Johnson counseled other southern states to ratify this relatively mild amendment, they might have listened. Instead, Johnson advised Southerners to reject the Fourteenth Amendment and to rely on him to trounce the Republicans in the fall congressional elections.

Johnson had decided to make the Fourteenth Amendment the overriding issue of the 1866 elections and to gather its white opponents into a new conservative party, the National Union Party. The president's strategy suffered a setback when whites in several southern cities went on rampages against blacks. Mobs killed thirty-four blacks in New Orleans and forty-six blacks in Memphis. The slaughter shocked Northerners and renewed skepticism about Johnson's claim that southern whites could be trusted. "Who doubts that the Freedmen's Bureau ought to be abolished forthwith," a New Yorker observed sarcastically, "and the blacks remitted to the paternal care of their old masters, who 'understand the nigger, you know, a great deal better than the Yankees can.'"

The 1866 elections resulted in an overwhelming Republican victory. Johnson had bet that Northerners would not support federal protection of black rights and that a racist backlash would blast the Republican Party. But the war was still fresh in northern minds, and as one Republican explained, southern whites "with all their intelligence were traitors, the blacks with all their ignorance were loyal."

Radical Reconstruction and Military Rule

When Johnson continued to urge Southerners to reject the Fourteenth Amendment, every southern state except Tennessee voted it down. "The last one of the sinful ten," thundered Representative James A. Garfield of Ohio, "has flung back into our teeth the magnanimous offer of a generous nation." After the South rejected the moderates' program, the radicals seized the initiative.

Each act of defiance by southern whites had boosted the standing of the radicals within the Republican Party. Radicals such as Massachusetts senator Charles

> CHRONOLOGY

1866
– Congress approves Fourteenth Amendment.
– American Equal Rights Association is founded.

1767
– Military Reconstruction Act.
– Tenure of Office Act.

1868
– Impeachment trial of President Johnson.

1869
– Congress approves Fifteenth Amendment.

| How radical was congressional reconstruction? | What brought the elements of the South's Republican coalition together? | Why did reconstruction collapse? | Conclusion: Was reconstruction "a revolution but half accomplished"? | ☑ LearningCurve Check what you know. bedfordstmartins.com /roarkunderstanding |

Military Reconstruction Act

▶ Congressional act of March 1867 that initiated military rule of the South. Congressional reconstruction divided the ten unreconstructed Confederate states into five military districts, each under the direction of a Union general. It also established the procedure by which unreconstructed states could reenter the Union.

Sumner and Pennsylvania representative Thaddeus Stevens united in demanding civil and political equality. Southern states were "like clay in the hands of the potter," Stevens declared in January 1867, and he called on Congress to begin reconstruction all over again.

In March 1867, Congress passed the **Military Reconstruction Act** and overturned the Johnson state governments and initiated military rule of the South.

> Military Reconstruction Act

- The ten unreconstructed Confederate states were divided into five military districts.
- Congress placed a Union general in charge of each district and instructed him to "suppress insurrection, disorder, and violence" and to begin political reform.
- After the military had completed voter registration, which would include black men, voters in each state would elect delegates to conventions that would draw up new state constitutions.
- Each constitution would guarantee black suffrage.
- When the voters of each state had approved the constitution and the state legislature had ratified the Fourteenth Amendment, the state could submit its work to Congress.
- If Congress approved the constitution, the state's senators and representatives could be seated, and political reunification would be accomplished.

Reconstruction Military Districts, 1867

Radicals proclaimed the provision for black suffrage "a prodigious triumph," for it extended far beyond the limited suffrage provisions of the Fourteenth Amendment. When combined with the disfranchisement of thousands of ex-rebels, it promised to cripple any neo-Confederate resurgence and guarantee Republican state governments in the South.

Despite its bold suffrage provision, the Military Reconstruction Act of 1867 disappointed those who also advocated the confiscation of southern plantations and their redistribution to ex-slaves. Thaddeus Stevens agreed with the freedman who said, "Give us our own land and we take care of ourselves, but without land, the old masters can hire us or starve us, as they please." But most Republicans believed they had provided blacks with what they needed: equal legal rights and the ballot. If blacks were to get land, they would have to gain it themselves.

Declaring that he would rather sever his right arm than sign such a formula for "anarchy and chaos," Andrew Johnson vetoed the Military Reconstruction Act, but Congress overrode his veto. With the passage of the Reconstruction Acts of 1867, congressional reconstruction was virtually completed. Congress left whites owning most of the South's land but, in a departure that justified the term "radical reconstruction," had given black men the ballot.

Impeaching a President

Despite his defeats, Andrew Johnson had no intention of yielding control of reconstruction. In a dozen ways, he sabotaged Congress's will and encouraged southern whites to resist. He issued a flood of pardons, waged war against the

CHAPTER LOCATOR | Why did Congress object to Lincoln's wartime plan for reconstruction? | How did the North respond to the passage of black codes in the southern states?

Freedmen's Bureau, and replaced Union generals eager to enforce Congress's Reconstruction Acts with conservative officers eager to defeat them. Johnson claimed that he was merely defending the "violated Constitution." At bottom, however, the president subverted congressional reconstruction to protect southern whites from what he considered the horrors of "Negro domination."

Radicals argued that Johnson's abuse of constitutional powers and his failure to fulfill constitutional obligations to enforce the law were impeachable offenses. According to the Constitution, the House of Representatives can impeach and the Senate can try any federal official for "treason, bribery, or other high crimes and misdemeanors." But moderates interpreted the Constitution to mean violation of criminal statutes. As long as Johnson refrained from breaking the law, impeachment (the process of formal charges of wrongdoing against the president or other federal official) remained stalled.

Then in August 1867, Johnson suspended Secretary of War Edwin M. Stanton from office. As required by the Tenure of Office Act, a law passed in March 1867 that demanded the approval of the Senate for the removal of any government official who had been appointed with Senate approval, the president requested the Senate to consent to Stanton's dismissal. When the Senate balked, Johnson removed Stanton anyway. "Is the President crazy, or only drunk?" asked a dumbfounded Republican moderate. "I'm afraid his doings will make us all favor impeachment."

News of Johnson's open defiance of the law convinced every Republican in the House to vote for a resolution impeaching the president. Supreme Court chief justice Salmon Chase presided over the Senate trial, which lasted from March until May 1868. When the vote came, thirty-five senators voted guilty and nineteen not guilty. The impeachment forces fell one vote short of the two-thirds needed to convict.

After his trial, Johnson called a truce, and for the remaining ten months of his term, congressional reconstruction proceeded unhindered by presidential interference. Without interference from Johnson, Congress revisited the suffrage issue.

The Fifteenth Amendment and Women's Demands

In February 1869, Republicans passed the **Fifteenth Amendment** to the Constitution, which prohibited states from depriving any citizen of the right to vote because of "race, color, or previous condition of servitude." The Reconstruction Acts of 1867 already required black suffrage in the South; the Fifteenth Amendment extended black voting nationwide.

Some Republicans, however, found the final wording of the Fifteenth Amendment "lame and halting." Rather than absolutely guaranteeing the right to vote, the amendment merely prohibited exclusion on grounds of race. The distinction would prove to be significant. In time, white Southerners would devise tests of literacy and property and other apparently nonracial measures that would effectively disfranchise blacks yet not violate the Fifteenth Amendment. But an amendment that fully guaranteed the right to vote courted defeat outside the South. Rising antiforeign sentiment — against the Chinese in California and

Fifteenth Amendment
▶ Constitutional amendment passed in February 1869 prohibiting states from depriving any citizen of the right to vote because of "race, color, or previous condition of servitude." It extended black suffrage nationwide. Woman suffrage advocates were disappointed that the amendment failed to extend voting rights to women.

| How radical was congressional reconstruction? | What brought the elements of the South's Republican coalition together? | Why did reconstruction collapse? | Conclusion: Was reconstruction "a revolution but half accomplished"? | ☑ LearningCurve Check what you know. bedfordstmartins.com /roarkunderstanding |

469

European immigrants in the Northeast — caused states to resist giving up total control of suffrage requirements. In March 1870, after three-fourths of the states had ratified it, the Fifteenth Amendment became part of the Constitution.

Woman suffrage advocates, however, were sorely disappointed with the Fifteenth Amendment's failure to extend voting rights to women. Elizabeth Cady Stanton and Susan B. Anthony condemned the Republicans' "negro first" strategy and pointed out that women remained "the only class of citizens wholly unrepresented in the government." The Fifteenth Amendment severed the early feminist movement from its abolitionist roots. Over the next several decades, feminists established an independent suffrage crusade that drew millions of women into political life.

Republicans took enough satisfaction in the Fifteenth Amendment to promptly scratch the "Negro question" from the agenda of national politics. Even Wendell Phillips, a steadfast crusader for equality, concluded that the black man now held "sufficient shield in his own hands. . . . Whatever he suffers will be largely now, and in future, his own fault." Northerners had no idea of the violent struggles that lay ahead.

> **QUICK REVIEW**

Why did Congress impeach President Andrew Johnson?

CHAPTER LOCATOR | Why did Congress object to Lincoln's wartime plan for reconstruction? | How did the North respond to the passage of black codes in the southern states?

Black Woman in a Cotton Field, Thomasville, Georgia

Few images of everyday black women during the Reconstruction era survive. This photograph was taken in 1895, but it nevertheless goes to the heart of the labor struggle after the Civil War. Before emancipation, black women worked in the fields; after emancipation, white landlords wanted them to continue working there. Freedom allowed some women to escape field labor, but not this Georgian, who probably worked to survive. Courtesy, Georgia Department of Archives and History, Atlanta, Georgia.

What brought the elements of the South's Republican coalition together?

NORTHERNERS BELIEVED they had discharged their responsibilities with the Reconstruction Acts and the amendments to the Constitution, but Southerners knew that the battle had just begun. Black suffrage established the foundation for the rise of the Republican Party in the South. Gathering together outsiders and outcasts, southern Republicans won elections, wrote new state constitutions, and formed new state governments.

Challenging the established class for political control was dangerous business. Equally dangerous were the confrontations that took place on southern farms and plantations, where blacks sought to give fuller meaning to their newly won legal and political equality. Freedom remained contested territory, and Southerners fought pitched battles with one another to determine the contours of their new world.

Freedmen, Yankees, and Yeomen

African Americans made up the majority of southern Republicans. After gaining voting rights in 1867, nearly all eligible black men registered to vote as Republicans. "It is the hardest thing in the world to keep a negro away from the polls," observed an Alabama white man. Southern blacks did not all have identical political priorities, but they united in their desire for education and equal treatment before the law.

> CHRONOLOGY

1866
– Ku Klux Klan is founded.

1867
– Southern African Americans gain voting rights under the Military Reconstruction Act.
– Southern states hold elections for delegates to state conventions.

1875
– One-half of South Carolina's and Mississippi's children, the majority black, attend school.
– Sharecropping is the dominant labor system for rural southern blacks.

How radical was congressional reconstruction?

What brought the elements of the South's Republican coalition together?

Why did reconstruction collapse?

Conclusion: Was reconstruction "a revolution but half accomplished"?

☑ LearningCurve
Check what you know.
bedfordstmartins.com
/roarkunderstanding

471

carpetbaggers
▶ Southerners' pejorative term for northern migrants who sought opportunity in the South after the Civil War. Northern migrants formed an important part of the southern Republican Party.

scalawags
▶ A derogatory term that Southerners applied to southern white Republicans, who were seen as traitors to the South. Most were yeoman farmers.

Ku Klux Klan
▶ A social club of Confederate veterans that quickly developed into a paramilitary organization supporting Democrats. With too few Union troops in the South to control the region, the Klan went on a rampage of violence to defeat Republicans and restore white supremacy.

Northern whites who made the South their home after the war were a second element of the South's Republican Party. Conservative white Southerners called them **carpetbaggers**, opportunists who stuffed all their belongings in a single carpet-sided suitcase and headed south to "fatten on our misfortunes." But most Northerners who moved south were young men who looked upon the South as they did the West — as a promising place to make a living. Northerners in the southern Republican Party supported programs that encouraged vigorous economic development along the lines of the northern free-labor model.

Southern whites made up the third element of the South's Republican Party. Approximately one out of four white Southerners voted Republican. The other three condemned the one who did as a traitor to his region and his race and called him a **scalawag**, a term for runty horses and low-down, good-for-nothing rascals. Yeoman farmers accounted for the majority of southern white Republicans. Some were Unionists who emerged from the war with bitter memories of Confederate persecution. Others were small farmers who wanted to end state governments' favoritism toward plantation owners. Yeomen supported initiatives for public schools and for expanding economic opportunity in the South.

The South's Republican Party, then, was made up of freedmen, Yankees, and yeomen — an improbable coalition. The mix of races, regions, and classes inevitably meant friction as each group maneuvered to define the party. But Reconstruction represents an extraordinary moment in American politics: Blacks and whites joined together in the Republican Party to pursue political change. Formally, of course, only men participated in politics — casting ballots and holding offices — but white and black women also played a part in the political struggle by joining in parades and rallies, attending stump speeches, and even campaigning.

Most whites in the South condemned southern Republicans as illegitimate and felt justified in doing whatever they could to stamp them out. Violence against blacks — the "white terror" — took brutal institutional form in 1866 with the formation in Tennessee of the **Ku Klux Klan**, a social club of Confederate veterans that quickly developed into a paramilitary organization supporting Democrats. The Klan went on a rampage of violence to defeat Republicans and restore white supremacy. Rapid demobilization of the Union army after the war left only twenty thousand troops to patrol the entire South. Without effective military protection, southern Republicans had to take care of themselves.

Republican Rule

In the fall of 1867, southern states held elections for delegates to state constitutional conventions, as required by the Reconstruction Acts. About 40 percent of the white electorate stayed home because they had been disfranchised or because they had decided to boycott politics. Republicans won three-fourths of the seats. About 15 percent of the Republican delegates to the conventions were Northerners who had moved south, 25 percent were African Americans, and 60 percent were white Southerners. As a British visitor observed, the delegate elections reflected "the mighty revolution that had taken place in America."

The reconstruction constitutions introduced two broad categories of changes in the South: those that reduced aristocratic privilege and increased democratic equality and those that expanded the state's responsibility for the general welfare. In the first

CHAPTER LOCATOR | Why did Congress object to Lincoln's wartime plan for reconstruction? | How did the North respond to the passage of black codes in the southern states?

472 CHAPTER 16 RECONSTRUCTING A NATION

category, the constitutions adopted universal male suffrage, abolished property qualifications for holding office, and made more offices elective and fewer appointed. In the second category, they enacted prison reform; made the state responsible for caring for orphans, the insane, and the deaf and mute; and exempted debtors' homes from seizure.

To Democrats, however, these progressive constitutions looked like wild revolution. Democrats were blind to the fact that no constitution confiscated and redistributed land, as virtually every former slave wished, or disfranchised ex-rebels wholesale, as most southern Unionists advocated. And they were convinced that the new constitutions initiated "Negro domination." In fact, although 80 percent of Republican voters were black men, only 6 percent of Southerners in Congress during reconstruction were black (**Figure 16.1**). The sixteen black men in Congress included exceptional men, such as Representative James T. Rapier of Alabama. No state legislature experienced "Negro rule," despite black majorities in the populations of some states.

Southern voters ratified the new constitutions and swept Republicans into power. When the former Confederate states ratified the Fourteenth Amendment, Congress readmitted them. Southern Republicans then turned to a staggering array of problems. Wartime destruction littered the landscape. Making matters worse, racial harassment and reactionary violence dogged Southerners who sought reform. In this desperate context, Republicans struggled to rebuild and reform the region.

Activity focused on three areas — education, civil rights, and economic development. Every state inaugurated a system of public education. Before the Civil War, whites had deliberately kept slaves illiterate, and planter-dominated governments rarely spent tax money to educate the children of yeomen. By 1875, half of Mississippi's and South Carolina's eligible children were attending school. Although schools were underfunded, literacy rates rose sharply. Public schools were racially segregated, but education remained for many blacks a tangible, deeply satisfying benefit of freedom and Republican rule.

State legislatures also attacked racial discrimination and defended civil rights. Republicans especially resisted efforts to segregate blacks from whites in public transportation. Mississippi levied fines and jail terms for owners of railroads and steamboats that pushed blacks into "smoking cars" or to lower decks. But passing color-blind laws was far easier than enforcing them. A Mississippian complained: "Education amounts to nothing, good behavior counts for nothing, even money cannot buy for a colored man or woman decent treatment and the comforts that white people claim and can obtain." Despite the laws, segregation — later called Jim Crow — developed at white insistence and became a feature of southern life long before the end of the Reconstruction era.

Republican governments also launched ambitious programs of economic development. They envisioned a South of diversified agriculture, roaring factories, and booming towns. State legislatures chartered scores of banks and industrial companies, appropriated funds to fix ruined levees and drain swamps, and went on a railroad-building binge. These efforts fell far short of solving the South's economic troubles, however. Republican spending to stimulate economic growth also meant rising taxes and enormous debt that siphoned funds from schools and other programs.

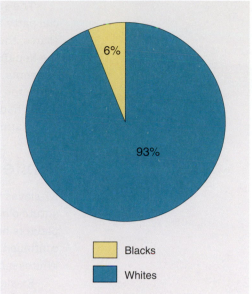

FIGURE 16.1 ■ Southern Congressional Delegations, 1865–1877

The statistics contradict the myth of black domination of congressional representation during reconstruction.

How radical was congressional reconstruction?

What brought the elements of the South's Republican coalition together?

Why did reconstruction collapse?

Conclusion: Was reconstruction "a revolution but half accomplished"?

✔ LearningCurve
Check what you know.
bedfordstmartins.com
/roarkunderstanding

The southern Republicans' record, then, was mixed. To their credit, the biracial party adopted an ambitious agenda to change the South. But money was scarce, the Democrats continued their harassment, and factionalism threatened the Republican Party from within. Moreover, corruption infected Republican governments. Nonetheless, the Republican Party made headway in its efforts to purge the South of aristocratic privilege and racist oppression. Republican governments had less success in overthrowing the long-established white oppression of black farm laborers in the rural South.

White Landlords, Black Sharecroppers

Ex-slaves who wished to escape slave labor and ex-masters who wanted to reinstitute old ways clashed repeatedly. Except for having to pay subsistence wages, planters had not been required to offer many concessions to emancipation. They continued to believe that African Americans would not work without coercion. Whites moved quickly to restore as much of slavery as they could get away with.

Ex-slaves resisted every effort to turn back the clock. They believed that land of their own would anchor their economic independence and end planters' interference in their personal lives. They could then, for example, make their own decisions about whether women and children would labor in the fields. Indeed, within months after the war, perhaps one-third of black women abandoned field labor to work on chores in their own cabins just as poor white women did. Black women also negotiated about work ex-mistresses wanted done in the big house. Hundreds of thousands of black children enrolled in school. But without their own land, ex-slaves had little choice but to work on plantations.

Although forced to return to the planters' fields, they resisted efforts to restore slavelike conditions. Instead of working for wages, a South Carolinian observed, "the negroes all seem disposed to rent land," which increased their independence from whites. Out of this tug-of-war between white landlords and black laborers emerged a new system of southern agriculture.

Sharecropping was a compromise that offered something to both ex-masters and ex-slaves but satisfied neither. Under the new system, planters divided their cotton plantations into small farms that freedmen rented, paying with a share of each year's crop, usually half. Sharecropping gave blacks more freedom than the system of wages and labor gangs and released them from day-to-day supervision by whites. Black families abandoned the old slave quarters and built separate cabins for themselves on the patches of land they rented (**Map 16.1**). Still, most black families remained dependent on white landlords, who had the power to evict them at the end of each growing season. For planters, sharecropping offered a way to resume agricultural production, but it did not allow them to restore the old slave plantation.

Sharecropping introduced the country merchant into the agricultural equation. Landlords supplied sharecroppers with land, mules, seeds, and tools, but blacks also needed credit to obtain essential food and clothing before they harvested their crop. Under an arrangement called a crop lien, a merchant would advance goods to a sharecropper in exchange for a *lien*, or legal claim, on the farmer's future crop. Some merchants charged exorbitant rates of interest, as much as 60 percent, on the goods they sold. At the end of the growing season, after the landlord had taken half of the farmer's crop for rent, the merchant took most of the rest. Sometimes,

sharecropping

▶ Labor system that emerged in the South during reconstruction. Under this system, planters divided their plantations into small farms that freedmen rented, paying with a share of each year's crop. Sharecropping gave blacks some freedom, but they remained dependent on white landlords and country merchants.

CHAPTER LOCATOR | Why did Congress object to Lincoln's wartime plan for reconstruction? | How did the North respond to the passage of black codes in the southern states?

474 CHAPTER 16
RECONSTRUCTING A NATION

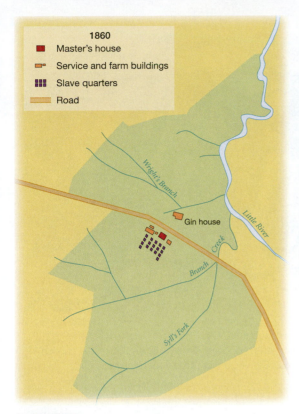

1860
- 🟥 Master's house
- ▱ Service and farm buildings
- ▦ Slave quarters
- ▬ Road

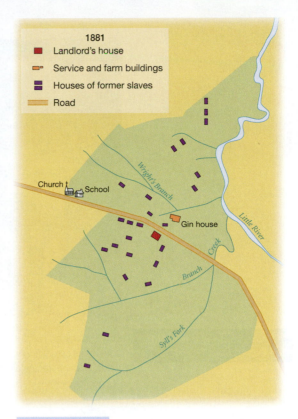

1881
- 🟥 Landlord's house
- ▱ Service and farm buildings
- ▪▪ Houses of former slaves
- ▬ Road

MAP 16.1 ■ **A Southern Plantation in 1860 and 1881**

These maps of the Barrow plantation in Georgia illustrate some of the ways in which ex-slaves expressed their freedom. Freedmen and freedwomen deserted the clustered living quarters behind the master's house, scattered over the plantation, built family cabins, and farmed rented land. The former Barrow slaves also worked together to build a school and a church.

> MAP ACTIVITY

READING THE MAP: Compare the number and size of the slave quarters in 1860 with the homes of the former slaves in 1881. How do they differ? Which buildings were prominently located along the road in 1860, and which could be found along the road in 1881?

CONNECTIONS: How might the former master feel about the new configuration of buildings on the plantation in 1881? In what ways did the new system of sharecropping replicate the old system of plantation agriculture? In what ways was it different?

the farmer did not earn enough to repay the debt to the merchant, and he would have to borrow more from the merchant and begin the cycle again.

An experiment at first, sharecropping soon dominated the cotton South. Lien merchants forced tenants to plant cotton, which was easy to sell, instead of food crops. The result was excessive production of cotton and falling cotton prices, developments that cost thousands of small white farmers their land and pushed them into the great army of sharecroppers. The new sharecropping system of agriculture took shape just as the political power of Republicans in the South began to buckle under Democratic pressure.

QUICK REVIEW

How did politics and economic concerns shape reconstruction in the South?

How radical was congressional reconstruction?

What brought the elements of the South's Republican coalition together?

Why did reconstruction collapse?

Conclusion: Was reconstruction "a revolution but half accomplished"?

☑ LearningCurve
Check what you know.
bedfordstmartins.com
/roarkunderstanding

Why did reconstruction collapse?

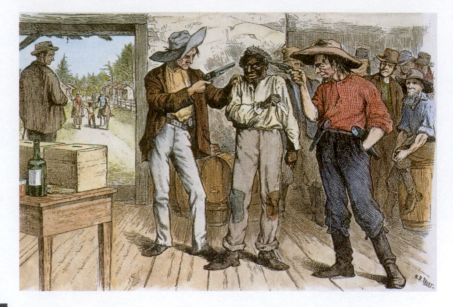

This Republican cartoon from the October 21, 1876, issue of *Harper's Weekly* comments sarcastically on the possibility of honest elections in the South. The caption reads, "You're free as air, ain't you? Say you are or I'll blow yer black head off." Granger Collection.

BY 1870, after a decade of war and reconstruction, Northerners wanted to put "the southern problem" behind them. Practical business-minded men came to dominate the Republican Party, replacing the band of reformers and idealists who had been prominent in the 1860s. Civil war hero Ulysses S. Grant succeeded Andrew Johnson as president in 1869 and quickly became an issue himself, proving that brilliance on the battlefield does not necessarily translate into competence in the White House. As northern commitment to defend black freedom eroded, southern commitment to white supremacy intensified. Without northern protection, southern Republicans were no match for the Democrats' economic coercion, political fraud, and bloody violence. One by one, Republican state governments fell in the South. The election of 1876 both confirmed and completed the collapse of reconstruction.

Grant's Troubled Presidency

In 1868, the Republican Party's presidential nomination went to Ulysses S. Grant, the North's favorite general. His Democratic opponent, Horatio Seymour of New York, ran on a platform that blasted reconstruction as "a flagrant usurpation of power . . . unconstitutional, revolutionary, and void." The

Candidate	Electoral Vote	Popular Vote	Percent of Popular Vote
Ulysses S. Grant (Republican)	214	3,012,833	52.7
Horatio Seymour (Democrat)	80	2,703,249	47.3
Nonvoting states (Reconstruction)			

MAP 16.2 ■ The Election of 1868

CHAPTER LOCATOR | Why did Congress object to Lincoln's wartime plan for reconstruction? | How did the North respond to the passage of black codes in the southern states?

476 CHAPTER 16 RECONSTRUCTING A NATION

Republicans answered by "waving the bloody shirt" — that is, they reminded voters that the Democrats were "the party of rebellion." Grant gained a narrow 309,000-vote margin in the popular vote and a substantial victory (214 votes to 80) in the electoral college (**Map 16.2**).

Grant was not as good a president as he was a general. The talents he had demonstrated on the battlefield — decisiveness, clarity, and resolution — were less obvious in the White House. Grant sought both justice for blacks and sectional reconciliation. But he surrounded himself with fumbling kinfolk and old friends from his army days and made a string of dubious appointments that led to a series of damaging scandals. Charges of corruption tainted his vice president, Schuyler Colfax, and brought down two of his cabinet officers. Though never personally implicated in any scandal, Grant was aggravatingly naive and blind to the rot that filled his administration.

In 1872, anti-Grant Republicans bolted and launched the Liberal Party. To clean up the graft and corruption, Liberals proposed ending the spoils system,

> CHRONOLOGY

1868
– Ulysses S. Grant is elected president.

1871
– Ku Klux Klan Act.

1872
– Liberal Party is formed.
– President Grant is reelected.

1873
– Economic depression sets in.
– *Slaughterhouse* cases.
– Colfax massacre.

1874
– Democrats win majority in House of Representatives.

1877
– In the disputed presidential election of 1876, Rutherford Hayes is declared the winner.

Grant and Scandal

This anti-Grant cartoon by Thomas Nast, the nation's most celebrated political cartoonist, shows the president falling headfirst into the barrel of fraud and corruption that tainted his administration. During Grant's eight years in the White House, many members of his administration failed him. Sometimes duped, sometimes merely loyal, Grant stubbornly defended wrongdoers, even to the point of perjuring himself to keep an aide out of jail. Library of Congress.

> **VISUAL ACTIVITY**

READING THE IMAGE: How does Thomas Nast portray President Grant's role in corruption? According to this cartoon, what caused the problems?

CONNECTIONS: How responsible was President Grant for the corruption that plagued his administration?

How radical was congressional reconstruction?

What brought the elements of the South's Republican coalition together?

Why did reconstruction collapse?

Conclusion: Was reconstruction "a revolution but half accomplished"?

✓ LearningCurve
Check what you know.
bedfordstmartins.com
/roarkunderstanding

by which victorious parties rewarded loyal workers with public office, and replacing it with a nonpartisan civil service commission that would oversee competitive examinations for appointment to office. Liberals also demanded that the federal government remove its troops from the South and restore "home rule" (southern white control). Democrats liked the Liberals' southern policy and endorsed the Liberal presidential candidate, Horace Greeley, the longtime editor of the *New York Tribune*. The nation, however, still felt enormous affection for the man who had saved the Union and reelected Grant with 56 percent of the popular vote.

Northern Resolve Withers

Although Grant genuinely wanted to see blacks' civil and political rights protected, he understood that most Northerners had grown weary of reconstruction and were increasingly willing to let southern whites manage their own affairs. Citizens wanted to shift their attention to other issues, especially after the nation slipped into a devastating economic depression in 1873. More than eighteen thousand businesses collapsed, leaving more than a million workers on the streets. Northern businessmen wanted to invest in the South but believed that recurrent federal intrusion was itself a major cause of instability in the region. Republican leaders began to question the wisdom of their party's alliance with the South's lower classes — its small farmers and sharecroppers. One member of Grant's administration proposed allying with the "thinking and influential native southerners . . . the intelligent, well-to-do, and controlling class."

Congress, too, wanted to leave reconstruction behind, but southern Republicans made that difficult. When the South's Republicans begged for federal protection from increasing Klan violence, Congress enacted three laws in 1870 and 1871 that were intended to break the back of white terrorism. The severest of the three, the Ku Klux Klan Act (1871), made interference with voting rights a felony. Federal marshals arrested thousands of Klansmen and came close to destroying the Klan, but they did not end all terrorism against blacks. Congress also passed the Civil Rights Act of 1875, which boldly outlawed racial discrimination in transportation, public accommodations, and juries. But federal authorities never enforced the law aggressively, and segregated facilities remained the rule throughout the South.

By the early 1870s, the Republican Party had lost its leading champions of African American rights to death or defeat at the polls. Other Republicans concluded that the quest for black equality was mistaken or hopelessly naive. In May 1872, Congress restored the right of office holding to all but three hundred ex-rebels. Many Republicans had come to believe that traditional white leaders offered the best hope for honesty, order, and prosperity in the South.

Underlying the North's abandonment of reconstruction was unyielding racial prejudice. Northerners had learned to accept black freedom during the war, but deep-seated prejudice prevented many from accepting black equality. Even the actions they took on behalf of blacks often served partisan political advantage. Northerners generally supported Indiana senator Thomas A. Hendricks's harsh declaration that "this is a white man's Government, made by the white man for the white man."

CHAPTER LOCATOR | Why did Congress object to Lincoln's wartime plan for reconstruction? | How did the North respond to the passage of black codes in the southern states?

The U.S. Supreme Court also did its part to undermine reconstruction. The Court issued a series of decisions that significantly weakened the federal government's ability to protect black Southerners. In the *Slaughterhouse* cases (1873), the Court distinguished between national and state citizenship and ruled that the Fourteenth Amendment protected only those rights that stemmed from the federal government, such as voting in federal elections and interstate travel. Since the Court decided that most rights derived from the states, it sharply curtailed the federal government's authority to defend black citizens. Even more devastating, the *United States v. Cruikshank* ruling (1876) said that the reconstruction amendments gave Congress the power to legislate against discrimination only by states, not by individuals. The "suppression of ordinary crime," such as assault, remained a state responsibility. The Supreme Court did not declare reconstruction unconstitutional but eroded its legal foundation.

The mood of the North found political expression in the election of 1874, when for the first time in eighteen years the Democrats gained control of the House of Representatives. As one Republican observed, the people had grown tired of the "negro question, with all its complications, and the reconstruction of Southern States, with all its interminable embroilments." Reconstruction had come apart. Rather than defend reconstruction from its southern enemies, Northerners steadily backed away from the challenge. By the early 1870s, southern Republicans faced the forces of reaction largely on their own.

White Supremacy Triumphs

Reconstruction was a massive humiliation to most white Southerners. Republican rule meant intolerable insults: Black militiamen patrolled town streets, black laborers negotiated contracts with former masters, black maids stood up to former mistresses, black voters cast ballots, and black legislators such as James T. Rapier enacted laws. Republican governments in the South attracted more hatred than did any other political regimes in American history. The northern retreat from reconstruction permitted southern Democrats to set things right.

Taking the name **Redeemers**, Democrats in the South promised to replace "bayonet rule" (a few federal troops continued to be stationed in the South) with "home rule." They promised that honest, thrifty Democrats would supplant corrupt tax-and-spend Republicans. Above all, Redeemers swore to save southern civilization from a descent into "African barbarism." As one man put it, "We must render this either a white man's government, or convert the land into a Negro man's cemetery."

Southern Democrats adopted a multipronged strategy to overthrow Republican governments. First, they sought to polarize the parties around color. They went about gathering all the South's white voters into the Democratic Party, leaving the Republicans to depend on blacks, who made up a minority of the population in almost every southern state. To dislodge whites from the Republican Party, Democrats fanned the flames of racial prejudice. A South Carolina Democrat crowed that his party appealed to the "proud Caucasian race, whose sovereignty on earth God has proclaimed." Local newspapers published the names of whites who kept company with blacks, and neighbors ostracized offenders.

Redeemers
▶ Name taken by southern Democrats who harnessed white rage in order to overthrow Republican rule and black political power and thus, they believed, save southern civilization.

How radical was congressional reconstruction?

What brought the elements of the South's Republican coalition together?

Why did reconstruction collapse?

Conclusion: Was reconstruction "a revolution but half accomplished"?

✔ LearningCurve
Check what you know.
bedfordstmartins.com
/roarkunderstanding

"White Man's Country"

This silk ribbon from the 1868 presidential campaign between Republican Ulysses S. Grant and his Democratic opponent, New York governor Horatio Seymour, openly declares the Democrats' goal of white supremacy. During the campaign, Democratic vice presidential nominee Francis P. Blair Jr. promised that a Seymour victory would restore "white people" to power by declaring the reconstruction governments in the South "null and void." Collection of Janice L. and David J. Frent.

Democrats also exploited the severe economic plight of small white farmers by blaming it on Republican financial policy. Government spending soared during reconstruction, and small farmers saw their tax burden skyrocket. "This is tax time," a South Carolinian reported. "We are nearly all on our head about them. They are so high & so little money to pay with" that farmers "[are] selling every egg and chicken they can get." In 1871, Mississippi reported that one-seventh of the state's land — 3.3 million acres — had been forfeited for nonpayment of taxes. The small farmers' economic distress had a racial dimension. Because few freedmen succeeded in acquiring land, they rarely paid taxes. In Georgia in 1874, blacks made up 45 percent of the population but paid only 2 percent of the taxes. From the perspective of a small white farmer, Republican rule meant that he was paying more taxes and paying them to aid blacks.

If racial pride, social isolation, and financial hardship proved insufficient to drive yeomen from the Republican Party, Democrats turned to terrorism. "Night riders" targeted white Republicans as well as blacks for murder and assassination. Whether white or black, a "dead Radical is very harmless," South Carolina Democratic leader Martin Gary told his followers.

But the primary victims of white violence were black Republicans. Violence escalated to an unprecedented ferocity on Easter Sunday in 1873 in tiny Colfax, Louisiana. The black majority in the area had made Colfax a Republican stronghold until 1872, when Democrats turned to intimidation and fraud to win the local election. Republicans refused to accept the result and eventually occupied the courthouse in the middle of the town. After three weeks, 165 white men attacked. They overran the Republicans' defenses and set the courthouse on fire. When the blacks tried to surrender, the whites murdered them. At least 81 black men were slaughtered that day. Although the federal government indicted the attackers, the Supreme Court ruled that it did not have the right to prosecute. And since local whites would not prosecute neighbors who killed blacks, the defendants in the Colfax massacre went free.

Even before adopting the all-out white supremacist tactics of the 1870s, Democrats had taken control of the governments of Virginia, Tennessee, and North Carolina. The new campaign brought fresh gains. The Redeemers retook Georgia in 1871, Texas in 1873, and Arkansas and Alabama in 1874. As Mississippi's election approached in 1876, Governor Adelbert Ames appealed to Washington for federal troops to control the violence, only to hear from the attorney general that the "whole public are tired of these annual autumnal outbreaks in the South." Abandoned, Mississippi Republicans succumbed to the Democratic onslaught in the fall elections. By 1876, only three Republican state governments survived in the South (**Map 16.3**).

CHAPTER LOCATOR | Why did Congress object to Lincoln's wartime plan for reconstruction? | How did the North respond to the passage of black codes in the southern states?

480 CHAPTER 16 RECONSTRUCTING A NATION

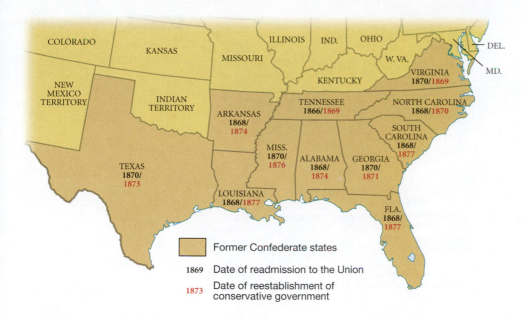

COLORADO

KANSAS

MISSOURI

ILLINOIS   IND.   OHIO

W. VA.

DEL.

MD.

NEW
MEXICO
TERRITORY

INDIAN
TERRITORY

ARKANSAS
1868/
1874

TENNESSEE
1866/1869

KENTUCKY

VIRGINIA
1870/1869

NORTH CAROLINA
1868/1870

SOUTH
CAROLINA
1868/
1877

TEXAS
1870/
1873

MISS.
1870/
1876

ALABAMA
1868/
1874

GEORGIA
1870/
1871

LOUISIANA
1868/1877

FLA.
1868/
1877

Former Confederate states

1869 Date of readmission to the Union

1873 Date of reestablishment of conservative government

MAP 16.3 ■ The Reconstruction of the South

Myth has it that Republican rule of the former Confederacy was not only harsh but long. In most states, however, conservative southern whites stormed back into power in months or just a few years. By the election of 1876, Republican governments could be found in only three states, and they soon fell.

> MAP ACTIVITY

READING THE MAP: List in chronological order the readmission of the former Confederate states to the Union. Which states reestablished conservative governments most quickly?
CONNECTIONS: What did the former Confederate states need to do in order to be readmitted to the Union? How did reestablished conservative governments react to reconstruction?

An Election and a Compromise

The year 1876 witnessed one of the most tumultuous elections in American history. The election took place in November, but not until March 2 of the following year did the nation know who would be inaugurated president on March 4. The Democrats nominated New York's governor, Samuel J. Tilden, who immediately targeted the corruption of the Grant administration and the "despotism" of Republican reconstruction. The Republicans put forward Rutherford B. Hayes, governor of Ohio. Privately, Hayes considered "bayonet rule" a mistake but concluded that waving the bloody shirt remained the Republicans' best political strategy.

On election day, Tilden tallied 4,288,590 votes to Hayes's 4,036,000. But in the all-important electoral college, Tilden fell one vote short of the majority required for victory. The electoral votes of three states — South Carolina, Louisiana, and Florida, the only remaining Republican governments in the South — remained in doubt because both Republicans and Democrats in those states claimed victory. To win, Tilden needed only one of the nineteen contested votes. Hayes had to have all of them.

Congress had to decide who had actually won the elections in the three southern states and thus who would be president. The Constitution provided no guidance for this situation. Moreover, Democrats controlled the House, and Republicans controlled the Senate. Congress created a special electoral

How radical was congressional reconstruction?	What brought the elements of the South's Republican coalition together?	**Why did reconstruction collapse?**	Conclusion: Was reconstruction "a revolution but half accomplished"?	✓ LearningCurve Check what you know. bedfordstmartins.com /roarkunderstanding

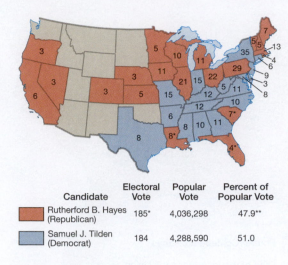

MAP 16.4 ■ The Election of 1876

Candidate	Electoral Vote	Popular Vote	Percent of Popular Vote
Rutherford B. Hayes (Republican)	185*	4,036,298	47.9**
Samuel J. Tilden (Democrat)	184	4,288,590	51.0

*19 electoral votes were disputed.

**Percentages do not total 100 because some popular votes went to other parties.

commission to arbitrate the disputed returns. All of the commissioners voted their party affiliation, giving every state to the Republican Hayes and putting him over the top in electoral votes (**Map 16.4**).

Some outraged Democrats vowed to resist Hayes's victory. Rumors flew of an impending coup and renewed civil war. But the impasse was broken when negotiations behind the scenes resulted in an informal understanding known as the **Compromise of 1877**. In exchange for a Democratic promise not to block Hayes's inauguration and to deal fairly with the freedmen, Hayes vowed to refrain from using the army to uphold the remaining Republican regimes in the South and to provide the South with substantial federal subsidies for railroads.

Stubborn Tilden supporters bemoaned the "stolen election" and damned "His Fraudulency," Rutherford B. Hayes. Old-guard radicals such as William Lloyd Garrison denounced Hayes's bargain as a "policy of compromise, of credulity, of weakness, of subserviency, of surrender." But the nation as a whole celebrated, for the country had weathered a grave crisis. The last three Republican state governments in the South fell quickly once Hayes abandoned them and withdrew the U.S. Army. Reconstruction came to an end.

Compromise of 1877

▶ Informal agreement in which Democrats agreed not to block Rutherford Hayes's inauguration and to deal fairly with freedmen; in return, Hayes vowed not to use the army to uphold the remaining Republican regimes in the South and to provide the South with substantial federal subsidies for railroads. The compromise brought the Reconstruction era to an end.

> ## QUICK REVIEW

How did the Supreme Court undermine reconstruction?

CHAPTER LOCATOR | Why did Congress object to Lincoln's wartime plan for reconstruction? | How did the North respond to the passage of black codes in the southern states?

482   CHAPTER 16   RECONSTRUCTING A NATION

Conclusion: Was reconstruction "a revolution but half accomplished"?

IN 1865, when General Carl Schurz visited the South, he discovered "a revolution but half accomplished." White Southerners resisted the passage from slavery to free labor, from white racial despotism to equal justice, and from white political monopoly to biracial democracy. The old elite wanted to get "things back as near to slavery as possible," Schurz reported, while African Americans such as James T. Rapier and some whites were eager to exploit the revolutionary implications of defeat and emancipation.

Although the northern-dominated Republican Congress refused to provide for blacks' economic welfare, it employed constitutional amendments to require ex-Confederates to accept legal equality and share political power with black men. Conservative southern whites fought ferociously to recover their power and privilege. When Democrats regained control of politics, whites used both state power and private violence to wipe out many of the gains of Reconstruction, leading one observer to conclude that the North had won the war but the South had won the peace.

The Redeemer counterrevolution, however, did not mean a return to slavery. Northern victory in the Civil War ensured that ex-slaves no longer faced the auction block and could send their children to school, worship in their own churches, and work independently on their own rented farms. Sharecropping, with all its hardships, provided more autonomy and economic welfare than bondage had. It was limited freedom, to be sure, but it was not slavery.

The Civil War and emancipation set in motion the most profound upheaval in the nation's history. War destroyed the largest slave society in the New World and gave birth to a modern nation-state. Washington, D.C., increased its role in national affairs, and the victorious North set the nation's compass toward the expansion of industrial capitalism and the final conquest of the West.

Despite massive changes, however, the Civil War remained only a "half accomplished" revolution. By not fulfilling the promises the nation seemed to hold out to black Americans at war's end, Reconstruction represents a tragedy of enormous proportions. The failure to protect blacks and guarantee their rights had enduring consequences. It was the failure of the first reconstruction that made the modern civil rights movement necessary.

| How radical was congressional reconstruction? | What brought the elements of the South's Republican coalition together? | Why did reconstruction collapse? | **Conclusion: Was reconstruction "a revolution but half accomplished"?** | ✓ **LearningCurve** Check what you know. bedfordstmartins.com /roarkunderstanding |

483

CHAPTER 16 STUDY GUIDE

 STEP 1 **GET STARTED ONLINE**

✓ **LearningCurve** ■ bedfordstmartins.com/roarkunderstanding

Now that you've read the chapter, make it stick by completing the LearningCurve activity.

 STEP 2 **EXPLAIN WHY IT MATTERS**

Put your reading into practice. Identify each term below, and then explain why it matters in U.S. history.

TERM	WHO OR WHAT & WHEN	WHY IT MATTERS
Freedmen's Bureau (p. 460)		
black codes (p. 463)		
Civil Rights Act of 1866 (p. 465)		
Fourteenth Amendment (p. 466)		
Military Reconstruction Act (p. 468)		
Fifteenth Amendment (p. 469)		
carpetbaggers (p. 472)		
scalawags (p. 472)		
Ku Klux Klan (p. 472)		
sharecropping (p. 474)		
Redeemers (p. 479)		
Compromise of 1877 (p. 482)		

 STEP 3 **MOVE BEYOND THE BASICS**

To demonstrate a more advanced understanding, indicate below how each phase of reconstruction addressed the key issues involved.

Phase of reconstruction	Requirements for readmission	Role/rights of freedmen	Achievements	Failures
Wartime reconstruction (Lincoln)				
Presidential reconstruction (Johnson)				
Congressional reconstruction				

STEP 4 — PUT IT ALL TOGETHER

Now, take a step back and try to explain the big picture. Remember to use specific examples from the chapter in your answers.

PRESIDENTIAL AND CONGRESSIONAL RECONSTRUCTION

▶ What role did the black codes play in shaping the course of reconstruction?

▶ What steps did Congress take between 1865 and 1869 to assist ex-slaves in their lives as freedmen? How effective were these actions?

SOUTHERN RECONSTRUCTION IN ACTION

▶ How did white Southerners respond during reconstruction? Consider both Democrats and Republicans in your response.

▶ How did southern African Americans attempt to shape their own lives during reconstruction?

THE END OF RECONSTRUCTION

▶ How and why did the decline of northern support for reconstruction help southern Democrats "redeem" the South?

▶ Why did white supremacy become the foundation of southern politics in the 1870s?

LOOKING BACKWARD, LOOKING AHEAD

▶ How did long-held racial views among whites, in both the South and the North, shape reconstruction?

▶ What were the lasting accomplishments of reconstruction? What were its most important failures?

> IN YOUR OWN WORDS

Imagine that you must give an oral report to the class answering the following question: **What were the achievements and failures of reconstruction?** What would be the most important points to include and why?

 Do it online at the Student Site ▪ bedfordstmartins.com/roarkunderstanding

APPENDIX I

DOCUMENTS

THE DECLARATION OF INDEPENDENCE

In Congress, July 4, 1776,

THE UNANIMOUS DECLARATION OF THE THIRTEEN
UNITED STATES OF AMERICA

When in the course of human events, it becomes necessary for one people to dissolve the political bands which have connected them with another, and to assume, among the powers of the earth, the separate and equal station to which the laws of nature and of nature's God entitle them, a decent respect to the opinions of mankind requires that they should declare the causes which impel them to the separation.

We hold these truths to be self-evident, that all men are created equal; that they are endowed by their Creator with certain unalienable rights; that among these, are life, liberty, and the pursuit of happiness. That, to secure these rights, governments are instituted among men, deriving their just powers from the consent of the governed; that, whenever any form of government becomes destructive of these ends, it is the right of the people to alter or to abolish it, and to institute a new government, laying its foundation on such principles, and organizing its powers in such form, as to them shall seem most likely to effect their safety and happiness. Prudence, indeed, will dictate that governments long established, should not be changed for light and transient causes; and, accordingly, all experience hath shown, that mankind are more disposed to suffer, while evils are sufferable, than to right themselves by abolishing the forms to which they are accustomed. But, when a long train of abuses and usurpations, pursuing invariably the same object, evinces a design to reduce them under absolute despotism, it is their right, it is their duty, to throw off such government and to provide new guards for their future security. Such has been the patient sufferance of these colonies, and such is now the necessity which constrains them to alter their former systems of government. The history of the present King of Great Britain is a history of repeated injuries and usurpations, all having, in direct object, the establishment of an absolute tyranny over these States. To prove this, let facts be submitted to a candid world: He has refused his assent to laws the most wholesome and necessary for the public good.

He has forbidden his governors to pass laws of immediate and pressing importance, unless suspended in their operation till his assent should be obtained; and, when so suspended, he has utterly neglected to attend to them.

He has refused to pass other laws for the accommodation of large districts of people, unless those people would relinquish the right of representation in the legislature; a right inestimable to them, and formidable to tyrants only.

He has called together legislative bodies at places unusual, uncomfortable, and distant from the depository of their public records, for the sole purpose of fatiguing them into compliance with his measures.

He has dissolved representative houses repeatedly for opposing, with manly firmness, his invasions on the rights of the people.

He has refused, for a long time after such dissolutions, to cause others to be elected; whereby the legislative powers, incapable of annihilation, have returned to the people at large for their exercise; the state remaining in the mean-time exposed to all the danger of invasion from without, and convulsions within.

He has endeavoured to prevent the population of these States; for that purpose, obstructing the laws for naturalization of foreigners, refusing to pass others to encourage their migration hither, and raising the conditions of new appropriations of lands.

He has obstructed the administration of justice, by refusing his assent to laws for establishing judiciary powers.

He has made judges dependent on his will alone, for the tenure of their offices, and the amount and payment of their salaries.

He has erected a multitude of new offices, and sent hither swarms of officers to harass our people, and eat out their substance.

He has kept among us, in times of peace, standing armies, without the consent of our legislature.

He has affected to render the military independent of, and superior to, the civil power.

He has combined, with others, to subject us to a jurisdiction foreign to our Constitution, and unacknowledged by our laws; giving his assent to their acts of pretended legislation:

For quartering large bodies of armed troops among us:

For protecting them by a mock trial, from punishment, for any murders which they should commit on the inhabitants of these States:

For cutting off our trade with all parts of the world:

For imposing taxes on us without our consent:

For depriving us, in many cases, of the benefit of trial by jury:

For transporting us beyond seas to be tried for pretended offences:

For abolishing the free system of English laws in a neighboring province, establishing therein an arbitrary government, and enlarging its boundaries, so as to render it at once an example and fit instrument for introducing the same absolute rule into these colonies:

For taking away our charters, abolishing our most valuable laws, and altering, fundamentally, the powers of our governments:

For suspending our own legislatures, and declaring themselves invested with power to legislate for us in all cases whatsoever.

He has abdicated government here, by declaring us out of his protection, and waging war against us.

He has plundered our seas, ravaged our coasts, burnt our towns, and destroyed the lives of our people.

He is, at this time, transporting large armies of foreign mercenaries to complete the works of death, desolation, and tyranny, already begun, with circumstances of cruelty and perfidy scarcely paralleled in the most barbarous ages, and totally unworthy the head of a civilized nation.

He has constrained our fellow citizens, taken captive on the high seas, to bear arms against their country, to become the executioners of their friends, and brethren, or to fall themselves by their hands.

He has excited domestic insurrections amongst us, and has endeavored to bring on the inhabitants of our frontiers, the merciless Indian savages, whose known rule of warfare is an undistinguished destruction of all ages, sexes, and conditions.

In every stage of these oppressions, we have petitioned for redress; in the most humble terms; our repeated petitions have been answered only by repeated injury. A prince, whose character is thus marked by every act which may define a tyrant, is unfit to be the ruler of a free people.

Nor have we been wanting in attention to our British brethren. We have warned them, from time to time, of attempts made by their legislature to extend an unwarrantable jurisdiction over us. We have reminded them of the circumstances of our emigration and settlement here. We have appealed to their native justice and magnanimity, and we have conjured them, by the ties of our common kindred, to disavow these usurpations, which would inevitably interrupt our connections and correspondence. They, too, have been deaf to the voice of justice and consanguinity. We must, therefore, acquiesce in the necessity which denounces our separation, and hold them as we hold the rest of mankind, enemies in war, in peace, friends.

We, therefore, the representatives of the United States of America, in general Congress assembled, appealing to the Supreme Judge of the world for the rectitude of our intentions, do, in the name, and by authority of the good people of these colonies, solemnly publish and declare, that these united colonies are, and of right ought to be, free and independent states: that they are absolved from all allegiance to the British Crown, and that all political connection between them and the state of Great Britain is, and ought to be, totally dissolved; and that, as free and independent states, they have full power to levy war, conclude peace, contract alliances, establish commerce, and to do all other acts and things which independent states may of right do. And, for the support of this declaration, with a firm reliance on the protection of Divine Providence, we mutually pledge to each other our lives, our fortunes, and our sacred honor.

The foregoing Declaration was, by order of Congress, engrossed, and signed by the following members:

JOHN HANCOCK

New Hampshire
Josiah Bartlett
William Whipple
Matthew Thornton

Massachusetts Bay
Samuel Adams
John Adams
Robert Treat Paine
Elbridge Gerry

Rhode Island
Stephen Hopkins
William Ellery

Connecticut
Roger Sherman
Samuel Huntington
William Williams
Oliver Wolcott

New York
William Floyd
Phillip Livingston
Francis Lewis
Lewis Morris

New Jersey
Richard Stockton
John Witherspoon
Francis Hopkinson
John Hart
Abraham Clark

Pennsylvania
Robert Morris
Benjamin Rush
Benjamin Franklin
John Morton
George Clymer
James Smith

George Taylor
James Wilson
George Ross

Delaware
Caesar Rodney
George Read
Thomas M'Kean

Maryland
Samuel Chase
William Paca
Thomas Stone
Charles Carroll, of
  Carrollton

North Carolina
William Hooper
Joseph Hewes
John Penn

South Carolina
Edward Rutledge
Thomas Heyward, Jr.
Thomas Lynch, Jr.
Arthur Middleton

Virginia
George Wythe
Richard Henry Lee
Thomas Jefferson
Benjamin Harrison
Thomas Nelson, Jr.
Francis Lightfoot Lee
Carter Braxton

Georgia
Button Gwinnett
Lyman Hall
George Walton

Resolved, That copies of the Declaration be sent to the several assemblies, conventions, and committees, or councils of safety, and to the several commanding officers of the continental troops; that it be proclaimed in each of the United States, at the head of the army.

THE CONSTITUTION OF THE UNITED STATES*

Agreed to by Philadelphia Convention, September 17, 1787. Implemented March 4, 1789.

Preamble

We the people of the United States, in order to form a more perfect union, establish justice, insure domestic tranquility, provide for the common defense, promote the general welfare, and secure the blessings of liberty to ourselves and our posterity, do ordain and establish this Constitution for the United States of America.

Article I

Section 1 All legislative powers herein granted shall be vested in a Congress of the United States, which shall consist of a Senate and a House of Representatives.

Section 2 The House of Representatives shall be composed of members chosen every second year by the people of the several States, and the electors in each State shall have the qualifications requisite for electors of the most numerous branch of the State Legislature.

No person shall be a Representative who shall not have attained to the age of twenty-five years, and been seven years a citizen of the United States, and who shall not, when elected, be an inhabitant of that State in which he shall be chosen.

Representatives and direct taxes shall be apportioned among the several States which may be included within this Union, according to their respective numbers, *which shall be determined by adding to the whole number of free persons, including those bound to service for a term of years and excluding Indians not taxed, three-fifths of all other persons.* The actual enumeration shall be made within three years after the first meeting of the Congress of the United States, and within every subsequent term of ten years, in such manner as they shall by law direct. The number of Representatives shall not exceed one for every thirty thousand, but each State shall have at least one Representative; *and until such enumeration shall be made, the State of New Hampshire shall be entitled to choose three, Massachusetts eight, Rhode Island and Providence Plantations one, Connecticut five, New York six, New Jersey four, Pennsylvania eight, Delaware one, Maryland six, Virginia ten, North Carolina five, South Carolina five, and Georgia three.*

*Passages no longer in effect are in italic type.

When vacancies happen in the representation from any State, the Executive authority thereof shall issue writs of election to fill such vacancies.

The House of Representatives shall choose their Speaker and other officers; and shall have the sole power of impeachment.

Section 3 The Senate of the United States shall be composed of two Senators from each State, *chosen by the legislature thereof*, for six years; and each Senator shall have one vote.

Immediately after they shall be assembled in consequence of the first election, they shall be divided as equally as may be into three classes. The seats of the Senators of the first class shall be vacated at the expiration of the second year, of the second class at the expiration of the fourth year, and of the third class at the expiration of the sixth year, so that one-third may be chosen every second year; and if vacancies happen by resignation or otherwise, during the recess of the legislature of any State, the Executive thereof may make temporary appointments until the next meeting of the legislature, which shall then fill such vacancies.

No person shall be a Senator who shall not have attained to the age of thirty years, and been nine years a citizen of the United States, and who shall not, when elected, be an inhabitant of that State for which he shall be chosen.

The Vice-President of the United States shall be President of the Senate, but shall have no vote, unless they be equally divided.

The Senate shall choose their other officers, and also a President *pro tempore*, in the absence of the Vice-President, or when he shall exercise the office of President of the United States.

The Senate shall have the sole power to try all impeachments. When sitting for that purpose, they shall be on oath or affirmation. When the President of the United States is tried, the Chief Justice shall preside: and no person shall be convicted without the concurrence of two-thirds of the members present.

Judgment in cases of impeachment shall not extend further than to removal from the office, and disqualification to hold and enjoy any office of honor, trust or profit under the United States: but the party convicted shall nevertheless be liable and subject to indictment, trial, judgment and punishment, according to law.

Section 4 The times, places and manner of holding elections for Senators and Representatives shall be prescribed in each State by the legislature thereof; but the Congress may at any time by law make or alter such regulations, except as to the places of choosing Senators.

The Congress shall assemble at least once in every year, and such meeting *shall be on the first Monday in December, unless they shall by law appoint a different day.*

Section 5 Each house shall be the judge of the elections, returns and qualifications of its own members, and a majority of each shall constitute a quorum to do business; but a smaller number may adjourn from day to day, and may be authorized to compel the attendance of absent members, in such manner, and under such penalties, as each house may provide.

Each house may determine the rules of its proceedings, punish its members for disorderly behavior, and with the concurrence of two-thirds, expel a member.

Each house shall keep a journal of its proceedings, and from time to time publish the same, excepting such parts as may in their judgment require secrecy; and the yeas and nays of the members of either house on any question shall, at the desire of one-fifth of those present, be entered on the journal.

Neither house, during the session of Congress, shall, without the consent of the other, adjourn for more than three days, nor to any other place than that in which the two houses shall be sitting.

Section 6 The Senators and Representatives shall receive a compensation for their services, to be ascertained by law and paid out of the treasury of the United States. They shall in all cases except treason, felony and breach of the peace, be privileged from arrest during their attendance at the session of their respective houses, and in going to and returning from the same; and for any speech or debate in either house, they shall not be questioned in any other place.

No Senator or Representative shall, during the time for which he was elected, be appointed to any civil office under the authority of the United States, which shall have been created, or the emoluments whereof shall have been increased, during such time; and no person holding any office under the United States shall be a member of either house during his continuance in office.

Section 7 All bills for raising revenue shall originate in the House of Representatives; but the Senate may propose or concur with amendments as on other bills.

Every bill which shall have passed the House of Representatives and the Senate, shall, before it become a law, be presented to the President of the United States; if he approve he shall sign it, but if not he shall return it with objections to that house in which it shall have originated, who shall enter the objections at large on their journal, and proceed to reconsider it. If after such reconsideration two-thirds of that house shall agree to pass the bill, it shall be sent, together with the objections, to the other house, by which it shall likewise be reconsidered, and, if approved by two-thirds of that house, it shall become a law. But in all such cases the votes of both houses shall be determined by yeas and nays, and the names of the persons voting for and against the bill shall be entered

on the journal of each house respectively. If any bill shall not be returned by the President within ten days (Sundays excepted) after it shall have been presented to him, the same shall be a law, in like manner as if he had signed it, unless the Congress by their adjournment prevent its return, in which case it shall not be a law.

Every order, resolution, or vote to which the concurrence of the Senate and House of Representatives may be necessary (except on a question of adjournment) shall be presented to the President of the United States; and before the same shall take effect, shall be approved by him, or being disapproved by him, shall be repassed by two-thirds of the Senate and House of Representatives, according to the rules and limitations prescribed in the case of a bill.

Section 8 The Congress shall have power

To lay and collect taxes, duties, imposts, and excises, to pay the debts and provide for the common defense and general welfare of the United States; but all duties, imposts and excises shall be uniform throughout the United States;

To borrow money on the credit of the United States;

To regulate commerce with foreign nations, and among the several States, and with the Indian tribes;

To establish an uniform rule of naturalization, and uniform laws on the subject of bankruptcies throughout the United States;

To coin money, regulate the value thereof, and of foreign coin, and fix the standard of weights and measures;

To provide for the punishment of counterfeiting the securities and current coin of the United States;

To establish post offices and post roads;

To promote the progress of science and useful arts by securing for limited times to authors and inventors the exclusive right to their respective writings and discoveries;

To constitute tribunals inferior to the Supreme Court;

To define and punish piracies and felonies committed on the high seas and offences against the law of nations;

To declare war, grant letters of marque and reprisal, and make rules concerning captures on land and water;

To raise and support armies, but no appropriation of money to that use shall be for a longer term than two years;

To provide and maintain a navy;

To make rules for the government and regulation of the land and naval forces;

To provide for calling forth the militia to execute the laws of the Union, suppress insurrections and repel invasions;

To provide for organizing, arming, and disciplining the militia, and for governing such part of them as may be employed in the service of the United States, reserving to the States respectively the appointment of the officers, and the authority of training the militia according to the discipline prescribed by Congress;

To exercise exclusive legislation in all cases whatsoever, over such district (not exceeding ten miles square) as may, by cession of particular States, and the acceptance of Congress, become the seat of the government of the United States, and to exercise like authority over all places purchased by the consent of the legislature of the State, in which the same shall be, for erection of forts, magazines, arsenals, dock-yards, and other needful buildings; —and

To make all laws which shall be necessary and proper for carrying into execution the foregoing powers, and all other powers vested by this Constitution in the government of the United States, or in any department or officer thereof.

Section 9 *The migration or importation of such persons as any of the States now existing shall think proper to admit shall not be prohibited by the Congress prior to the year one thousand eight hundred and eight; but a tax or duty may be imposed on such importation, not exceeding ten dollars for each person.*

The privilege of the writ of habeas corpus shall not be suspended, unless when in cases of rebellion or invasion the public safety may require it.

No bill of attainder or ex post facto law shall be passed.

No capitation, or other direct, tax shall be laid, unless in proportion to the census or enumeration herein before directed to be taken.

No tax or duty shall be laid on articles exported from any State.

No preference shall be given by any regulation of commerce or revenue to the ports of one State over those of another; nor shall vessels bound to, or from, one State be obliged to enter, clear, or pay duties in another.

No money shall be drawn from the treasury, but in consequence of appropriations made by law; and a regular statement and account of the receipts and expenditures of all public money shall be published from time to time.

No title of nobility shall be granted by the United States: and no person holding any office of profit or trust under them, shall, without the consent of the Congress, accept of any present, emolument, office, or title, of any kind whatever, from any king, prince, or foreign state.

Section 10 No State shall enter into any treaty, alliance, or confederation; grant letters of marque and reprisal; coin money; emit bills of credit; make anything but gold and silver coin a tender in payment of debts; pass any bill of attainder, ex post facto law, or law impairing the obligation of contracts, or grant any title of nobility.

No State shall, without the consent of Congress, lay any imposts or duties on imports or exports, except what may be absolutely necessary for executing its inspection laws: and the net produce of all duties and imposts, laid by any State on imports or exports, shall be for the use of the treasury of the United States; and all such laws shall be subject to the revision and control of the Congress.

No State shall, without the consent of Congress, lay any duty of tonnage, keep troops, or ships of war in time of peace, enter into any agreement or compact with another State, or with a foreign power, or engage in war, unless actually invaded, or in such imminent danger as will not admit of delay.

Article II

Section 1 The executive power shall be vested in a President of the United States of America. He shall hold his office during the term of four years, and, together with the Vice-President, chosen for the same term, be elected as follows:

Each State shall appoint, in such manner as the legislature thereof may direct, a number of electors, equal to the whole number of Senators and Representatives to which the State may be entitled in the Congress; but no Senator or Representative, or person holding an office of trust or profit under the United States, shall be appointed an elector.

The electors shall meet in their respective States, and vote by ballot for two persons, of whom one at least shall not be an inhabitant of the same State with themselves. And they shall make a list of all the persons voted for, and of the number of votes for each; which list they shall sign and certify, and transmit sealed to the seat of government of the United States, directed to the President of the Senate. The President of the Senate shall, in the presence of the Senate and House of Representatives, open all the certificates, and the votes shall then be counted. The person having the greatest number of votes shall be the President, if such number be a majority of the whole number of electors appointed; and if there be more than one who have such majority, and have an equal number of votes, then the House of Representatives shall immediately choose by ballot one of them for President; and if no person have a majority, then from the five highest on the list said house shall in like manner choose the President. But in choosing the President the votes shall be taken by States, the representation from each State having one vote; a quorum for this purpose shall consist of a member or members from two-thirds of the States, and a majority of all the States shall be necessary to a choice. In every case, after the choice of the President, the person having the greatest number of votes of the electors shall be the Vice-President. But if there should remain two or more who have equal votes, the Senate shall choose from them by ballot the Vice-President.

The Congress may determine the time of choosing the electors, and the day on which they shall give their votes; which day shall be the same throughout the United States.

No person except a natural-born citizen, *or a citizen of the United States at the time of the adoption of this Constitution,* shall be eligible to the office of President; neither shall any person be eligible to that office who shall not have attained to the age of thirty-five years, and been fourteen years a resident within the United States.

In cases of the removal of the President from office or of his death, resignation, or inability to discharge the powers and duties of the said office, the same shall devolve on the Vice-President, and the Congress may by law provide for the case of removal, death, resignation, or inability, both of the President and Vice-President, declaring what officer shall then act as President, and such officer shall act accordingly, until the disability be removed, or a President shall be elected.

The President shall, at stated times, receive for his services a compensation, which shall neither be increased nor diminished during the period for which he shall have been elected, and he shall not receive within that period any other emolument from the United States, or any of them.

Before he enter on the execution of his office, he shall take the following oath or affirmation: — "I do solemnly swear (or affirm) that I will faithfully execute the office of the President of the United States, and will to the best of my ability preserve, protect and defend the Constitution of the United States."

Section 2 The President shall be commander in chief of the army and navy of the United States, and of the militia of the several States, when called into the actual service of the United States; he may require the opinion, in writing, of the principal officer in each of the executive departments, upon any subject relating to the duties of their respective offices, and he shall have power to grant reprieves and pardons for offenses against the United States, except in cases of impeachment.

He shall have power, by and with the advice and consent of the Senate, to make treaties, provided two-thirds of the Senators present concur; and he shall nominate, and by and with the advice and consent of the Senate, shall appoint ambassadors, other public ministers and consuls, judges of the Supreme Court, and all other officers of the United States, whose appointments are not herein otherwise provided for, and which shall be established by law: but Congress may by law vest the appointment of such inferior officers, as they think proper, in the President alone, in the courts of law, or in the heads of departments.

The President shall have power to fill up all vacancies that may happen during the recess of the Senate, by granting commissions which shall expire at the end of their next session.

Section 3 He shall from time to time give to the Congress information of the state of the Union, and recommend to their consideration such measures as he shall judge necessary and expedient; he may, on extraordinary occasions, convene both houses, or either of them, and in case of disagreement between them, with respect to the time of adjournment, he may adjourn them to such time as he shall think proper; he shall receive ambassadors and other public ministers; he shall take care that the laws be faithfully executed, and shall commission all the officers of the United States.

Section 4 The President, Vice-President and all civil officers of the United States shall be removed from office on impeachment for, and on conviction of, treason, bribery, or other high crimes and misdemeanors.

Article III

Section 1 The judicial power of the United States shall be vested in one Supreme Court, and in such inferior courts as the Congress may from time to time ordain and establish. The judges, both of the Supreme and inferior courts, shall hold their offices during good behavior, and shall, at stated times, receive for their services a compensation which shall not be diminished during their continuance in office.

Section 2 The judicial power shall extend to all cases, in law and equity, arising under this Constitution, the laws of the United States, and treaties made, or which shall be made, under their authority; — to all cases affecting ambassadors, other public ministers and consuls; — to all cases of admiralty and maritime jurisdiction; — to controversies to which the United States shall be a party; — to controversies between two or more States; — between a State and citizens of another State; — *between citizens of different States;* — between citizens of the same State claiming lands under grants of different States, and between a State, or the citizens thereof, and foreign states, citizens or subjects.

In all cases affecting ambassadors, other public ministers and consuls, and those in which a State shall be party, the Supreme Court shall have original jurisdiction. In all the other cases before mentioned, the Supreme Court shall have appellate jurisdiction, both as to law and fact, with such exceptions, and under such regulations, as the Congress shall make.

The trial of all crimes, except in cases of impeachment, shall be by jury; and such trial shall be held in the State where said crimes shall have been committed; but when not committed within any State, the trial shall be at such place or places as the Congress may by Law have directed.

Section 3 Treason against the United States shall consist only in levying war against them, or in adhering to their enemies, giving them aid and comfort. No person shall be convicted of treason unless on the testimony of two witnesses to the same overt act, or on confession in open court.

The Congress shall have power to declare the punishment of treason, but no attainder of treason shall work corruption of blood, or forfeiture except during the life of the person attainted.

Article IV

Section 1 Full faith and credit shall be given in each State to the public acts, records, and judicial proceedings of every other State. And the Congress may by general laws prescribe the manner in which such acts, records, and proceedings shall be proved, and the effect thereof.

Section 2 The citizens of each State shall be entitled to all privileges and immunities of citizens in the several States.

A person charged in any State with treason, felony, or other crime, who shall flee from justice, and be found in another State, shall on demand of the executive authority of the State from which he fled, be delivered up, to be removed to the State having jurisdiction of the crime.

No Person held to service or labor in one State, under the laws thereof, escaping into another, shall, in consequence of any law or regulation therein, be discharged from such service or labor, but shall be delivered up on claim of the party to whom such service or labor may be due.

Section 3 New States may be admitted by the Congress into this Union; but no new State shall be formed or erected within the jurisdiction of any other State; nor any State be formed by the junction of two or more States, or parts of States, without the consent of the legislatures of the States concerned as well as of the Congress.

The Congress shall have power to dispose of and make all needful rules and regulations respecting the territory or other property belonging to the United States; and nothing in this Constitution shall be so construed as to prejudice any claims of the United States, or of any particular State.

Section 4 The United States shall guarantee to every State in this Union a republican form of government, and shall protect each of them against invasion; and on application of the legislature, or of the executive (when the legislature cannot be convened), against domestic violence.

Article V

The Congress, whenever two-thirds of both houses shall deem it necessary, shall propose amendments to this Constitution, or, on the application of the legislatures of two-thirds of the several States, shall call a convention for proposing amendments, which, in either case, shall be valid to all intents and purposes, as part of this Constitution, when ratified by the legislatures of three-fourths of the several States, or by conventions in three-fourths thereof, as the one or the other mode of ratification may be proposed by the Congress; provided *that no amendments which may be made prior to the year one thousand eight hundred and eight shall in any manner affect the first and fourth clauses in the ninth section of the first article;* and that no State, without its consent, shall be deprived of its equal suffrage in the Senate.

Article VI

All debts contracted and engagements entered into, before the adoption of this Constitution, shall be as valid against the United States under this Constitution, as under the Confederation.

This Constitution, and the laws of the United States which shall be made in pursuance thereof; and all treaties made, or which shall be made, under the authority of the United States, shall be the supreme law of the land; and the judges in every State shall be bound thereby, anything in the Constitution or laws of any State to the contrary notwithstanding.

The Senators and Representatives before mentioned, and the members of the several State legislatures, and all executive and judicial officers, both of the United States and of the several States, shall be bound by oath or affirmation to support this Constitution; but no religious test shall ever be required as a qualification to any office or public trust under the United States.

Article VII

The ratification of the conventions of nine States shall be sufficient for the establishment of this Constitution between the States so ratifying the same.

Done in convention by the unanimous consent of the States present, the seventeenth day of September in the year of our Lord one thousand seven hundred and eighty-seven and of the Independence of the United States of America the twelfth. In witness whereof we have hereunto subscribed our names.

GEORGE WASHINGTON
PRESIDENT AND DEPUTY FROM VIRGINIA

New Hampshire
John Langdon
Nicholas Gilman

Massachusetts
Nathaniel Gorham
Rufus King

Connecticut
William Samuel Johnson
Roger Sherman

New York
Alexander Hamilton

New Jersey
William Livingston
David Brearley

William Paterson
Jonathan Dayton

Pennsylvania
Benjamin Franklin
Thomas Mifflin
Robert Morris
George Clymer
Thomas FitzSimons
Jared Ingersoll
James Wilson
Gouverneur Morris

Delaware
George Read
Gunning Bedford, Jr.
John Dickinson

Richard Bassett
Jacob Broom

Maryland
James McHenry
Daniel of St. Thomas
   Jenifer
Daniel Carroll

Virginia
John Blair
James Madison, Jr.

North Carolina
William Blount
Richard Dobbs Spaight
Hugh Williamson

South Carolina
John Rutledge
Charles Cotesworth
   Pinckney
Charles Pinckney
Pierce Butler

Georgia
William Few
Abraham Baldwin

AMENDMENTS TO THE CONSTITUTION WITH ANNOTATIONS
(including the six unratified amendments)

Amendment I

Congress shall make no law respecting an establishment of religion, or prohibiting the free exercise thereof; or abridging the freedom of speech, or of the press; or the right of the people peaceably to assemble, and to petition the government for a redress of grievances.

Amendment II

A well-regulated militia being necessary to the security of a free State, the right of the people to keep and bear arms shall not be infringed.

Amendment III

No soldier shall, in time of peace, be quartered in any house without the consent of the owner, nor in time of war, but in a manner to be prescribed by law.

Amendment IV

The right of the people to be secure in their persons, houses, papers, and effects, against unreasonable searches and seizures, shall not be violated, and no warrants shall issue but upon probable cause, supported by oath or affirmation, and particularly describing the place to be searched, and the persons or things to be seized.

Amendment V

No person shall be held to answer for a capital, or otherwise infamous crime, unless on a presentment or indictment of a grand jury, except in cases arising in the land or naval forces, or in the militia, when in actual service in time of war or public danger; nor shall any person be subject for the same offence to be twice put in jeopardy of life or limb; nor shall be compelled in any criminal case to be a witness against himself, nor be deprived of life, liberty, or property, without due process of law; nor shall private property be taken for public use without just compensation.

Amendment VI

In all criminal prosecutions, the accused shall enjoy the right to a speedy and public trial, by an impartial jury of the State and district wherein the crime shall have been committed, which district shall have been previously ascertained by law, and to be informed of the nature and cause of the accusation; to be confronted with the witnesses against him; to have compulsory process for obtaining witnesses in his favor, and to have the assistance of counsel for his defence.

Amendment VII

In suits at common law, where the value in controversy shall exceed twenty dollars, the right of trial by jury shall be preserved, and no fact tried by a jury shall be otherwise reexamined in any court of the United States, than according to the rules of the common law.

Amendment VIII

Excessive bail shall not be required, nor excessive fines imposed, nor cruel and unusual punishments inflicted.

Amendment IX

The enumeration in the Constitution, of certain rights, shall not be construed to deny or disparage others retained by the people.

Amendment X

The powers not delegated to the United States by the Constitution, nor prohibited by it to the States, are reserved to the States respectively, or to the people.

Unratified Amendment

Reapportionment Amendment (proposed by Congress September 25, 1789, along with the Bill of Rights)

After the first enumeration required by the first article of the Constitution, there shall be one Representative for every thirty thousand, until the number shall amount to one hundred, after which the proportion shall be so regulated by Congress, that there shall be not less than one hundred Representatives, nor less than one Representative for every forty thousand persons, until the number of Representatives shall amount to two hundred; after which the proportion shall be so regulated by Congress, that there shall not be less than two hundred Representatives, nor more than one Representative for every fifty thousand persons.

Amendment XI

[Adopted 1798]

The judicial power of the United States shall not be construed to extend to any suit in law or equity, commenced or prosecuted against one of the United States by citizens of another State, or by citizens or subjects of any foreign state.

Amendment XII

[Adopted 1804]

The electors shall meet in their respective States, and vote by ballot for President and Vice-President, one of whom, at least, shall not be an inhabitant of the same State with them-selves; they shall name in their ballots the person voted for as President, and in distinct ballots the person voted for as Vice-President, and they shall make distinct lists of all persons voted for as President, and of all persons voted for as Vice-President, and of the number of votes for each, which lists they shall sign and certify, and transmit sealed to the seat of government of the United States, directed to the President of the Senate;—the President of the Senate shall, in the presence of the Senate and House of Representatives, open all the certificates and the votes shall then be counted;—the person having the greatest number of votes for President shall be the President, if such number be a majority of the whole number of electors appointed; and if no person have such majority, then from the persons having the highest numbers not exceeding three on the list of those voted for as President, the House of Representatives shall choose immediately, by ballot, the President. But in choosing the President, the votes shall be taken by States, the representation from each State having one vote; a quorum for this purpose shall consist of a member or members from two-thirds of the States, and a majority of all the States shall be necessary to a choice. And if the House of Representatives shall not choose a President whenever the right of choice shall devolve upon them, *before the fourth day of March* next following, then the Vice-President shall act as President, as in the case of the death or other constitutional disability of the President.

The person having the greatest number of votes as Vice-President shall be the Vice-President, if such number be a majority of the whole number of electors appointed; and if no person have a majority, then from the two highest numbers on the list the Senate shall choose the Vice-President; a quorum for the purpose shall consist of two-thirds of the whole number of Senators, and a majority of the whole number shall be necessary to a choice. But no person constitutionally ineligible to the office of President shall be eligible to that of Vice-President of the United States.

Unratified Amendment

Titles of Nobility Amendment (proposed by Congress May 1, 1810)

If any citizen of the United States shall accept, claim, receive or retain any title of nobility or honor or shall, without the consent of Congress, accept and retain any present, pension, office or emolument of any kind whatever, from any emperor, king, prince or foreign power, such person shall cease to be a citizen of the United States, and shall be incapable of holding any office of trust or profit under them or either of them.

Unratified Amendment

Corwin Amendment (proposed by Congress March 2, 1861)

No amendment shall be made to the Constitution which will authorize or give to Congress the power to abolish or interfere, within any State, with the domestic institutions thereof, including that of persons held to labor or service by the laws of said State.

Amendment XIII

[Adopted 1865]

Section 1 Neither slavery nor involuntary servitude, except as a punishment for crime whereof the party shall have been duly convicted, shall exist within the United States, or any place subject to their jurisdiction.

Section 2 Congress shall have power to enforce this article by appropriate legislation.

Amendment XIV

[Adopted 1868]

Section 1 All persons born or naturalized in the United States, and subject to the jurisdiction thereof, are citizens of the United States and of the State wherein they reside. No State shall make or enforce any law which shall abridge the privileges or immunities of citizens of the United States; nor shall any State deprive any person of life, liberty, or property, without due process of law; nor deny to any person within its jurisdiction the equal protection of the laws.

Section 2 Representatives shall be appointed among the several States according to their respective numbers, counting the whole number of persons in each State, excluding Indians not taxed. But when the right to vote at any election for the choice of Electors for President and Vice-President of the United States, Representatives in Congress, the executive and judicial officers of a State, or the members of the legislature thereof, is denied to any of the male inhabitants of such State, being twenty-one years of age and citizens of the United States, or in any way abridged, except for participation in rebellion, or other crime, the basis of representation therein shall be reduced in the proportion which the number of such male citizens shall bear to the whole number of male citizens twenty-one years of age in such State.

Section 3 No person shall be a Senator or Representative in Congress, or Elector of President and Vice-President, or hold any office, civil or military, under the United States, or under any State, who, having previously taken an oath, as a member of Congress, or as an officer of the United States, or as a member of any State legislature, or as an executive or judicial officer of any State, to support the Constitution of the United States, shall have engaged in insurrection or rebellion against the same, or given aid or comfort to the enemies thereof. Congress may, by a vote of two-thirds of each house, remove such disability.

Section 4 The validity of the public debt of the United States, authorized by law, including debts incurred for payment of pensions and bounties for services in suppressing insurrection or rebellion, shall not be questioned. But neither the United States nor any State shall assume or pay any debt or obligation incurred in aid of insurrection or rebellion against the United States, or any claim for the loss or emancipation of any slave;

but all such debts, obligations, and claims shall be held illegal and void.

Section 5 The Congress shall have power to enforce, by appropriate legislation, the provisions of this article.

Amendment XV

[Adopted 1870]

Section 1 The right of citizens of the United States to vote shall not be denied or abridged by the United States or by any State on account of race, color, or previous condition of servitude.

Section 2 The Congress shall have power to enforce this article by appropriate legislation.

Amendment XVI

[Adopted 1913]

The Congress shall have power to lay and collect taxes on incomes, from whatever source derived, without apportionment among the several States, and without regard to any census or enumeration.

Amendment XVII

[Adopted 1913]

Section 1 The Senate of the United States shall be composed of two Senators from each State, elected by the people thereof, for six years; and each Senator shall have one vote. The electors in each State shall have the qualifications requisite for electors of [voters for] the most numerous branch of the State legislatures.

Section 2 When vacancies happen in the representation of any State in the Senate, the executive authority of such State shall issue writs of election to fill such vacancies: Provided, that the Legislature of any State may empower the executive thereof to make temporary appointments until the people fill the vacancies by election as the Legislature may direct.

Section 3 This amendment shall not be so construed as to affect the election or term of any Senator chosen before it becomes valid as part of the Constitution.

Amendment XVIII

[Adopted 1919; repealed 1933 by Amendment XXI]

Section 1 After one year from the ratification of this article the manufacture, sale, or transportation of intoxicating liquors within, the importation thereof into, or the exportation thereof from the United States and all territory subject to the jurisdiction thereof, for beverage purposes, is hereby prohibited.

Section 2 The Congress and the several States shall have concurrent power to enforce this article by appropriate legislation.

Section 3 This article shall be inoperative unless it shall have been ratified as an amendment to the Constitution by the legislatures of the several States, as provided by the Constitution, within seven years from the date of the submission thereof to the States by the Congress.

Amendment XIX

[Adopted 1920]

Section 1 The right of citizens of the United States to vote shall not be denied or abridged by the United States or by any State on account of sex.

Section 2 Congress shall have the power to enforce this article by appropriate legislation.

Unratified Amendment

Child Labor Amendment (proposed by Congress June 2, 1924)

Section 1 The Congress shall have power to limit, regulate, and prohibit the labor of persons under eighteen years of age.

Section 2 The power of the several States is unimpaired by this article except that the operation of State laws shall be suspended to the extent necessary to give effect to legislation enacted by Congress.

Amendment XX

[Adopted 1933]

Section 1 The terms of the President and Vice-President shall end at noon on the 20th day of January, and the terms of Senators and Representatives at noon on the 3rd day of January, of the years in which such terms would have ended if this article had not been ratified; and the terms of their successors shall then begin.

Section 2 The Congress shall assemble at least once in every year, and such meeting shall begin at noon on the 3rd day of January, unless they shall by law appoint a different day.

Section 3 If, at the time fixed for the beginning of the term of the President, the President-elect shall have died, the Vice-President-elect shall become President. If a President shall not have been chosen before the time fixed for the beginning of his term, or if the President-elect shall have failed to qualify, then the Vice-President-elect shall act as President until a President shall have qualified; and the Congress may by law provide for the case wherein neither a President-elect nor a Vice-President-elect shall have qualified, declaring who shall then act as President, or the manner in which one who is to act shall be selected, and such person shall act accordingly until a President or Vice-President shall have qualified.

Section 4 The Congress may by law provide for the case of the death of any of the persons from whom the House of Representatives may choose a President whenever the right of choice shall have devolved upon them, and for the case of the death of any of the persons from whom the Senate may choose a Vice-President whenever the right of choice shall have devolved upon them.

Section 5 Sections 1 and 2 shall take effect on the 15th day of October following the ratification of this article.

Section 6 This article shall be inoperative unless it shall have been ratified as an amendment to the Constitution by the Legislatures of three-fourths of the several States within seven years from the date of its submission.

Amendment XXI

[Adopted 1933]

Section 1 The eighteenth article of amendment to the Constitution of the United States is hereby repealed.

Section 2 The transportation or importation into any State, Territory, or Possession of the United States for delivery or use therein of intoxicating liquors, in violation of the laws thereof, is hereby prohibited.

Section 3 This article shall be inoperative unless it shall have been ratified as an amendment to the Constitution by conventions in the several States, as provided in the Constitution, within seven years from the date of the submission thereof to the States by the Congress.

Amendment XXII

[Adopted 1951]

Section 1 No person shall be elected to the office of the President more than twice, and no person who has held the office of President, or acted as President, for more than two years of a term to which some other person was elected President shall be elected to the office of President more than once. But this article shall not apply to any person holding the office of President when this Article was proposed by the Congress, and shall not prevent any person who may be holding the office of President, or acting as President, during the term within which this Article becomes operative from holding the office of President or acting as President during the remainder of such term.

Section 2 This article shall be inoperative unless it shall have been ratified as an amendment to the Constitution by the legislatures of three-fourths of the several States within seven years from the date of its submission to the States by the Congress.

Amendment XXIII

[Adopted 1961]

Section 1 The District constituting the seat of Government of the United States shall appoint in such manner as the Congress may direct: A number of electors of President and Vice-President equal to the whole number of Senators and Representatives in Congress to which the District would be entitled if it were a State, but in no event more than the least populous State; they shall be in addition to those appointed by the States, but they shall be considered for the purposes of the election of President and Vice-President, to be electors appointed by a State; and they shall meet in the District

and perform such duties as provided by the twelfth article of amendment.

Section 2 The Congress shall have the power to enforce this article by appropriate legislation.

Amendment XXIV

[Adopted 1964]

Section 1 The right of citizens of the United States to vote in any primary or other election for President or Vice-President, for electors for President or Vice-President, or for Senator or Representative in Congress, shall not be denied or abridged by the United States or any State by reason of failure to pay any poll tax or other tax.

Amendment XXV

[Adopted 1967]

Section 1 In case of the removal of the President from office or of his death or resignation, the Vice-President shall become President.

Section 2 Whenever there is a vacancy in the office of the Vice-President, the President shall nominate a Vice-President who shall take office upon confirmation by a majority vote of both Houses of Congress.

Section 3 Whenever the President transmits to the President pro tempore of the Senate and the Speaker of the House of Representatives his written declaration that he is unable to discharge the powers and duties of his office, and until he transmits to them a written declaration to the contrary, such powers and duties shall be discharged by the Vice-President as Acting President.

Section 4 Whenever the Vice-President and a majority of either the principal officers of the executive departments or of such other body as Congress may by law provide, transmit to the President pro tempore of the Senate and the Speaker of the House of Representatives their written declaration that the President is unable to discharge the powers and duties of his office, the Vice-President shall immediately assume the powers and duties of the office as Acting President.

Thereafter, when the President transmits to the President pro tempore of the Senate and the Speaker of the House of Representatives his written declaration that no inability exists, he shall resume the powers and duties of his office unless the Vice-President and a majority of either the principal officers of the executive department[s] or of such other body as Congress may by law provide, transmit within four days to the President pro tempore of the Senate and the Speaker of the House of Representatives their written declaration that the President is unable to discharge the powers and duties of his office. Thereupon Congress shall decide the issue, assembling within forty-eight hours for that purpose if not in session. If the Congress, within twenty-one days after receipt of the latter written declaration, or, if Congress is not in session, within twenty-one days after

Congress is required to assemble, determines by two-thirds vote of both Houses that the President is unable to discharge the powers and duties of his office, the Vice-President shall continue to discharge the same as Acting President; otherwise, the President shall resume the powers and duties of his office.

Amendment XXVI

[Adopted 1971]

Section 1 The right of citizens of the United States, who are eighteen years of age or older, to vote shall not be denied or abridged by the United States or by any State on account of age.

Section 2 The Congress shall have power to enforce this article by appropriate legislation.

Unratified Amendment

Equal Rights Amendment (proposed by Congress March 22, 1972; seven-year deadline for ratification extended to June 30, 1982)

Section 1 Equality of rights under the law shall not be denied or abridged by the United States or by any State on account of sex.

Section 2 The Congress shall have the power to enforce, by appropriate legislation, the provisions of this article.

Section 3 This amendment shall take effect two years after the date of ratification.

Unratified Amendment

D.C. Statehood Amendment (proposed by Congress August 22, 1978)

Section 1 For purposes of representation in the Congress, election of the President and Vice-President, and article V of this Constitution, the District constituting the seat of government of the United States shall be treated as though it were a State.

Section 2 The exercise of the rights and powers conferred under this article shall be by the people of the District constituting the seat of government, and as shall be provided by Congress.

Section 3 The twenty-third article of amendment to the Constitution of the United States is hereby repealed.

Section 4 This article shall be inoperative, unless it shall have been ratified as an amendment to the Constitution by the legislatures of three-fourths of the several states within seven years from the date of its submission.

Amendment XXVII

[Adopted 1992]

No law, varying the compensation for the services of the Senators and Representatives, shall take effect, until an election of Representatives shall have intervened.

APPENDIX II

U.S. POLITICS AND GOVERNMENT

PRESIDENTIAL ELECTIONS

Year	Candidates	Parties	Popular Vote	Percentage of Popular Vote	Electoral Vote	Percentage of Voter Participation
1789	GEORGE WASHINGTON (Va.)*				69	
	John Adams				34	
	Others				35	
1792	GEORGE WASHINGTON (Va.)				132	
	John Adams				77	
	George Clinton				50	
	Others				5	
1796	JOHN ADAMS (Mass.)	Federalist			71	
	Thomas Jefferson	Democratic-Republican			68	
	Thomas Pinckney	Federalist			59	
	Aaron Burr	Dem.-Rep.			30	
	Others	—			48	
1800	THOMAS JEFFERSON (Va.)	Dem.-Rep.			73	
	Aaron Burr	Dem.-Rep.			73	
	John Adams	Federalist			65	
	C. C. Pinckney	Federalist			64	
	John Jay	Federalist			1	
1804	THOMAS JEFFERSON (Va.)	Dem.-Rep.			162	
	C. C. Pinckney	Federalist			14	
1808	JAMES MADISON (Va.)	Dem.-Rep.			122	
	C. C. Pinckney	Federalist			47	
	George Clinton	Dem.-Rep.			6	
1812	JAMES MADISON (Va.)	Dem.-Rep.			128	
	De Witt Clinton	Federalist			89	
1816	JAMES MONROE (Va.)	Dem.-Rep.			183	
	Rufus King	Federalist			34	
1820	JAMES MONROE (Va.)	Dem.-Rep.			231	
	John Quincy Adams	Dem.-Rep.			1	

*State of residence when elected president.

Year	Candidates	Parties	Popular Vote	Percentage of Popular Vote	Electoral Vote	Percentage of Voter Participation
1824	JOHN Q. ADAMS (Mass.)	Dem.-Rep.	108,740	30.5	84	26.9
	Andrew Jackson	Dem.-Rep.	153,544	43.1	99	
	William H. Crawford	Dem.-Rep.	46,618	13.1	41	
	Henry Clay	Dem.-Rep.	47,136	13.2	37	
1828	ANDREW JACKSON (Tenn.)	Democratic	647,286	56.0	178	57.6
	John Quincy Adams	National Republican	508,064	44.0	83	
1832	ANDREW JACKSON (Tenn.)	Democratic	687,502	55.0	219	55.4
	Henry Clay	National Republican	530,189	42.4	49	
	John Floyd	Independent			11	
	William Wirt	Anti-Mason	33,108	2.6	7	
1836	MARTIN VAN BUREN (N.Y.)	Democratic	765,483	50.9	170	57.8
	W. H. Harrison	Whig			73	
	Hugh L. White	Whig	739,795	49.1	26	
	Daniel Webster	Whig			14	
	W. P. Mangum	Independent			11	
1840	WILLIAM H. HARRISON (Ohio)	Whig	1,274,624	53.1	234	78.0
	Martin Van Buren	Democratic	1,127,781	46.9	60	
	J. G. Birney	Liberty	7,069		—	
1844	JAMES K. POLK (Tenn.)	Democratic	1,338,464	49.6	170	78.9
	Henry Clay	Whig	1,300,097	48.1	105	
	J. G. Birney	Liberty	62,300	2.3	—	
1848	ZACHARY TAYLOR (La.)	Whig	1,360,099	47.4	163	72.7
	Lewis Cass	Democratic	1,220,544	42.5	127	
	Martin Van Buren	Free-Soil	291,263	10.1	—	
1852	FRANKLIN PIERCE (N.H.)	Democratic	1,601,117	50.9	254	69.6
	Winfield Scott	Whig	1,385,453	44.1	42	
	John P. Hale	Free-Soil	155,825	5.0	—	
1856	JAMES BUCHANAN (Pa.)	Democratic	1,832,995	45.3	174	78.9
	John C. Frémont	Republican	1,339,932	33.1	114	
	Millard Fillmore	American	871,731	21.6	8	
1860	ABRAHAM LINCOLN (Ill.)	Republican	1,866,452	39.8	180	81.2
	Stephen A. Douglas	Democratic	1,375,157	29.4	12	
	John C. Breckinridge	Democratic	847,953	18.1	72	
	John Bell	Union	590,631	12.6	39	
1864	ABRAHAM LINCOLN (Ill.)	Republican	2,213,665	55.1	212	73.8
	George B. McClellan	Democratic	1,805,237	44.9	21	
1868	ULYSSES S. GRANT (Ill.)	Republican	3,012,833	52.7	214	78.1
	Horatio Seymour	Democratic	2,703,249	47.3	80	

Year	Candidates	Parties	Popular Vote	Percentage of Popular Vote	Electoral Vote	Percentage of Voter Participation
1872	ULYSSES S. GRANT (Ill.)	Republican	3,597,132	55.6	286	71.3
	Horace Greeley	Democratic; Liberal Republican	2,834,125	43.9	66	
1876	RUTHERFORD B. HAYES (Ohio)	Republican	4,036,298	48.0	185	81.8
	Samuel J. Tilden	Democratic	4,288,590	51.0	184	
1880	JAMES A. GARFIELD (Ohio)	Republican	4,454,416	48.5	214	79.4
	Winfield S. Hancock	Democratic	4,444,952	48.1	155	
1884	GROVER CLEVELAND (N.Y.)	Democratic	4,874,986	48.5	219	77.5
	James G. Blaine	Republican	4,851,981	48.3	182	
1888	BENJAMIN HARRISON (Ind.)	Republican	5,439,853	47.9	233	79.3
	Grover Cleveland	Democratic	5,540,309	48.6	168	
1892	GROVER CLEVELAND (N.Y.)	Democratic	5,555,426	46.1	277	74.7
	Benjamin Harrison	Republican	5,182,690	43.0	145	
	James B. Weaver	People's	1,029,846	8.5	22	
1896	WILLIAM McKINLEY (Ohio)	Republican	7,104,779	51.1	271	79.3
	William J. Bryan	Democratic-People's	6,502,925	47.7	176	
1900	WILLIAM McKINLEY (Ohio)	Republican	7,207,923	51.7	292	73.2
	William J. Bryan	Dem.-Populist	6,358,133	45.5	155	
1904	THEODORE ROOSEVELT (N.Y.)	Republican	7,623,486	57.9	336	65.2
	Alton B. Parker	Democratic	5,077,911	37.6	140	
	Eugene V. Debs	Socialist	402,283	3.0	—	
1908	WILLIAM H. TAFT (Ohio)	Republican	7,678,908	51.6	321	65.4
	William J. Bryan	Democratic	6,409,104	43.1	162	
	Eugene V. Debs	Socialist	420,793	2.8	—	
1912	WOODROW WILSON (N.J.)	Democratic	6,293,454	41.9	435	58.8
	Theodore Roosevelt	Progressive	4,119,538	27.4	88	
	William H. Taft	Republican	3,484,980	23.2	8	
	Eugene V. Debs	Socialist	900,672	6.1	—	
1916	WOODROW WILSON (N.J.)	Democratic	9,129,606	49.4	277	61.6
	Charles E. Hughes	Republican	8,538,221	46.2	254	
	A. L. Benson	Socialist	585,113	3.2	—	
1920	WARREN G. HARDING (Ohio)	Republican	16,143,407	60.5	404	49.2
	James M. Cox	Democratic	9,130,328	34.2	127	
	Eugene V. Debs	Socialist	919,799	3.4	—	
1924	CALVIN COOLIDGE (Mass.)	Republican	15,725,016	54.0	382	48.9
	John W. Davis	Democratic	8,386,503	28.8	136	
	Robert M. La Follette	Progressive	4,822,856	16.6	13	

Year	Candidates	Parties	Popular Vote	Percentage of Popular Vote	Electoral Vote	Percentage of Voter Participation
1928	HERBERT HOOVER (Calif.)	Republican	21,391,381	57.4	444	56.9
	Alfred E. Smith	Democratic	15,016,443	40.3	87	
	Norman Thomas	Socialist	881,951	2.3	—	
	William Z. Foster	Communist	102,991	0.3	—	
1932	FRANKLIN D. ROOSEVELT (N.Y.)	Democratic	22,821,857	57.4	472	56.9
	Herbert Hoover	Republican	15,761,841	39.7	59	
	Norman Thomas	Socialist	881,951	2.2	—	
1936	FRANKLIN D. ROOSEVELT (N.Y.)	Democratic	27,751,597	60.8	523	61.0
	Alfred M. Landon	Republican	16,679,583	36.5	8	
	William Lemke	Union	882,479	1.9	—	
1940	FRANKLIN D. ROOSEVELT (N.Y.)	Democratic	27,244,160	54.8	449	62.5
	Wendell Willkie	Republican	22,305,198	44.8	82	
1944	FRANKLIN D. ROOSEVELT (N.Y.)	Democratic	25,602,504	53.5	432	55.9
	Thomas E. Dewey	Republican	22,006,285	46.0	99	
1948	HARRY S. TRUMAN (Mo.)	Democratic	24,105,695	49.5	303	53.0
	Thomas E. Dewey	Republican	21,969,170	45.1	189	
	J. Strom Thurmond	States'-Rights Democratic	1,169,021	2.4	38	
	Henry A. Wallace	Progressive	1,156,103	2.4	—	
1952	DWIGHT D. EISENHOWER (N.Y.)	Republican	33,936,252	55.1	442	63.3
	Adlai Stevenson	Democratic	27,314,992	44.4	89	
1956	DWIGHT D. EISENHOWER (N.Y.)	Republican	35,575,420	57.6	457	60.6
	Adlai Stevenson	Democratic	26,033,066	42.1	73	
	Other	—	—		1	
1960	JOHN F. KENNEDY (Mass.)	Democratic	34,227,096	49.9	303	62.8
	Richard M. Nixon	Republican	34,108,546	49.6	219	
	Other	—	—		15	
1964	LYNDON B. JOHNSON (Tex.)	Democratic	43,126,506	61.1	486	61.7
	Barry M. Goldwater	Republican	27,176,799	38.5	52	
1968	RICHARD M. NIXON (N.Y.)	Republican	31,770,237	43.4	301	60.9
	Hubert H. Humphrey	Democratic	31,270,533	42.7	191	
	George Wallace	American Indep.	9,906,141	13.5	46	
1972	RICHARD M. NIXON (N.Y.)	Republican	47,169,911	60.7	520	55.2
	George S. McGovern	Democratic	29,170,383	37.5	17	
	Other	—	—		1	
1976	JIMMY CARTER (Ga.)	Democratic	40,830,763	50.0	297	53.5
	Gerald R. Ford	Republican	39,147,793	48.0	240	
	Other	—	1,575,459	2.1	—	

Year	Candidates	Parties	Popular Vote	Percentage of Popular Vote	Electoral Vote	Percentage of Voter Participation
1980	RONALD REAGAN (Calif.)	Republican	43,901,812	51.0	489	54.0
	Jimmy Carter	Democratic	35,483,820	41.0	49	
	John B. Anderson	Independent	5,719,722	7.0	—	
	Ed Clark	Libertarian	921,188	1.1	—	
1984	RONALD REAGAN (Calif.)	Republican	54,455,075	59.0	525	53.1
	Walter Mondale	Democratic	37,577,185	41.0	13	
1988	GEORGE H. W. BUSH (Tex.)	Republican	47,946,422	54.0	426	50.2
	Michael S. Dukakis	Democratic	41,016,429	46.0	112	
1992	WILLIAM J. CLINTON (Ark.)	Democratic	44,908,254	43.0	370	55.9
	George H. W. Bush	Republican	39,102,282	38.0	168	
	H. Ross Perot	Independent	19,721,433	19.0	—	
1996	WILLIAM J. CLINTON (Ark.)	Democratic	47,401,185	49.2	379	49.0
	Robert Dole	Republican	39,197,469	40.7	159	
	H. Ross Perot	Independent	8,085,294	8.4	—	
2000	GEORGE W. BUSH (Tex.)	Republican	50,456,062	47.8	271	51.2
	Al Gore	Democratic	50,996,862	48.4	267	
	Ralph Nader	Green Party	2,858,843	2.7	—	
	Patrick J. Buchanan	—	438,760	0.4	—	
2004	GEORGE W. BUSH (Tex.)	Republican	61,872,711	50.7	286	60.3
	John F. Kerry	Democratic	58,894,584	48.3	252	
	Other	—	1,582,185	1.3	—	
2008	BARACK OBAMA (Ill.)	Democratic	69,456,897	52.9	365	56.8
	John McCain	Republican	59,934,314	45.7	173	
2012	BARACK OBAMA (Ill.)	Democratic	65,909,451	51.02	332	58
	Willard Mitt Romney	Republican	60,932,176	47.16	152	
	Other	—	2,350,895	1.82	—	

ADMISSION OF STATES TO THE UNION

State	Date of Admission	State	Date of Admission
Delaware	December 7, 1787	Virginia	June 25, 1788
Pennsylvania	December 12, 1787	New York	July 26, 1788
New Jersey	December 18, 1787	North Carolina	November 21, 1789
Georgia	January 2, 1788	Rhode Island	May 29, 1790
Connecticut	January 9, 1788	Vermont	March 4, 1791
Massachusetts	February 6, 1788	Kentucky	June 1, 1792
Maryland	April 28, 1788	Tennessee	June 1, 1796
South Carolina	May 23, 1788	Ohio	March 1, 1803
New Hampshire	June 21, 1788	Louisiana	April 30, 1812

State	Date of Admission	State	Date of Admission
Indiana	December 11, 1816	West Virginia	June 19, 1863
Mississippi	December 10, 1817	Nevada	October 31, 1864
Illinois	December 3, 1818	Nebraska	March 1, 1867
Alabama	December 14, 1819	Colorado	August 1, 1876
Maine	March 15, 1820	North Dakota	November 2, 1889
Missouri	August 10, 1821	South Dakota	November 2, 1889
Arkansas	June 15, 1836	Montana	November 8, 1889
Michigan	January 16, 1837	Washington	November 11, 1889
Florida	March 3, 1845	Idaho	July 3, 1890
Texas	December 29, 1845	Wyoming	July 10, 1890
Iowa	December 28, 1846	Utah	January 4, 1896
Wisconsin	May 29, 1848	Oklahoma	November 16, 1907
California	September 9, 1850	New Mexico	January 6, 1912
Minnesota	May 11, 1858	Arizona	February 14, 1912
Oregon	February 14, 1859	Alaska	January 3, 1959
Kansas	January 29, 1861	Hawaii	August 21, 1959

INDEX

A note about the index: Names of individuals appear in boldface. Key terms and their locations are in boldface italic. Letters in parentheses following pages refer to: *(i)* illustrations, including photographs and artifacts as well as information in captions; *(f)* figures, including charts and graphs; *(m)* maps; *(t)* tables.

Race and racism. *See also* Abolition and abolitionism; African Americans; Segregation
  Fifteenth Amendment and, 469
  Fourteenth Amendment and, 467
  in middle colonies, 120
  mixed races and, 46, 47(i)
  Reconstruction and, 478–479
  in South, 129, 364
  southern Democratic Party and, 472, 479
  Wilmot Proviso and, 393
Race riots, in Memphis, 467
Racial segregation. *See* Segregation
Radical Reconstruction, 467–470
Radical Republicans, 467–468
Radicals and radicalism, in French Revolution, 250
Railroads
  in Civil War, 429–430
  expansion of, 298, 330–331, 331(m)
  segregation on, 473
  in South, 473, 482
  transcontinental, 400–401, 446
Raleigh, Walter, 50(t)
Rancheros, 341, 349
Ranchos, 341
Randolph, Edmund, 369
Rapier, James T., 473, 479, 483
Ratification
  of Articles of Confederation, 207–209
  of Constitution, 226, 227–230, 228(m), 237
Reader, Samuel J., 424(i)
Reapers, mechanical, 329, 446
Rebellions. *See* Protest(s); Revolts and rebellions
Reconquest (Spain), **32**
Reconstruction (1863–1877)
  carpetbaggers and, 472
  collapse of, 476–483
  congressional, 466–470
  Johnson impeachment and, 468–469
  Ku Klux Klan and, 472, 478
  labor code and, 459–460
  military rule during, 467–468, 468(m)
  North and, 478–479
  presidential, 458–459
  Radical, 466–470
  Redeemers and, 479, **479,** 480, 483
  scalawags and, 472
  South and, 481(m)
  southern Republican Party and, 472–473, 473(f)
  Union officers, 465(i)
  white supremacy and, 479–480, 479(f)
Reconstruction Acts (1867), 469, 471, 472
Reconstruction Amendments. *See* Thirteenth Amendment; Fourteenth Amendment; Fifteenth Amendment
Records
  archaeological, 4, 5
  written, 5
Redcoats, in Revolutionary War, 182
Redeemers, in South, 479, **479,** 480, 483
Redemptioners, in middle colonies, **119**
Red Hawk (Shawnee), 192
Reform and reform movements. *See also* Protestant Reformation; specific movements
  abolitionism, 317–318
  in education and training, 314

  of encomienda system, 45
  evangelicalism and, 350–351
  moral reformers and, 316
  in Second Great Awakening, 315–318
  temperance and, 316
Reformation. *See* Protestant Reformation
Refugees
  loyalist as, 187–188
  slaves as, 440(i)
Regions (U.S.). *See* specific locations
Regulation
  of British colonial trade, 102–104
  of passenger safety, 298
Religion(s). *See also* Churches; Missions and missionaries; specific groups
  in Chesapeake region, 66–67, 68(i)
  in colonies, 131
  evangelical, 315–316
  freedom of, 93
  in Maryland, 67
  in New England, 87–88, 90–92, 114
  in New Netherland, 99
  in Pennsylvania, 100, 101
  of plain folk, 380
  Reconquest and, 32
  of slaves, 374–375
  Taino, 35
Religious toleration, in Pennsylvania, 100–101
Removal policy, for Indians, 306, 308–310, 309(m)
Repartimiento reform, 45
Report on Manufactures (Hamilton), **244**
Report on Public Credit (Hamilton), **242**
Report on the Causes and Reasons for War, 276–277
Representation
  under Articles of Confederation, 207, 224
  in British colonies, 136, 154–155
  in Constitution, 225
  Continental Congress on, 165
  in Virginia, 60
  in Virginia and New Jersey plans, 224
  virtual, 151, 152
Republicanism, **210**–211
  vs. democracy, 225–226
  Jefferson and, 264–265
  women's roles and, 236
Republican Party, 279, 323, **406.** *See also* Elections; specific presidents
  on *Dred Scott* decision, 410–411
  ex-Confederates in Congress and, 464
  Fifteenth Amendment and, 469–470
  Fourteenth Amendment and, 467
  growth of, 406
  Klan and political violence against, 472, 478
  Liberal Party and, 477–478
  North and, 478–479
  presidential Reconstruction and, 462–463
  Radical Reconstruction and, 467–470
  on slavery, 406, 411
  in South, 464–465, 471–474, 473(f), 475, 476–477, 478, 479–480, 480(i)
  women in, 407
Republicans (Jeffersonian), **253,** 323
  election of 1796 and, 253–254
  election of 1800 and, 262–263

  election of 1804 and, 272
  election of 1808 and, 273
  Quasi-War and, 255
Republicans, election of 1824 and, 288
Republican wife and mother, 238–239
Republic of Texas, 342
Requisition, of 1785, 220
Resaca de la Palma, battle at (1846), 344(m), 345
Reservations (Indian), 338
Resistance. *See also* Revolts and rebellions
  to British taxation, 141(i)
  by Indians, 308
  by slaves, 127, 375–376
  to Stamp Act, 152–154
Resources. *See* specific resources
Revenue Act
  of 1764, 150–**151**
  of 1767, 157
Revere, Paul, 159(i)
Revivals and revivalism
  Great Awakening as, 133–134
  plain folk and, 380
  Second Great Awakening as, 315–316
Revolts and rebellions. *See also* Resistance
  at Acoma pueblo, 17, 42
  Bacon's Rebellion, 70–71
  Bear Flag Revolt, 341
  Gabriel's rebellion, 263
  by Leisler, 105
  by Native Americans, 73
  by Pontiac, 148–149
  Pueblo Revolt, 73
  Shays's Rebellion, 222
  by slaves, 78, 376
  in Spanish borderland, 135
  Stono rebellion, 127
  in Texas, 340(m), 341
  by Turner, Nat, 376(i)
Revolution(s). *See also* Market revolution; Revolutionary War
  in France, 250–251
  in Haiti, 251–252
Revolutionary War (1775–1783). *See also* Continental army; National debt; specific leaders and battles
  balance of power in, 194(i)
  British surrender at Yorktown, 198–199
  campaigns of 1777–1779 in, 190–197
  early battles of, 174, 175–176
  France and, 193–194, 195
  home front in, 185–189, 187(m)
  Indian country in, 192–193
  loyalists in, 178, 185, 186–188, 187(m), 198
  military forces during, 180–181
  Native Americans in, 186, 190(i)
  in North (1775–1778), 183(m)
  reasons for British loss, 201
  slaves and, 168
  in South, 195–199
Rhode Island, 92–93, 94, 136, 228
  emancipation in, 213
  western lands of, 207
Rice, 76, 124, 128–129, 365(m), 366
Richmond, Virginia, 448(i), 452
  Reconstruction in, 465(i)
  state convention at, 466(i)
Riflemen, 180(i)

About the Authors

James L. Roark (Ph.D., Stanford University) is Samuel Candler Dobbs Professor of American History at Emory University. In 1993, he received the Emory Williams Distinguished Teaching Award, and in 2001–2002 he was Pitt Professor of American Institutions at Cambridge University. He has written *Masters without Slaves: Southern Planters in the Civil War and Reconstruction* and coauthored *Black Masters: A Free Family of Color in the Old South* with Michael P. Johnson.

Michael P. Johnson (Ph.D., Stanford University) is professor of history at Johns Hopkins University. His publications include *Toward a Patriarchal Republic: The Secession of Georgia*; *Abraham Lincoln, Slavery, and the Civil War: Selected Speeches and Writings*; and *Reading the American Past: Selected Historical Documents*, the documents reader for *The American Promise*. He has also coedited *No Chariot Let Down: Charleston's Free People of Color on the Eve of the Civil War* with James L. Roark.

Patricia Cline Cohen (Ph.D., University of California, Berkeley) is professor of history at the University of California, Santa Barbara, where she received the Distinguished Teaching Award in 2005–2006. She has written *A Calculating People: The Spread of Numeracy in Early America* and *The Murder of Helen Jewett: The Life and Death of a Prostitute in Nineteenth-Century New York*, and she has coauthored *The Flash Press: Sporting Male Weeklies in 1840s New York*.

Sarah Stage (Ph.D., Yale University) has taught U.S. history at Williams College and the University of California, Riverside, and she was visiting professor at Beijing University and Szechuan University. Currently she is professor of Women's Studies at Arizona State University. Her books include *Female Complaints: Lydia Pinkham and the Business of Women's Medicine* and *Rethinking Home Economics: Women and the History of a Profession*.

Susan M. Hartmann (Ph.D., University of Missouri) is Arts and Humanities Distinguished Professor of History at Ohio State University. In 1995 she won the university's Exemplary Faculty Award in the College of Humanities. Her publications include *Truman and the 80th Congress*; *The Home Front and Beyond: American Women in the 1940s*; *From Margin to Mainstream: American Women and Politics since 1960*; and *The Other Feminists: Activists in the Liberal Establishment*.